Modern Trial Advocacy

Analysis and Practice

Fifth Edition

Modern Trial Advocacy

Analysis and Practice

Fifth Edition

Steven Lubet

Williams Memorial Professor of Law
Northwestern University School of Law
Chicago, Illinois

J.C. Lore

Director of Trial Advocacy and Clinical Professor of Law
Rutgers University School of Law
Camden, New Jersey

NITA®
National Institute for Trial Advocacy

Address inquiries to:

Reprint Permission
National Institute for Trial Advocacy
1685 38th Street, Suite 200
Boulder, CO 80301-2735
Phone: (800) 225-6482
Fax: (720) 890-7069
E-mail: permissions@nita.org

ISBN 978-1-60156-474-0
eISBN 978-1-60156-507-5
FBA 1474

Library of Congress Cataloging-in-Publication Data

Lubet, Steven, author.

Modern trial advocacy : analysis and practice / Steven Lubet, Williams Memorial Professor of Law, Northwestern University School of Law, Chicago, Illinois; J.C. Lore, Director of Trial Advocacy and Clinical Professor of Law, Rutgers University School of Law, Camden, New Jersey. -- Fifth edition.

pages cm

ISBN 978-1-60156-474-0

1. Trial practice--United States. I. Lore, J. C., author. II. Title.

KF8915.L82 2015

347.73'75--dc23

2015021906

Wolters Kluwer

Official co-publisher of NITA.
WKLegaledu.com/NITA

To Anne Miller

SL

To Melissa Lore

JCL

Contents

Chapter Five. Cross-Examination

To view the demonstrations noted throughout this text, please go to the Visuals Appendix at http://bit.ly/1FSfRXv.

Password: NITAModTriAd5

Chapter One

Case Analysis and Storytelling

1.1 The Idea of a Persuasive Story

1.1.1 Trials as Stories

The function of a trial is to resolve factual disputes. Trials are only held when the parties disagree on historical facts. These disagreements commonly involve the existence or occurrence of events or actions, but they may also turn on questions of sequence, interpretation, characterization, or intent. Thus, trials may be held to answer questions such as these: What happened? What happened first? Why did it happen? Who made it happen? Did it happen on purpose? Was it justified or fair? All of these questions are resolved by accumulating information about past events; if there is no dispute about past events the case should be resolved on summary judgment.[1]

Trials, then, are held to allow the parties to persuade the judge or jury by recounting their versions of the historical facts. Another name for this process is storytelling. Each party to a trial has the opportunity to tell a story, albeit through the fairly stilted devices of jury address, direct and cross-examination, and introduction of evidence. The framework for the stories—or their grammar—is set by the rules of procedure and evidence. The conclusion of the stories—the end to which they are directed—is controlled by the elements of the applicable substantive law. The content of the stories—their plot and mise-en-scène—is governed, of course, by the truth, or at least by so much of the truth as is available to the advocate. Thereafter, the party who succeeds in telling the most persuasive story should win.

But what is persuasive storytelling in the context of a trial? A persuasive story can establish an affirmative case if it has all, or most, of these characteristics: 1) it is told about people who have reasons for the way they act; 2) it accounts for or explains all of the known or undeniable facts; 3) it is told by credible witnesses; 4) it is supported by details; 5) it accords with common sense and contains no implausible elements; and 6) it is organized in a way that makes each succeeding fact increasingly

1. *See* FED. R. CIV. P. 56.

more likely. On the other hand, defense lawyers must often tell "counter-stories" that negate the above aspects of the other side's case.

In addition to persuasiveness, a story presented at trial must consist of admissible evidence, and it must contain all of the elements of a legally cognizable claim or defense.

An advocate's task when preparing for trial is to conceive of and structure a true story—comprising only admissible evidence and containing all of the elements of a claim or defense—that is most likely to be believed or adopted by the trier of fact. This is a creative process, since seldom will the facts be undisputed or capable of but a single interpretation. To carry through this process the lawyer must first "imagine" a series of alternative scenarios, assessing each for its clarity, simplicity, and believability, as well as for its legal consequences.

1.1.2 Planning a Sample Story

Assume, for example, that you represent a plaintiff who was injured in an automobile accident. You know from your law school torts class that to recover damages you will have to tell a story proving, at a minimum, that the defendant was negligent. You also know from your evidence class that the story will have to be built on admissible evidence, and you know from your ethics class that the story cannot be based on false or perjured testimony.[2] Your client knows only that when traffic slowed down to allow a fire truck to pass, she was hit from behind by the driver of the other automobile.

How can these basic facts be assembled into a persuasive trial story? First, we understand that the story must be about people who act for reasons. Your client slowed down for a fire truck, which explains her actions. But why didn't the defendant slow down as well? Your story will be more persuasive if you can establish his reason. True, a reason is not absolutely essential. Perhaps the defendant was such a poor driver that he simply drove about banging into other automobiles. On the other hand, consider what the absence of a reason implies. The plaintiff claims that traffic slowed for a fire truck, but the defendant—also part of traffic—did not slow down. Could it be that there was no fire truck? Perhaps there was a fire truck, but it was not sounding its siren or alerting traffic to stop. Is it possible that the plaintiff herself did not slow down, but rather slammed on her brakes? In other words, the very absence of a reason for the defendant's actions may make the plaintiff's own testimony less believable.

The skilled advocate will therefore look for a reason or cause for the defendant's actions. Was the defendant drunk? In a hurry? Homicidal? Distracted? You can choose from among these potential reasons by "imagining" each one in the context of your story. Imagine how the story will be told if you claim that the defendant was

2. *See* Model Rules of Prof'l Conduct R. 3.3 (2009).

drunk. Could such a story account for all of the known facts? If the police came to the scene, was the defendant arrested? Did any credible, disinterested witnesses see the defendant drinking or smell liquor on his breath? If not, drunkenness does not provide a persuasive reason for the defendant's actions.

Next, imagine telling your story about a homicidal defendant. Perhaps this wasn't an accident, but a murder attempt. Envision your impassioned plea for punitive damages. But wait, this story is too implausible. How would a murderer know that the plaintiff would be driving on that particular road? How would he know that a fire truck would be attempting to bypass traffic? How could he predict that the plaintiff would slow down enough, or that there would be no other cars in the way? Barring the unlikely discovery of additional facts that support such a theory, this story is unpersuasive.

Finally, imagine the story as told about a defendant who was in a hurry. This story accounts for the known facts, since it explains why traffic might slow while the defendant did not. Perhaps the defendant saw the fire truck, but was driving just a little too fast to stop in time; or he might have been so preoccupied with the importance of getting somewhere on time that he simply failed to notice the fire truck until it was too late. Moreover, there is nothing implausible or unbelievable about this theory. It is in complete harmony with everyone's everyday observations. Furthermore, details that support the story should not be hard to come by. Was the defendant going to work in the morning? Did he have an important meeting to attend? Was he headed home after a long day? The trial lawyer can find details in virtually any destination that will support the theory of the hurried defendant. Note, however, that while such additional evidence of the defendant's haste will be helpful, the story does not rest on any external witness's credibility. All of the major elements of the story may be inferred from the defendant's own actions.

How can this last story best be organized? Let us assume that the occurrence of the collision itself is not in issue and recall that it is important that each fact make every succeeding element increasingly more likely. Which aspect should come first—the presence of the fire truck or the fact that the defendant was in a hurry? Since the presence of the fire truck does not make it more likely that the defendant was in a hurry, that probably is not the most effective starting point. On the other hand, the defendant's haste does make it more likely that he would fail to notice the fire truck.

A skeletal version of our story, with some easily obtained details supplied, might go like this. We know there was a collision, but why did it happen? The defendant was driving south on Sheridan Road at 8:20 in the morning. It was the end of rush hour, and he had to be at work downtown. In fact, he had an important meeting that was to begin at 9:00 a.m. sharp. The defendant's parking lot is two blocks from his office. As traffic slowed for a passing fire truck, the defendant did not notice it. Failing to stop in time, the defendant ran into the plaintiff's car.

Other details might also be available to support this story. Perhaps, immediately following the collision, the defendant pulled out a cellular phone to call his office. Similarly, there might be "counter-details" for the plaintiff to rebut. The point, however, is to organize your story on the principle of successive supporting detail.

1.2 The Ethics of Persuasive Storytelling

In the preceding section we discussed the way in which an advocate imagines a persuasive theory or story. We also noted that lawyers are bound to the truth—we are not free to pick stories simply on the basis of their persuasive value. Within this parameter, exactly how much room is there for creative theory choice?

1.2.1 Assuming You "Know" the Truth

Let us begin with the proposition that in most cases neither the lawyer nor the client will know with certainty all of what we might call the "relevant truth." As in the scenario above, for example, the plaintiff knows her own actions, but has no special knowledge about the defendant. The lawyer, of course, is not free to persuade or coach the plaintiff to alter her own story simply to make it more effective.[3]

This is not to say, however, that legal ethics permit us to do nothing more than put the plaintiff on the witness stand. The lawyer's duty of zealous representation requires further inquiry into the existence of additional details, not to mention the artful use of sequencing and emphasis. For instance, let us assume that the plaintiff has informed her lawyer with certainty that the fire truck was flashing its lights, but not using its siren or bell. There is no doubt that an attorney absolutely may not coach the plaintiff to testify that the siren and bell were sounding. Such testimony would be false, perjurious, and unethical.

On the other hand, there is no requirement that the absence of bell and siren be made the centerpiece of the plaintiff's direct examination. Sequencing and emphasis may be used to minimize the adverse impact of this information. Therefore, the direct examination could be developed as follows: "The fire truck was the largest vehicle on the road. It was the standard fire-engine red. All of its lights were flashing brightly—headlights, taillights, and red dome lights. It could be seen easily from all directions. All of the traffic, save the defendant, slowed down for the fire truck. It was not necessary to hear a siren to notice the fire truck." Thus, the lawyer has held closely to the truth, while establishing the irrelevance of the potentially damaging information.

3. Model Rules of Prof'l Conduct R. 3.1, 3.4, and 4.1.

1.2.2 Assuming You Do Not Know the Truth

A different situation arises when the advocate is not able to identify truth so closely, as in the example above concerning the defendant's reasons for failing to notice the fire truck in time. Recall that we considered a variety of possible reasons, including inattention, drunkenness, and aggression. Some reasons have clear forensic advantages over others. What are the ethical limitations on the lawyer's ability to choose the best one?

First, it should be clear that we are not bound to accept the defendant's story in the same way that we must give credence to our own client. The duty of zealous representation requires that we resolve doubts in our client's favor.[4] Moreover, we speak to our client within a relationship of confidentiality, which not only protects her communication, but also gives her a strong incentive to speak candidly. Without her consent, what our client tells us will go no further, and this knowledge gives her every reason to make a full disclosure.[5] When our client gives us a damaging fact (such as the absence of the fire truck's siren), it is even more likely to be true, since she obviously has no reason to inject such information falsely. Statements that we obtain from an opposing party are not necessarily accompanied by comparable indicia of reliability, and we are entitled to mistrust them.

This is not to say that we must always accept information from our clients as revealed wisdom. Clients may mislead us as the result of misperception, forgetfulness, mistake, wishful thinking, reticence, or ignorance—and, unfortunately, they sometimes lie. Moreover, opposing parties in litigation usually tell what they perceive as the truth. As a tactical matter, therefore, trial lawyers must always examine every statement of every witness for potential error or falsehood. As an ethical matter, however, we should be more ready to assume that our client's words—both helpful and damaging—are likely to be true. It is, after all, the client's case.[6]

Recognizing, then, that we must go beyond the opposing party's version of the facts, we next evaluate the entire universe of possible stories. In our example we determined that the "in a hurry" story would be the most persuasive. Simultaneously, we must also determine whether it is an ethical story to tell.

The key to determining the ethical value of any trial theory is whether it is supported by facts that we know, believe, or have a good-faith basis to believe, are true.[7]

Returning to our fire truck case, assume that the defendant has denied that he was in a hurry. He has the right to make this denial, but as plaintiff's lawyers we

4. *See id.* 1.2.

5. *See id.* 1.6.

6. Note that a lawyer is generally required to accept the client's goals and objectives with regard to litigation. Model Rules of Prof'l Conduct R. 1.2(a) ("[A] lawyer shall abide by a client's decisions concerning the objectives of representation and . . . shall consult with the client as to the means by which they are to be pursued.").

7. *See* Model Rules of Prof'l Conduct R. 3.1, 3.4(e), and 4.1.

have no duty to accept it. Assume also that we have not been able to locate a witness who can give direct evidence that the defendant was in a hurry. We do know where and when the collision occurred, and it is safe to assume that we would be able to learn a number of facts about the defendant's home, automobile, occupation, and place of employment. The following story emerges, based strictly on facts that we would have no reason to doubt.

> The defendant lives sixteen miles from his office. He usually takes a commuter train to work, but on the day of the accident he drove. The accident occurred on a major thoroughfare approximately eleven miles from the defendant's office. The time of the accident was 8:20 a.m., and the defendant had scheduled an important, and potentially lucrative, meeting with a new client for 8:30 a.m. that day. The parking lot nearest to the defendant's office is over two blocks away. The first thing that the defendant did following the accident was to telephone his office to say that he would be late.

Our conclusion is that the defendant was in a hurry. Driving on a familiar stretch of road, he was thinking about his appointment, maybe even starting to count the money, and he failed to pay sufficient attention to the traffic. We are entitled to ask the trier of fact to draw this inference because we reasonably believe its entire basis to be true. The known facts can also support a number of other stories, or no story at all, but that is not an ethical concern. Perhaps the defendant was being particularly careful that morning, knowing how important it was that he arrive on time for his appointment. Perhaps the appointment had nothing to do with the accident. Those arguments can be made, and they may turn out to be more persuasive stories than our own. Our ultimate stories might be ineffective, but they are ethical as long as they are not built on a false foundation.

1.2.3 The Special Case of the Criminal Law

The analysis above, regarding both persuasion and ethics, applies to civil and criminal cases alike. In the criminal law, however, the prosecutor has additional ethical obligations, and the defense lawyer has somewhat greater latitude.

A criminal prosecutor is not only an advocate, but also a public official. It is the prosecutor's duty to punish the guilty, not merely to win on behalf of a client. Therefore, a public prosecutor must personally believe in the legal validity of each case and must refrain from bringing any prosecution that is not supported by probable cause.[8]

Conversely, a criminal defendant is always entitled to plead not guilty, thereby putting the government to its burden of establishing guilt beyond a reasonable

8. *See id.* 3.8.

doubt.[9] A plea of not guilty need not in any sense be "true," since its function is only to insist on the constitutional right to trial. Of course, a criminal defendant has no right to introduce perjury or false evidence. However, a criminal defendant need not present any factual defense, and in most jurisdictions a conviction requires that the prosecution exclude every reasonable hypothesis that is inconsistent with guilt. Thus, as long as she does not rely on falsity or perjury, a criminal defense lawyer may argue for acquittal—that is, tell a story—based only on "a reasonable hypothesis" of innocence.

1.3 Preparing a Persuasive Trial Story

Assume you have decided on the story that you want to tell. It is persuasive. It is about people who have reasons for the way they act. It accounts for all of the known facts. It is told by credible witnesses. It is supported by details. It accords with common sense. It can be organized in a way that makes each succeeding fact more likely.

How do you put your story in the form of a trial?

1.3.1 Developing Your Theory, Theme, and Frame

Your case must have both a theory and a theme, and it must appeal to the judge's or jurors' frame of understanding.

1.3.1.1 Theory

Your theory is the adaptation of your story to the legal issues in the case. A theory of the case should be expressed in a single paragraph that combines an account of the facts and law in such a way as to lead the trier of fact to conclude that your client must win. A successful theory contains these elements:

It is logical. A winning theory has internal logical force. It is based on a foundation of undisputed or otherwise provable facts, all of which lead in a single direction. The facts on which your theory is based should reinforce (and never contradict) each other. Indeed, they should lead to each other, each fact or premise implying the next, in an orderly and inevitable fashion.

It speaks to the legal elements of your case. All of your trial persuasion must be in aid of a "legal" conclusion. Your theory must not only establish that your client is good or worthy (or that the other side is bad and unworthy), but also that the law entitles you to relief. Your theory therefore must be directed to prove every legal element that is necessary to both justify a verdict on your behalf and preserve it on appeal.

9. *See id.* 3.1 ("[A] lawyer for the defendant in a criminal proceeding . . . [may] defend the proceeding as to require that every element of the case be established.").

It is simple. A good theory makes maximum use of undisputed facts. It relies as little as possible on evidence that may be hotly controverted, implausible, inadmissible, or otherwise difficult to prove.

It is easy to believe. Even "true" theories may be difficult to believe because they contradict everyday experience or because they require harsh judgments. You must strive to eliminate all implausible elements from your theory. Similarly, you should attempt whenever possible to avoid arguments that depend on proof of deception, falsification, ill motive, or personal attack. An airtight theory is able to encompass the entirety of the other side's case and still result in your victory by sheer logical force.

To develop and express your theory, ask these three questions: What happened? Why did it happen? Why does that mean that my client should win? If your answer is longer than one paragraph, your theory may be logical and true, but it is probably too complicated.

1.3.1.2 Theme

Just as your theory must appeal to logic, your theme must appeal to moral force. A logical theory tells the trier of fact the reason that your verdict must be entered. A moral theme shows why it should be entered. In other words, your theme—best presented in a single sentence—justifies the morality of your theory and appeals to the justice of the case.

A theme is a rhetorical or forensic device. It has no independent legal weight, but rather it gives persuasive force to your legal arguments. The most compelling themes appeal to shared values, civic virtues, or common motivations. They can be succinctly expressed and repeated at virtually every phase of the trial.

In a contracts case, for example, your theory will account for all of the facts surrounding the formation and breach of the contract, as well as the relevant law, say, of specific performance. Your theory will explain why a particular verdict is compelled by the law. Your theme will strengthen your theory by underscoring why entering that verdict is the right thing to do. Perhaps your theme will be: "The defendant would rather try to make money than live up to a promise." Or you might try: "This defendant tried to sell some property, and keep it too." Whatever the theme, you will want to introduce it during your opening statement, reinforce it during direct and cross-examinations, and drive it home during your final argument.

1.3.1.3 Frame

It is often said that compelling facts may speak for themselves, but that is not really accurate. Because no case occurs in a vacuum, every fact—and indeed, every argument—is subject to interpretation by the judge or jury. Lawyers must therefore pay careful attention to the fact finder's frame of reference, which in turn will be determined, at least in part, by his or her education, training, background, experiences, preferences, and biases. This is not to say that cases are decided on the basis of emotion or prejudice, but rather that facts will inevitably be differently understood by different people. A story frame provides the setting in which facts are received—the environment in which they are accepted, rejected, emphasized, or discounted.

The lawyer creates a case's theory and theme, but she does so within a framework that is determined by the fact finder. Nonetheless, every case has several (or more) potential frames, and it is the attorney's job to identify and appeal to the frame most favorable to her case.

In a case recently decided by the U.S. Supreme Court, for example, a thirteen-year-old girl sued a middle-school principal who subjected her to a strip search.[10] The plaintiff, who was an honor student, claimed that the search was unreasonably intrusive, while the principal argued that it was a necessary component of the school's zero tolerance policy regarding drugs. (No drugs were found in the search, but another student had reported that the plaintiff had given her some prescription strength Ibuprofen.) Without revisiting the Supreme Court's controversial ruling, it should be obvious that the "reasonableness" of the search is subject to interpretation, depending on one's general attitude concerning students' rights, school discipline, drug abuse, and privacy. A lawyer for the plaintiff, then, would want to frame the case as one that is primarily about good students and fair decision-making. The defense, however, would emphasize the dangers of drug use and the perils of lax discipline in schools. The attorneys would, in turn, paint very different pictures of the school environment—one stressing everything that the thirteen-year-old girl had done right, the other highlighting the principal's fears of everything that might go wrong. At a trial on the merits (if not in the Supreme Court), the case would likely be decided by the fact finder's ultimate perspective. Is the case about privacy and modesty, or is it about clear rules and discipline? Whoever controls the frame will probably win the trial.

1.3.2 Planning Your Final Argument

Good trial preparation begins at the end. It makes great sense to plan your final argument first, because that aspect of the trial is the most similar to storytelling; it is the single element of the trial where it is permissible for you to suggest conclusions, articulate inferences, and otherwise present your theory to the trier of fact as an uninterrupted whole.

In other words, it is during final argument that you are most allowed to say exactly what you want to say, limited only by the requirement that all arguments be supported by evidence contained in the trial record. Thus, by planning your final

10. Safford Unified School District v. Redding, 557 U.S. 364 (2009).

argument at the beginning of your preparation, you will then be able to plan the balance of your case in such a way that ensures the record contains every fact that you will need for summation.

Ask yourself these two questions: What do I want to say at the end of the case? What evidence must I introduce or elicit in order to be able to say it? The answers will give you the broad outline of your entire case.

1.3.3 Planning Your Case-in-Chief

Your goal during your case-in-chief is to persuade the trier of fact as to the correctness of your theory, constantly appealing to a compelling frame while invoking the moral leverage of your theme. To accomplish this, you have four basic tools: 1) jury address, which consists of opening statement and final argument; 2) testimony on direct examination (and to a somewhat lesser extent on cross-examination); 3) introduction of exhibits, including real and documentary evidence; and 4) absolutely everything else that you do in the courtroom, including the way you look, act, react, speak, move, stand, and sit. The skills involved in each of these aspects of a trial will be discussed at length in later chapters. What follows here is an outline of the general steps to take in planning for trial.

1.3.3.1 Consider Your Potential Witnesses and Exhibits

Your first step is to list the legal elements of every claim or defense that you hope to establish. If you represent the plaintiff in a personal injury case, then you must offer evidence on all of the elements of negligence: duty, foreseeability, cause-in-fact, proximate cause, and damages. Next, list the evidence that you have available to support each such element. Most likely the bulk of your evidence will be in the form of witness testimony, but some of it will consist of documents, tangible objects, and other real evidence. For each such exhibit, note the witness through whom you will seek its introduction.

You are now ready to make decisions concerning your potential witnesses by inverting the informational list that you just created.

1.3.3.2 Evaluate Each Witness Individually

Imagine what you would like to say in final argument about each witness you might call to the stand: What does this witness contribute to my theory? What positive facts may I introduce through this witness? Are other witnesses available for the same facts? Is this witness an effective vehicle for my theme? What can I say about this witness that will be logically and morally persuasive?

Once you have assembled all of the "positive" information about each witness, you must go on to consider all possible problems and weaknesses.

Factual Weaknesses

Are there likely to be inconsistencies or gaps in the witness's testimony? Does the witness have damaging information that is likely to be elicited on cross-examination? If the answer to either question is affirmative, how can you minimize these problems? Can you resolve the inconsistencies by reevaluating your theory? Can another witness fill the gaps? Can you defuse the potentially damaging facts by bringing them out on direct examination?

Evidentiary Problems

Each witness's testimony must be evaluated for possible evidentiary problems. Do not assume that any item of evidence or testimony is automatically admissible. Instead, you must be able to state a positive theory of admissibility for everything that you intend to offer during your case-in-chief. To prepare for objections ask yourself: "How would I try to keep this information out of evidence?" Then plan your response. If you are not absolutely confident of your ability to counter any objections, you have to go back to the law library.

Credibility Problems

How is the witness likely to be attacked? Is the witness subject to challenge for bias or interest? Will perception be in issue? Is there potential for impeachment by prior inconsistent statements? Can you structure your direct examination so as to avoid or minimize these problems?

1.3.3.3 Decide Which Witness to Call

Having evaluated the contributions, strengths, and weaknesses of all of your potential witnesses, you are now in a position to decide which ones you will call to the stand. Your central concern will be to make sure that all of your necessary evidence is admitted. You must call any witness who is the sole source of a crucial piece of information. Except in rare or compelling circumstances, you will also want to call any witness whose credibility or appearance is central to the internal logic or moral weight of your case.

All nonessential witnesses must be evaluated according to their strengths and weaknesses. You will want to consider eliminating those witnesses whose testimony will be cumulative or repetitive of each other, since this will increase the likelihood of eliciting a damaging contradiction. You must also be willing to dispense with calling witnesses whose credibility is seriously suspect or whose testimony has the potential to do you more harm than good.

Once you have arrived at your final list of witnesses, arrange them in the order that will be most helpful to your case. While there are no hard and fast rules for determining witness order, the following three principles should help you decide:

Retention. You want your evidence not only to be heard, but also to be retained. Studies have consistently suggested that judges and juries tend to best remember the evidence that they hear at the beginning and the end of the trial. Following this principle, you will want to call your most important witness first and your next most important witness last. Start fast and end strong.

Progression. The "first and last" principle must occasionally give way to the need for logical progression. Some witnesses provide the foundation for the testimony of others. Thus, it may be necessary to call "predicate" witnesses early in the trial as a matter of both logical development and legal admissibility. To the extent possible, you may also wish to arrange your witnesses so that accounts of key events are given in chronological order.

Impact. You may also order your witnesses to maximize their dramatic impact. For example, you might wish to begin a wrongful death case by calling one of the grieving parents of the deceased child. Conversely, a necessary witness who is also somewhat unsavory or impeachable should probably be buried in the middle of your case-in-chief. A variant on the impact principle is the near-universal practice of calling a criminal defendant as the last witness for the defense. This practice has arisen for two reasons. First, it postpones until the last possible moment the time when the lawyer must decide whether to call the defendant to the stand and allow her to be subjected to cross-examination. Second, and far more cynically, calling defendants last allows them to hear all of the other testimony before testifying. (While all occurrence witnesses are routinely excluded from the courtroom, the defendant has a constitutional right to be present throughout the trial.)

1.3.4 Planning Your Cross-Examinations

It is inherently more difficult to plan a cross-examination than it is to prepare for direct. It is impossible to safeguard yourself against all surprises, but the following four steps will help keep them to a minimum.

First, compile a list of every potential adverse witness. Imagine why the witness is likely to be called. Ask yourself: "How can this witness most hurt my case?" Always prepare for the worst possible alternative.

Second, consider whether there is a basis for keeping the witness off the stand. Is the witness competent to testify? Is it possible to invoke a privilege? Then consider whether any part of the expected testimony might be excludable. For every statement that the witness might make, imagine all reasonable evidentiary objections. Do the same with all exhibits that might be offered through the witness. For each objection plan your argument and prepare for the likely counterargument. You won't want to make every possible objection, but you will want to be prepared.

Third, consider the factual weaknesses of each opposing witness. Are there inconsistencies that can be exploited or enhanced? Is the witness's character subject to attack? Can the witness be impeached from prior statements? How can the witness be used to amplify your own theme?

Finally, catalog all of the favorable information that you will be able to obtain from each opposing witness.

1.3.5 Reevaluating Everything You Have Done

Now that you have planned your case-in-chief and cross-examinations, it is imperative that you go back and reevaluate every aspect of your case. Do your direct examinations fully support and establish your theory? Do they leave any logical gaps? Are you satisfied that all of your necessary evidence will be admissible? Will it be credible? Do the potential cross-examinations raise issues with which you cannot cope? Will you be able to articulate your moral theme during most or all of the direct and cross-examinations? If you are unable to answer these questions satisfactorily, you may need to readjust your theory or theme.

Assuming that you are satisfied with your theory, you should now have an excellent idea of what the evidence at trial will be. With this in mind, go back again and rework your final argument. Make sure that it is completely consistent with the expected evidence and that it makes maximum use of the uncontroverted facts.

Consider eliminating any parts of the argument that rest too heavily on evidence that you anticipate will be severely contested. Be sure that you structure your argument so that you can begin and end with your theme and invoke it throughout. Finally, outline your opening statement, again beginning and ending with your theme, and raising each of the points to which you will return on final argument.

1.4 Conclusion

The following chapters discuss all aspects of persuasion at trial, from the opening statement to the final argument. Trial lawyers must master numerous forensic skills, procedural rules, and examination techniques, but your starting point must always be your theory of the case—the story that you want to tell.

Chapter Two

Trial Tools

A lawyer's goal at trial is to persuade the fact finder. Certainly one hopes that this may be achieved primarily as a result of the accuracy of the evidence, the integrity of the witnesses, the clarity of communication, and the rightness of the cause. It would be naive, however, to suggest that the lawyer's skills do not play a part in convincing a judge or jury to enter a favorable verdict. While it is unlikely that an unsupportable case can be won solely through polished advocacy, it is also beyond question that a good case can truly be lost as a result of an inadequate, muddled, or confused presentation.

The lawyer's tools discussed in this chapter may be employed to clarify, underscore, and emphasize your presentations at trial. Most of the techniques can be employed throughout all of the various stages of the trial. For example, the concept of "primacy" teaches that opening statements, direct examinations, cross-examinations, and final arguments should all be organized so that the very first moments are as memorable and important as possible. Other tools—such as sequenced questioning—obviously have more limited uses. In either case, the rationales and the general outlines of the methods are covered in this chapter, leaving their specific applications to the substantive chapters that follow.

This chapter is an overview. It describes the ways in which lawyers use their skills to present a case to a judge or jury. Faced with the challenge of limited time and attention, it is crucial that the advocate maximize the value of every opportunity to communicate with the fact finder. Arguments must get to the point as efficiently as possible, without sacrificing necessary details. Cross-examinations must be structured to draw out the desired conclusions without allowing the witness to equivocate or beg the question. This chapter is intended to help you recognize the broad concepts that underlie much of the lawyer's art.

This chapter is not an inventory of secret ploys. There is nothing here (or anywhere else) that will teach you how to trick witnesses into saying things they do not mean. In truth, the material in this chapter can be used more powerfully than that. It is a guide to precise and efficient communication. These methods can be used to allow your witnesses to say what they really mean. They can prevent opposing witnesses from obscuring what they really said. And they can enable you to present and argue the case that you really prepared.

2.1 Advocacy Tools

2.1.1 Organization

In trial work, how information is ordered may often make a significant difference in its persuasive impact. As we saw in chapter one, a trial presentation is a story, supported by a theory and explained by a theme. In the course of developing a trial story, some facts are more important than others, some facts are meaningful only in relation to others, and some facts need to be discounted or deemphasized. The following are some of the organizational principles and methods that lawyers use to attain these ends.

2.1.1.1 Primacy and Recency

The principles of primacy and recency may be applied to almost everything that a lawyer does in the course of a trial. In jury selection, opening statement, witness examination, final argument, even in making and responding to objections, the axiom holds true that people tend most to remember the things that they hear first and last. Thus, as a general rule, the most important points should come at the beginning and end of every presentation.

In opening statements and final arguments, therefore, the preferred practice is to start strong and end strong. Lawyers structure their presentations so as to make the most important and memorable impression on the fact finder. In direct examination, too, it is useful to begin by addressing a critical or decisive issue and to return to one at the end of the witness's testimony.

The realities of cross-examination, however, may sometimes dictate a slightly different approach. Because of the need to "feel out" or "lull" an uncooperative witness, it is often impractical to expect a cross-examination to start strong. Rather, you may have to use the beginning of the examination to stake out ground rules or to develop areas of agreement or important, uncontested facts. It is certainly true, though, that every effort should be made to make sure that cross-examinations end on a high note.

There are other times, as well, when the principle of primacy must give way to other strategies. For example, it may turn out that the case's most important point cannot really be understood until certain predicate information has been established. Or you may want to delay revealing a key point until opposing counsel, or opposing witnesses, have become committed in one direction or another.

An interesting corollary to the idea of primacy and recency is what might be called "interment." If the first and last points are remembered best, then it follows that the midpoints will be remembered least. In every trial there will be information that you believe you must mention, but that is embarrassing or potentially counterproductive.

The principle of interment tells you that the safest approach, therefore, is to bury this material deeply in the middle of the examination or argument.

There are two things to be said about primacy and recency. First, do not take the idea too literally. The concept of primacy does not necessarily refer to the very first words out of your mouth. In many examinations or arguments there will be a sort of preamble where you introduce yourself, engage in pleasantries, and generally warm up before you really begin. Of course, you will not want to extend this stage beyond its natural usefulness, but you may not want to forego it entirely. Therefore, it may be helpful to think of primacy as applying to the substantive beginning of the argument or witness examination, not to the introduction.

Finally, bear in mind that the doctrines of primacy and recency may be applied many times within a single argument or examination. Your final argument, for example, will no doubt consist of many distinct subparts. In most cases, you will want to lay out your theory, establish a chronology, review the positive evidence, discount the contrary evidence, comment on the credibility of one or more witnesses, and conclude with a reasoned request for a favorable verdict. As you move through the subparts, each one will begin and end. Thus, each subpart (not to mention the subparts within subparts) will present a new opportunity to start strong and end strong.

2.1.1.2 Sequencing

The term "sequencing" refers to the arrangement of discrete items of information within a particular argument or examination. Since trial presentations are necessarily linear, it seems obvious that they will be sequenced. This truism may be used to best effect, however, only if you bear in mind the various advantages that can be achieved by purposefully ordering information.

Foundation. The most basic use of sequencing is to make certain that all of the necessary predicate facts have been established before moving on to the ultimate point. In other words, do not jump to conclusions and, more importantly, do not expect the fact finder to jump with you. Assume that you are trying a case in which you are about to argue that your client was too well trained to have made a foolish error. Simple logic dictates a sequence that reviews her educational and professional accomplishments before you proclaim her immunity to silly mistakes.

Clarity. A second use of sequencing follows directly from the example above. Facts and arguments may be arranged to maximize the fact finder's understanding of the information. Thus, an argument can be made that the lawyer should choose to begin by telling the jurors that the client was too good at her job to make careless errors and then lay out the details of her training. That way they will have a context for the information as they receive it. Otherwise, the rather bland details of the client's professional background might be too boring to hold the jury's attention. Clarity of purpose enhances attention.

The point is not that one sequence is right and the other wrong. Rather, the point is that good lawyers will understand the many potential tactical values of sequencing and will therefore make conscious choices about how to use it.

Impact. Sequencing can increase the impact of information. Imagine, for example, that you are about to cross-examine a witness in a commercial case. Your claim is that the witness forgot to obtain insurance on a valuable shipment of goods. Through discovery you have learned that the witness was responsible for a series of eight to ten much smaller shipping errors over the past several years. If the witness's entire examination is conducted in strict chronological order, including other details of the witness's work history, these mistakes will probably seem unrelated and trivial. If they are sequenced together, however, they will take on much greater significance. And if they are arranged (nonchronologically) in order of importance, going from least to most significant, the examination can conclude with a virtual crescendo as the cross-examiner finally confronts the fateful failure to obtain the crucial insurance coverage. That's impact.

Commitment. As every cross-examiner knows, it is sometimes necessary to obtain commitment from a witness before proceeding into riskier territory. Perhaps you will want a witness to acknowledge reading a document before you confront him with an inconsistency. Perhaps you will want him to admit being in a certain place or belonging to a particular organization. These techniques are dealt with at some length in chapter four. Here it is sufficient to point out that careful sequencing is often the key to constraining a witness. Begin with the least controversial piece of information and advance slowly, step by step, up the ladder of commitment, reducing at each stage the witness's latitude to deny your eventual point.

2.1.1.3 Contrast and Apposition

The related concepts of contrast and apposition refer to the pairing or comparison of two (or more) pieces of information. Apposition is a technique that shows the relationship of facts; contrast underlines factual differences.

For example, suppose that the plaintiff and defendant in a battery case testified to diametrically opposite versions of events, the plaintiff claiming to be the victim of an unprovoked attack and the defendant asserting that he acted in self-defense. In final argument, the plaintiff's lawyer might be tempted to deal separately with each party's testimony. Utilizing contrast, however, the attorney could choose instead to compare the witnesses' credibility:

> My client was the victim of an assault, but the defendant cries "self-defense." When you decide who to believe, consider that the plaintiff has held a responsible job for the last twelve years and regularly volunteers at soup kitchens and homeless shelters, while the defendant is a convicted felon who has done time for larceny. Whose testimony should you trust? Let's look at the details.

The comparisons need not be negative. The apposition of facts can lead to positive conclusions as well. Consider an automobile accident case in which the defendant driver claims to have been driving carefully and certainly not speeding. On direct examination, a chronological narrative could not directly address the question of due care. Apposition, however, could underscore the elements of caution.

Q: Who were your passengers?

A: My two children.

Q: How were they seated?

A: They were both in the back. The seven-year-old was belted, and the baby was in a car seat.

Q: Were you driving within the speed limit at the time of the accident?

A: Of course. My children were in the car.

In effect, the presence of the children spotlights the driver's incentive to avoid speeding. Apposition strengthens the defendant's denial of carelessness, which would otherwise stand alone as a self-serving assertion.

2.1.1.4 Repetition and Duration

Repetition and duration are also related concepts; they are used to emphasize the significance of certain information. Stated simply, the more time you spend on a topic, the more important it will seem. Likewise, the more times you say it, the more likely it is to be believed, remembered, and understood. The lesson follows inescapably in every phase of the trial: dwell on important matters; minimize unnecessary details.

Unlike other organizing principles, repetition and duration can easily be both overdone and misused. First, dwelling on something does not require beating it into the ground. Even the most crucial, compelling, climactic evidence can be trivialized by extended overtreatment. Use repetition and duration, but always use them with restraint.

Finally, take care in deciding what to emphasize. If too many facts are repeated, repetition will lose its impact. Emphasizing everything is the equivalent of emphasizing nothing.

See demonstrations 1.1 and 1.2 in the Visuals Appendix.

2.1.2 Content

The previous section discussed the arrangement and ordering of information during the phases of a trial. This section addresses content. Of course, the specific details of evidence are unique to every trial. Here the meaning of content is more generic; it refers to word choice, use of language, question formation, and the like.

2.1.2.1 Details

One of the most important aspects of content is the use of smaller details to support a greater whole. In brief, large conclusions tend to be more persuasive when they are broken down and presented in their component parts. Using details can turn a bald claim into a reasoned, logical, well-founded proposition.

In trial advocacy, this device is best used by considering the conclusions that you want to impress upon the fact finder. Whether you will be asserting the specific conclusions in argument or drawing them out from individual witnesses, the next step is to divide each conclusion into its inherent evidentiary parts. Those evidentiary elements, in turn, become the platform on which your broader conclusions will rest. Here is how it works.

Assume that you represent the defendant in a burglary case. Your client claims that he had consent to enter the complainant's warehouse yard and remove certain goods in satisfaction of a debt. Stated as a conclusion, the defense rings hollow: "Sure, that's what everyone says when they're caught." Supportive details, however, add credibility and weight. Consider how some details might be developed during the defendant's direct examination:

Q: How did you know the complainant?

A: We had done business together over the years.

Q: How many years?

A: About four years. I remember when she opened her business. It was right before Memorial Day.

Q: What sort of business did you do together?

A: I bought most of my landscaping supplies from her. She had good prices, and I prefer not to deal with chain stores if I don't have to.

Q: How often did you purchase supplies?

A: About every other week, during the good weather.

Q: Why do you say that she owed you a debt?

A: I bought a load of patio stone from her, but it turned out to be poor quality, and I couldn't use it.

Q: What did you do?

A: I asked her to replace it with an adequate product.

Q: What did she say?

A: She didn't have any more, or any replacement material, but she said she would refund my money.

Q: Were you able to replace the stone?

A: Yes, but I had to buy it from a different supplier.

Q: What did you do with the original stuff?

A: Well, I asked her if she wanted it back, and she said I should just dump it.

Q: Did you?

A: Sort of. I left it in a pile on my back lot.

Q: Did you ever get your money back from the complainant?

A: No. She just kept promising to repay me.

Q: What did you do?

A: I told her she had to make good.

Q: Then what happened?

A: She finally said she'd make it up to me by giving me some other products. She said I could pick what I wanted out of her lot.

Note that it was not until the last question in the example above that the defendant was asked to explain why he removed the items from the complainant's property. The specifics of the past relationship, the story of the defective product, the repeated requests for repayment, and the promise of replacement goods were all predicate details that were necessary to support the defendant's eventual claim of authorization.

The ability to provide details bolsters the defendant's contention that the sequence of events actually occurred the way he says it did. More details, perhaps including the specifics of the various conversations, could make the testimony even stronger. Moreover, once the defendant has provided a detailed context, he can proceed to call other, hopefully neutral, witnesses to provide corroboration. Perhaps another customer will testify to the poor quality of the patio stone or an adjoining property owner will confirm the continuing presence of the rock pile on the defendant's lot. While neither of these facts constitutes direct proof of the complainant's consent, they definitely enhance the circumstantial credibility of the defendant's case.

Of course, the defendant still has some explaining to do, especially since the complainant has obviously denied that any agreement ever existed. Still, the defendant's position is greatly benefited by his ability to provide a detailed account of the context of events. From the fact finder's perspective, the absence of details would amount to a telling admission.

Constituent details can be used to tell a story during opening statement or to press home a point during final argument. They can add credibility to a witness's testimony on direct examination, and they can be drawn out of an opposing witness on cross. The watchword, of course, is judgment. The well-conceived use of key details will add ballast to your case; an overwhelming tangle of pointless details will only sink your ship.

See demonstrations 2.1 and 2.2 in the Visuals Appendix.

2.1.2.2 Reflection

Your ultimate goal as a trial lawyer is to create for the fact finder a mental image that mirrors your theory of the case. You want the judge or jurors to be able to close their eyes and see a picture of events just the way your client described them. One technique for creating that picture is called "reflective questioning," an approach that uses the pacing of language to evoke time, distance, or intensity.

The basic premise is straightforward: Speaking rapidly makes events seem faster, closer together, more intense, and more disorganized. Speaking slowly makes things seem slower, further apart, more reasoned, and more relaxed. Thus, you can reflect the story that you want to tell by varying your pace as you proceed with your argument or questioning.

If you believe that events went by so quickly that the witness could not have seen all that he claims, a rapid-fire cross-examination consisting of a few short questions is most likely the best way to convey that impression. If, on the other hand, you want to underscore a witness's extended opportunity to observe, then a deliberate, drawn out, detailed examination is probably the way to go.

The same approach can be applied to location and intensity. If the distance was short, speak quickly to convey that image. If the discussion was informal and casual, a leisurely pace will emphasize that fact. These principles hold true (as long as you don't overdo it) whenever you are speaking—opening statement, witness examination, or final argument.

See demonstrations 3.1 and 3.2 in the Visuals Appendix.

2.1.2.3 Evocation

Evocation is a fancy way of saying "word choice." As a trial lawyer, words are your stock in trade. Choose them carefully for maximum effectiveness. Remember that you are using words the way an artist uses paints or ink—you hope to draw a virtual picture of events, one that is authentic, memorable, and compelling.[1]

---

1. Of course, you will avoid complex, arcane, pretentious, lawyerly gibberish. That point is so obvious that it has been relegated to this footnote.

Nouns and Verbs

The most evocative words are nouns and verbs. This may seem counterintuitive; many lawyers think that adjectives are the best words for conjuring a mental image. But the fact is that adjectives tend to convey judgments, which makes them argumentative, which in turn can make them seem (at least) somewhat undependable to the fact finder. Nouns and verbs, however, suggest not a belief about something but rather the thing itself. Thus, the fact finder can immediately picture exactly what you are saying.

Consider this example. Suppose that someone told you that a certain automobile was "ugly." The adjective "ugly" conveys an aesthetic judgment. Depending on the speaker and the circumstances, you might agree with the characterization and you might not. Adding an adverb doesn't help. The car was really ugly. The car was incredibly ugly. Even with inflection, adjectives and adverbs often lack intrinsically descriptive power. They convey opinions, but not the bases for the opinions.

Now suppose that the same person told you that the automobile's paint had peeled off the doors and that its hood was so rusted that you could see right through to the engine in several places. The windshield was covered by a spider web of fracture lines. The tailpipe dragged on the ground. One fender was missing, and another was replaced by a mismatched part from a different model. The hubcaps were gone, and the trunk was held down with bungee cords. These nouns and verbs (helped out by an occasional participle) tell the whole story—that car was ugly!

Powerful Language

Another method of evocation is through the use of active, powerful language. In ordinary conversation, most people tend to qualify or temper their ideas simply as a matter of politeness or convention. How many times have you heard someone say, "It's probably a bad idea," or, "I think it might take around ten or fifteen minutes to get there," or, "I'd have to guess, but I suppose there weren't any more than thirty people at the meeting"? Such tentative use of language hardly raises an eyebrow during a casual exchange.

Trials are different. Trials are about persuasion. Trials are about certainty. Trials are about asking a fact finder to reject the other party's claims and to enter a verdict in your client's favor.

It is not arrogant to speak as though you are entitled to the outcome that you seek. After all, you know more about the merits of your case than anyone else.[2] And if you appear uncertain, why should the fact finder grant you a verdict?

2. Be aware, however, that professional responsibility rules prohibit counsel from asserting personal knowledge of facts or stating a personal opinion as to the merits of the case. Model Rule of Prof'l Conduct R. 3.4(E).

2.1.2.4 Visual Aids

A lawyer's words can evoke a picture, but a visual aid can be a picture. At every stage of the trial you can enhance the impact of your case with photographs, diagrams, charts, drawings, models, transparencies, enlargements, videos, and computer-generated graphics.

For most people, visual memory is notably more acute than aural memory. People remember what they see far better than what they hear. Thus, for the truly important points in your case, ask yourself, "How can this idea be illustrated?"

2.1.2.5 Headlines and Transitions

Lawyers often find it surprising, but most parts of most trials are just plain dull. Argument is seldom gripping, and most witness examinations tend to drag on and on. While some of this monotony is caused by mediocre advocacy, much of it is unavoidable. It is the law, not the lawyer, that requires the establishment of a foundation for business records or predicate testimony for a witness's ability to perceive or the qualification of a child witness or the basis for a voice identification or a handwriting exemplar.

Burdened by this millstone of tedium, the attorney's task is twofold. First, you must do your utmost to make it all as interesting as possible. Second, you must develop means to let the fact finder know when something actually interesting (and truly important) is about to happen. This last responsibility can be aided by the use of headlines, transitions, and signals.

A newspaper or Web site headline is printed in bold type so it will draw the readers' attention to the story below. A lawyer's headline serves the same purpose. It alerts the fact finder to the significance of the information that is about to follow. Although lawyers lack the advantage of distinctive typeface, the phrasing of headlines can perform the same function. In direct examination, a relatively modest headline might take this form:

> Let's talk about your background and education.

A much bolder headline, say during an opening statement, could be:

> This case is about three broken promises. Let me tell you about the first one.

And the equivalent of a screaming banner might come in final argument:

> The defendant is a murderer—and here is the one fact that proves it.

A transition is a specific type of headline, one that signals the end of one subject and the beginning of another. Transitions are particularly helpful when the movement is from a boring or technical area into something more substantive. Imagine that you have just taken a witness through one of the admittedly monotonous foundations for a voice identification, showing that the witness placed a telephone call to the number that was listed for the defendant in the relevant directory. Now, as you proceed to the nontechnical heart of the matter, you can refocus the fact finder's attention with a transition question: "After you reached the defendant at his listed phone, did you have a reaction to anything that he said?" Now the fact finder knows 1) that the defendant was reached, 2) that he spoke, and 3) that his words drew a "reaction" from the witness. The transition has done its work. The fact finder should be ready to listen, eager to find out why and how a phone call could cause a "reaction."

See demonstration 4 in the Visuals Appendix.

2.2 Demeanor

In a very real sense, a lawyer is "on trial" from the first moment he steps in front of the fact finder. Judge and jury will constantly evaluate (and reevaluate) your credibility as they assess your behavior, appearance, bearing, and conduct. They will observe your interactions with your client, with opposing counsel, with witnesses, and with the court. They will be alert to signs of confidence, authority, and professionalism, as well as subtle displays of doubt, misgiving, weakness, or betrayal. All lawyers want to make the right impression, yet there is no formula that tells you how to act, much less how to react. There is a place in the courtroom for lawyers of every background, origin, appearance, temperament, and personality type.

Perhaps the only universal indicator of success is sincerity. Insincere lawyers may yet win cases, but they do it in spite of themselves.

This section is not intended as a one-size-fits-all guide to lawyers' preferred appearance. Rather, the following sections will point out three important components of demeanor that can be helpful to all lawyers.

2.2.1 Integrity

Throughout every trial you will be asking the fact finder to trust you, to believe you, to credit your witnesses, to accept your arguments, and, ultimately, to bring back the verdict you request. Why should a judge or jury do that? Certainly, the compelling nature of your evidence should provide one reason, but most trials feature cogent evidence on both sides. And when the evidence is most nearly equal, the credibility of the lawyers can play a large part in shaping the trial's outcome. Integrity inspires trust, and, in trial work, trust leads to success.

What does integrity have to do with demeanor? Isn't integrity something that you have rather than something that you do or show in front of a jury? In the deepest sense, of course, integrity is part of your character, your fiber. You live your life according to principles because they are right, not because their display will help you win a trial. But judges and juries are not blind, and they are not easily fooled. Lawyers who lack integrity almost inevitably reveal themselves in court.

The word integrity comes from the Latin integritas, meaning wholeness or soundness, complete in itself. Thus, our concept of integrity has come to mean unsullied, unbroken, undivided moral principle. In other words, it is a quality of the "whole lawyer." It refers to you and everything you do. When you are seen to depart from a principle, you diminish your standing as an honorable advocate. Thus, there are numerous courtroom behaviors that can add to or detract from your realization as a "whole lawyer."

If nothing else, integrity means honesty. An honest lawyer does not overstate her case, does not promise evidence that she cannot deliver, and does not make arguments that she cannot support. Most important, an honest lawyer does not try to sneak excluded evidence into the trial and does not misuse objections or argument as a means of presenting inadmissible material.

Courtesy is also an aspect of integrity. It means that you do not use bullying tactics to intimidate your opponent or to put a timid witness in a bad light. It means that you do not attempt to distract the fact finder during your opponent's case, and you do not try to disrupt opposing counsel's legitimate presentation. You do not use facial expressions, grimaces, or gestures to "argue" your case while other arguments or examinations are proceeding.

Much more can be said of integrity as demeanor. For now, suffice it to say that integrity cannot be "faked." It is not a face or costume that you put on and take off. If you are truly committed to trying a case with integrity, it will show. If you are not, it will also show.

2.2.2 Confidence

A lawyer demonstrates confidence by knowing and operating within the rules of the court, by understanding how the judge wants the trial to proceed, and by demonstrating her awareness of proper procedure. A confident lawyer has prepared her examinations, is ready to call and cross-examine witnesses, and can argue evidentiary objections on the basis of advance preparation. A confident lawyer enters the courtroom knowing what she wants to accomplish, why she wants to accomplish it, and how she intends to do it.

A competent lawyer is well-organized and well-prepared. He knows where his exhibits can be found, how they are supposed to be numbered, and which witnesses are necessary to introduce them. He understands which documents can be used to impeach which witnesses, as well as the difference between impeachment and refreshing recollection. He realizes that not every valid objection must be made, and he knows how to explain to the court why his objections have merit.

In short, competence leads to confidence, and confidence is apparent to the fact finder. Disorganization and incompetence lead to insecurity, which is also obvious and can be damning.

2.2.3 *Consideration*

Consideration is a third component of winning demeanor. In a sense, consideration is an aspect of confidence in that insecurity and thoughtlessness are surely companion traits. In another sense, consideration is a facet of integrity since the "whole lawyer" will be concerned about the impact of her work on the court, jurors, witnesses, and others in the courtroom. Consideration is discussed as a separate category because it sums up the need to recognize the limits of what a lawyer may do in the name of advocacy.

A considerate lawyer is a forceful advocate who nonetheless understands the impact that his advocacy may have on others. That depth of understanding can be made evident in many ways. He will not interrupt the court, the witnesses, or opposing counsel (other than for an extremely good reason). He will make certain that he can be heard throughout the courtroom. He will listen to the judge's rulings and instructions, and he will try in good faith to comply. (And if his duty to his client ever compels him to talk back to the court or to resist a ruling, he will respectfully explain why.)

A respectful lawyer will not wage a war of attrition against witnesses or other lawyers, and certainly not against the court or the jurors. She will know when to request breaks in the proceeding and when to proceed for the benefit of others despite her own preferences. She may attack witnesses, but only when they have shown themselves to deserve it. She may joust with opposing counsel over professional issues, but not over personalities. She will not back down from a fight, but she will not start one as a tactic.

Most importantly, a respectful lawyer will realize that the trial is being conducted for the benefit of the fact finder. She will not conduct a seemingly private dialogue between herself and the witnesses. Rather, she will be sure to structure her examinations (both rhetorically and physically) so that they include the fact finder. Her exhibits will be large enough to be seen. Her language will be straightforward and uncomplicated. Her pace will be intelligible. She will make certain (within her power) that the fact finder has plenty of time to hear, digest, understand, and appreciate her evidence.

Need it be said? Judges and juries appreciate considerate lawyers.

2.3 Witness Preparation

Witness preparation could easily be the subject of an entire chapter, or even a book, but why is it included in the discussion of advocacy techniques? Witnesses absolutely are not advocates, and there are clear ethical limits on what a lawyer may do to enhance a witness's persuasiveness. On the other hand, every trial ultimately rests on the shoulders of the witnesses. It is they who provide the evidence, and it is their testimony that will eventually be believed or disregarded. That is how it should be. A trial is about information, facts, truth—a lawyer is only the guide.

It would be somewhat remiss, then, to ignore the subject of witness persuasiveness. It would be more remiss, however, to fail to caution that the lawyer's job goes no further than assisting a witness in effective and truthful communication. What makes a witness effective?

In many recent psychological studies, two traits stand out as well-accepted indicators of believability. All things being equal, a fact finder is more likely to believe a witness who exhibits both certainty and credible mastery of detail. Of course, these characteristics cannot be grafted onto a witness. At bottom, a witness either knows or does not know the details; the witness is either certain or uncertain. But witness preparation has a legitimate part to play.

A witness is more likely to be certain about her testimony if she has had ample time to consider it before taking the stand. In the heat of trial, surprise may look very much like doubt. A witness who hears a question for the very first time may well appear unsure, even if she really has no misgivings whatsoever about her answer. Consequently, it is the lawyer's job to relieve her witness of the burden of surprise. This can easily be done by informing the witness of the topics to be covered on direct examination and by alerting them to the probable areas of cross-examination. The more specifics, the better.

The same sort of preparation can help a witness achieve mastery of detail. Recall from our earlier discussion that corroborative details are the indicators of credibility. As a lawyer, you will understand the evidentiary importance of details in a way that a lay witness may not. For example, a witness who observed a nighttime robbery might truthfully testify that the scene of the crime was brightly lit. Without preparation, however, he would be unlikely to focus on the details of the street lighting: How far was the nearest lamppost? In what direction? How tall was it? Was it blocked by trees or billboards? Did it have one of the newer, high-intensity lamps? And there can be more to lighting than street lamps: Were there stores nearby? Did they have exterior signs? Did any of the adjacent houses have outside lights? Where? How many? How far? A witness should know that these details are important and should not have to think about them for the first time after taking the stand.

Witness testimony—the process of recollection and description—involves a number of discreet steps, with opportunities for error at each stage. First, the witness must have been in a position to observe the relevant events, free from obstruction or distraction. In addition, the witness must have been able to observe the entire event (or at least its most relevant aspects) rather than a misleading or unrepresentative part. Even then, however, there is no guarantee that the witness perceived the events accurately—she might have seen things out of context or from a biased perspective, or she may have misconstrued certain words and gestures. Next, of course, she has to understand everything she perceived, drawing accurate conclusions and avoiding unwarranted suppositions. When she finally gets to court—months or years later—she has to remember the crucial facts, without gaps or embellishment. But even total recall is not enough, because the witness must also articulate her recollections with sufficient clarity and in coherent order. Finally, the witness must stress the most important facts, without dwelling on trivia or meandering through meaningless details.

For all of those reasons, and more, it is essential for an attorney to thoroughly prepare every witness for the hazards and pitfalls inherent in testimony. Accuracy in communication is elusive for even the most thoughtful and careful witness, and it is the lawyer's job to identify and help overcome lurking errors.

Chapter Three

Persuasion Theory

Persuasion can be defined as the exercise of influence on the decisions of another. In the real world, then, persuasion can take many forms, ranging from a benign moral appeal to brutal coercion. In the context of trial work, persuasion is used in a more confined, stylized sense. It means the marshaling of argument, evidence, and procedure in a way likely to cause the fact finder to make the desired decision. Or, more succinctly, persuasion is the trial lawyer's input designed to influence the judge or jury's output.

However defined, the concept of persuasion goes hand in hand with decision making. To persuade people, you must first determine how they make their decisions. Equipped with that knowledge, you may then shape your approach to utilize the most effective means. For example, you would choose one set of arguments to convince, say, a devotee of astrology and a markedly different set when speaking to an astronomer, although the language—planets, moons, degrees of rotation—might have much similarity.

Juror decision making may be divided into two components. First, there is the way that each person makes his own choices. This process is highly individualized, some might say idiosyncratic. In all but the most high-stakes or important trials it is unlikely that lawyers will be allowed the sort of extensive voir dire that would be necessary to develop a working insight into the mind of each individual juror.[1] On the other hand, it is possible to learn a great deal about the way that people generally go about making choices. Cognition theory has much to say about typical styles and modes of decision making.

The objective of this section is to explore some of the more functional aspects of cognition theory. It will not be possible, of course, to review in detail the extensive literature on the subject, nor would it be particularly helpful to attorneys to engage in an extended evaluation of mountains of scholarly research. A number of academic fields have devoted substantial attention to the study of decision making, ranging from the highly theoretical (cognitive psychology) to the intensely practical (advertising). Sociologists, communication theorists, political scientists, neurobiologists, philosophers, linguists, and others have all weighed in on the subject,

1. *See* chapter fourteen.

producing a variety of hypotheses—sometimes agreeing and sometimes disagreeing. The broader conclusions of cognition research, distilled into a form that can most readily be used by trial lawyers, may be referred to as "script theory."

3.1 Script Theory

A "script" is a person's mental image or understanding of a certain context or set of events. Script theory posits that human beings do not evaluate facts in isolation, but rather tend to make sense of new information by fitting each new fact into a preexisting picture. A simple thought experiment can make this concept clearer. Think about these words and phrases: popcorn, coming attractions, tickets, summer blockbusters. What do you see in your mind? Chances are good that you have envisioned an entire movie theater, and not just any movie theater, but probably one that you have attended recently or often. That theater is your script. You can "see" the box office, the candy counter, the lobby, the posters. Even if you attempt self-consciously to focus on "popcorn" to the exclusion of the theater, you will probably envision a particular bag or box or bucket of popcorn familiar from your past experience.

The essence of script theory is that people dislike uncertainty and want to reduce it as quickly as possible. New information is confusing, especially when presented piece by piece. Thus, people "call up" scripts to impose order on uncertainty or confusion.

This theoretical insight can be of great practical value to lawyers. Do not expect a fact finder to view facts as discrete units, holding conclusions in abeyance until all of the information has been received. Understand instead that the process of decision-making begins immediately, with each fact finder developing a mental picture virtually in step with the opening words of the trial. To be sure, that picture is subject to constant change and refinement as new information is received and initial information is contradicted. Script theory, nonetheless, underscores the importance to advocates of organization, coherence, and storytelling.

3.2 How Script Theory Works

As we have seen, the input of new information will tend to evoke a script in the mind of the fact finder. This knowledge alone can be a formidable tool in the hands of a trial lawyer, but there is yet more to script theory.

3.2.1 Harmonization

A further human tendency is to attempt to harmonize new information with previously envisioned scripts. Thus, new facts will tend to be interpreted as consistent with the script, and flatly inconsistent facts will tend to be discredited or rejected.

Consequently, much of the trial process may be seen as a competition for the fact finder's imagination.

Return to the movie theater example. Suppose that someone told you: "I went into the theater and had a snack." Although the type of food was not named, your mind would almost certainly interpret the new information—snack—to be consistent with the old information—movie theater. Therefore, you would probably envision a candy bar, popcorn, or similar movie fare. You would not imagine carrot sticks, cannoli, or stir-fried noodles because those snacks are inconsistent with a movie-theater script.

Assume instead that someone said, "I went into a movie theater and changed the oil in my car." You would assume that the person was joking or lying or speaking metaphorically. Your "movie theater" script rejects automobile repair. Now, there is nothing unusual or undependable about someone recounting the story of an oil change; the fact itself carries no indicia of unreliability. Following a movie theater context, however, it becomes questionable because it is out of place. In other words, the new information is discredited because it is inconsistent with the script.

Now try one more variation: "I went to the movie theater for a four-star meal." The "movie theater" script would discredit this information unless it was accompanied by an explanation. "It's a new concept—cinema dinner theater." Now the script can change; the information has been harmonized.

Judges and jurors engage in a constant process of harmonization. Once a script has been adopted, they will interpret new information in light of that script until they have been persuaded or educated to do otherwise. Take heed: just as it is harder to change someone's mind than it is to make an initial impression, it is harder to change a script than to invoke one in the first place.

3.2.2 Gaps

All stories have gaps. It is humanly impossible to tell a story that contains all the details one might observe in daily life. Consequently, all trials have gaps. The introduction of evidence is limited, by the rules of admissibility and the endurance of the fact finder, to a minute fraction of what the witnesses really saw and did. This must be so lest the trial of even the simplest case go on forever, eventually outlasting even the most determined fact finder's capacity to hear and comprehend.

But the existence of gaps in the evidence does not mean that there will be gaps in the fact finder's understanding. Instead, script theory informs us that many of the gaps will be filled by the fact finder's reconstruction (some would say imagination). Recall that you are telling a story whenever you present evidence or argue a case. You have, more or less, active control over the information that you choose to present. Whenever you leave out a detail, however, that void is likely to be filled—consistent with a script—by the fact finder's own supposition. This is a process over which you have little or no control.

Consider the presentation of this simple story: "I went to a racetrack to see the ponies run. I made a few bets, but I didn't win a single one, so I had a drink and went home." This account has more gaps than it has information. Many of them will be filled in by the reader who may, among other things, imagine the number of horses, the color of their "silks," the distance from the track to the grandstand, the crowd along the rail, the lines at the betting windows, and all manner of other obvious details. If those details are inconsequential to the story then there is no risk to leaving them out. Let the reader imagine them however he wishes.

On the other hand, suppose that a detail is important. Suppose that the story-teller truly cares about one of the elements. Suddenly there is great risk to leaving it out. Return to the racetrack story. The relater of the story mentions having a "drink." What does your experience tell you about people's drinking habits at race-tracks? Beer? Whiskey? Diet soda? Lemonade? Whatever the beverage, it is almost certain that the gap will be filled. And if the story is being told in a trial, the nature of the drink might matter very much.

The lesson to be learned is that the absence of evidence is not the same as the absence of information. It is only the absence of explicitly spoken information. Do not assume that the fact finder isn't thinking about something, or even relying on it, simply because there has been no evidence given. Of course, you cannot try a case without leaving gaps. That would be impossible to do and unbearable to attempt. Instead, your job is to fill the important gaps and set the stage for the fact finder to fill the others in your favor.

3.2.3 Inferences

How, exactly, do fact finders fill in gaps? One way is through the operation of inferences. In script theory, an inference is a mental conclusion that accept-ably ties together a series of facts or episodes. An inference tends to impose logic or a sense of relationship on information, whether or not that conclusion is justified in fact. People use inferences to solve problems or resolve puzzling situations, "inferring" solutions or results on the basis of the data presented. For example, if you received a never-ending series of invoices for a bill that had already been paid, you might resolve the mystery by resorting to a "computer error" inference, concluding that your problem was caused by an uncorrectable software glitch.

Unlike individual scripts, which vary from person to person according to experi-ence, there are a number of fairly common (if not quite universal) inferences that are frequently employed in decision-making. Be aware that these inferences are only habits of mind or well-recognized thought patterns. They explain how people may make decisions, but they do not always lead to factually correct results.

3.2.3.1 The Coherence Inference

The coherence inference suggests that stories that fit together are more likely to be true. A corollary is that stories are less likely to be true if they exhibit inconsistencies or unexplained contradictions. As every historian, journalist, and trial lawyer knows, inconsistency is no bar to truth. Given the extraordinary breadth of human perception, recall, and ability to relate, even the "truest" accounts may be rife with conflicting, even paradoxical, details. Still, the coherence inference is powerful and extremely difficult to overcome. It teaches us that trial counsel must strive for a theory that minimizes inconsistencies, accounts for those that cannot be eliminated, and exploits the ones left vulnerable by the other side's story.

3.2.3.2 The Causation Inference

The causation inference assumes that events in a sequence have caused each other to occur. This conclusion is a logical fallacy, often summed up in the Latin phrase post hoc ergo propter hoc—following this therefore because of this. There is no necessary or automatic relationship between sequence and cause, although there may be one in any particular factual situation. For example, because the air temperature usually feels colder after a summer rainstorm it is not uncommon for people to believe that the rain "cooled things off." Actually, the opposite is more often true: the arrival of a cold front causes condensation, which then makes it rain.

It is important for trial lawyers to understand the causation inference because it can have an important impact on how evidence is interpreted. Since trials are linear events, all facts are presented in some sequence or another. Recognizing that the fact finder will be inclined to attribute causation to each series, counsel may take the necessary steps either to enhance the phenomenon or to counteract it.

3.2.3.3 The Goal Inference

Under this inference, proof of a person's goal is taken as evidence of prior consistent action. In reality, this may or may not be the case. People often have multiple goals, and they are capable of tempering their activity for various reasons. For example, in an automobile accident case, assume it has been proven that the defendant driver was late for an important meeting. From his admitted objective (arriving on time for the meeting) the goal inference would lead to a conclusion that he acted consistently (by speeding). Of course, he may have had another goal as well, say, avoiding accidents and traffic violations, in which case the inference would be that he drove carefully. There is no guaranteed way to win this deductive battle, but you are certain to lose it if you are not constantly aware of the power of the goal inference.

3.2.3.4 The Availability Inference

The availability inference draws on the tendency to believe that a newly observed event falls into a frequently encountered or well-known category. A witness who has seen numerous traffic violations by, say, little red sports cars will tend to assume that every red convertible is likely to speed or change lanes abruptly. The image of an irresponsible or risk-taking sports-car owner is "available" and may therefore be used to categorize otherwise cautious drivers based only on the color and model of their automobiles.

3.2.3.5 Other Common Inferences

The pattern inference may create the illusion of relationships among isolated occurrences. Closely related is the hindsight inference, which suggests that an event was foreseeable (and therefore preventable) simply because it ultimately occurred. The representativeness inference leads to assessments based on generalities that overlook atypical or inconsistent factors, whereas the attribution inference does just the opposite by focusing on a single (usually negative) characteristic to the exclusion of everything else.

3.3 What Script Theory Does Not Do

Script theory does nothing more than provide us with a positive description of how people tend to think and make decisions. It is not a means of subliminal manipulation, nor is it a magic key that allows lawyers to invade and control the fact finder's innermost motivations. Indeed, scripts may often be called up intentionally as a method of arriving at rational decisions. For example, a physician's "decision tree," essential to the diagnosis and treatment of many illnesses, involves the rapid consideration of a series of evaluative scripts. It may be best, therefore, to think of script theory as a sort of language, an approach that best allows counsel to address the fact finder in terms that are most likely to be understood.

3.3.1 Overcoming Scripts

The most important thing to know about script theory is that it exists. The second most important thing is that scripts are far from immutable. People can be persuaded to reject or abandon scripts just as they can be persuaded to change their minds about other matters. The best way to neutralize a script is with a counter-script—provide the fact finder with a different and equally compelling context into which she can fit the trial's information. As with the construction of any initial narrative, a counter script can be made more compelling through harmonization and inference.

A further technique is what has been called "story framing" or the connection of your theory to a familiar narrative structure. Assume, for example, that you represent the defendant in the fire truck case, discussed in chapter one, and the plaintiff's opening statement successfully drew on a "hurried driver" script. It is probably safe to assume that the jurors have envisioned a scenario in which the driver (meaning your client) has taken dozens of small chances to get to his meeting on time. In your opening statement you could, of course, flatly deny each of the specifics: he didn't run the yellow light; he didn't speed; he didn't lane hop. But the harmonization principle tells us that such new information—by now inconsistent with the established script—stands a good chance of being rejected.

Story framing allows you to take a different approach by suggesting an alternative narrative—one that is, hopefully, even more familiar (or more acceptable) than the plaintiff's. What would constitute a "careful driver" story? If the facts support it, perhaps you could structure your opening statement around the idea that the defendant is a fastidious car owner, the type of person whose automobile is his prized possession and who dotes on it as most people would on a newborn. He keeps his car covered in a garage; he waxes it in the park every weekend; he allows no smoking, drinking, coughing, or dirty shoes in its interior; and he would cover it in bubble-wrap if that were an option. By the end of this story, you want the fact finder to imagine your client in a straw hat and bow tie, the sort of person who accelerates slowly (if at all) and brakes gently (at the slightest cause). Then you can explain that he was being his characteristically careful self on the day of the accident.

3.3.2 Active and Passive Processing

Reliance on scripts and inferences generally recedes when a decision maker engages in what is called "active processing" and intensifies during periods of "passive processing."

Active processing occurs when the decision maker displays a high level of interest and pays deliberate attention to the material being received. Passive processing occurs when active processing is suspended because of inattention, disinterest, overload, or some other reason. Courtroom fact finders, of course, are expected to engage in active processing at all times, but their ability to do so is limited. Judges, and jurors even more so, are ultimately passive participants in a trial. They are not allowed to leave their seats, they are not encouraged to ask questions, they cannot pursue ideas that seem interesting, they cannot request a certain order of evidence. They are, by and large, confined to sitting and listening—a virtual prescription for passive processing. Try as they might to stay focused, it is inevitable that jurors' minds will wander. That does not mean they have ceased receiving information or hearing the evidence, it simply means that they have suspended (for the moment) their full, active attention.

Active processing (also called systematic or high-level processing) engages the decision maker's sense of responsibility. When operating in this mode, a fact finder is most open to arguments based on plausibility, relevance, and logic and is less affected by nonverbal signals and unproven inferences. Conversely, passive processing (also called low-level or low-engagement processing) is more likely to employ intuitive decision-making tools such as deference to experts; reliance on popular opinion; and presumed, scripted, or imagined links between otherwise unrelated items of information.

As a trial lawyer you have considerably more control over active inputs than you do over a fact finder's passive assumptions. You should therefore strive to maintain active engagement, especially during the logic-dependent, less intuitive portions of your case. Active processing can be encouraged through a variety of techniques, many of which were discussed in the preceding chapter, such as pacing, organization, and using visual aids. Most importantly, it can be accomplished by self-consciously talking to the fact finder. That is, by regarding the decision-maker as a participant in the trial and not merely as a member of the audience.

Certainly no one has ever doubted that trial lawyers want judges and jurors to pay attention. What, if anything, does awareness of processing modes add to that truism? The answer is this. It is impossible for any fact finder to pay constant, close attention to everything that happens at trial. The opposite of attention, however, is not a thoughtless void. An inattentive juror has not completely tuned out the trial. If that were the case, the problem of inattention could be remedied simply through repetition. An understanding of passive processing, however, tells us that when concentration wanes, many other decision-making devices take over. The jurors do not stop thinking, rather they begin thinking differently. A successful trial lawyer, therefore, must intentionally plan each case in a way calculated to appeal to both the active and passive modes of decision making.

3.4 Credibility Factors

A number of variables in presentation have been found to affect the decision-maker's receptiveness to persuasion. Though hardly immutable, these tend to hold true whether the fact finder is engaged in active or passive processing and whether or not she is relying on prior scripts or inferences. A discussion of some of these factors—both positive and negative—follows.

3.4.1 Rapport

The existence of rapport exercises a strongly positive impact on openness to persuasion. All things being equal, a fact finder is more likely to accept the position of someone who is likable, engaging, interested, committed, and lively. All of these factors are more or less within the control of the advocate, so there is seldom an excuse for failing to attempt to develop rapport with the judge or jurors.

The rapport phenomenon also has its downside. Studies have shown that jurors are also somewhat more likely to credit the arguments of lawyers who are tall, "attractive," and, shall we say, demographically similar to the jurors themselves. Fortunately, these biases are often unconscious and can usually be neutralized through skillful, rapport-building advocacy.

3.4.2 Reporting Bias

The appearance of self-interest tends to negate credibility. Conversely, a communicator is more likely to be believed when violating apparent self-interest. Lawyers and parties, of course, are self-interested by definition. Nothing can be done to make a lawyer seem to be objective about his client's case. Any such efforts are likely to seem insincere or deceptive.

On the other hand, the phenomenon of reporting bias tells us much about how to present a case to a jury. First, we must understand that concessions will be taken very seriously. You must therefore be extremely careful about making admissions, because every concession will be given extraordinary evidentiary weight by the fact finder. This is not to say that you should contest every point to the bitter end. A prudent concession may have great persuasive force since it will counteract the reporting bias and make your other evidence seem more credible. Nonetheless, concessions should be made only after serious analysis and never as the result of carelessness or fatigue.

Recognize also that concessions may be made implicitly and through silence. Thus, for example, a promise to produce certain evidence may be taken as an implicit admission that the evidence is crucial to your case. If the evidence is not ultimately produced that silence may stand as an unspoken acknowledgment that you have failed in your proof.

Finally, always be mindful of the points your opponent may have conceded. The reporting bias phenomenon tells us that information favorable to your case will be deemed more reliable if it was produced by the other side. Thus, on cross-examination you should be alert to the possibility of establishing points that are positive for your case, even if you could bring out the same information through your own witnesses. In argument, of course, you will take care to point out all of the favorable evidence that was produced by the other side. And you will be doubly certain to exploit any inadvertent or implicit admissions that may have been made by the opposing party, counsel, or witnesses.

3.4.3 Knowledge Bias

An apparent command of relevant information correlates strongly with believability. Conversely, the appearance of limited knowledge tends to diminish the credibility of both witnesses and lawyers.

For counsel, this insight means only one thing: be prepared. Solid preparation is not only intrinsically valuable; it is also rhetorically powerful. A steady command of the facts provides counsel with an essential edge.

Witnesses, too, can benefit or be harmed by knowledge bias. Thus, on direct examination a witness's credibility may be bolstered by showing that he knows all that he ought to know. For example, the police officer who investigated an automobile accident might be asked to describe the surrounding intersection, even if that information is not strictly relevant to his report on the collision. By the same token, cross-examination could be used to emphasize a witness's lack of knowledge in circumstances where a credible person would be expected to know the answers.

3.4.4 Fluency

Fluency adds to credibility. Ease of communication, visible comfort level, the ability to speak without stammering or pausing—all of these seem to create an image of knowledge and reliability. Interestingly, a number of studies have concluded that rapid speaking (to a point) tends to increase believability. This seems counterintuitive given the generally poor reputation of the "fast-talking lawyer," and there certainly must be substantial regional variation in the way that rapid speaking is received. No doubt, unnaturally slow speech is taken as an indicator of uncertainty or worse. As pace increases, it will eventually reach an optimum level—fast enough to be convincing, but not so fast as to seem slick or devious.

3.4.5 Sleeper Effect

Over time people tend to forget the source of information, even while remembering what was said. Thus, high credibility and low credibility sources tend to converge in the fact finder's memory. While this phenomenon is far from absolute, it has significant implications for presenting evidence at trial. Perhaps the most important lesson is that evidence can be strengthened by using multiple witnesses for the same point, particularly if one witness has been impeached or contradicted.

The sleeper effect, however, can be overcome by reminding the fact finder of the source of the information. This is a lesson for final argument. It may not be sufficient to caution the jurors that a key opposing witness has been proven unreliable, because the sleeper effect may attribute that witness's testimony to other, more credible sources. Therefore, the jurors should be told precisely which information to reject and why.

3.4.6 Forewarning

A fact finder is less likely to accept information if she has been warned in advance of a reason to reject it. In other words, attacks on credibility (or plausibility) may be more effective if they are made before the challenged testimony rather than after it. This insight suggests that credibility-linked issues should be introduced during opening statements. It also suggests that one's case-in-chief (particularly for the plaintiff) ought to address the reliability of opposing witnesses. A third implication goes to the timing of so-called "defensive" direct examination. In a defensive direct, counsel prompts her own witness to reveal weaknesses or shortcomings so as to blunt the impact of cross-examination. The forewarning phenomenon, however, indicates that the fact finder, once alerted to the witness's flaws, may be inclined to devalue some or all of the following testimony. Consequently, defensive direct should come after the substantive testimony, not before. The same holds true for "defensive" segments of the opening statement or final argument.

3.4.7 Reciprocity

Many studies have shown that the human impulse to reciprocate can have enormous impact on an individual's actions and decisions. Put simply, we are all virtually hardwired to return favors and share obligations. The anthropologist Richard Leakey has gone so far as to posit that it was the reciprocation instinct that first allowed our hominid ancestors to develop social and cultural relationships. Modern advertisers and marketers understand this principle very well, realizing that the offer of a sample or so-called "free gift" can significantly increase sales. Charities too have discovered that the offer of a premium—even something as small as a coffee mug or tote bag—can dramatically raise contribution levels.

Needless to say, a lawyer may never offer a gift or favor to a judge or juror. Nevertheless, a lawyer may take advantage of the reciprocity phenomenon by extending his trust to the decision-maker. An attorney who demonstrates trust in the jury will be trusted in return. A lawyer who trusts the judge will likely be relied on by the court. Trust can be demonstrated in multiple ways: Do not ask for frequent side bars. Do not make repeated objections concerning unimportant evidence. Do not interrupt the judge or continue arguing after a ruling. Do not allow your face to show unhappiness or disagreement. Do not belabor minor points, or even major points once everyone has gotten the idea.

In short, a lawyer who expresses faith in the fact finder will usually be trusted in return.

3.4.8 Social Proof

It may not always be flattering to contemplate, but people often tend to follow the crowd. We like to read bestsellers, eat at trendy (and therefore crowded) restaurants, attend popular films, and cheer for winners. Psychologists refer to this phenomenon as "social proof," meaning that we tend to conform our ideas to the behavior and expectations of others and, more specifically, that we tend to "view a behavior as correct in a given situation to the degree that we see others performing it."[2]

2. R. Cialdini, Influence: Science and Practice 100 (4th ed. 2001).

Lawyers and witnesses, therefore, can enhance their credibility by conforming to social expectations. More importantly, a case theory can be made more persuasive by emphasizing the "normality" of your evidence and your claims. Of course, there is room in the legal world for unconventional lawyers and novel claims or defenses; and you must more or less take your witnesses as they come. Nonetheless, social proof will always exert powerful influence on the fact finder, and it is therefore a good idea to reinforce your case by showing that it accords with ordinary expectations.

3.4.9 Scarcity

It is an old but true observation that people place disproportionate value on scarce resources. From diamond jewelry to rare stamps to special deals that are offered "for a limited time only," there is almost nothing that will make an object more desirable than the fact that it is hard to get.

But how can lawyers take advantage of the scarcity principle? After all, don't we always want our evidence to be accessible and our witnesses to be easily understandable and forthcoming? In fact, the scarcity principle can play only a limited role at trial. Some witnesses—usually, but not always, experts—may have expended considerable effort gathering information. The evidence may have been hard to compile (as with a statistical survey), or deeply obscured (as in the case of an accident or fire), or even dangerous to obtain (for example, by an undercover police officer). In these and similar situations, it is important to emphasize the "scarcity" of the evidence, because that will almost certainly increase its perceived value.

3.4.10 Deception

Fact finders inevitably believe that they can determine the truthfulness of a witness based on the person's demeanor while testifying. Indeed, this principle is all but enshrined in our procedural law, which prevents appellate courts from second-guessing a trial judge or jury's superior opportunity to observe the witnesses. It is disquieting, however, to realize that most research indicates an extremely high error rate in distinguishing truth from deceit. Studies have consistently found that observers are wrong between 30 and 60 percent of the time when determining whether a witness is telling the truth or lying. Interestingly, it appears that almost no profession does better than any other when it comes to accurately evaluating the truthfulness of others. Judges, police officers, social workers, and psychiatrists all scored in the same range as the general population.

Nonetheless, people express great certainty in the belief that verbal and nonverbal conduct can provide clues that will reveal lying. Recent studies have identified a series of behaviors that are widely assumed to be indicators of deception. The verbal cues most closely associated with deceit include short responses, higher pitch, hesitation, speech errors (garbled, incomplete sentences), and resorting to generalizations instead of details. Additionally, constant use of self references—such as "to be honest with you" or "to tell the truth"—was perceived as indicating untruthfulness. Nonverbal manifestations of deceit were thought to include blinking, grinning, shifting posture, and frequent hand movements.

It is important to bear in mind that none of the supposed indicators have ever actually been shown to correlate generally with falsity. In any individual witness, the conduct may as easily demonstrate nervousness as untruthfulness. Still, fact finders cannot avoid judgments based on perception, so trial lawyers must be aware that certain behavior is likely to be perceived as signifying deceit. You will therefore want to purge all such behaviors from your own repertoire and do what you can to avoid it in your witnesses. In an extreme case, you might choose not to call a truthful witness who, for whatever reason, exhibits many of the external signs of dishonesty. You will certainly want to be alert to such negative signs in opposing witnesses, using them to highlight your own arguments about their credibility.

Chapter Four

Direct Examination

4.1 The Role of Direct Examination

Cases are won on direct examination.

Direct examination is your opportunity to present the substance of your case. It is the time to offer the evidence that will establish the facts you need to prevail. Having planned your persuasive story, you must now prove the facts on which it rests by eliciting the testimony of witnesses.

Direct examination, then, is the heart of your case. It is the fulcrum of the trial—the aspect on which all else turns. Every other aspect of the trial is derivative of direct examination. Opening statements and final arguments are simply the lawyer's opportunity to comment on what the witnesses have to say; cross-examination exists solely to allow the direct to be challenged or controverted. While we could easily imagine a reasonably fair trial system consisting solely of direct examinations, it is impossible to conceive of anything resembling accurate fact-finding in their absence.

Direct examinations should be designed to accomplish one or more of the following basic goals.

4.1.1 Introduce Undisputed Facts

In most trials there will be many important facts that are not in dispute. Nonetheless, such facts usually cannot be considered by the judge or jurors—and will not be part of the record on appeal—until and unless they have been placed in evidence through a witness's testimony.[1] Undisputed facts will often be necessary to establish an element of your case. Thus, failing to include them in direct examination could lead to an unfavorable verdict or reversal on appeal.

Assume, for example, that you represent the plaintiff in a case involving damage to the exterior of a building and that the defense in the case is consent. Even if the question of ownership of the premises is not in dispute, it is still an element of your

1. Undisputed facts may also be introduced through stipulation or by judicial notice.

cause of action. Thus, you must present proof that your client had a possessory or ownership interest in the building or run the risk of a directed verdict in favor of the defendant.

4.1.2 Enhance the Likelihood of Disputed Facts

The most important facts in a trial will normally be those in dispute. Direct examination is your opportunity to put forward your client's version of the disputed facts. Furthermore, you must not only introduce evidence on disputed points, you must do so persuasively. The true art of direct examination consists in large part of establishing the certainty of facts that the other side claims to be uncertain or untrue.

4.1.3 Lay Foundations for the Introduction of Exhibits

Documents, photographs, writings, tangible objects, and other forms of real evidence will often be central to your case. With some exceptions, it is necessary to lay the foundation for the admission of such an exhibit through the direct testimony of a witness. This is true whether or not the reliability of the exhibit is in dispute. It is not unusual for a witness to be called only for the purpose of introducing an exhibit. The "records custodian" at a hospital or bank may know absolutely nothing about the contents of a particular report, but nonetheless may be examined solely in order to qualify the document as a business record.

4.1.4 Reflect on the Credibility of Witnesses

The credibility of a witness is always in issue. Thus, every direct examination, whatever its ultimate purpose, must also attend to the credibility of the witness's own testimony. For this reason, most direct examinations begin with some background information about the witness. What does she do for a living? Where did she go to school? How long has she lived in the community? Even if the witness's credibility will not be challenged, this sort of information helps to humanize her and therefore adds weight to what she has to say.

You can expect the credibility of some witnesses to be attacked on cross-examination. In these situations, you can blunt the assault by bolstering the witness's believability during direct examination. You can strengthen a witness by eliciting the basis of her knowledge, her ability to observe, or her lack of bias or interest in the outcome of the case.

You may also call a witness to reflect adversely on the credibility of the testimony of another. Direct examination may be used, for example, to introduce negative character or reputation evidence concerning another witness. Alternatively, you may call a witness to provide direct evidence of bias or motive, to lay the foundation for an impeaching document, or simply to contradict other testimony.

4.1.5 Hold the Attention of the Trier of Fact

No matter which of the above purposes predominates in any particular direct examination, it must be conducted in a manner that holds the attention of the judge or jury. In addition to being the heart of your case, direct examination also has the highest potential for dissolving into boredom, inattention, and routine. Since it has none of the inherent drama or tension of cross-examination, you must take extreme care to prepare your direct examination in a way that maximizes its impact.

4.2 The Law of Direct Examination

The rules of evidence govern the content of all direct examinations. Evidence offered on direct must be relevant, authentic, not hearsay, and otherwise admissible. In addition, there is a fairly specific "law of direct examination" that governs the manner and means in which testimony may be presented.

4.2.1 Competence of Witnesses

Every witness called to testify on direct examination must be legally "competent" to do so. This is generally taken to mean that the witness possesses personal knowledge of some matter at issue in the case,[2] is able to perceive and relate information, is capable of recognizing the difference between truth and falsity, and understands the seriousness of testifying under oath or on affirmation.[3]

In the absence of evidence or other indications to the contrary, all individuals called to the stand are presumed competent to testify.[4] If the competence of a witness is reasonably disputed, it may be necessary to conduct a preliminary examination in order to "qualify" the witness. Such inquiries are usually conducted by the direct examiner, but may also be conducted by the trial judge. In either case, the examination must be directed to that aspect of competence that has been called into question.

In the case of a very young child, for example, the qualifying examination must establish that the witness is capable of distinguishing reality from fantasy, is able to perceive such relationships as time and distance, and appreciates that it is "wrong to tell a lie." Following the preliminary examination, the adverse party should be allowed an opportunity to conduct a "voir dire," which is a preliminary cross-examination limited to a threshold issue such as competence.[5]

Note that there are several exceptions to the general rules of competence. Expert witnesses, for example, are excused from the requirement of testifying exclusively

2. Fed. R. Evid. 602.
3. *Id.* 603.
4. *Id.* 601.
5. *See infra* section 9.2.3.1.

from personal knowledge.[6] Judges and jurors are generally disqualified from giving evidence in cases in which they are involved.[7]

4.2.2 Nonleading Questions

The principal rule of direct examination is that the attorney may not "lead" the witness.[8] A leading question is one that contains or suggests its own answer. Since the party calling a witness to the stand is presumed to have conducted an interview and to know what the testimony will be, leading questions are disallowed to ensure that the testimony will come in the witness's own words.

Whether a certain question is leading is frequently an issue of tone or delivery, as much as one of form. The distinction, moreover, is often finely drawn. For example, there is no doubt that this question is leading:

Q: Of course, you crossed the street, didn't you?

Not only does the question contain its own answer, its format also virtually demands that it be answered in the affirmative.

On the other hand, this question is not leading:

Q: Did you cross the street?

Although the question is highly specific and calls for a "yes" or "no" answer, it does not control the witness's response.

Finally, this question falls in the middle:

Q: Didn't you cross the street?

If the examiner's tone of voice and inflection indicate that this is meant as a true query, the question probably will not be considered leading. If the question is stated more as an assertion, however, it will violate the leading question rule.

There are, in any event, numerous exceptions to the rule against leading questions on direct examination. A lawyer is generally permitted to lead a witness on preliminary matters, on issues that are not in dispute, to direct the witness's attention to a specific topic, to expedite the testimony on nonessential points, and, in some jurisdictions, to refresh a witness's recollection. In addition, it is usually permissible to lead witnesses who are very young, extremely old, infirm, confused, or frightened. Finally, it is always within the trial judge's discretion to permit leading questions to make the examination effective for the ascertainment of the truth, avoid needless consumption of time, protect the witness from undue embarrassment, or as is otherwise necessary to develop the testimony.

---

6. Fed. R. Evid. 703.
7. *Id.* 605–606.
8. Fed. R. Evid. 611(c).

In the absence of extreme provocation or abuse, most lawyers will not object to the occasional use of leading questions on direct. It is most common to object to leading questions that are directed to the central issues of the case or that are being used to substitute the testimony of counsel for that of the witness.

4.2.3 Narratives

Another general rule is that witnesses on direct examination may not testify in "narrative" form. The term narrative has no precise definition, but it is usually taken to mean an answer that goes beyond responding to a single specific question. Questions that invite a lengthy or run-on reply are said to "call for a narrative answer."

An example of a non-narrative question is, "What did you do next?" The objectionable, narrative version would be, "Tell us everything that you did that day." As with leading questions, the trial judge has wide discretion to permit narrative testimony. Narratives are often allowed, indeed encouraged, when the witness has been qualified as an expert.[9]

4.2.4 The Nonopinion Rule

Witnesses are expected to testify as to their sensory observations. What did the witness see, hear, smell, touch, taste, or do?

Witnesses other than experts generally are not allowed to offer opinions or to characterize events or testimony. A lay witness, however, is allowed to give opinions that are "rationally based on the witness's perception."[10] Thus, witnesses will usually be permitted to draw conclusions on issues such as speed, distance, volume, time, weight, temperature, and weather conditions. Similarly, lay witnesses may characterize the behavior of others as angry, drunken, affectionate, busy, or irrational.

4.2.5 Refreshing Recollection

Although witnesses are expected to testify in their own words, they are not expected to have perfect recall. The courtroom can be an unfamiliar and intimidating place for all but the most experienced witnesses, and witnesses can suffer memory lapses due to stress, fatigue, discomfort, or simple forgetfulness. Under these circumstances the direct examiner may "refresh" the witness's recollection. While it is most common to rekindle a witness's memory by using a document such as her prior deposition or report, a photograph, an object, a leading question may also be used.

---

9. Many lawyers prefer to present expert testimony in narrative form, but this often interferes with effective communication. *See* section 8.5.3.
10. Fed. R. Evid. 701.

To refresh recollection with a document, you must first establish that the witness's memory is exhausted concerning a specific issue or event. You must then determine that her memory might be refreshed by reference to a certain writing. Next, show the writing to the witness, allow her time to examine it, and ask whether her memory has returned. If the answer is "yes," remove the document and request the witness to continue her testimony. Note that in this situation the testimony must ultimately come from the witness's own restored memory; the document may not be offered as a substitute.[11]

See demonstration 5 in the Visuals Appendix.

4.3 Planning Direct Examination

There are three fundamental aspects to every direct examination plan: content, organization, and technique.

Your principal tool in presenting a persuasive direct examination is, of course, the knowledge of the witness. If the underlying content of the examination is not accurate and believable, the lawyer's technique is unlikely to make any noticeable difference. Your primary concern, then, must be content—the existence of the facts that you intend to prove.

You can enhance the content of a direct examination through organization, language, focus, pacing, and rapport. Effective organization requires sequencing an examination in a manner that provides for logical development, while emphasizing important points and minimizing damaging ones. You should ask questions in language that directs the progress of the examination without putting words in the witness's mouth. A direct examination uses focus to underscore and expand on the most crucial issues, rather than allow them to be lost in a welter of meaningless details. Pacing varies the tone, speed, and intensity of the testimony to ensure that it does not become boring. Finally, the positive rapport of the direct examiner with the witness is essential to establish the witness's overall trustworthiness and believability.

4.3.1 Content

Content—what the witness has to say—must be the driving force of every direct examination. Recall that direct examination provides your best opportunity to prove your case. It is not meant merely as a showcase for the witness's attractiveness or for your own forensic skills. The examination must have a central purpose. It must either establish some aspect of your theory, or it must contribute to the persuasiveness of your theme. Preferably, it will do both.

Begin by asking yourself: "Why am I calling this witness?" To break it down further, which elements of your claims or defenses will the witness address? How

11. *Id.* 612.

can the witness be used to controvert an element of the other side's case? What exhibits can be introduced through the witness? How can the witness bolster or detract from the credibility of others who will testify? How can the witness add moral strength to the presentation of the case or appeal to the jurors' sense of justice?

Since a witness might be called for any or all of the above reasons, you must exhaustively determine all of the possible useful information. List every conceivable thing that the witness might say to explain or help your case.

Now you must begin to prioritize and discard. This is a ruthless process. In direct examination, length is your enemy. You must work to eliminate all nonessential facts that are questionable, subject to impeachment, cumulative, distasteful, implausible, distracting, or just plain boring.

4.3.1.1 What to Include

First, go through a process of inclusion. List the witness's facts that are necessary to establish your theory. What is the single most important thing that the witness has to say? What are the witness's collateral facts that will make the central information more plausible? What is the next most important part of the potential testimony? What secondary facts make that testimony more believable? Continue this process for every element of your case.

For example, assume that in our fire engine case you have located a witness who saw the defendant driver at an automobile repair shop just a few days before the accident. The witness told you that the defendant was advised that his brakes were in poor repair, but that he left without having them fixed. This is a fact of central importance, and you will no doubt present it in the direct examination. Collateral or supportive facts will include corroborative details such as the time of day, the witness's reason for being in the auto shop, the witness's location during the crucial conversation about the brakes, the reason that the witness can remember the exact language used, and why the witness can identify the defendant. These details, while not strictly relevant to your theory, give weight and believability to the crucial testimony.

You must also be sure to include those "thematic" facts that give your case moral appeal. Returning to the intersection case, perhaps you have an additional witness who will testify that at the time of the collision the defendant was already late for an important meeting. Your theme, then, might be that the defendant was "Too busy to be careful." How can this theme be developed in the testimony of the auto shop witness? The answer is to look for supportive details. Was the defendant curt or abrupt with the mechanic? Was he constantly looking at his watch? Was he trying to read "important-looking papers" while discussing the brakes? Did the defendant rush out of the shop? In other words, search for details that support your image of the defendant as busy, preoccupied, and unconcerned with safety.

In addition to central facts and supporting details, your "content checklist" should include consideration of the following sorts of information.

Reasons. Recall that stories are more persuasive when they include reasons for the way people act. A direct examination usually should include the reasons for the witness's own actions. Some witnesses can also provide reasons for the actions of another.

Explanations. When a witness's testimony is not self-explanatory, or where it raises obvious questions, simply ask the witness to explain. In the above repair shop scenario, it may not be immediately apparent that a casual observer would recall the defendant's actions in such detail. Ask for an explanation:

> Q: How is it that you can remember seeing and hearing what the defendant did that morning?
>
> A: I was at the shop to have my brakes fixed, and it really made an impression on me that he was leaving without taking care of his.

Credibility. The credibility of a witness is always in issue. Some part of every direct examination should be devoted to establishing the credibility of the witness. You can enhance credibility in a number of ways. Show that the witness is neutral and disinterested. Demonstrate that the witness had an adequate opportunity to observe. Allow the witness to deny any expected charges of bias or misconduct. Elicit the witness's personal background of probity and honesty.

4.3.1.2 What to Exclude

Having identified the facts that most support your theory and most strengthen your theme, you may now begin the process of elimination. It should go without saying that you must omit any facts that are not true. While you are not required to assure yourself beyond reasonable doubt of the truthfulness of each witness, neither may you knowingly elicit testimony that you believe to be false. By the time you are preparing your direct examinations you certainly will have abandoned any legal or factual theory that rests on evidence of this sort.

More realistically, unless you have an extraordinarily compelling reason to include them, you will need to consider discarding facts that fall into the following categories.

Clutter

This may be the single greatest vice in direct examination. Details are essential to the corroboration of important evidence, and they are worse than useless virtually everywhere else. Aimless detail will detract from your true corroboration. In the "auto shop" example, for instance, the witness's proximity to the service counter is an essential detail. The color of the paint in the waiting room is not.

How do you determine whether or not a certain fact is clutter? Ask what it contributes to the persuasiveness of your story. Does it supply a reason for the way that someone acted? Does it make an important fact more or less likely? Does it affect the credibility or authority of a witness? Does it enhance the moral value of your story? If all of the answers are negative, you're looking at clutter.

Unprovables

These are facts that can successfully be disputed. While not "false," they may be subjected to such vigorous and effective dispute as to make them unusable. Is the witness the only person who claims to have observed a certain event, while many other credible witnesses swear to the precise contrary? Is the witness herself less than certain? Is the testimony contradicted by credible documentary evidence? It is often better to pass up a line of inquiry than to pursue it and ultimately have it rejected. This is not, however, a hard-and-fast rule. Many true facts will be disputed by the other side, and your case will virtually always turn on your ability to persuade the trier of fact that your version is correct. Sometimes your case will depend entirely on the testimony of a single witness who, though certain and truthful, will come under massive attack. Still, you must be willing to evaluate all of the potential testimony against the standards of provability and need. If you can't prove it, don't use it. Especially if you don't need it.

Implausibles

Some facts need not be disputed to collapse under their own weight. They might be true, they might be useful, they might be free from possible contradiction, but they still just won't fly. Return to the auto shop witness and assume that she informed you that she recognized the defendant because they had once ridden in the same elevator fifteen years previously. You may have no reason to disbelieve the witness, and it is certainly unlikely that anyone could contradict or disprove her testimony. The testimony might even add some support to your theme, say, if the defendant rushed out of the elevator in an obvious hurry to get to work. Nonetheless, the testimony is simply too far-fetched. If offered, it will give the trier of fact something unnecessary to worry about; it will inject a reason to doubt the other testimony of the witness.

Note, however, that implausibility must be weighed against importance. If the case involved a disputed identification of the defendant, then proof of an earlier encounter might be of sufficient value to risk its introduction.

Impeachables

These are statements open to contradiction by the witness's own prior statements. By the time of trial, many witnesses will have given oral or written statements in the form of interviews, reports, and depositions. Many also will have signed or authored documents, correspondence, and other writings. With some limitations, the witnesses' previous words may be used to cast doubt on their credibility; this is called impeachment by a prior inconsistent statement. The demonstration that a witness has previously made statements that contradict her trial testimony is often one of the most dramatic, and damning, aspects of cross-examination. Unless you can provide an extremely good explanation of why the witness has changed, or seems to have changed, her story, it is usually best to omit impeachables from direct testimony.

Door Openers

Some direct testimony is said to "open the door" for inquiries on cross-examination that otherwise would not be allowed. The theory here is that fairness requires that the cross-examiner be allowed to explore any topic that was deliberately introduced on direct. For example, in the intersection case the defendant almost certainly would not be allowed to introduce the fact that the plaintiff had been under the care of a psychiatrist. On the other hand, assume that the plaintiff testified on direct that the accident had forced her to miss an important appointment with her doctor and that the appointment could not be rescheduled for a week due to the nature of the doctor's schedule. In these circumstances, the door would be opened, at a minimum, to a cross-examination that covered the nature of the appointment and the reason that it could not be rescheduled; in other words, that the plaintiff was on her way to see her psychiatrist.

Another common door opener is the misconceived "defensive" direct examination. It is considered a truism in many quarters that the direct examiner should defuse the cross by preemptively bringing out all of the bad facts. The danger, however, is that you will "defensively" bring out facts that would have been inadmissible on cross-examination. Assume, for example, that your client has a prior juvenile conviction for theft. While you might ordinarily want to raise a prior crime yourself to explain it or otherwise soften the impact of the evidence, juvenile convictions are almost never admissible.[12] Thus, a defensive direct examination would not only introduce otherwise excludable information, it could very well open the door to further exploitation of those facts on cross. You cannot always avoid door openers, but you must learn to recognize them.

4.3.2 Organization and Structure

Organization is the tool through which you translate the witness's memory of events into a coherent and persuasive story. This requires idiom, art, and poetry. An artist does not paint everything that she sees. Rather, she organizes shapes, colors, light, and texture to present a compelling image of a landscape. In the same manner, a trial lawyer does not simply ask a witness to "tell everything you know," but instead uses the placement and sequence of the information to heighten and clarify its value.

12. Fed. R. Evid. 609(d).

The keys to this process are primacy and recency, apposition, duration, and repetition.

Primacy and recency refer to the widely accepted phenomenon that people tend best to remember those things that they hear first and last. Following this principle, the important parts of a direct examination should be brought out at its beginning and again at its end. Less important information should be "sandwiched" in the middle. In our intersection case, the presence of the fire truck may well be the most important part of the plaintiff's testimony. It should therefore be introduced early in her direct examination and perhaps alluded to again at the end.

Apposition is the placement or juxtaposition of important facts in a manner that emphasizes their relationship. Again looking at the intersection case, a strictly chronological direct examination might have the plaintiff begin by explaining where she was headed on the morning of the accident. Assume now that she was going to an art exhibit that would not open for another hour. The importance and value of this seemingly innocuous fact can be heightened tremendously by "apposing" it to the conduct of the defendant immediately following the accident. Imagine the impact of contrasting the plaintiff's unhurried trip with the following information about the defendant:

> Q: Where were you going on the morning of the accident?
>
> A: I was going to the Art Institute.
>
> Q: Were you in any hurry to get there?
>
> A: It wasn't going to open for an hour, so I was in no hurry at all.
>
> Q: What did you do immediately after the accident?
>
> A: I asked the defendant if he was all right.
>
> Q: What did the defendant do immediately following the accident?
>
> A: He jumped out of his car and pulled out his cell phone. He shouted that he would talk to me later, but first he had to cancel an important appointment.

Duration refers to the relative amount of time that you spend on the various aspects of the direct examination. As a general rule, you should dwell on the more important points, using the very length of coverage to emphasize the significance of the topic. Less important matters should consume less of the direct examination. In the fire truck example, it should be obvious that the presence and noticeability of the fire engine is central to the plaintiff's case. Although the plaintiff's initial observation of the truck could be established in a single question and answer, the importance of the subject dictates that you spend more time on this part of the direct examination:

Q: What did you see as you drove south on Sheridan Road?

A: I saw a fire truck.

Q: Describe it, please.

A: It was your basic fire truck. It was red, and it had firefighters riding on it. It had lights and a bell.

Q: Were the lights flashing?

A: Yes, and it was sounding its siren.

Q: How far away were you when you first noticed the fire truck?

A: I would say almost a block away.

See demonstration 1.1 in the Visuals Appendix.

Repetition is a corollary of duration. Important points should be repeated, preferably throughout the direct examination, to increase the likelihood that they will be retained and relied on by the trier of fact.

Even when applying these principles, there is no set pattern for the structure of a direct examination, just as there is no correct way to paint a landscape. The following guidelines, however, will always be useful.

4.3.2.1 Start Strong, End Strong: The Overall Examination

Every direct examination, no matter how else it is organized, should strive to begin and end on strong points. The definition of a strong point will differ from trial to trial. It may be the most gripping and dramatic aspect of the entire examination; it may be the single matter on which the witness expresses the greatest certainty; it may be the case's most hotly disputed issue; or it may be a crucial predicate for other testimony. Whatever the specifics, the strong points of your overall examination should have some or all of the following features.

Admissibility. There is little worse than having an objection sustained right at the beginning, or end, of a direct examination. You must be absolutely certain of the admissibility of your opening and closing points.

Theory value. The very definition of a strong point is that it makes a significant contribution to your theory. What does the witness have to say that is most central to the proof of your case?

Thematic value. Ideally, your strongest points will reinforce the moral weight of your case. Try to phrase them in the same language you use to invoke your theme.

Dramatic impact. Dramatic impact at the beginning of an examination will keep the judge or jury listening. Dramatic impact at the end of the examination will help fix the testimony in their memories.

Undeniability. Choose strong points in the hope that they will be vividly remembered. It will do you little good if they are remembered as being questionable or controverted.

In most cases, of course, it will be necessary to use the opening part of the direct examination to introduce the witness and establish some of her background. Thus, the actual "beginning" of the examination should be understood as the beginning of the substantive testimony.

4.3.2.2 Start Strong, End Strong: The Subexaminations

Each full direct examination is actually a combination of many smaller subexaminations. As you move from topic to topic, you are constantly concluding and reinitiating the subparts of the direct testimony. The "start strong/end strong" rule should not be applied only to the organization of the full direct; it should also be used to structure its individual components.

In our intersection case, you might wish to begin and end the substantive part of the plaintiff's examination with evidence about the fire truck. In between, however, you will cover many other issues, including the plaintiff's background, the scene of the collision, and the plaintiff's damages. Each of these component parts of the direct should, if possible, begin and end on a strong point.

In something as simple as setting the scene, consider what elements of the description are most important to your case. Then begin with one and end with another. In the intersection case, you might want to lead off with the clarity of the weather conditions to establish visibility. Perhaps you would then conclude the scene-setting portion of the examination with this description of the traffic:

> Q: Of all of the cars that were present, how many stopped for the fire truck?
>
> A: All of them, except the defendant.

4.3.2.3 Use Topical Organization

Chronology is almost always the easiest form of organization. What could be more obvious than beginning at the beginning and ending at the end? In trial advocacy, however, easiest is not always best. In many cases it will be preferable to use a topical or thematic form of organization. In this way, you can arrange various components of the witness's testimony to reinforce each other, you can isolate weak points, and you can develop your theory in the most persuasive manner. The order in which events occurred is usually fortuitous. Your duty as an advocate is to rearrange the telling so that the story has maximum logical force.

Assume that you are the prosecutor in a burglary case. Your first witness is the police officer who conducted a stakeout and arrested the defendant on the basis of a description that she received from a superior officer. A strict chronology in such a case could be confusing and counterproductive. The witness would have to begin with the morning of the arrest, perhaps explaining the time that she came on duty, the other matters that she worked on that day, and her instructions in conducting the stakeout. She no doubt would have received the description somewhere in the middle of all this activity. Even if relevant, the importance of the surrounding details is not likely to be well understood at the outset of the examination. The officer, sticking to chronological order, would then describe the people she saw at the stakeout location whom she did not arrest. Finally, the witness would come to the defendant's arrival on the scene. Assume, however, that she did not immediately arrest him. Rather, she observed him for some time; perhaps he even left the scene (and returned) once or twice before the eventual arrest.

In plain chronological order, all of this can add up to a rather diffuse story. The officer's reasons for conducting the stakeout are separated from the activity itself; the receipt of the description has no immediate relationship to the apprehension of the suspect. The trier of fact is required to reflect both forward and back on the significance of the data.

A topical organization, however, could provide a framework that adds clarity and direction to the story. A structure based on the description of the defendant, rather than chronology, would begin with a description of the arrest itself; then:

> Q: Officer, why did you arrest the defendant?
>
> A: Because he fit a description that I had been given earlier of a wanted burglar.
>
> Q: Did you arrest him as soon as you saw him?
>
> A: No. I wanted to make sure that he fit the description completely, so I waited until he was standing directly below a street light.
>
> Q: Was there anyone else in the vicinity at that time?
>
> A: There had been a few people, but nobody who matched the description.
>
> Q: Officer, please go back and tell us how you received the description that led to the arrest of the defendant.

Even in a matter as simple as our automobile collision case, a strictly chronological direct examination of the plaintiff could fail to be either dramatic or persuasive.

Imagine an examination that begins with the plaintiff leaving home that morning. State her destination and her estimated travel time. Describe the weather and traffic conditions. Trace her route from street to street until she arrives at the fateful intersection. Describe the appearance of the fire truck, the plaintiff's reaction, and finally the collision. After slogging through a series of details, some important and some not, the direct examination finally arrives at the most important event—the accident itself.

It would be more dramatic to 1) begin with the collision, 2) explain why the plaintiff had stopped her car, 3) describe the fire truck, 4) describe the response of the surrounding traffic, and 5) contrast that with the actions of the defendant.

4.3.2.4 Do Not Interrupt the Action

Every direct examination is likely to involve one, two, or more key events or occurrences. The witness may describe a physical event such as an automobile accident, an arrest, the failure of a piece of equipment, or a surgical procedure. Alternatively, the witness may testify about something less tangible, such as the formation of a contract, the effect of an insult, the making of a threat, the breach of a promise, or the endurance of pain following an injury. Whatever the precise subject, it will always be possible to divide the testimony into "action" on the one hand and supporting details and descriptions on the other.

A cardinal rule for the organization of direct examination is never to interrupt the action. Do not disrupt the dramatic flow of your story—the description of the crucial events—to fill in minor details. There can be no more jarring or dissatisfying an experience during trial than when the witness, who has just testified to the sound of a gunshot or the screech of automobile tires, is then calmly asked the location of the nearest street light. The lighting conditions may be important, but they cannot possibly be important enough to justify the discontinuity created by fracturing the natural flow of occurrence testimony.

Many lawyers subscribe to the theory that you should "set the scene" before proceeding to the activity. Following this approach in our automobile case, you would first have the witness describe the intersection, the surrounding traffic, the condition of the streets, and the location of her car, all before proceeding to the events of the collision. This approach is based on the concept that the trier of fact can then place the activities within the framework that you have created.

An alternative approach is first to describe the events themselves and then to go back and redescribe them while filling in the details of the scene. Assume that the plaintiff in the automobile case has already testified about the events of the accident. You can now go back to set the scene, effectively telling the story a second time: "What were the weather conditions when you entered the block where the collision occurred?" "How much traffic was there when you first saw the fire truck?" "What direction were you traveling when the defendant's car struck yours?"

4.3.2.5 Give Separate Attention to the Details

We have seen that details add strength and veracity to a witness's testimony. Unfortunately, they can also detract from the flow of events. It is therefore often best to give separate attention to the details, an approach that also allows you to explain their importance.

Assume, for example, that you are presenting the testimony of a robbery victim and that the central issue in the case is the identification of the defendant. You know that you don't want to detract from the action, so you will present the events of the robbery without interruption. Then you will go back to supply the details that support the witness's ability to identify the defendant:

> Q: How far was the defendant from you when you first noticed him?
>
> A: About twelve or fifteen feet.
>
> Q: How much closer did he come?
>
> A: He came right up to me. His face wasn't more than a foot from mine.
>
> Q: Did you look at his face?
>
> A: Yes, absolutely. He stared right at me.
>
> Q: For how long?
>
> A: It was at least a minute.
>
> Q: Was it still light out?
>
> A: Yes, it was.
>
> Q: Could you see the color of his clothing?

There will be dozens of details available to support the witness's identification. Dispersing them throughout the description of events would both disrupt the testimony and diminish their cumulative importance. The remedy for this problem is to give the details separate attention.

4.3.2.6 Try Not to Scatter Circumstantial Evidence

Circumstantial evidence is usually defined as indirect proof of a proposition, event, or occurrence. The identity of a burglar, for example, could be proven directly through eyewitness testimony. It could also be proven indirectly through the accumulation of circumstantial evidence such as the following: The defendant was seen near the scene of the burglary on the evening of the crime; her scarf was found in the doorway of the burglarized house; she had been heard complaining about her need for a new MP3 player; two days after the crime she was found in possession of an MP3 player that had been taken in the burglary.

None of the above facts taken individually amount to direct proof that the defendant committed the crime. There could be a perfectly innocent explanation for each one. In combination, however, they raise an extremely compelling inference of guilt. In other words, the indirect circumstances accumulate to establish the likelihood of the prosecution's case.

Inferential evidence is at its strongest when a series of circumstances can be combined to lead to the desired conclusion. It is therefore effective to present all of the related circumstantial evidence at a single point in the direct examination, rather than scatter it throughout. This will not always be possible. The logic of a witness's testimony may require that items of circumstantial evidence be elicited at different points in the testimony. Chronological organization will dictate introducing the circumstances in the order that they occurred or were discovered. Even topical organization may require assigning individual circumstances to separate topics. In the burglary case, for example, a topical approach might divide the testimony into areas such as "condition of the premises" and "apprehension of the defendant." The discovery of the scarf and the recovery of the MP3 player would consequently be separated in the testimony.

Nonetheless, it is a good idea to attempt to cluster your circumstantial evidence. Abandon this technique only when you have settled on another that you believe will be more effective.

4.3.2.7 Defensive Direct Examination

From time to time it may be advisable to bring out potentially harmful or embarrassing facts on direct to blunt their impact on cross-examination. The theory of such "defensive" direct examination is that the bad information will have less sting if the witness offers it herself and, conversely, that it will be all the more damning if the witness is seen as having tried to hide the bad facts. As noted above, you should conduct a defensive direct examination only when you are sure that the information is known to the other side and will be admissible on cross-examination.

Assuming that you have determined to bring out certain damaging information, be sure not to do it at either the beginning or end of the direct examination. Remember the principles of primacy and recency. By definition, bad facts cannot possibly be the strong points of your case, so you will always want to bury them in the middle of the direct examination.

An extremely useful technique is to allow the trier of fact to "make friends" with your witness before you introduce harmful information. It is a normal human tendency to want to believe the best of people whom you like. Thus, you should give the judge or jurors every possible reason to like your witness before offering anything that might have a contrary effect. Recall the last time that you saw a television interview of the neighbors of an arrested crime suspect. They almost inevitably say something like, "He was such a nice man. I can't believe that he would do a thing like that."

If, for example, you have a witness who was previously convicted of a felony, you can reasonably assume that to be fair game for cross-examination. You will therefore want to bring out the conviction, in sympathetic terms, during your direct examination. Do not elicit such a fact until you have spent some time "personalizing" the witness. Give the trier of fact a reason to discount the conviction before you ever mention it.

4.3.2.8 Affirmation Before Refutation

Witnesses are often called both to offer affirmative evidence of their own and to refute the testimony of others. In such cases, it is usually best to offer the affirmative evidence before proceeding to refutation. In this manner you will accentuate the positive aspects of your case and avoid making the witness appear to be a scold. As with all principles, this one should not be followed slavishly. Some witnesses are called solely for refutation. Others are far more important for what they negate than for what they affirm. As a general organizing principle, it is useful to think about building your own case before destroying the opposition's.

4.3.2.9 Get to the Point

A direct examination is not a treasure hunt or murder mystery; there is seldom a reason to keep the trier of fact in suspense. Often, the best form of organization is to explain exactly where the testimony is headed and then to go directly there.

4.3.2.10 End with a Clincher

Every examination should end with a clincher, a single fact that capsulizes your trial theory or theme. To qualify as a clincher, a fact must be 1) absolutely admissible, 2) reasonably dramatic, 3) simple and memorable, and 4) stated with certainty. Depending on the nature of the evidence and the theory on which you are proceeding, the final question to the plaintiff in our automobile case might be any of the following:

> Q: How long was the fire engine visible before the defendant's car struck yours?
>
> A: It was visible for at least ten seconds, because I had already seen it and was stopped for a while when the defendant ran into me.

Or,

> Q: Did the defendant start using his cell phone before or after he checked on your injuries?
>
> A: He began talking on his telephone without even looking at me.

Or,

Q: Do you know whether you will ever be able to walk again without pain?

A: The doctors say that they can't do anything more for me, but I am still praying.

4.3.2.11 Ignore Any Rule When Necessary

By now you will no doubt have noticed that the above principles are not completely consistent with one another. In any given case you will probably be unable to start strong, organize topically, and separate the details, all while still getting to the point without interrupting the action. Which rules should you follow? The answer lies in your own good judgment and can only be arrived at in the context of a specific case. If you need another principle to help interpret the others, it is this: apply the rules that best advance your theory and theme.

4.4 Questioning Technique

Since content is the motive force behind every direct examination, you must use the questioning technique that focuses attention on the witness and the testimony. It is the witness's story that is central to the direct examination; the style and manner of your questioning should underscore and support the credibility and veracity of that story. The following questioning techniques can help you to achieve that goal.

4.4.1 Use Short, Open Questions

You want the witness to tell the story. You want the witness to be the center of attention. You want the witness to be appreciated and believed. None of these things can happen if you do all of the talking. Therefore, ask short questions.

Asking short questions will help you to refrain from talking, but not every short question will get the witness talking. To do that, you will need open questions.

Don't ask a witness, "Did you go to the bank?" The answer to that short question will probably be an even shorter "Yes." Instead, as much of your direct examination as possible should consist of questions that invite the witness to describe, explain, and illuminate the events of her testimony. Ask questions such as these:

Q: Where did you go that day?

Q: What happened after that?

Q: Tell us who was there.

Q: What else happened?

Q: Describe where you were.

Your witness will almost always be more memorable and believable if you can obtain most of her information in her own words. Short, open questions will advance that goal.

4.4.2 Use Directive and Transitional Questions

You cannot use open questions to begin an examination or to move from one area of the examination to another. To do so, you would have to start with "When were you born?" and then proceed to ask "What happened next?" in almost endless repetition.

A better approach is to ask directive and transitional questions. Directive questions, quite simply, direct the witness's attention to the topic that you want to cover. Suppose that you want the witness to address the issue of damages. Ask:

> Q: Were you in any pain after the accident?

Having directed the witness's attention, you can now revert to your short, open questions:

> Q: Please describe how you felt.
>
> Q: Where else did you hurt?
>
> Q: How has this affected your life?

You may need to ask more than one directive question during any particular line of testimony. To fill out the subject of damages, for example, you may need to ask additional questions such as:

> Q: Do you currently suffer any physical disabilities?

Or,

> Q: Did you ever have such pains before the accident?

Remember that the purpose of a directive question is to direct the witness's attention, not to divert the jurors'.

Another problem with short, open questions is that they are not very good at underscoring the relationship between one fact and another. The best way to do this is through "transitional" questions that use one fact as the predicate, or introduction, to another. Here are some examples of transitional questions:

> Q: After you saw the fire truck, what did you do?
>
> Q: Do you know what the defendant did as the other traffic slowed to a stop?
>
> Q: Once the defendant's car hit yours, did you see him do anything?

Note that directive and transitional questions will tend to be leading. As a technical matter, however, these questions are permissible as long as they are used to orient the witness, expedite the testimony, or introduce a new area of the examination. As a practical matter, objections to directive and transitional questions are not likely to be sustained as long as they are used relatively sparingly and are not asked in a tone that seems to insist on a certain answer. It is improper to abuse transitional or directive questions in a way that substitutes your testimony for that of the witness.

4.4.3 Reinitiate Primacy

The doctrine of primacy tells us that the trier of fact will pay maximum attention to the witness at the very beginning of the testimony. You can make further use of this principle by continuously "re-beginning" the examination. That is, every time you seem to start anew, you will refocus the attention of the judge or jurors. This technique can be called reinitiating primacy, and there are several ways to achieve it.

4.4.3.1 Ask General Headline Questions

Most direct examinations, including even those that are organized chronologically, will consist of a number of individual areas of inquiry. If you treat each such area as a separate examination, you can reinitiate primacy every time you move to a new topic. You can divide the direct into a series of smaller examinations through verbal headlines. Rather than simply move from area to area, insert a headline to alert the judge or jury to the fact that you are shifting gears or changing subjects.

The introduction should be overt. Don't ask:

> Q: What happened while you were driving south on Sheridan Road?

Instead, announce the new subject by asking:

> Q: Were you involved in an accident at the corner of Sheridan and Chase?

Similar headlines might include:

> Q: Had you kept your own car in good repair?

Or,

> Q: Were you hospitalized?

Or,

> Q: Are you still disabled today?

None of these introductory questions would really be necessary to begin the particular segment of testimony. You could simply proceed to the detailed questioning, relying on the witness to provide the necessary information. You could also write an entire novel without using chapter titles, paragraphs, or even punctuation. The headline question, however, serves the same function as a chapter heading in a book. It divides the "text" and reinitiates primacy.

See demonstration 4 in the Visuals Appendix.

4.4.3.2 Explain Where You Are Going

You can reinitiate primacy even more directly with a few, well-chosen, declaratory statements. Everything that you say during a direct examination does not have to be in the form of a question. You may say to the witness: "Let's talk about the aftermath of the accident"; or, "We need to move on to the subject of your injuries." Such statements are permissible as long as they are truly used to make the transition from one part of the testimony to another or to orient the witness in some other manner. You cannot, of course, use declaratory statements to instruct the witness how to testify.

4.4.3.3 Use Body Movement

Another way to segment your examination, and thereby reinitiate primacy, is through body movement. Most jurisdictions, although not all, allow lawyers to move somewhat freely about the courtroom as they conduct their examinations. Unless you are in a court that requires you to remain seated at counsel table or standing at a lectern, you can effectively announce the beginning of a new topic by pausing for a moment and then moving purposefully to a different part of the room. You needn't stride dramatically—a few short steps will usually suffice.

The key to this technique is to stop talking as you move. The silence and movement will reinforce each other, making it clear that one topic has ended and another is about to begin.

See demonstration 6 in the Visuals Appendix.

4.4.4 Ask Incremental Questions

Information usually can be obtained in either large or small pieces. Incremental questions break the "whole" into its component pieces so that the testimony can be delivered in greater, and therefore more persuasive, detail.

A large, nonincremental question might be:

> Q: What did the robber look like?

Even a well-prepared witness will probably answer this question with a fairly general description. A common response might be:

> A: He was a white male, about twenty or twenty-five years old, maybe six feet tall.

You might be able to go back to supply any omitted information, but in doing so you will risk giving the unfortunate impression of doing just that—filling in gaps in the witness's testimony. Furthermore, at some point in the backtracking a judge might sustain an objection on the ground that the question—"Describe the robber"—had been asked and answered.

An incremental approach to the issue of identification, on the other hand, would be built on a set of questions such as these:

Q: Were you able to get a good look at the robber?

A: Yes, I was able to see him clearly.

Q: How tall was he?

A: About six feet tall.

Q: How heavy was he?

A: He was heavy, almost fat, over 200 pounds.

Q: What race was he?

A: He was white.

Q: And his complexion?

A: He was very fair, with freckles.

Q: What color was his hair?

A: He was blond.

Q: How was his hair cut?

A: It wasn't really cut at all—just sort of long and stringy.

Q: Did he have any facial hair?

A: A small mustache.

Q: Could you see his eyes?

A: Yes, he came right up to me.

Q: What color were they?

A: Blue.

Q: Was he wearing glasses?

A: Yes, he was.

Q: What sort of frames?

A: Round wire rims.

Q: Did he have any scars or marks?

A: Yes, he had a birthmark on his forehead.

Q: Was he wearing a jacket?

A: He had on a Philadelphia Flyers jacket.

Depending on the witness's knowledge, further questions could inquire into other facts. Could the witness see the robber's shirt? What color was it? His trousers? His shoes? Any jewelry? Tattoos?

As you can plainly see, incremental questions, each seeking a single small bit of information, can drive home the accuracy of the identification without seeming to put words in the witness's mouth.

The incremental technique should be used sparingly. It will not work as an overall principle since the unrestrained use of details will quickly overwhelm the trier of fact. Use it only where the details are available, significant, and convincing.

First and foremost, the details must be available. It will only damage your case for you to ask a series of incremental questions that elicit negative or blank responses.

Second, the details must be significant. You will produce only boredom by providing every conceivable detail regarding every conceivable fact. No one will be interested in the location of the bell on the fire truck or the number of spots on the fire-house Dalmatian. Rather, you want the fine emphasis on small facts to come as a clear departure from the balance of the examination. What you are implying by the shift should be obvious: "Details weren't crucial before, but they are now. So pay close attention."

Finally, the incremental details have to be convincing; they have to lend verity to the larger point that you are trying to establish. Some details will be meaningless. It is unlikely to help an identification, for example, for the witness to testify that the robber was chewing gum. Other details may not be credible. Even if the witness claims absolute certainty, you probably won't want to offer testimony about the number of fillings in the assailant's teeth.

4.4.5 Reflect Time, Distance, Intensity

The very best direct examinations virtually re-create the incidents they describe, drawing verbal images that all but place the trier of fact at the scene of the events. Your pace and manner of questioning are essential to this process.

The timing or duration of an event, for example, is often crucial in a trial; one side claims that things happened quickly, while the other asserts that they were drawn out. It is possible to use the pace of questioning to support your particular theory. Assume that you represent the defendant in our fire truck case. His defense is that the fire engine appeared only a moment before the collision and that he just didn't have enough time to stop his car. The goal of the defendant's direct examination must be to re-create that scene by collapsing the time available to react to the fire truck. Hence, you will ask only a few, fast-paced questions:

Q: When did the fire truck first become visible?

A: It approached the intersection just as I did.

Q: What was the very first action that you took?

A: I slammed on my brakes.

Q: How much time did that take?

A: Less than a second.

Note that this direct examination proceeds quickly, emphasizing both shortness of time and immediacy of response. You can enhance this result if you fire off the questions and the witness doesn't pause before answering. Strive for the appearance of all but panting for breath.

In contrast, the plaintiff will claim that there was ample time for the defendant to stop. Her direct examination should therefore be drawn out to demonstrate exactly how much time there was:

Q: Where was the fire truck when you first saw it?

A: It was about a quarter of a block away from the intersection.

Q: How far away from you was it?

A: About one hundred yards.

Q: How many other cars were between you and the fire truck?

A: Three or four.

Q: What did they do in response?

A: They all stopped.

Q: How long did it take those other cars to stop?

A: Normal stopping time—a few seconds.

Q: What was the first thing that you did?

A: I started to pull over to the side.

Q: How long did that take?

A: Five seconds or so.

Q: What did you do after that?

A: I brought my car to a stop.

Q: How long did that take?

A: Well, I applied my brakes right away, and it took a few seconds for the car to stop.

Q: Then what happened?

A: That's when the other car rear-ended me.

Q: How much time elapsed between the moment when you first saw the fire truck and the time that the defendant's car hit yours?

A: At least ten or fifteen seconds.

There is every reason not to hurry through this part of the examination. The length, detail, and pace of your questions should be used to demonstrate the validity of your theory: the defendant had plenty of time to stop.

Similar techniques can be used to establish distance and intensity. Draw out your questions to maximize distance; move through them quickly to minimize it. Ask questions at a rapid pace to enhance the intensity of an encounter; slow down to make the situation more relaxed.

A word about ethics is important at this point. Lawyers are often accused of using verbal tricks to turn night into day. That is not what we are discussing here. Rather, the purpose of using "reflective" questioning is just the opposite—to ensure that the witness conveys her intended meaning. The techniques and examination styles discussed above are not deceptive, but they are useful to illuminate or underscore the content of a witness's testimony. If a witness says that an event took only moments, you can help the witness accurately present that testimony by using a questioning style that reflects suddenness and speed. Using the wrong style can actually inhibit the witness's communication and positively mislead the trier of fact.

4.4.6 Repeat Important Points

In every direct examination there will be several essential ideas that stand out as far more important than the rest. Do not be satisfied to elicit those points only once. Repeat them. Restate them. Then repeat them again. Then think of ways to restate them again. Since you are not allowed to ask the same question twice (*Objection: asked and answered*), you will need to employ your lawyer's creativity to fashion a number of slightly different questions, each stressing the same point. Repetition is the parent of retention, and your most important points should arise again and again throughout the testimony to ensure that they are retained by the trier of fact.

The corollary to this principle is that less important points should not be repeated in like manner. Emphasis that increases the fact finder's attention should be used to make key subjects stand out. If too many points are given this treatment, all points—essential and trivial—will be made to seem equally unimportant. How do you decide which facts are sufficiently important to bear repetition? The answer is to consider your theory and theme. You will want to repeat those facts that are basic to your logical theory as well as those that best evoke your moral theme.

In our automobile accident case, the gist of the plaintiff's theory is that she stopped for a passing fire truck whereas the defendant did not. Her single most important fact is definitely the observable presence of the fire truck. Thus, the words "fire truck" should be inserted at every reasonable point during the examination. At the close of her testimony, you want to have created the image that the fire truck dominated the scenery. How many different ways can the witness describe the fire truck? In how many locations can she place it? How many ways can she use it as a reference point for other testimony?

Thematic repetition may be more elusive or subtle. If the plaintiff's theme is that the defendant was "too busy to be careful," you will want to use repetition to emphasize how unbusy the plaintiff was.

Bench and jury trials differ significantly regarding the use of repetition. Juries consist of six or twelve individuals whose attention may sometimes drift. You can never be certain that every juror will have heard and retained every point, so repetition is particularly important. You not only need to drive your key points home, you need to drive them home to everyone. Judges are usually aware of this problem, and they typically will allow a fair amount of latitude for repetition during jury trials.

Bench trials are a different matter. Judges usually expect bench trials to move along swiftly. They don't want to be battered with constant reiteration of the same points. Of course, judges may also be inattentive, but they don't like to be reminded of it. In short, many judges do not like to be treated like jurors, and they will cut off attempts at repetition. Use this technique sparingly in bench trials.

4.4.7 Use Visual Aids

Seeing is believing. In daily life we are accustomed to receiving as much as 70 percent of our information through the sense of sight. Ordinary witness testimony is received primarily through the sense of hearing. This makes it hard to follow and harder to retain. You can enhance the effectiveness of almost any witness by illustrating the testimony with charts, photographs, maps, models, drawings, computer simulations, and other visual aids.

Always consider whether the witness's testimony can be illustrated. If the witness is going to testify about a pivotal document, determine whether it can be enlarged or projected on a screen in the courtroom. If the witness is going to testify about an event, create a map or produce an oversize photograph. If the witness will testify about a series of numbers or transactions, use a visual "timeline" as your visual aid.[13]

Demonstrations can also serve as visual aids. Ask the witness to reenact crucial events or to re-create important sounds. "Please show the jury exactly how the defendant raised his hand before he struck you." "Please clap your hands together

13. *See* chapter eleven for a full discussion of visual evidence.

to show us how loud the sound was." "Please repeat the plaintiff's words in exactly her tone of voice."

You must carefully prepare demonstrations. They have an inevitable tendency to backfire when ill-prepared. Be certain that your expectations are realistic. A witness will not be able to illustrate the loudness of a rifle shot by clapping her hands. Nor will a witness be able to demonstrate the movement of a vehicle by walking about the courtroom. Finally, make sure that your demonstration doesn't look silly. Many lawyers have lost more ground than they gained by asking witnesses to roll around on the floor, climb up on chairs, or dash from one end of the courtroom to the other.

4.4.8 *Avoid Negative, Lawyerly, and Complex Questions*

For reasons unknown and unknowable, many lawyers think that it makes them sound more professional when they phrase questions in the negative:

> Q: Did you not then go to the telephone?

No advocate, judge, juror, witness, English teacher, or speaker of our common language can possibly understand the meaning of that question. Even harder to understand are the two potential answers. What would "yes" mean? "Yes, I did not then go to the telephone?" Or, "Yes, I did." What would "no" mean? "No, I did then go to the telephone?" Or, "No, I didn't."

Furthermore, on direct examination your goal typically is to establish an affirmative case. It is therefore beneficial to phrase your questions so that your witnesses can answer them affirmatively. Avoid using negative questions.

You must also avoid "lawyer talk." Many jurors and witnesses will not understand lawyerese, and virtually all will resent it. On the other hand, everyone, including judges, will appreciate plain language. Do not ask:

> Q: At what point in time did you alight from your vehicle?

Ask instead:

> Q: When did you get out of your car?

Do not ask:

> Q: What was your subsequent activity, conduct, or response with regard to the negotiation of an offer and acceptance?

Opt for:

> Q: What did you agree to next?

Finally, do not pose questions that call for more than a single item or category of information. Although a witness may be able to sort through a fairly simple compound question—such as, "Where did you go and what did you do?"—many will become confused, and more will simply fail to answer the second part. Truly complex questions will almost certainly fail to elicit the answer that you seek.

4.5 Adverse and Hostile Witnesses

From time to time it may be necessary to call a witness, such as the opposing party, who will be hostile to your case. Because unfriendly witnesses cannot be expected to cooperate in preparation, most jurisdictions allow the use of leading questions for the direct examination of such witnesses.[14] They fall into two broad categories: adverse and hostile witnesses.

4.5.1 Adverse Witnesses

Adverse witnesses include the opposing party and those identified with the opposing party. Examples of witnesses identified with the opposing party include employees, close relatives, business partners, and others who share a community of interest. It is within the court's discretion to determine whether any particular witness is sufficiently identified with the opposition as to allow leading questions on direct examination.

It is important to alert the court to the fact that you are calling an adverse witness, lest the judge sustain objections to leading questions. In the case of the opposing party, counsel's right to ask leading questions on direct will be obvious. Nonetheless, there is no harm in stating that the witness is being called "as an adverse witness pursuant to Federal Rule 611(c)" or its local analog.

In the case of a nonparty adverse witness, it will usually be necessary at the outset to lay a foundation that establishes the witness's identification with the opposition. It may be as simple as in this example:

Q: Please state your name.

A: My name is Alex Rose.

Q: Mr. Rose, are you employed by the defendant, South Suburban Country Club?

A: Yes, I am.

Note that more foundation may be needed, depending on the nature of the witness's relationship to the adverse party.

In some jurisdictions, it may be necessary to request that the court specifically find that the witness is adverse. In others, one may lay the foundation and proceed to conduct the examination with leading questions.

14. Fed. R. Evid. 611(c).

4.5.2 Hostile Witnesses

A hostile witness is one who, while not technically adverse, displays actual hostility to the direct examiner or her client. The necessary characteristic may be manifested either through expressed antagonism or evident reluctance to testify. Additionally, a witness may be treated as hostile if his testimony legitimately surprises the lawyer who called him to the stand. Whatever the circumstances, it is generally necessary to have the court declare a witness to be hostile before proceeding with leading questions.

4.5.3 Strategy

There are only a few situations in which it may be advantageous to call an adverse witness. The first is where the adverse witness is the only person who can supply an essential element of your case. Thus, the witness will have to be called to prevent a directed verdict. For the same reason, an adverse witness might also be called to authenticate a necessary document or to lay the foundation for some other exhibit.

Finally, and most perilously, an adverse or hostile witness might be called solely for the purpose of making a bad impression on the trier of fact. Needless to say, this tactic has a strong potential to backfire.

In general, adverse (and potentially hostile) witnesses should not be called unless it is clearly necessary. As noted in the introduction to this section, direct examination provides counsel with an opportunity to build a case. There is therefore great risk involved in calling a witness who will be troublesome, uncooperative, or worse. Moreover, calling an adverse witness allows opposing counsel to conduct, in the midst of your case, a "cross-examination" that is very likely to resemble a final argument for the other side. The scope of adverse testimony should therefore be made as narrow as possible.

4.6 Ethics of Direct Examination

Most of the ethical issues in direct examination involve the extent to which it is permissible to "assist" a witness to prepare or enhance her testimony. Some issues are relatively easy to resolve. As was discussed earlier in this chapter, for example, it is not unethical to employ "reflective" questioning on direct examination to make events seem as though they occurred quickly or slowly.[15] At most, reflective questions will help a witness communicate accurately; they cannot alter the truth. A witness who testifies that an incident happened quickly can be helped, through reflective questioning, to make that point clear. If, on the other hand, the witness

15. *See* section 4.4.5.

states that the events were slow-paced, no amount of reflective direct will effectively change that conclusion.[16]

At the other end of the spectrum, it is absolutely unethical to participate in the creation of false testimony. Lawyers must not ever collude with witnesses in the invention of untrue facts. It is an underpinning of adversary justice that lawyers will act as guardians of the system to prevent the offer of perjured evidence. Without this safeguard, the very justification of adversary litigation is weakened if not destroyed.

The following subsections will discuss variations on this theme.

4.6.1 Witness Preparation

A recurring question is the extent to which lawyers may "coach" witnesses in preparation for their testimony. In many countries, it is considered unethical for a lawyer even to meet alone with a witness prior to the trial, such is the aversion to the possibility for contamination of the testimony. In the United States, however, we take a far different view. Here, a lawyer would be generally considered incompetent if he failed to meet with and prepare a witness in advance of offering her testimony.

The practice of witness preparation is so widespread and entrenched as to be unassailable. It is justified on the theory that witnesses, especially clients, are entitled to the lawyer's help to ensure that their testimony is presented accurately and persuasively. The justification is compelling. A witness, left to her own devices, might be forgetful, inarticulate, or unaware of the significance of the facts that she relates or omits. People come to lawyers precisely because they want—and are entitled to—assistance in presenting their claims and defenses. It smacks of abandonment to submit a client to examination without first reviewing the potential testimony.

Few would doubt that a lawyer's pretrial counsel should extend to advising a witness to be polite and well-dressed, to answer all of the questions, and to avoid losing her temper. In a sense, this advice might be seen as disguising an otherwise ill-mannered, boorish, and evasive client. The more realistic view, however, is that the lawyer is helping the client ensure that externalities do not obstruct effective communication. To be sure, there is a point where even recommendations on appearance can verge on fraud. It would, for example, be improper to urge a Muslim or Jewish client to wear a visible cross when testifying before an all-Christian jury.

More difficult issues arise when counsel attempts to refresh a witness's recollection, to fill in gaps in her story, or to suggest alternative possibilities. Again, this practice is usually justified on the ground that it is necessary to ensure that the truth emerges fully. Witnesses can be forgetful, especially when they are unaware of the legal importance of certain facts.

---

16. This is true of direct examination. On cross-examination, of course, the pacing of questions can be used to undermine a witness's conclusory testimony. Regarding the ethics of this sort of examination, *see* section 5.6.4.

Thus, a client complaining of a defective product would probably place greatest emphasis on the way that it malfunctioned; he might not think it important that the salesperson helped him select it. A lawyer, however, should know that the seller's participation in selection can result in an implied warranty of fitness for a particular use. It would be wrong to withhold this information from the client and equally wrong to avoid probing the client's memory for the nature and extent of the seller's representations. Most would agree that the following inquiries are proper:

> "Did you speak to a salesperson when selecting the product?"
>
> "What did the salesperson say?"
>
> "Did you tell the seller why you needed the product?"
>
> "Did you tell her the use to which you would put it?"
>
> "Did she recommend a particular product to you?"
>
> "Did the salesperson make any promises to you?"

While this line of questioning runs some slight risk of inducing memories, rather than simply recalling them, it is essential to adequate representation.

Now consider this scenario. The client was asked whether he spoke to the salesperson, and he replied, "Well, I pretty much picked the item out for myself. I really didn't want or need any help." The lawyer continued:

> I've shopped in those appliance stores, and my experience is that the salespeople just won't leave you alone. They're all on commission, and they pretty much stay with you until you buy something. You might not want their help, but sometimes you can't really avoid it. Did anything like that happen to you?

Is this an aid to the witness's memory or a not-so-subtle suggestion as to how to improve the story?

There is no good answer to the conundrum, as it essentially rests on the lawyer's intent.[17] It is permissible to invoke common experience to help a witness remember details that might have seemed unimportant when they occurred. It is flatly impermissible, even when "asking" an ostensible question, to prompt a witness to add facts that did not really take place.

The key is that counsel must, explicitly and implicitly, prepare the witness to give his or her own testimony and not the testimony that the lawyer would favor or prefer. Most efforts to help or empower the witness are ethical. Efforts at substitution or fabrication—no matter how well-cloaked—are not.

17. Needless to say, blatant efforts to influence the witness's testimony are unethical. The lawyer could not, for example, importune the witness this way: "You cannot win this case unless you testify that the salesperson assured you a specific level of performance. You need to tell me exactly how the seller induced you to buy and how you were promised that the product would meet your needs."

4.6.2 Offering Inadmissible Evidence

When evidence is admissible for only a limited purpose, it is unethical to attempt to put it to further use.[18] The obligation of zealous advocacy does not require counsel to ignore or evade the court's rulings with regard to the restricted admissibility of evidence.

By the same token, it is impermissible to prepare a witness to interject clearly inadmissible evidence. Where a motion in limine has been granted, for example, counsel cannot suggest or encourage a witness to use a narrative answer to volunteer the excluded information.[19]

Of course, counsel is not obligated to resolve all evidentiary doubts in favor of the opposition. It is ethical to offer any evidence with regard to which there is a reasonable theory of admissibility. In other words, it is proper to offer evidence as long as counsel can articulate at least one specific and recognizable argument in favor of its admission.[20]

4.6.3 Disclosing Perjury

The appropriate response to witness and client perjury has perplexed our profession endlessly. While no ethical lawyer would willingly be a party to perjury, questions arise as how best to prevent it without damaging the principles of confidentiality and zealous advocacy.

There is no doubt that a lawyer may not call a nonclient witness who is going to testify falsely and must "take reasonable remedial measures should nonclient perjury occur despite counsel's efforts to avoid it."[21]

The thorny problem is the client. An attorney must certainly take all reasonable steps to dissuade a client from presenting untrue testimony. But what if the client insists on presenting a story that the lawyer firmly believes is false? Or what if the client's perjury on the stand takes the lawyer by surprise and becomes a fait accompli before the lawyer can stop it?

The dilemma is especially acute in criminal cases. Many believe that a criminal defendant has a constitutional right to take the stand and "tell his story," whether

---

18. Regarding the misuse of evidence during final argument, *see* section 13.6.1.3.

19. *See* section 9.2.1.2.

20. This issue is discussed further section 9.3.1

21. A lawyer shall not "falsify evidence [or] counsel or assist a witness to testify falsely . . . ." Model Rules of Prof'l Conduct R. 3.4(b). Moreover, "[i]f a lawyer . . . has offered material evidence and the lawyer comes to know of its falsity, the lawyer shall take reasonable remedial measures . . . ." Model Rules of Prof'l Conduct R. 3.3(A)(3).
The Commentary to Rule 3.3 provides a three-step approach to "reasonable remedial measures." The lawyer must first remonstrate with the witness to correct the false testimony. If that fails, the lawyer should seek to withdraw "if that will remedy the situation." Since withdrawal will usually be inappropriate in the case of perjury by a nonclient, the final step is to make disclosure to the court.

the lawyer believes it or not. One commentator has gone so far as to urge that a lawyer's duties of loyalty and confidentiality require actively presenting a criminal defendant's perjured testimony.[22] The great majority of lawyers, judges, and scholars, however, reject this position. The U.S. Supreme Court has held that there is no constitutional right to testify falsely.[23] The Model Rules of Professional Conduct provide that counsel, in both civil and criminal cases, must take reasonable steps to remedy client perjury, even at the cost of revealing a confidential communication.[24]

The full dimension of the debate over responses to client perjury is beyond the scope of this text. A number of approaches have been suggested over the years, each supported by its own policies and justifications. It is fair to say, however, that the trend, as outlined in the preceding paragraph, is toward diminished latitude for the client and increased disclosure by counsel.

22. Monroe Freedman & Abbe Smith, Understanding Lawyers' Ethics, 159–94 (2004).
23. Nix v. Whiteside, 475 U.S. 157 (1966).
24. Model Rules of Prof'l Conduct R. 3.3(c).

Chapter Five

Cross-Examination

5.1 The Role of Cross-Examination

Cross-examination is hard. It is frequently dramatic, often exciting, and in many ways it defines our adversary system of justice. However it is described, cross-examination is the ultimate challenge for the trial lawyer. Can you add to your case or detract from your opponent's case by extracting information from your opponent's witnesses?

If direct examination is your best opportunity to win the case, cross-examination may provide you with a chance to lose it. A poor direct can be aimless and boring, but the witnesses are generally helpful. Your worst fear on direct examination is usually that you have left something out. A poor cross-examination, on the other hand, can be truly disastrous. The witnesses can range from uncooperative to hostile, and you constantly run the risk of actually adding weight or sympathy to your opponent's case. Moreover, most cross-examinations will inevitably be perceived by the trier of fact as a contest between the lawyer and witness. You can seldom afford to appear to lose.

In other words, cross-examination is inherently risky. The witness may argue with you. The witness may fill in gaps that were left in the direct testimony. The witness may make you look bad. You may make yourself look bad. And whatever good you accomplish may be subject to immediate cure on redirect examination.

None of these problems can be avoided entirely, but they can be minimized. Although some cross-examination is usually expected of every witness, and the temptation to do so is difficult to resist, as a general rule you should cross-examine sparingly. And you must always set realistic goals.

Brevity is an excellent discipline. Many trial lawyers suggest that cross-examinations be limited to a maximum of three points. While there may often be reasons to depart from such a hard and fast rule, there is no doubt that short cross-examinations have much to commend themselves. In terms of your own preparation, setting a mental limit for the length of the cross will help you to concentrate and organize your thinking. Actually conducting a short examination will minimize risk, add panache, and usually make the result more memorable.

This chapter discusses the general law, content, organization, and basic techniques of cross-examination. Several more advanced aspects of cross-examination—such as impeachment and the use of character evidence—are treated separately in later chapters.

5.2 The Law of Cross-Examination

Cross-examination is the hallmark of the Anglo-American system of adversary justice. Protected as a constitutional right in criminal cases, it is also understood as an aspect of due process in civil cases. The law of cross-examination varies somewhat from jurisdiction to jurisdiction, but the following rules are nearly universal.

5.2.1 Leading Questions Permitted

The most obvious distinction between direct and cross-examination is the permissible use of leading questions.[1] It is assumed that your adversary's witnesses will have little incentive to cooperate with you and that you may not have been able to interview them in advance. Consequently, virtually all courts allow the cross-examiner to ask questions that contain their own answers. Moreover, the right to ask leading questions is usually understood to include the right to insist on a responsive answer.

As we will see below, the ability to use leading questions has enormous implications for the conduct of cross-examination.

5.2.2 Limitations on Scope

The general rule in the United States is that cross-examination is limited to the scope of the direct.[2] Since the purpose of cross-examination is to allow you to inquire of your adversary's witnesses, the scope of the inquiry is restricted to those subjects that were raised during the direct examination.

Note that the definition of scope will vary from jurisdiction to jurisdiction, and even from courtroom to courtroom. A narrow application of this rule can limit the cross-examiner to the precise events and occurrences that the witness discussed on direct. A broader approach would allow questioning on related and similar events. For example, assume that the defendant in our collision case testified that his brakes had been inspected just a week before the accident. A strict approach to the "scope of direct" rule might limit the cross-examination to questioning on that particular inspection. A broader interpretation would allow inquiries into earlier brake inspections and other aspects of automobile maintenance.

1. FED. R. EVID. 611(c).
2. *Id.* 611(b).

A more generous approach to the scope of cross-examination is definitely the modern trend. Undue restriction of cross-examination can result in reversal on appeal. Nonetheless, there is no way to predict how an individual judge will apply the scope limitation in any given case; much will depend on the nature of the evidence and the manner in which the lawyers have been conducting themselves.

A few American jurisdictions have adopted the "English rule," which allows wide-open cross-examination concerning any issue relevant to the case. In the federal jurisdiction, and some others, the trial judge has discretion to allow inquiry beyond the scope of the direct examination, but the cross-examiner is then limited to nonleading questions. Also, in most states a criminal defendant who takes the stand and waives her Fifth Amendment rights is thereafter subject to cross-examination regarding all aspects of the alleged crime.

There are two general exceptions to the "scope of direct" rule. First, the credibility of the witness is always in issue. You may therefore always attempt to establish the bias, motive, interest, untruthfulness, or material prior inconsistency of a witness without regard to the matters that were covered on direct examination. Second, you may cross-examine beyond the scope of the direct once the witness herself has "opened the door" to additional matters. In other words, a witness who voluntarily injects a subject into an answer on cross-examination may thereafter be questioned as though the subject had been included in the direct.

5.2.3 Other Restrictions

Cross-examination is also limited by a variety of other rules, most of which involve the manner or nature of questioning.

Argumentative questions. You may ask a witness questions. You may suggest answers. You may assert propositions. But you may not argue with the witness. As you may have guessed, the definition of an argumentative question is elusive. Much will depend on your demeanor; perhaps an argumentative question is one that is asked in an argumentative tone. The following is a reasonable working definition: an argumentative question insists that the witness agree with an opinion or characterization as opposed to a statement of fact.

Intimidating behavior. You are entitled to elicit information on cross-examination by asking questions of the witness and insisting on answers. You are not allowed to loom over the witness; shout; make threatening gestures; or otherwise intimidate, bully, or (yes, here it comes) badger the witness.

Unfair characterizations. Your right to lead the witness does not include a right to mislead the witness. It is objectionable to attempt to mischaracterize a witness's testimony or to ask "trick" questions. If a witness has testified that it was dark outside, it would mischaracterize the testimony to begin a question: "So you admit that it was too dark to see anything . . . ." Trick questions cannot be answered accurately.

The most famous trick question is known as the "negative pregnant," as in Senator McCarthy's inquisitional, "Have you resigned from the Communist Party?"

Assuming facts. A frequently heard objection is that "Counsel has assumed facts not in evidence." Of course, a cross-examiner is frequently allowed to inquire as to facts that are not yet in evidence. This objection should only be sustained when the question uses the nonrecord fact as a premise rather than as a separate subject of inquiry, thus denying the witness the opportunity to deny its validity. Imagine in the fire truck case a witness who was standing on the sidewalk at the time of the accident. Assume that the witness testified on direct that the defendant never even slowed down before the impact and that the witness said absolutely nothing about having been drinking that morning. At the outset of the cross-examination, then, there would be no "facts in evidence" concerning use of alcohol. The cross-examiner is certainly entitled to ask questions such as, "Hadn't you been drinking that morning?" The cross-examiner should not be allowed, however, to use an assumption about drinking to serve as the predicate for a different question: "Since you had been drinking, you were on foot instead of in your car that morning?" The problem with this sort of bootstrapping is that it doesn't allow the witness a fair opportunity to deny that he had been drinking in the first place.

Compound and other defective questions. Compound questions contain more than a single inquiry: "Are you related to the plaintiff, and were you wearing your glasses at the time of the accident?" The question is objectionable because any answer will necessarily be ambiguous. Cumulative or "Asked and Answered" questions are objectionable because they cover the same ground twice (or more). Vague questions are objectionable because they tend to elicit vague answers.

5.3 The Content of Cross-Examination

The first question concerning any cross-examination is whether it should be brief or extensive. Although it is standard advice in many quarters that you should refrain from cross-examining a witness who hasn't hurt you, in practice almost every witness is subjected to at least a short cross-examination. You will seldom wish to leave the testimony of an adverse witness appear to go entirely unchallenged. Moreover, as we will see below, there will often be opportunities to use cross-examination to establish positive, constructive evidence. The most realistic decision, then, is not whether to cross-examine, but to what extent. This evaluation must be made at least twice: once in your pretrial preparation and again at the end of the direct examination.

In preparation, you must consider the potential direct examination. What do you expect the witness to say, and how, if at all, will you need to challenge or add to the direct? At trial you must make a further determination. Did the actual direct examination proceed as you expected? Was it more or less damaging than you anticipated? You must always reevaluate your cross-examination strategy in light of the direct testimony that was eventually produced. This process will often lead you to omit portions of your prepared cross because they have become unnecessary. It is considerably more dangerous to elaborate on or add to your plan, although this is occasionally unavoidable. In either situation always remember the risk inherent in cross-examination and ask yourself: "Is this cross-examination necessary?"

5.3.1 Consider the Purposes of Cross-Examination

Though often an invigorating exercise, cross-examination should be undertaken only to serve some greater purpose within your theory of the case. A useful cross-examination should promise to fulfill at least one of the following objectives.

Repair or minimize damage. Did the direct examination hurt your case? If so, can the harm be rectified or minimized? Can the witness be made to retract or back away from certain testimony? Can additional facts be elicited that will minimize the witness's impact?

Enhance your case. Can the cross-examination be used to further one of your claims or defenses? Are there positive facts that can be brought out that will support or contribute to your version of events?

Detract from their case. Conversely, can the cross-examination be used to establish facts that are detrimental to your opponent's case? Can it be used to create inconsistencies among the other side's witnesses?

Establish foundation. Is the witness necessary to the proper foundation for the introduction of a document or other exhibit, or for the offer of evidence by another witness?

Discredit direct testimony. Is it possible to discredit the witness's direct testimony by highlighting internal inconsistencies, demonstrating the witness's own lack of certainty or confidence, underscoring the witness's lack of opportunity to observe, illustrating the inherent implausibility of the testimony, or showing that it conflicts with the testimony of other, more credible witnesses?

Discredit the witness. Can the witness be shown to be biased or interested in the outcome of the case? Does the witness have a reason to stretch, misrepresent, or fabricate the testimony? Has the witness been untruthful in the past? Can it be shown that the witness is otherwise unworthy of belief?

Reflect on the credibility of another. Can the cross-examination be used to reflect, favorably or unfavorably, on the credibility of a different witness?

The length of your cross-examination will generally depend on how many of the above goals you expect to fulfill. It is not necessary, and it may not be possible, to attempt to achieve them all. You will often stand to lose more by overreaching than you can possibly gain by seeking to cover all of the bases in cross-examination. Be selective.

5.3.2 *Arrive at the "Usable Universe" of Cross-Examination*

5.3.2.1 The Entire Universe

In preparing to cross-examine any witness you must first determine the broadest possible scope, or universe, of the potential cross-examination. From a review of all of the available materials and documents, construct a comprehensive list of the information available from the witness. In keeping with the purposes of cross-examination, place each potential fact in one of the following categories:

- Does it make my case more likely?
- Does it make their case less likely?
- Is it a predicate to the admissibility of other evidence?
- Does it make some witness more believable?
- Does it make some witness less believable?

This process will give you the full universe of theoretically desirable information from which you will structure your cross-examination.

5.3.2.2 The Usable Universe

You must now evaluate all of the potential facts in order to arrive at your "usable universe." Ask yourself the following questions.

Is a friendly witness available to present the same facts? There may be no point in attempting to extract answers from an unwilling source if a friendly witness can provide you with the same information. On cross-examination you always run the risk that the witness will argue or hedge, or that the information will not be developed as clearly as you would like. Unless you stand to benefit specifically from repetition of the testimony, you may prefer to bypass cross-examination that will be merely cumulative of your own evidence.

Can the information be obtained only on cross-examination? You have no choice but to cross-examine on important facts that are solely within the knowledge or control of the adverse witness. Such information will range from the foundation for the admission of a document to evidence of the witness's own prior actions.

Will the facts be uniquely persuasive on cross-examination? Some information, though available from a variety of sources, will be particularly valuable when elicited on cross-examination. For example, evidence of past wrongdoing may be more credible if it is presented as an admission by the witness herself rather than as an accusation coming from another. In the automobile accident case, consider the different ways in which evidence of the defendant's driving habits could be admitted.

You could produce your own witness to testify that the defendant was a constant speeder. You would have to lay a foundation for this testimony, establishing both the witness's personal knowledge and the consistency of the defendant's "habit."[3] Additionally, your witness would then be subject to cross-examination not only on the foundation for the testimony, but also regarding issues such as bias, accuracy, and opportunity to observe. On the other hand, the defendant's own testimony that he loved driving fast cars would be virtually uncontrovertible. It would also bolster the testimony of your own witnesses to the same effect. When possible, it is generally desirable to obtain negative or contested evidence from the mouths of your opponent's witnesses.

How likely is it that the witness will agree with you? Certain information may be completely within the control of a witness for the other side, and it may be uniquely persuasive if elicited during the cross-examination of that witness. You must nonetheless consider the contingency that the witness will deny you the answer that you want. You may need to abandon or modify a promising line of cross-examination if you do not believe you will be able to compel the answers that you anticipate. Can the information be confirmed by the witness's own prior statements? Can it be documented through reports, photographs, tests, or other evidence? These and other devices for controlling a witness's testimony on cross-examination are discussed in later sections.

The construction of your usable universe depends almost entirely on your mastery of the case as a whole. To prepare for cross-examination, you must know not only everything that the particular witness is liable to say, but also every other fact that might be obtained from any other witness, document, or exhibit. Your effective choice of cross-examination topics will be determined by your ability to choose those areas that will do you the most good while risking the least harm.

5.3.3 Risk-Averse Preparation

There are many ways to prepare for cross-examination. The following is a "risk-averse" method designed to result in a solid, if generally unflashy, cross that minimizes the potential for damage to your case.

Risk-averse preparation for cross-examination begins with consideration of your anticipated final argument. What do you want to be able to say about this particular witness when you address the jury at the end of the case? How much of that information do you expect to be included in the direct examination? The balance is what you will need to cover on cross.

Next, write out the portion of a final argument that you would devote to discussing the facts presented by this particular witness. This will at most serve as a

3. FED. R. EVID. 406.

draft for your actual closing,[4] and you should limit this text to the facts contained in the witness's testimony. You need not include the characterizations, inferences, arguments, comments, and thematic references that will also be part of your real final argument. Depending on the importance of the witness, the length of this argument segment can range from a short paragraph to a full page or more.

It is important that you write your text using short, single-thought, strictly factual sentences. You are not attempting to create literature. Do not worry about continuity, style, or transition. Simply arrange the declarative sentences one after another in the order that you believe will be the most persuasive, referring to the witness in the third person. For example, your argument concerning the defendant in the fire truck case might, assuming that all of these facts were readily available (in the defendants' deposition, for example), include the following:

> The defendant awoke on the morning of the accident at 7:00 a.m. He had to be downtown later that morning. He was meeting an important new client. He wanted to get that client's business. He stood to make a lot of money. The meeting was scheduled for 9:00 a.m. The defendant lives sixteen miles from his office. He rents a monthly parking spot. That spot is in a garage located two blocks from his office. He left his home at 7:55 a.m. There was a lot of traffic that morning. The accident occurred at an intersection seven miles from downtown. It happened at 8:20 a.m.

An effective paragraph will include the facts that underlie your theory of the case. It should now be a simple matter to convert the text into a cross-examination plan. You merely need to take each sentence and rephrase it into a second-person question. In fact, it is often best to leave the sentence in the form of a declaration, technically making it a question through voice inflection or by adding an interrogative phrase at the end. The above paragraph then becomes the following cross-examination of the defendant:

> Q: You awoke at 7:00 a.m. on the morning of the accident, isn't that right?
>
> Q: You had to be downtown later that morning, correct?
>
> Q: You were meeting an important new client?
>
> Q: You wanted to get that client's business?
>
> Q: You stood to make a lot of money?
>
> Q: The meeting was scheduled for 9:00 a.m., correct?
>
> Q: You live sixteen miles from your office?

4. Final argument is treated in chapter thirteen. At this point it is sufficient to note that while it may be a useful exercise to write out a draft, it is a mistake to read your closing argument from a prepared text.

Q: You rent a monthly parking spot?

Q: That spot is in a garage located two blocks from your office?

Q: You left your home at 7:55 a.m., right?

Q: There was a lot of traffic that morning?

Q: The accident occurred at an intersection seven miles from downtown?

Q: It happened at 8:20 a.m., isn't that right?

Note that the above questions also fit neatly into the "usable universe." Many of the facts are not likely to be available from friendly witnesses. Most others are of the sort that will be most valuable if conceded by the defendant himself. Finally, the facts are nearly all of the sort that can be independently documented or that the defendant is unlikely to deny.

This technique is useful for developing the content of your cross-examination. The organization of the examination and the structure of your individual questions will depend on additional analysis.

5.4 The Organization of Cross-Examination

5.4.1 Organizing Principles

As with direct examination, the organization of a cross-examination can be based on the four principles of primacy and recency, apposition, repetition, and duration. Unlike direct examination, however, on cross-examination you will often have to deal with a recalcitrant witness. You may therefore have to temper your plan in recognition of this reality, occasionally sacrificing maximum clarity and persuasion to avoid "telegraphing" your strategy to the uncooperative witness. Thus, we must include the additional organizing principles of indirection and misdirection when planning cross-examinations.

Three further concepts are basic to the organization, presentation, and technique of virtually every cross-examination.

First, cross-examination is your opportunity to tell part of your client's story in the middle of the your opponent's case. Your object is to focus attention away from the witness's direct testimony and onto matters that you believe are helpful. On cross-examination, you want to tell the story. To do so, you must always be in control of the testimony and the witness.

Second, cross-examination is not the time to attempt to gather new information. Never ask a witness a question simply because you want to find out the answer. Rather, cross-examination must be used to establish or enhance the facts that you have already discovered.

Finally, an effective cross-examination often succeeds through implication and innuendo. It is not necessary, and it is often harmful, to ask a witness the "ultimate question." Final argument is your opportunity to point out the relationship between facts, make characterizations, and draw conclusions based on the accumulation of details. Do not expect an opposing witness to do this for you.

Lay the groundwork for your eventual argument, then stop. This technique is premised on the assumption that many witnesses will be reluctant to concede facts that will later prove to be damaging or embarrassing. Thus, it may be necessary to avoid informing the witness of the ultimate import of the particular inquiry. You can do this through indirect questioning, which seeks first to establish small and incontrovertible factual components of a theory and only later addresses the theory itself.

For example, a witness may be loath to admit having read a certain document before signing it; perhaps the written statement contains damaging admissions that the witness would prefer to disclaim. Direct questioning, therefore, would be unlikely to produce the desired result. The witness, if asked, will deny having read the item in question. Indirect questioning, however, may be able to establish the point:

Q: You are a businessman?

Q: Many documents cross your desk each day?

Q: It is your job to read and respond to them?

Q: Your company relies on you to be accurate?

Q: You often must send written replies?

Q: Large amounts of money can change hands on the basis of the replies that you send?

Q: You have an obligation to your company to be careful about its money?

Q: So you must be careful about what you write?

Q: Of course, that includes your signature?

By this point you should have obtained through indirection that which the witness would not have conceded directly. The final question should be superfluous.

Misdirection is an arch-relative of indirection, used when the witness is thought to be particularly deceptive or untruthful. Here the cross-examiner not only conceals the object of the examination, but actually attempts to take advantage of the witness's own inclination to be uncooperative. Knowing that the witness will tend to fight the examination, the lawyer creates, and then exploits, a "misdirected" image. In our fire truck case, for example, the defendant is extremely unlikely to admit that he should have seen the fire engine; perhaps he would go so far as to deny the obvious. The lawyer may therefore misdirect the defendant's attention, as follows:

Q: Isn't it true that you expected to see a fire truck at that corner?

A: Certainly not, I never expected a fire truck.

Q: You weren't looking for a fire truck?

A: No.

Q: You didn't keep your eye out for one?

A: No.

Q: And you never saw one?

A: No.

Q: Until, of course, after it was too late?

To be effective in the use of this technique, the cross-examination must be organized first to obtain the "misdirected" denial. Note that the above example would not work at all if the questions were asked in the opposite order. In other words, the principle of misdirection works best with an intentionally elusive witness who needs only to be given sufficient initial rope with which to hoist himself.

5.4.2 Guidelines for Organization

There are many ways in which you can employ the principles discussed above.

5.4.2.1 Do Not Worry About Starting Strong

It would be desirable to be able to begin every cross-examination with a strong, memorable point that absolutely drives home your theory and theme. Unfortunately, this will not always be possible. Many cross-examinations will have to begin with an introductory period in which you acclimate yourself to the tenor of the witness's responses and you also attempt to put the witness in a cooperative frame of mind. Unless you are able to start off with a true bombshell, it will usually be preferable to take the time necessary to establish predicate facts through indirection.

5.4.2.2 Use Topical Organization

Topical organization is essential in cross-examination. Your goal on cross-examination is not to retell the witness's story, but rather to establish a small number of additional or discrediting points. A topical format will be the most effective in allowing you to move from area to area. Moreover, topical organization allows you to take maximum advantage of apposition, indirection, and misdirection. You can use topical organization to cluster facts in the same manner that you would on direct examination or to separate facts to avoid showing your hand to the witness.

Assume that you want to use the cross-examination of the defendant in the automobile accident to show how busy he was on the day of the collision. You know that he had an important meeting to attend that morning, but he will be unlikely to admit that he might lose the client (and a lot of money) if he arrived late. You can solve this problem by using topical organization to separate your cross-examination into two distinct segments: one dealing with the nature of the defendant's business and the other covering his appointment on the fateful morning.

In the first topical segment you will show that the defendant is an independent management consultant. It is a very competitive business in which client relations are extremely important. Part of his work involves seeking out potential new clients, who he is always anxious to please. Since he is a sole proprietor, every client means more money. As a consultant, he must pride himself on professionalism, timeliness, and efficiency. He bills his clients by the hour. Time is money. In short, examine the witness on his business background without ever bringing up the subject of the accident. (The defendant's own lawyer almost certainly will have introduced his stable, businesslike background; your examination on the same issue would then be within the scope of the direct.)

Later in the examination, after covering several other areas, you will shift topics to the defendant's agenda on the day of the accident. Now it is time to establish the details of his planned meeting and the fact that he was still miles from downtown shortly before it was scheduled to begin. You do not need to obtain an admission that he was running late or that he was preoccupied. Topical organization has allowed you to develop the predicate facts for that argument before the witness was aware of their implications.

There is another advantage to topical organization on cross-examination. Assume in the example above that the witness was well-prepared and that he immediately recognized your reasons for asking about his business practices. Because your examination was segmented, however, he could scarcely deny the facts that you suggested. In a portion of the examination limited to the operation of his business, it would be implausible for him to deny that his clients value "professionalism, efficiency, and timeliness." Denying your perfectly reasonable propositions would make him look either untrustworthy or defensive. Note that you would not obtain the same result without topical organization. In the middle of the discussion of the morning of the accident, it would be quite plausible for the defendant to testify that this particular new client was not dominating his thoughts.

5.4.2.3 Give the Details First

Details are, if anything, more important on cross-examination than they are on direct. On direct examination, a witness will always be able to tell the gist of the story; details are used in a secondary manner to add strength and veracity to the basic testimony. On cross-examination, however, the witness will frequently disagree with the gist of the story that you want to tell, and details therefore become the primary method of making your points. You may elicit details to lay the groundwork for future argument, to draw out internal inconsistencies in the witness's testimony, to point out inconsistencies between witnesses, to lead the witness into implausible assertions, or to create implications that the witness will be unable to deny later.

Within each segment of your cross-examination, it will usually be preferable to give the details first. No matter what your goal, the witness will be far more likely to agree with a series of small, incremental facts before the thrust of the examination becomes apparent. Once you have challenged, confronted, or closely questioned a witness, it will be extremely difficult to go back and fill in the details necessary to make the challenge stick.

Assume that the weather conditions turn out to be of some value to you in the automobile accident case. If you begin your examination of the defendant with questions about the weather, you will be likely to obtain cooperative answers. As a preliminary matter, you may have no difficulty establishing that it was clear and sunny that day. Perhaps you will have additional details available—the defendant left home without an umbrella, he wasn't wearing overshoes, he didn't turn on his headlights. Conversely, imagine a first question such as, "Isn't it true that you never even tried to stop before the collision?" Now what is the witness likely to say when you ask whether the pavement was dry? Suddenly, the witness may remember all manner of fog and puddles; of course he tried to stop, but the street was just too wet.

There is an additional advantage to beginning a cross-examination with details. It allows you to learn about the witness with a minimum of risk. We know that cross-examination is not the time to gather new information about the case. You should only ask questions to which you know the answer, or where you at least have a good reason to expect a favorable answer. On the other hand, you frequently will not know how a particular witness will react to your questions. Will the witness be cooperative or compliant, or can you expect a struggle every inch of the way? Worse, is the witness slippery and evasive? Even worse, is the witness inclined to mislead and prevaricate? Worst of all, have you misinterpreted the information or made some other blunder in your own preparation? You must learn the answers to these questions before you proceed to the heart of your cross-examination. While it may be mildly uncomfortable to receive an unexpectedly evasive answer to a question about a preliminary detail, it can be positively devastating to discover that you are unable to pin down a witness on a central issue. Beginning with details will allow you to take the witness's measure (and to evaluate your own preparation) at a time of minimum impact and risk.

5.4.2.4 Scatter the Circumstantial Evidence

Inferential or circumstantial evidence[5] is most persuasive when a series of facts or events can be combined in such a way as to create a logical path to the desired conclusion. Unfortunately, facts arranged in this manner on cross-examination will also be highly transparent to the witness. As you stack inference on inference, your direction will become increasingly clear. A hostile or unfriendly witness will then become increasingly uncooperative, perhaps to the point of thwarting your examination. A far safer approach is to scatter the circumstantial evidence throughout the examination, drawing it together only during final argument.

5.4.2.5 Save a Zinger for the End

The final moment of cross-examination may well be the most important. No matter how low-key or friendly your style, almost every cross-examination will in some sense be viewed as a contest between you and the witness. Were you able to shake the adverse testimony? Were you able to help your client? In short, did you do what you set out to do? In this regard the final impression that you leave is likely to be the most lasting. Were you able to finish on a high note, or did you simply give up?

It is therefore imperative that you plan carefully the very last point that you intend to make on cross-examination. It must be a guaranteed winner, the point on which you are willing to make your exit. Indeed, you should write this point down at the very bottom of your note pad, underlined and in bold letters. It should stand alone with nothing to obscure it or distract you from it. Then, if your entire examination seems to fail, if the witness denies every proposition, if the judge sustains every objection, if the heavens fall and doom impends, you can always skip to the bottom of the page and finish with a flourish. Satisfied that you have made this single, telling, case-sealing point, you may proudly announce, "No further questions of this witness," and sit down.

How do you identify your fail-safe zinger? The following guidelines should help.

It Must Be Absolutely Admissible

There can be no doubt about the admissibility of your intended final point. Nothing smacks more of defeat than ending a cross-examination on a sustained objection. If you suspect even for a moment that your zinger might not be allowed, abandon it and choose another. In fact, you should make an entry in the margin of your notes that reminds you of your theory of admissibility. Why is the point relevant? Why isn't it hearsay? How has the foundation been established? Why isn't it speculation?

5. Circumstantial evidence is defined and described in section 4.3.2.6.

It Should Be Central to Your Theory

Since your closing point is likely to be the most memorable, you would be best served to make it one of the cornerstones of your theory. If there are eight facts that you must establish to prevail, you would like to end each cross-examination on one of them. This may not always be possible. Not every opposing witness will testify about an essential matter, and it is important to ensure admissibility by keeping your zinger well within the scope of the direct. Or it may be possible to undermine the witness's credibility by ending on a point that is collateral to your basic theory.

It Should Evoke Your Theme

The very purpose of a trial theme is to create a memorable phrase or invocation that captures the moral basis of your case. The closing moments of cross-examination, therefore, constitute the perfect time to evoke your theme. Attention will never be more focused and memorability will never be higher. Imagine that the plaintiff in the fire truck case was taken directly to a hospital, but the unhurt defendant went on to his office after filling out a police report. If your theme is "Too busy to be careful," you can close your cross-examination with these two questions: "You made it to your office later that morning, didn't you? Taking care of business, I suppose?" You know that the answer to the first question will be "Yes." You don't care about the answer to the second one.

It Must Be Undeniable

It should be obvious by now that your final question must be undeniable. The end of your cross is not the time to argue or quibble with the witness. There are two good ways to ensure undeniability.[6]

First, choose a fact that you can document. Look for something that can be proven from a prior statement of the witness or some other tangible exhibit or writing. If evidence of that sort is unavailable, select a point that has already been made in the testimony of other opposition witnesses, thereby making a denial either implausible or inconsistent with the balance of your opponent's case.

Second, phrase your question in terms of bedrock fact, making sure that it contains nothing that approaches a characterization. The more "factual" your question, the less possible it is for the witness to deny you a simple answer. In the automobile accident case, for example, a purely factual closing question would be: "You arrived at your office later that morning?" The same point, but made with a characterization, would be: "You were so busy that you went straight to your office?" The witness can argue with you about the interpretation of the word "busy," but arrival at his office is a fact.

6. The subject of controlling the witness and ensuring favorable answers is discussed at greater length in section 5.5.

Remember that cross-examination may be followed immediately by redirect examination. Your closing question on cross may provide the opening subject for redirect. Thus, another aspect of undeniability is that the point must not be capable of immediate explanation. For example, the fire truck defendant may have gone straight to his office, but only to retrieve medicine for his heart condition. After that he might not have worked for the next three days. You can omit those facts on cross-examination, but you can be sure that they will be developed on redirect. Since that point can be explained, it is not sufficiently "undeniable" for use as a closing question.

It Must Be Stated with Conviction

No matter what your closing question, you must be able to deliver it with an attitude of satisfied completion. If the subject makes you nervous, worried, or embarrassed, then you must choose another. It is neither necessary nor desirable to smirk, but you must exhibit confidence that your parting inquiry has done its work.

5.4.3 A Classic Format for Cross-Examination

Because almost all cross-examinations will be topical, there can be no standard or prescribed form of organization. The following "classic format" is designed to maximize witness cooperation. Of course, you may have a goal in mind for your cross-examination other than witness cooperation; in that case, feel free to ignore or alter this approach. As a rule of thumb, however, you can best employ principles such as indirection and "detail scattering" by seeking information in this order.

See demonstrations 7.1 and 7.2 in the Visuals Appendix.

5.4.3.1 Friendly Information

Be friendly first. Begin by asking questions that the witness will regard as nonthreatening. These will often be background questions. For example, medical malpractice cases are often based on errors of omission, and you may intend to argue in closing that the defendant physician, by virtue of her extraordinary training, should have known about certain available tests. You can start your cross-examination, then, by asking friendly questions about the defendant's medical education, residency, fellowships, and awards. Most people, even defendants on trial, like to talk about their achievements. There is little doubt that a witness will be the most forthcoming when asked about aggrandizing information at the very outset of the cross-examination.

5.4.3.2 Affirmative Information

After exhausting the friendly information, ask questions that build up the value of your case rather than tear down the opposition's. Much of this information will fill in gaps in the direct testimony. In fact, a good way to plan this portion of the cross is to list the information that you reasonably hope will be included in the direct. Whatever is omitted from the witness's actual testimony will form the core of your affirmative information section. Although adverse witnesses may not be enthusiastic about supplying you with helpful information, they will be unlikely to fight you over answers that might logically have been included in their own direct.

5.4.3.3 Incontrovertible Information

You can now proceed to inquire about facts that damage the opposition's case or detract from the witness's testimony, as long as they are well-settled or can be documented. On these questions, a witness may be inclined to hedge or quibble, but you can minimize this possibility by sticking to the sort of information that ultimately must be conceded.

5.4.3.4 Challenging Information

It is unlikely that a witness will cooperate with you once you begin challenging her memory, perception, accuracy, conduct, or other aspects of her testimony. Therefore, it is usually desirable to proceed through friendly, affirmative, and uncontroverted information before you begin to take sharper issue with the witness. At some point, of course, you will have to ask most witnesses questions that they will recognize as challenges: "Mr. Defendant, the fact is that the first thing you did after the collision was to telephone your office?" Such questions are necessary. When used in their proper place, they will not prevent you from first exploiting the other, more cooperative testimony from the witness.

5.4.3.5 Hostile Information

Hostile information involves confronting the witness directly. You may be able to extract the necessary answers to hostile questions, but certainly you can eliminate all hope of cooperation both then and thereafter. Hostile questions involve assaults on the witness's honesty, probity, peacefulness, character, or background. "Didn't you spend time in prison?" "You never intended to live up to the contract?" "That was a lie, wasn't it?"

5.4.3.6 Zinger

Always end with a zinger. You know why.

5.5 Questioning Technique

You know what you want to cover on cross-examination, and you know the order in which you want to cover it. How do you ask questions that will ensure your success?

The essential goal of cross-examination technique is witness control. As we noted above, your object on cross-examination is to tell your client's story. This requires that you set the agenda for the examination, that you determine the flow of information, and that you require answers to your questions. In short, you must always be in control of the witness and the testimony. This does not, by the way, mean that you must appear to be in control, and it certainly does not mean that you must be domineering, rude, or overbearing toward the witness. In this context, control means only that the examination follows the course that you have selected and that the information produced be only that which you have determined to be helpful.

Control, therefore, can be either nonassertive or assertive. With a cooperative or tractable witness, control may mean nothing more than asking the right questions and getting the right answers. A hostile, evasive, or argumentative witness may require that you employ more assertive means.

There are a number of questioning techniques, to be discussed below, that you can employ to ensure witness control. At a minimum, however, every question on cross-examination should have all of the following bedrock characteristics.

Short. Questions on cross-examination must be short in both concept and execution. If a question contains more than a single fact or implication, it is not short in concept. Divide it. If a question is more than ten words long, it is not short in execution. Try to shorten it.

Leading. Every question on cross-examination should be leading. Include the answer in the question. Tell the witness exactly what to say. Cross-examination is no time to seek the witness's interpretation of the facts. It is the time for you to tell a story by obtaining the witness's assent. A nonleading question invites the witness to wander away from your story.[7]

Propositional. The best questions on cross-examination are not questions at all. Rather, they are propositions of fact that you put to the witness in interrogative form. You already know the answer—you simply need to produce it from the witness's mouth. Every question on cross-examination should contain a proposition that falls into one of these three categories: 1) you already know the answer; 2) you can otherwise document or prove the answer; or 3) any answer will be helpful. An example of the last sort of question would be the classic inquiry to a witness who must admit having previously given a false statement: "Were you lying then, or are you lying now?"

7. There are a few situations in which you may want to ask a nonleading question on cross-examination. This chiefly occurs when you are absolutely sure that the witness must answer in a certain way and you believe that the dramatic value of the answer will be enhanced by having it produced in the witness's own words. If, for example, you are cross-examining a witness with a prior felony conviction, you might ask the nonleading question: "How many years did you spend in prison after you were convicted of perjury?" Even in low-risk situations such as this, however, the technique has been known to backfire. Use it sparingly, if at all.

5.5.1 Planning for Control

Control of a witness on cross-examination begins with your plan and is achieved, in large measure, on your notepad. In other words, a cross-examination is only as good as your outline.

5.5.1.1 Avoid Written Questions

Many beginning lawyers like to write out all of the questions they intend to ask on cross-examination. This can be an excellent drill since it will concentrate your thinking and sharpen your specific questions. As we will see below, much of the art of cross-examination involves asking short, incremental, closely sequenced questions. Since this is an unnatural style for many lawyers, it can be useful indeed to write out the questions first to make sure that they conform to this ideal.

When it comes to the actual examination, however, it is usually a mistake to read from a prepared list of questions. The great majority of lawyers use notes, of course, but not in the form of written questions. Reading your questions will deprive your examination of the appearance of spontaneity. For all but the most accomplished thespians, reading from a script will sound just like reading from a script, or worse, a laundry list. It will be almost impossible to develop any rhythm with the witness.

Reading from a set of questions will also deprive you of the control that comes from eye contact with the witness. The witness will be less likely to follow your lead, and you will be less able to observe the witness's demeanor of telltale signs of nervousness or retraction. Witnesses often betray themselves or open doors during cross-examination, and you must constantly be ready to exploit such an unplanned opportunity. Needless to say, that will not happen if you are tied to a set of written questions.

There are even drawbacks simply to keeping your notes in the form of a set of written questions. First, this format encourages bobbing your head up and down from pad to witness. Even if you do not read the questions, you will spend an inordinate amount of time looking away from the witness. A more serious difficulty is the increased likelihood of losing your place. This is not a small problem. Notes based on written questions will be much longer than an outline, and the questions will all tend to look alike. The possibility of losing your place on a page, or being unable to find the page that you need, is extreme. Almost nothing is more embarrassing or damaging than being unable to continue a cross-examination because your notes have become disorganized.

Written questions are best used as a pre-examination device. Write them out, study them, hone them, rearrange them, and then discard them in favor of a topical outline.

5.5.1.2 Using an Outline

The purpose of your outline should be to remind yourself of the points that you intend to make on cross-examination and to ensure that you do not inadvertently omit anything. Do not regard your notes as a script, but rather as a set of cues or prompts, each of which introduces an area of questioning. Beneath each of the main prompts you will list the key details that you intend to elicit from the witness.

Your outline can follow the same format that you have used since high school. Principal topics are represented by Roman numerals, subtopics are denoted by capital letters, and smaller points or component details are represented by Arabic numerals. Although the form for academic outlines goes on to involve lower case letters, small Roman numerals, and other levels ad infinitum, the outline for a cross examination will become too complex if it extends beyond the third level.

The main topics for the cross-examination of the defendant in the fire truck case would probably include the defendant's background, the events of the accident, and his post-accident conduct. In abbreviated form, an outline for that cross-examination might look like this:

I. Background
   A. Business consultant
      1. Sole proprietor
      2. Clients are important
      3. Timeliness and efficiency
   B. Locations and distances
      1. His home
      2. His office
      3. Parking lot

II. Accident
   A. Plans for day
      1. Left home at 7:55 a.m.
      2. Meeting at 8:30 a.m.
   B. Weather
   C. Fire truck
      1. Didn't see
      2. Didn't hear
      3. Didn't stop

III. Post-accident

A. Phoned office/important client

B. Didn't call ambulance for plaintiff

Note that the use of subparts will vary according to the importance of, and your need to remember, discrete details. Depending on your level of confidence, for example, you might want to fill in additional details for the weather conditions. On the other hand, you can usually expect to remember what was important to your case about the weather.

More importantly, note that the indented headings make it very easy to follow an outline in this form. It is not organized merely to tell the story, but also to provide a visual pattern that allows you to keep your place. Even when you lose your place, the sparsity of words makes recovery that much simpler. Moreover, using single-word or short-phrase headings should allow you to keep your outline short. It may be possible to limit your notes to a single sheet of paper or a single screen, and it should almost never be necessary to use more than a few pages.

Finally, your zinger has to be the very last Roman numeral at the bottom of the final page of your outline. It is a good idea to write the zinger in bold print so that it will have maximum visual impact. You will want it to stand out when you need it.

5.5.1.3 "Referencing" Your Outline

Add references

Once you have drafted the outline for your cross-examination, you should proceed to "reference" it. Referencing allows you to refresh the recollection of forgetful witnesses and to impeach or contradict witnesses who give you evasive, unexpected, or false answers.

Across from every important subtopic and crucial detail, make a note that records the source for the point that you intend to make. You need not reference the major topic headings, but other than that it will often prove useful to reference your notes line by line. At a minimum, you must reference every point that you consider essential to your case, as well as those that you expect to be controverted by or challenging to the witness. For example, assume that you know about the defendant's meeting plans because he testified to them at his deposition. At the point in your outline where you reach the defendant's intended destination on the morning of the accident, make a note of the page and line in his deposition where he testified that he had an 8:30 a.m. meeting with an important client.

In addition to deposition transcripts, reference sources can be letters, reports, memoranda, notes, and even photographs. The best sources, of course, are the witness's own prior words. Adequate secondary sources may include documents that the witness reviewed, acted on, or affirmed by silence. In most circumstances, the testimony of a different person, though perhaps useful, will not be a reliable source for referencing a cross-examination.

Many lawyers prepare their outlines (whether on paper or on a laptop) by first drawing a vertical line slightly to the right of the center of the page. They then write the outline for the examination on the left side of the line, while references are noted on the right side. The right column may also be used for note-taking during the witness's direct examination. The first part of such a note pad would look like this:

Cross-Examination of Defendant

I. Background	
A. Business consultant	Dep., p. 6, line 11
1. Sole proprietor	Dep., p. 7, line 2
2. Clients important	Dep., p. 26, line 23
3. Timeliness	Dep., p. 19, line 4
B. Locations and distance	
1. His home	Dep., p. 2, line 16
2. His office	Lease
3. Parking lot	Rental contract

It is also useful to devote the top of your first page to a sort of mini-reference chart, where you list all of the important times, dates, and addresses in the case. Although by the time of trial you may think that you know these details as well as your own name, no lawyer is forever safe from "drawing a blank" on crucial details at crucial moments. The last thing you want to do is cross-examine a witness as to her whereabouts for the wrong date. Cautious lawyers have even been known to write the names of the key witnesses—including their own clients—at the top of the first page.

5.5.2 Questions That Achieve Control

Having organized and outlined the cross-examination, we are now ready to consider the precise techniques that provide maximum control over a witness's testimony. Many of the following rules will seem familiar since most are based on the principles of apposition, duration, indirection, and misdirection. As with all of trial advocacy, it will seldom be possible to apply every rule in any given examination (although some lawyers have managed somehow to break every rule during a single examination). Rather, you must use your own good judgment to determine which principles will be most effective in your particular situation.

5.5.2.1 Use Incremental Questions

Cross-examination should proceed in a series of small, steady steps. No matter how certain you are that a witness must grant you an answer, there is always a risk that she will disagree.

Disagreement can hurt. While it is true that you may often bring a witness back under control, at a minimum that effort will generally waste time and distract attention from your more important goals.[8]

The larger the scope of your question, the more likely you are to give the witness room to disagree. It is therefore preferable to divide areas of questioning into their smallest component parts. For example, assume that you are about to cross-examine the defendant in the fire truck case. You want to establish the distance from his parking garage to his office to show that he was in a hurry to get to his meeting that morning. You could ask one question: "Your parking garage is located three blocks from your office, isn't it?" If the witness says "yes," you will have achieved your purpose, but what will you do if the witness says "no"? Make no mistake about it—no matter how carefully you have planned your cross-examination, some witnesses will find a way to say "no." In the above scenario, for example, the defendant may decide that the distance is somewhere between two and three blocks, because his office building is not exactly on the corner. Or he may quibble with you over whether you can call the parking lot "his" garage. You may even have made a mistake about the facts. In any event, you can head off such potential problems by asking incremental questions, such as these:

> Q: You have a monthly parking contract at the Garrick garage?
>
> Q: The Garrick is located at the northwest corner of Randolph and Dearborn?
>
> Q: Your office is located at 48 South Dearborn?
>
> Q: The shortest distance from the Garrick to your office is to go south on Dearborn?
>
> Q: First you must cross Randolph? Then you must cross Washington? Then you must cross Madison?
>
> Q: And your office is further south on that block, isn't it?

This technique allows you to do two things. First, it cuts off the escape route for a witness who is inclined to argue or prevaricate. The incremental questions provide small targets for a witness's inventiveness. More importantly, it lets you know early in the sequence whether the witness is likely to disagree with you. The use of incremental questions allows you to test the witness for cooperation and to

8. Techniques for reasserting control are discussed in section 5.5.4.

determine whether your own factual assumptions are correct before you reach an embarrassing point of no return.

5.5.2.2 Use Sequenced Questions for Impact

Sequencing may be used on cross-examination for a variety of purposes. First, as on direct, you may use sequencing (or apposition) to clarify your story or enhance its impact on the trier of fact. Eliciting two facts in close proximity can underscore relationships, contrasts, inconsistencies, connections, or motives. In the fire truck case, you may sequence your cross-examination so that the defendant testifies within a very short time about the important meeting that he had to attend on the morning of the accident and his earlier decision to leave the auto repair shop without servicing his brakes. The apposition of these otherwise disparate facts can help develop your theme: "Too busy to be careful."

The defendant, of course, will not want to draw the connection for you that his busy professional life leads him to neglect safety. You may be able to control the witness, however, by sequencing your examination in a way that multiplies the impact of two otherwise unconnected facts.

5.5.2.3 Use Sequenced Questions for Indirection

What is clear to the jury will also be clear to the witness. Alerted that you have decided to exploit his busy schedule, the defendant may decide not to concede so readily the key details of his visit to the mechanic. In such situations, you may use sequencing not for clarity and impact, but for indirection. You may therefore decide simply to abandon apposition and instead to "scatter" the information about the defendant's busy schedule.

Alternatively, however, you may still use sequencing to make your point. The key lies in the order of the examination. Assume that you still want to elicit in close proximity the information about the repair shop and the client meeting. Neither event is a necessary predicate to the other, so which one should you establish first?

Although it may seem counterintuitive, the answer is to save the "surest" topic for last. In the above example, you can probably be the most "sure" that the defendant will admit going directly to his office following the accident. The issue is purely factual, and there are, no doubt, other witnesses who will place him at the office that morning. You can also be fairly sure that the witness will admit having been at the repair shop, since again there will be witnesses to place him there.

On the other hand, you must be decidedly less sure that he will concede that he opted not to have his brakes fixed because he was busy that day. The defendant's motivations are his own, and they can seldom be established from a collateral source.[9]

9. This discussion assumes that you do not have available a prior statement from the defendant that admits the facts that you are seeking to establish.

Thus, motivation is your touchiest subject. It should therefore come at the beginning of your sequence, for two reasons. First, recall that the witness will be most cooperative before he understands where the examination is headed. Since proof of motivation depends most on the witness's own cooperation, you will want to address that issue at the beginning of that part of the examination. Second, you know that you want to conclude every area of the examination successfully. You will therefore save your more "provable" points for last.

How will this particular exercise in sequencing work? Assume that the brake shop incident occurred on Monday and that the accident was on Friday. Begin by asking the witness about his business schedule on that Monday. Do not bring up automobile repairs until you have completely established all of his appointments and time commitments for that day. Then ask him about his visit to the mechanic, concluding with the fact that he did not leave his car there. You may now go on to the day of the accident, establishing that the defendant went on to his office following the collision. Through careful sequencing you should be able to maintain sufficient control of the witness and keep both events in close apposition.

5.5.2.4 Use Sequenced Questions for Commitment

Using sequenced questions in combination with incremental questions may occasionally allow you to compel an unwilling witness to make important concessions. Facts can often be arranged in a manner that gives their progression a logic of its own. When the initial facts in a sequence are sufficiently small and innocuous, a witness may be led to embark on a course of concessions that will be impossible to stop.

Suppose that you represent the defendant in the fire truck case, and you want to prove that the plaintiff was not as seriously injured as she claims. There is, of course, absolutely no possibility that the witness will admit flatly to having exaggerated her injuries. On the other hand, she may initially admit the accuracy of a series of smaller, more innocuous assertions. Note that the sequencing of the following questions commits the witness to a premise that will later be expanded in a way that she will not be able to deny.

> Q: You have testified that the accident has interfered with your enjoyment of life?
>
> Q: For example, you have given up playing tennis?
>
> Q: Tennis, of course, requires considerable physical exertion?
>
> Q: Because of that, you have dropped your membership in the North Shore Tennis Club?
>
> Q: One of your other interests is the fine arts, isn't that right?
>
> Q: In particular, you admire the French impressionists, correct?

Q: Of course, the accident has not diminished your appreciation for the French impressionists?

Q: In fact, you are a fairly serious student of nineteenth century art?

Q: You share that interest with your friends and children, don't you?

Q: You have maintained your membership in the Art Institute, haven't you?

Q: You attended the special Monet exhibition, didn't you? And your membership allowed you to bring along some friends as guests, correct?

Q: And in fact, you have continued to serve as a guide for schoolchildren?

Q: Being a guide, of course, involves accompanying the children throughout the museum?

Sequencing was used in this example to commit the witness to several premises that were later expanded in a way that she would be unable to deny. Tennis is strenuous. She continues to enjoy the French impressionists. She was able to keep up with her friends at a crowded museum exhibit. And eventually, she is still capable of chasing children around the Art Institute.

5.5.2.5 Create a "Conceptual Corral"

As we have seen, the purpose of cross-examination is often to "box in" a witness so that crucial facts cannot be averted or denied. It is often useful to think of this process as building a "conceptual corral" around the witness. After building the first three sides of the corral, you may then close the gate with your final proposition.

Each side of the conceptual corral is formed by a different sort of question. One side consists of the witness's own previous admissions or actions, another is formed by undeniable facts, and the third is based on everyday plausibility. The length of any particular side, or the extent to which you will rely on any of the three sorts of information, will differ from case to case. With almost every witness, however, the three sides of the corral can be constructed to form an enclosure from which the witness cannot escape.

Suppose that you want to prove that the defendant in the accident case ignored the fire truck. That proposition will be the gate of your corral; you won't make it obvious until all three sides have been put into place.

The first side is formed by the witness's own admissions, gathered from his deposition, documents in the case, or his earlier testimony on direct: he was driving south on Sheridan Road, he was late for an appointment, he had over ten miles yet to go, he had to park a few blocks from his office, and he didn't hit his brakes before the collision.

Side two consists of undeniable facts that have already been established or that can readily be proved by other witnesses: the fire truck was the largest vehicle on the road; it was red; the other traffic stopped; the weather was clear.

The last side is based on plausibility. A fire truck can be seen at a distance of over one hundred yards. Fire trucks have red lights to increase their visibility. A car traveling at thirty miles per hour takes only about ninety feet to stop.

The three sides having been constructed, the gate will simply fall into place: the defendant could only have missed the fire truck by ignoring the roadway.

Note that the fourth side of the corral often will not require any questions at all. Admissions, facts, and plausibility will frequently be all that you need to establish your ultimate point. And, as we will discuss below, it is usually preferable not to confront the witness with your ultimate proposition.

5.5.2.6 Avoid Ultimate Questions

It will often be tempting to confront an adverse witness with one last conclusory question: "So you just ignored the fire truck, didn't you?" Resist this temptation. If you have already established all of the incremental facts that lead to your conclusion, then you will have little to gain by making the question explicit. At best you will repeat what has become obvious, and at worst you will give the witness an opportunity to recant or amend the foundational testimony.

Even worse, you may not have established the incremental facts as fully as you thought. Under these circumstances, you can expect the witness not only to disagree with your ultimate proposition, but to be prepared to explain exactly why you are wrong.

The classic approach to cross-examination calls for the lawyer to elicit all of the facts that lead to the ultimate conclusion, and then stop. The final proposition is saved for final argument. By saving the ultimate point for final argument, you ensure that the witness will not be able to change or add to the testimony. To a certain extent, you also avoid informing opposing counsel of your argument, and you diminish the likelihood of having your position refuted either on redirect or through another witness.

While some writers state flatly that you should always save your ultimate point for argument, a more flexible rule is more realistic. Perhaps it could best be stated as "Save the ultimate point for argument unless you are certain that it will be inescapable." For example, the witness may already have admitted your ultimate point during her deposition. Or your proposition might have been so firmly established by the evidence as to be undeniable. Occasionally, you might even want the witness to disagree with your conclusion so that you may exploit the sheer implausibility of the denial. Short of these circumstances, however, the safest route is generally to be satisfied with establishing a chain of incremental facts and to reserve the capstone for argument.

5.5.2.7 Listen to the Witness and Insist on an Answer

There is more to controlling a witness on cross-examination than asking the right questions. You must also make sure that you have gotten the correct answers. This requires you to listen to the witness. Even the most painstakingly prepared question can elicit the wrong answer. The witness may not have understood you, or she may have detected an ambiguity in your inquiry. Some witnesses will argue with you for the sake of argument, some will try to deflect your examination, and some will simply answer a question different from the one that you asked. In any event, you must always recall that it is the witness's answer that constitutes evidence, not your question, and you must listen carefully to ensure that the evidence is what you expected.

You can often correct an answer by restating your question. Consider the following scenario from the fire truck case:

> Q: Isn't it true that all of the other traffic stopped for the fire truck?
>
> A: How would they know to stop? There was no siren.
>
> Q: You didn't answer my question. All of the other cars did stop?
>
> A: Yes.

In the preceding example, the defendant apparently decided that he did not want to respond to the cross-examiner's question, so he deflected it by answering a different question. An inattentive lawyer might have interpreted that answer as a denial or otherwise let it go by. The advocate listened more carefully, however, and was able to obtain the precise information sought.

Note as well that the cross-examiner in this situation would be equally satisfied with either an affirmative or negative answer. If the defendant admitted that all of the other traffic stopped, then the point is made. If the defendant insisted that the traffic hadn't stopped, he would be subject to contradiction by many other witnesses. Either way, the cross-examination would be successful. The greater problem, then, is the non-answer. There are many techniques for requiring difficult or evasive witnesses to answer your questions,[10] but the first step is always to listen to the witness and to insist on an answer.

---

10. *See* section 5.5.4.

5.5.3 *Questions That Lose Control*

The pitfalls of cross-examination are well known: refusals to answer, unexpected answers, argumentative witnesses, evasive and slippery witnesses. Significantly, virtually all of these problems derive from the same basic error on the part of the cross-examiner—failure to control the testimony.

Control of testimony on cross-examination means ensuring that 1) all of your questions are answered with the information that you want, and 2) no information is produced other than what you have requested. In other words, the witness must answer your questions and only your questions. An examination goes slightly out of control when a witness hedges or withholds answers. It goes seriously out of control when a witness begins to spout entirely new information.

While some witnesses are intractable by nature, lawyers often bring these problems on themselves. Certain questions and styles of questioning constitute virtual invitations to a witness to set up an independent shop. The most common of these are detailed below. From time to time, there may be a reason to use one of the following sorts of questions, but as a general proposition they are all to be avoided.

5.5.3.1 Nonleading Questions

The cardinal rule on cross-examination is to use leading questions. The cardinal sin is to abandon that tool. We have discussed at length the advantages of stating your questions in the form of leading propositions. For some reason, however, many lawyers seem impelled to drift into nonleading questions once an examination has begun. You can control a witness this way:

> Q: You were thirty feet away from plaintiff's car when you first applied your brakes, correct?

But you lose control when you ask:

> Q: How far from the plaintiff's car were you when you applied your brakes?

Why would a lawyer make such an elementary mistake? The principal reason no doubt lies in lack of confidence. It is awkward to put words in another person's mouth. We do not generally conduct conversations by telling others exactly what to say. It is even more uncomfortable when you are uncertain about the content yourself. How odd it feels to tell the driver of an automobile exactly where and when he applied his brakes. An easy response mechanism to this unease is to revert to a more natural style of discourse—just ask what happened. We all occasionally fall into the trap of turning control of the examination over to the witness.

The solution to this problem is preparation. If you are unsure of where the witness applied his brakes, of course you will not tell him that it was thirty feet. So be sure. Read his deposition, scour the police report, measure the skid marks, talk to other witnesses, calculate his speed and stopping distance. Then, once you are certain that there is no plausible denial, tell him exactly what he did. Because your leading question is based on verifiable facts, the great likelihood is that the witness will agree with you. If the witness disagrees, all is still well and good. After all, you have the facts to use in further cross-examination or to introduce through another witness.

There are two legitimate reasons to suspend temporarily the use of leading questions. Neither is without its risks, and both should be used with care. First, you will occasionally need to learn a bit of information from a witness to continue a cross-examination. For example, there might have been two routes available for the fire truck defendant to reach his office from the scene of the accident. Having prepared thoroughly, you know that you will be able to show that he was already so late that neither route would have gotten him to his appointment on time. Thus, even if you don't know the answer to the question, you can safely ask a nonleading question: "What road did you intend to take downtown?" You need that information to structure the balance of your examination, and you can handle whichever answer you are given. Never employ this approach because you are curious or because you hope that the answer will be helpful. The potential for backfiring is great. You must truly be certain that you need to ask an informational question and that you have prepared alternate examinations to meet whichever answer you are given.

Second, and even less frequently, you may believe that an answer will have more impact if it comes in the witness's words instead of yours. Sometimes this works, but often it does not. Suppose that you are cross-examining the fire truck plaintiff on the extent of her injuries. You know that she is still able to work at her job and that she recently went on a three-day camping trip. It would indeed heighten the drama of the moment if you could obtain the damning testimony in her own words:

> Q: Ma'am, please tell us all of the things that you were able to do on your recent camping trip.
>
> A: Oh, I was able to hike, fish, swim, pitch the tent, carry my backpack, and sleep on the ground.

Perhaps the witness testified to all of that during her deposition. By the time of trial, however, the more likely scenario will be:

> Q: Ma'am, please tell us all of the things that you were able to do on your recent camping trip.
>
> A: I was hardly able to do anything. Everything I tried caused me pain, even sleeping.

Nonleading questions might have a terrific potential impact, but leading questions have the incalculable advantage of greater safety. Consider:

> Q: Ma'am, you went on a three-day camping trip?
>
> A: Yes.

Q: You went hiking?

A: Yes, but it caused me pain.

Q: You went fishing and swimming?

A: Yes.

Q: You pitched the tent?

A: Yes, but that hurt, too.

Q: You stayed out in the woods for three days?

A: Yes.

Note that the witness may be able to argue with you notwithstanding your use of leading questions. The difference, however, is that short leading questions limit her ability to do so while increasing your ability to bring her back under control. Furthermore, the "yes, but" nature of her embellishments necessarily makes them less convincing.

Still, there may be times when it is truly advantageous to extract cross-examination testimony in a witness's own words. This technique is most likely to work when the information you are after is well-documented, factual, and short. In the above example, assuming that you have adequate deposition testimony, you might be able to use nonleading questions to the following extent:

Q: Where did you spend last Labor Day weekend?

A: At Eagle River Falls.

Q: What is Eagle River Falls?

A: It is a campground.

That is enough—do not push your luck. Since the last thing you want to do is lose control of the testimony, now is the time to go back to leading questions.

5.5.3.2 "Why" or Explanation Questions

It is almost impossible to imagine a need to ask a witness to explain something on cross-examination. If you already know the explanation, then use leading questions to tell it to the witness. If you do not already know the explanation, then cross-examination surely is not the time to learn it. No matter how assiduously you have prepared, no matter how well you think you understand the witness's motives and reasons, a witness can always surprise you by explaining the unexplainable.

The greatest temptation to ask for an explanation arises when a witness offers a completely unexpected answer. The dissonance between the expectation and the actual response cries out for resolution. The natural reaction is to resolve the inconsistency by asking the witness: "Please explain what you mean by that."

Unfortunately, the witness will be more than happy to explain, almost always to the detriment of the cross-examiner. The following scenario is not unrealistic:

Q: Your parking garage was located three blocks from your office, correct?

A: Yes.

Q: And the sidewalks are always very crowded between 8:00 and 8:30 in the morning?

A: That's right.

Q: You usually have to wait for one or more traffic lights between the garage and your office, don't you?

A: I do.

Q: So you have to plan on at least ten minutes to get from your garage to your office, right?

A: No, that is not right. I usually make it in three to five minutes.

Q: Please explain how you can travel that distance, under those circumstances, in only three to five minutes.

A: It's simple. There is an express bus that travels that route in a bus lane. I get on in front of the garage, and its next stop is right in front of the office. Even in heavy traffic it never takes more than five minutes since the bus lane is always clear and the traffic lights are coordinated.

There are many common questions that invite such long, unwelcome answers. They should all be excised from your cross-examination vocabulary. Do not ask a witness to explain. Do not ask a "why" question. Do not ask a question that begins with "How do you know" or "Tell us the reason." If you receive an unexpected answer, the fault probably lies with the original question. The best solution is usually to move on or rephrase your inquiry.[11] Allowing the witness to dig the hole a little deeper cannot help you.

Asking a witness to explain is the equivalent of saying, "I've grown tired of controlling this cross-examination. Why don't you take over for a while?"

5.5.3.3 "Fishing" Questions

Fishing questions are the ones that you ask in the hope that you might catch something. It has been said before, and it is worth repeating here: do not ask questions to which you do not know the answers. For every reason that you have

11. Reasserting control in such situations is discussed in greater detail below at section 5.5.4.

to think that the answer will be favorable, there are a dozen reasons you haven't thought of, all of which suggest disaster.

Very few lawyers actually intend to go fishing during cross-examination; most lawyers plan only to elicit information that they have developed during preparation for trial. Nonetheless, temptation has been known to strike. A witness, during either direct or cross, may expose an enticing, but incomplete, morsel of information. It is difficult to resist exploring such an opening, just to see if anything is really there. That is how the fishing starts.

In our fire truck case, for example, suppose that during discovery the plaintiff produced medical reports indicating that she would need to participate in extensive physical therapy for the next several years. During her direct testimony at trial, however, she has unexpectedly stated, "My doctor said that I did not need to go to physical therapy any longer, and I ended it several months ago." The suggestion seems obvious; her injuries are not as severe as was previously thought and she is now well on the way to resuming her normal life. Defense counsel immediately sees a vision of reduced damages. The temptation to go fishing on cross is now nearly irresistible; the defendant's lawyer wants to make sure that the record is clear as to the plaintiff's recovery.

Unfortunately, defendant's counsel is likely to "catch" information sharply different from that which was sought:

Q: You have told us that your doctor terminated your physical therapy.

A: That is correct.

Q: Isn't that because your recovery has been quicker than was expected, and you don't need the therapy any longer?

A: No. It is because the therapy was too painful, and I wasn't making any progress.

The defendant's lawyer in the above scenario had a good reason to hope that the "therapy" questions would produce helpful information. The most important part of the answer, however, was unknown. Counsel simply had no way of predicting what the witness would say about why the physical therapy ended. Reasonably hoping to turn up a good answer, counsel instead made the plaintiff's case stronger. That is what can happen when you go fishing.

5.5.3.4 Long Questions

Long questions have an almost limitless capacity to deprive a cross-examiner of witness control. Recall that short, single-fact, propositional questions give a witness the least room to take issue with your point. By contrast, long questions, by their very nature, multiply a witness's opportunity to find something with which to disagree. The more words you use, the more chance there is that a witness will refuse to adopt them all.

A second problem with long questions is that they are easily forgotten or misunderstood. Even a witness with every reasonable intention to honestly and forthrightly answer can be misled or baffled by a lengthy question. Thereafter, the witness may insist on answering the question that she thought you asked rather than the one that you meant to ask.

Finally, long questions diminish your ability to enlist the judge in your efforts to control a witness. It is a little-known, and even less-acknowledged, characteristic of trial judges that they do not all tend to pay close attention to attorneys' questions, particularly in jury trials. It is, after all, the answer that constitutes evidence. Given the principle of primacy, long questions have the greatest potential to lose a judge's attention. In ordinary circumstances, this is not of great moment, since the judge's impression, or even understanding, of the question may not be essential. Once a witness has avoided answering, however, the judge's perception of the question can become crucial.

Counsel will often want to request the judge to direct a witness to answer a question "yes" or "no." Understandably, a judge will only be inclined to do this if she has heard and comprehended the entire question. Even if your question is completely susceptible of a "yes" or "no" answer, a judge who has tuned out the last two-thirds of your inquiry is extremely unlikely to restrict the witness's answer.

There is no fixed point at which a question becomes "long." Some inquiries, depending on the nature of the concept and the cooperativeness of the witness, may call for more words than others. A useful rule of thumb is that any question of ten words or fewer may be considered "short." You may wish to exceed this length, but only for a good reason.

5.5.3.5 "Gap" Questions

"Gap" questions constitute an especially enticing subset of explanation questions. Interestingly, they are often most irresistible to lawyers who are particularly well prepared or attentive.

Imagine that you are the prosecutor in a hit-and-run case. You know the date on which the crime occurred, but because there were no eyewitnesses, you have been able to narrow the time of the crime only to a six-hour window. The defendant has raised the defense of alibi. You have thoroughly researched the law and meticulously prepared the facts of your case, which is based entirely on circumstantial evidence. The defendant has taken the stand and testified in his own defense. Listening carefully, you were surprised to notice that he left several half-hour gaps in his alibi.

The defendant is now available for cross-examination. The temptation may be overwhelming to alert the jury to the gaps in the defendant's alibi: "Mr. Defendant, you told us where you were at 2:00 p.m., but you didn't say anything about 2:30 p.m., did you?" Do not ask that question—you will lose control. It is an unspoken invitation to the witness to fill in the gap. Even if the witness does not take the opportunity to complete his alibi, you can be certain that opposing counsel will do it for him on redirect. The far better tactic is to allow the omission to remain unexplained and then to point it out during final argument.

Gaps are found in direct testimony more often than one might expect. A witness may neglect to testify about one of a series of important events or may omit testimony concerning a crucial document. Alternatively, a witness might leave out important evidence on damages or may fail entirely to testify as to an element, such as proximate cause, of your opponent's case.

How can you avoid the temptation to ask "gap" questions? The key is to remember that it is your opponent's burden to prove their case. Everything that they leave out of their case works in your favor. In most circumstances the absence of proof can be interpreted as negative proof.[12]

Of course, your opposition may also create gaps in their testimony by design, purposely leaving out facts that damage their case, but are helpful to yours. Needless to say, you will want to address these omissions during your cross-examination. The fatal "gap" questions are the ones that are directed at omissions in the other side's case. A useful way to keep this distinction in mind is the following: Do not cross-examine on omissions in testimony. Do cross-examine on the absence of facts.

Thus, when your opposition has failed to prove something, simply allow the gap to remain. Comment on it during final argument, not cross-examination.

5.5.3.6 "You Testified" Questions

Another common method of surrendering control to a witness is by asking questions that seem to challenge the witness to recall the content of her earlier direct testimony. These can be referred to as "you testified" questions because they inevitably contain some variant on those words. Each of the following is a "you testified" question:

> Q: You testified that the assailant had brown hair?
>
> Q: Wasn't it your testimony that you left your house at 8:00 a.m.?
>
> Q: On direct examination you testified that the last possible delivery date was May 17, didn't you?

---

12. The most obvious exception to this rule is a criminal defendant's decision not to testify at all, from which no negative inference may be drawn.

What is wrong with these questions? In each instance they seem to call for relevant information. They are all leading. They are all short. They are all propositional. The problem with "you testified" questions is that they invite the witness to quibble over the precise wording used on direct examination. The exact language of the witness's earlier answer is seldom essential, but the "you testified" format inflates its apparent importance, often almost to the point of seeming to pick a fight.[13] Imagine these answers to the above questions, with the witness's unspoken thoughts given in parentheses:

> Q: You testified that the assailant had brown hair?
>
> A: No. (I testified that he had sort of sandy brown hair.)
>
> Q: Wasn't it your testimony that you left your house at 8:00 a.m.?
>
> A: That was not my testimony. (I said that I believed that I left my house at approximately 8:00 a.m.)
>
> Q: On direct examination, you testified that the last possible delivery date was May 17, didn't you?
>
> A: I do not believe that is correct. (I think I said that we could not accept delivery any later than May 17.)

Even if you have correctly remembered the witness's precise testimony down to the last word, there is no guarantee that the witness will remember it equally well. At best, you may end up with a response on the order of: "I cannot remember whether those were my exact words." At that point you have lost control, since the examination has now shifted away from your agenda and onto the issue of the superiority of your memory. The court reporter can be called on to resolve the dispute, but that exercise, at a minimum, will disrupt your pace. Besides, you might turn out to be embarrassingly wrong.

It is far less risky, and generally much more effective, to cross-examine witnesses on facts and events, rather than on prior testimony: "You left your home at 8:00 a.m.?" "You expected delivery no later than May 17?" In situations where you want to make it clear that you challenge the witness's version of events, use a formulation such as this one: "You now claim that the assailant had brown hair?"

13. The precise wording of a witness's previous answer can be essential when you intend to impeach the witness through the use of a prior inconsistent statement. In that situation it is usually necessary, and indeed some courts require, that you "recommit" the witness to the testimony that you intend to impeach. Thus, the classic foundation for impeachment by a prior inconsistent statement includes a preliminary "you testified" question. Note, however, that the subject of the impeachment is the witness's earlier testimony and not the actual underlying events. For further information on the specifics of impeachment, *see* section 6.2.

It may be helpful to think of possible cross-examination questions using the following hierarchy. As a general rule, you should prefer questions that are higher on the list:

- Best, direct your questions to what happened.
- Next, direct your questions to what the witness claims happened.
- Last, direct your questions to what the witness said happened.

The closer you can stay to "real life," the less likely you are to lose control of the witness.

5.5.3.7 Characterizations and Conclusions

Another way to risk losing control on cross-examination is to request that a witness agree with a characterization or conclusion. Assume that you are cross-examining the complaining witness in a robbery case. The witness testified on direct that the crime occurred at midnight on a seldom-traveled country road. Your defense is misidentification. Wishing to take advantage of the time and place of the events, you ask this question:

It was too dark to see very well, wasn't it?

You have just asked the witness to agree with your characterization of the lighting conditions. The witness, being nobody's fool, answers:

I could see just fine.

Instead, you should have asked the witness about the facts that led you to the characterization: the sun had gone down, there was no moon that night, there were no street lamps, there were no house lights, and there were no illuminated signs. The characterization could then be saved for final argument.

Some outstanding trial lawyers, through force of personality, splendid preparation, or stunningly good luck, have been quite successful in obtaining a witness's agreement to their characterizations. In the above example, it would be of inestimable value to have the witness concede that it was too dark to see very well. For most lawyers, however, the risk to these questions usually outweighs the gain.

Bear in mind that it may be difficult to draw the line between characterization and fact. It will depend on the specifics of the case, the inclinations of the witness, the context of the question, and many other factors. On the one hand, a question such as, "It was midnight?" is clearly one of fact. On the other hand, a question such as, "Your identification was mistaken?" is no doubt a characterization. There are numerous possibilities in between. Even the question, "It was too dark to see?" might be regarded as either characterization or fact, depending on the witness's background. While most people would regard that statement as conclusory—who is to say when it becomes too dark to see?—a photo-physicist, or perhaps a forensic ophthalmologist, might regard the inquiry as calling for an absolute fact.

Recognizing the impossibility of stating an absolute rule, the wisest course is to examine your questions for their potential to be taken as characterizations. Then make sure that you phrase them as facts.

5.5.4 Reasserting Control

Notwithstanding your best efforts and preparation, some witnesses will inevitably wander beyond your control. Your perfectly reasonable question may result in an absolute torrent of unwelcome, and uncalled for, information. While your first reaction to such testimony may range from anger to panic, the better response is to ask yourself, "Why is this witness out of control?" Once you have answered that question, you can proceed to apply the techniques for reasserting witness control.

A witness typically falls out of control in one of three ways: 1) she has refused to agree with you; 2) she has been invited to explain an answer; or 3) she is being impermissibly uncooperative.[14] In the first two instances the problem is your fault, and you can usually cure it with further questions. In the third case the witness is at fault, and you may need help from the judge.

5.5.4.1 Refusal to Agree

Determine Why the Witness Has Refused to Agree

What happens when you ask a short, propositional, leading question and the witness simply disagrees with you? You are well prepared, you have done your homework, your question is in good form, you know what the answer should be—but the witness will not give you the right answer. The witness is clearly beyond your control, but why?

Imagine that you have asked a purely factual leading question but that the witness will not give you the answer you expect. Perhaps things have gone along the line of one of the following scenarios:

Q: You are the plaintiff's next door neighbor, aren't you?

A: No, I am not.

Or,

Q: When you entered the operating room the chief surgeon was already there, wasn't she?

A: That is not correct.

14. A fourth circumstance, where the witness has changed her testimony, will be covered in the discussion of impeachment. *See* chapter six.

Or,

Q: Wasn't the gun sitting on the desk?

A: No.

In each of these situations you expected an affirmative answer, but you received a resounding negative. Why did it happen? As Shakespeare's Cassius remarked, "The fault, dear Brutus, is not in our stars, but in ourselves." Unless the witness is lying,[15] intentionally uncooperative,[16] or sincerely mistaken,[17] you received the wrong answer because of the nature of your question. This usually happens for one of three reasons: 1) you were wrong about your facts; 2) you included a "compound detail"; or 3) your question contained an "embedded" characterization.

In the first example above, it is possible that you were simply wrong on the facts. This happens to everyone. Perhaps the witness lives across the street or down the block from the plaintiff. Perhaps your investigator gave you erroneous information. Perhaps the police report that you relied on was incorrect. Perhaps you simply got two witnesses confused. These are all common occurrences.

In the second example, it is likely that the cross-examiner included what we will call a compound detail. Recall the question: "When you entered the operating room the chief surgeon was already there, wasn't she?" The chief surgeon's presence in the operating room exactly at the time of the witness's entry is an extra detail. It may be superfluous, but it gives the witness the opportunity to seize on that nuance as a reason for answering "No" to the entire question. The witness is not disagreeing about the chief surgeon's presence, but only about the timing of her arrival. Note, by the way, that the question is not technically compound in form; it asks only for a single fact. Still, the inclusion of an unnecessary detail has the effect of "compounding" the question and releasing the witness from control.

Finally, the question in the third example, while appearing factual on its face, may have been interpreted by the witness as including a characterization. This sort of "embedded characterization" is frequently the reason for an unexpected negative answer. How could a question so purely factual be taken as an embedded characterization? The witness, after all, was asked whether the gun was on the desk. That question calls only for a simple observation; there is no room for interpretation. If all the facts point to the gun's location on the desk, how can this witness respond otherwise? The answer is that one person's fact may indeed be another's characterization. Although you may be quite confident that the piece of furniture in question is a desk, the witness may regard it as a vanity or computer table. Moreover,

15. If the witness is lying or otherwise changing her testimony you will, of course, impeach her through the use of her own prior statement. We know that you have access to a prior statement or other impeaching material, because otherwise you would not have asked the question in the first place. Regarding the mechanics of impeachment, *see* chapter six.
16. Methods for dealing with impermissibly uncooperative witnesses are discussed in section 5.5.4.3.
17. If the witness is mistaken, you will refresh her recollection.

the distinction may be important to the witness, if, for example, there had been several similar pieces of furniture in the room.

Retreat to Constituent Facts

Once you have determined why a witness has refused to agree with you, you can generally bring the witness back under control simply by asking further questions. Of course, you will never ask a witness for an explanation or elaboration. Rather, your following questions should retreat to constituent facts. This method can work regardless of the reason the witness has chosen to disagree. It involves breaking your original question into a series of ever-smaller "constituent facts" until the basis of the witness's disagreement can be eliminated.

The retreat to constituent facts is a retreat only in the tactical sense. By using this method you are not giving up or abandoning your line of questioning. You are "retreating" from an insistence that the witness adopt your exact language. By changing your wording while maintaining the substance of your question, you can effectively reassert control over the witness. In other words, you can accomplish your advocacy objective without the need for direct confrontation.

Mistaken Facts

In retreating to constituent facts, you must first consider that you may have been mistaken in the first place. If your facts were wrong, then the witness obviously will not agree. Reconsider your question. Are you certain of its premise? Are you depending on a reliable source? Is the answer you want truly beyond controversy? If you conclude that the witness may have disagreed with you because of misinformation, then rephrase your question to include only those facts of which you are the most certain.

In the next-door-neighbor example above, for instance, your retreat might take the following form:

Q: You are the defendant's next door neighbor, aren't you?

A: No, I am not.

Q: It is true that you know the defendant?

A: Yes, that is true.

Q: And you do live near the defendant?

A: Yes, I do.

At this point, having established the constituent facts of which you are the most certain, you will stop. Of course, if the witness denies knowing or living near the defendant, then it is obvious that something else is wrong with your cross-examination. Under those circumstances your best recourse is to move on to another line of questioning and to reexamine your notes and files during a break in the testimony.

Compound Details

Compound details are those that are unnecessary to the question, but which have the effect of compounding the inquiry and making possible a denial or disagreement. You can usually reassert control over the witness simply by rephrasing your question without the superfluous detail. Note, however, that not all details are "compound"; some may be quite necessary, even crucial, to your case. Consider the two following examples:

Q: You saw a red car run the stop light, didn't you?

Q: The next car that you saw was red, correct?

In the first question the car's color may well be irrelevant. As long as the witness saw a car run the stop light, it may not matter what color it was. If your case does not depend on the color of the automobile, you may rephrase the question by omitting the detail and retreating to a constituent fact: "You did see a car run the stop light?"

In the second question, on the other hand, it seems apparent that the color of the car does matter, since the cross-examiner has taken pains to point out that the very next automobile was red. Thus, the detail is probably not compound. You can proceed to ask another question to establish that the witness did indeed see a car, but at some point the color will have to be established as well.

Identifying compound details, then, calls for the exercise of judgment. Only the lawyer who prepared the case will know whether a particular detail is essential or unnecessary. In either event, however, you can begin to reassert control over the witness by disaggregating the details and continuing your examination on the basis of constituent facts. Consider the operating room example from the previous section:

Q: When you entered the operating room the chief surgeon was already there, wasn't she?

A: That is not correct.

Q: Well, you did enter the operating room?

A: I did.

Q: You and the chief surgeon were present in the operating room at the same time?

A: We were.

Q: You observed the operation?

A: Yes.

Q: The chief surgeon was there when the procedure began?

A: She was.

Note that the cross-examiner was able to elicit all of the important facts while omitting the compound detail. Of course, if the exact time of the surgeon's entry was relevant to the case, another approach would have to be taken. Such an approach, as used with "embedded characterizations," is discussed in the next section.

Embedded Characterizations

"Embedded characterizations" are statements that appear to be factual, but which, on examination, turn out to contain unspoken characterizations or assumptions. In the example in the introductory section above we saw that even a simple noun like "desk" can contain an embedded characterization, since the term expresses an assumption about the intended use of the piece of furniture.

Our language, as imprecise as it is, is filled with opportunities to use embedded characterizations. They may arise through the use of technical language, professional or occupational jargon, slang, or as we saw above, simply as the result of a differentiated understanding of an otherwise simple noun or verb.

Imagine, for example, that a murder was committed on a Hollywood soundstage just as a studio tour was passing through. A member of the cast was charged with the crime and has raised the SODDI[18] defense. One of the tourists has testified on direct and is now being cross-examined:

Q: You were on the set when you heard a shot?

A: I was.

Q: You looked over and saw a gun on the floor?

A: I did.

Q: It was at the feet of the best boy?

A: No, I don't think so.

As it happens, "best boy" is the professional term for the first assistant electrician on a film crew. The lawyer, apparently a Los Angeles native, thought nothing about using this term. The tourist-witness, however, gave the term its ordinary meaning and therefore gave the cross-examiner the wrong answer.

18. Some Other Dude Did It.

Of course, the "best boy" story is a fanciful example, since only the most star-struck lawyer would fail to recognize it immediately as containing an ambiguity. Even still, the characterization can be unpacked via retreat to constituent facts:

Q: You were on the set when you heard a shot?

A: I was.

Q: You looked over and saw a gun on the floor?

A: I did.

Q: It was at the feet of the best boy?

A: No, I don't think so.

Q: Well, it was at the feet of a member of the film crew?

A: Yes, that's right.

Q: And that person was holding a tool box?

A: Yes, I believe he was.

Q: He was wearing an apron?

A: Yes.

Q: And he was off to the side, away from the actors?

A: Correct.

At this point the constituent facts have been established: the weapon was seen near a member of the crew, not in the vicinity of the defendant-actor. It is not necessary to insist that the witness adopt the lawyer's language or even define the term "best boy." Facts are more important than words, and it is almost always possible to rephrase a question so as to employ more basic facts.

How would one retreat to constituent facts concerning a more realistic question? Assume that you are cross-examining an eyewitness to a crime that occurred at 8:30 p.m. on May 21. You want to establish that it was too dark for anyone to see clearly, but the witness will not agree with your embedded characterization. Therefore, you retreat to constituent facts:

Q: It was already dark at the time of the crime, wasn't it?

A: No, I wouldn't say so.

Q: Well, it was 8:30 p.m., wasn't it?

A: Yes.

Q: And it was still May?

A: Of course.

Q: The sun had set?

A: Yes.

Q: The street lights had gone on?

A: I think that is right.

Q: The cars had their headlights on?

A: I believe so.

Q: Certainly it was no longer daylight, correct?

A: Correct.

At this point you will stop. You have elicited the constituent facts that establish "darkness." It is not necessary to drag a concession out of the witness that it was too dark to see; the facts, and your final argument, will speak for themselves. Note also that most of the constituent facts can be proven through other means. The time of the sunset can be shown from Weather Bureau publications, and the time of street light illumination should be available from municipal records. Thus, a witness who disagrees with your constituent facts can be shown as untrustworthy during your case-in-chief.

Embedded characterizations lurk everywhere. They are particularly tricky precisely because they generally involve a witness's unforeseen interpretation of a term or idea. It is important, therefore, not to become obsessed with avoiding embedded characterizations. To do so would turn your cross-examination into an interminable series of overwhelming details. You should never ask, "Was the gun on a piece of furniture with a flat horizontal surface and four vertical legs?" Go ahead and ask whether it was on the desk. By the same token, go ahead and ask the witness whether it was dark. Maybe she will agree with you, in which case there will be no need to retreat to constituent facts.

It is only when the witness unexpectedly disagrees that you must break your reasonable question into its smallest factual components. This places a premium on quick reaction. Since you cannot plan a response to a witness's unexpected answer, how can you know which constituent facts to use? It is impossible to list constituent facts for every noun and verb in your cross-examination, just in case you might need them.

The answer lies in your theory of the case. You may not anticipate a witness's answer to your question, but you should always know why you asked the question. Why was the question necessary? How will it contribute to your final argument? What did you want to prove? The answers to these questions should almost always supply you with more than sufficient constituent facts.

5.5.4.2 Invited Explanation

Determine Why the Witness Has Explained

Most witnesses launch into unsolicited explanations because they think that they have been requested, or at least allowed, to do so. Whenever a witness begins to answer you at length, you must ask yourself what it was about the question that the witness took as a cue. Certainly you did not directly ask the witness to explain something, but perhaps the question was long, compound, fishing, or asked to fill a "gap."

In addition to those enumerated in the previous section,[19] many questions contain implicit invitations to explain. Questions that use words such as "yet" and "still" are often regarded by witnesses as challenges that call for explanations. Consider this example, in which the last question uses both of the challenging words:

> Q: Immediately before the accident you were waiting for a bus?
>
> A: That's right.
>
> Q: The bus was coming from the north, wasn't it?
>
> A: Correct.
>
> Q: You had to look north for your bus?
>
> A: I did.
>
> Q: The accident took place to the south of the intersection?
>
> A: I guess it did.
>
> Q: Yet you still say that you could see the accident clearly?
>
> A: Well, I turned my head when I heard the brakes screech.

Note that the "yet/still" question added virtually nothing to the examination, other than to alert the witness to the need for an explanation.

Other questions that frequently evoke explanations include those that are argumentative or unfair. Every time you take issue with or confront a witness, and especially when you mischaracterize testimony, you are inviting the witness to offer an explanation. This is not to say that you should never confront a witness during cross-examination; indeed, it frequently is essential that you do so. Rather, you must be aware that confrontation will not always result in meek acquiescence on the witness's part. On the other hand, you should not knowingly mischaracterize a witness's testimony, for reasons both tactical and ethical.

---

19. *See* "Questions That Lose Control," section 5.5.3.

In any event, the first step toward reasserting control of an explaining witness is to understand why the witness has begun to explain. This knowledge is crucial so that you may avoid perpetuating your mistake in your subsequent questions.

Reasserting Control, Part One

See demonstration 8 in the Visuals Appendix.

How do you reassert control over a witness whom you have, even if unintentionally, invited to explain an answer? For many lawyers, the initial reaction to the beginning of an explanation lies somewhere between panic and fury. It is not hard to imagine the mental response when the unwanted explanation begins to emerge: The witness is not supposed to be doing this! The witness is just supposed to be giving the answer that I want! The witness is being unfair !

In these circumstances it is not surprising that the first tendency is to try to get the witness to shut up. Most lawyers try to achieve this in one of two ways: the impolite and the not-so-polite.

The rude way to terminate a witness's explanation is simply by interrupting with an instruction to the witness on the order of "Please just answer the question." Slightly more polite is the common interjection that begins, "Thank you, you have answered my question." Both interruptions ignore the fact that the witness was invited to explain. While the lawyer may not have recognized the invitation as it was issued, there is no guarantee that the judge or jurors will take the attorney's side of the dispute. In fact, there is every reason to think that the judge and jurors will take the witness's side. Nobody likes to see a witness interrupted.

As a rule of thumb, it is best to avoid interrupting a witness. Not only will you appear rude, but the tactic is likely to be ineffective. The witness may persist in explaining, or the judge may insist that you allow the explanation to go forward. More to the point, even when your interruption is successful, the explanation is almost certain to be elicited on redirect examination. You will have lost "rudeness" points for no reason.

There are really only two situations that call for interrupting a witness. The first is when you believe that the witness is about to blurt out some devastating fact that is otherwise absolutely inadmissible. Under these circumstances, redirect examination is not a concern, and you do indeed need to silence the witness. The second situation in which you may want to interrupt a witness is when the witness deserves it, and you consequently have earned the right to interrupt. This occurs when the witness, despite your valiant efforts to be reasonable and precise, insists on continuing to volunteer collateral information. This witness is actually being impermissibly uncooperative, and the techniques for resolving this problem are discussed below.[20]

20. *See* section 5.5.4.3 regarding the reassertion of control over an impermissibly uncooperative witness.

Suffice it to say here that you should hesitate to interrupt, even when you are dealing with a flagrantly uncooperative witness.

Well, if you are not going to interrupt the witness, what can you do? As a first line of defense, there are a fair number of nonverbal techniques that can be used to get a witness to stop talking. A stern look can be surprisingly effective, especially when the witness knows that she has gone beyond the legitimate bounds of your original question. Guilt, even for those on the witness stand, plays its part in human motivation. A second approach is to raise your hand in the universal "stop" symbol. This works particularly well if you do it at a natural pause in the witness's testimony or when the witness displays some hesitancy about continuing.

A pause or hesitation by the witness is an excellent opportunity to recover the initiative by putting an entirely new question to the witness. Artfully done, this will not seem like an interruption, but rather as though you simply moved on after allowing the witness to finish the reply. This technique works best when it can be accomplished unobtrusively. Try to "slide" your question into the space where the witness is catching her breath or visibly deciding whether to continue. You do not need to change the subject entirely, but your question should be new. Be certain that it does not resuggest the subject of the explanation that you are attempting to abort.

These first three techniques—glare, upraised hand, and fill-in-the-blank—will sometimes work. Sometimes they will not. Their effectiveness depends in large part on the level of control that you established at the outset of your examination of the witness. A witness who has become accustomed to answering short, leading, propositional questions will be more likely to stop explaining. In contrast, a witness who repeatedly has been given latitude to explain will be inclined to keep it up. Additionally, your own level of confidence, not to mention the witness's natural degree of loquaciousness, will play a large part in your ability to reassert control through these means.

Reasserting Control, Part Two

Assuming that you cannot stare or "slide" the witness back under control, what are your remaining alternatives? While this may seem counterintuitive or insufficiently activist, the best approach for coping with invited explanations may well be to do nothing. Allow the witness to finish the answer and then proceed to another question that does not invite explanation.

Recall that we are dealing here with a witness who has been allowed or invited to explain. It is therefore unnecessary, and may be counterproductive, to attempt to prove that the witness took unfair license. Many lawyers attempt to discipline the witness or otherwise make a point by saying something such as:

> Q: You haven't answered my question. Can you please answer yes or no?

Or,

> Q: Are you finished? Would you like to answer my question now?

Or,

> Q: Please listen carefully. I am going to ask you a very simple question.

While these questions, and others like them, may be satisfying to the ego, they accomplish little and may actually result in making the witness more combative. It is very unlikely that the witness will retract the previous answer. "Was I explaining? I'm sorry. The answer should have been that I could not really see." That simply will not happen. Once an invited explanation has been given, it is almost certain to stand. Do not argue about it or attempt to undo it; your time will be better spent making sure that it does not happen again. There is no reason to announce that you are going to ask a simple question. Just ask one.

The best way to bring an "invited" witness back under control is to terminate the invitation. Make sure that the next question is short, propositional, and leading. Ask yourself what it was about the previous question that was taken as an invitation, and then cure the problem with your next question. Recall the witness to the intersection accident who was invited to explain with a "yet/still" question. Instead of arguing with her, bring her back under control by reverting to controlling questions:

> Q: Immediately before the accident you were waiting for a bus?
>
> A: That's right.
>
> Q: The bus was coming from the north, wasn't it?
>
> A: Correct.
>
> Q: You had to look north for your bus?
>
> A: I did.
>
> Q: The accident took place to the south of the intersection?
>
> A: I guess it did.
>
> Q: Yet you still say that you could see the accident clearly?
>
> A: Well, I turned my head when I heard the brakes screech.
>
> Q: So before you turned your head you were looking to the north.
>
> A: Yes.
>
> Q: And the accident occurred to the south of where you were standing.
>
> A: That is right.

A witness who is inclined to play fairly will generally be brought back under control if you ignore the explanation and proceed with leading questions. Some witnesses will continue to interject information and explain every answer, whether invited to or not. These witnesses are impermissibly uncooperative, and the techniques for dealing with them are discussed in the next section.

5.5.4.3 Impermissible Lack of Cooperation

Not all witnesses are inclined to play fairly. Some witnesses are overtly partisan, some are subtly uncooperative, and some are just plain ornery. While there is no requirement that a witness facilitate or enhance the goals of your cross-examination, there is a requirement that the witness, within her ability, provide fair answers to fair questions. Unfair answers take a number of forms, including speechmaking, deflection, and obstinance.

Speechmaking occurs when a witness insists on responding to a question with an uninvited explanation. In contrast to the invited explanation, where some aspect of the question encouraged the witness to explain the answer, a speechmaking witness is actually attempting to take control of the cross-examination by inserting an explanation where none has been called for:

> Q: Didn't the accident occur at 8:20 a.m.?
>
> A: Yes, it did.
>
> Q: You had a business meeting scheduled for 9:00 that same morning, didn't you?
>
> A: It really wasn't a very important meeting. We were just going to exchange a few papers. One of my partners could easily have taken care of it, and, in fact, I had pretty much decided to skip it by the time I left home.

The witness in this example believes that he has figured out where the cross-examination is headed, and he has determined to cut off the line of questioning by offering an explanation in advance. There was nothing about the question that prompted or suggested the need for an immediate explanation, but the witness's own agenda nonetheless impelled one.

Deflection occurs when the witness decides to answer a question other than the one that was asked:

> Q: You know that traffic must stop for fire trucks, don't you?
>
> A: There was no bell and no siren; I had no reason to stop.

Here the witness ignored the question, interjecting instead the information that he believes will be most helpful to his case.

Finally, a witness is obstinate when he simply refuses to answer the question, either by hedging the answer or by arguing with the cross-examiner:

> Q: You left home at 7:55 that morning?
>
> A: I guess so.
>
> Q: It is a sixteen-mile drive to your office?
>
> A: You could say that.
>
> Q: You had a business meeting that morning?
>
> A: It depends on what you mean by business.
>
> Q: It was important that you be on time?
>
> A: Don't you try to be on time for your meetings?

This witness, in essence, has refused to participate in the cross-examination. He does not want to answer any questions, so he responds with a series of non-answers. In each of the above examples, the witness was impermissibly uncooperative. The questions were simple, straightforward, and easily capable of "yes" or "no" answers. The witnesses, however, intentionally sought to thwart the cross-examination. How can such witnesses be brought back under control?

There are two basic methods for reasserting control over intentionally uncooperative witnesses. The preferred way is to do it yourself; the other way is to ask the judge for help.

Obtaining Help from the Judge

As a cross-examiner, you are entitled to reasonably responsive answers from a witness. It is the judge's obligation to ensure not only that the witness respond to your questions, but also to "strike" any answers that are unresponsive. Thus, the ultimate solution to the problem of the impermissibly uncooperative witness is to seek the judge's intervention:

> Q: Your Honor, could you please instruct the witness to answer my question?
>
> Q: Your Honor, could you please direct the witness to answer that question "yes" or "no"?
>
> Q: I move to strike that answer as nonresponsive to my question, and I request that the court instruct the jury to disregard it.

There are a number of reasons, however, to be wary of seeking the judge's help to control your witness on cross-examination.

First, early recourse to the judge may seem petty or picky. Just as lawyers do not object to every conceivably objectionable question, there is no reason to go running to the judge every time a witness fails to answer in precisely the manner that you expected. It looks bad, maybe even childish, to go looking for outside help when circumstances do not really call for it.

Moreover, many judges dislike interceding in cross-examinations. They expect the lawyers to handle their own questioning, and they do not want to appear to take sides between a lawyer and a witness. Some judges, regrettably, have a nasty habit of not paying attention during jury trials, and they will be unable to tell whether your request is reasonable. For these reasons, a request for help from the judge is often met with something like "Proceed, counsel" or "Just ask another question."

Finally, never underestimate the possibility that the judge might disagree with you. You may think that the question can be answered "yes" or "no," and you might think that the witness was clearly nonresponsive, but the judge might have an entirely different view of things. Imagine the difficulty of returning to a cross-examination following this scenario:

Lawyer:	Your Honor, will you please direct the witness to give me a "yes" or "no" answer?
Court:	I don't think that your question can be answered "yes" or "no." The witness is entitled to explain.

Or,

Lawyer:	I move to strike the last answer as unresponsive to my question.
Court:	I think that the answer was perfectly responsive, given the nature of your question. Proceed, counsel.

How, then, can you be certain of obtaining the court's help when you ask for it? And in the process, how can you avoid appearing petty or ineffectual when you finally resort to the judge? The answer is to earn the right to seek outside assistance with the witness by first attempting to reassert control by yourself. This method will not only validate your later attempt to invoke judicial authority, it will also have the added benefit of demonstrating to the witness the futility of any subsequent efforts to evade your questions.

If your own attempts to control the witness do not succeed, there will still be an opportunity to turn to the judge. By that time, of course, you will have demonstrated that you are not being petty and, with luck, you also will have ensured that you have the judge's full attention.

Reasserting Control by Yourself

The one thing that you can always do in cross-examination is ask more questions.

Pointed Repetition

You can frequently reassert control over even a recalcitrant witness simply by repeating your original question, while using your voice or demeanor to emphasize the need for a direct answer:

Q: You had a business meeting scheduled for 9:00 that same morning, didn't you?

A: It really wasn't a very important meeting. We were just going to exchange a few papers. One of my partners could easily have taken care of it, and, in fact, I had pretty much decided to skip it by the time I left home.

Q: You did have a business meeting scheduled for 9:00 that morning, didn't you?

Many witnesses will provide you with an answer at this point. Some will continue to resist. In these circumstances, an explanation from you may help:

Q: You did have a business meeting scheduled for 9:00 that morning, didn't you?

A: Like I said, it wasn't very important.

Q: We will discuss importance in a little while. Right now I am asking you whether you had a meeting scheduled for 9:00 that morning.

If the witness refuses to answer at this point, he has obviously decided never to answer. There is little to be gained by squabbling with the witness, although there are a few additional rhetorical flourishes that work from time to time:

Q: Mr. Witness, surely you do not deny that you had a business meeting scheduled for 9:00 that morning?

In any event, assuming that the information is important to your case, you have by this time earned the right to go to the judge.

Discipline

A witness who deflected your question can frequently be brought back under control if you restate the question firmly. If this doesn't work, there are a variety of ways to "discipline" the witness by pointing out the flaw in the deflection:

Q: You know that traffic must stop for fire trucks, don't you?

A: There was no bell and no siren; I had no reason to stop.

Q: But my question was this: you know that traffic must stop for fire trucks?

A: What I am trying to tell you is that there was no siren, so why should I stop?

Q: Mr. Witness, you are thirty-five years old, aren't you?

A: Yes, I am.

Q: You have been driving an automobile for over fifteen years?

A: That seems right.

Q: You took driver's education in high school?

A: I did.

Q: You passed the written test to get your license?

A: Of course.

Q: And you passed subsequent written tests for periodic renewals?

A: I did.

Q: So can't you agree with me that the rules of the road require you to stop for fire trucks?

A: I guess so.

Q: And you have known that for years, haven't you?

Note that the cross-examiner in the above example earned the right to discipline the witness. The original question was short and factual; it did not invite an explanation. The witness was then given a second chance to answer. Only after the repeated deflection did the cross-examiner set out to bring the witness to heel. The identical technique would have been considerably less useful under other circumstances. If the witness had not persisted in the refusal to answer, or if the question had been less precise, the lawyer's "disciplinary" line of questions might have appeared to be nasty or bullying.

There are a number of ways to "discipline" a witness. One of the surest is to confront the witness with his own previous words or actions. While impeachment through the use of prior statements is covered in the next chapter,[21] the following is a short example of using the witness's own prior actions to reassert control:

Q: You know that traffic must stop for fire trucks, don't you?

A: There was no bell and no siren; I had no reason to stop.

21. *See* chapter six.

Q: Well, you did eventually hit your brakes, didn't you?

A: Yes.

Q: As soon as you saw the fire truck?

A: Yes.

Q: And that was because you knew that traffic had to stop for fire trucks, isn't that right?

This technique involves the use of short, factual questions that combine to demonstrate the utter reasonableness of the original question. By painstakingly eliciting the logical basis for the inquiry you, in a sense, shame the witness into providing you with a direct answer.

More aggressive means are also available. A final method of reasserting control, short of seeking the court's assistance, is through the judicious use of what we might call semi-sarcasm. Sarcasm is always risky in the courtroom, especially for beginning lawyers, and it should be used only when the witness clearly deserves it. Save this approach for the truly evasive, partisan, or oily witness—the witness who has resisted your every well-moderated effort to extract a plain answer:

Q: You left home at 7:55 that morning?

A: I guess so.

Q: Well you know that you left home, don't you?

A: Yes.

Q: And you testified earlier that you left at about 7:55 a.m., right?

A: Yes.

Q: So it isn't a guess at all when I say that you left home at 7:55 on the morning of the accident?

Similarly,

Q: It is a sixteen-mile drive to your office?

A: You could say that.

Q: Is there a reason that you don't want to say that?

A: No.

Q: Then it is sixteen miles to your office?

Or,

Q: You had a business meeting that morning?

A: It depends on what you mean by business.

Q: You were wearing your jacket and tie, weren't you?

A: Yes.

Q: You weren't going golfing at 8:30 that morning?

A: No.

Q: You were headed toward your office?

A: Yes.

Q: Toward your place of business, right?

And finally,

Q: It was important that you be on time?

A: Don't you try to be on time for your meetings?

Q: Unfortunately, the rules of evidence do not allow me to answer your questions, but I would like you to answer mine. You don't have a problem with that, do you?

A: No.

Q: Good. You do try to be on time for your business meetings, don't you?

Semi-sarcasm, as illustrated above, is a questioning technique that is aimed at exposing the groundless obstinacy of the witness's answers. It is called "semi-sarcasm" precisely because its goal is not to demonstrate the lawyer's superior wit and intelligence, but rather to underline the witness's unreasonable lack of cooperation. Such sarcasm comes more easily to some lawyers than to others. Some judges and jurors receive it well; others do not. The decision to use semi-sarcasm is a personal one, with one near-universal requirement. You can only use this technique on a witness who truly deserves it.

5.6 Ethics of Cross-Examination

While lawyers generally consider cross-examination to be an engine of truth-seeking, we are often criticized for using cross as a device for distortion and obfuscation. And in truth, as with all powerful rhetorical tools, cross-examination can be used to mislead and deceive. Accordingly, certain ethical principles have developed that circumscribe a lawyer's use of cross-examination.

5.6.1 Basis for Questioning

5.6.1.1 Factual Basis

Effective cross-examinations contain inherent assertions of fact. Indeed, many of the best cross-examination questions are strictly "propositional." Consider these examples from the fire engine case:

Q: You did not have your brakes fixed, did you?

Q: You slept on the ground while on your camping trip, correct?

Q: You were on your way to an important business meeting, right?

Q: You have continued to work as a guide at the Art Institute, haven't you?

Each question contains a single fact that counsel is urging to be true. The danger arises that counsel might also propose baseless or knowingly false points. The witness, of course, can deny any untrue assertions, but the denials may ring hollow in the face of an attorney's presumably superior persuasive skills. Enormous damage can be done by false or groundless accusations. Imagine the impact of this examination:

Q: Isn't it true that you had been drinking on the morning of the accident?

A: No, not at all.

Q: Didn't you arrive at Ricky's Bar at 7:00 a.m.?

A: Certainly not.

Q: Well, the truth is that you ran up a $22.00 tab that morning, didn't you?

A: No.

Q: $22.00 would cover at least four drinks, right?

A: I'm telling you that I wasn't drinking.

The precision of the details in the questions appears to add reliability to the cross-examination, while the denials can be made to appear superficial. The cross-examiner's ability to control the interchange puts the witness at an extreme disadvantage. This cross-examination raises no problems if the witness was indeed drinking at Ricky's Bar, but it is intolerable if the charge is untrue.

To protect against the unscrupulous use of cross-examination, every question must have a "good-faith basis" in fact.[22] Counsel is not free to make up assertions

22. A lawyer shall not "in trial, allude to any matter that the lawyer does not reasonably believe is relevant or that will not be supported by admissible evidence." MODEL RULES OF PROF'L CONDUCT R. 3.4(e).

or even to fish for possibly incriminating material. Rather, as a predicate to any "propositional" question, counsel must be aware of specific facts that support the allegation.

5.6.1.2 Legal Basis

The "good-faith basis" for a cross-examination question cannot consist solely of inadmissible evidence. Counsel cannot allude to any matter "that will not be supported by admissible evidence."[23] Thus, a good-faith basis cannot be provided by rumors, uncorroborated hearsay, or pure speculation.

Allegations lacking a basis in admissible evidence may lead to a sustained objection, an admonition by the court, or even a mistrial. Moreover, many jurisdictions require counsel to offer admissible extrinsic evidence to "prove up" certain assertions made on cross-examination, such as past conviction of a felony.

5.6.2 Assertions of Personal Knowledge

It is unethical to "assert personal knowledge of facts in issue . . . or state a personal opinion as to the justness of a cause, the credibility of a witness, the culpability of a civil litigant or the guilt or innocence of an accused."[24] While this problem most frequently occurs during final argument,[25] it also arises during cross-examination.

Cross-examination questions sometimes take a "Do you know?" or "Didn't you tell me?" format. Both types of question are improper because they put the lawyer's own credibility in issue. "Do you know?" questions suggest that the lawyer is aware of true facts that, while not appearing on the record, contradict the witness's testimony. "Didn't you tell me?" questions argue that the witness and the lawyer had a conversation and that the lawyer's version is more believable. In either case, the questions amount to an assertion of personal knowledge.[26]

5.6.3 Derogatory Questions

It is unethical to ask questions that are intended solely to harass, degrade, or humiliate a witness, or to discourage him from testifying.

---

23. *Id.*
24. *Id.*
25. *See* section 13.6.1.1.
26. "Do you know?" questions may be permissible in limited circumstances. A witness claiming compendious knowledge, for example, could legitimately be questioned as to her lack of certain information. Similarly, a character witness could be questioned concerning unknown facts about a witness's reputation. In each situation, however, the question must have a good-faith basis.

5.6.4 Discrediting a Truthful Witness

To what extent may cross-examination be used to discredit the testimony of a witness whom counsel knows to be telling the truth?

The answer to this question is reasonably straightforward in criminal cases. Defense counsel is entitled to insist that the government prove its case through evidence that is persuasive beyond a reasonable doubt. Thus, witnesses must not only be truthful, they must also be convincing to the required degree of certainty. A discrediting cross is simply an additional safeguard.

Conversely, a criminal prosecutor has a public duty to avoid conviction of the innocent. A truthful witness, therefore, should not be discredited simply for the sake of the exercise.

The rule is less certain in civil cases. It is clear, however, that a witness cannot be degraded or debased simply to cast doubt on otherwise unchallenged testimony. On the other hand, true factual information may be used to undermine the credibility of a witness whose testimony is legitimately controverted.

5.6.5 Misusing Evidence

The same rules apply on cross as on direct with regard to misusing evidence that has been admitted for a limited purpose.[27]

27. *See* section 4.6.2.

Chapter Six

Impeachment

6.1 Introduction

6.1.1 Categories of Impeachment

While much cross-examination consists of demonstrating inaccuracies or rebutting a witness's testimony, impeachment is intended to actually discredit the witness as a reliable source of information.[1] Successful impeachment renders the witness less worthy of belief, as opposed to merely unobservant, mistaken, or otherwise subject to contradiction. There are three basic categories of witness impeachment, each of which provides a reason to place less credence in a witness's testimony.

Perhaps the most common method of impeachment is the use of a prior inconsistent statement, action, or omission. The elicitation of a prior inconsistency demonstrates that the witness's current testimony is at odds with her own previous statements or actions. In essence, this examination says: "Do not believe this witness because her story has changed."

A second method of impeachment is the use of character, or "characteristic" evidence. This form of impeachment is aimed at demonstrating that the witness possesses some inherent trait or characteristic, unrelated to the case at hand, that renders the testimony less credible. Perhaps the witness is a convicted felon or suffers a memory defect. This examination says: "This witness is not trustworthy on any matter, because of who he is."

Finally, "case-data" impeachment involves the establishment of facts that make the witness less reliable, although only within the context of the case at trial. The witness might have a financial interest in the outcome of the case or might

1. It was once considered improper for a lawyer to "impeach one's own witness" on the theory that a lawyer who called a witness to the stand for direct examination had "vouched" for the witness's credibility. The techniques of impeachment, therefore, arose in the context of cross-examination. The rule against impeaching your own witness has been abolished. *See* Fed. R. Evid. 607. As a technical matter, impeachment may now occur during either direct or cross-examination. As a practical matter, however, impeachment during direct examination is unusual. This chapter, therefore, will treat impeachment as a device to be used on cross-examination.

be prejudiced against one of the parties. In other words: "Give less weight to the witness because of her relationship to the case."

6.1.2 Tactical Considerations

Impeachment is a powerful tool. Unlike "standard" cross-examination, which may rely on unspoken premises and subtle misdirection, there should be no mistaking or hiding the intended impact of impeachment. All three kinds of impeachment are inherently confrontational. They challenge the witness's believability, perhaps even her veracity. For this reason, it is best to use the techniques of impeachment sparingly, both to preserve the potency of the method and to avoid crying wolf over unimportant details.

6.1.2.1 Impeach the Witness Only on Significant Matters

It is important to avoid impeaching witnesses on irrelevant, trivial, or petty inconsistencies. The process of impeachment, particularly through the use of prior inconsistency, can become so confrontational that there is a great risk of creating an annoying dissonance between expectation and reward. If the "punch line" fails to justify the buildup, the result can be embarrassing or damaging to your case. Imagine this scenario, for example, in the trial of the fire truck case that we have been using throughout; the plaintiff is being cross-examined:

> Q: You testified on direct examination that you heard the siren, saw the flashing lights, and then slowed down, correct?
>
> A: Correct.
>
> Q: You have given an earlier statement?
>
> A: Why, yes I did.
>
> Q: You spoke to the investigating police officer?
>
> A: That is right.
>
> Q: You knew that you had to be truthful with the police officer?
>
> A: Of course.
>
> Q: Didn't your earlier statement say, "I saw the flashing lights, then I heard the siren, which caused me to slow down at once"?
>
> A: Yes, I believe that is what I said.

Although the plaintiff has, in some technical sense, been impeached, the inconsistency involved is so slight as to be inconsequential. What difference does it make whether the witness first heard the siren or saw the lights? The essential point—that the fire truck was using its warning signals and that traffic slowed down—remains completely intact. The cross-examiner, however, has squandered valuable capital by confronting the witness, wasting time, and emerging with nothing to show for those efforts. A juror's near-certain response would be, "Is that all you can do?" A judge's response would be even less charitable.

This principle of "significance" does not apply only to prior inconsistencies. Other forms of impeachment also should only be used on important matters. Charges of prejudice or bias, for instance, should only be made when they are truly likely to make a difference to the way in which the witness will be perceived.

6.1.2.2 Impeach the Witness Only on True Inconsistencies

The purpose of impeachment through the use of a prior inconsistency is to show that the witness has made contradictory statements. The technique works only when the two statements cannot both be true. If the two statements can be harmonized, explained, or rationalized, the impeachment will fail. For example:

> Q: You testified on direct that the bank robbers drove away in a blue car, correct?
>
> A: Yes.
>
> Q: You gave a statement to the police right after the robbery, didn't you?
>
> A: Yes, I did.
>
> Q: You told the police that the robbers drove off in a turquoise car, didn't you?

Although different words were used, the two statements are not inconsistent. It does not detract from the witness's credibility that she once referred to the car as turquoise and that she later called it blue.

6.1.2.3 Impeach the Witness Only When Success Is Likely

Failed impeachment can be disastrous. A lawyer who begins an assault that cannot be completed will look ineffective at best and foolishly overbearing at worst. Impeachment can succeed only when the source of the impeachment is readily available. For that reason, the outline of your cross-examination must be indexed to the sources of your information, including all of the witness's prior statements. Do not begin your impeachment until you have the prior statement firmly in hand and have located the precise page and line that you intend to use to contradict the current testimony.

Do not rely on your memory. Even your clear recollection that the witness's deposition was diametrically contrary to her new testimony will have a way of betraying you when you turn to the transcript and read her exact words. It makes much more sense to pause and review your notes before attempting to impeach a witness than it does to have to stop in the middle when you cannot find the right material.

6.1.2.4 Do Not Impeach Favorable Information

Impeachment is not like climbing a mountain. It should not be undertaken simply because it is there. The purpose of impeachment is to cast doubt on the credibility of some or all of a witness's testimony. There is nothing to be gained by casting doubt on testimony that was helpful to your own case. Thus, even if an opposing witness has given a prior inconsistent statement, it should not be used to impeach favorable trial testimony.

Assume that the defendant in the fire engine case testified at trial that immediately after the accident he picked up his cell phone to call his office. In contrast, at deposition he testified that his first action was to check the damage to his BMW and that he called his office only after making sure that the plaintiff was not seriously injured.

The two statements are clearly inconsistent, and the witness is technically open to impeachment. The trial testimony, however, is actually more helpful to the cross-examiner's case. Recall the possible plaintiff's theme that the defendant was "too busy to be careful." The defendant's admission that his first thought was to telephone his office fits beautifully into that theme. While his hard-heartedness in checking on his BMW before looking into the plaintiff's injuries might also be useful to the cross-examiner's case, this information does not go directly to any theory of liability or damages. The cross-examiner therefore will not want to undercut the trial testimony (about the immediate phone call) by impeaching it with the deposition transcript (about checking on his BMW).

6.1.2.5 Consider the Impact of Multiple Impeachment

In some cases, a witness may have made a number of potentially impeaching statements. Though no single statement may be of great significance, it is possible that the sheer volume of self-contradiction may be sufficient to take on a life of its own. Thus, it may be worthwhile to impeach a witness on a series of relatively minor facts. Consider this, somewhat truncated, impeachment of a bystander witness in the fire engine case:

> Q: You testified today that you were standing on the northeast corner, correct?
>
> Q: But you told the police officer that you were standing on the southeast corner, didn't you?
>
> Q: You told the jury that you saw the accident while you were waiting for a bus?

Q: But your pretrial statement said that you were out for a walk.

Q: Today you said that you were on your way to work that day.

Q: In your deposition, though, you said you were going to the beach.

Q: Today's testimony was that you were the only person on the corner.

Q: You told thc policc, however, that there was a jogger standing right next to you.

In isolation, none of the above details would make much difference to the witness's credibility. In aggregation, however, they paint a picture of a confused person who is very likely confused about precisely what he saw.

Multiple impeachment is a refined tool. It can be overdone, and the point may be easily lost. On the other hand, when deftly executed and well-conceived, the whole of the impeachment can actually turn out to be much greater than the sum of its parts.

6.1.2.6 Consider the "Rule of Completeness"

The "Rule of Completeness" provides that once a witness has been impeached from a prior inconsistent statement, opposing counsel may request the immediate reading of additional, explanatory portions of the same statement. Under the Federal Rules of Evidence, for example, the adverse party may introduce any other part of the statement "that in fairness ought to be considered at the same time."[2]

Thus, even a true gem of an impeaching statement may be immediately undercut if some other part of the impeaching document explains or negates the apparent contradiction. Assume that the following impeachment of the plaintiff has taken place in our fire truck case:[3]

Q: You testified on direct examination that as a result of the accident you are no longer able to ride your bicycle, correct?

A: Correct.

Q: On deposition, however, didn't you testify as follows: "Just last week I rode my bicycle over four miles to the Botanic Garden"?

A: Yes, I did say that.

The above impeachment obviously hurts the plaintiff's claim for damages. The effectiveness of the impeachment will be undercut, if not entirely destroyed, however,

2. Fed. R. Evid. 106.

3. The form of the impeachment has been truncated to emphasize the point about the Rule of Completeness.

if the following statement from the same deposition is immediately admitted into evidence:

> I try to do everything I can to minimize the limitations of my injury. Sometimes I try too hard. That bike trip to the Botanic Garden put me back in the hospital for two days; I'll never try that again.

There is little to gain and much to lose by impeaching a witness only to see the impeachment come completely undone within a matter of minutes. Always scour the impeaching document for other information "that in fairness ought to be considered at the same time" with the impeachment.

6.1.2.7 Consider Refreshing the Witness's Recollection

Not every gap or variation in a witness's testimony is the result of an intentional change. Witnesses often become confused or forgetful. A witness may have testified inconsistently with her prior statements quite innocently or inadvertently. In these circumstances, it will often be possible to use the prior statement to refresh the witness's recollection, rather than to impeach her credibility. The technique for refreshing recollection is the same on cross-examination as it is on direct.[4] In many courts, however, a cross-examiner will be allowed to refresh a witness's recollection without first being required to establish that the witness's memory has been exhausted. For example:

Q: You testified on direct examination that you went directly from the scene of the accident to the hospital.

A: That is right.

Q: You also testified to these matters when your deposition was taken, didn't you?

A: I am sure that I did.

Q: Please look at page 725 of your deposition, which I am now handing to you, and tell me when you have finished reading it.

A: I am done.

Q: Does that refresh your recollection as to whether you did anything before going to the hospital?

A: Yes, it does.

Q: In fact, you used your cell phone to call your office first, didn't you?

A: Yes, I did.

---

4. *See* section 4.2.5.

The strict requirements for refreshing recollection are usually somewhat relaxed on cross-examination because the cross-examiner cannot expect much cooperation from the witness. It is one thing on direct examination to refresh the recollection of a witness who admits to a memory lapse, but it is quite another on cross-examination to refresh the memory of a witness who has omitted some fact without realizing it. Judges therefore tend to leniency, and opposing counsel often abstain from objecting, if only to avoid the unpleasant necessity of impeachment.

6.1.3 Evidentiary Considerations

Prior inconsistent statements that were given under oath are admissible as substantive evidence—they can be used to prove the truth of the original statement.[5] Prior inconsistent statements that were not given under oath are generally admissible for the limited purpose of impeachment—they can be used only to reflect on the credibility of the witness.[6]

Under traditional theories of evidence, prior out-of-court statements of witnesses are hearsay and therefore not admissible as substantive evidence. They are admissible, however, as impeachment under the theory that the offer is intended only to reflect on the witness's credibility and not actually as proof of the facts contained in the statement. Consider the following example:

Q: You testified on direct examination that the southbound traffic had the green light?

A: Yes.

Q: In your statement to the police officer, didn't you say that the southbound traffic had a red light?

A: I did.

The witness's earlier statement to the police officer was obviously made out of court. It therefore would be hearsay if offered to prove that the light actually was red since that would go to the "truth of the matter asserted."[7] The statement is not hearsay, however, if it is only offered to show that the witness has changed her testimony. Under those circumstances, the statement is not offered to prove that the light was red, but only that the witness is an unreliable source for the color of the light.

5. Fed. R. Evid. 801(d)(1)(A).

6. Prior inconsistent statements that were not given under oath may occasionally be used as substantive evidence if they qualify for some exception to the hearsay rule. For example, the prior statement of a party is admissible as an opposing party's statement (formerly known as a party admission) whether or not it was made under oath. *See* Fed. R. Evid. 801(d)(2). The same would be true of declarations against interest, excited utterances, or present sense impressions. Fed. R. Evid. 803.

7. *See* Fed. R. Evid. 801(c).

The traditional rule has been altered somewhat by modern practice. Under the Federal Rules of Evidence, a prior inconsistent statement is not considered hearsay if it was originally made under oath at a trial, hearing, other proceeding, or in a deposition.[8] Thus, if the witness in the example above had made the earlier statement at her deposition, rather than to a police officer, it would then be admissible as substantive proof that the light was indeed red.

What is the importance of this distinction? Isn't the difference between substantive evidence and impeaching evidence simply too fine for most jurors to comprehend? It is true that judges' limiting instructions are frequently ignored or misunderstood. In some situations, however, it may make a difference if the judge instructs the jurors to "consider the witness's prior statement only as impeachment, and not as substantive evidence."

More frequently, the difference between impeaching and substantive evidence will be relevant to the determination of issues of law. For example, only substantive evidence should be considered when deciding whether the plaintiff has made out a prima facie case. Similarly, a reviewing court should not consider strictly impeaching evidence when deciding whether a verdict was supported by sufficient evidence. Finally, a court may restrict a lawyer's final argument if evidence that was admitted for a limited purpose is sought to be used as substantive proof.

In consequence, it is usually preferable to impeach a witness through the use of a sworn statement if one is available, since that approach allows the greatest latitude for later use of the evidence.

6.2 Prior Inconsistent Statements

One of the most dramatic aspects of any trial is the confrontation of a witness with his own prior inconsistent statement. This is the moment that cross-examiners live for—the opportunity to show that the witness's current testimony is contradicted by his own earlier words. Properly conducted, this form of impeachment is not only effective on cross-examination, it also can provide extremely fruitful final argument:

> Ladies and gentlemen, Mr. Kaye is simply unworthy of belief. He couldn't even keep his story straight himself. Right after the accident he told Officer Berkeley that the light was red. By the time of trial, it had mysteriously changed to green. The best you can say about Mr. Kaye is that he doesn't know what color the light was.

Prior inconsistent statements damage a witness's credibility because they demonstrate that the witness has changed his story. Depending on the nature and seriousness of the change, the witness may be shown to be evasive, opportunistic, error-prone, or even lying. To accomplish any of these goals, of course, it is necessary

8. Fed. R. Evid. 801(d)(1)(A).

that the prior statement be clearly inconsistent with the current testimony and that it be directed to a subject of true significance to the case. Semi-inconsistencies concerning tangential matters will have little or no impact.

There are three steps necessary to impeach a witness with a prior inconsistent statement: 1) recommit, 2) validate, and 3) confront. Each of the three steps will be treated in detail below. Before proceeding to consider the separate elements of impeachment, the following illustration, though somewhat truncated, will place the entire process in perspective.

Recommit:

Q: Mr. Kaye, you testified during your direct examination that the traffic light was green for the southbound traffic.

A: That is right.

Validate:

Q: Immediately after the accident you spoke to Officer Berkeley?

A: I did.

Q: You understood that it was important to tell Officer Berkeley exactly what you saw?

A: Yes.

Q: You spoke to the police officer on the very day of the accident?

A: Correct.

Q: So obviously the events were fresh in your mind?

A: Yes.

Q: Since then over a year has gone by?

A: Yes.

Q: After you spoke to Officer Berkeley, she asked you to sign a statement, didn't she?

A: Yes, she did.

Q: You read and signed the statement, didn't you?

A: Yes.

Confront:

Q: Please look at Exhibit Number 39 for identification and tell me if you recognize your signature at the bottom of the page.

A: I do.

Q: Isn't this the statement that you signed for Officer Berkeley?

A: It is.

Q: Please read it through and tell me when you have finished.

A: I am finished.

Q: Doesn't your statement say the following: "At the time of the accident, the traffic light was red for the southbound traffic."

A: Yes, that is what the statement says.

Q: That is the statement that you signed for Officer Berkeley?

A: Yes.

This illustration contains all of the elements of impeachment with a prior inconsistent statement. We will discuss each of those elements in considerably more detail below.

6.2.1 The Process of Impeachment

See demonstrations 9.1 and 9.2 in the Visuals Appendix.

6.2.1.1 Recommit the Witness

The first step in impeaching a witness with a prior inconsistent statement is to recommit the witness to his current testimony:

Q: Mr. Kaye, you testified on direct examination that the light was green for the southbound traffic, correct?

The purpose of recommitting the witness is to underscore the gulf between the current testimony and the prior statement. There is no evidentiary requirement that the witness be allowed to repeat the direct testimony. On the other hand, it is difficult to imagine how the two statements could be effectively contrasted without restating the testimony that is about to be impeached.

There are two ways to recommit a witness to the about-to-be-impeached testimony. One is traditional, and one is elegant.

The Traditional Way

The traditional method of recommittal is to restate the witness's direct testimony and then ask the witness to reaffirm it. Thus, the witness's current statement is made absolutely clear so that there can be no doubt about its content when it is eventually impeached. To use this method, you must restate the direct testimony as accurately as possible. Paraphrases or summaries may result in a series of arguments or quibbles with the witness that can detract from the impeachment.

It is equally important, however, for the cross-examiner to avoid giving the witness an unbridled opportunity simply to repeat the direct testimony. It is therefore crucial to use short, leading questions during this phase of recommittal. Do not, as in the example that follows, ask a witness to repeat his direct testimony:

> Q: Mr. Kaye, what color did you say that the light was for the southbound traffic?

Instead, tell the witness what his previous testimony was:

> Q: Mr. Kaye, you testified on direct examination that the light was green for the southbound traffic.

The difference between these two approaches is that the leading question retains control over the witness and prevents the witness from embellishing or improving his answer. Moreover, the second approach allows you to use vocal inflection and facial expression to inject a note of doubt as to the accuracy of the testimony that you are repeating. When you ask a witness to repeat his testimony, there is an inevitable suggestion that the testimony is important. On the other hand, when the cross-examiner repeats the testimony, it is possible to inject a note of skepticism that will convey just the right measure of doubt.

Depending on the severity of the impending impeachment, it may be possible to ask the question in a form that is doubtful indeed:

> Q: Mr. Kaye, on direct examination you told defendant's counsel that the light was green for the southbound traffic?

Or in extreme cases:

> Q: Mr. Kaye, the story that you told on direct examination was, and I quote, that "the light was green for the southbound traffic."

The traditional approach has the benefit of predictability and recognizability. By quoting the direct examination, you are almost assured that the witness will agree with you and thereby allow you to proceed with the impeachment. Furthermore, since impeachment has been accomplished in this manner for generations, virtually all judges will recognize what you are doing, and this alone may obviate any lurking evidentiary problems.

The inescapable drawback to the traditional approach is that, by definition, it restates the witness's direct testimony. Furthermore, the repeated testimony will almost always be damaging, since you wouldn't bother impeaching it if it had not damaged your case. Sometimes the repetition can seem endless:

> Q: Mr. Kaye, you testified on direct examination that the light was green for the southbound traffic.
>
> A: The light was definitely green for the southbound traffic.

Q: And that was your testimony on direct examination?

A: Yes. The light was green for the southbound traffic.

Now the testimony has been repeated three times, although the cross-examiner will only be allowed to impeach it once.

The Elegant Way

An elegant alternative to the traditional approach avoids this difficulty by rephrasing the direct examination in language that is beneficial to the cross-examiner's own case. As we noted above, there is no strict rule of evidence that requires a cross-examiner to repeat verbatim the witness's about-to-be-impeached testimony. The purpose of recommitment is only to focus attention on the inconsistency between the courtroom testimony and the prior statement. It is therefore possible to recommit the witness to the content of the current testimony without repeating it word for word. The content, in turn, can be phrased in a virtually unlimited number of ways.

Consider the simple traffic light example that was used in the previous section. The witness testified on direct examination that the light was green for the southbound traffic, but his statement to the police was just the opposite. It is your theory that the light was red for the southbound traffic. Rather than repeat the direct testimony, the cross-examiner can recommit the witness as follows:

Q: Mr. Kaye, the light was red for the southbound traffic, correct?

A: No, that is not true.

Q: Mr. Kaye, I would like to show you the statement that you gave to Officer Berkeley.

You can now proceed to impeach the witness with his own prior statement. This format for recommittal avoids repetition of the direct testimony. It also allows you to describe your own case in affirmative language: "Wasn't the light red for the southbound traffic?" Since your case rests on the proposition that the light was red for the southbound traffic, you profit from stating that affirmative fact as often as possible.

The impeachment that follows will not be directed at the witness's direct testimony that the light was green, but rather at his denial during cross-examination that the light was red. The effect, of course, will be the same.

There is a further benefit to the elegant method of recommittal. It creates an outside opportunity that the witness will agree with you. Should lightning strike and the witness agree that the light was indeed red, impeachment will be unnecessary. What's more, the witness's revised testimony about the color of the light will be admissible as substantive evidence, not merely as impeachment.

Even in the far more likely situation, where the witness does not agree to change his testimony, the elegant approach to recommittal can make it appear as though you expected the witness to agree. This, in turn, will give greater credence to your own case. There is little risk to this approach since you will have the impeaching document firmly in hand.

There are two difficulties with the elegant approach. First, precise phrasing becomes extremely important, since you cannot rely simply on repeating the witness's own testimony. Counsel must find a way of restating the witness's earlier testimony that not only puts the cross-examiner's case in an affirmative light, but is also faithful to the direct examination. Finally, the witness's denial must be subject to immediate contradiction by the impeaching document. This is a far more daunting task, particularly when it arises unexpectedly in the heat of trial, than simply confronting a witness with his own earlier direct examination.

The second difficulty is one that always confronts an elegant technique. Judges may not recognize it. Lawyers and judges have been taught that repetition of the direct testimony is a necessary prelude to impeachment via prior inconsistent statement. We have seen that recommittal is really nothing more than a rhetorical technique that is intended to focus attention on the disparity between the two statements. Many older practitioners, however, may tend to view traditional recommittal as a mandatory litany, or even as an evidentiary foundation. With some judges, this problem may be acute, since they will tend to allow the familiar and to disallow what they do not recognize.

6.2.1.2 Validate the Prior Statement

Once the witness has been recommitted, the next step in the impeachment is to validate the prior statement. The initial purpose of validation is to establish that the witness actually made the impeaching statement. Depending on the circumstances of the case, further validation may be employed to accredit or demonstrate the accuracy of the earlier statement.

Basic Validation of Written Statements

The basic format for validating a witness's prior written statement is simply to establish when and how the earlier statement was made:

> Q: Did you give a statement to Officer Berkeley immediately after the accident?

Or,

> Q: Your deposition was taken at my office in March of last year, correct?

Although the basic process of validation is straightforward, care must still be taken to avoid ambiguity. For example, while lawyers understand what is meant by "giving" a statement, to some witnesses that may suggest a level of formality that was not actually present. Remedy this problem by eliciting constituent facts:

> Q: You spoke to Officer Berkeley immediately after the accident?
>
> Q: Officer Berkeley was taking notes during your conversation?
>
> Q: At the end of the conversation Officer Berkeley gave you a handwritten statement to read?
>
> Q: That statement contained a description of what you had seen that day?
>
> Q: You read the statement?
>
> Q: After reading it, you signed it?

In the same fashion, the witness's deposition can be validated without the use of compound questions and also in a manner that explains the deposition process to a jury:

> Q: You came to my office in March of last year?
>
> Q: There was a court reporter present?
>
> Q: Your attorney was also there?
>
> Q: You were placed under oath?
>
> Q: I asked questions, and you gave answers, correct?
>
> Q: While you were being questioned, the court reporter was taking down your testimony?
>
> Q: Several weeks later you were given a copy of the transcript?
>
> Q: You read and signed the transcript?

The final step in basic validation is to show the written statement to the witness to have her confirm that it is indeed her own. As with all exhibits, the statement must be marked and shown to opposing counsel.[9] The validation may then proceed as follows:

> Q: Let me show you Exhibit 9; please tell me when you are done examining it.
>
> Q: Isn't this the statement that you signed after speaking to Officer Berkeley?

9. Regarding the handling of exhibits, *see* chapter ten.

This method can be used to validate business documents, memoranda, signed depositions and interrogatories, letters, and other writings that carry the witness's signature. In the case of an unsigned deposition transcript,[10] other means of final validation will have to be used, such as:

> Q: At the end of the deposition you were asked if you wanted to read and sign it, correct?
>
> Q: And you stated that you would waive your right to read and sign the deposition transcript?

As we will see below, the witness will later be given an opportunity to admit or deny having given the specific deposition testimony being used for impeachment.

Accreditation of Prior Statements

The fact that a witness has made a prior inconsistent statement is impeaching, but it does not necessarily demonstrate that the witness's current testimony is false or inaccurate. After all, the earlier statement may have been erroneous and the direct testimony correct. It is therefore frequently advantageous to show that the first statement was made under circumstances that make it the more accurate of the two. Since the two statements are by definition mutually exclusive, there is a natural syllogism: if the earlier statement is true, then the current testimony must be wrong. Thus, the "accreditation" of the prior inconsistent statement can further detract from the witness's credibility.

Of course, no witness is likely to admit that her out-of-court statement was more accurate than her sworn testimony. It is therefore usually necessary to accredit the prior statement through circumstantial evidence. Many indicia of accuracy can be attributed to the witness's earlier statement, including importance, duty, and proximity in time.

Accreditation through Importance

A witness's earlier statement can be accredited by showing that the witness had an important reason to be accurate when giving it. Assume that the victim of a robbery testified on direct examination that the robber was wearing a Chicago Bulls sweatshirt:

> Q: Immediately after the robbery you called the police?
>
> Q: Officer Marbley came to your home?

---

10. Depositions may be recorded in audio or video, in which case, even if later transcribed, they may not result in a signed transcript. FED. R. CIV. P. 30(b)(4). In any event, the signing of a transcript can be, and frequently is, waived by the witness and the parties. FED. R. CIV. P. 30(e). Finally, a witness may have failed, neglected, or refused to sign the transcript. In these circumstances, the transcript generally can still be used as though it had been signed. *Id.*

Q: At that time, the robber was still at large?

Q: Of course, you wanted to help Officer Marbley catch the criminal?

Q: So it was very important that you give Officer Marbley a full and complete description?

Q: A careless or incomplete description would make Officer Marbley's job harder, wouldn't it?

Q: You certainly didn't want anyone else to be robbed?

Q: So you gave Officer Marbley the best information that you could?

Q: Didn't you tell Officer Marbley that the robber was wearing a Philadelphia Flyers shirt?

This form of validation establishes the witness's reason to be as accurate and truthful as possible at the time that the original description was given. The inconsistent later description will therefore be less credible.

Circumstantial importance can be shown in a wide variety of situations. Assume that the plaintiff in a contract case has testified on direct examination that he had agreed orally with the defendant that a large shipment of vegetables would be delivered no later than May 17:

Q: Your company receives deliveries on its loading dock?

Q: The loading dock is run by the dock supervisor?

Q: The receipt of deliveries is very important to your company?

Q: So the dock supervisor must have accurate information about which deliveries are expected?

Q: Refrigeration space must be available for perishables?

Q: Dock hands have to be there to unload the merchandise?

Q: It is very important that you not take possession of the wrong goods, because that could result in liability?

Q: That is why you always communicate with the dock supervisor in writing?

Q: On May 11, you sent an e-mail to the dock supervisor, correct?

Q: Doesn't that e-mail state, "Our next shipment of vegetables will arrive on May 19. Please be sure that sufficient refrigeration space is available"?

By establishing the importance of the written communication with the dock supervisor, the cross-examiner has also established the greater likelihood that the goods really were expected on May 19, as opposed to May 17 as the witness claimed during direct examination.

The importance of some prior statements can only be demonstrated indirectly. Assume that the owner of a nearby gas station witnessed the accident in our fire truck case. The witness later signed a statement prepared by an insurance investigator,[11] which stated that the fire engine was not sounding its siren. On direct examination, however, the witness testified that he heard a siren. Because the statement to the insurance investigator was of no special importance to the witness, the cross-examiner will accredit it indirectly:

> Q: The gasoline business operates on a very small margin?
>
> Q: As owner, you are responsible for the bottom line?
>
> Q: Small mistakes can be costly?
>
> Q: You wouldn't want to write a check for the wrong amount?
>
> Q: You wouldn't want to sign an invoice that charged you too much?
>
> Q: You wouldn't want to accept a bill of lading for the wrong supplies?
>
> Q: So you have to be careful about what you sign?

Since the witness cannot realistically deny taking care with his signature, the signed statement to the investigator has been circumstantially accredited. The contrary testimony has therefore been discredited.

Accreditation through Duty

A prior statement can also be accredited by showing that the witness was under either a legal or business duty to be accurate. The most common example of a statement given under a legal duty is prior testimony, either at trial or deposition. Here is an example of accrediting deposition testimony:

> Q: You came to my office in March of last year?
>
> Q: There was a court reporter present?

---

11. The cross-examiner will refer to the statement as having been taken only by an "investigator," taking pains to ensure that the testimony omits the word "insurance." A jury's knowledge of the existence of liability insurance is usually regarded as so devastating to the defendant's case that it is generally inadmissible. *See* FED. R. EVID. 411. In circumstances such as the instant example, most courts would grant a motion in limine excluding evidence that the investigator worked for an insurance company. Before the witness took the stand, he would be instructed to omit the word "insurance" from his testimony. Regarding motions in limine, *see* section 9.2.1.2.

Q: Your attorney was also there?

Q: You were sworn to tell the truth?

Q: That was the same oath that you took here today?

Q: You did tell the truth at your deposition?

Q: You promised to give accurate answers?

Q: You promised to tell me if there were any questions that you did not understand?

Q: I asked questions and you gave answers, correct?

Q: All of your answers at the deposition were under oath?

An even greater duty can often be shown if the prior testimony occurred in court:

Q: You testified in an earlier hearing in this case?

Q: That testimony took place right here in this courtroom?

Q: Judge Rubinowitz was presiding, just as he is here today?

Q: You were sworn to tell the truth?

Q: You knew that Judge Rubinowitz wanted you to tell the truth?

Business duties may also be used to accredit a prior statement. Assume that a high-school student has been charged with a crime and that one of her teachers has testified that the student was present in his class at the time of the offense. The attendance report, however, has the student marked absent.

Q: One of your jobs as a high-school teacher is to take attendance?

Q: You fill out an attendance form and send it down to the school office?

Q: Your attendance figures are entered onto a master roll?

Q: And that roll is eventually sent on to the superintendent's office?

Q: Attendance figures are used to determine state funding for your school?

Q: They are also used to determine allocation of resources?

Q: The filing of attendance reports is considered in your own annual review?

Q: The filing of attendance reports is part of your job description?

Q: The filing of attendance reports is included in your union contract?

Q: A teacher could be suspended for serious errors in his attendance reports, isn't that right?

This accreditation creates a circumstantial basis for preferring the information in the attendance report to the witness's later inconsistent testimony.

Accreditation through Proximity in Time

Because human memory inevitably fades, an earlier statement can be accredited because it was given closer in time to the events being described. This source of accreditation can be employed whether the impeaching material is a written statement, a deposition transcript, or a business document. Recall the robbery victim from the earlier example:

Q: Immediately after the robbery you called the police?

Q: Officer Marbley came to your home?

Q: You spoke to Officer Marbley about the events of the robbery?

Q: This was less than an hour after the robbery occurred?

Q: The events of the robbery were obviously very fresh in your mind when you spoke to Officer Marbley?

Q: And now over a year has gone by, correct?

The value of proximity in time can be emphasized by pointing out intervening events that may have caused the witness's memory to dim. In the same robbery case, assume that Officer Marbley testified on direct testimony that she arrested the defendant, who was wearing a Chicago Bulls sweatshirt. Her police report, however, states that the defendant was wearing a Philadelphia Flyers shirt:

Q: Officer Marbley, immediately after you arrested the defendant you filled out a police report, correct?

Q: You completed your report within an hour of making the arrest?

Q: At the time that you wrote your report, the defendant was still in a holding cell?

Q: The defendant was still available to you, if you had wanted to confirm any of the details of your report?

Q: In any event, when you wrote the report, the events of the arrest were still fresh in your mind?

Q: And now over a year has gone by, correct?

Q: During the intervening year you have made at least fifty additional arrests?

Q: You have had to write reports concerning each of those fifty arrests?

Q: And you always try to write arrest reports as soon as you can, while the events are fresh in your mind, correct?

Proximity in time will only accredit a statement that was given significantly earlier than the trial testimony. You can scarcely use this method to accredit a deposition that was taken two weeks before trial.

Evidentiary and Ethical Considerations

Recall that a prior inconsistent statement, unless given under oath, is generally not admissible as substantive evidence.[12] Thus, no matter how strongly accredited, an unsworn prior statement may be used only to detract from the credibility of the witness's current testimony.

Why, then, would a lawyer want to go to such lengths to accredit a statement by showing importance, duty, or proximity in time? Isn't the witness sufficiently impeached once it is established that a prior inconsistent statement was made?

The answer is that the accreditation of the first statement reflects negatively on the accuracy of the witness's testimony. If the statement to the investigator is accurate and the filling station owner did not hear a siren, then the witness's later testimony that there was a siren must necessarily be incorrect. On the other hand, if the circumstances surrounding the statement to the investigator suggest unreliability, then the trial testimony may be credible after all. The strength of the original statement contributes directly to the weight of the impeachment.

The contents of the unsworn prior statement cannot be used to establish an affirmative fact. The prior statement may be used to discount the testimony of the gas station owner, but not to prove the actual absence of the siren. Furthermore, the prior statement cannot be considered in ruling on the sufficiency of the evidence for the purposes of a motion for a directed verdict.

Thus, on the basis of the impeachment counsel can argue:

> The service station owner has testified that the fire engine was sounding its siren, but that testimony is not worthy of your belief. Just days after the accident, when the events were fresh in his mind, the witness gave a reliable statement that he heard no siren at all. The station owner is a careful man who reads what he signs. There is no reason on earth for him to have given such a statement if there actually had been a siren.

12. A prior inconsistent statement may be admissible as a party admission or perhaps as a present sense impression or an excited utterance. If there is such an independent basis for the statement's admissibility, then it can be used as substantive evidence whether or not it was also offered as impeachment.

Counsel cannot argue:

> We know that the fire engine was not sounding its siren. We know that because the service station owner said so in the statement that he gave just days after the accident. Let me read you the statement: "I saw the fire truck's lights, and I was surprised that there was no siren." This proves that the siren was not sounding.

A judge will often allow the use of a prior inconsistent statement subject to a limiting instruction that it can be considered only for the purpose of reflecting on the witness's credibility. Even when such an instruction has not been given, the evidentiary limitation on the use of prior statements is often implicit in the circumstances of their admission into evidence.

Attorneys will often seek to avoid the impact of the "substantive evidence" rule by cleverly structuring their arguments to the jury in a way that intimates that an impeaching statement should be accepted as substantive proof. Nonetheless, if an out-of-court statement has been admitted for a limited purpose, it is improper to attempt to convert it into substantive proof through the "back door." Indeed, if the judge has actually instructed the jury not to consider a statement as substantive evidence, it is unethical to attempt to evade the judge's ruling in the hope that the court and opposing counsel will not notice.

6.2.1.3 Confront the Witness with the Prior Statement

The final stage of impeachment is to confront the witness with the prior statement. The purpose of this confrontation is to extract from the witness an admission that the earlier statement was indeed made; recall that it is the fact of the prior inconsistency that is admissible as impeachment. This confrontation need not always be "confrontational." It can be sufficient merely to require the witness to admit making the impeaching statement, particularly when the impeachment is based on the witness's forgetfulness, confusion, or embellishment. Hostility or accusation should be reserved for those situations when the witness can be shown to be lying or acting out of some other ill motive.

To be effective, the confrontation must be accomplished in a clear and concise manner that leaves the witness no room for evasion or argument. The classic approach is simply to read the witness's own words. In confronting the gas station owner from the fire truck case, the cross-examiner will end the impeachment by reading from the witness's statement:

> Q: Now just after the accident, didn't you tell the investigator, "I saw the fire truck's lights, and I was surprised that there was no siren"?
>
> A: Yes, I did.

The confrontation can be enhanced, and counsel can be more assured of agreement from the witness, by directing the witness to read along from the impeaching statement. Give a copy to the witness and proceed:

> Q: Please take a look at Exhibit 14; isn't that the statement that you signed?
>
> A: Yes, it is.
>
> Q: Now please look at the first sentence of the last paragraph and read along with me. Doesn't your statement say, "I saw the fire truck's lights, and I was surprised that there was no siren"?

There are two rules to be followed in confronting a witness with a prior inconsistent statement: 1) do not ask the witness to read the statement aloud, and 2) do not ask the witness to explain the inconsistency. Both of these rules are applications of basic principles of cross-examination.

Asking a witness to read aloud from an impeaching document is the same as asking a wide-open, nonleading question—it surrenders control of the examination to the witness. The cross-examiner has no way of knowing how clearly, loudly, or accurately the witness will read the statement. It is not unknown for a witness, either mistakenly or intentionally, to read from an entirely different portion of the document. It is nearly certain that the witness will not read with inflection that emphasizes the inconsistency.

Impeachment will be more effective when the cross-examiner reads the impeaching matter in a loud, clear, contrasting tone of voice. While some attorneys believe that they can make a dramatic point by eliciting the words from the witness's own mouth, for most lawyers the risk of this approach will far outweigh the possible gain.

An even riskier way to lose control of the examination is to ask the witness to explain the inconsistency between a prior statement and the trial testimony. There is almost never a reason to ask a witness to explain something on cross-examination, and the middle of impeachment is no time to experiment with exceptions to this rule. At best, the witness will take the opportunity to muddle the clarity of the impeachment; at worst, the witness will launch into a facile explanation that undercuts the entire line of examination. A variety of questions might function as invitations to explain. Do not ask a witness to agree that the two statements are inconsistent or different. Except in unusual circumstances, do not ask a witness to concede that she has "changed her story." Questions of this sort are likely only to produce argument, and argument is likely to engender explanation.

Properly conducted, each line of impeachment will conclude on a lawyer's highlight. You will read the impeaching statement in a manner that underscores the inconsistency between the witness's own previous words and the testimony just given in court. There will be no mistaking the implication, and the witness will necessarily concede that the prior statement was indeed given.

6.2.1.4 Variations

As we have seen, there is a standard, well-recognized model for impeachment—recommit, validate, confront. Judges and lawyers all recognize this pattern as soon as it begins. Judges in particular take comfort in familiarity. As soon as they hear the opening phrase of recommittal, they reflexively begin listening for the technical requirements of impeachment. Thus alerted, the judge will not worry about hearsay, for example, once mention is made of the impeaching document or conversation. That is the benefit of following the standard format.

There are reasons as well, however, to depart from the standard format. Lawyers understand impeachment and are therefore impressed by it. Jurors, unacquainted with the process, may not immediately realize its significance. This is especially the case when the impeachment is drawn out or where the contradictions are something less than startling.

The value of impeachment, therefore, can sometimes be maximized by drawing as much contrast as possible between the trial testimony and the original statement. This can be accomplished by presenting one immediately after the other. Thus, instead of "recommit, validate, confront," it can be more striking to proceed "validate, recommit, confront." In that way, the replay of the challenged trial testimony is placed in direct comparison to the prior inconsistent statement rather than being separated by the technical validation. In brief, such an impeachment would go like this:

> Q: Immediately after the accident, you gave a statement to the police, didn't you?
>
> Q: You tried to be as accurate as possible in that statement, correct?
>
> Q: When you spoke to the police officer, the events of the accident were fresh in your mind?
>
> Q: Today you testified that the stoplight was green for the southbound traffic, correct?
>
> Q: But in your statement to the police you said the light was red for the southbound traffic, didn't you?

In a situation involving multiple impeachments from a single document there is a further reason to "validate" before "recommitting"—you can validate the document a single time at the outset of the impeachment and then proceed to reel off the contradictory statements without interruption.

6.2.1.5 Special Cases

The Denying Witness

Some witnesses may deny some or all of the predicates to impeachment. They may refuse to reconfirm their own direct testimony, they may resist validating the circumstances of the impeaching statement, or they may deny ever having made the prior statement. Most of these difficulties can be dealt with by using basic cross-examination principles.

The simplest problem is the witness who refuses to reaffirm the direct testimony. The easy remedy is to have the court reporter read back the original testimony and then put the question to the witness again. In any but the shortest trial, however, it may take the court reporter some time to find the precise place in the transcript where the testimony can be found. Indeed, if the testimony to be impeached occurred on an earlier day of the trial, a different court reporter may be present. Unfortunately, not every trial judge will have the patience to wait while the exact testimony is located.[13]

There are a number of solutions to this problem. The first solution is to avoid the problem entirely by making sure that your notes contain a word-for-word rendition of the testimony that you intend to impeach. That will make it more difficult for the witness to deny your accuracy, and it will also make the judge and jury more inclined to view a denying witness as a quibbler. Second, as with any cross-examination that runs into a compound detail or embedded characterization,[14] you can break the question into its constituent parts. Imagine that the filling station owner in the fire truck case refused to reaffirm his direct testimony. Rather than take the time to search through the court reporter's notes, counsel could proceed as follows:

Q: You testified on direct testimony that you clearly heard the siren of the fire engine, correct?

A: I do not believe that I said that.

Q: You did testify about the fire engine?

A: Yes, I did.

Q: Are you telling me that you did not hear the siren?

A: No.

Q: All right, so your current testimony is that you did hear the siren?

A: That is right.

---

13. This problem is obviated if counsel has been able to afford the purchase of "daily copy" of the transcript. Testimony likely to be impeached can be marked by the court reporter. In that case, you need only turn to the appropriate page and read the testimony to the witness. The court reporter's certification at the end of the transcript is sufficient proof of authenticity. *See* section 5.5.4.
14. *See* section 5.5.4.

Note that use of the "elegant" method of recommittal would prevent this problem. If the cross-examiner asked, "You did not hear a fire truck siren, did you?," the witness would either have to agree or disagree with the assertion. If the witness agrees, then there is no need to proceed with impeachment. If the witness denies the assertion, then that denial can be impeached without regard to his exact words on direct examination.

A witness who will not validate the circumstances of a prior statement can be handled in the same manner. Break the cross-examination into small, constituent facts that the witness cannot deny. Confronting the witness with the negative implications of the denial is also effective. In the robbery scenario, for example, imagine that the witness will not agree to the importance of the description given to Officer Marbley:

Q: Immediately after the robbery Officer Marbley came to your home?

A: Yes.

Q: At that time the robber was still at large?

A: I guess so.

Q: Of course, you wanted to help Officer Marbley catch the criminal?

A: I just wanted to get my things back.

Q: Well, the robber had your things, didn't he?

A: Yes.

Q: So it was very important that you give Officer Marbley a full and complete description?

A: I did the best I could under the circumstances.

Q: You did the best you could to give a good description, right?

A: Yes.

Q: You certainly wouldn't have intentionally misled Officer Marbley?

A: No, of course not.

Q: And you wouldn't have left anything out?

A: Not on purpose.

Q: You certainly didn't want anyone else to be robbed?

A: Of course not.

Q: And you were the only one that Officer Marbley could talk to about a description?

A: Yes.

Q: So you gave Officer Marbley the best information that you could, didn't you?

A: I did.

Since the true circumstances of the statement contribute to its validity, the witness cannot avoid supplying the cross-examiner with the accrediting information.

Finally, some witnesses will disclaim ever having made the impeaching statement:

Q: Didn't you tell Officer Marbley that the robber was wearing a Philadelphia Flyers shirt?

A: No, I never said that.

If the prior statement was in writing, the witness can then be confronted with the impeaching document. Further denial will lead to the admission of the impeaching document into evidence.

A stickier problem arises when the prior statement was oral rather than written. Assume that the robbery victim spoke to Officer Marbley, but did not sign a written statement. Even if Officer Marbley included verbatim notes in the police report, that document cannot be used to complete the impeachment because it is not a prior statement of the witness. Thus the officer would have to be called to the stand and examined about the description that the witness gave orally during the investigation:

Q: Didn't you interview the victim immediately after the robbery?

A: Yes.

Q: And he told you that the robber was wearing a Philadelphia Flyers shirt?

A: Yes, he did.

Should Officer Marbley also deny the cross-examiner's assertion, then the police report can be used either for impeachment or to refresh recollection.

The Lying Witness

Prior inconsistent statements are generally used to cast doubt on witnesses' credibility, but not to accuse them of outright falsehood. It is usually enough to argue that a witness has forgotten the facts or has exaggerated her testimony without attempting to paint her as a liar. Viewed purely as a matter of persuasion, it is easier to get a jury to accept that a witness is in error than it is to establish that the witness is guilty of deliberate falsehood. The witness may have a tolerable explanation for the inconsistency, or she may have other redeeming personal qualities that can create juror sympathy if she is attacked too harshly.

Nonetheless, some witnesses are liars. Some of the liars can be exposed by their own prior inconsistent statements. Some witnesses even admit having contradicted their testimony by lying in the past.

Lying witnesses can be confronted directly, since almost nothing will be more damaging to a witness's credibility than proof of past deceit. Perhaps the most frequently encountered admitted liar is the criminal defendant who has become the government's witness against a codefendant:

Q: You testified on direct that you participated in the crime with Mr. Snyder?

A: I did.

Q: You were arrested for that crime on December 19?

A: Yes, I was.

Q: Right after your arrest you were questioned by Officer Hernandez?

A: That is right.

Q: You told Officer Hernandez that you didn't know anything about the crime?

A: Yes, but that was not true.

Q: You claim now that you were lying to Officer Hernandez?

A: That is right.

Q: You claim that you lied to Officer Hernandez to keep yourself out of trouble?

A: Yes.

Q: So you admit to being a liar?

A: I guess so.

Note that the cross-examiner has taken care not to validate the witness's claim that the original denial was a lie. Defense counsel wants the original denial of involvement to be true and the current testimony, which implicates the defendant, to be false. Thus, the cross-examiner uses the prior inconsistent statement only to establish the witness's willingness to lie.

6.2.1.6 The Timing of Impeachment

To be used effectively, impeachment should fit into the overall strategy of your cross-examination. If you intend to impeach a statement that was made during the witness's direct examination, you can decide where to place it in your own cross-examination. Assuming that you have multiple points to make, at what stage of the cross-examination should you make use of the prior inconsistent statement?

The basic principles for the organization of cross-examination also apply to impeachment. It is usually advisable to maximize cooperation by beginning with inquiries that do not challenge or threaten the witness. For the same reason, initial questions are usually employed to build up your own case as opposed to controverting the opposition's. These are not hard and fast rules, but they do form a sound framework within which to begin thinking about organization.

Since impeachment can easily become threatening or confrontational, it is usually advisable to save it until you have exhausted the favorable information that you intend to obtain from the witness.

Only once the witness's cooperation is no longer important to your success should you move on to the past inconsistency.

There is such a thing as gentle impeachment, where a witness is reminded nicely that she made a contrary statement in the past. A close cousin to refreshing recollection, this form of impeachment can be used safely at almost any point in the cross-examination.

A third approach to timing is to "discipline" the witness by conducting a good, strong impeachment at the very beginning of the cross-examination. This technique should be used when you anticipate some difficulty in controlling the witness. By teaching the witness right from the start of the examination that you have the tools to compel the answers that you are entitled to, the witness's tendency to wander or argue may be minimized. You will sacrifice cooperation, but this is a witness from whom you had not expected cooperation in the first place.

It is crucial to consider impeachment within the context of the entire cross-examination. If you are using topical organization, then you will probably want to impeach the witness on any relevant matter at some point during that aspect of the examination. In the fire truck case, for example, assume that the defense attorney is cross-examining the filling station owner on his ability to see and hear the fire engine. Even though there is a fair amount of favorable information to be gathered on this issue, it also makes sense during this portion of the examination to impeach the witness with his earlier statement that he did not hear a siren. The clarity and continuity of the examination is more important than preserving the witness's good will. Of course, there is nothing to prevent you from saving the impeachment on the sound and appearance of the fire truck until the very end of your examination.

The technique of apposition is also relevant to impeachment. Recall from our discussion of the trial as a persuasive story that good stories are told about people who act for reasons. Impeachment, then, is most effective when the examination also provides a motive for the witness's inconsistency. Perhaps intervening facts led to a convenient memory lapse. Or perhaps the witness had an opportunity to confer with other interested parties. In suitable cases the use of apposition can make it clear that the witness's inconsistency is due to something other than coincidence or mistake. The classic example of apposing impeachment to an intervening event is the cross-examination of a criminal defendant who has agreed to testify for the government:

Q: You testified on direct that you participated in the crime with Mr. Snyder?

A: Yes, I did.

Q: You were arrested for that crime on December 19?

A: Yes, I was.

Q: Right after your arrest you were questioned by Officer Hernandez?

A: That's right.

Q: You were then charged with the crime, and you pleaded "not guilty"?

A: Yes.

Q: About three weeks later you had a conversation with the prosecutor, right?

A: Right.

Q: The prosecutor offered you a plea bargain?

A: She did.

Q: You agreed to plead guilty and to testify against Mr. Snyder?

A: Yes.

Q: And in exchange you would receive a sentence of probation?

A: Yes.

Q: That was your deal?

A: I guess so.

Q: But you spoke to Officer Hernandez before you ever made any deals, right?

A: Yes.

Q: And before you made any deals you told Officer Hernandez that you didn't know anything at all about the crime.

A: Yes.

Q: It was only after your deal that you came into court to testify that you participated in the crime along with someone else.

A: That's right.

The cross-examiner has not only shown that the witness told inconsistent stories, but she has also established the witness's motive for making the change.

Although lacking the drama of a plea bargain, other examples of intervening events that might be tied into impeachment can include contact with an attorney or investigator; becoming a party to the lawsuit; changes of employment; discussions with family members; exposure to media accounts of the underlying events; or anything else that might, overtly or subtly, influence a witness to change his story.

Thus far we have been discussing the impeachment of a witness's direct testimony. This situation allows counsel the maximum opportunity to plan and organize for the later impeachment. The need to impeach a witness, however, will frequently arise for the first time during cross-examination. The cross-examiner asks a reasonable question, and, surprise, the witness provides a wholly unexpected answer. At that point there is no reason to wait or experiment with the niceties of fine organization. If you have the ammunition, impeach the witness on the spot.

6.2.2 *Ethical Concerns*

Two primary ethical issues arise in the context of impeaching a witness through the use of a prior inconsistent statement. The first issue, attempting to use the statement for a purpose other than that for which it was admitted, was discussed at some length earlier.[15] It bears repeating.

It is unethical for a lawyer to "allude to any matter that the lawyer does not reasonably believe is . . . supported by admissible evidence."[16] Once a judge has ruled that certain evidence is admissible only for a limited purpose, it is inadmissible on those issues for which it has been excluded. In light of a limiting instruction, no lawyer can reasonably believe otherwise. Thus, it is unethical to "allude" to a purely impeaching statement as though it had been admitted as substantive evidence.[17]

The second ethical issue in impeachment involves the admonition not to allow a witness to explain the inconsistency. Assuming that there may be a perfectly

15. *See* section 6.2.1.2.
16. Model Rules of Prof'l Conduct R. 3.4(e).
17. As has been noted previously, many prior statements may be admitted both for impeachment and as substantive evidence.

reasonable explanation for the discrepancy between two statements, is it ethical to prevent the witness from explaining?

The answer lies in the fact that it is not truly possible for a cross-examiner to prevent a witness from providing an explanation. It will always be possible for opposing counsel to ask the witness to elaborate during redirect examination. No admissible evidence can ultimately be excluded as the result of cross-examination tactics. Thus, the most that the cross-examiner can accomplish will be to prevent the witness from explaining an inconsistency during cross-examination. As an advocate, it is the cross-examiner's task to present the evidence that is favorable to her client; the very purpose of redirect is to allow the other side to fill in gaps, remedy errors, and correct misperceptions. Leaving potential explanations to redirect is perfectly permissible under the adversary system.

An explanation would carry more weight if it could be given in the midst of cross-examination. It will necessarily seem somewhat hollow and apologetic occurring after the fact during redirect. That again is a consequence of advocacy. Recall that the witness had an opportunity during direct examination to offer the earlier statement and explain its seeming inconsistency with current testimony. Having passed up the chance to offer that testimony during direct examination, a witness can hardly complain that it is unethical for the cross-examiner not to allow it during cross.

6.3 Other Prior Inconsistencies

In addition to prior inconsistent statements, witnesses may also be impeached through the use of prior omissions or silence as well as on the basis of prior inconsistent actions.

6.3.1 Impeachment by Omission or Silence

See demonstration 10 in the Visuals Appendix.

Impeachment by omission generally follows the same theory as impeachment with a prior inconsistent statement. The witness's current testimony is rendered less credible because when she told the same story earlier it did not contain facts that she now claims are true. In essence, the impeachment is saying: "Do not believe this witness because she is adding facts to her story." Or, in other words: "If those things are true, why didn't you say them before?"

To be impeaching, the witness's prior omission must be inconsistent with the current testimony. A prior omission is not impeaching, or even admissible, if it occurred in circumstances that do not render it incompatible with the witness's testimony from the stand. The following example, as should be obvious, does not constitute impeachment by omission:

Q: You have testified today that the fire engine was sounding its siren, correct?

A: Yes.

Q: You took a final examination in your Property class last week, didn't you?

A: Yes, I did.

Q: Nowhere on your final exam did you write that you heard a fire engine's siren, did you?

The cross-examination misses the mark because the omission is entirely consistent with the witness's testimony about the siren. There was no reason for the witness to include the facts of the accident on a final examination. Impeachment by omission, then, rests on the establishment of circumstances that create a dissonance between the witness's previous silence and the story that is now being told. The stronger the dissonance, the more effective the impeachment. What circumstances create the necessary discontinuity between omission and testimony? We can begin by looking at opportunity, duty, and natural inclination.

6.3.1.1 Opportunity

The first requirement is opportunity. A witness cannot be impeached by virtue of previous silence if she was not given the opportunity to speak. Moreover, this must include the opportunity to provide the information that is now being challenged at trial. Thus, a witness cannot be impeached on the basis of omission at a deposition unless a question was asked that reasonably called for that information. The following example illustrates the minimum necessary for impeachment:[18]

Q: You have testified that you heard the fire truck siren?

A: Yes.

Q: During your deposition I asked you this question: "After you first saw the fire truck, what else did you see or hear?"

A: That's right.

Q: And you answered, "I heard the screech of brakes, and I saw the BMW slam into the back of the other car."

A: I believe that was my testimony.

The witness was impeached, if not devastated, by the omission of the sound of the siren in response to a question that reasonably called for it. In contrast, the following example is not impeaching:

---

18. For the sake of brevity, most of the buildup for the use of the deposition has been omitted.

Q: During your entire deposition you never once mentioned hearing the fire truck's siren, did you?

A: I do not believe that anyone asked me about what I heard.

Proof of opportunity, however, is not always sufficient to allow impeachment by omission. A witness who neglects the opportunity to provide information may have misunderstood the question or may have been temporarily forgetful or confused. The cross-examiner must usually go further to show that the absent statement would have been made if it had been true. This can be shown by virtue of either duty or natural inclination.

6.3.1.2 Duty

A witness who was under a duty to provide or record information cannot easily be forgiven its absence. Under these circumstances, the natural conclusion to be drawn from the omission of a fact is that the fact did not occur. Impeachment by omission can be tremendously enhanced by building up the obligation involved in the witness's prior statement. In the context of a deposition, the accreditation might proceed as follows:

Q: You recall having your deposition taken?

Q: You came to my office along with your own attorney?

Q: There was a court reporter present who placed you under oath?

Q: That was the same oath that you took here in court today?

Q: I asked you to tell me if you did not understand any of my questions?

Q: I asked you to tell me if you were unable to give full and complete answers?

Q: And you agreed to answer all of my questions to the best of your ability?

Q: After the deposition was concluded, you had the opportunity to read it over?

Q: You were able to make any corrections or additions that you wanted?

Q: You signed the transcript without making any additions?

Q: Didn't I ask you the following question: "After you noticed the fire truck, what else did you see or hear?"

A: That's right.

Q: You did not ask me to rephrase that question?

A: I guess not.

Q: Nothing prevented you from giving a full answer?

A: No.

Q: And your only answer was, "I heard the screech of brakes, and I saw the BMW slam into the back of the other car."

A: I believe that was my testimony.

Q: Nowhere else in your deposition did you say or add anything about hearing a siren?

A: I do not believe that I did.

Duty is easily established when the witness previously testified under oath. Duty can also be shown in a wide variety of other circumstances. A prime example is the police report. Assume that the officer in the scenario below arrested the defendant on a charge of narcotics possession; on direct examination the officer testified that the defendant also vigorously resisted arrest:

Q: Officer, immediately after the arrest you filled out a police report, correct?

Q: It is one of your official duties to fill out such a report?

Q: In fact, police reports are required by both municipal statute and state law, isn't that right?

Q: There are also departmental regulations on the manner in which the reports are to be filled out?

Q: Doesn't one of those regulations state, quote, "Every felony arrest report must contain all information relevant to the apprehension and prosecution of the offender"?

Q: So it is your duty to include in your report "all information relevant to the apprehension and prosecution of the offender," right?

Q: On the day that you arrested the defendant, you certainly wanted to do your duty?

Q: Now, you testified here today that the defendant resisted your arrest and even took a swing at you?

A: Yes, that is right.

Q: Resisting a police officer is a crime, isn't it?

A: Yes, it is.

Q: And trying to hit a police officer can surely lead to "prosecution of the offender," can't it?

A: It can.

Q: Please look at your police report, which has been marked as Exhibit 6. Read it through carefully, and tell me when you are finished.

A: I am done reading.

Q: Isn't this the report that you were under a duty to complete?

A: Yes.

Q: A duty imposed both by law and departmental regulations?

A: Yes.

Q: There is not a single word in your report about the defendant resisting arrest?

A: No.

Q: And there is not a single word in your official report about the defendant taking a swing at you, is there?

A: No, there is not.

Note that it is impossible to use the elegant method of recommittal when impeaching by omission. The witness's exact testimony must be used to illustrate the importance of the omission.

Business duty can also be used as a predicate to impeachment by omission. It can be shown that a witness did not include facts in a docket entry, a sales record, a service report, a transmittal letter, a bill of lading, an invoice, or any of numerous other documents that are expected to contain complete records of transactions. In the intersection case that we have frequently used as an example, assume that an automobile mechanic testified that she had examined the defendant's brakes and recommended that they be repaired, but that he declined to have any work done:

Q: Ms. Nelson, you testified that you examined the defendant's brakes and recommended that they be repaired?

A: Yes, I did.

Q: When the defendant brought his car in for repairs, you filled out a work sheet, didn't you?

A: Yes.

Q: The work sheet is the record that your shop keeps of all the work that is done on any car, correct?

A: Yes.

Q: It is also the form that you use to calculate charges for labor and parts?

A: It is.

Q: You do charge for the labor involved in making inspections, don't you?

A: Yes, we do.

Q: So it is an important part of your job to record all of the work that you do?

A: That's right.

Q: Let me show you Defendant's Exhibit 4. Please tell me when you have finished reading it.

A: I am done.

Q: That is your work sheet for the defendant's car on the day he brought it in to you, correct?

A: It is.

Q: The work sheet includes an entry for "replace windshield wiper blades," correct?

A: It does.

Q: And that is because you did replace the wiper blades, right?

A: We did.

Q: It contains an entry for "change oil and filters," right?

A: Right.

Q: Because you did change the oil?

A: We changed it.

Q: There is no entry whatsoever on that work sheet that says anything about inspecting brakes, is there?

A: It isn't on here.

The witness's business duty to include an entry on brake inspection, if an inspection was indeed performed, is established by the question regarding labor charges for inspections. The other entries on the form are used to underscore the glaring absence of anything concerning the purported brake inspection. This is the syllogism of impeachment by omission: the witness appears to have written down everything she did; she wrote nothing down about a brake inspection; therefore, she did not perform a brake inspection.

6.3.1.3 Natural Inclination

Even if no duty can be established, impeachment by omission can still be accomplished. Previous silence can be inconsistent with a current statement if the earlier omission occurred in circumstances where the witness should have been naturally inclined to speak. Imagine that a witness testified at trial that he had seen several children break into a neighbor's garage and steal a bicycle. It would impeach the witness to point out that he had never mentioned this occurrence to either the neighbor or to the children's parents since a natural inclination is to report such matters to the persons affected. In other words, "If you really saw the kids steal a bicycle, why didn't you say anything at the time?" While it is true that the witness was under no legal or business duty to alert his neighbor to the theft, it is nonetheless a reasonable inference that he would have told his neighbor if the theft had really happened. It is a natural inclination to help your friends and neighbors.

Natural inclination can be found in a wide variety of circumstances and relationships. A crime victim should be naturally inclined to give the police a complete description of the criminal. Parents should be naturally inclined to give safety warnings to their children. Employees should be naturally inclined to complain about adverse working conditions to their employers. The key to this form of impeachment by omission is accreditation of the circumstances that give rise to the inclination to speak. Consider the case of a crime victim.

> Q: You testified on direct that you were able to identify the defendant because of the scar on his forehead?
>
> A: Yes.
>
> Q: Immediately after the crime you were interviewed by a police officer?
>
> A: Yes, I was.
>
> Q: You knew that the officer wanted your help in catching the criminal?
>
> A: I did.
>
> Q: And you knew that you were the only one who could give a description of the criminal?
>
> A: Yes, I was the only one who was robbed.

Q: Of course, you didn't want anyone else to be robbed?

A: Certainly.

Q: So you gave the officer all the help that you could?

A: Yes, I did.

Q: But you never once told the officer that the criminal had a scar on his forehead?

A: No, I guess I didn't.

Can the witness in this example deflect the impeachment by replying that the officer never asked whether the robber had a scar? Obviously not, since a crime victim should be naturally inclined to volunteer that sort of information, whether directly asked about it or not.

Another example can be found in "missing complaint" situations. Assume that the tenant in a commercial lease case seeks to break a tenancy on the ground that the building did not provide adequate security. The plaintiff's testimony about poor security could be impeached if there had been no previous complaints about conditions.

Q: You testified on direct that the security situation in the building makes it impossible for you to do business there?

A: That is absolutely correct.

Q: That is because security is very important to you and your customers, right?

A: Yes, it obviously is.

Q: You have never written a letter or sent a message to building management complaining about security, have you?

A: No.

Q: You never requested a meeting to discuss security, did you?

A: Well, no.

Q: You paid your rent by check each month?

A: Yes.

Q: But you never sent a note complaining about security along with the rent check, did you?

A: No, we didn't.

The absence of complaints is impeaching because a business owner would naturally be inclined to complain about something so important to business. Since there were no complaints, the logic of the impeachment is that conditions could not have been so bad as the plaintiff is now claiming.

6.3.2 Prior Inconsistent Actions

Finally, a witness may be impeached on the basis of prior inconsistent actions. The witness's current testimony is rendered less credible by pointing out that she did not act in conformity with her own story on some previous occasion: "If what you are saying now is true, why did you act inconsistently in the past?"

Unlike impeachment through prior inconsistent statements or omissions, no elaborate setup is necessary for the use of prior inconsistent actions. It is sufficient simply to put the questions to the witness. Return to the commercial lease case from the preceding section and assume that the business owner testified about the poor security in the building. With no further elaboration, the cross-examiner may proceed as follows:

Q: Your business hours are 9:00 a.m. to 10:00 p.m.?

Q: You have not shortened your hours?

Q: You have not installed closed-circuit television cameras?

Q: You have not put in additional lighting?

Q: You have allowed your own teenage children to work the evening shift?

Each of these instances of the witness's own conduct, if admitted or otherwise proven, detracts from the credibility of the plaintiff's testimony that security conditions were intolerable.

The impeachment might be enhanced further still by using a setup that takes advantage of the principle of apposition:

Q: You testified on direct examination that security conditions are intolerable?

A: That's right.

Q: You claim to be in fear for your customers' safety?

A: Absolutely.

Q: You keep your store open until 10:00 p.m.?

A: Yes.

> Q: And security conditions are so bad that you have had your own teenage children work the evening shift?

The witness's claim of danger is flatly inconsistent with his actions in allowing his children to work in the store at night. Note, however, that the use of sarcasm is often risky. Many lawyers would prefer simply to make this point during final argument.

See demonstration 21 in the Visuals Appendix.

6.4 Character and "Characteristic" Impeachment

Character impeachment refers to the use of some inherent trait or particular characteristic of the witness, essentially unrelated to the case at hand, to render the testimony less credible. The thrust of the impeachment is to show that the witness, for some demonstrable reason, is simply not trustworthy.

The most common forms of characteristic impeachment include conviction of a crime, defect in memory or perception, and past untruthfulness.

6.4.1 Conviction of a Crime

A witness may be impeached on the basis of his past conviction of certain crimes. While the specifics vary from state to state, under the Federal Rules of Evidence a conviction is admissible as impeachment only if the crime

> (1) . . . was punishable by death or imprisonment for more than one year . . . and . . . if the probative value of the evidence outweighs its prejudicial effect to the defendant, [or] (2) regardless of the punishment . . . the elements of the crime required proving—or the witness's admitting—a dishonest act of false statement.[19]

In addition, the federal rules provide that convictions generally may not be used if they are more than ten years old[20] and that juvenile adjudications are inadmissible under most circumstances.[21]

The theory behind impeachment on the basis of conviction of a crime is that criminals are less trustworthy than other witnesses. Thus, the characteristic of having been convicted of a qualifying crime may be admissible to discredit a witness, without regard to the issues in the particular case. This makes great sense with regard to crimes such as perjury, forgery, and theft by deception, but it is somewhat less compelling concerning crimes such as assault or criminal damage to

19. Fed. R. Evid. 609(a).
20. Specifically, "if more than 10 years have passed since the witness's conviction or release from confinement for it whichever is later[,] [e]vidence of a conviction under this rule is admissible only if: (1) its probative value, supported by specific facts and circumstances, substantially outweighs its prejudicial effect . . . ." Fed. R. Evid. 609(b).
21. Fed. R. Evid. 609(d).

property. Why would a six-year-old conviction for, say, vandalism have any bearing on a witness's credibility in a current contract dispute? It is for this reason that Rule 609(a)(1) provides that before allowing the impeachment to proceed the court must determine whether the probative value of admitting the evidence outweighs its prejudicial effect. Note, however, that the balancing test is not required if the impeaching crime involved dishonesty or false statement.

Once it has been determined that a conviction can be used for impeachment, relatively little technique is involved in the cross-examination:

Q: Isn't it true, Ms. O'Reilly, that you were once convicted of the crime of aggravated battery?

A: Yes.

Q: You were convicted on October 12, 2011, correct?

A: Yes.

Q: That was a felony?

A: It was.

Q: And you were sentenced to two years of probation?

A: I was.

Q: That conviction took place in this very courthouse?

A: It did.

As a rule, the impeachment is limited to the details of the conviction; the facts and circumstances of the crime are generally inadmissible.[22] Because of this, the importance of the impeachment can easily be lost if the cross-examiner collapses it all into one or two questions. It is far more effective to draw out the impeaching information, as in the above example, into a series of short questions, each of which deals with a single fact. Repetition of terms such as "crime," "conviction," and even "convicted felon" will add weight to the impeachment.

If the witness denies having been convicted, the cross-examiner must be able to complete the impeachment by introducing a certified copy of the judgment or order of conviction.

See demonstration 22 in the Visuals Appendix.

6.4.2 Past Untruthfulness and Other Bad Acts

We have discussed the rules governing impeachment on the basis of a criminal conviction. What about a witness's bad acts that were not the subject of a conviction? A witness who has lied in the past, whether or not prosecuted and whether or

22. The facts and details of the crime may become admissible, however, if the witness or opposing counsel "opens the door."

not under oath, may well be likely to lie during current testimony. On the other hand, past misconduct of some sort is a near-universal human condition, and trials could easily become bogged down if lawyers are allowed free rein to cross-examine witnesses on any and all of their old misdeeds.

The Federal Rules of Evidence strike a balance by allowing the impeachment of witnesses on the basis of specific instances of past misconduct, apart from criminal convictions, only if they are probative of untruthfulness. Thus, a witness can be impeached with evidence that he has lied on a specific previous occasion, but generally not on the basis of previous violence. Moreover, the trial judge has discretion to exclude evidence even of past untruthfulness. Finally, incidents of prior untruthfulness may not be proven by extrinsic evidence.[23] The cross-examiner is stuck with the witness's answer.

Impeachment on the basis of past untruthfulness is therefore a very tricky matter. You must be certain that the witness will "own up" to the charge since you will be unable to prove it otherwise.

6.4.3 Impaired Perception or Recollection

A witness can also be impeached on the basis of inability to perceive or recall events.

Perception can be adversely affected by a wide variety of circumstances. The witness may have been distracted at the time of the events, or his vision may have been obscured. The witness may have been sleepy, frightened, or intoxicated. The witness may have poor eyesight or may suffer from some other sensory deficit. Any of these, or similar, facts can be used to impeach the credibility of a witness's testimony.

As with so much else in cross-examination, this form of impeachment is usually most effective when counsel refrains from asking the ultimate question. Assume, for example, that a witness in a burglary case identified the defendant during direct examination. The cross-examiner is primed for impeachment, knowing that the witness had just awakened from a nap when he observed the burglar. The focus of the impeachment will be on the witness's diminished ability to perceive.

Q: The burglary occurred in the middle of the afternoon?

A: Yes.

Q: You had been taking a nap on the couch?

A: Yes.

23. Fed. R. Evid. 608(b).

Q: It was light outside?

A: It was.

Q: But you were still able to sleep, correct?

A: Yes.

Q: Then you heard a sound?

A: I did.

Q: It must have taken a moment to awaken you?

A: I suppose so.

Q: You couldn't have known right away where the sound was coming from?

A: No, I guess not.

Q: So you had to orient yourself?

A: Yes.

Q: Then you sat up?

A: I did.

Q: Then you looked around?

A: That's right.

Q: You saw someone by the window?

A: Right.

Q: That must have come as quite a shock?

A: It certainly did.

Q: The man had his back to the window?

A: Yes.

Q: And the light was coming through the window?

A: Yes, it must have been.

At this point the cross-examiner will stop. The constituent facts of the impeachment have been established—the witness's perception was obviously impeded. Any further questioning is likely to be taken by the witness as an invitation to explain, thus threatening counsel's control of the examination. The argument is certainly clear: The witness was groggy, surprised, and a little frightened; the burglar's face was in a shadow; the identification is therefore suspect. The point is to save these conclusions for final argument rather than to attempt to extract them directly from the witness.

The concept of impaired perception relates to the witness's ability to perceive at the time of the original events. In contrast, the concept of impaired recollection involves the occurrence of intervening events that damaged the witness's recall. Such events can be as mundane as the mere passage of time or as dramatic as a head injury.

See demonstration 20 in the Visuals Appendix.

6.5 "Case-Data" Impeachment

Some facts are impeaching only within the circumstances of a particular case. They would be innocuous, or perhaps even helpful, in any other context. The most common forms of case-data impeachment are based on the witness's personal interest, motive, and bias or prejudice.

6.5.1 Personal Interest

A witness who is personally interested in the outcome of a case may be inclined to testify with less than absolute candor. Whether it occurs consciously or subconsciously, it is a well-recognized human tendency to shape one's recollection in the direction of the desired outcome.

Impeachment on the basis of personal interest is therefore geared to take advantage of this phenomenon by pointing out just how the witness stands to gain or lose as a consequence of the resolution of the case. The technique is common in both civil and criminal cases, and it may be applied to both party and nonparty witnesses.

Perhaps the clearest example of impeachment on the basis of personal interest arises when the witness is the defendant in a serious criminal case. The following example belabors an obvious point:

> Q: You are the defendant in this case?
>
> A: Yes.
>
> Q: You understand that if you are found guilty you can be sentenced to many years in the penitentiary?
>
> A: I guess so.
>
> Q: The penitentiary is a terrible place?
>
> A: That's what I hear.

Q: No one would ever willingly spend years in jail?

A: Certainly not.

Q: Of course, if you have an alibi, then you might not have to go to prison?

A: I guess not.

Q: But only if the jury believes you?

A: That is right.

Q: As it turns out, you do have an alibi, don't you?

A: I was not there when the crime was committed.

Q: And your testimony will keep you out of prison if the jury believes it?

The defendant's interest in his own testimony is so transparent that the point is often best left for final argument.

In civil matters the parties often stand to receive (or lose) great amounts of money depending on the verdict in the case. As with the criminal defendant, the interest of both civil plaintiffs and defendants is generally apparent. Moreover, since there is always a plaintiff and defendant in each case, this form of interest will usually cancel itself out. The financial interest of nonparty witnesses, however, may not be quite so obvious and therefore frequently becomes the target of impeachment.

In the following example, assume that the witness has been called to the stand on behalf of the plaintiff in a will contest. The witness testified on direct that the testator did not appear to be "of sound mind" at the time that the challenged will was executed.

Q: You are not a party to this case, are you?

A: I am not.

Q: But you are the plaintiff's business partner?

A: Yes, I am.

Q: You will receive no funds directly if the will is thrown out?

A: Right. I am not involved at all.

Q: But your business partner is involved.

A: Yes, I suppose so.

Q: He will become the sole beneficiary if the will is found invalid.

A: I believe that is true.

Q: Your business showed a large loss last year, didn't it?

A: Yes, we did.

Q: You lost over $1,000,000, didn't you?

A: Something like that.

Q: You have loaned over $400,000 to the business yourself, haven't you?

A: I have.

Q: You could lose that money if the business enters bankruptcy?

A: Yes.

Q: Your business needs an infusion of capital?

A: We do.

Q: And if that doesn't come from someone else, it might have to come from you?

A: I suppose that is right.

Q: If this will is upheld, your business partner will not receive a penny?

A: I guess that's right.

Q: And you have testified that the testator was not of sound mind when she left her estate to someone other than your business partner?

Two things about this example are noteworthy. First, the value of the impeaching fact depends strictly on the circumstances of this case. This impeachment would be impossible, even laughable, if it were attempted in a case that did not involve this unique confluence of events: challenged will, business partner, failing company, and personal loan. Unlike "characteristic" impeachment, which can be used in virtually any matter, "case-data" impeachment is limited to its particular circumstances.

This observation leads to the second point. Case-data impeachment is most valuable when the cross-examiner takes full advantage of the technique of apposition. The impeaching facts have the most weight when they are developed in conjunction with the other "case data" that explain their significance. The above witness's status as the plaintiff's business partner might be viewed as mildly impeaching standing alone. The witness's credibility is eroded far more significantly, however, when the additional facts—failing business, cash shortage, and outstanding personal loan—are elicited in close succession.

The most effective use of case-data impeachment requires the advocate to search the record, and often to search beyond the record, for specific bits of information that can be accumulated to challenge some witness's credibility. This is true, as we have just seen, for impeachment on the basis of interest. It is also true, as we shall see below, for impeachment on the basis of motive, bias, or prejudice.

6.5.2 Motive

A witness's testimony may be affected by a motive other than financial interest. The witness may have a professional stake in the issues being litigated or may have some other reason to prefer one outcome to another. In the will contest from the previous section, imagine that the lawyer who drew the will was called to the stand to testify with regard to its validity:

Q: You are the lawyer who drew the will?

A: Yes.

Q: You also arranged for it to be executed?

A: I did.

Q: You were there at the signing?

A: I was.

Q: You called your secretary and receptionist into your office to act as witnesses?

A: That is correct.

Q: You could not have done those things if the testator had been incompetent?

A: Of course not.

Q: You could not arrange for an incompetent person to execute a will?

A: No, I couldn't.

Q: It would be unprofessional for you not to notice a person's obvious lack of mental faculties?

A: It would be a mistake.

Q: So the challenge to this will is also a challenge to your own professional observations?

A: I suppose you could put it that way.

Q: And, of course, your testimony today is that the testator was perfectly lucid at all times?

This witness may be inclined to testify in such a way as to vindicate her earlier judgment. While she has no direct interest in the distribution of the estate, she is still impeachable on the basis of motive. Other commonly encountered motives include emotional attachment, revenge, chauvinism, preexisting belief, or adherence to a school of thought.[24] In all cases, apposition is the key.

6.5.3 Bias or Prejudice

Bias and prejudice generally refer to a witness's relationship to one of the parties. A witness may be well-disposed, or ill-inclined, toward either the plaintiff or the defendant. Sadly, some witnesses harbor prejudices against entire groups of people. Bias in favor of a party is often the consequence of friendship or affinity.

Q: You are the defendant's younger brother?

Q: You grew up together?

Q: You have helped each other out throughout your lives?

Q: Now your brother is charged with a crime?

Q: He is in trouble?

Q: He needs help?

Q: And you are here to testify?

Nothing is more case specific than this sort of impeachment. It has forensic value if and only if the witness's brother is the defendant in the case. Nothing can be presumed about case data; research and exploration are always required. When it comes to bias and prejudice, even close familial relationships have the potential to cut both ways:

Q: You are the defendant's younger brother?

Q: You grew up together?

Q: He was always beating you up?

Q: He seemed to have all of life's advantages?

Q: It was hard to follow in his successful footsteps?

Q: Everyone was always comparing you to him?

Q: He teased you and called you names?

Q: You were always resentful of him?

---

24. This last motive is most frequently used to impeach expert witnesses.

Q: You swore that you would get even?

Q: Now your older brother is charged with a crime?

Q: After all these years, his success seems to have run out?

Q: And you have come to court today to testify against him?

As with all case-data impeachment, the establishment of bias or prejudice requires careful development through the use of small, individual facts. This sort of impeachment is made doubly difficult by the fact that it is hard to avoid "telegraphing" your strategy. Once the witness realizes that you intend to impugn his objectivity, he will very naturally attempt to avoid admitting the component facts of your impeachment. In the fraternal scenario above, for example, the typical witness would do everything possible to deny the existence of lifelong resentment of his older brother. Thus, the cross-examiner would not risk this line of examination unless the witness's grudge could be sufficiently documented through letters, prior statements, or the testimony of other witnesses.

Witnesses are similarly reluctant to admit to racial, ethnic, or other group prejudices. Effective impeachment on this basis therefore depends on the initial establishment of incontrovertible facts such as prior statements, organizational memberships, or other provable past actions.

Chapter Seven

Redirect Examination and Rehabilitation

7.1 Purpose of Redirect

Redirect examination, which allows counsel an opportunity to respond to the cross-examination, may be used for a number of purposes. The witness may be asked to explain points that were explored during the cross, to untangle seeming inconsistencies, to correct errors or misstatements, or to rebut new charges or inferences. In other words, the purpose of redirect is to minimize or undo the damage, if any, that was effected during the cross-examination.

Cross-examiners are universally cautioned not to ask "one question too many." In a nutshell, redirect is the time to ask exactly those additional questions that the cross-examiner purposefully left out.

7.2 Law and Procedure

7.2.1 Scope

Because redirect is allowed for counteracting or responding to the cross-examination, the material that can be covered on redirect is technically limited to the scope of the cross. The interpretation of this rule varies from court to court; some are quite strict, and others are fairly lenient. Almost all courts, however, insist that counsel is not free to introduce a wholly new matter on redirect. The redirect must always have some reasonable relationship to the cross-examination.

The scope rule adds considerable hazard to the tactic of "sandbagging" or withholding crucial evidence from the direct examination to raise it following the cross. Counsel who reserves an important item of testimony from direct runs the risk that the issue will not be covered on cross and that it will therefore be excluded from redirect as well. Accordingly, there is little to be gained and much to lose by sandbagging, especially since redirect examination is usually followed by recross. Even when successful in deferring certain testimony to redirect, counsel cannot succeed in insulating the witness from recross-examination.

There is, however, one situation in which reserving evidence until redirect may be helpful. A witness may have an effective response to a potential line of cross-examination. Counsel, however, may have no way of knowing whether the cross-examiner will pursue those particular issues. Thus, it can be prudent to withhold the explanation until redirect rather than to insert it defensively during the main direct.[1]

7.2.2 Rules of Evidence

All of the rules of direct examination apply equally to redirect examination. Leading questions are prohibited, witnesses may not testify in narrative form, testimony must come from personal knowledge, lay opinions are limited to sensory perceptions, and the proper foundation must be laid to refresh recollection.

Many courts, however, allow a certain amount of latitude during redirect, especially with regard to leading questions. Even without indulgence, leading questions are always permissible to direct the witness's attention or to introduce a new area of questioning. A certain amount of leading may be necessary on redirect to focus the examination on the segment of the cross-examination that you wish to explain or rebut.

7.2.3 Recross Examination and Additional Redirect

Redirect examination may be followed by recross, which may be followed by additional redirect, and so on into the night. Each additional examination is limited to the scope of the one that immediately preceded it. Thus, recross is restricted to the scope of the redirect, and a second redirect would be confined to the scope of the recross. There is no right to continue an infinite regression of successive "re-examinations." Rather, it is within the court's discretion to allow or deny a request for, say, re-recross. Most judges routinely allow at least one redirect and one recross.

7.2.4 Reopening Direct Examination

Reopening direct examination is an alternative to redirect. It can be employed where counsel needs to pursue a line of questioning that is beyond the scope of the cross-examination. It is strictly within the court's discretion to allow counsel to reopen a direct examination.

7.3 Planned Redirect

Most redirect examinations cannot be thoroughly planned, since each must be closely responsive to the preceding cross-examination. Nonetheless, it is possible

1. Situations that may call for this approach are addressed in 7.3.

to anticipate that certain areas will have to be covered on redirect and to prepare accordingly.

It is not always possible to know which lines of cross-examination will actually be pursued. Counsel would not want to use the direct examination to explain away a cross that might never materialize. Thus, an explanation may be best reserved for redirect in the event that the cross-examination ultimately probes that particular area. It is both possible and necessary to plan for such contingencies.

For example, a witness may have given a prior statement that is arguably impeaching. While there may be a perfectly reasonable response to any apparent inconsistency, it would undermine the witness to bring up the earlier statement during the direct. An explanation would only make sense once the cross-examiner actually effected the impeachment. Consequently, the best approach in this situation is probably to defer the explanation until the redirect.

A similar situation arises where there is a credible objection to the anticipated cross-examination. A witness's past criminal act, for example, might be excludable.[2] The direct examiner certainly would not want to bring up a prior crime or other bad act, even to justify the circumstances, without first determining whether an objection to the cross-examination will be sustained. Again, the wisest approach may be to hold the explanation for redirect.

In both of these situations, and others like them, it is possible to plan a segment of the redirect—including preparation of the witness—just as one would plan a direct examination. Note, however, that both examples involve only rejoinders to potential cross-examination. The technique of withholding testimony until redirect is not recommended for affirmative evidence or elements of your case.

7.4 Waiving Redirect

Redirect examination is not always necessary. As with all witness examinations, redirect should only be pursued if it will contribute to your theory of the case.

There is no need to ask additional questions if the witness was not appreciably hurt by the cross-examination. Additionally, some damage cannot be repaired; it is a mistake to engage in redirect examination if the situation cannot be improved. The worst miscalculation, however, is to surprise the witness with a redirect question. Do not ask for an explanation unless you are certain that the witness has one.

As a further hazard, redirect exposes the witness to recross. If redirect is waived, there can be no additional cross-examination. Even a single question on redirect, however, can subject the witness to significant further cross-examination, as long as it stays within the applicable scope.

2. Fed. R. Evid. 404(b).

Finally, an unnecessary redirect risks repeating, and therefore reemphasizing, the cross-examination. It can also trivialize the effect of the direct by rehashing minor points.

7.5 Conducting Redirect

Content is the most important aspect of redirect examination. The redirect should concentrate on a few significant points that definitely can be developed. As noted above, these can typically include explanations, clarifications, or responses.

7.5.1 Explanations

Explanations are best obtained by asking for them. Focus the witness's attention on the pertinent area of the cross-examination and then simply ask her to proceed.

> Q: Defense counsel pointed out that you did not visit your doctor immediately following your camping trip at Eagle River Falls. Why didn't you go to the doctor right away?

This approach can also be used to bring out clarifying facts, made relevant by the cross-examination:

> Q: How soon after the camping trip did you visit the doctor?

A witness may have been frustrated by the control exerted by the cross-examiner. If the level of control seemed unfair or unjustified, this can be pointed out during the redirect. Consider:

> Q: Defense counsel seemed very concerned that you did not go to the doctor immediately after your camping trip, but she didn't ask you for an explanation. Would you like to explain?

Or,

> Q: I noticed that defense counsel cut you off when you tried to continue your answer about the camping trip. What was it that you wanted to say?

Or,

> Q: There was a lot of cross-examination about your camping trip, but counsel didn't ask you anything about what your doctor eventually prescribed for you. What treatment did you get?

While the introductions in the above examples are arguably leading, they are probably permissible efforts to direct the witness's attention. Nonetheless, do not overuse preambles of this sort. They are likely to be effective only where the cross-examination truly was overbearing or oppressive.

7.5.2 Rehabilitation

Redirect can be used specifically for rehabilitation of a witness who has been impeached with a prior inconsistent statement.

7.5.2.1 Technique

The technique for rehabilitation is similar to that used for any other explanation. Direct the witness's attention to the supposed impeachment and request a clarification. It may be that the alleged inconsistency can be easily resolved or that the earlier statement was the product of a misunderstanding or misinterpretation. Whatever the explanation, it is important to conclude the rehabilitation with an affirmative statement of the witness's current testimony.

In the following example, the plaintiff in the fire truck case testified on direct examination that the fire engine had been sounding its siren and flashing its lights. On cross-examination, she was impeached with her deposition in which she stated that the fire truck "had not been using all of its warning devices." She might be rehabilitated on redirect as follows:

Q: In your deposition, you said that the fire truck was not using all of its warning signals. Can you explain how that fits in with your testimony today about the lights and the siren?

A: When I answered the deposition question, I was thinking about the horn as an additional warning signal, and as far as I can recall the fire truck was not sounding its horn.

Q: Which warning devices was the fire truck using?

A: It was definitely sounding its siren and flashing all of its red lights.

7.5.2.2 Prior Consistent Statements

A witness can also be rehabilitated by introducing a prior consistent statement. Although a witness's own previous out-of-court account would ordinarily be hearsay, a prior consistent statement is admissible to "rebut an express or implied charge that the declarant recently fabricated it or acted from a recent improper influence or motive in so testifying."[3]

Accordingly, once the cross-examiner suggests that the witness has changed her story, the direct examiner may show that the witness's testimony is consistent with an earlier report or other statement. Note that in some jurisdictions, a prior consistent statement is admissible only if it predates the inconsistent statement used for impeachment.

---

3. Fed. R. Evid. 801(d)(1)(B).

Chapter Eight

Expert Testimony

8.1 Introduction

Most witnesses are called to the stand because they have seen, heard, or done something relevant to the issues in the case. Such persons are often referred to as fact witnesses, ordinary witnesses, lay witnesses, or percipient witnesses. Whatever the term used, the testimony of witnesses is generally limited to those things they have directly observed or experienced, as well as reasonable conclusions that can be drawn on the basis of their sensory perceptions. In short, lay witnesses must testify from personal knowledge, and they may not offer opinions.

Expert witnesses comprise an entirely different category. An expert witness is not limited to personal knowledge and may base her testimony on information that was gathered solely for the purpose of testifying in the litigation. Moreover, under the proper circumstances an expert witness may offer an opinion that goes well beyond her direct sensory impressions. An expert may opine on the cause or consequences of occurrences; interpret the actions of other persons; draw conclusions on the basis of circumstances; comment on the likelihood of events; and may even state her beliefs regarding such seemingly nonfactual issues as fault, damage, negligence, avoidability, and the like.

Expert witnesses may be helpful in a wide variety of cases. Experts can be used in commercial cases to interpret complex financial data, in tort cases to explain the nature of injuries, or in criminal cases to translate underworld slang into everyday language. Properly qualified, an expert can be asked to peer into the past, as when an accident reconstructionist re-creates the scene of an automobile collision. Other experts may predict the future, as when an economist projects the expected life earnings of the deceased in a wrongful death case. In some cases, expert testimony is required as a matter of law. In legal or medical malpractice cases, for example, it is usually necessary to call an expert witness to establish the relevant standard of care; in narcotics cases, the prosecution usually must call a chemist or other expert to prove that the substance in question is actually an illegal drug.

Given the extraordinarily broad scope of expert testimony, and its extreme potential for influencing the judgment of the trier of fact, certain rules have developed regarding the permissible use, extent, and nature of expert testimony.

8.2 Standards for Expert Testimony

8.2.1 Areas of Expertise

Rule 702 of the Federal Rules of Evidence provides that expert opinions may be admissible where the expert's "scientific, technical, or other specialized knowledge will help the trier of fact to understand the evidence or to determine a fact in issue." Thus, there are two threshold questions: Does the witness possess sufficient scientific, technical, or other specialized knowledge? If so, will that knowledge be helpful to the trier of fact?

The U.S. Supreme Court has held that a trial judge must also make a preliminary assessment of the validity of the reasoning and methods that support proffered expert testimony.[1] The Federal Rules of Evidence subsequently codified that requirement, specifying that opinion testimony is admissible only if

> (b) the testimony is based on sufficient facts or data, (c) the testimony is the product of reliable principles and methods, and (d) the expert has reliably applied the principles and methods to the facts of the case.[2]

In the federal system, then, the trial judge has become a gatekeeper and makes an initial determination whenever the validity of opinion evidence is challenged. A number of states have also adopted this approach. In other jurisdictions, however, the soundness of an expert's methodology will still be a question for the jury. Needless to say, it is always essential to determine which test for admissibility will be used for scientific or other expert evidence.

8.2.2 Scope of Opinion

It was once considered improper for an expert to offer an opinion on the "ultimate issue" in the case, as this was regarded as "invading the province of the jury." This restrictive convention often led to extremely elliptical testimony, with the expert testifying to a series of inferences and opinions, but not drawing the most obvious factual conclusions. This process was further complicated by the difficulty of determining exactly what were the ultimate issues in a case.

---

1. Daubert v. Merrell Dow Pharmaceuticals, Inc., 509 U.S. 579 (1993); Kumho Tire v. Carmichael, 526 U.S. 137 (1999).
2. Fed. R. Evid. 702.

The Federal Rules of Evidence now provide that expert testimony, if otherwise admissible, "is not objectionable just because it embraces an ultimate issue."[3] The only exception is that an expert in a criminal case may not state an opinion as to whether the defendant "did or did not have a mental state or condition that constitutes an element of the crime charged or a defense."[4]

Judges vary on their interpretations of the "ultimate issue" rule. Some courts will allow experts to opine on virtually any issue, including such case-breakers as whether the plaintiff in a personal injury case was contributorily negligent or whether the defendant in a tax evasion case had unreported income. Other judges draw the line at what they consider to be legal conclusions. So, for example, a medical expert in a malpractice case would no doubt be allowed to state that certain tests were indicated and that the defendant had not performed them. Many judges would also allow the expert to testify that the failure to order the tests fell below the standard of care generally exercised by practitioners in the relevant community, although this might be considered an "ultimate issue" in the case. Most judges, though not all, would balk at permitting the expert to testify that the defendant's conduct constituted malpractice, on the theory that malpractice is a legal conclusion that is not within the specialized knowledge of a medical expert.

8.2.3 Bases for Opinion

Under the Federal Rules of Evidence, an expert can testify about her opinion with or without explaining the facts or data on which the opinion is based.[5] In theory, then, an expert, once qualified, could simply state her opinion on direct examination, leaving the cross-examiner to search for its basis.[6] In practice this approach is rarely followed since the expert's opinion could hardly be persuasive until its foundation is explained. The practical effect of the rule is to allow the witness to state her opinion at the beginning of the examination, followed by an explanation, rather than having to set forth all of the data at the outset.

A related issue is the nature of the information that an expert may rely on in arriving at an opinion. At common law, experts could give opinions only on the basis of facts that were already in evidence. One way for an expert to comply with this requirement was to observe the actual testimony by sitting through the trial. The only alternative to this expensive and cumbersome routine was for the attorney offering the expert testimony to precede it with an elaborate "hypothetical question" that recited all of the facts—either admitted or eventually to be admitted—needed by the expert as the basis for an opinion.

3. *Id.* 704(a).
4. *Id.* 704(b).
5. *Id.* 705.
6. "But the expert may be required to disclose those [underlying] facts or data on cross-examination." FED. R. EVID. 705.

The Federal Rules of Evidence abolished the need for this highly stylized ritual. An expert witness may now testify on the basis of facts "that the expert has been made aware of or personally observed."[7] Moreover, those facts or data need not be admissible as long as they are "of a type reasonably relied on by experts in the particular field."[8]

While it is certain that an expert may rely on inadmissible date, it is less clear when the expert may recite that data as support for her testimony. For example, forensic pathologists regularly rely on toxicology reports in determining the cause of death. A pathologist could presumably reach an opinion based on such a written report even if it would be hearsay when offered at trial. The question, however, is whether the expert, having accepted the report, may also testify as to its contents.

According to Rule 703, otherwise inadmissible facts or data may not be disclosed to the jury by the proponent of the opinion "only if their probative value in helping the jury evaluate the opinion substantially outweighs their prejudicial effect." Thus, the pathologist in the above example could read the language of the toxicology report to the jury only if the court first determines that it is substantially more helpful than it is prejudicial. Otherwise, the witness would be limited to stating how and why she relied on the report, but would not be allowed to testify about its contents. Note, however, that there is no such limitation on the opponent of the proffered opinion, who may always require an expert "to disclose those [underlying] facts or data on cross-examination."[9]

8.3 The Expert's Overview

Just as a lawyer cannot succeed without developing a comprehensive theory of the case, neither will an expert be effective without a viable, articulated theory. An expert's theory is an overview or summary of the expert's entire position. The theory must not only state a conclusion, but must also explain, in commonsense terms, why the expert is correct. Why did she settle on a certain methodology? Why did she review particular data? Why is her approach reliable? Why is the opposing expert wrong? In other words, the expert witness must present a coherent narrative that provides the trier of fact with reasons for accepting, and, it is hoped, internalizing, the expert's point of view.

The need for a theory is especially true in cases involving "dueling experts." It is common for each of the opposing parties in litigation to retain their own expert witnesses. The trier of fact is then faced with the task of sorting through the opinion testimony and choosing which witness to believe. It is likely that both experts will

7. Fed. R. Evid. 703.

8. *Id.*

9. *Id.* 705. The requirements of the Sixth Amendment's Confrontation Clause are beyond the scope of this discussion. *See* Melendez-Diaz v. Massachusetts, 577 U.S. 305 (2009).

be amply qualified, and it is unlikely that either will make a glaring error in her analysis or commit an unpardonable faux pas in her testimony. The trier of fact will therefore be inclined to credit the expert whose theory is most believable.

Consider the following case. The plaintiff operated a statewide chain of drive-in restaurants, but was put out of business by the defendant's allegedly unfair competition. Assume that summary judgment was granted in favor of the plaintiff on the issue of liability and that the court set the case for trial on damages. Each side retained an expert witness, each of whom generated a damage model.

Not surprisingly, the plaintiff's expert opined that the restaurants, had they not been driven out of business, would have earned millions of dollars over the following five years. The defendant's witness, however, held the view that the stores would have been marginally profitable, with total profits amounting to no more than a few hundred thousand dollars. Each witness backed up her opinion with computer printouts, charts, and graphs. Both used reliable data, and all of their figures were rigorously accurate.

The rival experts reached different conclusions because they followed different routes. The plaintiff's expert calculated lost profits as a function of population growth and driving habits, opining that the revenues at drive-in restaurants would rise in proportion to expected increases in population and miles driven. The defendant's witness, on the other hand, estimated damages on a "profit-per-store" basis, taking the plaintiff's average profit for the existing restaurants and multiplying them by the number of outlets that the plaintiff planned to build.

Faced with this discrepancy, the task for counsel is to present the expert testimony in its most persuasive form. Whichever side you represent, it should be obvious that a simple recitation of your expert's methods will be unlikely to carry the day. After all, we have assumed that both experts were meticulously careful within the confines of their respective approaches. For the same reason, the trier of fact will probably be unimpressed by an expert who reviews in detail all of her calculations. Numbers are boring in any event, and both experts are sure to have been accurate in their arithmetic.

Instead, the key to this case is to persuade the trier of fact that your expert chose the correct approach. The plaintiff's expert must be asked to explain why lost profits can be determined on the basis of population growth; the defendant's expert has to support her reliance on profits-per-store. The prevailing expert will not be the one with the greatest mastery of the details, but rather the one who most successfully conveys the preferability of her theory. The most painstakingly prepared projection of population growth cannot succeed in persuading a jury if they ultimately decide that only profits-per-store can give them an accurate assessment of damages.

The importance of theory extends to all types of expert testimony. It is necessary, but not sufficient, for your expert to be thorough, exacting, highly regarded, incisive, honorable, and well-prepared. Her testimony will suffer if she cannot support her opinion with commonsense reasons.

8.4 Offering Expert Testimony

There is a certain logic to the direct examination of most experts. While the particulars and details will vary, there are a limited number of possible patterns for organizing the testimony. It is absolutely necessary, for example, to qualify the expert before proceeding to her opinion. The following is a broad outline that can accommodate the specifics of most expert testimony.

See demonstration 11 in the Visuals Appendix.

8.4.1 Introduction and Foreshadowing

The first step is to introduce the expert and explain her involvement in the case. Since expert testimony is qualitatively different from lay testimony, it is a good idea to clarify its purposes for the jurors so that they will understand what they are about to hear.[10] Ask the witness how she came to be retained and why she is present in court.

Moreover, the technical requirements of presenting expert testimony often result in a considerable time gap between the introduction of the witness and the substantive high points of her testimony. Thus, it is generally desirable to foreshadow the expert's opinion at the very outset of the examination.

The plaintiff's damages expert in the example from the preceding section might be introduced as follows:

> Q: Please state your name.
>
> A: Dr. Andrea Longhini.
>
> Q: Dr. Longhini, have you been retained to reach an expert opinion in this case?
>
> A: Yes.
>
> Q: Did you reach an opinion concerning the plaintiff's lost profits?
>
> A: Yes, I have calculated the amount of money that the plaintiff would have earned.
>
> Q: We'll talk about your opinion in detail in a few minutes, but right now we have to talk about your qualifications to testify as an expert in this case.

10. It is obviously unnecessary to explain the purpose of expert testimony in bench trials.

8.4.2 Qualification

To testify as an expert, a witness must be qualified by reason of knowledge, skill, experience, training, or education. This is a threshold question for the judge, who must determine whether the witness is qualified before permitting her to give opinion testimony. The qualification of the witness, then, is a necessary predicate for all of the testimony to follow. Care must be taken to qualify the expert in a manner that is both persuasive and technically adequate.

8.4.2.1 Technical Requirements

The technical requirements for qualifying an expert witness are straightforward. It is usually adequate to show that the witness possesses some specialized skill or knowledge, acquired through appropriate experience or education, and that the witness is able to apply that skill or knowledge in a manner relevant to the issues in the case.

Thus, the minimal qualifications for the financial expert in the restaurant case could be established as follows:

Q: Dr. Longhini, could you please tell us something about your education?

A: Certainly. I have an undergraduate degree in business from the University of Michigan and a PhD in economics from the University of California.

Q: What work have you done since receiving your doctorate?

A: I was a professor in the economics department at Washington University for six years. Then I left to start my own consulting firm, which is called Longhini & Associates.

Q: Do you have a specialty within the field of economics?

A: Yes, my specialty is business valuation.

Q: Has business valuation been your specialty both at Washington University and at Longhini & Associates?

A: Yes.

Q: What is the field of business valuation?

A: It is the study of all of the components that contribute to the fair value of a business, including anticipated future profits, assets, receivables, good will, and investment potential.

The above examination confirms the expert's qualifications by reason of both education and experience. Dr. Longhini should now be able to give an opinion about the projected profits for the restaurant chain.

There are, of course, many other areas of basic qualification beyond education and business experience. Examples include specialized training, continuing education courses, teaching and lecturing positions, licenses and certifications, publications, consulting experience, professional memberships, awards, and other professional honors.

The establishment of basic qualifications, however, should not be counsel's entire objective. It is equally if not more important to go on to qualify the witness as persuasively as possible.

8.4.2.2 Persuasive Qualification

The technical qualification of an expert merely allows the witness to testify in the form of an opinion. Counsel's ultimate goal is to ensure that the opinion is accepted by the trier of fact. Persuasive qualification is particularly important in cases involving competing experts, since their relative qualifications may be one basis on which the judge or jury will decide which expert to believe.

It is a mistake, however, to think that more qualifications are necessarily more persuasive. An endless repetition of degrees, publications, awards, and appointments may easily overload any judge or juror's ability, not to mention desire, to pay careful attention to the witness. It is often better to introduce into evidence the witness's detailed résumé or curriculum vitae and to use the qualification portion of the actual examination to focus in on several salient points.[11]

It is usually more persuasive to concentrate on a witness's specific expertise as opposed to her more generic or remote qualifications. Every economist, for example, is likely to hold a doctorate, so there is comparatively little advantage to be gained by spending valuable time expounding your expert's academic degrees. Similarly, there is usually scant reason to go into matters such as the subject of the witness's doctoral thesis, unless it bears directly on some issue in the case.

On the other hand, an expert's credibility can be greatly enhanced by singling out qualifications that relate specifically to the particular case. Thus, it would be important to point out that the witness has published several articles directly relevant to the issues in the case. It would be less useful to take the witness through a long list of extraneous articles, even if they appeared in prestigious journals. Other case-specific qualifications may include direct experience, consulting work, or teaching that is connected to an issue in the case.

11. An expert's résumé might be considered hearsay. Expert qualifications, however, are notoriously boring, and most judges will jump at the chance to move things along by allowing the introduction of a résumé. For the same reason, it is common for counsel to stipulate to the introduction of résumés for all expert witnesses. Alternatively, a résumé might be admissible as a business record. The expert's résumé should rarely be used as a complete substitute for examination on qualifications since this would deprive counsel of the opportunity to emphasize the witness's most compelling virtues.

Experience is often more impressive than academic background. So, for example, a medical expert may be more impressive if she has actually practiced in the applicable specialty as opposed to possessing knowledge that is strictly theoretical. When presenting such a witness, then, counsel should typically dwell on her experience, pointing out details such as the number of procedures she has performed, the hospitals where she is on staff, and the numbers of other physicians who have consulted her.

Finally, it is frequently effective to emphasize areas of qualification where you know the opposing expert to be lacking. If your expert has a superior academic background, use the direct examination to point out why academic training is important. If your expert holds a certification that the opposing expert lacks, have her explain how difficult it is to become certified.

8.4.2.3 Tender of the Witness

In some jurisdictions it is necessary, once qualifications have been concluded, to tender the witness to the court as an expert in a specified field. The purpose of the tender is to inform the court that qualification has been completed and to give opposing counsel an opportunity either to conduct a voir dire examination of the witness or to object to the tender. In the restaurant example above, the financial expert would be tendered as follows:

Counsel: Your Honor, we tender Dr. Andrea Longhini as an expert witness in the field of business valuation and the projection of profits.

It may be an effective tactic to tender an expert witness to the court even in jurisdictions where a formal tender is not required. First, tendering the witness signals that the qualification segment has been completed and requires opposing counsel either to object or accede to the witness's qualifications. By forcing the issue early in the examination, the direct examiner can avoid being interrupted by an objection to the witness's qualifications at some more delicate point in the testimony. Additionally, assuming that the judge rules favorably on the tender, counsel in effect has obtained the court's declaration that the witness is, indeed, an expert. This will give additional weight to the opinions that follow.

8.4.3 Opinion and Theory

Following qualification, the next step in the direct examination of an expert witness is to elicit firm statements of opinion and theory.

8.4.3.1 Statement of Opinion

The Federal Rules of Evidence provide that "[u]nless the court orders otherwise, an expert may state an opinion—and give the reasons for it—without first testifying to the underlying facts or data."[12] Consequently, once the witness has been qualified (and accepted as an expert in jurisdictions requiring a formal tender and ruling), she may proceed to express her opinion without additional foundation. In other words, she may state her conclusions without first detailing the nature or extent of her background work or investigation.

Many attorneys believe strongly in taking advantage of the "opinion first" provision. Expert testimony tends to be long, arcane, and boring. The intricate details of an expert's preparation are unlikely to be interesting or even particularly understandable. They will be even less captivating if they are offered in a void, without any advance notice of where the details are leading or why they are being explained. On the other hand, a clear statement of the expert's conclusion can provide the context for the balance of the explanatory testimony. Compare the two following vignettes, each taken from the "fast food" example above:

> Q: Dr. Longhini, what did you do to arrive at your opinion in this matter?
>
> A: My first step was to gather all of the available data regarding vehicle registrations and anticipated population growth in the state.
>
> Q: Then what did you do?
>
> A: I correlated population growth with expected vehicle miles to arrive at a reasonable estimate of "miles per person" over each of the next five years.
>
> Q: How was that calculation performed?

Even the most diligent and attentive juror would be baffled by this examination. What is the relevance of vehicle miles and population growth to fast-food profits? The nature of the witness's computation is meaningless in the absence of some connection to her opinion in the case. Indeed, the more thoroughly the witness explains her calculations, the more incomprehensible they will become. In contrast, consider the following:

> Q: Dr. Longhini, do you have an opinion as to the profits that the plaintiff's restaurant chain would have made, if they hadn't been forced out of business?
>
> A: Yes, I do.
>
> Q: What is your opinion?
>
> A: I believe that the restaurant chain would have earned at least $8.2 million over the next five years, if they had been able to stay in business.

---

12. FED. R. EVID. 705.

Q: How did you reach that opinion?

A: I based my calculations on the state's projected population growth, combined with the probable demand for fast-food, drive-in restaurants.

This examination is far more understandable. By providing her opinion at the outset, the expert allows the trier of fact to comprehend the significance of the following details. The jury will be much more able to understand the relationship between lost profits and the data on vehicle registration and population growth.

8.4.3.2 Statement of Theory

Once the expert's opinion has been stated, immediately provide the underlying theory. The theory should furnish the nexus between the expert's conclusion and the data used to support the conclusion.

In other words, the examination should follow this pattern: 1) here is my opinion; 2) here are the principles that support my opinion; 3) here is what I did to reach my final conclusion.

In the fast food example, the expert's theory should explain why population growth and vehicle miles are reliable indicators of projected profits:

Q: Dr. Longhini, why did you base your calculations on the state's projected population growth?

A: The demand for fast food will rise as population grows. This is particularly true because teenagers and parents of young children are the largest purchasers of fast food, and they are also two of the groups that increase most rapidly as population goes up.

Q: Why did you also consider growth in vehicle miles?

A: Drive-in restaurants are especially sensitive to vehicle miles. As people drive more, they are exposed to more drive-in restaurants, and they therefore buy more meals.

Q: What did you conclude from these relationships?

A: I concluded that the profitability of a drive-in restaurant chain will rise in proportion to a combination of general population growth and increases in miles driven.

Q: Did you consider only population growth and vehicle miles?

A: Of course not. I began by determining the chain's profits under current conditions, and I used those figures as a base. Then I projected them forward for five years, using the government's statistics for population and driving.

Q: Please tell us now exactly how you did that.

Note how this examination provides the context for the explanation to follow.

8.4.4 Explanation and Support

Having stated and supported her theory choice, the expert can now go on to detail the nature of her investigation and calculations. The trier of fact cannot be expected to take the expert at her word, so the validity and accuracy of her data and assumptions must be established.

8.4.4.1 Data

The expert should be asked how she chose and obtained her data. She should also explain why her information is reliable. In the scenario above, for example, the expert could point out that government statistics on population and vehicle miles are used to make many crucial decisions, such as the configuration of traffic lights, the expansion of highways, and even the construction of schools. The expert should also be asked to describe any tests or computations that she performed.

The treatment of underlying data is one of the trickiest aspects of expert testimony. Many experts will be in love with their data, and they will be anxious to lay them out in excruciating detail. Unfortunately, most judges and jurors will have little tolerance for lengthy descriptions of enigmatic scientific or technical processes. Counsel must therefore strike a balance, eliciting a sufficiently detailed treatment of the data to persuade the jury of its reliability, but stopping well short of the point where their attention span is exhausted.

It is not sufficient for the expert simply to relate the nature of the data. Rather, the expert should go on to explain how and why the data support her conclusions.

8.4.4.2 Assumptions

Most experts rely on assumptions. The financial expert in the fast-food case, for example, would no doubt assume that the relationship between sales and population growth would continue at historical rates. The expert would also probably assume a certain financial "discount rate" for reducing the dollars in her projection to present value. There is obviously nothing wrong with using appropriate presumptions, but their validity should be explained:

Q: Dr. Longhini, did you make any assumptions in reaching your opinion that the plaintiff's restaurant chain would have earned $8.2 million in profits?

A: Yes, I assumed that fast food sales would continue to increase in proportion to population at the same rate as they had in the past.

Q: Why did you make that assumption?

A: The restaurant chain was put out of business, so there were no actual sales to look at. I therefore had to project their most likely sales, and for that I had to assume a base figure to project forward.

Q: What did you use as your base figure?

A: I used the average growth for the entire industry.

Q: Why did you use the industry average?

A: I used the industry average precisely because it is an average of all of the companies in that particular business. That way I could be sure that I wasn't using a figure that was abnormally high or abnormally low.

It is not necessary to explain or outline every hypothesis used by your expert, but the more important assumptions should be noted and supported.

8.4.5 Theory Differentiation

In cases involving dueling experts, there will also be competing theories. With properly prepared and presented theories, each expert will attempt to explain to the trier of fact why her theory ought to be accepted. It can be particularly effective, therefore, to ask your expert to comment on the opposing expert's work. This technique can be called theory differentiation because it is most convincing when your expert discusses the shortcomings of the opposition theory.

In the previous sections we have seen illustrations taken from the testimony of the plaintiff's financial expert in a case involving lost profits. Now consider this example of theory differentiation, offered by the expert witness for the defendant.[13]

Q: Please state your name.

A: Benjamin Haruo.

Q: Dr. Haruo, have you had an opportunity to review the work done in this case by Dr. Andrea Longhini?

A: Yes, I have.

Q: Do you agree with Dr. Longhini's damage projections?

A: No, I do not.

Q: Why not?

13. For the purpose of this example, assume that the witness has been identified and qualified.

A: Dr. Longhini based her estimate on a combination of population growth and mileage assumptions, and this approach cannot yield a reliable result.

Q: Why is that?

A: Because it assumes too much. Dr. Longhini's theory is that restaurant revenues will inevitably rise along with population and automobile miles. While this might possibly be true for the entire restaurant industry, there is no reason to think that it would be true for any particular chain of restaurants. To reach a dependable result for an individual chain you would have to consider many other factors.

Q: What factors are those?

A: At a minimum you would have to consider location, market niche, product recognition, potential competition, specific demographics, and general economic climate.

Q: Did Dr. Longhini consider any of those factors?

A: No, she did not.

Q: Could you please give us an example of how location could affect the profit projections?

A: Certainly. Population always grows unevenly. Even if the overall population rises in a state or a city, it might stay constant or fall in certain areas. Therefore, a restaurant chain might not be able to take advantage of population increases if all of their outlets were placed in stagnant or declining locations.

The defense expert has deftly exposed the flaws in the plaintiff's theory. There are two advantages to such theory differentiation. First, it enables the expert to concentrate on major issues as opposed to picking out petty mistakes. Second, it allows the expert to avoid personal attacks. In essence, the above example has Dr. Haruo saying: "I have no personal quarrel with Dr. Longhini; she simply chose an inadequate theory." This "high road" approach will contribute to the dignity and persuasiveness of the witness.

The timing of theory differentiation can be important. Plaintiff's counsel generally will want to establish her own theory first before proceeding to criticize the defense expert. Depending on the circumstances of the case, plaintiff's counsel might even want to forego theory differentiation entirely during her case-in-chief and recall her expert for that purpose on rebuttal.

The defense, on the other hand, should address the plaintiff's expert's theory at some point during the direct examination of the defendant's own expert. This can be done early in the examination (to rebut the plaintiff's expert immediately and forcefully), or it can be done toward the end of the testimony (to allow the defense expert to build up the positive aspects of his own theory before turning his attention to the opposition).

8.4.6 Conclusion

An expert's direct examination should conclude with a powerful restatement of his most important conclusions.

8.5 Persuasive Techniques for Direct Examination

Most of the direct examination methods discussed in chapter two can be used effectively with expert witnesses. In addition, the following techniques are specifically applicable to expert testimony.

8.5.1 Humanize the Witness

Many experts from scientific, technical, or financial backgrounds may appear aloof, intimidating, or even arrogant to jurors who do not share their special expertise. It is therefore important to humanize these witnesses as much as possible in the course of the direct examination. If permitted in your jurisdiction, this can be done by bringing out personal and family background information and by allowing the witness to talk about more than strictly professional matters.

8.5.2 Use Plain Language

Virtually every field of expertise creates its own technical and shorthand terms, and expert witnesses will often be inclined to use arcane and jargon-laden speech without even thinking about it. It is counsel's job to guide the witness away from the use of jargon and into the realm of everyday speech. There are three basic ways to accomplish this task.

First, thoroughly prepare the witness to avoid complex, professional terms. Spend sufficient time with the witness before trial so that she will understand the importance of plain, simple language.

Second, ask for an explanation when your witness lapses into her native tongue, whether it is finance-talk, engineeringese, or accounting-speak. Do this gently and without reprimand or condescension, as in this example:

> Q: Dr. Merkys Gomez, do you have an opinion as to why the pressure plate failed?
>
> A: Yes. My tests indicate that the fastening bolts were over-torqued.

Q: What do you mean when you say over-torqued?

A: I mean that the bolts were turned too far when they were tightened.

Finally, and possibly most important, counsel must avoid the temptation to adopt the expert's word choices. Too many lawyers, perhaps out of a desire to appear erudite or knowledgeable, tend to examine expert witnesses using the expert's own jargon. Such examinations can take on the characteristics of a private, and completely inaccessible, conversation between the lawyer and the witness. It is bad enough when lawyers use legalese; it is worse when they embrace the private speech of another profession. Consider the following:

Q: Dr. Clarke, what injuries did you observe?

A: I observed multiple contusions on the anterior upper extremities.

Q: Was there anything remarkable about the contusions?

A: Yes. They varied in color, which indicated that they had been inflicted at different times.

Q: Did the anterior location of the contusions indicate anything further to you?

A: Yes. Their anterior location suggested that they had been inflicted from a superior position.

The lawyer and doctor are talking about bruises. The witness chose to use the term "contusions" because it is medically precise, and the lawyer's adoption of the term encouraged the doctor to continue using it. While the lawyer may have succeeded in demonstrating his medical sophistication, he may have done so at the cost of the jury's comprehension.

8.5.3 Avoid Narratives

Most judges will allow expert witnesses considerable freedom to testify in narrative fashion. Many lawyers believe that they should take advantage of this leeway, and they therefore encourage their experts to present their testimony in long, uninterrupted segments. This is a mistake. Long narratives are hard to follow and harder to digest. Anyone who ever sat through a long lecture or speech should understand how difficult it is to pay attention to a speaker for an extended period of time. This is particularly true of expert testimony, which often concentrates on complex or intricate details. Allowing an expert to testify in a long, unbroken stretch invites juror inattention.

Recall the discussion of the importance of primacy in basic direct examination—the judge and jury remember best what they hear first. This concept applies to individual answers as well as to complete examinations. A new answer begins every time counsel asks a question. In other words, every question to the expert reinitiates primacy and refocuses the listeners' attention. Unless the expert is an extraordinarily skilled speaker, a narrative answer will have no comparable points of reinitiation. The opportunity to continuously highlight the testimony will be lost.

Counsel can avoid narrative answers and reinitiate primacy by punctuating the expert's testimony at logical breaking points.

> Q: Dr. Haruo, what is the significance of location in projecting profits for a chain of drive-in restaurants?
>
> A: Location is probably the single most important factor when it comes to profitability in any retail business. Even if the overall trend in an industry is upward, a poorly located business is unlikely to benefit. This is especially true of the restaurant business.
>
> Q: Please explain.
>
> A: The restaurant business is intensely local in nature. There are very few restaurants that attract people from great distances. Most people eat near their homes, their places of work, or their shopping destinations. So a restaurant in an undesirable neighborhood or in a declining business district simply will not draw customers.
>
> Q: Why is that?
>
> A: Many restaurants depend heavily on luncheon trade. People on their lunch break usually do not have more than an hour, so a restaurant will not be able to draw this business unless it is located near a fairly large number of employers. No matter how well the economy is doing, a restaurant will not do well at lunchtime if it is located in an area that happens to have experienced a downturn.

Note that the lawyer in this example did not cut off the witness and did not limit the expert to unnaturally short answers. The lawyer did, however, use strategically interjected questions to break up the narrative, thereby continually reemphasizing the expert's testimony.

8.5.4 Use Examples and Analogies

Many complex ideas can be made understandable with examples, analogies, or metaphors. Expert witnesses should be encouraged to clarify their testimony with such imagery. Consider the following use of an example to flesh out a relatively abstract concept:

> Q: Dr. Haruo, please give us an example of how a restaurant chain might do poorly, even in a state with an expanding population and increasing vehicle miles?

A: Certainly. Many urban areas have experienced population growth that is basically limited to the suburbs. A restaurant chain that was concentrated in the central city would show almost no increased profitability as a result of that growth. In fact, its profits might well decline because of the population shift. That is why location is such an important factor.

An analogy could serve the same purpose.

Q: Dr. Haruo, could you please explain the importance of location a little further?

A: Well, maybe it would help to think about it this way. Imagine a baseball league with eight teams. If the top two or three pennant contenders are all located in big cities, they will obviously draw a lot of fans. On the other hand, a cellar-dwelling team in a small city would probably play to an empty stadium. So even if the league's overall attendance went up, that wouldn't help to fill the seats for the last place team. A poor location is a lot like being stuck in last place.

Do not take the witness by surprise with a request for an example or metaphor. The time to consider using these explanatory tools is during preparation, not on the spur of the moment in the midst of direct examination.

8.5.5 Use Visual Aids

The direct examination of almost every expert can be enhanced by using visual displays. Since expert testimony may be hard to follow, it can be particularly effective to portray the expert's concepts with charts, graphs, drawings, animations, or models. A physician's testimony, for example, can be brought to life with an anatomical model or a series of colored overlays. Financial experts should illustrate their testimony with graphs or tables. An architectural or engineering expert should use diagrams or scale models. In an age of computerized presentations, the possibilities for visual aids are practically infinite, limited only by counsel's (and the expert's) imagination and budget.

8.5.6 Use Internal Summaries

Because of the potential length and complexity of expert testimony, it is important to highlight significant points with internal summaries. Ask the expert to point out the relevance of the most critical steps in his analysis. Request that he summarize the implications of his findings.

Think of the expert's testimony as containing a series of steps or elements. At the conclusion of each step the expert should explain how he got there, why it is important, and where he is going next, as in the following example from the testimony of the defendant's expert in the drive-in case:

Q: Dr. Haruo, please summarize your objections to Dr. Longhini's methodology?

A: The problem with Dr. Longhini's approach is that she failed to consider several of the most important factors in determining profitability. Her reliance on population and vehicle miles led her to dramatically overestimate the restaurant chain's likely profitability. Her study was especially deficient because it did not account for either location or potential competition.

Q: Were you able to conduct a more comprehensive study?

A: Yes. I conducted a study that included the six most important factors, all of which were omitted by Dr. Longhini.

8.5.7 Use Leading Questions When Called For

Two recurring problems in expert testimony are boredom and pomposity. Many experts are inclined to drone on at length over unimportant details. Others present themselves with an air of overweening self-importance, especially in the course of presenting their credentials. Both of these difficulties can be resolved through the judicious use of leading questions.

Counsel can often cut through a welter of details by using a leading question to direct the witness to the heart of the matter. Consider the examination of a chemist, called to testify as to the composition of substance. The process used by the witness may have been comprised of many steps. The judge or jurors, however, would quickly become bored with a blow-by-blow recitation of the entire procedure. Counsel can shorten the questioning by using a few leading questions:

Q: Did you perform a chemical analysis?

A: Yes.

Q: Did that analysis consist of a six-step process?

A: Yes, it did.

Q: Did you perform all six steps in accordance with accepted procedures?

A: Yes.

Q: What were your results?

Leading questions were permissible in the above example because they were preliminary. If the adequacy or scrupulousness of the chemist's tests were in issue, however, leading questions would neither be allowed nor advisable. While it is a useful technique to use leading questions to skip over minor details, they should never be used as a substitute for the witness's own testimony concerning important issues.

Leading questions can also be used to make the witness seem less haughty or pretentious. Even an inherently modest witness may have some difficulty testifying to a list of glowing qualifications without appearing arrogant. Other witnesses do not even try to tone down the self-laudation. Imagine a series of answers along this line: "I am the author of *Principles of Business Valuation*, which is widely regarded as the leading treatise in the field. My book won three national awards, and it is regularly assigned at over forty business schools." While the witness is no doubt justly proud of this achievement, the recitation may sound too self-important.

In contrast, counsel can elicit the same information through leading questions:

Q: Are you the author of *Principles of Business Valuation*?

A: Yes, I am.

Q: I understand that your book is widely regarded as the leading treatise in the field.

A: Well, I think others would have to make that judgment.

Q: Let me put it this way. Your book won three national awards, didn't it?

A: Yes, it did.

Q: And isn't it regularly assigned at over forty business schools?

A: I believe that it is.

Again, the leading questions in this example may be considered preliminary because they are directed solely at the witness's qualifications.

8.5.8 Encourage Powerful Language

There is a tradition in many technical fields of hedging or qualifying the language in which conclusions are expressed. This makes great sense when discussing research since one's results are always subject to further inquiry. Thus, it is not uncommon for professionals to use terms such as "to the best of my knowledge," or "according to current indications," or "as far as we can tell." While this language is meant to convey open-mindedness as opposed to uncertainty, it can be fatal to a witness's testimony in a courtroom.

To prevent inadvertent miscommunication, expert witnesses should be prepared to testify in straightforward, unequivocal terms. Caution experts to avoid language that unintentionally qualifies or hedges their results, using instead wording that emphasizes accuracy and certainty.

Here is an example of weak language:

> A: My best estimate at this time is that the restaurant chain would have earned approximately $8.2 million.

In fact, the witness has conducted an exhaustive study and is completely certain, within the bounds of professional competence, that $8.2 million is the correct figure. That certainty can be better expressed through more powerful language:

> A: I have calculated lost profits at $8.2 million.

Or,

> A: My projections show that the restaurant chain would have earned $8.2 million.

Or,

> A: The result of my study is a determination of lost profits in the amount of $8.2 million.

Substituting authoritative terminology for weak language may require a process of education for the witness. Of course, if the expert's conclusions really are tentative or provisional, counsel should not attempt to persuade the witness to testify otherwise.

8.5.9 Use Enumeration

Audiences most often pay closer attention to information presented in numbered lists. Expert witnesses should therefore be encouraged to introduce concepts in terms of factors or considerations rather than launching into extended explanations. The following is a good example of enumeration:

> Q: Dr. Haruo, what is your opinion of Dr. Longhini's study?
>
> A: There are three basic problems with Dr. Longhini's study.
>
> Q: What are those problems?
>
> A: First, she projected profits on the basis of only two factors. Second, she failed to consider location, which should have been the most important element. Third, she doesn't seem to recognize that population growth can be extremely uneven.

Counsel can now ask the witness to explain each of the three points. Note that the introduction of each point will reinitiate primacy and therefore heighten the jurors' attention.

8.5.10 Consider Inoculation

Expert witnesses may be open to several distinct lines of cross-examination. Counsel should therefore consider conducting a certain amount of explanatory or defensive direct examination to "inoculate" the witness against cross-examination on such matters as the payment of fees, the use of presumptions, reliance on secondary sources, and the like.

8.5.11 Do Not Stretch the Witness's Expertise

It may be tempting to try to stretch a witness's expertise, either as a cost-saving measure or in an effort to enlarge the scope of her testimony. Both of these undertakings are misguided. It is risky, bordering on unethical, to seek to have an expert testify outside her legitimate field.

In the restaurant scenario, we have seen examples of testimony from financial experts on the question of lost profits. Although the plaintiff's expert was called and qualified solely with regard to the issue of damages, some attorneys might venture to have the witness offer an opinion on liability as well. Perhaps the witness might do double duty by testifying that the defendant's pricing practices were predatory. There are two immediate problems with this approach. First, it is unlikely that a single economist would really possess expertise with regard both to damage modeling and pricing practices. Second, even assuming sufficient expertise, once the witness takes a position on liability she will be compromised as an impartial arbiter of damages. A witness who advances too many favorable opinions may quickly come to be seen as a shill or hired gun.

More troubling is the possibility that some lawyers might try to inveigle the expert to offer opinions that are truly beyond the scope of her expertise. Such testimony, if given, puts the witness out on a limb that may well be sawed off during cross-examination. Tactics aside, experts are intended to be both qualified and independent. It is therefore unethical to attempt to persuade a witness to exaggerate her qualifications or to tamper with the independence of her views. Honorable experts will not allow attorneys to influence their opinions, and counsel must always respect this position. If an expert's ultimate conclusions are not sufficiently favorable, one need not call her as a witness.

8.6 Cross-Examination of Expert Witnesses

Most of the basic approaches to cross-examination discussed in chapter three can also be adapted to expert testimony. In addition, there are certain tools that can be used primarily or most effectively with expert witnesses.

Research, as much as technique, lies at the heart of expert witness cross-examination. Counsel cannot conduct an adequate cross-examination without first thoroughly investigating all of the technical aspects of the expected testimony. It is often said that you cannot cross-examine an expert without first becoming an expert yourself.

Moreover, your research should extend beyond the expert's subject matter area and into the witness's own professional background. Counsel should read everything the witness has ever published and should also attempt to obtain transcripts of prior trial or deposition testimony. There is nothing so effective as impeaching an expert with his own prior assertions. Other fruitful areas of investigation may include the expert's professional affiliations, past clients, governmental positions, and the like. Such research should not be viewed as an effort to dig up dirt (although once in a lifetime you might stumble across something juicy), but rather as an attempt to obtain a rounded picture of the expert's professional status. Many experts have become closely associated with certain positions over the course of their careers, and this knowledge can be of considerable assistance in shaping a cross-examination.

The research necessary to cross-examine an expert witness will necessarily vary considerably from case to case. The balance of this section is therefore limited to techniques that can be applied to expert witnesses in general.

8.6.1 Challenge the Witness's Credentials

An expert witness's credentials are subject to challenge either on voir dire or during cross-examination. Voir dire may be used to object to the legal sufficiency of the expert's qualifications, while cross-examination is the time to attack their weight.

8.6.1.1 Voir Dire on Credentials

Once the proponent of an expert has concluded the qualification segment of the direct examination, opposing counsel is entitled to conduct a voir dire of the witness. A voir dire examination temporarily suspends the direct so that the opponent of the proffered evidence can inquire as to its evidentiary sufficiency. With regard to the qualification of experts, this means that opposing counsel can interrupt the direct examination in order to conduct a mini-cross limited to the issue of the witness's credentials.

In jurisdictions that require the tender of expert witnesses, voir dire typically proceeds once the witness is proffered to the court:

Proponent:	Your Honor, we tender Dr. Benjamin Haruo as an expert on the subject of lost profits.
Court:	Any objection, counsel?
Opponent:	Your Honor, we would like the opportunity to conduct a voir dire examination.
Court:	You may examine the witness on the subject of his qualifications to testify.

In jurisdictions where tender is not used, it is necessary for opposing counsel to interpose an objection at the point where the witness begins to offer an opinion. Do not wait to be invited by the court:

Proponent:	Dr. Haruo, do you have an opinion as to the profits that the plaintiff would have earned if the restaurant chain had not been driven out of business?
Opponent:	Objection. Your Honor, we would like an opportunity for voir dire of this witness before he is allowed to give opinion testimony.
Court:	You may examine the witness on the subject of his qualifications to testify.

Note that voir dire is limited generally to the question of the admissibility of evidence. Thus, voir dire regarding an expert's credentials is restricted to the foundation for the witness's ability to opine on the issues in the case. In other words, is the witness "qualified as an expert by knowledge, skill, experience, training, or education"?[14] Voir dire is not the time to launch into a wide-ranging attack on the expert's integrity.

It may be an uphill battle to persuade a judge that a proffered witness should not be allowed to testify as an expert. Many judges respond to such objections by ruling that they go only to the weight and not the admissibility of the expert testimony. Other judges, however, have become increasingly willing to bar expert testimony, especially in areas thought to comprise "junk science."

Nonetheless, it is possible to disqualify an expert through voir dire. Purported experts can be disqualified by establishing the remoteness in time of their credentials, the inapplicability of their specialties, the lack of general acceptance of their purported expertise, or the unreliability of their data.

8.6.1.2 Cross-Examination on Credentials

The court's ruling that a witness may testify as an expert means only that the witness possesses sufficient credentials to pass the evidentiary threshold. It still may be possible to diminish the weight of the witness's qualifications during cross-examination. There are three basic methods for discrediting the value of a witness's credentials.

---

14. Fed. R. Evid. 702. It may be possible to challenge the reliability of an expert's "principles and methods" or to question the "facts of the case." *Id.* 702(c)–(d). Such objections are frequently raised prior to trial in so-called *Daubert* hearings, which are named after the U.S. Supreme Court case in which the rule was articulated.

Limit the Scope of the Witness's Expertise

Although a witness may be well-qualified in a certain area or subspecialty, it may be possible to recast the issues of the case in such a way as to place them beyond the witness's competence. Assume, for example, that the plaintiff's expert in the restaurant scenario was tendered and accepted as an expert on lost profits:

Q: Dr. Longhini, your primary consulting work involves business valuation, correct?

A: That is my profession.

Q: Issues of valuation usually involve an existing business, right?

A: That is the usual case.

Q: People come to you when they want to buy or sell a business, or when they have to value it for estate tax purposes, or perhaps when there is a divorce?

A: Yes, those are all typical situations for business valuation.

Q: You wouldn't call yourself a management consultant, would you?

A: No, I do not get involved in operations.

Q: Because your work is basically evaluative?

A: Exactly.

Q: So someone who wanted assistance in expanding a business would need to go to a different consultant, wouldn't they?

A: Correct.

Q: For example, there are consultants who specialize in site evaluation, correct?

A: Yes, there are.

Q: But you do not do that yourself?

A: No, I do not.

Q: So if I wanted to evaluate the best possible locations for my business outlets, you would recommend that I consult someone else, isn't that right?

A: Yes, I suppose that I would refer you.

Counsel may now argue that the crucial issue of location is beyond Dr. Longhini's expertise and that her opinion regarding lost profits should therefore be discounted.

Stress Missing Credentials

An expert witness may be minimally qualified to testify, but still lack certain important certifications, degrees, or licenses. Assume for example that the plaintiff in a personal injury case has called his psychotherapist to testify on the issue of damages. The witness was tendered and accepted as an expert and has completed his direct testimony. This cross-examination followed:

Q: Mr. Linzer, your degree is in social work, correct?

A: Yes, I have an MSW, and I am a licensed psychotherapist.

Q: You do not have a doctorate in clinical psychology, do you?

A: No, I do not.

Q: And of course you are not a psychiatrist?

A: That is correct.

Q: I notice that your stationery lists your name as Merlin Linzer, MSW.

A: Yes, that is right.

Q: I have seen other social workers with the letters ACSW after their names. What does ACSW stand for?

A: It stands for Accredited Clinical Social Worker.

Q: That is an additional certification that some social workers earn, correct?

A: Yes, that is correct.

Q: But you have not achieved that certification, have you?

Contrast Your Expert's Credentials

It is most effective to point out an adverse witness's missing credentials when their absence can be contrasted with your own expert's superior qualifications. In the following example, assume that the plaintiff called a practicing attorney as an expert witness in a legal malpractice case. This scenario is taken from the defendant's cross-examination:

Q: Mr. Wylie, I understand that you are a member of the American Bar Association Section of Litigation, correct?

A: Yes, I am.

Q: The American Bar Association Section of Litigation is open to any lawyer who is willing to pay the dues, correct?

A: That is right.

Q: So you were not elected or chosen by your peers for membership in that section, were you?

A: Nobody is.

Q: I assume that you are familiar with the American College of Trial Lawyers?

A: I am.

Q: That organization consists of lawyers who specialize in litigation and the trial of cases, correct?

A: I believe so.

Q: Membership in the American College is limited to two percent of the lawyers in any given state, isn't that right?

A: I think that is right.

Q: And individuals have to be proposed and elected to membership in the American College of Trial Lawyers?

A: I understand that to be the process.

Q: You are not a member of the American College, are you?

A: No, I am not.

Q: Are you aware that Colin O'Donovan, the defendant's expert witness, is a member of the American College of Trial Lawyers?

A: I understand that he is.

Experts' credentials can be contrasted on bases other than certification. It is fair game to point out your own witness's greater or more specific experience, your witness's teaching or publication record, or any other disparity that will enhance your expert and diminish the opposition.

Note, however, that all of the rules of basic cross-examination apply here as well. You must be satisfied to elicit the fact of the contrasting qualifications. It will do you little good to argue with the opposing witness or to try to extract a concession that his credentials are inadequate.

8.6.2 Obtain Favorable Information

It will often be possible to obtain favorable concessions from the opposing party's expert witness. As with all cross-examination, it is usually wisest to attempt to extract such information near the beginning of the examination. Needless to say, one must be positive of the answers before launching into this sort of cross-examination.

In general, the helpful material available from opposing experts will fall into the following categories.

8.6.2.1 Affirm Your Own Expert

Even experts who ultimately disagree may have many shared understandings. You may therefore contribute to the accreditation of your own expert by asking the opposing expert to acknowledge the reliability of your expert's data, the validity of her assumptions, or the caliber of her credentials.

8.6.2.2 Elicit Areas of Agreement

In addition, it may be possible to elicit concessions from the opposing expert that go to the merits of the case. The adverse expert may, for example, be willing to agree with several of your major premises, even while disagreeing with your ultimate conclusion. Consider this cross-examination of the defense expert in the drive-in restaurant case:

Q: Dr. Haruo, you are dissatisfied with the nature of Dr. Longhini's study of lost profits, correct?

A: Yes, I have trouble with Dr. Longhini's methodology.

Q: But you do agree, don't you, that the chain had been operating as a going concern?

A: Yes, I do.

Q: In fact, the restaurant chain had made a profit every year they were in business?

A: I believe that is correct.

Q: And every one of their outlets was profitable, correct?

A: I think that is right.

Q: So someone must have been able to select profitable locations, right?

A: I suppose so.

Q: Dr. Longhini assumed that the chain would continue to choose good locations, isn't that right?

A: That is implicit in her model.

Q: And you did not conduct an independent study of favorable or unfavorable restaurant locations, did you?

A: No, I did not.

Q: So you have no data that you can point to that would contradict Dr. Longhini's assumption?

A: I do not.

8.6.2.3 Criticize the Opposing Party's Conduct

Finally, it may be possible to draw from an opposing expert significant criticism of her own party's conduct. Though the expert reached a final conclusion favorable to the party, she may be unwilling to approve of all of their underlying actions. For example:

Q: Dr. Longhini, in order for you to reach your opinion on damages it was necessary for you to review all of the plaintiff's financial records, correct?

A: Yes, that is correct.

Q: Isn't it true that the plaintiff company did not keep accurate store-by-store records?

A: Yes, they aggregated their financial information, rather than breaking it down store-by-store.

Q: The absence of store-by-store information must have made your job more difficult.

A: I found that I was able to achieve accurate results on the basis of statewide projections.

Q: I understand your position. Still, you could have projected profits for each individual restaurant if the available financial data had been more precise, isn't that true?

A: Yes, that is true.

Q: But because of the plaintiff's aggregate record keeping, you were not able to do that?

A: No one could have made such projections on the basis of that data.

8.6.3 Use of Learned Treatises

One form of cross-examination unique to expert witnesses is impeachment through the use of a learned treatise. Under the Federal Rules of Evidence, an expert witness may be confronted with "a statement contained in a treatise, periodical, or pamphlet," as long as the publication is established as reliable authority.[15]

15. Fed. R. Evid. 803(18).

Contrary to the beliefs of many lawyers and judges, it is not necessary to establish that the witness has relied on the particular treatise, or even to have the witness acknowledge it as authoritative. Under the federal rules, the reliability of a learned treatise may be established by admission of the witness, by other expert testimony, or by judicial notice.[16] Impeachment, then, could conceivably take this form:

Q: Are you familiar with Lubet's *Modern Trial Advocacy*?

A: Certainly.

Q: Do you regard it as authoritative in the field?

A: Absolutely not.

Q: I want to read you a passage from Lubet's *Modern Trial Advocacy.*

Opponent: Objection, your Honor. The witness testified that Lubet is not regarded as an authority.

Q: Your Honor, we will produce other expert testimony that Lubet's *Modern Trial Advocacy* is regarded as an authoritative text.

Court: You may proceed.

Of course, it is far more persuasive when the witness agrees that the treatise is indeed recognized as a leading authority. You can ensure such a favorable response by restricting your impeachment to widely recognized sources. Alternatively, you can use the expert's deposition to determine exactly what treatises she will accept as reliable.

In either case, once the reliability of the treatise is confirmed, the impeachment may proceed one of two ways. You may read a passage from the treatise into evidence without asking the expert any questions about it; the federal rules require only that the passage be called to the witness's attention. The more traditional approach is to ask the witness whether she agrees with the particular quotation. At that point, the witness must either accede or disagree. If she accepts the statement, your job is done. If she disagrees, you may argue later that she is out of step with recognized authority.

Finally, note that this rule allows an excerpt from a learned treatise to be read into evidence, but that the treatise itself may not be received as an exhibit.

8.6.4 Challenge the Witness's Impartiality

Expert witnesses are supposed to be independent analysts, not advocates. The worst accusation you can make against an expert witness is that he has altered his opinion to fit a party's needs. Accordingly, it can be very effective to cross-examine an

16. *Id.*

expert on the issue of bias if the material is there to be exploited. Cross-examination on bias falls into three basic categories.

8.6.4.1 Fees

Most experts in litigation are retained and paid significant fees. While the acceptance of money in exchange for testimony would initially seem to be a fruitful area for cross-examination, the reality is somewhat less promising. First, the trier of fact is likely to understand that no witness could afford to perform extensive tests or analyses without being compensated. Second, all experts in the case are probably being paid, so there is little ground to be gained by making a point of it on cross-examination when your own expert is equally vulnerable. Finally, most experienced experts will be adept at turning such challenges aside.

It is generally productive to cross-examine an expert concerning her fee only in fairly limited circumstances. For example, it may demonstrate bias if the fee is extraordinarily large. Similarly, it may be evidence of something less than objectivity if the witness has a large unpaid fee outstanding at the time that she testifies. Certain fee arrangements are unethical; these will be discussed in the section on ethics and expert testimony.[17]

8.6.4.2 Relationship with Party or Counsel

An expert's relationship with a party or with counsel may also indicate a lack of impartiality. Some witnesses seem to work hand in glove with certain law firms, testifying to similar conclusions in case after case. While such an ongoing relationship is not proof of bias, it does suggest that the association may have been sustained for a reason.

The extent of the repeated retention is important. It will usually be of little significance that an expert worked on two or three cases for one law firm over a fairly lengthy period. After all, the firm might prize the witness precisely for her independence. On the other hand, it can become questionable when a firm has engaged the same expert on a dozen or more occasions. While there may be a perfectly innocent explanation for this constancy, it is certainly reasonable to bring it out on cross-examination. The same analysis applies to witnesses who have testified repeatedly for the same party, although retained by different law firms.

Finally, some cases may involve testimony by in-house experts, perhaps a company's own accountant or engineer. In most cases, such experts are susceptible to no more suggestion of bias than would be any other employee. In some situations, however, the in-house expert's own judgment will be at issue in the case. An accountant, for example, may have failed to see that a debt was undercollateralized; an engineer may not have foreseen the need for more exacting tolerances. In these

17. *See* section 8.7.

circumstances, the cross-examination must bring out the witness's personal stake in the outcome of the litigation.

8.6.4.3 Positional Bias

With or without regard to past retention, some experts seem wedded to certain professional, scientific, or intellectual positions. Experts frequently come to testify only for plaintiffs or only for defendants. Others reach only one of a range of conclusions. For example, it is said that some psychiatrists have been known never to find a single criminal defendant to be sane or competent. Where they exist, these rigidly held positional biases can be exploited effectively on cross-examination.

8.6.5 Point Out Omissions

An expert may be vulnerable on cross-examination if she has failed to conduct essential tests or procedures, or if she has neglected to consider all significant factors. The question of neglected tests or experiments will depend on the unique factors of each case. You must pursue thorough discovery to determine whether processes were shortcut or slighted, preferably after first consulting your own expert.

Other sorts of omissions are more commonplace. Witnesses are frequently asked to give evaluations concerning the validity or accuracy of other experts' work. A consulting pathologist, for example, might be asked to reevaluate the protocol of an autopsy conducted by the local medical examiner. No matter how prominent, a "second-opinion" witness can almost always be undermined by the fact that she did not conduct the primary investigation:

Q: Dr. Elliot, you reach a conclusion quite different from the conclusions reached by Dr. Arlington, correct?

A: Yes.

Q: Of course, you did not perform an autopsy yourself, did you?

A: No, I did not.

Q: In fact, your information comes exclusively from Dr. Arlington's autopsy protocol?

A: That's right.

Q: So you have relied on Dr. Arlington for all of your factual information, isn't that right?

A: Yes, I have.

Q: You know nothing of the actual circumstances of the autopsy, other than what you have learned from Dr. Arlington's report?

A: Correct.

Q: So at least with regard to gathering information, you have trusted Dr. Arlington's work.

This technique is not limited to "reevaluating" experts. It can be employed, in different form, with regard to any witness who relies exclusively on information provided by others:

Q: Dr. Elliot, you base your opinion solely on an examination of hospital records, correct?

A: Correct.

Q: You did not examine the decedent yourself, did you?

A: No, I did not.

Q: So your opinion can only be as good as the information you received, right?

A: I suppose so.

Q: If any of that information were faulty, that could affect the basis for your opinion, correct?

A: Yes, depending on the circumstances.

Q: The same would be true of missing information, right?

A: Right.

Q: You'll agree with me, won't you, that firsthand observation is preferred for the purpose of diagnosis?

A: Yes, it is preferred.

Finally, many experts will testify on the basis of statistics or studies compiled from other sources. Frequently, such experts will not have investigated the reliability of the underlying data, and this can leave them vulnerable to cross-examination.

8.6.6 Substitute Information

8.6.6.1 Change Assumptions

As we have seen, almost all experts must use assumptions of one sort or another in the course of formulating their opinions. An expert's assumptions, however, might be unrealistic, unreliable, or unreasonably favorable to the retaining party. It can be extremely effective, therefore, to ask the witness to alter an assumption, substituting one that you believe to be more in keeping with the evidence in the case. Consider this scenario from the drive-in restaurant case:

Q: Dr. Longhini, your lost-profits calculation includes an assumption that vehicle miles will continue to grow at the rate of 4 percent, correct?

A: Yes, that is the figure I used.

Q: Will you agree that numerous factors can influence the growth of vehicle miles?

A: Yes, I think that is obvious.

Q: For example, vehicle miles usually fall when oil prices rise sharply, correct?

A: I believe that is true.

Q: And if vehicle miles were to rise at a rate of less than 4 percent, your estimate of lost profits would have to be reduced, correct?

A: Yes, that is right.

Q: In fact, if we used an assumption of 2 percent, your estimate of lost profits would have to be reduced by over $1.5 million?

A: I haven't done the calculation, but it should be something in that range.

When the substituted assumption calls for recalculation, it is generally most effective to do the math in advance rather than asking the witness to do it on the spot. A request that the witness perform the computation is an invitation to quibble.

8.6.6.2 Vary the Facts

A related technique is to vary the facts on which the expert has relied or to suggest additional facts, as in this example from the restaurant case:

Q: Dr. Longhini, you are aware that the plaintiff's most profitable outlet was in the Lincoln Walk Mall, correct?

A: Yes.

Q: And the continued existence of that outlet was a fact that you relied on in calculating your result, right?

A: That is right.

Q: But if the entire Lincoln Walk Mall were to close due to bankruptcy, then you would have to change your conclusion, isn't that right?

A: I suppose that is correct.

Q: Well, you couldn't have a profitable restaurant in a closed mall, could you?

A: Of course not.

As with all cross-examination questions, counsel must have a good-faith basis for asserting new or varied facts to an expert witness.

8.6.6.3 Degree of Certainty

It is also possible to challenge an expert's degree of certainty by suggesting alternative scenarios or explanations:

Q: Dr. Haruo, you believe that the plaintiff's history of profitability is largely attributable to location, correct?

A: Yes, I think that location is, and has been, the most important factor.

Q: But there are other factors that contribute to profitability, correct?

A: Certainly.

Q: Some of those factors would be product quality, value, or market demand, correct?

A: Yes.

Q: You are surely familiar with the term "destination shopping," aren't you?

A: Of course.

Q: That means that people will travel to seek out value or quality or amenities, regardless of the location, correct?

A: That does happen.

Q: Well, you didn't interview the plaintiff's customers, did you?

A: Of course not.

Q: So you cannot be sure that location was of primary importance to them, can you?

A: I can't look into their minds.

Q: Isn't it possible that the plaintiff's customers sought out their restaurants because of value or quality?

A: It is possible.

Q: So it is also possible that location was not the primary factor in plaintiff's profitability?

8.6.6.4 Dependence on Other Testimony

The opinion of an expert witness often depends on facts to be established by other witnesses. Thus, the expert's testimony may be undermined, not by anything you ask the expert directly, but rather by challenging its factual underpinnings during the cross-examination of the fact witnesses. It is necessary only to obtain the expert's concession that the other witness's facts are essential to her opinion:

Q: Dr. Longhini, part of your opinion is based on Ms. Nelson's statement that she was certain that the restaurant chain would have been able to obtain funding for continued expansion, correct?

A: Correct.

Counsel need examine the expert no further, as long as Ms. Nelson's certainty of funding can later be shaken or refuted. The connection—that the expert's opinion is weakened—may be drawn during final argument. Alternatively, counsel could ask the expert to concede that the opinion would have to be changed if the expansion money were not available.

8.7 Ethics of Expert Testimony

8.7.1 Fees

Unlike other witnesses who can be reimbursed only for expenses, an expert may be paid a fee for preparing and testifying in court.[18] There is authority that an expert's fee must be "reasonable," but that limit has never been well defined. In any event, an unreasonably large fee could render the witness vulnerable on cross-examination.

A more salient restriction is the rule against paying contingent fees to expert witnesses, which is found in virtually every jurisdiction.[19] Contingent fees are prohibited because they provide the expert with an unacceptable incentive to tailor her opinion to the interests of the party retaining her.

---

18. Model Rules of Prof'l Conduct R. 3.4(b), comment 3.

19. The rule was explicit in the Model Code of Professional Responsibility: "A lawyer shall not pay, offer to pay, or acquiesce in the payment of compensation to a witness contingent upon the content of his testimony or the outcome of the case." Model Code of Prof'l Responsibility DR 7-109(C). The Comments to the Model Rules of Professional Conduct point out that "[t]he common rule in most jurisdictions is that it is . . . improper to pay an expert witness a contingent fee." Model Rules of Prof'l Conduct R. 3.4, comment 3.

8.7.2 Influencing Testimony

Lawyers typically retain experts for one reason only—to help win the case. Given the expense involved, there may be a temptation to view the expert as simply another member of the team who can be enlisted to provide whatever advocacy is necessary. Thus, it is not unknown for attorneys to attempt to persuade experts to alter the content of their opinions. This is wrong. It is no more acceptable to attempt to persuade an expert to change his opinion than it would be to try to convince a percipient witness to change his account of the facts. The entire system of expert testimony rests on the assumption that experts are independent of the retaining attorneys. Counsel must take care not to attempt or appear to use the fee relationship to corrupt the expert's autonomy.[20] It is similarly unethical to attempt to color an expert's testimony by withholding damaging facts or by providing false information or data.

As with other witnesses, it is not unethical to assist an expert to prepare for trial. Counsel may inform the witness of the questions to be asked on direct examination and may alert the witness to potential cross-examination. An expert may be advised to use powerful language, avoid jargon, use analogies, refrain from long narratives, or use other means that will help her convey her opinion accurately.

8.7.3 Disclosure and Discovery

The Federal Rules of Civil Procedure, and the corresponding rules in most states, contain limitations on discovery and disclosure with respect to expert witnesses.[21] In brief, experts are divided into two categories: those who are expected to testify and those who are retained only as consultants. Although there are exceptions, only testifying experts are generally subject to discovery. Purely consulting experts, other than in extreme circumstances, are exempt from discovery.[22]

The question that arises is whether it is ethical to attempt to interview an opposing party's consulting expert, from whom formal discovery is not available. The courts are divided on this issue. Some jurisdictions hold that Rule 26, or its equivalent, is intended to shield nontestifying experts from all disclosure, formal or informal. Other courts have held that the discovery rules apply only to discovery and that extramural interviews are permissible. There is also a third approach that allows supervised interviews, but only with leave of court. Counsel must therefore take care to determine the relevant jurisdiction's law on this issue before attempting to interview the opposition's nontestifying expert.

---

20. Model Rules of Prof'l Conduct R. 3.4(b) provides that a lawyer shall not "counsel or assist a witness to testify falsely." An expert's opinion can be false if it is induced by a desire to please counsel or obtain compensation as opposed to an objective investigation of the facts and circumstances of the case.
21. Fed. R. Civ. P. 26(b)(4).
22. *Id.* 26(b)(4)(B).

Chapter Nine

Objections

9.1 Making the Record

There is a technical, as well as an artistic, side to trial advocacy. The laws of evidence and procedure govern the manner in which a trial proceeds. It is not sufficient for information to be persuasive and elegant, or even true; it must also be admissible under the law of evidence and presented properly under the rules of trial procedure. The process of bringing and contesting information before the court and jury is called making the record.

Making the record involves a series of steps. Attorneys offer evidence in the form of testimony and exhibits. Some of this evidence may become the subject of objections, in which case the trial judge is called on to make rulings on admissibility. The admissible evidence is presented before the fact finder. If properly preserved, both the evidence and the objections may eventually be reviewed by an appellate court.

To make a record, it is necessary to internalize the rules of evidence and procedure. It is not enough to understand the theory of the hearsay rule; one must also be able to recognize hearsay on an almost instinctual level and to articulate a persuasive objection at almost any given moment. It is not enough to comprehend the foundation for the admission of a past recollection; it is also necessary to be able to elicit the foundation in a manner that will be persuasive to the trier of fact. In other words, making the record calls for knowledge, judgment, decisiveness, adaptability, and quick reflexes.

This chapter will discuss the use of objections. The next chapter will cover two related aspects of making a trial record—exhibits and foundations. Objections are the means by which evidentiary disputes are raised and resolved. Objections may be made to an attorney's questions, to a witness's testimony, to the introduction or use of exhibits, to a lawyer's demeanor or behavior, and even to the conduct of the judge.

Most of a trial advocate's energy is understandably devoted to the content of her case. What do the witnesses have to say? What facts are available to prove the case? How can the opposition be undermined? Which events are central to the proof? Is it possible for several different stories to be harmonized? A persuasive story rests on the manner in which facts can be developed, arranged, and presented to the trier of fact. It is equally and sometimes more important however, that the advocate also be well-versed in the technical side of trial advocacy. A well-conceived and tightly constructed story cannot persuade a jury if its crucial elements are not admitted into the record or if the opposition has had the benefit of using substantial amounts of inadmissible evidence.

9.2 Objections

9.2.1 Purpose and Function

9.2.1.1 Use of Objections at Trial

An objection is a request that the court rule on the admissibility of certain testimony or evidence. The purpose of objecting is to prevent the introduction or consideration of inadmissible information. Our adversary system relies on opposing attorneys to present evidence and the judge to decide on its admissibility. An objection, then, is nothing more than a signal to the judge that there is a disagreement between counsel concerning the rules of evidence or procedure. When there are no objections, which is the overwhelming majority of the time, the judge can allow evidence to come into the record without the need for a specific ruling. If we had no process of objecting, the trial judge would have to rule on every separate answer and item of evidence. Unless the process is abused or misused, trials are actually expedited by the judge's ability to rely on counsel to object to questionable evidence.

Objections can be made to questions, answers, exhibits, and virtually anything else that occurs during a trial.

An attorney's question may be objectionable because of its form or because it calls for inadmissible evidence. A question is objectionable as to form when it seeks to obtain information in an impermissible way. For example, a leading question on direct examination is improper because it tells the witness what answer is expected. Even if the answer itself would be admissible, the question is disallowed because of its suggestiveness. Compound questions, vague questions, and argumentative questions, to name a few, are also objectionable as to form.

Conversely, a question phrased in proper form may nonetheless call for inadmissible evidence. The information sought may be irrelevant, privileged, or hearsay. An objection may be made when it is apparent from the question itself that the answer should not be admitted. The question, "What is your religious belief?" is in proper form. Any answer, however, would be inadmissible under most circumstances by virtue of the Federal Rules of Evidence.[1] The question is therefore objectionable.

1. "Evidence of a witness's religious beliefs or opinions is not admissible to attack or support the witness's credibility." FED. R. EVID. 610.

Even in the absence of an objectionable question, a witness may respond with an inadmissible answer. The answer might volunteer irrelevant information, it might contain unanticipated hearsay, or it might consist entirely of speculation. For example, a direct examiner could ask the perfectly allowable question, "How do you know that the traffic light was red?" only to receive the hearsay reply, "Because someone told me just last week." Opposing counsel would no doubt object to the answer and move that it be stricken from the record.

Finally, objections may be made to anything else that might have an impermissible impact on the trier of fact. A lawyer can object if opposing counsel raises her voice to a witness or approaches the witness in an intimidating manner. Objections can be made to the manner in which exhibits are displayed or to the position of chairs and tables in the courtroom. Even the judge's words and actions are not immune to objection, although it is admittedly awkward to ask the court to rule on the permissibility of its own conduct.

9.2.1.2 Use of Objections before Trial

It is not always necessary to wait until trial to move for the exclusion of evidence. Motions in limine are available to obtain pretrial rulings on evidence that is potentially so harmful that even mention of it may prejudice the jury. A motion in limine asks the judge to rule that the offending evidence be found inadmissible and that it not be offered or introduced at trial.[2]

A motion in limine can be based on any of the substantive rules of evidence. Note, however, that the motion usually will not be granted merely because the subject evidence is objectionable. An additional showing is usually required that the evidence is so damaging that once it is mentioned a sustained objection at trial will not be sufficient to undo its prejudicial impact.

Effect of Granting a Motion in Limine

Once granted, a motion in limine excludes all references to the subject evidence. Not only is the evidence itself disallowed, but counsel may not offer it or refer to it in a question. Evidence excluded in this manner may not be mentioned during jury selection, opening statements, or closing arguments. In the appropriate situation, witnesses may be instructed not to volunteer testimony concerning the excluded evidence.

For example, assume that the plaintiff in a contract action had been convicted of disorderly conduct while participating in a peace demonstration during the 1960s.

2. A motion in limine may also be used to obtain an advance ruling that evidence is admissible. With such a ruling in hand, counsel can better frame her trial theory and can also plan witness examinations so as to avoid the possibility of reversible error. Nonetheless, this "reverse" use of the motion in limine is fairly unusual.

The conviction is clearly not admissible under the Federal Rules of Evidence.[3] An order granting plaintiff's motion in limine would prevent defense counsel from inquiring about the conviction during the cross-examination of the plaintiff. It would also bar mention of the conviction during jury selection, opening statement, and closing argument. Finally, the defense attorney could be required to instruct all of her witnesses to refrain from mentioning the plaintiff's past conviction.

Alternatively, the court might grant only some portion of a motion in limine. The court may exclude some, although not all, of the subject evidence, or could enter an order limiting its use. In the above example, it is conceivable that the judge might rule that the conviction is admissible for impeachment, but only if the plaintiff first offers evidence of his own good character.[4] In that case, the conviction could still not be mentioned during jury selection or opening statement, but it might become admissible once the plaintiff took the stand.

Effect of Reserving Ruling on a Motion in Limine

Judges may reserve ruling on motions in limine, as it is often difficult or impossible to determine whether evidence should be excluded until the trial is under way. The admissibility of some evidence may depend on the foundational testimony that precedes it. In such circumstances the judge might want to delay ruling until the trial evidence is more fully developed.

To prevent prejudice to the moving party, many judges will instruct counsel to refrain from mentioning the subject evidence until the reserved motion can be ruled on. This will generally require the offering attorney to wait until she believes the foundation has been established and then approach the bench for a decision on the motion in limine.

Effect of Denying a Motion in Limine

The denial of a motion in limine does not necessarily mean that the subject evidence is absolutely admissible. It may mean only that there are insufficient grounds to take the step of excluding it before the trial begins. Thus, even where a pretrial motion has been denied, an objection to the same evidence at trial might be sustained. If possible, the court should be asked to clarify the meaning of an order denying a motion in limine. Has the evidence been found admissible, or is it simply too soon to decide?

9.2.1.3 Preservation of the Record on Appeal

Appellate courts typically will not consider issues that were not originally raised in the trial court. The admission of evidence generally cannot be reviewed unless it

3. Fed. R. Evid. 609.
4. *Id.* 404(a)(1).

was the subject of a motion in limine or a timely objection was made at trial.[5] Thus, objections serve not only to alert the trial judge to the need for a ruling, they also define the scope of the evidentiary issues that can be considered on appeal.

9.2.2 The Decision to Object

9.2.2.1 The Process of Decision-Making

In the heat of trial the decision on whether to object to some item of evidence must usually be made literally on a split-second basis. A question on either direct or cross-examination typically lasts less than ten seconds; a long question will go on for no more than twenty seconds. Yet within that time counsel must recognize, formulate, and evaluate all possible objections. The concentration required is enormous, and there is no opportunity for letup; counsel must pay exquisite attention to every question and every answer, lest some devastating bit of inadmissible evidence sneak its way into the record. There is no room for even the slightest lapse.

The decision-making process consists of three distinct phases. Counsel must first recognize the objectionability of the particular question, answer, or exhibit. This is often the easiest step since many questions simply "sound wrong." In addition, it is often possible to rely on certain key words and phrases to jog the objection reflex. Questions that use words such as "could," "might," or "possible" commonly call for speculation. Questions that ask about out-of-court statements or conversations must clear the hearsay hurdle.

Following recognition, the next task is to formulate a valid objection. Does the question truly call for speculation, or is it an acceptable lay opinion? Is the out-of-court statement inadmissible hearsay, or does it fall within one of the many exceptions? Even if there is a potentially applicable exception, is it possible to present a counterargument in favor of excluding the evidence? This is the sort of analysis that can fill pages in an appellate opinion or an evidence casebook, but trial counsel must undertake it within the five or ten seconds during which a viable objection can be made.

Finally, counsel must evaluate the tactical situation in order to determine whether the objection is worth making. It is well worth noting that not every valid objection needs to be made. There is little point to objecting if opposing counsel will be able to rectify the problem simply by rephrasing the question or if the information is not ultimately harmful to your case. Moreover, there are often good reasons to refrain from objecting.

---

5. Fed. R. Evid. 103. The only exception is in the case of "plain error," in which case the appellate court can take notice of egregious errors affecting substantive rights, even if they were not brought to the attention of the trial judge. Fed. R. Evid. 103(e). On the other hand, once the court has made a definitive ruling, either before or at trial, "a party need not renew an objection or offer of proof to preserve a claim of error for appeal." *Id.* 103(b).

9.2.2.2 Reasons Not to Object

Jurors' Reactions

Objections are tiresome. They interrupt the flow of the evidence, they distract attention from the real issues at hand, and they have an awful tendency to degenerate into posturing or whining. It is always possible that the objecting lawyer will lose points with the judge or jury by constantly interrupting her opponent.

It was once widely believed that jurors hate objections and that this alone was reason enough to avoid objecting in all but the most pressing circumstances. More recent thinking on the subject is that jurors understand the need for lawyers to object and see it as part of counsel's job, as long as it is not overdone. Juror reaction, then, becomes a reason to utilize objections wisely and sparingly, but not a reason to stand in fear of making them at all.

Judge's Reaction

Fear of losing remains a substantial reason to refrain from objecting. No lawyer can predict with certainty that a judge will agree with her objections. A judge may overrule an objection because she misunderstood it, because her knowledge of the law of evidence is inadequate, or because she just wants to move the trial along without interruption. A judge might also overrule an objection because it was meritless, foolish, or contemptuous. Whatever the reason, it hardly enhances counsel's stock to be overruled regularly when making objections. It is therefore necessary to evaluate the risk of losing when deciding whether to object.

Bear in mind, however, that an unmade objection cannot preserve the record for appeal. Only an objection that is presented and overruled can later be considered by the appellate court. Reticence in objecting can therefore result in the waiver of important issues. Fear of being overruled should never be the sole determining factor in deciding whether to object. It can even be tactically advantageous to make and lose an objection, since this may lay the groundwork for a successful appeal.

Opponent's Reaction

What goes around comes around. Counsel who objects at every turn will eventually find her own examinations punctuated by the intercessions of her opponent. This sort of interchange serves no good end and can only detract from the dignity and value of the adversary system.

In a well-prepared trial involving experienced counsel it would not be surprising for hours, even days, to go by without a single objection. When objections are made, they are directed at important items of evidence whose admissibility is seriously in doubt. While this standard cannot be achieved in every case, it is one to which we all might aspire.

9.2.2.3 Deciding to Object

The decision to object must be made in reference to your theory of the case. Concerning every potential objection, always ask: will the exclusion of the evidence contribute to my theory of the case? Unless the exclusion of the evidence actually advances your theory, there is probably no need to raise an objection.

The principal contribution that an objection can make to your theory of the case is to prevent the admission of truly damaging evidence. Hence the maxim, "Do not object to anything that doesn't hurt you." You can refine the decision even further by asking these two additional questions: Even if the information is harmful, can it be accommodated by other means? Even if the objection is sustained, will the information eventually be admitted after another question or through another witness?

Accommodating Harmful Evidence

Harmful information can often be accommodated through explanation or argument. Indeed, the function of the theory of the case is precisely to anticipate the use of harmful information and to develop a story that both accounts for and devalues it. Consider the case of a plaintiff in a personal injury case being cross-examined on the issue of damages. She testified on direct that the injuries to her hand prevented her from engaging in many activities that she previously had enjoyed, including oil painting. The cross-examiner, armed with information gained in discovery, has determined to show that plaintiff's inability to paint is of no great value:

> Q: You used to engage in oil painting, and now you can't? Correct?
>
> Q: You even considered becoming a professional artist?
>
> Q: You tried to sell your paintings in a local gallery?
>
> Q: But not a single person ever bought one, right?
>
> Q: You even gave up painting several times out of frustration, didn't you?
>
> Q: In fact, just before the accident the gallery owner told you that your paintings could not even be displayed there any longer, isn't that right?
>
> Q: The fact is, you were never any good at all at painting, were you?

Should the plaintiff's counsel have objected to these questions? Her inability to sell her paintings seems irrelevant to her current injuries, since she did not claim loss of income. The gallery owner's statement appears to be hearsay. The parting shot was surely argumentative. And the purpose of the examination was to damage the plaintiff.

On the other hand, the information can be accommodated. Imagine the plaintiff's own explanation, either during cross-examination or on redirect:

A: I never painted for money. It was just my way of relaxing and enjoying myself.

A: Being in the gallery was nice, but the real joy came from holding the brush and creating the images.

A: I suppose I wasn't that good in some people's eyes, but just standing at the easel and creating was enough for me. Now I can never do that again.

Or imagine the final argument of plaintiff's lawyer:

> Maybe my client wasn't the best painter in the world, but it was a hobby that brought her inner peace. It was a way for her to lose the troubles of the day. Even if the paintings were bad, that harmed no one. She seeks damages not from the loss of a profession or job, but from the loss of her enjoyment of life. So what if she was a poor painter? Does that give the defendant the right to crush her hand so that she can no longer even hold a brush? And who knows, perhaps she would have improved. Perhaps she would have been discovered. Now she will never know.

In other words, the plaintiff's theory of damages can accommodate, perhaps even benefit from, the nasty cross-examination. Counsel therefore must choose. Is it better to object in the hope of terminating the line of questioning, or is there more to be gained by weaving the cross-examination into the plaintiff's own case? There is no definitive answer to this question, other than to note that reflexive objection is not always the optimum solution.

Eventual Admissibility

A further consideration is the eventual admissibility of the information. When a question is improper solely as a matter of form, it can generally be cured simply with rephrasing. An objection, therefore, is quite unlikely to result in the actual exclusion of any evidence. This is particularly true of leading questions on direct examination:

Q: Isn't it true that you had the green light as you approached the intersection?

Objection: Counsel is leading his own witness.

Court: The objection is sustained.

Q: What color was the traffic light as you approached the intersection?

A: It was green.

In this example the objection to the leading question accomplished nothing in the way of excluding evidence and may actually have emphasized the witness's testimony that the light was green. Counsel would have been just as well off not making it. Of course, the persistent use of leading questions to feed answers to a witness is quite another matter. In those circumstances an objection should almost always be made. The use of an occasional leading question, however, is so easily cured that experienced counsel seldom object.

A variation on this theme occurs when information is objectionable coming from one witness, but conceivably admissible if elicited from another. Hearsay provides a good example, as in this direct examination of the defendant driver in an intersection case:

Q: Did you speak to anyone following the accident?

A: Yes, I spoke to a crossing guard who was standing on the corner.

Q: Did the crossing guard tell you what he saw?

A: Yes.

Q: What did the crossing guard tell you that he saw?

Objection: Hearsay.[6]

Court: Sustained.

Here, the objecting lawyer has succeeded in keeping the crossing guard's observations out of evidence, but only for the time being. What will happen when the crossing guard testifies?

Q: What is your occupation?

A: I am a crossing guard.

Q: Did you see the accident?

A: Yes, I did.

Q: What did you see?

No objection is possible since the crossing guard will be testifying about his own direct observations.

Most situations are hardly so clear-cut. The crossing guard may not be available to testify, or he might give testimony that is much less favorable to the defendant. The guard might be subject to impeachment or might suffer a memory lapse. There is no hard-and-fast rule that counsel should refrain from objecting simply because another witness is available to give unobjectionable testimony. On the other hand,

6. Note that no objection was made to the earlier question, "Did the crossing guard tell you what he saw?" An objection at that point would have been premature since only the content of the statement will be hearsay. Regarding the timing of objections, *see* section 9.2.3.1.

the ultimate admissibility of the information is definitely a factor to be considered when deciding whether to object.

If the harmful information cannot be accommodated and if it is unlikely to be admitted later, then objecting is a no-risk proposition. All other situations call for the exercise of judgment.

9.2.2.4 Planning

We have just cataloged a long list of factors to be considered when deciding whether or not to raise any particular objection. Even in the computer age it is difficult to imagine anyone actually running through all of these factors in the five or so seconds available between question and response. How, then, can full consideration be given to the objection decision?

The answer, as in so much of trial advocacy, lies in planning. Given the scope of modern pretrial discovery, there is no reason to postpone the objection decision until the very moment when the answer is falling from the witness's lips. The general content, if not the precise words, of most important testimony is known to all counsel before the witness ever takes the stand. Most documents and tangible exhibits must be tendered to opposing counsel in advance of trial.

Objection strategy should therefore be planned in the same manner as is direct or cross-examination. For each opposition witness, counsel's preparation should include consideration of all possible objections to every reasonably anticipated area of testimony. The potential objections should be weighed against the standards discussed in the above sections, and counsel should come to at least a tentative conclusion as to whether an objection is worth making. The same process should be applied to every expected exhibit and document. It is also necessary to consider the likely content of the opposition's cross-examination of your own witnesses and to determine the value of any possible objections.

The best of planning, of course, will not free counsel from the need to make split-second decisions. The evidence will rarely come in exactly as was expected, and the context of the trial may require last-minute adjustments to strategy and approach. Nonetheless, a good deal of the evidentiary background work can and should be done prior to trial.

9.2.3 Making and Meeting Objections

The format for making and meeting objections differs somewhat from state to state and even from courtroom to courtroom, so you will need to tailor your approach to objections to local practice. If in doubt about the requirements in a particular jurisdiction, you should always inquire. What follows here is a generalized description of the majority approach.

See demonstrations 19.1 and 19.2 in the Visuals Appendix.

9.2.3.1 Making an Objection

The standard method of raising an objection is to stand and state the grounds for the objection:

> "Objection, your Honor, relevance."
>
> "Objection, counsel is leading the witness."
>
> "Your Honor, we object on the ground of hearsay."
>
> "Objection, no foundation."

In a jury trial, it may also be advisable to add a descriptive tag line so that the jurors will understand the basis of the objection:

> "Objection, hearsay, your Honor. The witness cannot testify about what somebody else said."
>
> "We object to the leading questions; counsel is testifying instead of the witness."

In any event, it is necessary to give the precise basis for the objection to preserve the issue for appeal. In most jurisdictions, simply stating "objection" is understood only to raise the ground of relevance. If such a "general objection" is made and overruled, all other possible grounds are waived for appeal.[7]

Speaking Objections

A speaking objection goes beyond the simple "state-the-grounds" formula described above. Some attorneys find it necessary or fulfilling to launch into an extended discourse on the bases for their objections before allowing the judge to rule or opposing counsel to speak:

> Objection, your Honor, that question calls for hearsay. The witness's personal notes constitute an out-of-court statement even though the witness is present on the stand. They do not qualify either as business records or as past recollection recorded, and in any event there has been no foundation.

While there is no absolute rule against speaking objections, most judges do not like them. Since the judge is often ready to rule as soon as the initial objection is made, speaking objections are seen as time-wasting and laborious. Judges generally consider it their prerogative to request argument and may resent it when counsel fails to wait for the invitation.

7. Note, however, that a "general objection" that is sustained may be affirmed on appeal if there is any valid basis for the objection.

Repeated Objections

It is often necessary to raise the same objection to a number of questions in a row. Perhaps your initial objection was sustained, but your opponent is persistent in attempting to introduce the inadmissible evidence through other means. Perhaps your initial objection was overruled, and you feel bound to protect your record for appeal as opposing counsel asks a series of questions in elaboration.[8] In any event, an awkward feeling inevitably arises when it is necessary to object repeatedly, on the same ground, to question after question.

If your objections are being sustained, the judge will no doubt tire of reiterating her ruling and will eventually instruct opposing counsel to move on to another line of questioning. If your "same objections" are being consistently overruled, the judge is likely to tire of them even sooner. At some point, she will probably inform you that "I have ruled on that issue, counsel. There is no need for you to continue to object." Now you will risk the judge's ire if you continue to object, but you also risk waiving an issue on appeal if some future question expands on the theme in a way that was not covered by your earlier objections.

The solution to this conundrum, which will often be suggested by the trial judge, is the "standing objection." The theory of the standing objection is that a single objection will be considered to "stand" or apply to an entire line of questioning without the need for repeated interruptions. The problem with standing objections is that it may be difficult in the future to determine exactly which questions and answers were covered. Although the meaning of the standing objection may be apparent to everyone present in the courtroom, the cold transcript presented to the appellate court may seem to tell an entirely different story. Should a judge require that you proceed by way of standing objection, it is imperative that the objection be articulated as clearly as possible.

Timing

Having determined what to say when initiating an objection, one must consider when to say it. The general rule is that an objection must be made as soon as it is apparent that it is called for. On the other hand, an objection may be premature if it interrupts an incomplete question or if it anticipates testimony that may or may not be given. To be timely, an objection must come neither too early nor too late.

Most objections to questions should be held until the examiner has had the opportunity to complete the question. Not only is it rude to interrupt, but the final version may turn out not to be objectionable. On a more pragmatic level, many judges will refuse to rule on an objection until the question has been completed. An

8. Renewed objections are not required once the court "rules definitively on the record," but it will not always be obvious (or certain) that the court's ruling extends to an ensuing series of questions. FED. R. EVID. 103(b).

interrupting objection, then, merely ensures that the question will be stated twice, thereby emphasizing its objectionable information or implications.

There are times, however, when it is necessary to interrupt the questioner. Some questions are objectionable not because of what they will elicit, but because of what they assert. A question may contain a damaging suggestion or proposition which, once heard by the jury, cannot be wholly remedied by objection. Such questions must be interrupted to cut off the interrogator's inadmissible statement. For example, a cross-examiner may be about to question a witness about an inadmissible criminal conviction. Imagine this scenario:

Q: Isn't it true that you were convicted of the crime of selling heroin?

Objection: Objection, your Honor, that was a juvenile offense. It is inadmissible under Rule 609(d).

Court: Sustained.

Although the objection was sustained, the jury has already heard the inadmissible, though nonetheless damning, truth about the witness.[9] It would obviously have been far more effective to cut off the question earlier:

Q: Isn't it true that you were con—

Objection: Objection, your Honor. Counsel is seeking information that is prohibited under Rule 609(d).

Court: Sustained.[10]

Even if it does not interrupt a question, an objection may be premature if the examination has not yet reached the point where the inadmissibility of the answer has become certain. An objection must be made immediately before the inadmissible answer, not in anticipation of it. It is not uncommon for a diligent and eager lawyer to object one question too soon, as in the following example:

Q: Did you have a conversation with Mr. Isaacs?

Objection: Objection, your Honor, hearsay.

Court: Overruled. At this point the only question is whether a conversation occurred. The witness may answer.

A: Yes, I had a conversation with Mr. Isaacs.

---

9. In reality, it is most likely that this information would have been the subject of a pretrial motion in limine. For the purposes of this illustration, assume that for some reason no pretrial motions were made.

10. If the judge does anything other than immediately sustain the objection, the objecting lawyer will want to approach the bench for argument.

Q: Did Mr. Isaacs tell you anything about the investigation report?

Objection: Hearsay, your Honor.

Court: Still too soon, counsel. Proceed.

A: Yes, he did.

Q: What did Mr. Isaacs tell you about the investigation report?

Objection: Objection on the ground of hearsay.

Court: Sustained.

The first two objections were overruled because under the hearsay rule, only the content of the out-of-court statement is inadmissible. The fact of the conversation is admissible evidence.

Timing the objections to questions is relatively easy. Often, however, a witness will respond to a seemingly proper question with a wholly inadmissible response. The timing in these situations is trickier since, by definition, the answer was not foreshadowed by the question. The general rule is that an objection must be made as soon as the inadmissible nature of the answer becomes apparent. This necessarily means interrupting the witness. For example:

Q: When did you begin your investigation of the defendant's financial situation?

A: I began the investigation as soon as I received an anonymous letter charging that—

Objection: We object on the grounds of hearsay and foundation.

Court: Sustained.

It will not do to allow the witness to finish the answer because by then the jurors would have heard the testimony and the harm would be done.

Unfortunately, it is not always possible to recognize and respond to inadmissible testimony before it happens. Counsel may be momentarily distracted or may suffer from rusty reflexes. And some witnesses, either innocently or by design, just have a way of slipping improper testimony into the record. When this happens counsel's only recourse is the motion to strike:

Q: Are you the comptroller of the defendant corporation?

A: The only thing I knew about skimming funds came through the rumor mill.

Objection: Objection, hearsay. We move to strike that answer.

Court:	Sustained. The answer will be stricken from the record.[11]

In a jury trial it is also important that the judge instruct the jury to disregard the inadmissible answer:

Counsel:	Will your Honor please instruct the jury to disregard that last answer?
Court:	Yes, certainly. Ladies and gentlemen, you are to disregard the answer that the witness just gave. Proceed.

While this sort of curative instruction is hardly a satisfying remedy, it is the best that can be done under the circumstances. In many jurisdictions the request for a curative instruction is a necessary predicate to raising the issue on appeal.

Witness Voir Dire

The basis for an objection may not always be apparent from the question or even the answer. Counsel may have access to information that is not yet in the record, but which negates the admissibility of some part of a witness's testimony. This information can be brought to the judge's attention through witness voir dire. The term voir dire is derived from "law French," which was once in use in English courts; it means "speak the truth."

In the context of witness examination, voir dire refers to a limited cross-examination for the purpose of determining the admissibility of evidence. The voir dire examination interrupts the direct and gives the opposing lawyer a chance to bring out additional facts that bear directly on the admissibility of some part of the balance of the testimony. Counsel who wishes to conduct voir dire must ask permission of the judge:

Q: Whose signature is on that document?

A: It appears to be the defendant's.

Objection:	Your Honor, we object to that testimony and ask leave to conduct a limited voir dire of the witness.
Court:	You may proceed with voir dire of the witness.

[*By Objecting Counsel*]

11. Note that the "stricken" testimony will not actually be deleted from the transcript. For the purpose of review on appeal, it is necessary that all of the witness's testimony, as well as all of the rulings of the court and the arguments of counsel, appear on the transcript. Thus, the testimony is stricken only in the legal sense, not literally.

Q: You did not see the document being signed, did you?

A: No.

Q: You have never seen the defendant sign his name, have you?

A: No.

Q: You have never received any signed correspondence from the defendant, have you?

A: No.

Q: Your Honor, it is obvious that the witness cannot identify the signature from her own personal knowledge. We renew our objection to the testimony and move to strike the previous answer.

Voir dire examination is most commonly used with regard to the qualifications of an expert witness or the foundation for a document or exhibit, but it can be used in other situations as well. Note that following voir dire, the offering attorney is entitled to conduct additional examination aimed at reestablishing the admissibility of the evidence.

9.2.3.2 Responding to Objections

Many judges like to rule on objections as soon as they hear them, without even a response from opposing counsel. Believing that they know the law and have been attentive to the proceedings, judges often consider it a waste of time to entertain argument. In truth, a majority of evidentiary objections present no great problems in jurisprudence. A judge can sustain or overrule a good many objections without recourse to counsel's views.

It is common, therefore, for opposing counsel to make no response to an objection unless invited to do so by the judge:

Q: What did the police officer say to you?

Objection: Objection, hearsay.

Court: What about it, counsel?

Q: It is not hearsay because . . . .

The judge might also use a nonverbal signal to prompt a response, perhaps by looking at counsel or by nodding in counsel's direction. It is important to be on the alert for such gestures, since failure to respond might be interpreted by the judge as waiver.

Requesting Argument

Many objections will not be readily susceptible of summary disposition because they raise subtle or complex legal issues. Aspects of an objection may escape the judge or may require consideration of additional information that is not apparent from the record. In these circumstances, counsel cannot rely on an invitation to argue from the judge and will need to inform the court, as politely as possible, that argument is necessary. It is preferable to do this before the judge has ruled, if that can be accomplished without interrupting. An effective signal is to stand while the objection is being made, to alert the judge that argument is desired. Despite counsel's best efforts, the judge may rule on a disputed objection without input from the opposing side. If the point is important, counsel cannot be shy about letting the judge know that there is another side to the objection:

Q: What did the police officer say to you?

Objection:	Objection, hearsay.
Court:	Sustained.
Counsel:	Your Honor, we would like to be heard on that.
Court:	Very well, what do you have to say?
Counsel:	The statement falls under the "present sense impression" exception.
Court:	I see. Overruled. The witness may answer.

Specific Responses

The key to responding to any objection is specificity. A judge who has agreed to listen to argument on an objection has indicated that she may be persuaded. A good argument will result in the admission of the evidence only if it provides the judge with a good reason to overrule the objection. Tell the judge exactly why the proffered evidence is admissible. Some lawyers, for reasons known only to themselves, respond to objections by repeating the evidence and exhorting the judge to admit it. The following scenario is not at all unusual:

Q: What did the defendant do immediately after the accident?

A: He began yelling at his eight-year-old son.

Objection:	Objection. The defendant's relationship with his son is irrelevant.
Court:	It does seem irrelevant. What do you have to say, counsel?
Counsel:	It is very relevant, your Honor. It shows that he was yelling at his child.

This response communicates very little to the judge. What is the probative value of the defendant's conduct? Note how much more effective it is when counsel explains why the evidence is being offered to the court:

Q: What did the defendant do immediately after the accident?

A: He began yelling at his eight-year-old son.

Objection:	Objection. The defendant's relationship with his son is irrelevant.
Court:	It does seem irrelevant. What do you have to say, counsel?
Counsel:	The defendant's anger at his son tends to show that he was distracted by the child just before the accident. It goes directly to negligence, your Honor.

The judge may or may not agree with your assessment of the case, but at least he will have the benefit of your analysis.

Limited Admissibility

Evidence may be inadmissible for some purposes yet admissible for others. When responding to objections, it is extremely important to advise the judge of the precise purpose for which the evidence is offered.

For example, evidence that a dangerous condition has been repaired is generally inadmissible to prove negligence.[12] Counsel cannot argue to the jury, "Of course the owner of the car took inadequate care of the automobile; he had his brakes repaired just two days after the accident." On the other hand, evidence of the repair is admissible to prove ownership of the automobile. Counsel can argue, "The defendant denies that he was responsible for the upkeep of the car, but he was the one who ordered and paid for the repair of the brakes just two days after the accident." With this dichotomy in mind, consider the possible objections and responses in the cross-examination of the defendant:

Q: Didn't you have your brakes repaired just two days after the accident?

Counsel:	Objection, your Honor, this testimony violates Rule 407.
Court:	What do you have to say, counsel?
Counsel:	We are offering it only to prove ownership and control, your Honor.

12. *See* Fed. R. Evid. 407.

Court: The evidence will be received, but only for that limited purpose. Ladies and gentlemen of the jury, you are to consider this evidence only for the purpose of showing ownership and control of the automobile. You must not consider it as proof of any negligence on the part of the defendant.

If the court does not immediately give a limiting instruction, one should be requested by the attorney whose objection was overruled.

Conditional Offers

The admissibility of certain testimony, particularly with regard to relevance, may not always be immediately clear. This is a frequent occurrence on cross-examination since counsel may be using the technique of indirection or otherwise attempting to avoid being too obvious about the direction of the cross. Nor is such subtlety unknown on direct examination. In either case, the ultimate admissibility of the evidence might depend on other testimony to be developed through later witnesses.

In these circumstances, counsel may respond to an objection by making a "conditional offer." This is done either by promising to "tie it up later" or, preferably, by explaining to the court the nature of the evidence that is expected to follow. For example:

Q: Isn't it true that you had an important meeting scheduled for the morning of the accident?

Objection: Objection. The witness's business schedule is not relevant.

Court: What is the relevance of that inquiry, counsel?

Counsel: We intend to introduce evidence that the defendant had a meeting scheduled with a prospective client, that he was already late for the meeting at the time of the accident, and that he stood to lose a great deal of money if he didn't arrive on time. The question is therefore directly relevant to show that he was speeding and inattentive.[13]

Court: Based on that representation I will allow the testimony, subject to a motion to strike if you don't tie it up.

13. Depending on the sensitivity of the information, it would be appropriate to request that the argument on such an objection be conducted outside the presence of the witness.

A conditional offer is always subject to the actual production of the later evidence. The testimony can, and should, be stricken if counsel's representations are not fulfilled.[14]

Anticipating Objections

Being specific is a challenge. When you are interrupted in mid-examination by a maddening objection, the precise, and hopefully devastating, reply may not spring spontaneously to mind. It is therefore essential to plan for likely objections as part of the overall preparation for trial.

Planning for relevance objections should be nearly automatic since it is really part and parcel of developing your theory of the case. Recall that every question you ask, indeed every item of evidence you put forward, should be calculated to advance your theory of the case. By definition, then, you will have considered the probative value of each question before the trial ever starts. To respond to a relevance objection, you will really need to do nothing more than explain to the judge why you offered the evidence in the first place. In other words, "The testimony is relevant, your Honor, because it contributes 'X' to my theory of the case."

Other objections may not be as easy to anticipate. At a minimum, however, trial preparation should include an evaluation of the admissibility of every tangible object, document, or other exhibit that you intend to offer into evidence or use for demonstrative purposes. It is similarly necessary to do an "admissibility check" on all testimony involving conversations, telephone calls, meetings, and other out-of-court statements. Finally, potential objections should be considered for all opinions, conclusions, calculations, and characterizations you expect to elicit. Why is the evidence relevant? What is the necessary foundation for its authenticity? Does the witness have sufficient personal knowledge? Is there a hearsay problem? Might it be privileged?

Judicious Nonresponses

It is not necessary to fight to the death over every objection. Counsel can frequently avoid an objection by rephrasing the offending question, either before or after the judge rules.

Since the precise language of a question is seldom of vital importance, it should be possible to circumnavigate virtually any objection as to form. Leading questions, compound questions, and vague questions can all be cured. Even if your original question was perfectly fine, you may be able to move the trial along, and earn the gratitude of judge and jury, by posing the same inquiry in different words.

Other objections that can be undercut through rephrasing include personal knowledge, foundation, and even relevance. For example:

---

14. *See* Fed. R. Evid. 104(b).

Q: Did the plaintiff follow his doctor's advice?

Objection: Objection. Lack of personal knowledge.

Q: Let me put it this way. Did the plaintiff say anything to you about his doctor's advice?

A: Yes.

Q: What did he say?

A: He said that he would rather risk the consequences than stay in bed all day.

Note that in this scenario, the examination was made stronger by rephrasing the question in response to the objection.

Making and meeting objections involves a certain amount of gamesmanship. No lawyer likes to be seen as an evidentiary pushover. From time to time, it may be tactically important to stand behind a question, if only to establish your mastery of the rules. Another alternative is to rephrase a question without saying so. In the above example, the attorney neither withdrew the question nor overtly rephrased it, but rather said, "Let me put it this way." Problem solved.

9.2.4 Arguing Objections

9.2.4.1 Where

As an initial matter, lawyers usually argue objections from wherever they happen to be standing or sitting when the issue first arises. Even in a jury trial most objections are resolved without anyone moving from their location. The language of objecting is arcane, and in most circumstances it does no harm to have the discussion in the presence of the jury.

Occasionally, however, it is important that the jury not hear the content of the argument. It may be necessary to recite the expected testimony so the judge can rule on the objection or to refer to other evidence that has not yet been admitted. In these circumstances, either side may request that the argument take place out of the presence of the jury.

The most common way of insulating the jury from the attorneys' argument is for counsel to approach the bench and hold, in whispered tones, a sidebar conference. Alternatively, the jury can be excused from the courtroom while counsel argue. This latter approach is used fairly infrequently, and only in the case of extended arguments, since it is cumbersome and time-consuming to shuffle the jury in and out of the courtroom.

A sidebar can be called by the court or requested by either the party making or the party responding to the objection. Typically, the lawyer whose case is most likely to be harmed by disclosures in the course of the argument requests the sidebar. Ethical counsel, however, will volunteer the need for a sidebar whenever she realizes that her own argument may prejudice the other side. The opposition's failure to ask for argument outside the jury's presence should not be taken as license to make statements containing potentially inadmissible evidence. Unfortunately, this practice is all too common. It has no place in a trial conducted by professionals.

9.2.4.2 How

Arguments on objections should be conducted as a conversation between counsel and the court. The general scenario is for objecting counsel to argue first, followed by the attorney who offered the evidence, and concluding with a reply from the objector. In practice, however, the format is often much less formal, with the judge asking questions and counsel responding.

If there is one essential rule in arguing objections, it is that counsel should not argue with, or even address, each other. It is the judge who will make the ruling, and the judge who must be convinced. It is ineffective, distracting, and even insulting to the court when counsel turn to each other to argue their objections:

Plaintiff's Counsel:	Your Honor, our objection to the testimony is lack of foundation.
Defendant's Counsel:	What more foundation could you want, counselor?
Plaintiff's Counsel:	Well, you could start with a basis for personal knowledge.
Defendant's Counsel:	He already testified that he is the comptroller. Isn't that enough for you?

No matter how foolish, trite, or easily disposed of the other side's position seems, avoid speaking directly to opposing counsel. All of your arguments should be made to the court. If, in the course of an argument, you are ever tempted to turn to opposing counsel, remember that she is being paid to disagree with you. There should be nothing in the world that you can say to make her alter her position. Her job is to take the other side of the issue. The judge, by contrast, is employed to keep an open mind. The judge can be persuaded, but only if you take the trouble to address the court directly.

Your evidentiary arguments will be most convincing if they are delivered with a tone of firm conviction. When you argue an objection, you are asking the judge to do something—either to admit or exclude evidence. The wrong decision can lead to reversal, a matter of at least passing professional concern to the judge. Your argument, then, should give the judge a reason for ruling in your favor. Emotive histrionics will be counterproductive. The sort of diffidence or lassitude often displayed by attorneys when arguing to the bench is also unlikely to succeed. A judge, despite the robe, is human. If you do not believe in your argument, why should she?

Finally, counsel must be certain actually to obtain a ruling on every objection. Judges may often prefer to avoid ruling on objections, either because they didn't hear them, don't understand them, or simply because they want to reduce the possibility of being reversed on appeal. In some courtrooms this practice has been raised to the level of a fine art

The remedy to this sort of decision by default is simply to insist politely on a ruling:

> "Before we proceed, your Honor, I have an objection pending."
>
> "Has the court ruled on counsel's objection?"
>
> "May we please have a ruling, your Honor?"

Here and there a judge may be chagrined, but few will ever be offended by an attorney's request that evidence either be admitted or not. A clear record is in everyone's best interest.

9.2.5 *Once the Judge Has Ruled*

The judge's ruling on an objection is not necessarily the end of that particular discourse. Counsel must remain alert to protect and develop the record. Both the proponent of the evidence (offering lawyer) and the opponent (objecting lawyer) may have more yet to do.

9.2.5.1 Objection Overruled

Proponent's Job

The proponent's job when an objection is overruled is to ensure that the evidence actually makes its way into the record. In other words, the proponent must make sure that the witness answers the question that the judge has just ruled to be permissible. The following is an all-too-frequent scenario:

> Q: After the accident, what did the crossing guard say to you?

Objection:	Objection, your Honor, the question calls for hearsay.
Counsel:	Your Honor, it has already been established that the crossing guard observed the accident immediately before making the declaration, so it qualifies as either an excited utterance or a present sense impression.

Court: Yes, I think there is a hearsay exception there. Overruled.

Q: What is the next thing that you did?

A: I took out my phone and called 911.

Despite the court's ruling, the witness was never given an opportunity to answer the original question. The proponent, apparently flushed with victory, just went on to another subject.

A variation on this theme occurs when the witness's answer has been interrupted or when the arguments on the objection overlap the testimony. Moreover, even when the witness was able to get an answer out, the import of the testimony may have been drowned out by the subsequent wrangling over the objection.

Some lawyers use the dubious tactic of having the court reporter read back the prior question and answer (if there was one) following an overruled objection. While this approach is technically correct, it is usually a bad idea. Presumably, the lawyer has prepared an examination that is designed for maximum impact. Counsel knows which words to emphasize and knows how the witness is likely to respond. Why would an attorney choose to forego the persuasive force of her own examination in favor of turning it over to the inevitably monotonous reading of a court reporter? It is the lawyer, not the stenographer, who has been retained to represent the client.

Following an overruled objection, the proponent's safest course is to repeat the question and to be sure to get a clear answer from the witness.

Opponent's Job

The opponent's job following an overruled objection is to stay alert to the possibility of excluding all or some of the offending evidence.

In the first instance the opponent of the evidence should not withdraw an objection. Many lawyers, perhaps out of embarrassment or obsequiousness, seem to think that they can gain points with the trial judge by withdrawing an objection once it has been overruled. In fact, the opposite is probably true. Having already taken the court's time by making and arguing an objection, one can only convey indecision or lack of seriousness by withdrawing it immediately thereafter. Even more to the point, withdrawing an objection has the effect of waiving the issue for appeal.

In any event, once an objection has been overruled, the objecting lawyer must continue to scrutinize the subsequent testimony. Perhaps the witness will not testify in the manner that was promised by the proponent of the evidence in her argument to the court. For example:

Q: After the accident, what did the crossing guard say to you?

Objection:	Objection, your Honor, the question calls for hearsay.
Counsel:	Your Honor, it qualifies as either an excited utterance or a present sense impression.
Court:	Yes, I think there is a hearsay exception there. Overruled.

A: She said that she didn't really see what happened, but that it looked as though . . .

Objection:	Your Honor, I renew my objection. If the witness didn't really see the accident then she can't have a present sense impression.
Court:	Yes. The objection will be sustained on those grounds.

Alternatively, other grounds for objection may become clear in the course of the testimony, or perhaps the witness will begin volunteering evidence that is inadmissible for some additional reason. In the above scenario counsel could also have objected on the ground that the declarant's statement ("it looked as though . . .") was speculative.

9.2.5.2 Objection Sustained

Proponent's Job

A sustained objection means that the proponent of the evidence has been denied the opportunity to place the testimony or exhibit into the record. This ruling leaves the proponent with two tasks.

Offer of Proof

The proponent's first task is to protect the record by making an offer of proof. When a witness is not allowed to testify, the record is silent as to the content of the evidence. An appellate court reviewing the record, however, must know the content of the omitted material to determine whether the judge's ruling was reversible error. The offer of proof is the means by which counsel can place into the record a description of the excluded testimony so that the right to an effective appeal may be preserved.[15] An offer of proof also gives the trial court an opportunity to reconsider its ruling on the basis of a more complete description of the excluded evidence.

15. Fed. R. Evid. 103(a)(2). Note that an offer of proof need not be renewed following a "definitive" ruling by the court. When a proffered exhibit is not admitted, it usually remains part of the record as an exhibit "for identification" as opposed to an exhibit "in evidence." Thus, exhibits can generally be reviewed by an appellate court without the need for an offer of proof.

There are three generally accepted ways to present an offer of proof. The first method is to excuse the jury and proceed with the examination of the witness. This approach has the obvious benefit of accuracy since the witness's actual testimony will be preserved. It is also time-consuming and somewhat awkward, and for those reasons it is only employed in exceptional circumstances.

The most frequently used method of presenting an offer of proof is for counsel to summarize the excluded testimony. For example:

Q: What did the crossing guard say to you immediately after the accident?

Objection:	Hearsay, your Honor.
Court:	Sustained.
Counsel:	May I make an offer of proof?
Court:	Certainly. Proceed.
Counsel:	If the witness were allowed to testify, he would state that the crossing guard made the following statement to him: "I saw the fire truck and heard the siren. All of the traffic stopped except for the red car in the left lane, which just ran right into the back of the blue car without even slowing down."
Court:	Very well, the ruling stands. Ask another question.

Although certainly time-efficient, the summarization method has its drawbacks. One problem is that it is very easy to leave out crucial information. In the above scenario, for example, the offer of proof contains nothing to show that the crossing guard's statement would qualify under an exception to the hearsay rule.[16] A further problem is that enterprising and less than scrupulous lawyers have been known to pad their summaries with "testimony" far more favorable than the witness ever would have produced.

The third approach to offers of proof is the submission to the court of witness statements, reports, or deposition transcripts. This method can have the benefit of both thoroughness and brevity, as follows:

> Your Honor, we submit as an offer of proof pages 12–21 of the witness's deposition, which we have marked for identification as Plaintiff's Exhibit 8.

---

16. *See* Fed. R. Evid. 803(1)–(2).

Or,

> Your Honor, this witness gave a written statement to Officer Lucas, which has been marked as Defendant's Exhibit 8.
>
> If we were allowed to proceed the witness would testify to the facts contained in that statement, which we present as an offer of proof.

This method is used relatively infrequently, however, due at least in part to the difficulty of assembling the right written materials at exactly the right time.

Keep Trying

The proponent's second task in the face of a sustained objection is to keep trying to have the evidence admitted. When a judge sustains an objection, the ruling usually applies only to the specific question (or answer) and grounds that were then before the court. Unless the judge says so explicitly, the ruling does not extend to the ultimate admissibility of the underlying evidence. In other words, a sustained objection says only that "the evidence cannot be admitted based on the testimony and arguments heard so far." It does not say that "the evidence cannot ever be admitted no matter what you do." Counsel generally has the option to offer the evidence through other means.

These "other means" may consist of nothing more than rephrasing a question. Any objection as to form—leading, compound, vague, argumentative—can be cured by altering the language of the inquiry. Leading questions on direct examination can easily be restated:

> Q: You had the green light when the defendant's car hit yours, didn't you?
>
> Objection: Objection, leading.
>
> Court: Sustained.
>
> Q: What color was your light when the defendant's car hit yours?
>
> A: It was green.

Objections are frequently sustained not because of the form of the question, but because of some missing predicate in the testimony. Objections to foundation can be cured by eliciting additional foundation. Objections to a witness's lack of personal knowledge can be remedied with further questions showing the basis of the witness's information. Relevance objections can be overcome through continued questioning aimed at demonstrating the probative value of the original question. In the following cross-examination, the witness is the defendant in an intersection accident case:

> Q: Immediately after the accident you started yelling at your twelve-year-old son, didn't you?
>
> Objection: Objection, relevance.

Court: Sustained.

Q: Well, your twelve-year-old son was in the car at the time of the accident, wasn't he?

A: Yes.

Q: He was sitting in the front seat?

A: Yes, he was.

Q: He was playing the radio, wasn't he?

A: He was.

Q: The music was awfully loud, wasn't it?

A: I suppose so.

Q: Most drivers find that extremely annoying, don't they?

A: I couldn't really say.

Q: Are you aware that the police report says that the radio was still playing in your front seat when they arrived at the scene?

A: I remember something like that.

Q: And immediately after the accident you yelled at your son, didn't you?

Objection: Same objection.

Counsel: Your Honor, I believe we have established the likelihood that the defendant was distracted by his son's music. Yelling at the child is probative on that issue.

Court: Yes, I see your point. Overruled.

The same approach can work for hearsay objections. Additional facts can often be established that will qualify a statement for an exception to the hearsay rule. Moreover, out-of-court statements may sometimes be recast in the form of conduct or observations. In the following example a police officer has just testified on direct examination that she received a radio dispatch that a crime had been committed:

Q: What was the content of the radio bulletin from the dispatcher?

Objection: Objection, hearsay.

Court: Sustained.

Q: What did you do immediately after receiving the alert?

A: I drove to the corner of Grand Avenue and State Street.

Q: What did you do there?

A: I began looking for a suspect wearing glasses and a white lab jacket.

The effect of the sustained hearsay objection was avoided by continuing the examination on the admissible subject of the witness's actions as opposed to the inadmissible subject of the dispatcher's out-of-court statement.

It is not always possible to overcome a sustained objection. Some testimony will be flatly inadmissible no matter how many approaches counsel attempts. On the other hand, there are often numerous routes to admissibility, and a sustained objection usually closes off only one. Keep trying.

Opponent's Job

When an objection is sustained, the opponent of the evidence has been successful. This should bring satisfaction to the objector, and in some cases even rejoicing, but it is never a reason to rest on your laurels. The very next question may ask for the identical evidence, in which case an additional objection must be made. A sustained objection will be a temporary victory indeed if the proponent of the evidence succeeds in having it admitted later in the witness's testimony. This is not uncommon. Successful objections can come undone as soon as the objector relaxes vigilance.

Q: Who told you to begin your financial investigation?

A: I received an anonymous note charging that—

Objection: Objection, hearsay.

Court: Sustained.

Q: What caused you to begin investigating?

A: There was a charge that money had been skimmed from one of the trust accounts.

Q: How did you learn of the charge?

A: I received a note.

The opponent of the evidence in this case let down his guard. When the first hearsay objection was successful he allowed his attention to lapse. He therefore failed to notice that the identical testimony was being introduced as the "cause" of the investigation. The information, of course, is no less hearsay (and no less anonymous) the second time around. A second objection should have been made.

9.2.5.3 Evidence Admitted for a Limited Purpose

If the evidence is admitted for a limited purpose, the opponent's job is to ask for a limiting instruction that explains the nature of the court's ruling. Most judges give such an instruction as a matter of course. Counsel may occasionally want to forego the limiting instruction on the theory that it will only call attention to the harmful evidence.

9.2.5.4 Theory Reevaluation

Rulings on objections govern the flow of evidence at trial. The availability of evidence forms the underpinning of every attorney's theory of the case. Theory planning, in turn, involves calculated predictions about the admissibility of evidence. It may be, therefore, that the court's ruling on a particularly important objection will require counsel to reevaluate her theory of the case.

Evidentiary rulings must be understood in the context of the entire case. They are not merely passing successes or failures; they can be crucial turning points in the progress of the case. If an essential item of evidence is excluded, or if some controversial proof is admitted, counsel may have to switch theories, or abandon a claim or defense, even if this occurs in midtrial.

In some instances the effect of an evidentiary ruling may be only to strengthen or weaken your case. If the court excludes some testimony of one of your witnesses, you might be able to proceed as planned, but with a lesser volume of evidence. Recall the fire engine/intersection case that we have been using as an example. The plaintiff's theory was that the defendant caused the accident because he was hurrying to a business meeting for which he was already late. Assume that the court, for whatever reason, sustained an objection to testimony that the defendant was seen rushing from his home that morning with his tie undone and a coffee cup in his hand. This ruling diminishes the proof available to the plaintiff, but as long as other evidence is available, the "hurrying to work" theory can remain intact.

Other missing testimony might vitiate entirely one of your claims. Return to the fire engine case and assume now that an objection was sustained to evidence that the defendant had declined to have his brakes repaired despite a mechanic's advice to the contrary. Following this ruling, the entire claim of negligent maintenance will probably have to be scrapped. Plaintiff's counsel will be in trouble indeed if she does not have a back-up theory available.

Theory alterations cannot be well made on the spur of the moment. As a consequence, during trial preparation counsel must always take into consideration the possible effects of evidentiary rulings. It is not enough to plan to make objections. Counsel must go further to determine the impact on her theory if the objection is overruled and the evidence is admitted. By the same token, it is not sufficient to anticipate one's response to the opposition's objections. It is also necessary to plan conceivable theory adaptations in the event that those objections are sustained.

9.3 Ethics and Objections

Ethical issues frequently arise in the context of making and meeting objections. Because the objecting process is one of the most confrontational aspects of the trial, it often tests counsel's reserves of good will, civility, restraint, and sense of fair play. The three most common problems are discussed below.

9.3.1 Asking Objectionable Questions

As we have discussed previously, assessing the likely admissibility of evidence is an essential component of trial preparation. There is no question that counsel may offer any evidence that she believes is either clearly or probably admissible. What about evidence that is probably inadmissible? Is it ethical to offer such testimony in the hope that either opposing counsel will fail to object or that the judge will make an erroneous ruling?

It is ethical to offer any evidence over which there is a reasonable evidentiary dispute. Our adversary system calls on each attorney to make out the best case possible and relies on the judge to rule on disputed issues of law. Valuable evidence should not be preemptively excluded on the basis of counsel's own assessment, as long as there is a reasonable basis in the law for its admission.

As we have seen, an attorney is usually wise to refrain from objecting to every objectionable question or answer. This raises the possibility that opposing counsel may choose not to object to testimony even if its admissibility is open to debate. That decision is the opposition's to make, and there is no need for an attorney to save them from having to make it.

By the same token, the judge is the arbiter of the law. If her evaluation of admissibility is different from counsel's, then the judge is correct, at least until the matter reaches an appellate court.[17] This is not a novel concept. Boswell reported that Dr. Johnson took the same position with regard to arguing a case that he knew to be weak:

> Sir, you do not know it to be good or bad till the Judge determines it. * * * An argument which does not convince yourself, may convince the Judge to whom you urge it: And if it does convince him, why, then, Sir, you are wrong and he is right.[18]

This principle does not, however, relieve counsel of all responsibility to cull inadmissible evidence from the case. A corollary to counsel's right to offer evidence for which there is a reasonable basis is the obligation to refrain from offering evidence

17. There may be purely tactical reasons to abstain from offering proof of questionable admissibility. If the trial judge admits the evidence over objection, and counsel relies on it in winning her case, that same evidence may later become the basis for reversal on appeal.
18. 2 Boswell, The Life of Johnson 47 (Hill Ed. 1887).

for which there is no reasonable basis. As stated in the Model Rules of Professional Conduct, "a lawyer shall not . . . in trial, allude to any matter that the lawyer does not reasonably believe is relevant or that will not be supported by admissible evidence . . . ."[19]

In other words, it is unethical to offer evidence knowing that there is no reasonable basis for its admission. Even though opposing counsel might neglect to object, and even though the court might err in its ruling, the adversary system does not extend so far as to allow the intentional use of improper evidence. Indeed, one of the justifications for the adversary system is precisely that counsel can be relied on to perform this minimum level of self-policing.

When does counsel have a reasonable belief as to the admissibility of evidence? This determination lies within the thought processes of the individual lawyer. For this reason it is unlikely that any single proffer would ever result in discipline, although repeated efforts to offer clearly inadmissible evidence could lead to sanctions in an extreme case.

The test of ethical conduct, however, cannot be found in the likelihood of punishment. An appropriate rule, therefore, is that it is improper to offer evidence that cannot be supported by an articulable and coherent theory of admissibility. Counsel should be able to complete, with specific and recognizable legal arguments, the sentence that begins, "This evidence is admissible because . . . ." If the only conclusion for the sentence is, "because it helps my case," then there is not a reasonable basis for the offer.

Finally, it is unethical to attempt to use the information contained in questions as a substitute for testimony that cannot be obtained. Some lawyers apparently believe that the idea of zealous advocacy allows them to slip information before a jury by asserting it in a question, knowing full well that the witness will not be allowed to answer. The usual scenario is something as follows:

Counsel:	Isn't it true that you were once fired from a job for being drunk?
Objection:	Objection, relevance.
Counsel:	I withdraw the question. (*Sotto voce:* Who cares about the ruling? I never expected to get it in, but now the jury knows that the witness is a drunk.)

This conduct, even if the information is true, is absolutely unethical. Testimony is to come from witnesses, with admissibility ruled on by the court. It subverts the very purpose of an adversary trial when lawyers abuse their right to question witnesses to slip inadmissible evidence before the jury.

19. Model Rules of Prof'l Conduct R. 3.4(e).

9.3.2 Making Questionable Objections

The same general analysis applies to the use of objections as it does to the offer of evidence. Counsel need not be positive that an objection will be sustained, but must only believe that there is a reasonable basis for making it. Again, under the adversary system it is up to the judge to decide whether to admit the evidence.

The license to make questionable objections is available only if counsel is truly interested in excluding the subject evidence. That is, an attorney may make a reasonable or plausible objection, but only as long as the purpose of the objection is to obtain a ruling on the evidence. As we will see in the following section, objections may also be employed for a variety of ulterior purposes, most of which are unethical.

9.3.3 Making "Tactical" Objections

Many lawyers tout the use of so-called "tactical" objections. Since an objection is the only means by which one lawyer can interrupt the examination of another, it is suggested that objections should occasionally be made to "break up" the flow of a successful examination. An objection can throw the opposing lawyer off stride, or give the witness a rest, or distract the jury from the content of the testimony. This advice is usually tempered with the admonition that there must always be some evidentiary basis for the objection, but the real message is that an objection may be used for any purpose whatsoever as long as you can make it with a straight face.

This view is unfortunate. It amounts to nothing more than the unprincipled use of objections for a wholly improper purpose. No judge would allow a lawyer to object on the ground that the opposition's examination is going too well. The fact that disruption can be accomplished *sub silentio* does not justify it. The same is true of other "tactical" uses of objections. It is unethical to use a speaking objection to communicate with the jury or to suggest testimony to a witness.

The tactical use of objections is widespread and seldom punished. The use of "colorable" objections to accomplish impermissible goals can insulate a lawyer from discipline, but it does not make the practice right.[20] The "true exclusion" standard being urged here may well be unenforceable by judges; it is virtually impossible to evaluate a lawyer's thought process to determine the underlying reason for any particular objection. However, that standard may be attained by any honorable lawyer who is committed to practice in good faith.

20. Just as racial or religious discrimination can also be accomplished, at least on a small scale, through undetectable means. One can often find an arguable excuse for bad actions. In this context, it is easily recognizable that hiding one's motivation does not justify the result.

9.4 A Short List of Common Objections

A complete discussion of evidentiary objections is beyond the scope of this book. The following list of some frequently made objections (and responses) is intended only as a reference or guide, not as a substitute for a thorough knowledge of evidence and procedure.

This section provides a brief description of the grounds for each objection followed by an equally brief statement of some possible responses. Where appropriate, citations are made to the Federal Rules of Evidence.

9.4.1 Objections to the Form of the Question (or Answer)

9.4.1.1 Leading Question

A leading question suggests or contains its own answer. Leading questions are objectionable on direct examination. They are permitted on cross-examination. *See* Rule 611.

Responses. The question is preliminary, foundational, directing the witness's attention, or refreshing the witness's recollection. The witness is very old, very young, infirm, adverse, or hostile. Leading questions can most often be rephrased in non-leading form.

9.4.1.2 Compound Question

A compound question contains two separate inquiries that are not necessarily susceptible of a single answer. For example, "Wasn't the fire engine driving in the left lane and flashing its lights?"

Responses. Dual inquiries are permissible if the question seeks to establish a relationship between two facts or events. For example, "Didn't he move forward and then reach into his pocket?" Other than to establish a relationship, compound questions are objectionable and should be rephrased.

9.4.1.3 Vague Question

A question is vague if it is incomprehensible, or incomplete, or if any answer will necessarily be ambiguous. For example, the question, "When do you leave your house in the morning?" is vague since it does not specify the day of the week to which it refers.

Responses. A question is not vague if the judge understands it. Many judges will ask the witness whether he understands the question. Unless the precise wording is important, it is often easiest to rephrase a "vague" question.

9.4.1.4 Argumentative Question

An argumentative question asks the witness to accept the examiner's summary, inference, or conclusion rather than to agree with the existence (or nonexistence) of a fact. Questions can be made more or less argumentative depending on the tone of voice of the examiner.

Responses. Treat the objection as a relevance issue and explain its probative value to the court: "Your Honor, it goes to prove . . . ." (It will not be persuasive to say, "Your Honor, I am not arguing." It might be persuasive to explain the nonargumentative point that you are trying to make.) Alternatively, make no response, but wait to see if the judge thinks that the question is argumentative. If so, rephrase the question.

9.4.1.5 Narratives

Witness examinations are required to proceed in question and answer form. This requirement ensures that opposing counsel will have the opportunity to frame objections to questions before the answer is given. A narrative answer is one that continues at some length in the absence of questions. An answer that is more than a few sentences long can usually be classified as a narrative. A narrative question is one that calls for a narrative answer, such as, "Tell us everything that you did on December 19." Objections can be made both to questions that call for a narrative and answers in narrative form.

Responses. The best response is usually to ask another question that will break up the narrative. Note that expert witnesses are often allowed to testify in narrative fashion since technical explanations cannot be given easily in question-and-answer format. Even then, however, it is usually more persuasive to interject questions to break up long answers.

9.4.1.6 Asked and Answered

An attorney is not entitled to repeat questions and answers. Once an inquiry has been "asked and answered," further repetition is objectionable. Variations on a theme, however, are permissible, as long as the identical information is not endlessly repeated. The asked-and-answered rule does not preclude inquiring on cross-examination into subjects that were covered fully on direct. Nor does it prevent asking identical questions of different witnesses. (Judges do, however, have the inherent power to exclude cumulative testimony. *See* Rule 611(a).)

Responses. If the question has not been asked and answered, counsel can point out to the judge the manner in which it differs from the earlier testimony. Otherwise, it is best to rephrase the question in a way that varies the exact information sought.

9.4.1.7 Assuming Facts Not in Evidence

A question, usually on cross-examination, is objectionable if it includes as a predicate a statement of fact that has not been proven. The reason for this objection is that the question is unfair; it cannot be answered without conceding the unproven assumption. Consider, for example, the following question: "You left your home so late that you only had fifteen minutes to get to your office?" If the time of the witness's departure was not previously established, this question assumes a fact not in evidence. The witness cannot answer "yes" to the main question (fifteen minutes to get to the office) without implicitly conceding the unproven predicate (that he was late).

Responses. A question assumes facts not in evidence only when it uses an introductory predicate as the basis for another inquiry. Simple, one-part cross-examination questions do not need to be based on facts that are already in evidence. For example, it would be proper to ask a witness, "Didn't you leave home late that morning," whether or not there had already been evidence as to the time of the witness's departure. As a consequence of misunderstanding this distinction, "facts not in evidence" objections are often erroneously made to perfectly good cross-examination questions. If the objection is well taken, most questions can easily be divided in two.

9.4.1.8 Nonresponsive Answers

It was once hornbook law that only the attorney who asked the question could object to a nonresponsive answer. The theory for this limitation was that opposing counsel had no valid objection as long as the content of the answer complied with the rules of evidence. The more modern view is that opposing counsel can object if all, or some part, of an answer is unresponsive to the question, since counsel is entitled to insist that the examination proceed in question-and-answer format. Jurisdictions that adhere to the traditional view may still recognize an objection that the witness is "volunteering" or that there is "no question pending."

Responses. Ask another question.

9.4.2 Substantive Objections

9.4.2.1 Hearsay

The Federal Rules of Evidence define hearsay as "a statement that: (1) the declarant does not make while testifying at the current trial or hearing; and (2) a party offer in evidence to prove the truth of the matter asserted in the statement."[21] Thus, any out-of-court statement, including the witness's own previous statement, is potentially hearsay. Whenever a witness testifies, or is asked to testify, about what she or someone else said in the past, the statement should be subjected to hearsay

21. Fed. R. Evid. 801(c).

analysis. Statements are not hearsay if they are offered for a purpose other than to "prove the truth of the matter asserted." For example, consider the statement, "I warned him that his brakes needed work." This statement would be hearsay if offered to prove that the brakes were indeed defective. On the other hand, it would not be hearsay if offered to prove that the driver had notice of the condition of the brakes and was therefore negligent in not having them repaired. There are also numerous exceptions to the hearsay rule.

Responses. Out-of-court statements are admissible if they are not hearsay or if they fall within one of the exceptions to the hearsay rule. In addition to statements that are not offered for their truth, the Federal Rules of Evidence define two other types of statements as nonhearsay. The witness's own previous statement is not hearsay if (A) it was given under oath and it is inconsistent with the current testimony; or (B) it is consistent with the current testimony and it is offered to rebut a charge of recent fabrication; or (C) it is a statement of past identification. In addition, an statement of a party opponent is defined as nonhearsay if offered against that party.[22]

Some of the more frequently encountered exceptions to the hearsay rule are as follows:

Present Sense Impression. A statement describing an event made while the declarant is observing it. For example, "Look, there goes the President." Rule 803(1).

Excited Utterance. A statement relating to a startling event made while under the stress of excitement caused by the event. For example, "A piece of plaster fell from the roof, and it just missed me." Rule 803(2).

State of Mind. A statement of the declarant's mental state or condition. For example, "He said that he was so mad he couldn't see straight." Rule 803(3).

Past Recollection Recorded. A memorandum or record of a matter about which the witness once had knowledge, but which she has since forgotten. The record must have been made by the witness when the events were fresh in the witness's mind and must be shown to have been accurate when made. Rule 803(5).

Business Records. The business records exception applies to the records of any regularly conducted activity. To qualify as an exception to the hearsay rule, the record must have been made at or near the time of the transaction by a person with knowledge or transmitted from a person with knowledge. It must have been made and kept in the ordinary course of business. Rule 803(6). The foundation for a business record may be provided by "certification," making it unnecessary to call a witness. Rule 902(11).

Reputation as to Character. Evidence of a person's reputation for truth and veracity is an exception to the hearsay rule. Note that there are restrictions other than hearsay on the admissibility of character evidence (discussed below). Rule 803(21).

22. *Id.* 801(d).

Prior Testimony. Testimony given at a different proceeding, or in deposition, qualifies for this exception if 1) the testimony was given under oath; 2) the adverse party had an opportunity to cross-examine; and 3) the witness is currently unavailable. Rule 804(b)(1).

Dying Declaration. A statement by a dying person as to the cause or circumstances of what she believed to be impending death. Admissible only in homicide prosecutions or civil cases. Rule 804(b)(2).

Statement Against Interest. A statement so contrary to the declarant's pecuniary, proprietary, or penal interest that no reasonable person would have made it unless it were true. The declarant must be unavailable, and certain other limitations apply in criminal cases. Rule 804(b)(3).

Catch All Exception. Other hearsay statements may be admitted if they contain sufficient circumstantial guarantees of trustworthiness. Advance notice must be given to the adverse party. Rule 807.

9.4.2.2 Irrelevant

Evidence is irrelevant if it does not make any fact of consequence to the case more or less probable. Evidence can be irrelevant if it proves nothing or if it tends to prove something that does not matter. Rules 401, 402.

Responses. Explain the relevance of the testimony.

9.4.2.3 Unfair Prejudice

Relevant evidence may be excluded if its probative value is substantially outweighed by the danger of unfair prejudice. Note that evidence cannot be excluded merely because it is prejudicial; by definition, all relevant evidence must be prejudicial to some party. Rather, the objection only obtains if the testimony has little probative value and it is unfairly prejudicial. The classic example is a lurid and explicit photograph of an injured crime victim offered to prove some fact of slight relevance, such as the clothing that the victim was wearing. The availability of other means to establish the same facts will also be considered by the court. Rule 403.

Responses. Most judges are hesitant to exclude evidence on this basis. A measured explanation of the probative value of the testimony is the best response.

9.4.2.4 Improper Character Evidence, Generally

Character evidence is generally not admissible to prove that a person acted in conformity with his character. For example, a defendant's past burglaries cannot be offered as proof of a current charge of burglary. A driver's past accidents cannot be offered as proof of current negligence. Rule 404(a).

Responses. A criminal defendant may offer proof of her own good character, which the prosecution may then rebut. Rule 404(a)(1).

Past crimes and bad acts may be offered to prove motive, opportunity, intent, preparation, plan, knowledge, identity, or absence of mistake. Rule 404(b).

9.4.2.5 Improper Character Evidence, Conviction of Crime

As noted above, the commission, and even the conviction, of past crimes is not admissible to prove current guilt.

The credibility of a witness who takes the stand and testifies, however, may be impeached on the basis of a prior criminal conviction, but only if the following requirements are satisfied: the crime must have been either 1) a felony, or 2) one which involved dishonesty or false statement, regardless of punishment. With certain exceptions, the evidence is not admissible unless the conviction occurred within the last ten years. Juvenile adjudications are generally not admissible. Rule 609.

Note that the impeachment is generally limited to the fact of conviction, the name of the crime, and the sentence received. The details and events that comprised the crime are generally inadmissible.

Responses. If the crime was not a felony, the conviction may still be admissible if it involved dishonesty. If the conviction is more than ten years old, it may still be admissible if the court determines that its probative value, supported by specific facts and circumstances, substantially outweighs its prejudicial effect. Rule 609.

9.4.2.6 Improper Character Evidence, Untruthfulness

As noted above, the past bad acts of a person may not be offered as proof that he committed similar acts. Specific instances of conduct are admissible for the limited purpose of attacking or supporting credibility. A witness may therefore be cross-examined concerning past bad acts only if they reflect on truthfulness or untruthfulness. Note, however, that such bad acts (other than conviction of a crime) may not be proved by extrinsic evidence. The cross-examiner is stuck with the witness's answer. Rule 608(b).

Responses. Explain the manner in which the witness's past bad acts are probative of untruthfulness.

9.4.2.7 Improper Character Evidence, Reputation

Reputation evidence is admissible only with regard to an individual's character for truthfulness or untruthfulness. Moreover, evidence of a truthful character is admissible only after the character of the witness has been attacked. Rule 608(a).

Responses. Explain the manner in which the reputation evidence is probative of truthfulness or untruthfulness.

9.4.2.8 Lack of Personal Knowledge

Witnesses (other than experts) must testify from personal knowledge, which is generally defined as sensory perception. A witness's lack of personal knowledge may be obvious from the questioning, may be inherent in the testimony, or may be developed by questioning on voir dire. Rule 602.

Responses. Ask further questions that establish the witness's personal knowledge.

9.4.2.9 Improper Lay Opinion

Lay witnesses (nonexperts) are generally precluded from testifying as to opinions, conclusions, or inferences. Rule 701.

Responses. Lay witnesses may testify to opinions or inferences if they are rationally based on the perception of the witness. Common lay opinions include estimates of speed, distance, value, height, time, duration, and temperature. Lay witnesses are also commonly allowed to testify as to the mood, sanity, demeanor, sobriety, or tone of voice of another person.

9.4.2.10 Speculation or Conjecture

Witnesses may not be asked to speculate or guess. Such questions are often phrased as hypotheticals in a form such as, "What would have happened if . . ."

Responses. Witnesses are permitted to make reasonable estimates rationally based on perception.

9.4.2.11 Authenticity

Exhibits must be authenticated before they may be admitted. Authenticity refers to adequate proof that the exhibit actually is what it seems or purports to be. Virtually all documents and tangible objects must be authenticated. Since exhibits are authenticated by laying a foundation, objections may be raised on the ground of either authenticity or foundation. This subject is discussed in greater detail in chapter ten.

Responses. Ask additional questions that establish authenticity.

9.4.2.12 Lack of Foundation

Nearly all evidence, other than a witness's direct observation of events, requires some sort of predicate foundation for admissibility. An objection to lack of foundation requires the judge to make a preliminary ruling as to the admissibility of the evidence. Rule 104. The evidentiary foundations vary widely. For example, the foundation for the business records exception to the hearsay rule includes evidence that the records were made and kept in the ordinary course of business. The foundation for the introduction of certain scientific or physical evidence requires the establishment of a chain of custody. The following list includes some, though by no means all, of the sorts of evidence that require special foundations for admissibility: voice identifications, telephone conversations, writings, business records, digital data, the existence of a privilege, dying declarations, photographs, scientific tests, expert and lay opinions, and many more. This subject is discussed in greater detail in chapter ten.

Responses. Ask additional questions that lay the necessary foundation.

9.4.2.13 Best Evidence

The "best evidence" or "original document" rule refers to the common-law requirement that copies or secondary evidence of writings could not be admitted into evidence unless the absence of the original could be explained. Under modern practice, most jurisdictions have significantly expanded on the circumstances in which duplicates and other secondary evidence may be admitted.

Under the Federal Rules of Evidence, "duplicates" are usually admissible to the same extent as originals. Duplicates include carbons, photocopies, photographs, duplicate printouts, or any other copies that are made by "techniques which accurately reproduce the original." Rules 1001–1003.

Other secondary evidence, such as oral testimony describing the contents of a document, is admissible only if the original has been lost or destroyed, is unavailable through judicial process, or if it is in the exclusive possession of the opposing party. Rule 1004.

Responses. Ask additional questions demonstrating either that the item offered is a duplicate or that the original is unavailable.

9.4.2.14 Privilege

Numerous privileges may operate to exclude otherwise admissible evidence. Among the most common are attorney-client, physician-patient, marital, clergy, psychotherapist-patient, and a number of others that exist either by statute or at common law. Each privilege has its own foundation and its own set of exceptions. Rule 501 did not change the common-law privileges, but note that state statutory privileges may not obtain in federal actions.

Responses. Virtually all privileges are subject to some exceptions, which vary from jurisdiction to jurisdiction.

9.4.2.15 Liability Insurance

Evidence that a person carried liability insurance is not admissible on the issue of negligence. Rule 411. This exclusion is necessary because it is generally assumed that jurors will be promiscuous in awarding judgments that they know will ultimately be paid by insurance companies. The improper mention of liability insurance may be considered so prejudicial as to warrant a mistrial.

Responses. Evidence of liability insurance may be admissible on some issue other than negligence, such as proof of agency, ownership, control, or bias or prejudice of a witness. Rule 411.

9.4.2.16 Subsequent Remedial Measures

Evidence of subsequent repair or other remedial measures is not admissible to prove negligence, product defect, or other culpable conduct. Rule 407. The primary rationale for this rule is that parties should not be discouraged from remedying dangerous conditions and should not have to choose between undertaking repairs and creating proof of their own liability.

Responses. Subsequent remedial measures may be offered to prove ownership, control, or feasibility of precautionary measures, if controverted. Evidence of subsequent repair may also be admissible in strict liability cases as opposed to negligence cases.

9.4.2.17 Settlement Offers

Offers of compromise or settlement are not admissible to prove or disprove liability. Statements made during settlement negotiations are also inadmissible. Rule 408.

Responses. Statements made during settlement discussions may be admissible to prove bias or prejudice of a witness or to negate a contention of undue delay.

Chapter Ten

Foundations and Exhibits

10.1 Evidentiary Foundations

10.1.1 The Requirement of Foundation

Before any evidence can be considered at trial there must be some basis for believing it to be relevant and admissible. This basis is called the foundation for the evidence. Depending on the nature of the evidence, the foundation may be painfully complex or strikingly simple. The law of evidence determines exactly which facts form the predicate for the admission of all testimony and exhibits. In any event, the question of foundation is directed to the judge, who must make a preliminary determination as to whether the particular evidence will be received.[1]

Regarding much testimony, foundation is so obvious that it is almost overlooked as a formal aspect of the trial. For example, the basic foundation for eyewitness, or percipient, testimony is that the witness observed relevant events and is able to recall them. This foundation is typically established as a means of introducing the witness, virtually as a matter of course. For example:

> Q: Where were you on the afternoon of December 19?
>
> A: I was at the corner of Central and Ridge.
>
> Q: What did you see?
>
> A: I saw an automobile collision.

It has now been shown that the witness has personal knowledge of relevant facts. On the basis of this foundation, and in the absence of some objection that is not apparent from the example, the witness should be allowed to describe the collision. Of course, not all foundations are so straightforward. Many require the proof of substantial predicate facts, as will be discussed below.

Foundations are required in the interest of both efficiency and fairness. To conserve the court's time, evidence will not be heard unless there is first a threshold

---

1. *See* Fed. R. Evid. 104.

showing of relevance and admissibility. In the above example, for instance, there would be no reason for a court to hear a narrative about the accident from a witness who was not qualified to describe it.

Similarly, fairness dictates that an adversary be given notice of the basis for offering evidence before it is actually received. Imagine this scenario at the very beginning of a direct examination:

Q: What is your name?

A: Ari Madison.

Q: Please describe the automobile accident that occurred at the corner of Central and Ridge last December 19.

In the absence of some basis for the witness's testimony, opposing counsel has no way of knowing whether the proffered evidence will be competent or inadmissible. The witness may be about to testify on the basis of speculation or hearsay. Foundation is therefore required in order to prevent unfair prejudice.

10.1.2 Components of Foundation

There are three universal aspects to virtually all evidentiary foundations. To be received, evidence must be shown to be 1) relevant, 2) authentic, and 3) admissible under the applicable laws of evidence. While the discrete elements of foundation will differ according to the nature of the evidence and the purpose for which it is offered, these three considerations must always apply.

10.1.2.1 Relevance

Relevance defines the relationship between the proffered evidence and some fact that is at issue in the case. Evidence will not be admitted simply because it is interesting or imaginative. Rather, it must be shown to be probative in the sense that it makes some disputed fact either more or less likely. The relevance of most evidence is generally made apparent from the context of the case, but occasionally it must be demonstrated by the establishment of foundational facts.

In the intersection example above, the relevance of the testimony is made clear by the recitation of the date and place of the witness's observation. The witness is about to testify concerning the collision at issue, not just any accident. Note, however, that this basic foundation might not always be adequate. Had there been more than one accident on December 19 at the corner of Central and Ridge, the witness would have to provide additional identifying facts before testifying to the events. What time was the witness there? What colors were the automobiles involved?

10.1.2.2 Authenticity

The concept of authenticity refers to the requirement of proof that the evidence is actually what the proponent claims it to be.[2] In other words, evidence is not to be admitted until there has been a threshold showing that it is "the real thing." The judge decides whether an item of evidence has been sufficiently authenticated, and the criteria vary according to the nature of the evidence involved. In many jurisdictions the strict rules of evidence do not apply to the court's preliminary determination of admissibility.[3]

We generally think of authentication as it applies to tangible evidence such as documents, physical objects, or photographs. Is that really the contract that the parties executed? Is this actually the machine part that caused the injury? Does the photograph fairly and accurately depict the scene of the accident? Before any exhibit can be received, a foundation must be established that adequately supports the proponent's claim of authenticity. Note that the court's initial ruling on authenticity is preliminary. It bears only on admissibility and is not binding as a factual determination. Opposing counsel may continue to controvert the genuineness of the exhibit, and the trier of fact (either judge or juror) remains free ultimately to reject the exhibit.

The requirement of authenticity is not, however, limited to tangible objects. It also applies to certain testimonial evidence. For example, a witness generally may not testify to a telephone conversation without first establishing her basis for recognizing the voice of the person on the other end of the line.[4] That is, the identity of the other speaker must be authenticated.

10.1.2.3 Specific Admissibility

While evidence will generally be received if it is relevant and authentic, the law of evidence contains a host of specific provisions that govern the admissibility of various sorts of proof. In many cases, evidence can be admitted only after foundational facts have been established. Most exceptions to the hearsay rule, for example, require such a preliminary showing. Similarly, a foundation must be laid for the admission of evidence of habit or routine practice[5] or for the admission of evidence of subsequent remedial measures.[6] It is impossible to generalize about such prereq-

2. *See* FED. R. EVID. 901(a), which provides: "To satisfy the requirement of authenticating or identifying an item of evidence, the proponent must produce evidence sufficient to support a finding that the item is what the proponent claims it is."
3. *See, e.g.*, FED. R. EVID. 104(a): "The court must decide any preliminary questions about whether . . . evidence is admissible. In so deciding, the court is not bound by evidence rules, except those on privilege."
4. Alternative means for authenticating telephone conversations are discussed in section 10.2.2.2.
5. *See* FED. R. EVID. 406.
6. *See id.* 407.

uisites except to say that the advocate must be aware of the rule of evidence under which each item of evidence is proffered. As is discussed in detail below, a foundation can then be tailored to meet the rule's requirements.

10.1.3 Establishing Foundations

10.1.3.1 Using a Single Witness

The most common approach to establishing a foundation is simply to call a witness who can provide the necessary facts and then offer the evidence after that testimony has been elicited. Consider this example from the direct examination of the plaintiff in our fire engine case:[7]

> Q: Do you recognize the object that I am showing you, which has been marked as Plaintiff's Exhibit 12?
>
> A: Yes, it is the neck brace that I got from my doctor.
>
> Q: When did you get it from your doctor?
>
> A: When I was discharged from the hospital following the accident.
>
> Q: What is it made of?
>
> A: Stiff plastic.
>
> Q: Do you still wear it?
>
> A: Yes, I have to wear it at least eight hours a day.

Counsel may now offer the neck brace into evidence. Its relevance to the issue of damages is apparent from the context of the case, its authenticity as the actual neck brace has been established by the witness, and there are no special evidentiary considerations that govern the admission of this real evidence.

10.1.3.2 Using Multiple Witnesses

Some foundations cannot be laid by a single witness. In such cases, counsel must establish separate parts of the foundation from each of several witnesses before offering the evidence. In a purse-snatching case, for example, it may be necessary to call two witnesses to lay the foundation for the admission of the stolen purse. First, the arresting officer:

> Q: Officer, do you recognize Prosecution Exhibit 1?
>
> A: Yes. It is a lady's purse that was in the possession of the defendant when I arrested him.

7. This example is slightly truncated. A fuller discussion of the steps for offering real evidence is found in section 10.3.2.1.

The officer has laid some of the foundation, but not all of it. The defendant's possession of a purse is not relevant until it is shown to have been stolen. It is therefore necessary to call the crime victim:

> Q: Ma'am, do you recognize prosecution exhibit 1?
>
> A: Yes. It is my pocketbook.
>
> Q: Before today, when was the last time that you saw it?
>
> A: The last time I saw it was when it was ripped off of my shoulder by a purse snatcher.

Now the purse is admissible. The victim provided the missing aspect of relevance, and she also authenticated the purse as the object that was stolen.

Note that it is possible to combine both direct and cross-examinations to lay a single foundation. Thus, defense counsel can begin to lay a foundation during the cross-examination of a plaintiff's witness and can conclude the foundation during the defendant's case-in-chief. Assume, for example, that the defendant wants to introduce a letter from the plaintiff. To be admissible, it must be shown both that the plaintiff wrote the letter and that the defendant received it. Defense counsel can begin the foundation during the plaintiff's case by having the plaintiff authenticate his own signature on cross-examination. The foundation can later be completed by having the defendant testify during her own case that the letter was actually received.

10.1.3.3 Conditional Admissibility

It is not always possible to complete a foundation during the testimony of a single witness. However, a witness who is responsible for part of the foundation will in many cases have other important information concerning the exhibit. In the absence of a special rule, this witness could not testify about the exhibit until a second witness had been called to complete the foundation. Only then could the first witness return to the stand to complete his testimony about the exhibit.

Fortunately, such an awkward and inefficient procedure is generally not necessary. The courts have developed the doctrine of conditional admissibility, which allows the temporary or conditional admission of the evidence based on counsel's representation that the foundation will be completed through the testimony of a subsequent witness.[8]

In the above purse-snatching case the prosecution might want to elicit further testimony about the purse from the arresting officer:

---

8. Fed. R. Evid. 104(b) provides: "When the relevance of evidence depends on whether a fact exists, proof must be introduced sufficient to support a finding that the fact does exist. The court may admit the proposed evidence on the condition that the proof be introduced later."

Prosecutor: Officer, do you recognize Prosecution Exhibit 1?

A: Yes. It is a lady's purse that the defendant was concealing under his jacket when I arrested him.

Prosecutor: Officer, please show us how the defendant was concealing the purse when you arrested him.

Defense: Objection. There is no foundation for this demonstration.

Prosecutor: Your Honor, we will complete the foundation when we call the victim, who will testify that Exhibit 1 is the same purse that was stolen from her.

Court: On the basis of counsel's representation, the objection is overruled.

The further testimony of the officer has been conditionally allowed, subject to the perfection of the foundation. In the event that the victim does not identify the purse, all of the conditionally accepted testimony will be subject to a motion to strike.

10.1.3.4 Using Adverse Witnesses

Potentially complex foundations can often be simplified through adverse examination. In a case where executed contracts have been exchanged through the mail, for example, it may be extremely difficult for one party to authenticate the other party's signature. This problem can be completely alleviated, however, simply by calling the opposing party as an adverse witness:

Q: Are you the defendant in this case?

A: I am.

Q: Is this your signature at the bottom of Plaintiff's Exhibit 1?

A: Yes, it is.

The signature has now been authenticated.

10.1.3.5 Cross-Examination

Foundation requirements apply equally during cross- and direct examinations. Testimonial foundations must be laid on cross-examination for personal knowledge, voice identification, hearsay exceptions, and in every other circumstance where a foundation would be necessary on direct examination. In addition, there are special foundations for certain cross-examination techniques such as impeachment by past omission or prior inconsistent statement.

It is also often necessary to use cross-examination to lay the foundation for the admission of exhibits. Defense counsel in particular can avoid the need to call adverse witnesses by attempting to establish foundations for her own exhibits while cross-examining a plaintiff's witness.

In some jurisdictions, however, exhibits cannot actually be offered other than in counsel's case-in-chief. In such jurisdictions, you may proceed to elicit the appropriate foundational testimony during cross-examination, but you must delay actually offering the exhibits until the other side has rested. Following this rule, a plaintiff's attorney who develops the foundation for exhibits while cross-examining defense witnesses must wait until the defense has rested, and may then offer the exhibits on rebuttal.

The "case-in-chief" rule is very difficult to justify analytically. Counsel can develop affirmative testimonial evidence on cross-examination, and there is no good reason to treat real or documentary evidence any differently. Moreover, delaying the offer of an exhibit until after cross-examination also delays any objections to the exhibit. This may prove awkward in situations where an objection is sustained for some technical reason and the witness is no longer on the stand to cure the defect.

It is far preferable to be able to offer exhibits on cross-examination. Nonetheless, the case-in-chief rule must be followed where it exists.

10.2 Foundations for Testimonial Evidence

10.2.1 Personal Knowledge

Witnesses are expected to testify from personal knowledge.[9] The most common sort of personal knowledge is direct sensory perception—information gained through sight, hearing, touch, taste, and smell. Witnesses may also have personal knowledge of more subjective information, such as their own intentions or emotions or the reputation of another person.

Whatever the content of the witness's testimony, it is necessary to lay a foundation showing that the witness is testifying either from personal knowledge or on the basis of an acceptable substitute, as in the case of expert testimony.[10]

9. *See* Fed. R. Evid. 602: "A witness may testify to a matter only if evidence is introduced sufficient to support a finding that he has personal knowledge of the matter. Evidence to prove personal knowledge may consist of the witness's own testimony."

10. Expert witnesses are not required to testify from personal knowledge. The foundation for expert testimony is discussed in section 8.2.

In the case of sensory perception, the basic foundation is simply that the witness was in a position to observe or otherwise experience the relevant facts:

Q: Where were you on the afternoon of March 17?

A: I was at the corner of State and Madison.

Q: What were you doing?

A: I was watching the St. Patrick's Day parade.

Q: Please tell us what you saw.

Or,

Q: What was your last meal before you went to the hospital?

A: I had a tuna sandwich at a restaurant called Kate's Corner.

Q: How did it taste?

A: It was warm, and it tasted sort of sour.

Q: Did you finish it?

A: No, because of the way it tasted.

In ordinary circumstances it is not necessary to establish more than the witness's general basis for testifying. Witnesses are assumed to have all of their senses in order, so, for example, counsel is not required to show that the witness's eyesight is unimpaired or that the witness was familiar with right-tasting tuna sandwiches. In some situations, however, additional foundation may be called for to establish fully the basis of the witness's testimony:

Q: Where were you on the afternoon of March 17?

A: I was in my office on the twenty-eighth floor of the National Bank Building.

Q: What were you doing?

A: I was watching the St. Patrick's Day parade.

Q: Were you able to see the people on the floats?

A: Yes.

Q: How is that?

A: I was using binoculars.

Or,

Q: What happened when you were standing in the workshop?

A: I heard a high-pitched, mechanical, whining sound in the next room.

Q: Could you tell what it was?

A: Yes.

Q: How could you tell?

A: I have worked in the workshop before, and I heard that sound when I saw the machines operating.

Q: What was the sound?

The foundations in the above scenarios are actually slightly overdone. In simple cases such as these, most witnesses will be allowed to provide the basis of the perception either before or after testifying to the facts. Thus, in the machine-shop example, most judges would allow the witness first to identify the noise and then to explain why she could recognize it.

Apart from the personal knowledge rule, special foundations are required for certain sorts of testimony. Special foundations may also be necessary to bring testimony within an exception to the hearsay rule. These foundations are discussed in the following sections.

10.2.2 Special Foundations for Certain Testimonial Evidence

While most testimony requires a showing of personal knowledge, certain testimony calls for the establishment of additional foundational facts.

10.2.2.1 Conversations

Witnesses are often called on to testify to conversations between two or more parties. To authenticate the conversation, and thereby allow opposing counsel to conduct a meaningful cross-examination, testimony concerning a conversation generally must be supported by a foundation establishing the date, time, and place of the conversation, as well as the persons present at the time. For example:

Q: Did you complain to anyone about the quality of the printing job?

A: Yes, I spoke to the store manager, Alex Rose.

Q: When did you speak to the manager?

A: On April 18, the same day that I refused to accept the product.

Q: About what time was that?

A: I believe that it was just before noon, but it may have been somewhat later.

Q: Where were you when you spoke?

A: We were at the service counter.

Q: Was anybody else present?

A: There was a clerk nearby, but she wasn't involved in the conversation.

Q: Please tell us what was said during that conversation.

This foundation demonstrates the authenticity of the conversation. The witness's ability to relate the time, date, place, and participants provides sufficient evidence that the conversation happened as she says it did. It is not necessary to lay the foundation with minute precision. In the above scenario, the witness would not be required to provide the clerk's name or the exact time of the conversation. The foundation is sufficient as long as it fulfills its purpose of providing opposing counsel with reasonably sufficient information with which to challenge or contest the witness's testimony.

Note, however, that the authentication of the conversation does not resolve any hearsay or other evidentiary problems that may be raised by its content. Those issues must be addressed separately, often necessitating the development of additional foundation.

10.2.2.2 Telephone Conversations and Voice Identification

The foundation for a telephone conversation includes the additional element of voice identification or of a reasonable circumstantial substitute.

Voice Identification

Voice identification can be based on personal familiarity that either precedes or postdates the telephone conversation in question.[11] For example:

Q: Did you complain to anyone about the quality of the printing job?

A: Yes, I telephoned the store manager, Alex Rose, as soon as I opened the first package.

Q: How do you know that you were speaking to Mr. Rose?

A: I recognized his voice. I have been going to that print shop for years, and I have spoken to Alex many times in person.

11. *See* Fed. R. Evid. 901(b)(5).

The witness could also base voice identification on a subsequent contact with the store manager:

Q: Did you complain to anyone about the quality of the printing job?

A: Yes, I telephoned the store manager, Alex Rose, as soon as I opened the first package.

Q: Had you ever met Mr. Rose?

A: Not at that time.

Q: How do you know that you were speaking to Alex Rose on the phone?

A: I spoke to him in person the next day, and I recognized his voice as the same person from the phone call.

There is no strict time limit for voice identification based on subsequent contact, although a lengthy time lapse will obviously detract from the weight to be given to a contested identification.

Circumstantial Evidence; Listed Numbers

In the absence of a basis for voice identification, circumstantial evidence can be used as the foundation for a telephone conversation. A telephone call placed by the witness can be authenticated by showing that the call was made to a listed number.[12] Again:

Q: Did you complain to anyone about the quality of the printing job?

A: Yes, I telephoned the store as soon as I opened the first package.

Q: How did you obtain the number?

A: I looked it up in a Web directory.

Q: Did you dial the number that was listed in the directory?

A: Yes.

Q: What did you say when the telephone was answered?

A: I said that I wanted to complain about the quality of the printing job that I had just picked up.

Under the Federal Rules of Evidence, the above foundation is sufficient in the case of a business, as long as the conversation related to "business reasonably trans-

12. *See* FED. R. EVID. 901(b)(6), which uses the phrase "the number assigned at the time to: (A) a particular person . . .; or (B) a particular business . . . ."

acted over the telephone."[13] There is a presumption that the person who answers a business telephone is authorized to speak for the business.

In the case of an individual, however, the foundation must also include "circumstances, including self-identification, [that] show that the person answering was the one called."[14]

Other Circumstantial Evidence

Many other circumstances can be used to authenticate telephone conversations. Subsequent verifying events can form the foundation for telephone calls either placed or received by the witness. In the following example, the witness both placed and received a telephone call:

Q: Did you ever speak to Mr. Hill after the incident?

A: Yes, I looked up his number, and I called his home.

Q: Did you speak to Mr. Hill?

A: No, a woman answered the telephone.

Q: What did you do?

A: I left my name and number, and I asked for Mr. Hill to call me back.

Q: Did you ever receive a return call?

A: Yes, I received a call the next day.

Q: What did the party say?

A: He said, "This is Arthur Hill. I am returning your call from yesterday."

Note that the placement of a call to an individual's listed number is not alone sufficient to lay the foundation for a conversation. Additional verifying facts must be established. In this example, both the first and second conversations are verified by the following circumstances of the return call: 1) Hill's self-identification; 2) the stated response to the initial message; and 3) the listing of Hill's number in the telephone directory.

Circumstantial evidence authenticating telephone calls received by a witness must include specific information that tends to identify the caller. Calls placed by the witness are commonly authenticated circumstantially on the basis of the number dialed. Such evidence can include reference to listings other than in the telephone directory, perhaps on company stationery or advertising material.

13. *Id.* 901(b)(6)(B).
14. *Id.* 901(b)(6)(A).

10.2.2.3 Prior Identification

Under the Federal Rules of Evidence a witness may testify to his previous out-of-court identification of an individual.[15] While such evidence is most commonly offered in criminal cases to bolster the in-court identification made at trial,[16] it also has its uses in civil matters. The foundation for this testimony is that the out-of-court identification was made by the witness after perceiving the person identified:

Q: Were you able to see the person who stole your car?

A: Yes. He was driving away in it just as I got home from work. I saw him from the shoulders up.

Q: How far away were you when you first saw him?

A: I was about thirty feet away.

Q: Did you ever see him again?

A: Yes, I picked him out of a lineup.

Q: Where and when was that?

A: About four days later at the police station.

Q: Please describe the circumstances of the lineup.

A: There were five men standing in a row. They were all about the same height, and they were all wearing blue jeans and flannel shirts. I identified the man who was second from the left.

Q: Was that the same man whom you identified here in court today?

A: Yes.

10.2.2.4 Habit and Routine

Testimonial evidence of habit or routine practice may be admitted as circumstantial evidence that a person or organization acted in a similar fashion on a particular occasion.[17] The subject matter of such testimony can range from an individual's clothing preferences to a business's routine for sending packages. In each case, the evidence of a regular custom or practice is offered to prove that the individual or business acted in the same way at a time relevant to the issues at trial.

15. Fed. R. Evid. 801(d)(1)(C). Note that statements of prior identification are excluded from the definition of hearsay and therefore are admissible to "prove the truth of the matter asserted."

16. In-court identifications may be less than compelling since the physical arrangement of the courtroom will often serve to point the witness in the direction of the party to be identified. In criminal cases, for example, the defendant will usually be seated at counsel table next to the defense lawyer. Out-of-court identifications, on the other hand, are more likely to test the witness's initial observation. Proof that the witness picked the defendant out of a lineup, for example, will significantly bolster the subsequent in-court identification.

17. Fed. R. Evid. 406.

To lay the foundation for evidence of habit or routine practice it is necessary to call a witness with personal knowledge of the regular conduct of the person or organization involved. Furthermore, counsel must establish that the asserted conduct was, in fact, of a consistently repeated nature. This can be accomplished through proof of either extended observation or the existence of a formal policy or procedure.

Individual Habit

The most common foundation for an individual's habit is through evidence of a pattern of conduct repeated over a substantial period of time. The alleged habit must be clearly differentiated from independent or distinct activities.

In the following example, assume that the defendant is charged with stabbing a man to death. Pleading self-defense, the defendant claims that it was the victim who attacked him with a knife, which he took away and used to defend himself. Habit evidence will be offered by the prosecution to show that the defendant always carried a knife:

Q: How long have you known the defendant, Richard Levin?

A: About five years.

Q: In what context do you know him?

A: We are neighbors. He lives next door to me.

Q: During the last five years, how often have you seen the defendant?

A: On average, I would say that I have seen him at least twice a week.

Q: On those occasions, did you ever see the defendant carry a knife?

A: Yes. He always carried a hunting knife strapped to his belt.

Q: How often did you see the defendant with a hunting knife?

A: Whenever he went out of the house, he always had that knife on his belt.

Q: Did you ever see him go out of the house without a knife on his belt?

A: Only once.

Q: What was that occasion?

A: He was going to a wedding in a tuxedo.

The evidence of the defendant's constant habit over an extended period of time is admissible to prove that he was carrying a knife on the date in question.

Business Practice

The routine practice of a business or organization may be established through either direct observation or evidence of an existing policy or practice. In the following example, assume that a dispute exists over whether an employee's references were checked before she was hired by a large corporation. Although the employee's file was marked "OK," no one can specifically remember making the reference checks. The company must therefore rely on proof of their business practice. First, through direct experience:

Q: What is your position at the Judson Corporation?

A: I work in personnel. I am in charge of checking references.

Q: How long have you held that position?

A: Six years.

Q: How do you go about checking references?

A: Once a potential employee has been approved by the department head, the next step is to check references. The file comes to me, and I personally telephone every listed reference.

Q: What happens after you telephone the references?

A: If all of the references are positive I mark the file "OK" and send it on to the personnel manager. If they are negative I mark it "failed" before I send it on.

Q: Have you ever marked a file "OK" when you haven't telephoned the references?

A: No. Not in my entire six years at the Judson Company.

Q: Was that the practice that you followed during April of last year?

A: Absolutely.

Q: Did anyone else handle reference checks during that period?

A: No. I was the only one.

The witness's testimony of her own business routine is proof that she adhered to that custom during the time period in question.

Now assume that there were a number of employees who did reference checks during the relevant time period and that several of them have left the company. Furthermore, the "OK" notation on the file was made by a rubber stamp:

Q: What is your position at the Judson Corporation?

A: I work in personnel. I am in charge of checking references.

Q: How long have you held that position?

A: Six years.

Q: Do other employees also check references?

A: Yes. Over the years there have been four or five of us who have made the actual telephone calls.

Q: Does the Judson Company have a written policy regarding reference checks?

A: Yes. Once a potential employee has been approved by the department head, the next step is to check references. The file comes to our department, and someone personally telephones every listed reference. If all of the references are positive, the file is stamped "OK" and sent on to the personnel manager. If they are negative, it is stamped "failed" before it is sent on.

Q: Was that policy provided in writing to every employee in your department?

A: Yes.

Q: Does the written policy of the Judson Company permit a file to be stamped "OK" if the references have not been telephoned?

A: Definitely not.

Q: Was that policy in effect during April of last year?

A: Yes it was.

Even without personal observation, the witness's knowledge of the company's business policy[18] provides a sufficient foundation for the introduction of the routine practice.

10.2.2.5 Character and Reputation

Evidence of a person's character generally is not admissible to prove "that on a particular occasion the person acted in conformance with the character or trait."[19] For example, counsel may not offer proof of a person's dislike of children as evidence that he committed a kidnapping. There are, however, a number of exceptions that allow the admission of character evidence for a variety of purposes.[20] Each exception requires the establishment of its own foundation.

---

18. Since the witness testified to the content of a written policy, further foundation might be necessary to comply with the "best evidence" or "original writing" rule. *See* section 10.5.2.

19. Fed. R. Evid. 404(a).

20. The uses of character evidence for impeachment are discussed in section 6.4.

Other Crimes or Past Misconduct

Following the general rule, evidence of past crimes or other wrongful conduct is not admissible to prove the occurrence of a specific event. Three previous burglaries cannot be offered to show that a defendant is a burglar, nor can three previous automobile accidents be used to prove that a tort plaintiff was guilty of contributory negligence. Past misconduct—including uncharged crimes—may, however, be admitted for other purposes "such as proving motive, opportunity, intent, preparation, plan, knowledge, identity, absence of mistake, or lack of accident."[21]

The foundation for such evidence must include the specifics of the past act as well as the circumstances that make it usable for a permissible purpose in the case at trial. Assume that the defendant in the following example is an employer who is being prosecuted for intentionally failing to pay the previous year's employee withholding taxes to the government. The defendant admits the conduct, but claims that it was an unintentional oversight. The prosecution has called a tax examiner to the stand:

Q: What is your occupation?

A: I am an auditor for the Internal Revenue Service.

Q: Have you audited the records of the defendant's business?

A: Yes, I audited the records for the last seven years.

Q: Exactly what records did you review?

A: I looked at all of the payroll records, including the time sheets and check stubs for every employee.

Q: Were you able to determine anything with regard to withholding taxes?

A: Yes. In each of the last seven years, the amount of money withheld from employees' paychecks was more than the amount paid over to the government.

Q: What was the difference last year?

A: Last year, the defendant withheld $55,000 more from employees than was paid to the government for their withholding taxes.

Q: And in the preceding six years?

A: The amounts for the previous six years were $40,000; $32,000; $51,000; $39,000; $46,000; and $42,000.

Q: Did the defendant submit withholding tax returns in each of the last seven years?

21. Fed. R. Evid. 404(b).

A: Yes. They were submitted and signed by the defendant in each of the last seven years, but they never accurately reflected the amount of money deducted from employees' paychecks.

The defendant has not been charged with failing to pay withholding taxes other than in the most recent year. The government may not offer the other tax records to show that the defendant was an habitual tax cheat. Nonetheless, evidence of the past misconduct is admissible to show either intent or absence of mistake in filing last year's return.

Note that the foundation included the basis of the witness's knowledge, the precise records that were reviewed, the relationship of the records to the withholding return, the years in which underpayments were made, and the defendant's personal involvement in signing the returns.

Reputation for Untruthfulness

Once a witness has testified, it is permissible for the opposing party to offer evidence of the witness's reputation in the community for untruthfulness. This is typically done by calling another witness to the stand who has knowledge of the first witness's reputation in the community. This evidence can be offered only to reflect on the credibility of the first witness's testimony.

The foundation for such reputation evidence includes identification of the relevant community, the basis of the witness's knowledge, and the nature of the first witness's reputation during a relevant time period. Note that the "community" involved may be residential, professional, social, or the like. Assume that the plaintiff has already testified in our fire engine case. The defendant has now called a witness to testify regarding the plaintiff's reputation for untruthfulness:

Q: Do you know the plaintiff?

A: Yes, I have known her for four years.

Q: In what context do you know her?

A: We belong to the same hiking club. It's called the Campside Walkers.

Q: Are you familiar with the plaintiff's reputation for truth and veracity among the Campside Walkers?

A: Yes. Her reputation is very bad. She is regarded within the club as an untruthful person.

Q: Was that her reputation as of last Tuesday when she testified?

A: Yes, it was.

In many jurisdictions, a witness may also testify about her opinion of a previous witness's untruthfulness.[22] The foundation is similar to that for reputation testimony:

Q: Do you know the plaintiff?

A: Yes, I have known her for four years.

Q: In what context do you know her?

A: We belong to the same hiking club, the Campside Walkers.

Q: How often have you spoken to the plaintiff during those four years?

A: Well, the club meets once a month, and both of us usually attend the meetings. In addition, we have gone on many long hikes together, and on at least three occasions we went on weekend camping trips.

Q: Based on your contacts with the plaintiff, do you have an opinion concerning her truthfulness?

A: Yes, I do. My opinion is that she is not a truthful person.

Once a witness has given reputation or opinion evidence concerning another's untruthfulness, the cross-examiner may then inquire as to "relevant specific instances of the person's conduct."[23] Additionally, once the character of a witness has been attacked, the proponent of the witness may proceed to offer evidence of the witness's good reputation for truthfulness.

Character Traits of Criminal Defendant or Crime Victim

Notwithstanding the general rule, a criminal defendant may always offer evidence of a pertinent character trait such as honesty, truthfulness, or peacefulness. This evidence may come in the form of reputation or opinion. Courts have also been known to allow evidence of specific incidents of good conduct, often under the rubric of "foundation" for the witness's opinion or reputation testimony. Once the accused has offered evidence of good character, the prosecution may offer the same sorts of evidence in rebuttal.[24] It is up to the defendant to initiate the admissibility of character evidence; the prosecution may not launch a preemptive attack.

In the same vein, a criminal defendant may offer evidence of a relevant character trait of the crime victim, which may then be rebutted in similar fashion by the

22. Fed. R. Evid. 405(a).
23. *Id.*
24. *Id.* 404(a)(1).

prosecution.[25] Finally, even in the absence of initial evidence from the defense, the prosecution may use reputation, opinion, or specific conduct evidence of the "peaceful" character traits of a homicide victim in order to prove that the victim was not the "first aggressor."[26]

10.2.3 Foundations for Hearsay Statements

The rule against hearsay excludes evidence of out-of-court statements if offered to prove the truth of the matter asserted.[27] Numerous exceptions to the hearsay rule allow for the admissibility of out-of-court statements, provided that the necessary foundation is established. The foundations for those exceptions that apply primarily to testimonial evidence are discussed below. Foundations for hearsay exceptions that typically apply to documentary evidence are discussed in a later section.[28] The following sections are intended only as an outline of the foundations for the various hearsay exceptions, not as a complete treatment of the complexities or rationale for the hearsay rule itself.

10.2.3.1 Opposing Party Statements (Party Admissions)

Out-of-court statements made by the opposing party are generally admissible to prove the truth of the matter asserted. Opposing party statements (sometimes called party admissions) constituted a hearsay exception at common law and are excluded from the definition of hearsay under the Federal Rules of Evidence.[29] Notwithstanding the approach of the federal rules, most lawyers continue to find it convenient to refer to the "exception" for statements by a party-opponent.

In brief, the previous statements of the opposing party are admissible if: 1) the witness can authenticate the statement, 2) the statement was made by the party against whom it is offered, and 3) the statement is adverse to the opposing party's claim or defense.[30] In the following example the witness is a police officer who

25. Note that Fed. R. Evid. 412 places severe restrictions on the admissibility of evidence concerning the past conduct or reputation of victims of rape or sexual assault. Specifically, "evidence offered to prove a victim's sexual predisposition" is not admissible. A similar provision applies to direct evidence of the victim's past conduct. Virtually every state has adopted some version of this important and beneficial rule.
26. Fed. R. Evid. 404(a)(2).
27. *Id.* 801.
28. *See* section 10.5.3.
29. Fed. R. Evid. 801(d)(2). Prior to the 2011 revisions, the Federal Rules of Evidence used the term "admission by a party opponent," which is still in use in most states and will be readily recognized by lawyers and judges for years to come. The new language, however, avoids the ambiguity inherent in the word "admission," thus making it clearer that the principle applies quite generally to the statements of an opposing party and not only to so-called "admissions" (however that might be characterized).
30. Opposing party statements may be received in written as well as testimonial form. The foundation for a written party statement—such as a letter, memorandum, or report—is the same as that for an oral one. Where the statement is contained in a document, however, all of the other general requisites for the admissibility of an exhibit must be present.

investigated an automobile accident. The direct examination is being conducted by plaintiff's counsel:

Q: Officer, did you speak to anyone after you arrived at the scene of the accident?

A: I spoke to both drivers, Mr. Weiss and Ms. Gable.

Q: Was that the same Mr. Weiss who is the defendant in this case?

A: Yes.

Q: Who was present when you spoke with Mr. Weiss?

A: Only the two of us.

Q: When did that conversation take place?

A: At approximately 10:00 a.m. on December 19.

Q: Where did it take place?

A: At the intersection of Ridge and Central.

Q: Did Mr. Weiss say anything about the cause of the accident?

A: Yes. He said that he never saw the other automobile until just before the impact.

The defendant's out-of-court statement is admissible. The witness heard the statement and can identify it as having been made by the party against whom it is being offered. The content of the statement itself demonstrates its adverse nature.

The opposing party statement doctrine applies only to statements offered against the party-declarant. The plaintiff in the above example could not elicit her own favorable statements to the investigating police officer.[31]

The opposing party statement exception also applies to statements made by certain agents or employees of a party. In these situations the exception is available when 1) a party has adopted the statement or manifested a belief in its truth; 2) a party has authorized the declarant to make a statement concerning the subject; or 3) the statement was made by a party's agent or servant, during the existence of the relationship, concerning a matter within the scope of agency or employment.[32] In the following example, assume that the plaintiff is the Quickset Printing Company, which has sued the defendant for nonpayment on a large duplicating order. The defendant is testifying on direct examination:

31. The plaintiff's statements to the officer might, however, be admissible on some other theory such as "excited utterance" or state of mind. *See* sections 10.2.3.–4.
32. Fed. R. Evid. 801(d)(2)(B)–(D).

Q: Did you speak to anyone at Quickset after you received the order?

A: Yes. I went back to the shop, and I spoke to the manager.

Q: How do you know that you were speaking to the manager?

A: I have been doing business with Quickset for years, and I have spoken to the manager many times.

Q: What did you say to the manager?

A: I said that the order was defective and that I would not pay for it.

Q: Did the manager respond?

A: Yes. He said that he didn't expect anyone to pay for defective work and that he would speak to the owner of the company.

Agency and scope having been established, the manager's out-of-court statement is admissible. Note that the testimony also contained a reference to the defendant's own out-of-court statement concerning the defective nature of the order. While the defendant could not offer her own statement as an opposing party statement, it is admissible to provide the context for the manager's response.

10.2.3.2 Present Sense Impression

The present sense impression exception allows the admission of out-of-court statements "describing or explaining an event or condition made while the declarant was perceiving the event or condition, or immediately thereafter."[33] The foundation for the exception, then, is that: 1) the declarant perceived an event; 2) the declarant described the event; and 3) the description was given while the event occurred or immediately afterward. A witness may testify to her own previous statement of a present sense impression, as in this example taken from the fire engine case:

Q: Where were you at about 8:20 a.m. last March 17?

A: I was at the corner of Sheridan and Touhy, walking west on Touhy.

Q: Were you with anyone?

A: Yes, I was with my two children, who are four and six years old. My neighbor was also with us.

Q: Was your attention drawn to a vehicle at that time?

A: I saw a fire engine headed west on Touhy Avenue.

Q: Was the fire engine using its warning signals?

33. *Id.* 803(1).

A: It was flashing its lights and sounding its siren.

Q: Did you say anything about the fire engine to anyone?

A: Yes. I told my children to listen to the siren and to look for the fire truck. I think that my exact words were something like, "Listen kids, whenever you hear a siren like that it means that you have to look out for a fire engine."

Q: When did you say that to your children?

A: Right as the fire truck was passing.

A witness also can often testify to a present sense impression statement made by another. It is generally necessary for the statement to have been made in the witness's presence to satisfy the foundational requirement of personal knowledge.[34]

10.2.3.3 Excited Utterance

The excited utterance exception is quite similar to the present sense impression rule, allowing for the admission of hearsay when the statement relates "to a startling event or condition, made while the declarant was under the stress of excitement that it caused."[35]

The foundation for an excited utterance is that 1) the declarant perceived a startling event or experienced a stressful condition; 2) the declarant made a statement concerning the event or condition; and 3) the statement was made while the declarant was under the stress of the event or condition. As with present sense impressions, a witness may testify to her own excited utterance or to that of another.

---

34. It is possible, however, to "stack" hearsay exceptions to allow testimony concerning secondhand statements. Imagine, for instance, the following chain of events in the fire truck case: a passenger in the defendant's car heard the siren and described it to the defendant, saying, "Listen, I think I hear a fire truck siren." The defendant later mentioned the passenger's remark to the investigating police officer. The officer would be allowed to testify as follows:

Q: Did the defendant say anything to you about a siren?

A: Yes. The defendant said that his passenger told him something like, "Listen, I think I hear a fire truck siren."

The passenger's statement is a present sense impression, and the defendant's recounting of it is an opposing party statement. Each out-of-court statement falls under an independent exception to the hearsay rule. Assuming that the proper foundations are laid, the police officer's testimony is therefore admissible. *See* FED. R. EVID. 805.

The further intricacies of the treatment of "hearsay within hearsay" are beyond the scope of this chapter and will not be discussed in any greater detail.

35. FED. R. EVID. 803(2).

10.2.3.4 State of Mind

"State of mind" provides one of the broadest exceptions to the hearsay rule, as it allows the admission of statements concerning the declarant's "then-existing state of mind (such as motive, intent, plan) or emotional, sensory, or physical condition (such as mental feeling, pain, or bodily health)."[36]

The foundation for this exception is that the statement actually be probative of the declarant's mental, emotional, or physical condition. This can best be demonstrated by the content of the statement itself. Apart from the content of the statement, there is no special foundation for the state of mind exception. However, the witness still must establish the authenticity of the statement by testifying about 1) when the statement was made, 2) where it was made, 3) who was present, and 4) what was said.

Note also that the statement must have been made during the existence of the mental, emotional, or physical condition that it describes.

10.2.3.5 Statement Made for Medical Treatment

The foundation for this exception is that the declarant made a statement for the purpose of obtaining medical care or diagnosis. The statement may be made to a physician, medical worker, or other person, as long as its purpose was to obtain or facilitate treatment. The statement may include medical history or past symptoms, but it must relate to a present bodily condition.[37]

10.2.3.6 Dying Declaration

The hearsay exception for dying declarations requires the following foundation: 1) the declarant made a statement while believing that her death was imminent, 2) concerning what she believed to be the cause of death. At common law it was also required that the declarant had actually died, but under the federal rules it is sufficient that the declarant be unavailable as a witness.[38]

The declarant's belief that death was imminent can be established by surrounding circumstances, such as the nature of an illness or injury or by the declarant's own words. The content of the statement will generally be sufficient to show that it related to the declarant's belief as to the cause of death.

Under the federal rules, dying declarations are admissible only in civil cases or homicide prosecutions. The exception is not available in criminal cases other than homicides.

---

36. *Id.* 803(3).
37. *Id.* 803(4).
38. *Id.* 804(b)(2).

10.3 Exhibits

10.3.1 The Role of Exhibits

Exhibits are the tangible objects, documents, photographs, video and audiotapes, digital recordings, and other items that are offered for the jury's consideration. Exhibits are the only form, apart from the testimony of witnesses, in which evidence can be received. Spoken testimony typically presents the jury with a recitation of the witness's memories and perceptions. As effective as testimony might be, it remains a secondhand account that is, at best, once removed from the jurors' own experiences. Exhibits, on the other hand, allow the jurors to use their own senses and perceptions. It is one thing to hear somebody describe, for example, the texture of a piece of cloth; it is far more striking actually to run your hand over the material itself. Your direct experience will be infinitely more informative than listening to another person's description. Having touched the cloth, you will remember it better, you will appreciate more of its texture, and you will be much less likely to change your mind about it in the future.

Life is full of experiences that cannot truly be described, and exhibits bring reality into the courtroom in a way that spoken testimony will never approach. Imagine the melody of the last popular song that you heard on the radio. No matter how simple the tune, even the most gifted critic cannot recapture it in words. The use of a CD or MP3 player, however, can re-create the experience almost exactly. The same is true of visual exhibits. Think of a scene as commonplace as the street immediately outside the room in which you are sitting. It would take hours to describe everything that you could see there, and even then you would be unable to capture all of the colors, distances, spatial relationships, angles, and other particulars.

A photograph can depict these details, and numerous others, all at once. At trial, exhibits enhance or supplement the testimony of the witnesses. Exhibits can make information clearer, more concrete, more understandable, and more reliable. The sections immediately following will discuss the general procedures for the introduction of exhibits.

10.3.2 Types of Exhibits

Although the categories tend to overlap and the lines cannot be drawn with precision, it is often helpful to think of exhibits as falling into these three categories: 1) real or tangible evidence, 2) demonstrative evidence, and 3) documentary evidence.

10.3.2.1 Real Evidence

The term "real evidence" generally refers to tangible objects that played an actual role in the events at issue in the trial.

The proceeds or instrumentalities of the crime are often introduced in criminal cases. Typical examples might include the "marked money" recovered in a suspect's possession, the bullet casing found at the scene of the crime, an item of clothing that the defendant was wearing when arrested, or a quantity of narcotics seized by the police.

Real evidence is also used in all categories of civil cases. In personal injury cases, it is common for plaintiff's counsel to introduce objects that allegedly caused or contributed to the injury. Such real evidence might include a frayed wire that led to a steering failure or a rusty canister that failed to contain a corrosive liquid. Similarly, defense counsel in a tort case would be expected to introduce the actual safety devices that were available to, but ignored by, the plaintiff. Real evidence in a commercial dispute might include samples of allegedly nonconforming goods.

Photographs and videos, while obviously different from tangible objects, are so close to reality that they are also often treated as real evidence. Documents such as contracts, memoranda, letters, and other primary writings can also be considered real evidence, although the special rules that apply to out-of-court writings generally make it more convenient to treat "documentary evidence" as a separate category.

10.3.2.2 Demonstrative Evidence

The term "demonstrative evidence" refers to exhibits that did not play an actual role in the events underlying the case, but that are used to illustrate or clarify a witness's testimony. Demonstrative evidence can take the form of models, animations, graphs, diagrams, charts, drawings, or any other objects that can explain or illustrate issues in the case.

A familiar form of demonstrative evidence is the simple intersection diagram on which a witness can indicate the locations of the automobiles involved in an accident. The intersection itself, not the diagram, would constitute real evidence of the configuration of the streets. The diagram, however, may be used to demonstrate the relative positions of the cars, traffic signals, and witnesses. It is easy to see why demonstrative evidence can be superior to real evidence—the intersection cannot be transported into the courtroom. And even if the jurors were to be taken to the scene of the accident, it would still be extremely difficult for the lawyers to push real automobiles around at the instruction of the witnesses.

Another common type of demonstrative evidence is the "comparison" object. In many cases, it is not possible to produce the original objects involved—they may have been destroyed, lost, or concealed. It is therefore permissible to use a similar object for the purpose of illustration. Imagine an automobile accident in which a young child was injured. If the child's safety seat was destroyed in the crash, either party could use an identical seat to demonstrate, for example, how the child fit into it and how it was fastened.

More complex displays are also possible. An anatomical model of a human shoulder can be used to show the effects of surgery on an individual's ability to move or work. "Day in the life" videos have been used with great impact to demonstrate the limitations and obstacles faced by accident victims and the extraordinary effort and expense that is necessary to cope with severe injuries. Computer simulations can rotate or enlarge objects; animations can virtually re-create past events or depict complex interactions.

The distinguishing feature of demonstrative evidence is that it is lawyer-generated. Real evidence exists by virtue of the activities of the parties and witnesses in the case. Counsel can search for it, discover it, preserve it, and use it, but a lawyer can never create real evidence. Demonstrative evidence is not intrinsic to the case. It is never handed to counsel, but must be developed by the attorneys as an aspect of the presentation of the case.

The production of demonstrative evidence is a creative task. It allows counsel, in effect, to dream about ways of presenting a case and then to fashion those dreams into a persuasive reality. The attorney must constantly ask, "How can I make this testimony more concrete?" Or, "How can I help the jury visualize this point?" Or, "Is there a way to accentuate the relationship between these two ideas?" The answer will often be found in the development of demonstrative exhibits.

10.3.2.3 Documentary Evidence

"Documentary evidence" is the term used to refer to virtually all writings, including letters, contracts, leases, memoranda, reports, ledgers, printouts, and business records. Written documents, almost by definition, contain out-of-court statements, and they are typically offered because their contents are relevant to the case. Thus, most documents face hearsay hurdles in a way that real and demonstrative exhibits do not. Tangible objects are admitted into evidence because of what they are; documentary exhibits are admitted because of what they say.

The value of documentary evidence cannot be overstated. Intrinsic writings can provide proof of past events in a way that mere testimony cannot. Imagine a criminal case in which the defendant has raised an alibi defense, claiming that on the day of the crime he was visiting relatives in a distant city. The testimony of the defendant and his family is relevant and admissible to establish the alibi, but it will be subject to vigorous attack on cross-examination. A signed hotel receipt for the date in question stands to be far more persuasive than any witness as to the defendant's whereabouts.

Documentary evidence has the power to document past events. Barring fraud or forgery, contemporaneous writings often provide the best proof possible. For that reason counsel must always take pains to ensure that all potentially relevant documents are discovered. Thorough searches must be made not only of the client's files, but also of every conceivable third-party source. Many businesses, institutions, and even individuals keep copious records and notes. It is the lawyer's job to inquire into and investigate every conceivable source of favorable documentary evidence.

Perhaps more than any other form of evidence, however, documents have the potential to overwhelm the trier of fact. Only the most determined judge or juror will have the patience to wade through a foot-tall stack of reports to extract some evidentiary gem. Thus, while your search for documents should be exhaustive, your presentation of documents must be judicious. Truly important exhibits can be emphasized effectively only if trivial or repetitive ones are omitted. The final section of this chapter deals in greater depth with the persuasive use of documentary evidence and other exhibits.

10.3.3 Pretrial Procedures for the Admission of Exhibits

The foundations for various exhibits can be lengthy and cumbersome even when the eventual admissibility of the exhibit is not really in doubt. At trial, foundation testimony can be boring and repetitive; worse, it can distract attention from the truly contested issues in the case. For this reason the courts have developed a number of streamlined procedures that allow pretrial rulings on the admissibility of exhibits, including real, demonstrative, and documentary evidence.

10.3.3.1 Pretrial Conferences and Orders

Most jurisdictions now require pretrial conferences, especially in large or complex cases. Under the Federal Rules of Civil Procedure, for example, parties may be required to attend one or more pretrial conferences at which the court may rule in advance "on the admissibility of evidence."[39]

Many federal judges have adopted a routine practice of requiring the parties to submit written pretrial orders identifying every exhibit that they anticipate offering at trial. Counsel must also indicate whether or not they object to each other's proposed exhibits, giving the basis for the objection. Where there is no objection, the exhibit will automatically be received. Rulings on contested exhibits may be made at a pretrial conference or may be reserved until trial.

In jurisdictions that use extensive pretrial practice, every exhibit may be ruled on in advance of the trial. Lawyers will therefore know exactly which exhibits have been admitted and which have been refused, thereby freeing counsel of the necessity of expending valuable trial time on unnecessary foundations.

---

39. Fed. R. Civ. P. 16(c)(2)(C).

10.3.3.2 Motions in Limine

Even in the absence of a formalized pretrial process it is possible to secure advance decisions on the admissibility of exhibits with the motion in limine.[40] Contrary to some opinion, the motion in limine is not merely the civil analog to the motion to suppress evidence in criminal cases. Although the motion in limine is most commonly used to obtain the exclusion of evidence, there is no reason that it cannot also be used affirmatively to seek a ruling that certain evidence is admissible. "In limine" means "at the threshold," and there is nothing about the motion that restricts its use to excluding evidence.

The reason to object to evidence before trial is obvious. An order barring the use of an exhibit will prevent opposing counsel from referring to it during the opening statement or from displaying it to the jurors while ostensibly laying a foundation.

It can be equally useful to obtain a pretrial ruling allowing an exhibit into evidence. Advance knowledge that an exhibit will be admissible allows counsel to prepare an opening statement that takes full advantage of the exhibit, but which does not risk a reprimand from the court or reversible error. By the same token, knowing that an exhibit has been admitted will permit the attorney to work it more easily into direct and cross-examinations.

10.3.3.3 Stipulations

In situations where judicial involvement is unavailable, impractical, or unnecessary, pretrial admissibility of an exhibit may still be obtained by stipulation. A stipulation is an agreement between counsel about some aspect of the case. Lawyers may stipulate, for example, to the filing of an amended pleading or to the existence of a certain set of facts. While judges are technically free to reject stipulations, this is seldom done other than in the case of over-reaching or abuse.[41]

Stipulations to the admissibility of exhibits are almost uniformly honored by the courts since they really amount to nothing more than a pretrial agreement not to object to certain evidence. Since the stipulating attorney would be equally free to refrain from objecting at trial, the end result of the stipulation is to save time for all concerned.

There is no formal procedure for obtaining a stipulation.[42] Any lawyer may request a stipulation from opposing counsel, who may either refuse or accede. This can be done by letter, telephone conversation, at a meeting, or in court. Informal stipulations, however, and especially oral ones, have a maddening way of dissolving or becoming ambiguous at trial. It is therefore desirable to reduce stipulations to

40. *See* section 9.2.1.2.

41. It was once common practice for attorneys to cooperate with one another by stipulating to numerous continuances or extensions of time. Most courts now attempt to curtail this abusive practice.

42. Note that a judge may require proposed stipulations to be presented as part of a pretrial order or at a pretrial conference. FED. R. CIV. P. 16(c). This does not, however, prevent the parties from arriving at stipulations on their own.

writing, preferably in the form of a signed document. Even when oral stipulations between counsel have been stenographically recorded, either in court or at a deposition, it is wise to review a transcript before relying too heavily on the stipulation during trial preparation.

Finally, it is important for all parties that stipulations be as precise as possible. If the stipulation is to the admissibility of an exhibit, the object or writing must be specifically identified, and the stipulation should also include any understood limitations on the exhibit's use.

10.3.3.4 Requests to Admit

Modern discovery practice allows counsel to obviate the need to lay many foundations at trial. Under the Federal Rules of Civil Procedure,[43] and comparable provisions in most states, any party may serve "Requests for Admission" on any other party. The opposing party must then either admit or deny the request and may suffer sanctions for making false denials.

The federal rules specifically provide for a request to admit "the genuineness of any described documents."[44] Once opposing counsel has admitted the genuineness of a document, no objection on that ground can be made to its admissibility at trial. Additionally, counsel may serve requests to admit the "truth" of virtually any fact relevant to the case. Such facts definitely include all of the elements of the foundations for exhibits. A carefully drafted request to admit can result in the admissibility of even an otherwise contested exhibit.

Opposing counsel is free to deny any of the facts presented in a request for admission. Significant sanctions, however, may attend false or dilatory denials or other evasive replies.[45] Moreover, failure to respond to such a request is, under the federal rules, treated as an admission.

10.3.4 Offering Exhibits at Trial

See demonstration 12 in the Visuals Appendix.

Whether they consist of real, demonstrative, or documentary evidence, there is one basic protocol for offering exhibits at trial. Although the details vary somewhat from jurisdiction to jurisdiction, the following steps form a nearly universal procedure.[46]

---

43. Fed. R. Civ. P. 36(a).
44. *Id.* 36(a)(1)(B).
45. *Id.* 37(c).
46. Subsequent sections of this chapter will discuss the foundations for various sorts of exhibits. Most sections will include examples of these foundations. For the sake of brevity, these examples will be limited to the evidentiary foundations and will not include the technical protocol for offering the exhibits. Readers should assume that in each example the sponsoring attorney would go on to follow the general procedure for offering exhibits as is outlined below.

10.3.4.1 Mark the Exhibit for Identification

Every exhibit should be marked for identification before it is offered into evidence or even referred to in the course of a trial. Marking the exhibit identifies it for the record so that it will be uniquely recognizable to anyone who later reads a transcript of the proceedings. References to "this letter" or "the first broken fastener" may be understood in the courtroom, but they will be meaningless to an appellate court. "Defendant's exhibit three," on the other hand, can mean only one thing, assuming that the exhibit was appropriately marked and identified.

Exhibits are generally marked sequentially and further identified according to the designation of the party who has first offered them. Thus, the exhibits in a two-party trial will be called plaintiff's exhibit one, plaintiff's exhibit two, defendant's exhibit one, defendant's exhibit two, and so forth. In multiple-party trials it is necessary to identify an exhibit by the name, and not merely the designation, of the party who offers it. Accordingly, you will see references to plaintiff Bennett exhibit one or Weber exhibit two. In some jurisdictions, plaintiffs are expected to use sequential numbers for their exhibits, while defendants are requested to use letters. Hence, plaintiff's exhibit one and defendant's exhibit A. The details of the particular marking system are unimportant as long as it produces a clear and understandable indication of which exhibit is which.

The "mark" itself usually takes the form of a sticker placed directly on the object or document. Stickers are available in a variety of forms. Many attorneys use color-coded sets that already contain the words plaintiff or defendant, with a space left blank for the number assigned to each exhibit.

It was once the prevailing practice to have the court reporter or clerk mark each exhibit in open court. Often counsel was required to ask the judge's permission to have an exhibit marked. This time-consuming procedure has been widely replaced by the premarking of exhibits either at a pretrial conference or in the attorney's office. The term "marked for identification" means that the exhibit has been marked and can be referred to in court, but has not yet been admitted into evidence. Exhibits that have been marked for identification may be shown to witnesses and may be the subject of limited examinations for the purpose of establishing a foundation, but they usually may not be shown to the jury.

The distinction between exhibits that have and have not been admitted is crucial. Many jurisdictions, however, have abolished the "for identification" notation as redundant. All exhibits need to be marked, and the record will show which have been allowed into evidence even in the absence of a special inscription.[47]

47. Moreover, the presence or absence of the "for identification" notation can be misleading. The judge's decision on admissibility is determinative, as shown by the trial record. Examining an exhibit to see if the clerk has stricken the words "for identification" can lead to disastrous results if the clerk misunderstood or failed to hear the court's ruling.

10.3.4.2 Identify the Exhibit for Opposing Counsel

Exhibits should be identified for opposing counsel before they are shown to the witness. This may be done by referring to the exhibit number or by indicating its designation in the pretrial order, if one has been prepared. In some jurisdictions, you may be expected to hand or display the exhibit to opposing counsel before proceeding. In any event, these common courtesies allow opposing counsel to confirm that the exhibit is the same one that was produced during discovery or that was discussed and marked at the pretrial conference. Opposing counsel is also afforded an opportunity to make an early objection to the use of the exhibit.

10.3.4.3 Examine the Witness on the Foundation for the Exhibit

Having identified the exhibit, you may now proceed to lay the foundation for its admission.

Show the Exhibit to the Witness

The first step is to show the exhibit to the witness. This is typically done by handing it to the witness.[48] If the exhibit is something as large as a life-sized model or an enlarged photograph, you may point to it and direct the witness's attention. In either case you should announce for the record what you are doing, using a shorthand description of the exhibit as well as its identification number:

Counsel:	Ms. Harris, I am handing you Defendant's Exhibit 11, which is a letter dated July 26.

The description ensures clarity. The term "defendant's exhibit eleven" will mean nothing to the jury and even less to someone reading the transcript. Many lawyers prefer to have the witness give the initial description of the exhibit, but this approach unnecessarily cedes control of the examination. The witness, especially on cross-examination, might give a misleading or inadmissible description. In any event, the witness will have plenty of opportunity to describe the exhibit during the identification phase of the testimony.

Your initial description of the exhibit must be scrupulously neutral. While you are allowed to ask a leading question on preliminary matters, you are not allowed to begin arguing your case under the pretext of laying a foundation. Thus, you cannot say:

Counsel:	Ms. Harris, I am handing you Defendant's Exhibit 11, which is the letter in which the plaintiff agreed to provide repair service at no additional cost.

48. In some jurisdictions, you must obtain the court's permission before you approach the witness. In other courtrooms, you may simply walk up to the witness, as long as you do it politely.

The date of the letter, and perhaps the name of its author, would be sufficient. If the very description of the exhibit is in issue, you may briefly describe what it "purports" to be.

Identify the Exhibit

The next step is to have the witness identify the exhibit. The witness should state the basis for her familiarity with the exhibit and then describe it in some detail:

Q: Have you ever seen Plaintiff's Exhibit 7 before?

A: Yes, I have seen it many times.

Q: What is Plaintiff's Exhibit 7?

A: It is a piece of the stationery that I received when my order was delivered from Quickset Printing.

Q: How is it that you recognize it?

A: I remember how it looked when I took it out of the box.

Numerous variations are possible once the witness has examined the exhibit: "Are you familiar with the exhibit? Do you recognize the exhibit? Are you able to identify the exhibit?" While it is technically necessary to establish initially that the witness has a basis for giving a description, it is often possible to elicit the description first:

Q: What is it?

Q: How do you know?

Complete the Foundation for the Exhibit

In some situations, particularly those involving real evidence, the identification of the exhibit will provide a sufficient foundation for admission. In other circumstances, the foundation will be much more elaborate, perhaps calling for chain of custody or the establishment of a hearsay exception. These and other foundations for the introduction of real, demonstrative, and documentary evidence are discussed at length in subsequent sections of this chapter.

10.3.4.4 Offer the Exhibit into Evidence

Once the foundation has been completed, the exhibit can be offered into evidence. Jurisdictions vary as to the formality with which this must be done. In the simplest version:

Counsel: Your Honor, we offer Plaintiff's Exhibit 3

Some courts, however, expect a more highly mannered presentation:

Counsel:	Your Honor, we move that the identifying mark be stricken and that Plaintiff's Exhibit 3 be received as Plaintiff's Exhibit 3 in evidence.

In any case, the exhibit must be shown to the judge who will then ask opposing counsel if there are any objections to its admission.[49] At this point, it is sufficient to recall that objecting counsel is entitled to request a limited cross-examination of the witness (voir dire), which will be restricted to the subject of the admissibility of the exhibit.

10.3.4.5 Publish and Use the Exhibit

Once an exhibit has been received, it can be "published" to the jury and also used as a basis for further testimony.

See demonstration 14 in the Visuals Appendix.

Publication

The term "publication" refers to the communication of the exhibit to the jurors. Exhibits may be published in a variety of ways. Large objects and oversize graphics are usually turned toward the jurors. Smaller objects typically are handed to the jurors and passed among them. Documents can be enlarged and displayed, passed among the jurors, or read aloud. The choice of publication method is customarily left to counsel, although the court may deny leave to use overly dramatic, prejudicial, or dangerous means.[50]

While the right of publication follows inherently from the admission of the document, the court still exercises discretion over the timing and manner of publication. Consequently, it is necessary to obtain the judge's permission to communicate an exhibit to the jurors:

Counsel:	Your Honor, may I show Defendant's Exhibit 6 to the jury?

Or,

Counsel:	May I have leave to publish Plaintiff's Exhibit 3 by passing it among the jurors?

Or,

Counsel:	Your Honor, may the witness read Prosecution Exhibit 9 to the jury?

49. The process for arguing objections is discussed in chapter nine.

50. Section 10.5 discusses the persuasive use of exhibits, including effective methods of publication to the jury.

There is no requirement that the entire exhibit be published. In the case of a lengthy document or voluminous record, it is appropriate to ask a witness to read only the portions that you deem most important. The entire exhibit, however, must be made available to the jury for inspection as well as to opposing counsel for use on cross-examination.

Using the Exhibit

Once an exhibit has been admitted into evidence it can be used to illustrate or amplify a witness's testimony. In addition to publishing it to the jury, a witness can give further testimony that interprets or otherwise explains the significance of the exhibit.

Tangible objects can be used in demonstrations. A witness can show how a gun was aimed or how a tool was used. Maps, diagrams, and photographs can be used to illustrate the movement of persons and vehicles, the locations of incidents, or the relationship and distances between stationary objects. It is permissible to have a witness mark directly on the exhibit or to use velcro "stick-ons" to elaborate on her testimony. These techniques will be discussed further in the section below on demonstrative evidence.

Additionally, once an exhibit is in evidence, a witness can testify about its contents:

Q: Do the words in Defendant's Exhibit 9 have a particular meaning in your profession?

Q: Why was the color of the stationery, Plaintiff's Exhibit 1, so important to you?

Q: What did you do once you received Plaintiff's Exhibit 12?

Q: What was your reaction when you saw Mr. Castillo holding Defendant's Exhibit 4?

The right to testify about an exhibit is constrained by the applicable rules of evidence. Contrary to a frequently heard objection, however, an exhibit is not required to "speak for itself."

Finally, be aware that once an exhibit has been admitted, it may be used, subject to the rules of evidence, in the examination of any witness, not only the witness who introduced it.

10.4 Foundations for Real and Demonstrative Evidence

10.4.1 Real Evidence/Tangible Objects

Real evidence must be shown to be relevant and authentic. Did the object actually play a role in the facts of the case? Does it tend to prove (or disprove) some issue in contention? Is the object in court really the one that we are talking about? If these conditions are met, the evidence will usually be admitted.[51]

See demonstration 12 in the Visuals Appendix.

The relevance of real evidence is typically established by the context of the case and often requires no additional attention when it comes to laying the foundation. Authenticity, on the other hand, must always be carefully established, as it is the fact of authenticity that qualifies the exhibit as real evidence.

In many cases, the authenticity of real evidence can be shown by a witness's recognition of the exhibit. Other cases require a more detailed and complex foundation, usually referred to as chain of custody.

10.4.1.1 Recognition of the Exhibit

The authenticity of real evidence can be established through the testimony of a witness who is able to recognize the item in question. Many objects can be identified by virtue of their unique features. Others may have been given some identifying mark in anticipation of litigation. In either case, the witness must testify 1) that she was familiar with the object at the time of the underlying events, and 2) that she is able to recognize the exhibit in court as that very same object.

In the following example, the plaintiff in a property damage case will be asked to lay the foundation for an item of personal property:

> Q: Do you recognize Plaintiff's Exhibit 1?
>
> A: Yes, it is an oil painting that was left to me by my grandmother.
>
> Q: How is it that you can recognize it?
>
> A: Until the fire, it hung over our mantle, and I used to look at it almost every day.
>
> Q: Was it in your house at the time of the fire?
>
> A: Yes it was. It was one of the first things that I tried to salvage after we were allowed back into the house.
>
> Q: Is Plaintiff's Exhibit 1 the same oil painting that you removed from your house after the fire?
>
> A: Yes.

51. Fed. R. Evid. 403 provides an exception: "The court may exclude relevant evidence if its probative value is substantially outweighed by the danger of one or more of the following: unfair prejudice, confusing the issues, misleading the jury, undue delay, wasting time, or needlessly presenting cumulative evidence." This provision is often applied to real evidence.

Q: Is Plaintiff's Exhibit 1 in the same condition as it was when you removed it from your house after the fire?

A: Yes, it is.

While an oil painting is likely to be unique and easily recognizable, other exhibits are more fungible. Police officers and others who are familiar with litigation often solve this problem by placing identifying marks on tangible objects. In the following example, a police officer will lay the foundation for a child's safety seat that was found at the scene of an automobile accident:

Q: Officer, did you recover any personal property at the scene of the accident?

A: Yes, I removed a child's safety seat from the back seat of the plaintiff's automobile.

Q: What did you do with the car seat after you removed it?

A: I wrote my initials on the back of the seat, along with the date of the accident.

Q: Showing you Defendant's Exhibit 6, is this the same child's safety seat that you removed from the back of the plaintiff's automobile on the date of the accident?

A: Yes, it is.

Q: How do you know?

A: Because it has my initials and the date written on the back, in my own handwriting.

Q: Is Defendant's Exhibit 6 in the same condition as it was when you retrieved it from the plaintiff's automobile?

A: Yes, it is.

The above foundation is sufficient for the admission of the car seat as long as the exhibit is being offered only to prove the presence of the child seat in the plaintiff's automobile. The question on condition is technically superfluous unless the condition of the car seat is in issue. Nonetheless, judges are accustomed to hearing the "same condition" question, so it is usually a good idea to include it in the foundation for any tangible object.

An exhibit may still be admissible even if its physical condition has changed between the incident and the time of the trial. Under those circumstances, the foundation must include an explanation of any changes:

Q: Have there been any changes to the car seat since the time that you retrieved it from the plaintiff's automobile?

A: Yes. It is now much dirtier, and some of the plastic has been chipped or scratched.

Q: Other than those changes, is Defendant's Exhibit 6 in the same condition as it was when you removed if from the plaintiff's car?

A: Yes.

In both the oil painting and the car seat examples, it was unnecessary for the witness to account for the whereabouts of the exhibit between the incident and the trial. This is because the witnesses were able to supply all of the information necessary to authenticate the exhibits. In other circumstances, however, a foundation will need to include a chain of custody.

10.4.1.2 Chain of Custody

A chain of custody establishes the location, handling, and care of an object between the time of its recovery and the time of trial. A chain of custody must be shown whenever 1) the exhibit is not uniquely recognizable and has not been marked, or 2) when the exhibit's physical properties are in issue.

The Need for a Chain of Custody

Many objects are not inherently identifiable. A case might involve a defective piece of industrial machinery, a damaged automobile part, a contaminated food product, or a misapplied hospital dressing. In none of these situations is a witness likely to recognize the relevant object with any certainty. While it is possible that some of these items might have been marked for later use in litigation, most people (other than police officers and trial lawyers) do not go around scratching their initials on objects to ensure their admissibility. Furthermore, some exhibits cannot be marked at all. For example, vegetation samples, tissue samples, liquids, and narcotics all have physical properties that defy marking.

A chain of custody is also necessary when the exhibit has been subjected to testing or analysis or when other aspects of its condition or composition are at issue in the case. An object that has been tested is likely to have passed through many hands on its way to the courtroom. Because the test results can be invalidated by mishandling, tampering with, or altering the exhibit, counsel must account for its possession and care at least between the time that it was recovered and the time that it was analyzed. The same holds true for an item that is used to display some physical property in the courtroom; a chain must be established to show possession of the exhibit from the time of the underlying incident until its production in court.

Establishing a Chain of Custody

A chain of custody must, at a minimum, be sufficient to show that the object in the courtroom is the same one that was involved in the events being considered at trial. This can usually be accomplished by tracing the possession of the item as it passed from hand to hand. In some situations, it is also necessary to show that the object was stored during the intervening period in a manner that secured it from tampering or inadvertent change. In either case, it may be necessary to call more than one witness to complete the chain.

In the following example, an automobile mechanic was injured when a tire exploded as it was being mounted. The tire manufacturer has been sued, and the allegedly defective tire will be offered solely to show that it was manufactured by the defendant. The first witness is the garage manager:

Q: Where were you when the plaintiff was injured?

A: I was standing about thirty feet away when I heard the noise of a loud explosion.

Q: What did you do?

A: I ran over to where the plaintiff was lying on the ground. He was covered with blood, and there was a ragged tire lying right next to him.

Q: Were there any other tires nearby?

A: No, that was the only one.

Q: Did you do anything with the tire?

A: Yes. I picked it up and put it in my office.

Q: Were there any other tires in your office at the time?

A: No.

Q: Did you ever do anything else with the tire that you found next to the plaintiff?

A: Yes. About a week later, a company superintendent came to investigate the injury. He asked to take the tire, and I gave it to him.

Q: Had the tire been in your office the entire time between the injury to the plaintiff and the time that you gave it to the company superintendent?

A: Yes.

Q: Were there any other tires in your office during that time?

A: No.

The garage manager has completed the first part of the chain. Note that the tire has not yet been produced in court. The next witness is the company superintendent:

Q: Did you obtain a tire in the course of your investigation of this injury?

A: Yes. I went to speak to the garage manager about two weeks after the incident, and he gave me a tire that he had kept in his office.

Q: What did you do with that tire?

A: I brought it back to company headquarters and placed it in my office.

Q: From that day until today, were there any other tires in your office?

A: No.

Q: Did the tire that you got from the garage manager ever leave your office?

A: Yes, I brought it with me to court today.

Q: Showing you plaintiff's exhibit one, is this the tire that you obtained from the garage manager and that you brought with you to court today?

A: Yes, it is.

The chain of custody is now sufficient to establish the identity of the tire. Even though the company superintendent did not witness the accident or initially recover the tire, there is enough evidence to show the continuity of possession. Since in this example the tire is being offered only to prove who manufactured it, physical properties are not in issue. It is therefore unnecessary to show that the tire was kept under lock and key during the intervening period. While it is remotely conceivable that someone could have sneaked into either office and affixed a fraudulent logo to the tire, it is usually unnecessary for a chain of custody to exclude all such unlikely possibilities.[52]

If the tire had been given to an engineering consultant for stress analysis, a more elaborate foundation would be required. It would be necessary to show that measures were taken to safeguard the condition of the tire from the time it was recovered to at least the time it reached the laboratory for testing. With most exhibits this is accomplished by placing the item in a sealed container, usually marked with a date and a person's initials or some other distinctive notation. If the exhibit is removed

52. If there were evidence of such tampering, however, a more elaborate chain would be required.

for testing, the container is typically resealed and re-marked once the test has been completed. Organizations that frequently collect evidence, such as police departments and hospitals, generally have developed routine chain-of-custody procedures for isolating and preserving potential exhibits.

10.4.2 Photography and Other Recording Devices

Photographs and other recordings bridge the gap between real and demonstrative evidence. While a visual or audio recording of any sort is, strictly speaking, an illustration of a past event, its capacity to portray a scene with accuracy is so great that many courts treat photographs and other recordings as tantamount to real evidence.

10.4.2.1 Still Photographs

The basic foundation for the admission of a still photograph is that it "fairly and accurately" portrays the scene shown. In all but a few situations it is not necessary to call the photographer to the stand. It is generally possible to introduce a photograph through the testimony of any witness who is familiar with the scene as it appeared at a relevant time. In the following example, the witness is the owner of a home that was destroyed by fire. A photograph of the house will be offered as evidence of damages.

Q: Were you the owner of the house located at 208 Oak Street?

A: Yes.

Q: How long did you live there?

A: About eight years, until the fire.

Q: So, of course, you are familiar with the appearance of your home before the fire.

A: Yes, certainly.

Q: Does Plaintiff's Exhibit 11 fairly and accurately show your home at 208 Oak Street as it appeared on the day before the fire?

A: Yes, it does.

Because the witness is familiar with the appearance of the house, it is not necessary to call the photographer or to inquire into the circumstances under which the photo was taken. Nor is it necessary to show that the photo was taken on the day before the fire as long as the picture "fairly and accurately" depicts the house as it appeared on the relevant day.

If there had been any alterations in the appearance of the house, the photo could still be admitted once the changes had been explained. The admissibility of the photo will depend on the significance of the changes.

Q: Were there any changes in the appearance of your house between the time of Exhibit 11 and the time of the fire?

A: Yes. The house had been painted, so the color was blue instead of white.

Because the value of the destroyed property will not be affected by the color of the paint, this foundation is sufficient. It is certainly possible, however, for the admission of a photograph to be refused because of discrepancies between the scene at the time it was taken and the scene at the time of the relevant events.

In some circumstances, it may be necessary to call the photographer to the stand, as in cases where the photograph was taken using special equipment or unusual techniques. Additionally, while most photographs are offered to show how something looked at a particular time, some photographs are offered to prove that an event occurred at a certain time. It is usually necessary to produce the testimony of the photographer if the date or occasion of the occurrence in the photograph is in issue.

One last word about magic words. It has become a virtual reflex for lawyers to introduce photographs by asking whether they "fairly and accurately" depict the scene portrayed. Many judges have come to rely on the phrase "fairly and accurately depict" as a required part of the foundation for a photograph. It is not. Any language should be acceptable as long as it authenticates the photograph as a reliable representation of a relevant scene. Nonetheless, it may be advisable to use the words. Judges often expect them, and opposing counsel will be less likely to object if they are used.

10.4.2.2 Video Recordings

As with photographs, a video recording may be authenticated by any witness who is familiar with the scene or scenes portrayed. It is necessary to call the operator of the camera only if special features were employed or if the date of the filming is in issue.

A more difficult problem arises in the case of remote recording—for example, by a security camera—when no witness actually observed the events as they occurred. In these circumstances, the foundation must include additional information about operating procedures as well as the condition of the equipment.

10.4.2.3 Audio Recordings

The foundation for an audio recording depends on the purpose for which it is offered. A recording that is submitted merely as a voice exemplar, for example, may be authenticated by any witness who is able to recognize the voices of the various speakers. The same holds true for recorded music, as might be offered in a copyright dispute. The foundation can be laid by any witness who is familiar with the material recorded.

Audio recordings are perhaps most commonly offered to prove the content of a conversation. Such recordings have often been made surreptitiously, as in the case of police wiretaps.[53] As might be expected, the foundation for these recordings may be quite involved. The simplest case is presented when it was made by a participant to the conversation, or where the conversation was overheard by a person who may be called as a witness:

Q: Did you have a conversation with Lawrence Pinsky on September 21?

A: Yes, I did.

Q: Was that conversation recorded?

A: Yes, I recorded it myself.

Q: Is Prosecution Exhibit 8 the recording that you made of that conversation?

A: Yes.

Q: How do you know?

A: Because I have listened to it several times.

Q: Does Prosecution Exhibit 8 contain an accurate recording of the conversation that you had with Lawrence Pinsky on September 21?

A: Yes, it does.

While this foundation is generally adequate,[54] many lawyers prefer to elicit more extensive testimony concerning the reliability of the equipment used in the recording and the safekeeping (chain of custody) of the recording between the time it was made and the time of trial. Such a foundation may be necessary if authenticity is in issue or if no witness is available to testify to the content of the conversation as it occurred.

10.4.2.4 Medical Imaging

Medical images such as x-rays, computerized axial tomography (CT scans), positron emission tomography (PET scans), and magnetic resonance imaging (MRIs) are comparable to photographs of the body's internal composition. While it is a scientifically reliable fact that x-rays generally produce a "fair and accurate" representation of the bone structure, there is no person who can provide eyewitness

53. Note that the legality of surreptitious audio recording differs from jurisdiction to jurisdiction. In some states it is illegal to record a conversation without the consent of every person involved. In other states, "one-party" consent is sufficient. Law enforcement recording and wiretaps, of course, must comply with search and seizure law.

54. Note that the authentication of a recording does not obviate the need for the recorded conversation to be brought within an exception to the hearsay rule.

testimony comparing an x-ray and a live patient's actual skeleton. Fortunately, courts have long been willing to take judicial notice of the validity of x-rays, and the same now holds true for CT scans, PET scans, MRIs, and other imaging methods.

Consequently, the foundation for the admission of these technologies has been streamlined since the time when it was considered necessary to prove the scientific basis for the process, the competency of the technician, and the good working condition of the particular machine.

It is now generally considered sufficient for a physician or other qualified person to testify that an x-ray, CT scan, or MRI is a fair representation of the internal structure of a given patient's body. The identifying marks on the film (which allow the physician to recognize which x-ray belongs to which patient) are usually considered to be business records of the hospital or clinic.[55]

10.4.3 Demonstrative Evidence

Demonstrative evidence is used to illustrate, clarify, or explain other testimony or real evidence. When such an exhibit is sufficiently accurate or probative, it may be admitted into evidence and even given to the jury when they retire to deliberate. A closely related type of exhibit is the "illustrative aid," which may be used to assist a witness in explaining testimony but cannot be given to the jury as evidence.

The line between "evidence" and "aid" cannot be clearly drawn, but it is possible to imagine a continuum based on accuracy. Scale exhibits, such as models, maps, and diagrams, are extremely accurate and are usually considered demonstrative evidence; rough freehand drawings may be useful devices, but their lack of precision makes them more likely to be limited to use as visual aids.

10.4.3.1 Admissible Demonstrative Evidence

Maps, Charts, and Diagrams

The foundation for a map, chart, blueprint, or other diagram is essentially the same as that for a photograph. The witness must be familiar with the scene, location, or structure as it appeared at a relevant time and must testify that the exhibit constitutes a fair representation.

Additional foundation is necessary if the exhibit is drawn to scale. If the witness prepared the exhibit herself, she may testify to the manner in which she prepared it and the steps she took to ensure its accuracy. If counsel follows this approach, it may be necessary to call two witnesses: one who prepared the exhibit, and another who can testify regarding the facts or events in issue. Note that in many cases, wit-

55. Fed. R. Evid. 901(b)(9) allows authentication of "a process or system" via evidence "describing a process or system and showing that it produces an accurate result." Regarding the foundation for the business records exception to the hearsay rule, *see* section 10.5.3.1.

ness testimony will not be necessary to establish scale since the notation on official maps, plats, and surveys may be self-authenticating,[56] and the court may take judicial notice of the accuracy of commercially produced maps and charts.[57]

See demonstration 14 in the Visuals Appendix.

Models and Reproductions

The foundation for a model or reproduction is similar to that for a photograph. The witness must be familiar with the real location or object and must testify to the model's accuracy. Issues regarding scale are identical to those concerning maps and diagrams.

Litigation often calls for the use of generic, as opposed to specific, models. A medical expert in a personal injury case might want to use an anatomical model to illustrate her testimony. A scale representation of a human shoulder joint will not be an exact model of the plaintiff's own shoulder joint. Nonetheless, it is possible to authenticate such a model with adequate sufficiency. To do so, the witness must testify that the model will be useful in explaining her testimony:

> Q: Doctor, what is Plaintiff's Exhibit 12?
>
> A: It is a scale model of a human shoulder joint.
>
> Q: Would the use of Plaintiff's exhibit 12 assist you in explaining the injury to the plaintiff's shoulder?
>
> A: Yes. All human shoulder joints are basically the same.

A final type of model is the "similar" object. If the actual object is unavailable, a similar object may be used to illustrate a witness's testimony. A defective product, for example, might be destroyed in the same accident that causes an injury. A defect could be "modeled," however, by using an identical product produced by the same company.

See demonstration 14 in the Visuals Appendix.

10.4.3.2 Illustrative Aids

Exhibits that are insufficiently accurate to be allowed into evidence may often still be used for illustrative purposes. The foundation includes a witness's testimony that the exhibit will assist in explaining her testimony as well as a general explanation or description of the inaccuracy. In the following example, the witness has produced a freehand drawing of an intersection:

> Q: What is Defendant's Exhibit 5?
>
> A: It is a drawing of the intersection of Forest and Main.

---

56. *See* FED. R. EVID. 902(5).
57. *See id.* 201(b).

Q: Did you make that drawing yourself?

A: Yes, I did.

Q: Does Defendant's Exhibit 5 generally show the configuration of the streets at Forest and Main as they appeared on the date of the accident?

A: Yes, it shows the location of the streets and the locations of the traffic signs.

Q: Is Defendant's Exhibit 5 drawn to scale?

A: It is the best I could do, but it is not drawn to scale.

Q: Would Defendant's Exhibit 5 still help you to explain your testimony about the accident?

A: Yes, it would.

The above foundation is sufficient to allow the witness to use the diagram in the course of her testimony. The eventual admissibility of the diagram, however, will depend on the court's assessment of its accuracy. Freehand drawings are often inadmissible because they tend to distort distances, spatial relationships, angles, sight lines, and similar information. For that reason, as well as the notorious unreliability of witness-produced drawings, it is generally preferable to use professionally prepared diagrams.

10.5 Foundations for Documents

In addition to the issues of relevance and authenticity, the foundation for a document usually includes two other elements. Because documents invariably contain out-of-court statements, they must be brought within an exception to the hearsay rule. Additionally, the proffer must comply with the "best evidence" or "original writing" rule.

See demonstration 13 in the Visuals Appendix.

10.5.1 Authentication

The authentication of documents typically requires proof of authorship or origin and may also call for proof of transmission or receipt. The existence of a lease, for example, may not be probative unless it can be shown that it bears the signatures of the contending parties. Similarly, the existence of a product recall letter is likely to be meaningless unless it was transmitted to the affected consumers. Thus, unlike tangible objects, the foundation for documentary evidence may include more than simple recognition.

On the other hand, it is unusual for the physical condition or safekeeping of a document to be in issue. Chain of custody, therefore, is seldom a component of the foundation for documentary evidence, although it may be required if the paper has been subjected to testing or if the writing appears to have been altered or amended.

10.5.1.1 Handwriting and Signature

The signature or other handwriting on a document can be authenticated through a variety of means. A witness may recognize a signature based on past observation or may authenticate it on the basis of circumstantial evidence. Other possibilities include expert testimony and in-court comparison by the trier of fact.

A witness may always authenticate her own handwriting or signature. A witness may also authenticate the handwriting of another if sufficient familiarity can be shown:

> Q: Please examine Defendant's Exhibit 2 and tell me if you recognize the signature at the bottom of the page.
>
> A: Yes, I do recognize the signature.
>
> Q: Whose signature is it?
>
> A: It is Ann Nelson's.
>
> Q: How are you able to recognize it?
>
> A: I have seen Ann sign her name many times, and I recognize the handwriting as hers.

It is not necessary, however, for the witness actually to have seen the person sign her name. Circumstantial evidence can also support the required degree of familiarity:

> Q: How is it that you are able to recognize Ann Nelson's signature?
>
> A: We have corresponded over the years, and it is the same signature that I have seen on her letters.
>
> Q: How do you know that those letters came from Ms. Nelson?
>
> A: Because she would usually answer questions that I had written to her in my letters.

Note that extended correspondence is not a requisite. A nonexpert witness can identify a signature on the basis of a single past event or sample as long as familiarity was not acquired for the purpose of litigation.[58]

58. Fed. R. Evid. 901(b)(2).

An expert witness can authenticate a signature on the basis of comparison to a single identified specimen, and the trier of fact, either court or jury, can make its own comparison on the basis of an authenticated exemplar.[59] In the case of comparison to be made by an expert or the trier of fact, the known specimen must still be authenticated. This can be accomplished through the testimony of a witness, as above, by stipulation, or by having the alleged signer write out an exemplar in open court.

10.5.1.2 Circumstantial Evidence of Authorship or Origin

Many documents are printed or typewritten and do not contain signatures or other handwriting. Unless such a document is somehow uniquely marked, it will need to be authenticated via circumstantial evidence. Such evidence can be in the form of a letterhead, seal, or stamp, or it can be provided by the context of the case:

Q: Do you recognize Defendant's Exhibit 6?

A: Yes, it is a price list that I received from Quickset Printing.

Q: How do you know that Defendant's Exhibit 6 came from Quickset Printing?

A: Well, it is on stationery that says Quickset Printing at the top of the page.

Q: Is there any other reason that you know that Defendant's Exhibit 6 came from Quickset Printing?

A: Yes. I called the telephone number listed for Quickset in the directory, and I asked the person who answered the phone to send me a price list. This price list arrived as an e-mail attachment later that day.

The above foundation is more than sufficient to authenticate the document. Note that, notwithstanding the admission of the document, the opposing party remains free to controvert its origin or authorship. Authentication is a threshold question, and it is not dispositive of the ultimate issue.

10.5.1.3 Mailing or Delivery

The admissibility of a document will often depend on its receipt by, or at least transmission to, another party. This is an authenticity issue because the document is made admissible only by its status as one that was actually or constructively received. In other words, proof of mailing authenticates the document as truly having been sent to the other party.

---

59. *Id.* 901(b)(3).

Mailing can be proven either directly or through evidence of a routine business practice.[60] Direct proof of mailing can be given in a single sentence: "I placed the document in an envelope, with the correct address, and I deposited it in the U.S. mail with sufficient postage." The following is an example of the "business practice" approach to proof of mailing:[61]

Q: Does your organization have a routine practice for the handling of outgoing mail?

A: Yes, we do.

Q: Please tell us, step by step, what that practice is.

A: The secretary prepares an envelope as soon as a letter is typed, taking the address from the address block on the letter itself.

Q: What is the next step?

A: Then the letter and the envelope are given back to the person who wrote it. That person proofreads the letter and signs it if there are no corrections.

Q: What happens next?

A: The letter is given back to the secretary, who makes any necessary corrections. If there are no corrections, or once any corrections have been made and approved, the secretary seals the letter in the envelope and places it in the out box.

Q: What is the next step?

A: The letters in the out box are picked up twice each day by someone from the mail room. The letters are taken to the mail room where they are weighed and run through the postage meter. The metered mail is taken to the local post office twice each day, once at about noon and once at 5:00 p.m.

Q: Was that procedure in place on December 19?

A: Yes, it was.

The postal service was once the only common means of transferring documents. Today there are numerous others, including messengers and overnight express services. The basic foundation for proof of transmission is the same no matter which

60. *See* section 10.2.2.4 for a discussion of the foundation for habit and routine practice evidence.
61. In a real trial, the witness would probably be permitted to explain the entire mailing procedure in a single, narrative answer. This example uses multiple questions and answers to underscore the individual elements of the foundation, as well as to avoid giving the impression that narratives are generally allowed.

mode of communication is used. A witness may provide direct proof of transmission or may testify as to the organization's practice for handling outgoing documents.

10.5.1.4 Faxes

Various forms of electronic transmission have become increasingly common, and in some areas virtually dominate communications. The foundations for telefaxes and e-mails vary somewhat from standard letters and telephone calls, but rely on the same basic principles. In both cases, the technologies have become sufficiently well known that courts will take judicial notice of their reliability, making it unnecessary (except in unusual circumstances) to introduce evidence that the "process or system . . . produces an accurate result."[62]

For faxed documents, then, it is sufficient to provide either direct evidence ("I put it in the fax machine and entered the listed number"), or to offer proof of an organization's practice for outgoing documents ("I filled out a fax sheet and handed it to my secretary"). In addition, most fax machines now provide documentation for all transmissions, which may be offered as business records.[63]

Incoming faxes present a slightly different problem since the sender's identity will usually need to be authenticated. If the sender's fax number appears on the document (as is required by a federal statute), that will usually provide sufficient authentication—as long as the number itself can be linked to the sender through a directory or other means. In the alternative, a fax may be authenticated circumstantially, as with any other document.

10.5.1.5 E-mails

The authentication of e-mails is somewhat trickier. For outgoing correspondence, it must be shown that the e-mail was actually sent to the intended recipient. Thus, the e-mail address must be linked to the recipient, either through a directory or some other means. Many businesses and other organizations publish such directories, but in other situations the validity of the address may have to be established circumstantially, as in this example in a simple contract case:

Q: How did you transmit your acceptance of the offer?

A: I sent an e-mail to Louis Robbins.

Q: What e-mail address did you use?

A: It was louis-dot-robbins-at-jacksonville-dot-net.

---

62. *See* Fed. R. Evid. 901(b)(9).
63. *See* section 10.5.3.1.

Q: How do you know that was the correct address?

A: Louis and I had corresponded by e-mail for several months, and all of his replies came from that address.

Traditionally, the "mailbox rule" provided a rebuttable presumption that properly mailed letters were in fact received. That presumption may have to be relaxed a bit in the case of e-mails, however, since some transmissions "bounce" and others may be mistakenly deleted as unwanted spam. In the absence of a reply or an automatic receipt, therefore, it may be necessary to call the recipient as a witness or to subpoena her computer (or to achieve the same result through a request to admit facts.)

Incoming e-mails will have to be authenticated the same way, either by establishing reliable knowledge of the sender's e-mail address or through other circumstantial evidence. In the case of both outgoing and incoming messages, the proponent's printout of the e-mail will usually have to qualify as an exception to the hearsay rule, perhaps as a business record (outgoing) or party admission (incoming).

In an extreme case, it might be necessary to prove in detail that a particular e-mail was actually transmitted from one computer to another. Though complex, this can be done by establishing the routing chain as the e-mail (or rather, the electronic impulses) passed through various servers en route from sender to recipient. Fortunately, the documentation at each stage will usually qualify as a business record, and authentication may be made by certification, thus making it unnecessary to call a series of witnesses.[64]

See demonstrations 15 and 16 in the Visuals Appendix.

10.5.1.6 Web Sites and Posts

Web site postings have become increasingly important in commercial and consumer litigation. Information that was once found in catalogs and brochures, or on price lists and other printed documents, is now disseminated even more broadly over the Internet. Proof of a Web site's content may therefore be relevant in contract, warrantee, consumer fraud, and even tort cases.

It is a fairly simple matter for a proponent to prove the content of its own Web site, as the necessary documentation will generally qualify as a business record. It will usually be sufficient, therefore, for a witness to testify that a certain page was posted on the date in question. As with faxes and e-mails, most courts will accept the reliability of the technology and not require proof of the process by which the postings actually appear at a given Web address.

Extra steps are required when the proponent offers evidence from someone else's Web site. In that case, it must be shown that the site is actually operated at a certain

64. Fed. R. Evid. 902(11).

URL (universal resource locator) by a particular person, organization, or entity. Such proof may be readily available if the site has an easily identifiable inscription or logo. Otherwise, circumstantial evidence (or a party admission) may be necessary. Consider the following example:

Q: Where did you find the pricing information that you relied on?

A: It was posted on the Web site for Quickset Printing, which was quicksetprinting-dot-com.

Q: How do you know that was Quickset's Web site?

A: It had their logo, street address, and telephone number.

Q: Anything else?

A: Yes. I have frequently ordered products through that Web site. My payments were always accepted and the products always arrived.

Because Web sites are not static, it will often be necessary to establish the date of the posting as well, either through documentation (a printout or "screenshot" of the page in question) or specific testimony.

10.5.2 The Original Writing ("Best Evidence") Rule

The so-called "best evidence" rule was once a formidable obstacle to the admission of documentary evidence. In its harshest form, the rule excluded all but the original copy of any writing unless certain conditions could be met. Today, the rule has been softened considerably and now allows for the easy admissibility of most copies.[65] The rule constitutes an authenticity requirement, but its terms are sufficiently unique so as to call for separate treatment.[66]

The essence of the original writing rule is that the content of a document can be proved only by producing the original, or an acceptable duplicate, unless the original is lost, destroyed, or unavailable. Because under most circumstances a duplicate is admissible on the same terms as the original, the rule now operates primarily to exclude testimonial summaries or paraphrases of a document. Note also that the original writing rule applies only to proof of a document's content, not its signing, acknowledgment, or delivery.

---

65. Fed. R. Evid. 1002 states the basic original writing requirement: "An original writing, recording, or photograph is required in order to prove its content unless these rules or a federal statute provides otherwise." Rule 1003, however, goes on to allow the admissibility of most duplicates: "A duplicate is admissible to the same extent as an original unless a genuine question is raised about the original's authenticity or the circumstances make it unfair to admit the duplicate."

66. As everyone knows, the "best evidence" rule has nothing to do with whether or not a document is the highest quality evidence of any particular proposition, which is why most commentators now choose to refer to it as the "original writing" or "original document" rule. Judges and lawyers, perhaps because they thrive on confusion, have persisted in using the "best evidence" terminology.

A duplicate may be substituted for the original in most situations. The Federal Rules of Evidence define the term "duplicate" quite broadly to include essentially all accurate reproductions, including carbons, photocopies, telefaxes, and computer-generated duplicates.[67]

Duplicates are not admissible, however, where "a genuine question is raised about the original's authenticity."[68] Thus, for example, a photocopy of a contract cannot be offered if one of the parties can support a claim that her signature was forged on the original.

In any event, there are exceptions to the original writing rule. The original is not required if it 1) has been lost or destroyed, 2) is unobtainable, or 3) is in the possession of an opponent who has refused to produce it.[69] Invocation of an exception requires the establishment of a foundation.

In the following example, the witness claims to have received a threatening letter from the defendant:

Q: Did you receive a letter from the defendant?

A: Yes, I did.

Q: How do you know that it was from the defendant?

A: I recognized his handwriting, which I have seen many times.

Q: Do you still have the letter?

A: No, I do not.

Q: What happened to it?

A: I lost it when I moved to a new apartment.

Q: What did the letter say?

The witness, having explained the loss of the original, may now testify about the letter's content.[70] Similar foundations are necessary for the other exceptions to the rule.[71]

---

67. *See* FED. R. EVID. 1001(e), which provides as follows: "A 'duplicate' means a counterpart produced by a mechanical, photographic, chemical, electronic, or other equivalent process or technique that accurately reproduces the original."

68. FED. R. EVID. 1003.

69. *Id.* 1004.

70. Note that compliance with the original writing rule goes only to authenticity. A document may still be excluded if it is otherwise hearsay. In this example, however, the letter, having been written by the defendant, qualifies as an opposing party statement.

71. The most involved foundation is necessary when the original is asserted to be in the possession of a party opponent. The federal rules allow secondary evidence if "the party against whom the original would be offered had control of the original; was at that time put on notice, by pleadings or otherwise, that the original would be a subject of proof at the trial or hearings; and fails to produce it at the trial or hearing . . . ." FED. R. EVID. 1004(c).

10.5.3 Foundations for Hearsay Exceptions

The offer of a document inevitably sets the hearsay bell ringing in opposing counsel's mind. While writings may be admissible for nonhearsay purposes, such as proof of notice or acceptance, they are frequently submitted precisely to prove that their contents are true. Various exceptions are available to allow the use of such documents, each requiring its own foundation. The more common exceptions are discussed in the following sections.

10.5.3.1 Business Records

Business records can include ledgers, accounts, calendar entries, memoranda, notices, reports, statements, and similar writings. All of these documents constitute hearsay if they are offered to prove that their contents are true. Thus, the entries in a loan company's account book would be hearsay if submitted as proof that a certain loan was not repaid in time.

Fortunately for the world of commerce, the "business records" exception to the hearsay rule allows for the admission of most such records, as long as they can be shown to meet certain requirements. Under the federal rules, the records of any regularly conducted activity are admissible if they 1) were made at or near the time of a transaction or event; 2) were made by, or based on information transmitted from, a person with knowledge; 3) were kept in the course of a regularly conducted business activity; and 4) were made as a part of the regular practice of that business activity.[72]

It is not uncommon to use the approximate words of the rule in order to lay a foundation for the exception, as in this classic example:

Q: Are you employed by the Quickset Printing Company?

A: Yes, I am the accountant and bookkeeper.

Q: Do you recognize Plaintiff's Exhibit 3?

A: Yes, I do. It is our ledger book.

Q: What is the function of your ledger book?

A: We use it to record all of our credit sales and all of the payments that we receive.

Q: Are the entries in Plaintiff's Exhibit 3 made at or near the time of the sales or payments?

A: Yes.

Q: Are the entries made by or transmitted from a person with knowledge of the sales and payments?

72. Fed. R. Evid. 803(6).

A: Yes.

Q: Are those entries made as a part of the regular business practice of Quickset Printing?

A: Yes.

Q: Is the ledger book, Plaintiff's Exhibit 3, kept in the regular course of business?

A: Yes, it is.

The foundation for the exception is now complete. Note that the witness does not need to be the keeper or custodian of the records, but may be merely "someone with knowledge." The term "business" is defined broadly to include any "business, organization, occupation, or calling, whether or not conducted for profit."[73] Furthermore, the absence of an entry is also admissible on the basis of the same foundation as long as it is the type of matter of which a record was regularly kept.[74]

The basic foundation for the business records exception can be expanded on as circumstances dictate. When dealing with records that are more complex, intricate, questionable, digital, or exotic than ledger books, it is often desirable to have the witness spend more time explaining their use and reliability. It is worth keeping in mind, however, that judges are accustomed to hearing the foundation's magic words and that objections are less likely to be made or sustained when you use them too.

10.5.3.2 Computer Records and Printouts

Computer-generated printouts have become a common form of business record. In the early days of computing, it was considered necessary to prove that computer data entry and retrieval systems were reliable means for storing information, but this is no longer the case.

The federal rules specifically recognize "data compilations" as an acceptable form of business record. Thus, the foundation for a computer printout is basically the same as that for any other business record:

Q: Are you employed by the Quickset Printing Company?

A: Yes, I am the accountant and data manager.

Q: Do you recognize Plaintiff's Exhibit 3?

A: Yes, I do. It is a printout of our accounts receivable.

Q: How was Plaintiff's Exhibit 3 generated?

73. Fed. R. Evid. 803(6).
74. *Id.* 803(7).

A: We use a computer program to record all of our credit sales and all of the payments that we receive. We can then print out the information whenever we need it.

Q: Are the entries made on your computer system at or near the time of the sales or payments?

A: Yes.

Q: Are the computer entries made by or transmitted from a person with knowledge of the sales and payments?

A: Yes.

Q: Are those entries made as a part of the regular business practice of Quickset Printing?

A: Yes.

Q: Are your computer records kept in the regular course of business?

A: Yes, they are.

Note that only the computer entries, and not the printout, need to have been made "at or near the time of the transactions."

10.5.3.3 Summaries

Many business records or other sets of data are so lengthy and ponderous that they cannot be conveniently produced in court. Even if they could be produced, they may be so extensive and technical as to be impenetrable. In these circumstances, it is permissible to substitute a "summary, chart, or calculation" that fairly presents the relevant information in a usable or understandable form.[75]

The foundation for such a summary includes these elements: 1) the original documents are so voluminous that they cannot be conveniently examined in court; 2) the witness has examined the original data; 3) the witness is qualified to produce a summary of the information; and 4) the exhibit is a fair and accurate summary of the underlying information. The witness in the following example is an economist who has been called to testify regarding a company's net worth:

Q: What is your occupation?

A: I am an economist.

Q: Have you examined certain records of the Quickset Printing Company?

A: Yes.

75. Fed. R. Evid. 1006.

Q: Please describe all of the documents that you examined.

A: I looked at all of the records of the company, including their pay records, tax records, fringe benefit records, insurance records, accounts payable, accounts receivable, inventories, mortgages, and appraisals of their real property.

Q: Why did you examine those records?

A: It was necessary to look at all of that information to arrive at a figure for their net worth.

Q: Can you describe the volume of the materials that you examined?

A: All in all, I would say that printouts would fill three or four large binders.

Q: Do you recognize Plaintiff's Exhibit 19?

A: Yes, it is a summary that I prepared of the Quickset records.

Q: What does Plaintiff's Exhibit 19 contain?

A: It shows their outstanding assets and liabilities, which then gives us their net worth.

Q: Is Plaintiff's Exhibit 19 a fair and accurate summary of the corporate records of Quickset Printing?

A: Yes.

It is also necessary for the original records to be made available for examination by the other parties. This aspect of the foundation can be established through testimony or by stipulation.

10.5.3.4 Recorded Recollection

A witness's written notes or other recorded recollection may be admitted into evidence only if the witness, at the time of trial, "cannot recall well enough to testify fully and accurately."[76] The foundation for this exception to the hearsay rule comprises these elements: 1) the witness once had personal knowledge of the relevant facts or events; 2) the witness cannot currently recall the events fully and accurately; 3) the witness previously made an accurate memorandum or record of the facts; 4) at a time when the events were fresh in her memory.

The witness in the following example has sued an insurance company for failure to pay a property damage claim:

76. Fed. R. Evid. 803(5).

Q: Is it possible for you to name all of the items that were destroyed in the fire at your home?

A: No, we lost everything. I am sure that I would not be able to name every item, or even most of them.

Q: Before the fire, had you ever made a list of your belongings?

A: Yes, I inventoried all of the more valuable or significant items, and I put the list in my safe deposit box.

Q: How did you make that list?

A: It was easy. I went from room to room and wrote down each thing as I saw it.

Q: Was the list accurate when you made it?

A: Yes, it was.

Q: Showing you Plaintiff's Exhibit 1, is this the list of belongings that you made?

A: It is.

Q: After reviewing the list, would it be possible for you to remember all of the items on it?

A: No, there are too many.

The foundation for the witness's recorded recollection is now complete. Note that the witness testified that she could not recall all of the items even after reviewing the list. This testimony fulfills the requirement that the witness be unable to testify "fully and accurately." If the witness could recall all of the items, then her recollection would be "refreshed," and this particular hearsay exception would not be available. The witness would, of course, be able to testify as to her renewed recollection.[77]

Under the federal rules, a document containing a recorded recollection may only be read into evidence; the record itself cannot be received as an exhibit unless offered by the adverse party.[78] Some state jurisdictions simply allow the admission of the document.

10.5.3.5 Public Records

There are a number of hearsay exceptions that allow for the admissibility of public records, statistics, and reports. Such records are generally admissible if they were made by a public office or agency and they set forth 1) the activities of the office or agency; or 2) matters observed pursuant to a duty imposed by law; or

77. The techniques for refreshing recollection are discussed in section 4.2.5.
78. Fed. R. Evid. 803(5).

3) in limited circumstances, certain investigative findings; or 4) officially required records of vital statistics.[79]

Because most government records are "self-authenticating," it is not usually necessary to call a witness to testify to their authenticity.[80] While it is technically necessary to call a witness to establish the "governmental duty" elements of the foundation, most courts will take judicial notice of the fact that agencies are required by law to record their activities and observations, particularly where the obligation is imposed by a statute or regulation.

Note that the federal rule places two limits on the use of this hearsay exception in criminal cases. First, "a matter observed by law-enforcement personnel" do not qualify for the exception, even if contained in a report made pursuant to a duty imposed by law. Second, investigative findings are admissible in criminal cases only if offered against the government.[81]

10.5.3.6 Absence of Public Record or Entry

Public records may also be used to show the nonoccurrence of events. The foundation for this evidence is 1) that such events, occurrences, or matters were regularly recorded in some form; 2) by a public office or agency; and 3) that a diligent search has failed to disclose a record of a particular fact or event. This evidence may be offered by certification from the appropriate official, in which case no witness needs to be called. The evidence may also be offered via testimony:

Q: Do you hold a public position in this state?

A: Yes, I am the chief clerk at the Liquor Control Commission.

Q: Does your agency keep records of the liquor licenses issued in this state?

A: Yes, we keep a record of every license as it is issued, as well as the payment of each annual licensing fee.

Q: Are those records regularly made and preserved as part of the public business of your agency?

A: They are.

Q: Have you conducted a diligent search to determine whether this state has ever issued a liquor license to an organization called the Park City Club?

A: Yes, I have.

79. *See id.* 803(8)–(9).
80. *Id.* 902.
81. *Id.* 803(8).

Q: What was the result of that search?

A: No such license has ever been issued.

10.5.3.7 Previous Testimony

The transcript of a person's previous testimony may be admitted into evidence if 1) the declarant is currently unavailable to testify; 2) the testimony was given under oath in court or at a deposition; 3) the party against whom the testimony is being offered had a fair opportunity to examine the witness when the testimony was originally given.[82] Note that this exception allows the admission of the earlier statement as a substitute for current testimony. Unlike the use of prior testimony for impeachment, there is no requirement that the previous testimony be inconsistent with the declarant's current position.

Under the federal rule a witness can be deemed unavailable for a variety of reasons, including: 1) the valid assertion of a privilege; 2) persistent refusal to testify; 3) inability to attend the hearing due to illness; 4) death; 5) failure of memory; or 6) absence from the hearing notwithstanding the efforts of the proponent of the testimony to procure attendance.

The elements of the foundation for this exception will frequently be established through judicial notice. The court, for example, will usually take notice of the fact that a party had an opportunity to cross-examine the declarant at the earlier hearing or deposition. It may occasionally be necessary to produce proof of unavailability, as in the case of a witness who failed to respond to a subpoena.

10.5.3.8 Opposing Party Statements

The party admission exception applies to documents as well as to oral statements. A party admission can be contained in a letter, e-mail, report, memorandum, journal, progress chart, or virtually any other form of writing or recordation. Once the exhibit has been authenticated, the only remaining foundation is that it was made or adopted by a party against whom it is being offered or by an agent, servant, or employee of such a party.

10.6 Persuasive Use of Exhibits

The previous sections dealt with the technical aspects of offering exhibits. The admission of an exhibit, however, is only part of counsel's task. It is equally important to ensure that exhibits are presented and used as persuasively as possible. The following sections cover traditional courtroom exhibits, such as physical objects, photographs, and drawings. Computer-generated visuals will be discussed in chapter eleven.

---

82. Fed. R. Evid. 804(b)(1).

10.6.1 Persuasive Foundations

Because foundations are technical matters that are principally directed to the court, it is easy to lose sight of their impact on the jury. There are two approaches that can be used to keep jurors from being confused, bored, or annoyed by foundations.

10.6.1.1 Minimalism

Whenever possible, use stipulations and pretrial rulings to avoid the need for developing foundations in court. If foundational testimony must be presented, keep it as short as possible. Leading questions, permissible on preliminary matters, can be used to move the testimony along.

Several elements of a foundation can frequently be combined in a single sentence. The business records foundation, for example, can be summed up in only two questions:

> Q: Were the entries made at or near the time of the transaction by a person with knowledge, or transmitted by a person with knowledge, of the transaction?
>
> Q: Were the records made and kept in the ordinary course of business?

These questions are technically compound, but few lawyers or judges will be concerned with that nicety at the expense of expediting such a boring aspect of the trial. The above language will be unfathomable to most jurors, but it will be over with in a hurry. It is not usually important for the jurors to understand a technical foundation, and it may well be better to have them baffled and happy than well-educated and resentful.

10.6.1.2 Maximalism

Foundations are not always rote technicalities. Particularly where the authenticity of the exhibit is in issue, the thoroughness of the foundation can play an important role in juror persuasion. In such circumstances, it is important to develop the foundation fully, taking care to use language that the jurors will understand.

Using another business records situation, assume that the defendant company in the following example is being sued for nonpayment of a bill for supplies. The defendant's records show that payment was made in cash, and the plaintiff contests the accuracy of the entry. The witness is the defendant's bookkeeper:

> Q: What are your duties as bookkeeper for the Alyssa Carlton Gallery?
>
> A: I am in charge of all purchase, payment, and receipt records.
>
> Q: Does your job require you to keep a record of payments?
>
> A: Yes, every time we make a payment I make an entry on a spreadsheet.

Q: Showing you Defendant's Exhibit 1, is this ledger printout of the spreadsheet that you referred to?

A: Yes, it is.

Q: What do the entries in Defendant's Exhibit 1 show?

A: They show the amount, the form of payment, the person or company we paid, and the name of the person who made the payment.

Q: How soon after each payment do you make the entries?

A: Within twenty-four hours.

Q: How do you get the information?

A: Each person who makes a payment reports it directly to me, and I enter it in the database.

Q: Were the entries in Defendant's Exhibit 1 made in any particular order?

A: They are entered in the order of the date on which each payment was made.

Q: Is it a regular part of your job to make the entries in Exhibit 1?

A: Yes.

Q: Is it a regular part of your job to keep Defendant's Exhibit 1 up to date?

A: Yes, it is.

Q: Does Defendant's Exhibit 1 contain an entry for a payment to Quickset Printing last January 4?

A: Yes, it does.

Q: At the time of that entry, were you aware of any dispute between your employer and Quickset?

A: No, it was just another regular entry.

The above foundation was long, but it was necessary to show the reliability of the entry. As with any direct examination, details add credibility.

A detailed foundation can make an exhibit more persuasive even when its authenticity is not in dispute. The following example is a battery prosecution in which the defendant is alleged to have struck the victim with a length of pipe. The original pipe was not recovered, and the prosecution is seeking to introduce a similar pipe as demonstrative evidence. A sufficient foundation could be laid by the victim's testimony that the exhibit is "identical" to the one with which he was hit. A longer foundation, however, could be much more effective:

Q: Please take prosecution Exhibit 5 in your hand, and tell me when you have finished examining it.

A: I have finished.

Q: Is Exhibit 5 similar to the pipe that the defendant hit you with?

A: Yes, it is.

Q: Is it the same weight as the defendant's weapon?

A: Yes, it is the same weight.

Q: Is it the same length as the defendant's pipe?

A: Yes.

Q: Is it as big around as the pipe that the defendant used?

A: Yes.

Q: Are there any differences at all between Prosecution Exhibit 5 and the pipe that the defendant used to beat you?

A: They are exactly alike.

Following this foundation, the jurors should have a full appreciation of the exhibit not merely as a model, but as a dangerous weapon. Further demonstrations with the pipe, once it is admitted into evidence, will drive the point home even more.

10.6.1.3 Magic Words

Whether using the minimalist or maximalist approach to foundations, counsel must always reckon with the potency of magic words. Many foundations—including those for photographs, business records, and the authenticity of conversations—have become routine to the point that convenient phrases are now frequently confused with legal requirements. No matter what some judges may think, though, it is not necessary to introduce every photograph by asking whether it "fairly and accurately depicts" the scene involved. As far as the law of evidence is concerned, it would be just as acceptable to ask whether the photograph "shows everything in the scene just as it appeared on the date in question." Hundreds of other variations would serve just as well.

Nonetheless, there is not much advantage to be gained by arguing with judges or opposing lawyers who are determined to hear the magic words. In the end, it is just easier to say "fairly and accurately depict" than it is to convince the court that your more thoughtful version of the foundation is legally sufficient.

Magic words get results and must therefore be part of every attorney's repertoire. For the benefit of a jury, you will often want to lay a foundation in more readily understandable language, but this should not prevent you from falling back on the expected jargon, either in response to an objection or as an extra "fail-safe" line of questions at the end of your preferred foundation.

10.6.2 Creative Exhibits

The most valuable exhibits in any case seldom step forward and present themselves. Rather, they must be sought after, searched out, and discovered. Often they must be developed and created. Even those exhibits that are simply handed to counsel by the client can be presented in an enhanced form. The following sections discuss creative means of finding, developing, and presenting exhibits.

10.6.2.1 Developing Exhibits

All exhibits fall essentially into two categories: those that predate the litigation and those created by the attorneys. The prelitigation, or integral, exhibits must be taken as they are found, but counsel has wide latitude in shaping and developing other exhibits for use at trial. Some of the more common sorts of lawyer-generated exhibits are discussed below (electronic visuals are discussed in the next chapter). The creation of these, and similar, exhibits should be considered in virtually every case.

Deposition Transcripts

Although not commonly thought of as exhibits, deposition transcripts are indeed physical objects that did not exist before the litigation. They come into being only as a consequence of arrangement and questioning by counsel. The words on the printed page can under some circumstances be shown to, as well as read to, the jury. An enlargement of a key section of an adverse witness's testimony can make an extremely effective exhibit when used on cross-examination.

Photographs and Videos

As we noted in the foundation section, it is extremely easy to have photographs admitted in evidence. They only need to portray accurately a relevant scene to be received. With this in mind, you will almost always want to photograph important objects or locations that bear on your theory of the case.

Although it is not necessary to call the photographer to authenticate a photograph, it is often a good idea to employ a professional photographer to take any desired photographs. Amateurs, even working with good equipment, can make errors in focus, lighting, or composition. A professional will understand how to capture the desired scene while avoiding extraneous or misleading information.

It is also possible to use video recordings in much the same way that still photography has been used for years. Instead of photographing the scene of an accident, for example, counsel should consider making a video or digital recording not only the scene, but also the viewpoints of the parties as they approached the scene. A still photograph can capture only a limited amount of information about a physical space, while a video can more accurately convey information concerning perspective, spatial relationships, and even speed.

Models

Models can be simple or elaborate, but they are almost always useful in explaining a series of events. Depending on the size of the case and the available litigation budget, models can range from to-scale duplicates of entire buildings to commercially available reproductions of human organs or joints.

Diagrams and Maps

Diagrams are perhaps the simplest and most ubiquitous form of lawyer-generated exhibit. Virtually no automobile accident case would be complete without an intersection drawing, and many other cases use street grids, floor plans, or other diagrams on which to place the occurrence of physical events. One of the advantages of a diagram is that it can be marked to indicate the locations of signs, objects, or witnesses, as well as the movement of persons and things.

Explanatory Graphs and Charts

Photographs, models, and diagrams all represent physical objects and occurrences. Graphs and charts, on the other hand, help explain concepts and ideas. A simple "timeline," for example, can clarify the sequence in which crucial events occurred. Similarly, a pie chart can help a witness explain loss of income or allocation of damages. It is entirely permissible for a witness to illustrate her testimony in addition to describing it in words. Counsel can help the witness communicate by helping the witness develop graphs and charts.

10.6.2.2 Presenting Exhibits

The presentation of an exhibit can be as important as its composition or foundation. No matter how well thought out, no matter how solidly admissible, an exhibit will not accomplish its purpose if the trier of fact does not understand and accept it. As with any aspect of witness examination, there are certain principles that can generally be applied to the presentation of exhibits at trial.

Advance Preparation

The best exhibits are usually those prepared in advance of trial. This principle applies to both selection and design.

While some cases involve only two or three exhibits, many cases will see the production of dozens, if not hundreds, of documents. A careful trial plan will determine precisely which of these exhibits are the most significant and will treat them in such a way as to emphasize their importance. As with direct examination, clutter is the enemy of coherent document presentation. Even if thirty or forty documents are necessary to establish every element of your case, the advocate's duty is to cull out the three or four (or perhaps even five or six) that have the most impact. This must be done in advance of trial. It will not do to wait for the witnesses' testimony before you decide which exhibits to highlight. First, your decision about the value of the exhibits should drive the preparation of your witness examinations, not the other way around. Second, the documents that you intend to rely on most should be scanned for electronic presentation, photographically enlarged, or otherwise prepared for an impressive display.

In addition to selecting key integral documents for enhanced presentation, effective trial preparation also involves the design of lawyer-generated exhibits. Particularly when it comes to diagrams and graphs, an ounce of professional preparation is usually worth several pounds of courtroom drawing. The lawyer must decide whether a witness's testimony can be improved with a chart, graph, or diagram. If so, the desired exhibit should be developed in advance of trial.

While witnesses may be allowed to draw on blackboards or poster boards while testifying, this approach usually should be avoided. Freehand drawing is unreliable under the best circumstances, and witnesses are notoriously prone to make embarrassing mistakes when called on to draw in a courtroom. Using a blackboard, in particular, seldom leads to a satisfying result. Whether the blackboard drawing is made by the witness or the attorney, it will often be either too small to be seen or so large as to run out of space. The time spent drawing will be wasted at best and distracting at worst. Lighting conditions may make even the boldest lines difficult to see, and the chalk will inevitably squeak at the most dramatic moment of the testimony.

Essential features of an exhibit such as scale, perspective, and proportion can only be assured when entrusted to a professional illustrator or designer. If professional assistance is not an alternative, then counsel must take care to create the best diagram possible. (The next chapter discusses the various means for creating electronic visuals.)

Size

Exhibits must be seen to be appreciated. When creating an exhibit, create a big one. When using integral exhibits such as preexisting documents, make enlargements, either physically or on a digital display.

There is no reason for a lawyer-produced exhibit to be visually inaccessible. When using physical enlargements, charts, graphs, and diagrams should be made on oversize pieces of stiff poster board. Thin tagboard is unacceptable since even a masterpiece will be useless if it cannot be made to stand up. It is also necessary to ensure that a display easel will be available in the courtroom.

While it is neither necessary nor desirable to enlarge every document, the crucial few should be blown up to poster size and mounted for display. The most important exhibits to enlarge are those that support your theory of the case. In a case involving extended correspondence over the terms of a contract, for example, counsel may want to enlarge only the two letters showing the final offer and acceptance. Alternatively, trial strategy might dictate enlarging letters that contain certain terms or conditions. In any event, the enhanced presentation of a limited number of exhibits can underscore their importance and drive home your trial theory.

Photographs, whether preexisting or taken at counsel's direction, should also be enlarged. Even an 8×10 photograph cannot easily be seen from the usual distance between the jury box and the witness stand. If the film quality permits, crucial photographs should be further enlarged to poster size or reproduced as 35-mm slides.

Copies

Counsel should enter the courtroom with enough copies of every exhibit. At a minimum, this should include an original, additional copies for the witness and the judge, and copies for each opposing attorney if they have not already been produced. Distributing copies at the appropriate time in the examination will prevent delays and can forestall objections. There is little more awkward and distracting than a lawyer leaning over a witness's shoulder while they attempt to share an exhibit.

When enlargements or digital displays are impractical or unavailable, counsel should also make enough copies of the exhibits, whether documents or photographs, to distribute to the jurors. With the court's permission, the copies can be given to the jurors as the witness testifies about the foundation. Alternatively, counsel might wish to delay passing out the copies until the exhibit has been admitted, or even until the end of the examination, to avoid having the jurors' attention distracted during the witness's testimony.

It is increasingly common for documents to be admitted at the pretrial conference. When this occurs, it is possible to assemble all of the documents into a bound or loose-leaf "exhibit book," copies of which can be provided to court, to each juror, and to witnesses as necessary.

Chapter Eleven

Electronic Visuals

To view the visuals and simulations noted in this chapter, please go to the Visuals Appendix at http://bit.ly/1FSfRXv.

Password: NITAModTriAd5

11.1 Introduction

Electronic visuals, when properly used, can be a powerful tool of persuasion in the courtroom. As technology has continued to evolve in the past decade, attorneys have become more willing to use its new tools, and courts have become more accommodating of electronic visuals and technology in the courtroom. In fact, many courtrooms are now equipped with monitors, electronic whiteboards, document cameras, appropriate electrical outlets, and hook-ups for equipment.

Electronic visuals can help attorneys move quickly and effortlessly from exhibit to exhibit or from document to document, a far better state of affairs than the laborious, distracting, and time-wasting practice of changing large pieces of foam board or searching through boxes or binders for relevant documents.

Courts have continued to adjust to the use of electronic visuals, and many have enacted specific local rules to control how they are handled and used. You should consult each court's local rules for guidance on matters such as available equipment and protocols for exchanging exhibits.

11.2 How Electronic Visuals Make an Impact

11.2.1 Meeting Jurors' Expectations

Electronic visuals present evidence to jurors in a familiar manner. With the proliferation of smartphones and interaction through social media on electronic devices, most jurors receive a high percentage of their information in electronic form. Because they are accustomed to receiving information in this format, electronic visuals often help them feel at ease, which in turn makes them receptive to your message.

11.2.2 Establishing Attorney Credibility

By using electronic visuals, you appear prepared and confident in your case, and even more so when opposing counsel does not employ these tools. The fact finder may be quick to recognize this disparity and have a more favorable impression of the attorney who effectively uses technology than of the attorney who ignores it.

11.2.3 Engaging Fact Finder via Change

Presenting an electronic visual changes the momentum of the proceedings, which allows you to both engage and re-engage the fact finder. Oral testimony can drag on, even when it is well presented, and the fact finder may be inclined to tune out a witness who has testified at length. However, when you project an electronic visual onto a screen in the midst of that oral presentation, the fact finder will engage the change in the environment and pay additional attention to what the witness has to say. By the same token, if you rely on electronic presentations too heavily and for too long, they will no longer be the "change," and the fact finder will again begin to disengage—so be cautious about overusing these—or any other—tools. Keep mixing it up.

11.2.4 Learning Theory: Retention and Understanding

When you present information in multiple formats, you increase the likelihood that the judge or jurors will understand and be able to recall the information at a later point, such as jury deliberations.

Learners tend to fall into one of three categories: auditory, visual, or kinesthetic. Auditory learners process best through hearing and can remember conversations and lectures. Lawyers usually communicate with fact finders in this way. Most jurors, however, are visual learners who rely on their sense of sight to understand and process information. Therefore, using electronic visuals in conjunction with oral testimony allows you to engage more jurors than through oral testimony alone. Electronic visuals do not provide easy opportunities to reach kinesthetic learners, who learn more by doing and interacting than through hearing or seeing. Where possible, you should consider passing around pieces of evidence that jurors can touch and interact with to reach the kinesthetic learners. Regardless of what type of learner the fact finders may be, studies strongly support that after hours, days, or even months of hearing testimony, they are much more likely to retain information presented in more than one format when they leave the courtroom to deliberate.

11.2.5 Support and Clarification

Timelines, charts, and summaries are examples of simple, yet effective, electronic visuals that can make information clear, comprehensible, and memorable, especially in complex cases. When fact finders don't understand something or are confused, they have a strong tendency to simply ignore the information. Electronic visuals are an important tool you can use to avoid an advocate's worst fear—being ignored.

Electronic visuals are frequently the most effective tool to convey precise and clear information about an event or scene. Oral testimony alone can't achieve the clarity and precision that the addition of an electronic visual can provide. There are two primary reasons for this. First, you cannot reach the same level of detail with oral testimony as you can with a picture or video. Second, and perhaps more crucially, the fact finder filters information through her own personal experiences, a process which may be difficult to overcome through oral testimony alone. For example, imagine a case in which an incident occurred at a movie theater. Each juror will immediately picture the movie theater with which they are most familiar, whether it's the one they went to as a child or the one they frequent as an adult. As you present information about the incident to them, all of that information will be filtered through the lens of that memorable movie theater. Oral testimony alone won't be able to fully overcome the filtering bias; however, showing the jurors a video or floor plan of the inside of the actual movie theater where the incident took place can usually solve the problem by superimposing the new image over the old.

11.3 Avoid Overuse and Complication

Electronic visuals should be simple and used sparingly. By overusing them or making them unnecessarily complicated, you can actually damage your credibility. Each time you use a visual, you direct the jurors' attention away from you and toward that visual. If you rely on visuals too heavily, especially during an opening statement or closing argument, the jury can quickly become disconnected from you—or worse, fail to connect with you in the first place.

Complicated visuals are self-defeating. If your electronic visual appears cluttered or intricate, consider using multiple exhibits. For example, if your timeline covers thirty years, you could separate it into three separate timelines of ten-year increments. If you find yourself trying to squeeze too many events into a single graph or chart, think about creating a separate visual for each event.

As useful as they can be, electronic visuals are not for every case or for all situations. Because their primary function is to persuade by presenting information in a simple, familiar, and understandable format, the more complex the trial or issue at trial is, the more likely you are to benefit from their use.

11.3.1 The Exception

On the other hand, sometimes an electronic visual that emphasizes complexity may be just the thing to help your case. For example, if you are representing an employee who is denying responsibility for a particular action, a complicated organizational flow chart could help show that your client could not have been responsible because of all the other people involved above, below, and sideways on the chart.

11.4 Common Electronic Visuals in the Courtroom

11.4.1 Introduction

You can use many different types of electronic visuals during a trial. Some are created solely for the purpose of a trial, such as animations or simulations. Other electronic visuals simply display substantive evidence by projecting an image in an enlarged electronic format, such as the contract in dispute or a close up of a bullet found at the scene of a crime.

As we discuss the examples below, it is important to understand that the rules related to the admission and use of these visuals differ for substantive or demonstrative evidence. You will have to follow the appropriate evidentiary rules and courtroom procedures relating to substantive and demonstrative evidence in your jurisdiction as discussed in section 10.4. Even if your electronic visual is admitted into evidence, it may be logistically difficult or impossible to have it taken into the jury room so plan accordingly and consider whether you should also present that evidence via nonelectronic means.

11.4.2 Animations and Simulations

11.4.2.1 Overview

As costs continue to decrease and technology is more readily accessible, the use of a variety of computer-generated animations and simulations is becoming more and more common. These visuals can sometimes approach Hollywood quality in terms of lifelike appearance and visual detail. As a result, there is also the inherent danger that jurors will overly rely on flashy videos, which may make these flashy visuals vulnerable to exclusion under Federal Rule of Evidence 403 as being unfairly prejudicial, confusing, or misleading. The most common types of cases in which animations and simulations are useful are criminal, medical and surgical malpractice, product liability, environmental, aviation, construction, personal injury, transportation, and accidents.

Various terms are used to describe such exhibits, including "animation," "simulation," and "re-creation." No matter which term you use, however, the evidentiary foundation depends on whether you are offering the exhibit as substantive or demonstrative evidence. Generally, the more the exhibit purports to be a recreation of the actual scene or event, the more likely the evidentiary requirements are to be heightened, thus requiring additional foundation. Conversely, when you use computer animations as illustrative or demonstrative evidence, the foundation is usually simpler.

Animations

Computer animations usually illustrate the testimony of an expert, but you can use them to illustrate the testimony of any witness. As with all demonstrative or illustrative evidence, the admissibility of an animation depends on whether you can show that it is a fair and accurate depiction of the events described by the witness and, if so, that it will help the fact finder understand the witness's testimony. Therefore, the four foundation steps for admitting animations are:

1. Authentication (Rule 901).
2. Relevance (Rules 401 and 402).
3. Fair and accurate depiction of what the witness is testifying about.
4. Satisfies the balancing test pursuant to Rule 403 that it is not unfairly prejudicial, confusing, misleading, or a waste of time.

The more closely the animation used as demonstrative evidence resembles the actual incident, the more detailed a foundation may be required. Many courts also require the proponent to establish that the demonstrative evidence shares substantial similarity with incident conditions, limiting the concern that it could be misleading.

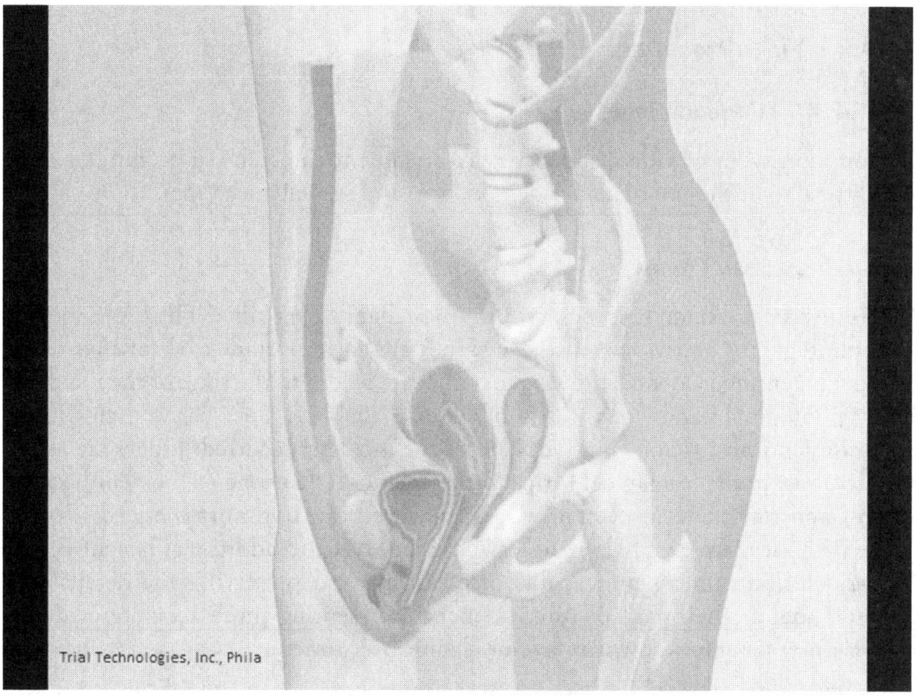

Figure 1 is a screenshot of an animation used help an expert explain how an infection can spread due to a uterine prolapse surgery. To see the full animation, go to the Visuals Appendix.

Simulations

Simulations have a higher evidentiary standard for use and admission because they usually involve entering data into a computer program that generates a visualization of some type of event or action; that visualization is produced by applying technical principles to the data. For example, an expert can create a simulation of an automobile accident by entering data such as speed, skid marks, resting position of the cars, and other factors. Simulations produce a result—from which the fact-finder will draw a conclusion—based on scientific or engineering principles as applied by a particular computer program. Because such a result is the functional equivalent of an expert's opinion and generally requires the testimony of an expert, it must satisfy the requirements for expert testimony set forth in Rule 702. Therefore, depending on your jurisdiction, you must satisfy either the *Frye* or *Daubert* standard to use the simulation, and a pretrial hearing may be required to determine its admissibility. The foundation is described in section 8.2, but the main variation with simulations is the foundation requirement that the underlying computer program is reliable pursuant to Rule 702.

***See* Figure 2 on the Visuals Appendix for an example of animation of an accident between a car and truck that incorporates motion data produced by an expert witness.**

11.4.3 Video Evidence

11.4.3.1 Common Types

Common types of video evidence may document the scene of a crime or incident, the day-in-the-life of an accident victim, and surveillance tapes.

Site-Inspection Videos

Crime scenes, accident scenes, and injuries change over time. Thus, site-inspection photographs and videos of those scenes are an important tool for preserving and documenting evidence in the state it appeared close to the time of the incident. These photographs and videos can also be more reliable and persuasive than witness testimony months, if not many years, after the incident occurred. Judges are reluctant to allow jurors to take field trips to the location of a crime or incident because of cost and time. Site inspection videos, however, can transport the jurors to the scene without them ever having to leave the jury box. An additional benefit is that high-resolution cameras are capable of capturing and preserving the details of a scene as well as the broad picture, frequently presenting more accurate evidence than witness's memories, which fade or change over time.

***See* Figure 3 on the Visuals Appendix for an example of a site-inspection video of a home that was damaged by fire and the water used to extinguish the flames.**

Day-in-the-Life Videos

Day-in-the-life videos are often used to show how a plaintiff—in a personal injury or medical malpractice case—has been damaged. These videos can transport the fact finder into the home or workplace of the plaintiff without ever having to leave the courtroom. In this way, jurors can see for themselves how the plaintiff is unable to care for himself and the sort of assistance or accommodation he needs on a daily basis.

You must handle this type of evidence with care and caution. Videos that are clearly exaggerated or that include nontypical activities can backfire, immediately detracting from your credibility and damaging your case. Moreover, the final video will virtually always, for the sake of brevity and coherence, contain selective portions of the entire recorded material. If the opposing party requests and is granted access to the raw footage, which usually happens, the outtakes may appear to contradict the video you presented in court.

See Figure 4 on the Visuals Appendix for an example of a day-in-the-life video of an injured man and how he now struggles to get in and out of a car.

Surveillance Video

The proliferation of smartphones with video capability and the decreased cost of surveillance cameras have led to increased presentation of surveillance video in the courtroom. Such videos can be used as substantive evidence regarding liability in civil cases and guilt in criminal cases, frequently playing the role of a "silent witness" when no one was around to observe the event.

Video Enhancement

Surveillance video is frequently of poor quality because of camera angle, lighting, camera movement, and low-quality recording settings or equipment. Poor video quality can be improved through video enhancement, most commonly by using a series of filters that make the image appear clearer. This process can make the original image clearer without changing any of its content. Improvements can be as simple as sharpening the edges of images or stabilizing a video with a lot of movement. If a video has been enhanced, you must explain the method and its reliability as part of the foundation.

Figure 5 is an example of video enhancement.

11.4.4 Video Depositions

You can use video depositions at trial either as substantive evidence or for impeachment. In either case, the fact finder frequently finds video testimony more persuasive and interesting than listening to you read from a transcript of the deposition. A video deposition also allows the fact finder to view the demeanor of a witness, which is impossible to observe from the simple reading of a transcript.

11.4.4.1 Depositions as Substantive Evidence

Video depositions are admissible as substantive evidence during trial in certain circumstances: the witness is unavailable to provide live testimony; witness is a party[1]; and by agreement of the parties. Using video deposition can not only save time and expense, but can also eliminate the potential for scheduling conflicts. Despite these advantages, video deposition testimony will never engage the fact finder as live testimony does, so use it cautiously, especially when the testimony is important or credibility is an issue.

When appropriate, showing a video deposition at trial rather than reading a transcript is also advantageous when a witness is referring to a particular exhibit, recreating an important moment in the case, or enacting any type of demonstration. You can use a split-screen view to show the exhibits simultaneously with the witness performing the demonstrations. The video deposition is now interactive, so that when a witness discusses a document or exhibit, it will simultaneously appear on the screen, and the picture of the witness will be moved to the side or minimized to the corner of the screen.

1. Fed. R. Civ. P 32; Fed. R. Evid. 804.

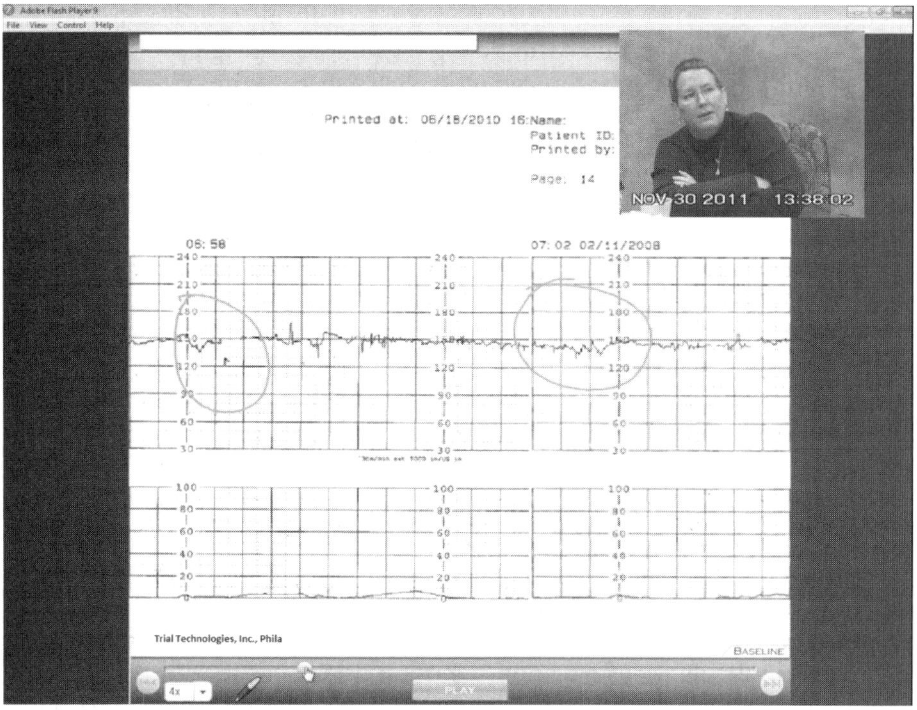

Figure 6 is a screenshot of an interactive deposition where an expert is shown testifying about a fetal monitoring strip—the printout from a fetal heart rate monitor is onscreen, and the witness is shown circling the moments where there were variations and possible times of distress. To see the full video of this interactive deposition, go to the Visuals Appendix.

Even when a video deposition is admissible as substantive evidence, the testimony is still subject to other evidentiary objections—such as relevance, hearsay, and unfair prejudice—just as if the witness were on the stand in the courtroom. When necessary, you can simply edit out the inadmissible portions of the testimony. You should resolve these issues with opposing counsel and, if necessary, with court intervention well ahead of trial.

11.4.5 Depositions for Impeachment

Depositions are more commonly used to impeach a witness whose trial testimony differs from the deposition. A video of a witness making a contradictory statement can be more damaging to her credibility than simply reading the prior inconsistent statement from a transcript. The jurors will experience the drama of watching the witness's negative reaction as she watches her own contradictory statement when it is shown in court.

Depositions go on for many hours, so the most difficult part of impeachment with a video deposition is quickly retrieving the impeaching segment. Long delays while you or your assistant try to cue up the relevant part can seriously limit the effectiveness of impeachment.

Fortunately, it is possible to move quickly to targeted parts of the video by creating a synchronized deposition. Many commercial firms provide this service—you provide them with the video deposition, which is then linked to a written transcript. The linked transcript allows you to easily create small video clips simply by pointing your cursor at the portion of the transcript in question. And you can do this before trial or even on the fly at trial. By clicking on or scanning part of the linked written transcript, you are taken directly to a specific part of the video deposition. Synchronized depositions also enable you to show scrolling text beneath the video so that the fact finder can both hear and read the statement.

11.4.6 Displaying Substantive Evidence Visually

You can and should show many types of substantive evidence as electronic visuals. Jurors are sometimes distracted when individual exhibits and pieces of evidence are passed around. Moreover, when a juror is closely examining an exhibit, she is unable to pay simultaneous attention to critical details in the witness testimony. And most judges will not allow the long delay caused by waiting for each juror individually to complete her review of the item.

You will often want each juror and the judge to be able to view a piece of evidence at the same time, especially while a witness is testifying about it, but this is difficult or impossible to achieve when an object is small or needs close examination. If an expert witness is describing specific markings on the side of a bullet found at a crime scene, it is not possible for all jurors to examine the bullet at a close enough range as the expert describes it. Projecting a large image of the bullet solves this problem. In addition to small objects, common types of evidence that are projected electronically are documents; contracts; checks; photographs; business or hospital records; email and text messages; and medical images, such as x-rays, computerized axial tomography (CT scans), positron emission tomography (PET scans), and magnetic resonance imaging (MRI) images.

An additional advantage of projecting the exhibit is that you can easily highlight, annotate, or draw direct attention to particular parts of the evidence. Thus, in the above example, you could ask the expert to draw an arrow on the projected image of a bullet as she describes a specific marking. You can save any projected images with annotations on a computer through presentation software, print it immediately (or at a later time), and preserve the printed copy as an exhibit. Some courts require that the printed versions be admitted as a separate exhibit or as a subset of the original exhibit. This ensures an accurate record. As part of your advance preparation, make sure you have access to a printer in the courtroom and confer with the court before trial about how they prefer to handle annotated exhibits.

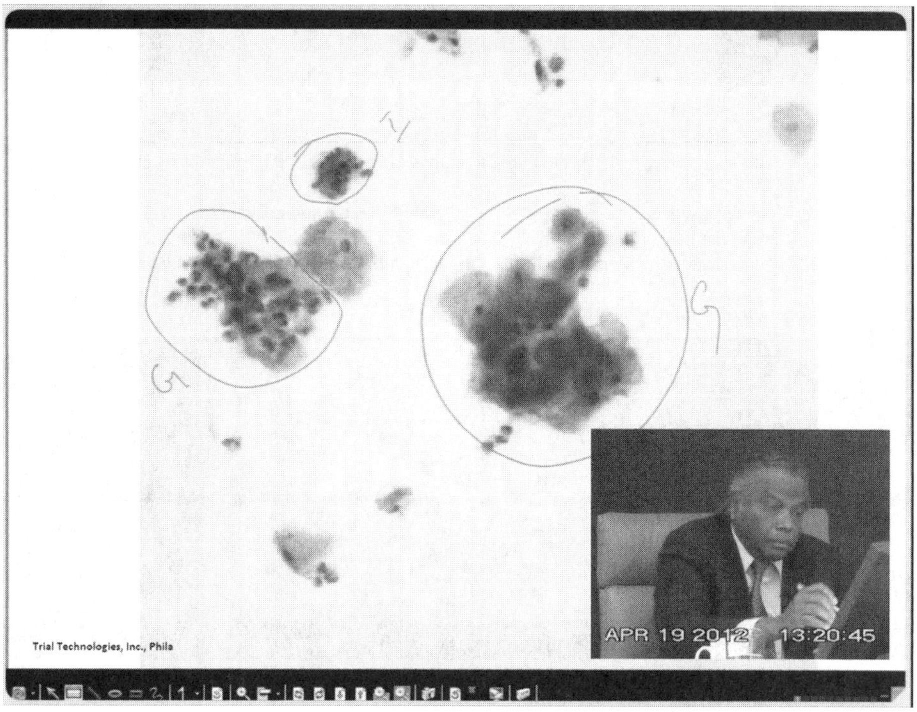

Figure 7 is a screen shot of a video showing a witness testifying while circling images of cells as he identifies their types. To see full video, go to the Visuals Appendix.

Presenting an entire document filled with much irrelevant information will unnecessarily distract the fact finder, who may be tempted to read the entire document rather than focus on the relatively few important details. You can use call-out boxes (sometimes called text-pulls) or other forms of highlighting to effectively direct the fact finder to the crucial parts of the document.

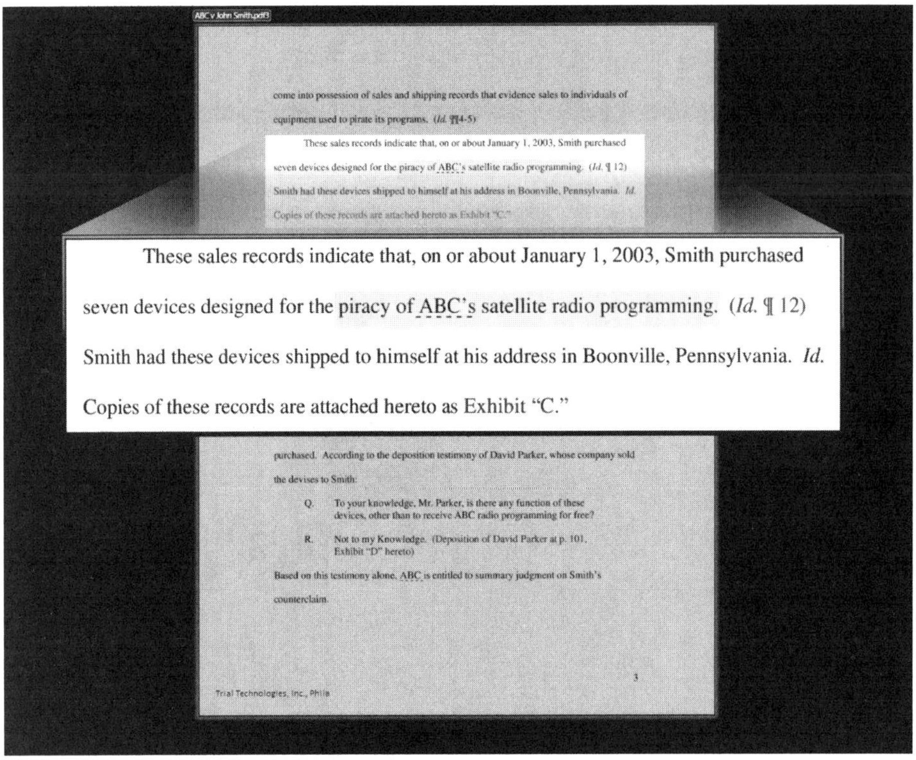

Figure 8 is an example of a call-out.

11.4.7 Charts, Graphs, and Diagrams

11.4.7.1 Overview

Trials often involve vast amounts of complex information. Electronic visuals, such as diagrams, charts, graphs, and maps, provide ways to clarify, simplify and organize the evidence.

11.4.7.2 Common Examples

Timelines

Evidence at trial is seldom delivered in strictly chronological order. That can be a problem, especially when timing is an essential part of your case. Timelines are helpful in situations when there are numerous dates or the sequence of events is important. You may need to clearly demonstrate the order of events to establish an alibi defense or to show how a series of occurrences led to someone's motive. You can place a large number of events on a single timeline to provide visual clarity that you could not readily accomplish in oral testimony, opening statement, or closing argument.

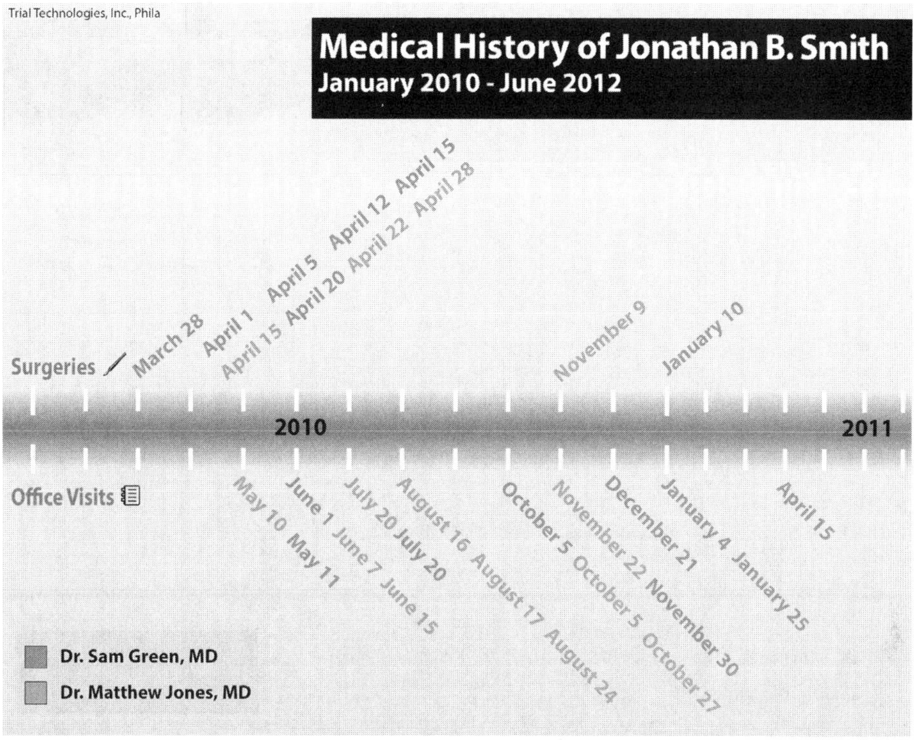

Figure 9 is a timeline that illustrates when a patient had received various treatments and when he saw a doctor.

Interactive Timelines

It is impossible in most cases to display all the supporting evidence or even the key evidence on a single timeline. Such an exhibit would quickly become cluttered and unreadable. Therefore, you can use digital or interactive methods to create expanded timelines. An interactive timeline allows you to click on a particular event in coordination with a witness's testimony or during your opening statement or closing argument. Thus, you can display the evidence precisely when you, or the witness, are explaining it.

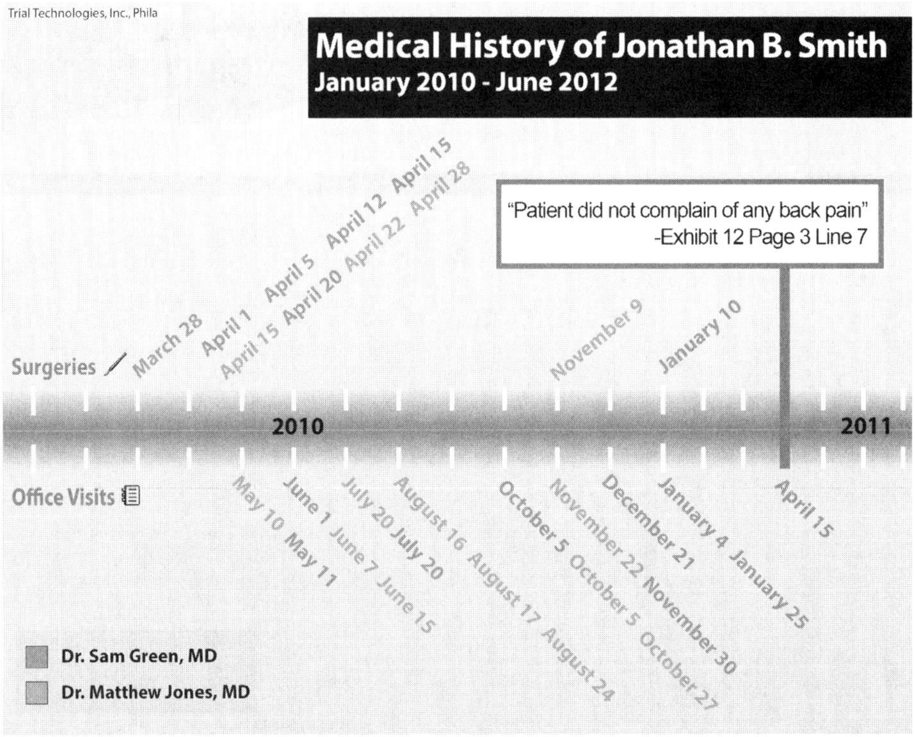

Figure 10 is an example of an interactive timeline.

Remember, however, that you are using a timeline to show the relationships among a series of important events—but not every event—in your case. Too many entries on a single timeline will make it confusing and less effective.

Lists

Simple lists can be effective visuals. They are used at all stages of a trial, but most commonly during opening statements and closing arguments.

You can use a checklist during closing argument to help show the jurors how you have proven every element of your claim. A simple slide listing two or three trial themes can be a memorable way of connecting with the fact finder during opening statement. You can also use lists to support one of your major arguments. For example, you could show the fact finder a visual that lists the proper method for handling a chainsaw.

Was Mr. Jones working safely?

Fueling a Chain Saw	YES	NO
• Use approved containers for transporting fuel to the saw.		
• Dispense fuel at least 10 feet away from any sources of ignition when performing construction activities. **No smoking during fueling.**		✓
• Use a funnel or a flexible hose when pouring fuel into the saw.		✓
• Never attempt to fuel a running or HOT saw.		✓

Source: https://www.osha.gov/Publications/3269-10N-05-english-06-27-2007.html

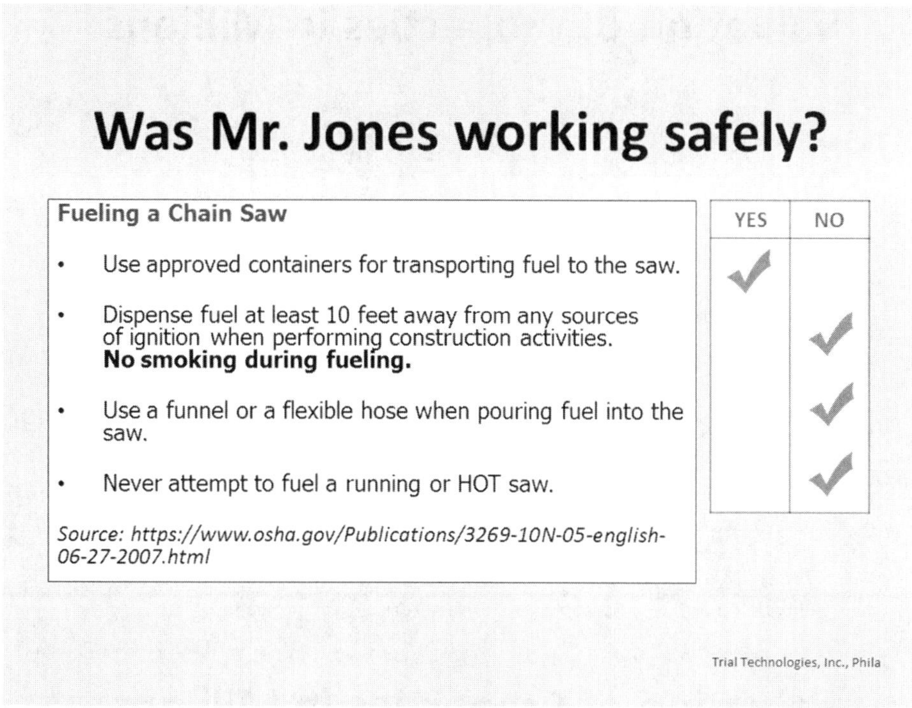

Figure 11 is an example of a list.

Line Charts

Line charts are the most useful visual aids for demonstrating trends over time. For example, if you are trying to show price changes over a period of ten years, a simple chart—recognizable as a Cartesian plane from high school algebra—would plot the years along the x-axis and the cost along the y-axis. The connecting line will then show upward or downward trends or other fluctuations. You must be aware, however, that line charts can be easily manipulated to make trends appear more or less dramatic. This is usually done by increasing or decreasing the space between the points on either the x- or y-axis. Two examples of a line chart are shown below. They demonstrate how the same information can be presented in different ways to be more persuasive, but also more misleading.

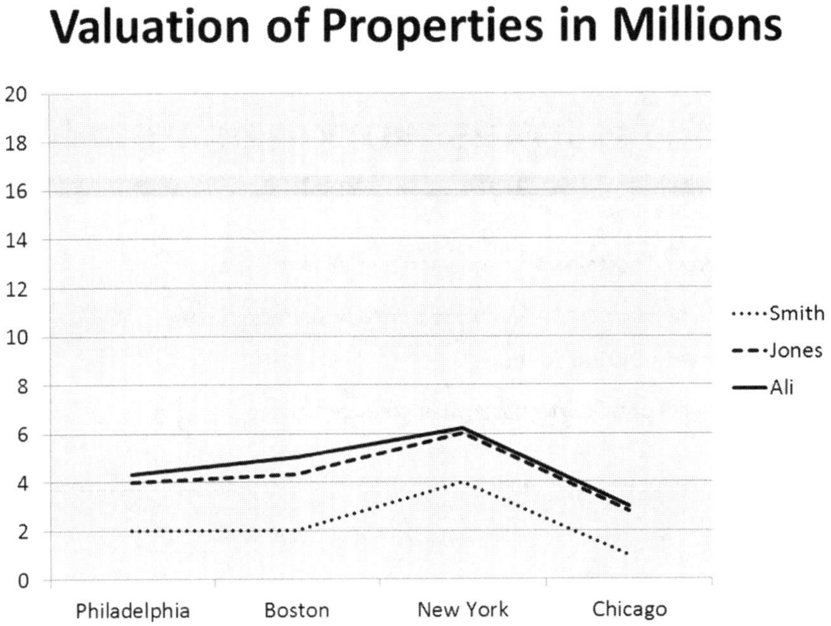

Trial Technologies, Inc., Phila

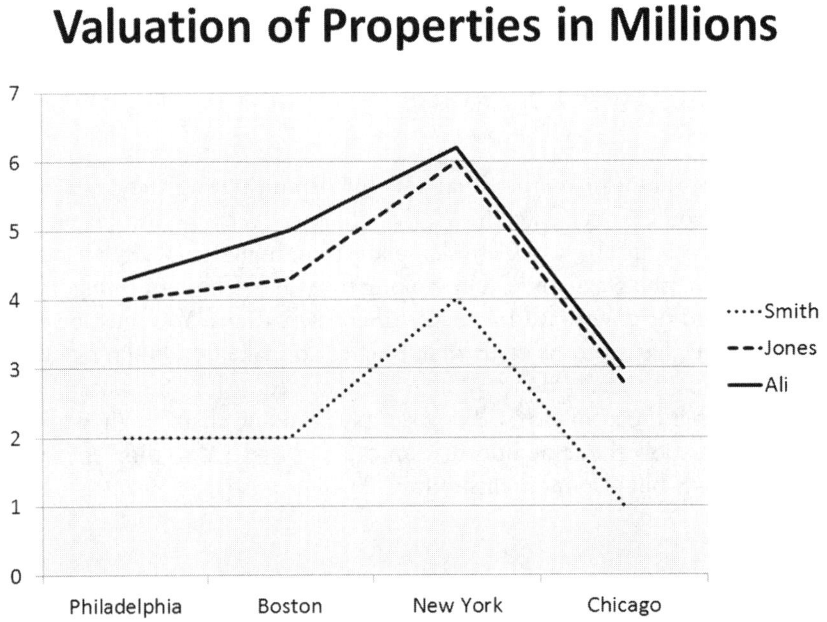

Trial Technologies, Inc., Phila

Figures 12 and 13 are examples of two line charts that present the same information—the value of a product over several years. In Figure 12 you can clearly see the change in value. However, that same information appears much more dramatic in Figure 13 because one axis has been manipulated.

A word of caution: you must not only review your opponent's charts to catch such manipulation, you must also review your own to make sure you didn't inadvertently introduce an exaggeration—your opponent will surely point out such exaggerations to the jurors, thus diminishing your credibility.

Witness Relationships

One of your goals during opening statement is to introduce key witnesses, and your goal during closing argument is to make sure the fact finder remembers who they are, what they said, and their relationship to the case. You can use witness relationship charts to make that information more clear and comprehensible, and you can refer to it as your story unfolds.

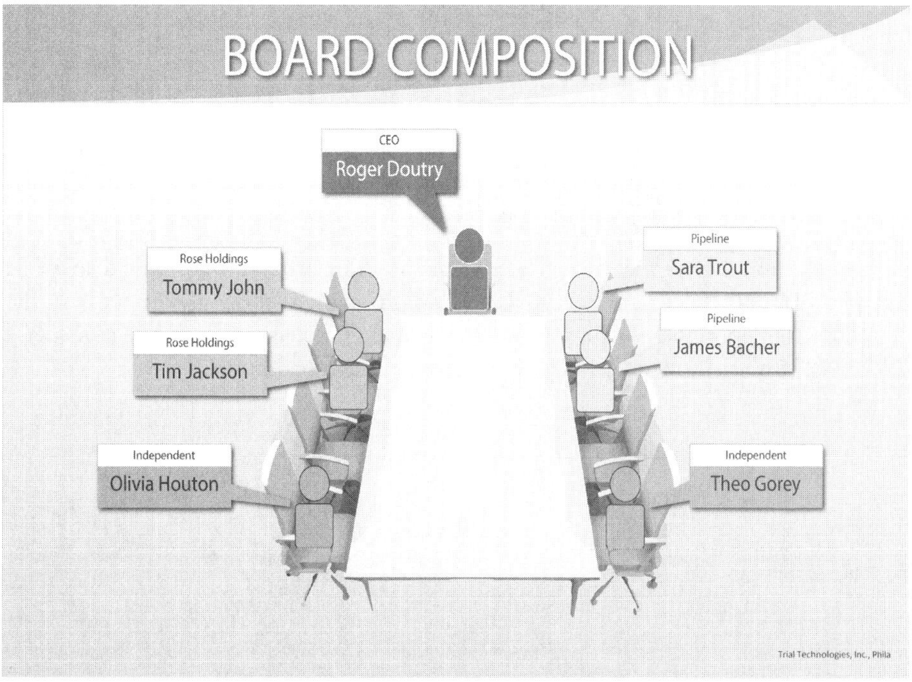

Figure 14 is an example of a witness chart that can be used to introduce members of the Board of Directors.

You can use more complicated charts to show the relationship between witnesses. Numerous witnesses can be placed at different levels on the same chart or with lines connecting them to each other. Remember to not overcomplicate such charts—unless, of course, that is your goal.

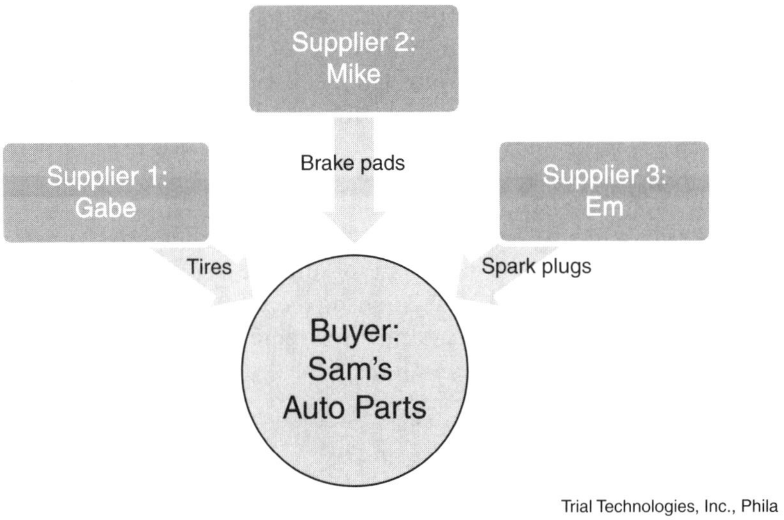

Figure 15 is an example of a chart showing the multiplicity of suppliers to a retailer.

Flow Charts

Flow charts are generally used to depict a system or process in a single display. In a products liability case, for example, you might want to show all the steps in the manufacture and delivery of a particular product. Likewise, you might consider a flow chart to show how decisions are made within a corporation.

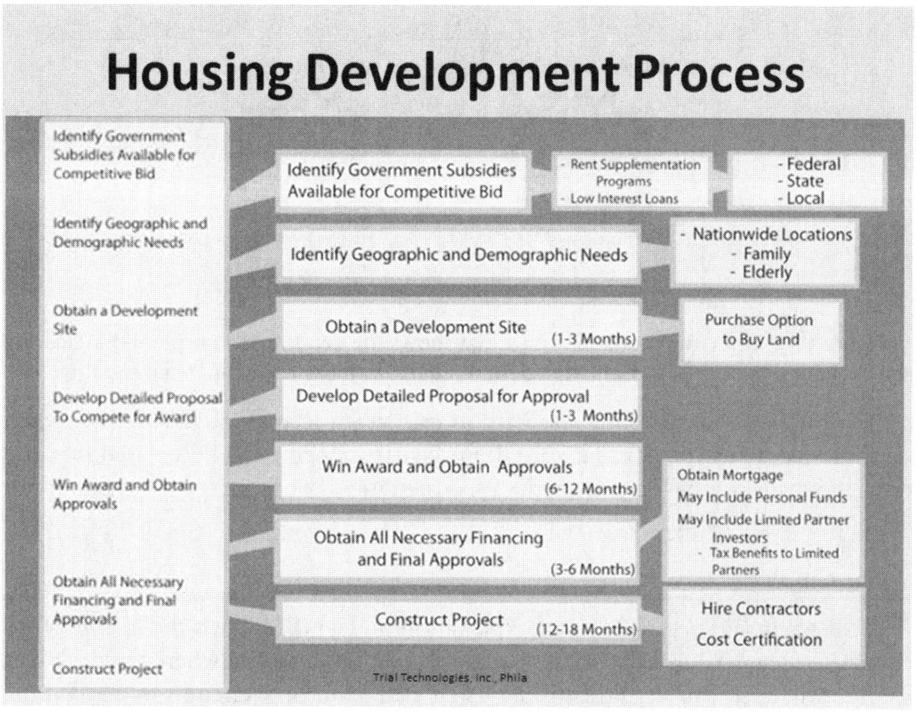

Figure 16 is an example of the process for developing affordable housing.

Be careful not to include unnecessary and irrelevant steps, as this will make your chart cluttered and confusing. If you want to explain more than one process, consider using a separate flow chart for each.

Pie Charts

Pie charts are used to demonstrate percentages, proportions, and representative amounts. A pie chart would be helpful, for example, to show how the assets of a company have been distributed following bankruptcy or how damages should be allocated among defendants.

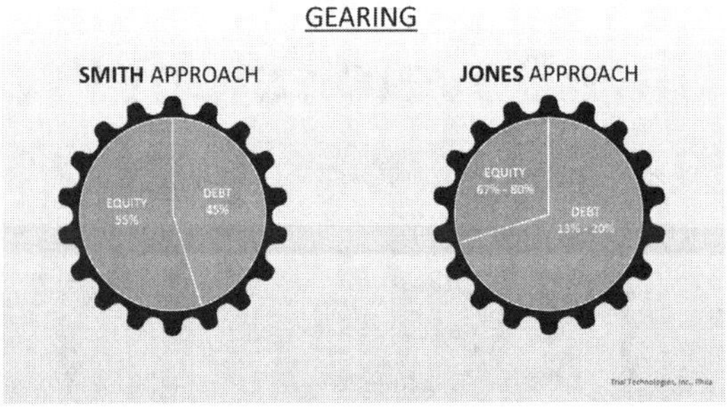

Figure 17 is an example of a pie chart that shows the gearing of a corporation. Gearing shows the proportion of a company's debt to equity to measure its financial stability.

Pie charts can be confusing and hard to read when sectors are too small or when there are too many categories involved. Pie charts generally should be used in situations in which you have no more than six categories. For more complex situations, consider using a bar graph.

Bar Graph

A bar graph can provide a visual explanation of data that allows the fact finder to compare categories or see a trend. Bar graphs are less effective when precise values are important, so you should consider using a table in those circumstances.

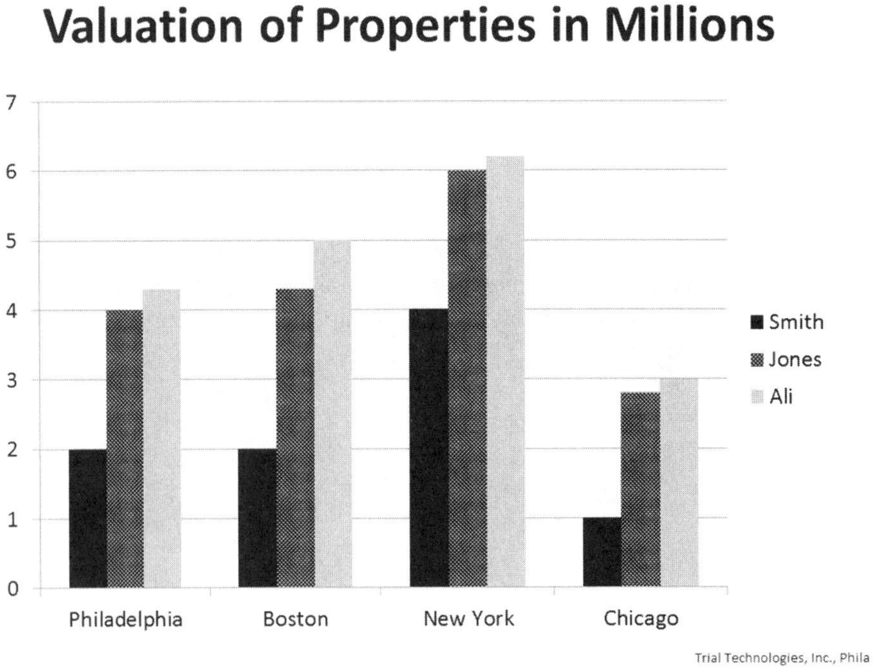

Figure 18 is an example of a vertical bar graph.

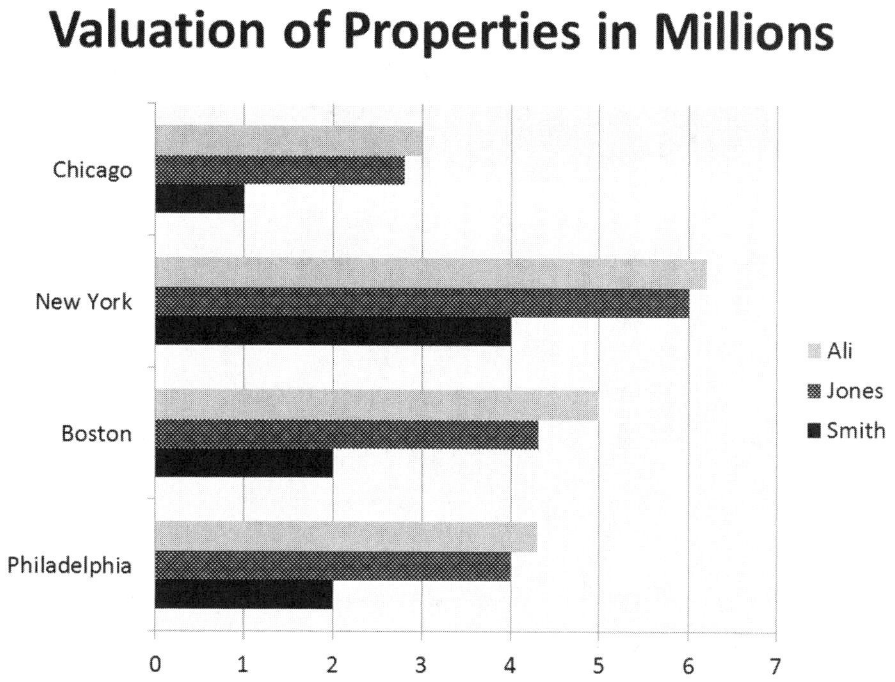

Trial Technologies, Inc., Phila

Figure 19 is an example of a horizontal bar graph.

Table

Tables are an effective method to visually display precise, specific, or numerical data. They do not clearly show trends or comparisons of several categories, but are ideal when specificity is important. Attorneys frequently use tables when discussing damages.

Plaintiff's Income 2014

Month	Dollars
January	$4,166.72
February	$4,022.45
March	$4,348.23
April	$4,602.12
May	$4,343.11
June	Accident Occurs

Trial Technologies, Inc., Phila

Figure 20 is an example of a table.

As discussed in section 10.5.3.3, many business records or other sets of data are so lengthy and ponderous that they cannot be conveniently produced in court. Therefore, you may substitute a "summary, chart, or calculation" that fairly presents the relevant information in a usable or understandable form.[2] Summaries are commonly displayed as tables. Unlike many other graphics, summaries may be admissible as substantive evidence.

2. Fed. R. Evid. 1006.

Trial Technologies, Inc., Phila

Male/Female Employees

	2009	2010	2011	2012	2013	2014
Company X						
Total number of employees	8,013	7,468	7,253	7,021	7,196	7,731
Total number of men	5,611	5,207	5,058	4,942	5,082	5,402
Total number of women	2,402	2,261	2,195	2,079	2,114	2,329
Average salary of men	$85,321	$81,022	$79,152	$79,008	$80,309	$82,417
Average salary of women	$59,027	$58,111	$56,087	$57,155	$58,219	$57,351
Company Y						
Total number of employees	10,106	9,202	9,104	9,386	9,595	10,067
Total number of men	6,005	5,490	5,343	5,522	5,691	6,047
Total number of women	4,101	3,712	3,761	3,864	3,904	4,020
Average salary of men	$ 98,102	$ 97,224	$ 95,022	$ 97,419	$ 98,386	$100,253
Average salary of women	$ 65,985	$ 63,179	$ 60,154	$ 63,007	$ 63,658	$ 66,044

Figure 21 is an example of a summary chart.

Unlike exhibits that make an immediate visual impact, summaries must be read to be understood. It is therefore important to give the fact finder adequate time to read through the visual before proceeding to your next point. As always, be careful not to include too much information on one table, as that will make it confusing and hard to read.

Maps

You can use maps to show location, distance, relationships between multiple locations, direction of travel, and terrain type. More broadly, they can also set the scene for the relevant action in your case. Commercially made maps are readily available in stores, on the Internet, and through government agencies, although they vary greatly in color, size, and degree of detail. Therefore, you should explore multiple options and consider a custom-made map if none of the ready-made maps meet your needs.

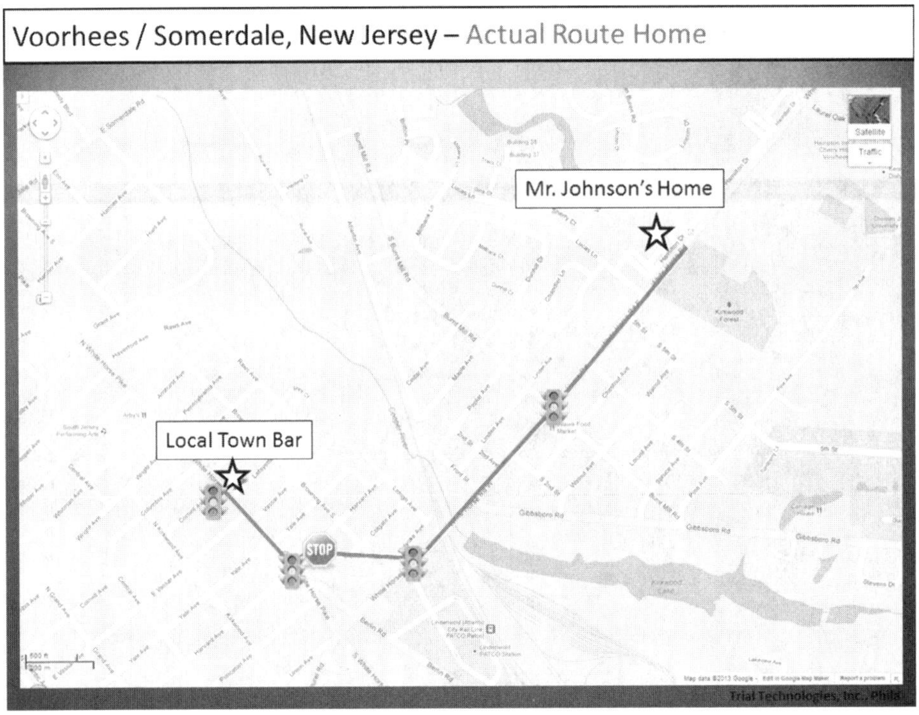

Figure 22 is an example of using a map to clearly illustrate the route between two locations.

Virtually all maps include distortions and inaccuracies, which may draw objections in situations where precise location and distance are important (*see* section 10.4.3.1). Electronic projection can sometimes add to the distortion of that map, potentially creating a valid basis for objection. It is therefore important to preview any map in its projected version and to prepare for any potential problems.

11.4.8 Interactive Demonstrative Exhibits

One of the primary advantages to using electronic exhibits is your ability to adapt, change, and annotate your exhibits in the course of your presentation. An interactive exhibit allows you and the witness to do this with movement, sound, and additional content. All of the exhibits previously discussed can be made to be interactive in one way or another: you can move graphics around while a witness is testifying, hyperlink additional information, and enhance or highlight aspects of the visual. In our fire engine case, for example, you might ask a witness to position the cars and fire truck on the map as they were at the time of the accident, showing them in motion as the collision occurred. In a timeline, your exhibit could be set up so that a click will take you to a photograph or chart that is relevant to a specific event.

See Figure 23 on the Visuals Appendix for an example of an interactive demonstrative accident exhibit from an automobile accident case. The exhibit allows the witness to move the witnesses around and place them where they were at the time of the accident.

11.5 When to Use Electronic Visuals

11.5.1 Opening Statements

The opening statement is your chance to tell a persuasive story, simplify and make clear the important parts of your case, develop your credibility, and capture the attention of the fact finder.

11.5.1.1 Establishing Credibility

A well-developed, and sometimes simple, electronic visual can impress the fact finder because it shows that you care about and believe in your case enough to have taken the time to create such a visual.

11.5.1.2 Making It Memorable

Using electronic visuals will enable you to highlight key evidence and make it memorable. Jurors are used to receiving information in a visual format in their everyday lives, so presenting information in this way may help to make them feel at ease, which increases their ability to process the information and allows them to better comprehend and recall it.

11.5.1.3 Common Examples

Electronic visuals can play an important role during the opening statement to clarify, simplify, and explain. Common electronic visuals used to accomplish these goals are charts, graphs, timelines, maps, video surveillance, photographs, diagrams, key documents, and lists.

When cases involve large numbers of people or complicated relationships between people and parties, a witness chart can introduce witnesses and illustrate their relationship to the other parties.

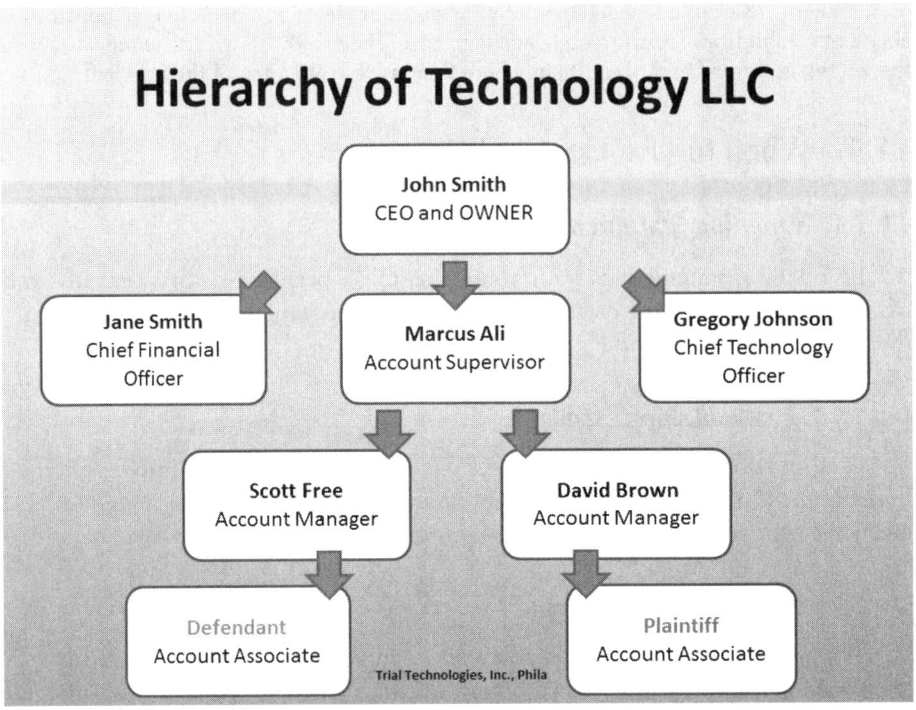

Figure 24 is an example of a witness flow chart.

When timing is critical, a simple timeline highlighting the key events can help the fact finder understand and remember the timing of those events.

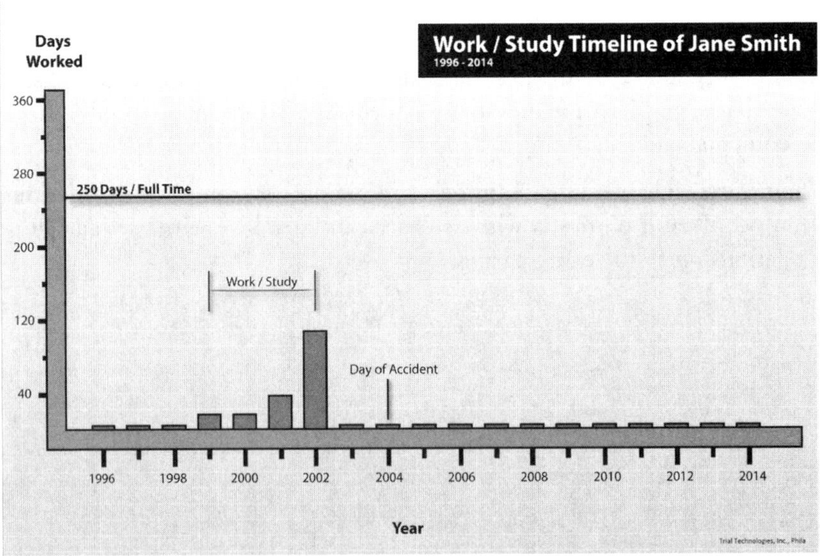

Figure 25 is an example of timeline.

Electronic visuals can effectively highlight key documents, or parts of documents.

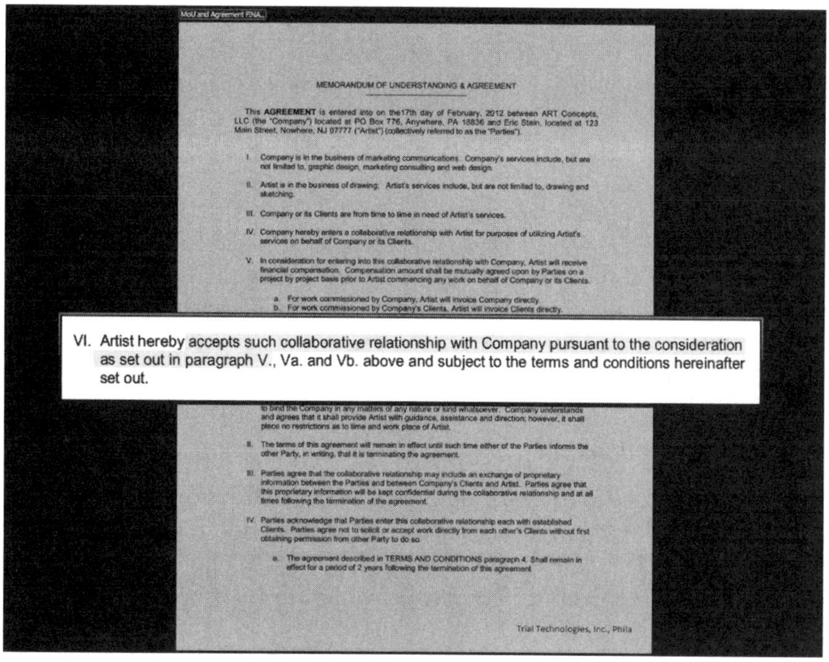

Figure 26 is an example of a call-out.

Keep in mind that when you want to project an electronic visual of potential evidence, such as a gun or a contract, you must have a good-faith belief that it will be admitted in evidence at trial. If you are using an electronic visual that you have created to simply explain something, such as a timeline or witness chart, you must be sure that it isn't misleading.

11.5.1.4 Risks and Dangers

Backfire

Although electronic visuals can be effective during opening statements, you should proceed with caution because you never know exactly how the evidence will unfold and what witnesses will actually say. Be careful not to lock yourself into something that you cannot later prove; presenting a memorable visual during opening that turns out to be inaccurate can be devastating to your case and your credibility.

Although electronic visuals can go a long way toward establishing your credibility, a poorly executed visual can do the opposite. You must therefore practice and prepare in advance. Likewise, you must have an alternate plan in case the electronic visual does not work out as intended.

Getting in the Way

Using too many visuals in the opening statement tends to distract the fact finder during one of their first opportunities to assess your credibility. Moreover, presenting confusing visuals has the potential to be even more damaging because the jury may form negative impressions of your advocacy, which will diminish your credibility from the start.

Avoiding Argument

Your use of electronic visuals must be consistent with the prohibition against argument during opening statements. When electronic visuals draw conclusions or include interpretation of the evidence you are in the dangerous territory of impermissible argument.

Opponent Objections

Even if you are careful to avoid argument, using an electronic visual during your opening statement opens up the potential for an objection from the opposing side. You can ameliorate this concern by showing the visual to opposing counsel ahead of time and seek a ruling from the court on any objections, if necessary.

11.5.2 Closing Argument

11.5.2.1 Don't Forget to Use Them

You have just spent a great deal of time creating and admitting exhibits throughout the trial. Now use them! Ask yourself the question, why did I offer this exhibit? Was it to support the testimony or credibility of a witness? If so, consider displaying the exhibit when you talk about a particular witness. Did you enter the exhibit to help establish an element of your claim or defense? Consider displaying it electronically when discussing the law and explaining why the fact finder should rule for your client.

You can be very creative with electronic visuals during the closing argument because the fact finder has now seen and heard all of the evidence. Unlike the opening statement, you are no longer constrained by the prohibition against argument, nor do you need to be concerned about admissibility. The possibilities are almost limitless.

11.5.2.2 Empower the Jury

Some jurors may already be on your side by the end of the evidence, and your closing argument may therefore provide them with the tools to convince their fellow jurors to rule in your favor. A persuasive electronic visual can provide a resource or roadmap for a favorable juror to influence the others.

11.5.2.3 Common Examples

In addition to replaying some or all of your animation or simulation, other common forms of electronic visuals during closing argument include presenting your tangible evidence; replaying audio and video evidence; and displaying key documents, lists, photos, charts, or diagrams. You might use a simple slide that displays a few key points made by a particular witness, or you could use one that lists some of the key reasons why a witness should or should not be believed.

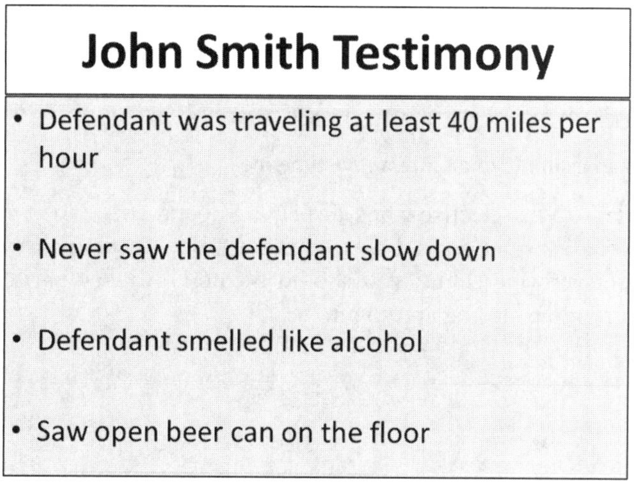

John Smith Testimony
• Defendant was traveling at least 40 miles per hour
• Never saw the defendant slow down
• Defendant smelled like alcohol
• Saw open beer can on the floor

Trial Technologies, Inc., Phila

Figure 27 is an example of a slide that highlights a witness's key testimony.

Timelines are an effective way to organize and remind the fact finder of important dates. Closing argument is a perfect time to use an interactive timeline because it will allow you to bring up detailed information as you address key points in your case.

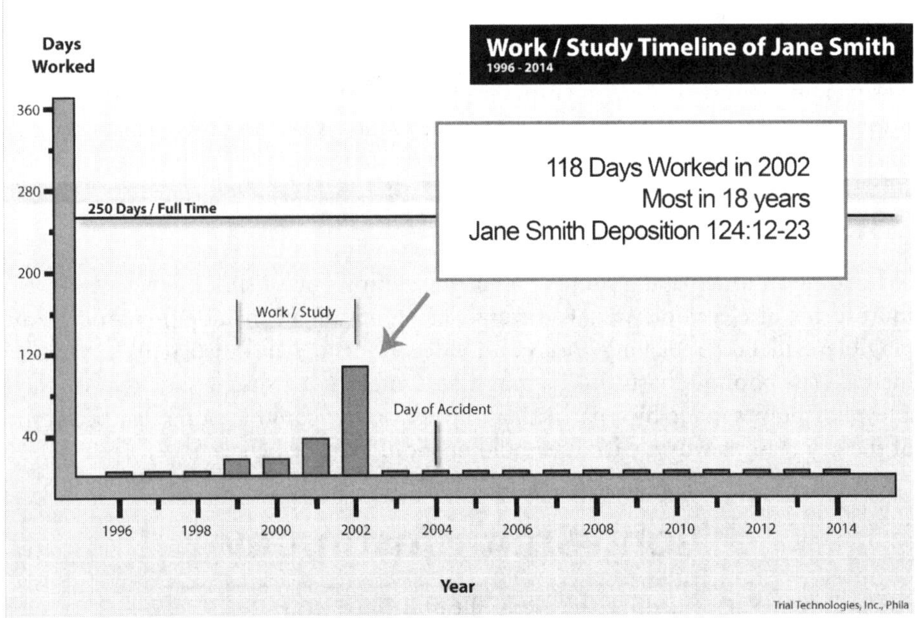

Figure 28 is an example of an interactive timeline.

It is important to be selective when displaying documents. Not every document is a critical piece of evidence, and even important documents will usually include much irrelevant verbiage. Thus, you should include only key parts of important documents during the closing argument.

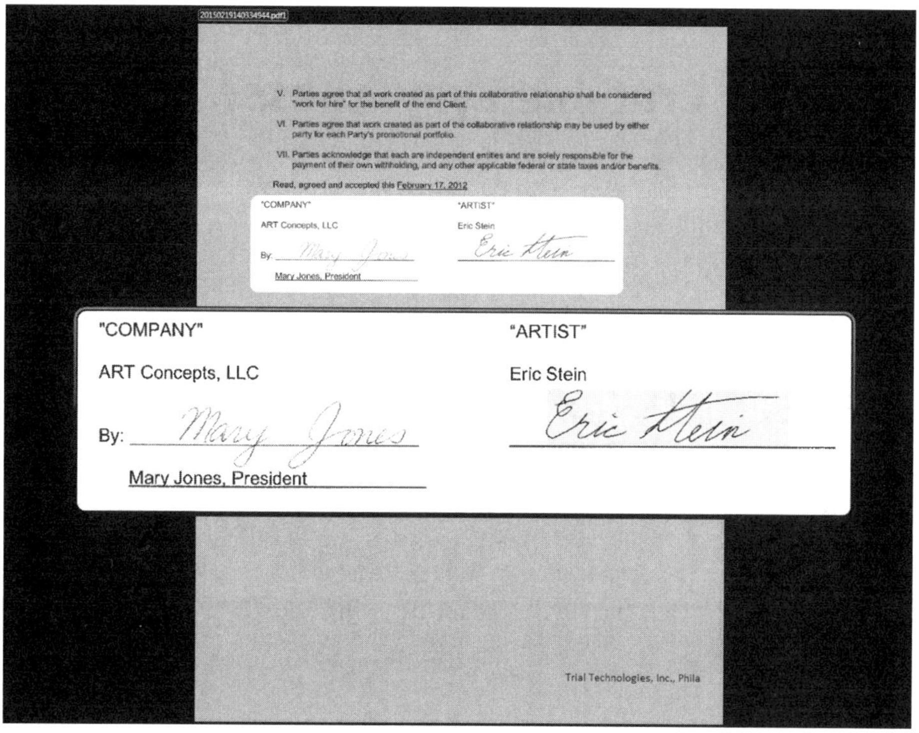

Figure 29 is an example of a way to display a call-out of an element of a contract that is important to the case.

You can also use slides to contrast and compare testimony and evidence. If a witness has made multiple inconsistent statements, you can show the contrasting testimony side-by-side in a single visual. In a related technique, you can also use contradictory statements between witnesses to attack the credibility of an opponent's witness or their entire case.

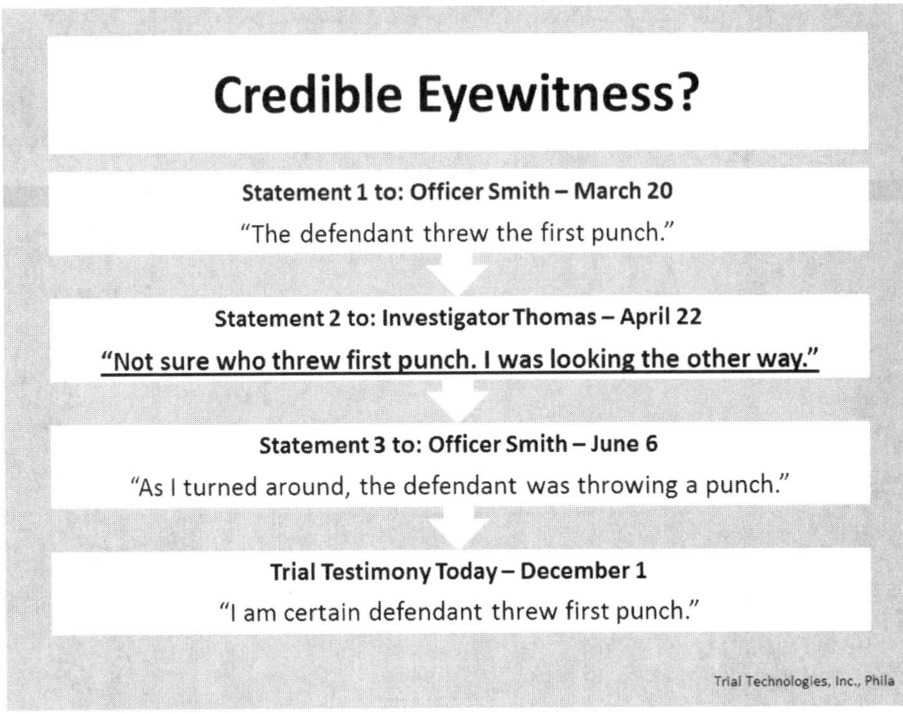

Credible Eyewitness?
Statement 1 to: Officer Smith – March 20
"The defendant threw the first punch."
Statement 2 to: Investigator Thomas – April 22
"Not sure who threw first punch. I was looking the other way."
Statement 3 to: Officer Smith – June 6
"As I turned around, the defendant was throwing a punch."
Trial Testimony Today – December 1
"I am certain defendant threw first punch."
Trial Technologies, Inc., Phila

Figure 30 is an example of a slide with witness's contrasting statements.

When you bear the burden of proof in either a civil or criminal case, you must be sure to convince the fact finder that you have proven all of the elements of a claim or defense. Conversely, if you are on the other side, you will want to demonstrate that your opponent failed to meet that burden. In either scenario, you can use a slide to list the relevant elements and to show how they have (or have not) been established by the evidence.

Robbery Elements
The taking of personal property of another;
with the intent to permanently deprive;
from his or her person or in their presence;
against his or her will;
by violence, intimidation or the threat of force.
Trial Technologies, Inc., Phila

Figure 31 is an example of a checklist with elements.

11.5.2.4 Risks and Dangers

Be wary of distractions. Make sure that electronic visuals support your closing argument rather than distract from it. Each time you present an electronic visual, the fact finders will turn their attention toward the display and potentially away from you. If you use electronic visuals that contain too much information, the fact finder may ignore what you are saying, thinking you have nothing more to add. So keep your visual aids simple and supportive of your position.

Although argument is permissible during closing, judges still have discretion over the use of electronic visuals and may disallow them when they appear misleading. Therefore, be certain that your electronic visuals are founded on fair inferences, characterizations, and conclusions that are based on the admitted evidence.

11.5.2.5 Using Your Opponent's Electronic Visuals

Consider whether you can take advantage of any of your opponent's electronic visuals. It can be devastating to display your opponent's visual and point out where it is wrong or incomplete. And it can be a triumph to show that one of your opponent's visuals is actually persuasive evidence of one of your own positions.

11.5.3 Witness Examinations

Witness examinations present many opportunities to use electronic visuals. However, it is essential that you plan carefully and consider many questions. Will you need to ask the court for permission to have the witness step down from the witness stand and point to the exhibit? Will that require a laser pointer? Is the witness going to add annotations to the exhibit and will that be permitted by the court? How will you preserve such annotations? Will opposing counsel want her witnesses to mark the exhibit?

The interaction between a witness and an electronic visual can be extremely powerful, but it can also be undermined by insufficient preparation.

11.5.3.1 Expert Witnesses

Electronic visuals are commonly used during the direct examination of expert witnesses to make complicated and technical information more comprehensible. An electronic visual can help the expert assume the role of teacher, which is almost always the most effective way to present her testimony. Experts commonly use slides to define or explain key terms, to list their conclusions, or to summarize their opinions.

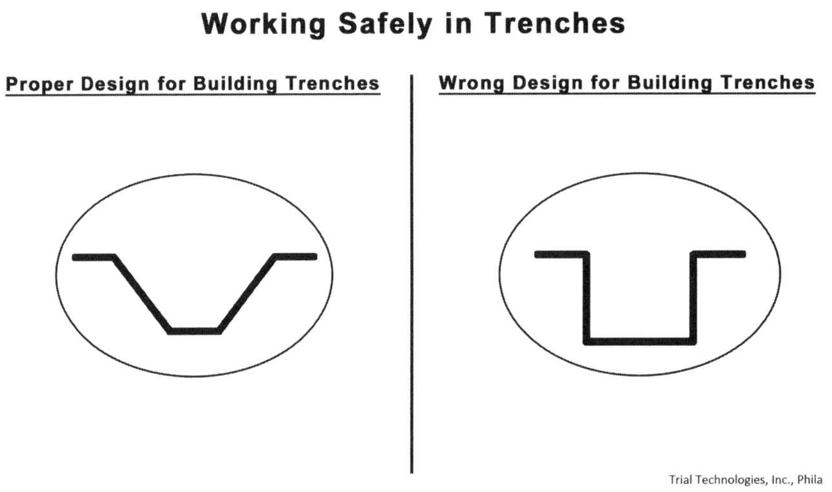

Figure 32 is an example of an expert's explanatory slide.

Common Examples

An electronic visual can be used to explain an expert's damage calculations.

ECONOMIC DAMAGES – Lost Earnings and Fringe Benefits	
Past Loss of Earnings Capacity	$406,500
Past Loss of Fringe Benefits	$90,110
Future Loss of Earnings Capacity	$2,485,320
Future Loss of Fringe Benefits	$590,800
Future Health-Related Goods and Services	$18,394,437
Total Economic Damages:	**$21,967,167**

Trial Technologies, Inc., Phila

Figure 33 is example of a damages calculation by an expert.

An expert's flow chart can explain a process.

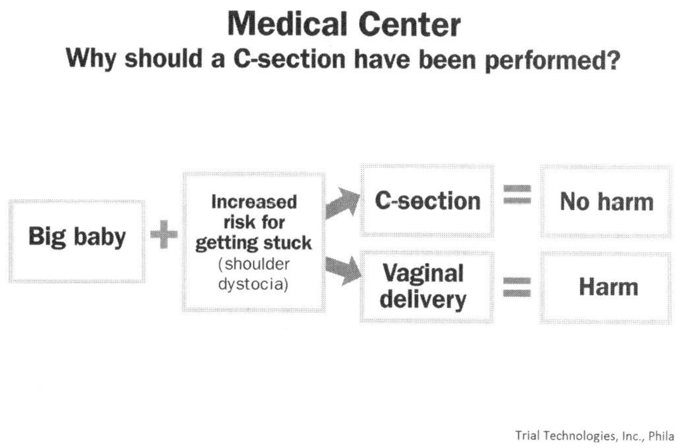

Figure 34 is an example of an expert's flow chart.

11.5.3.2 Lay Witness Testimony

Supporting and reinforcing a lay witness's direct examination with an electronic visual, such as a diagram or a document, can make that testimony more memorable and believable. Electronic visuals commonly used on direct examination include maps, photos, or diagrams. You can also use electronic visuals on cross-examination.

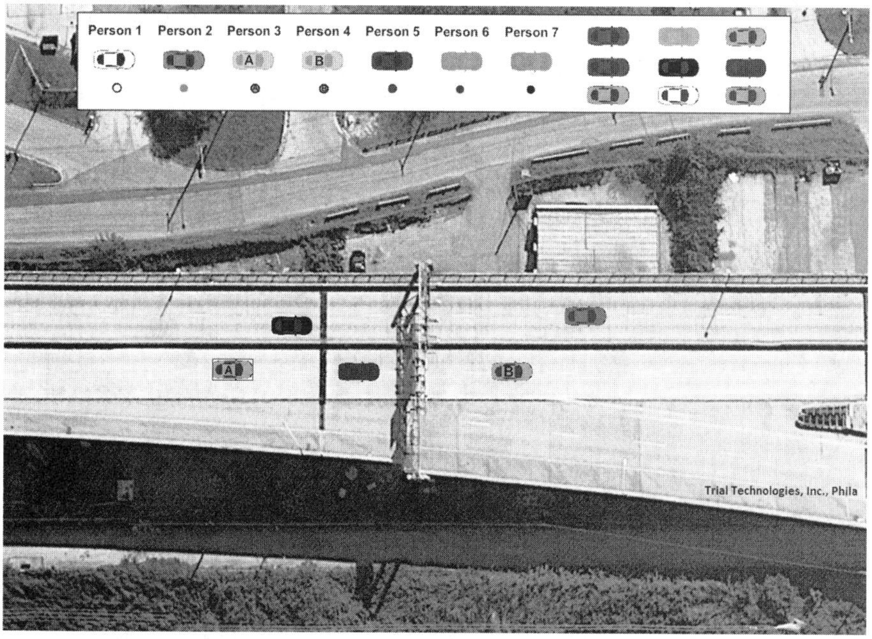

Figure 35 is an example of a map with the location of vehicles.

During her testimony, a lay witness may take you (and the jurors) through the organizational flow chart of a corporation to explain how company decisions are made. You can make even a simple contract more compelling by highlighting a specific clause as the witness explains its importance.

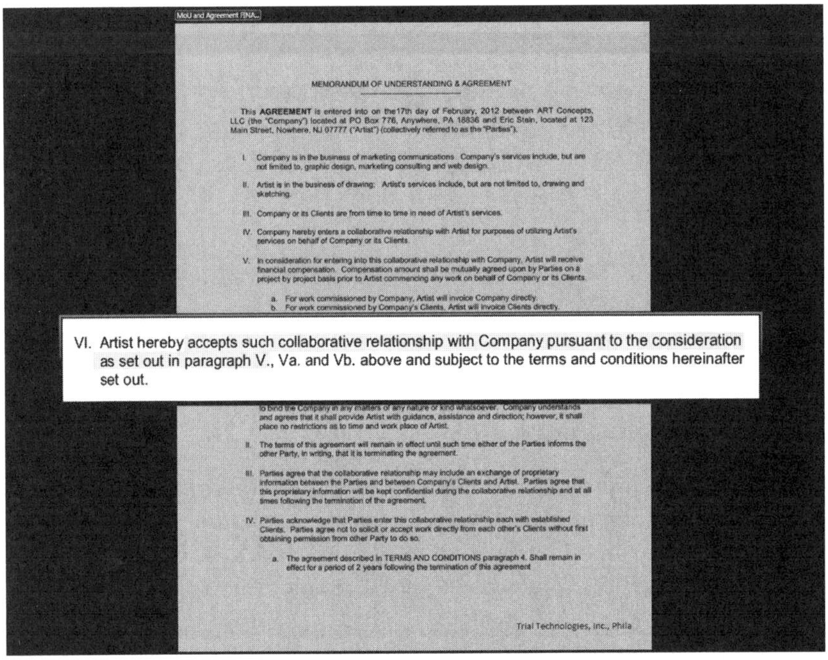

MoU and Agreement FINA...

MEMORANDUM OF UNDERSTANDING & AGREEMENT

This **AGREEMENT** is entered into on the17th day of February, 2012 between ART Concepts, LLC (the "Company") located at PO Box 776, Anywhere, PA 18836 and Eric Stain, located at 123 Main Street, Nowhere, NJ 07777 ("Artist") (collectively referred to as the "Parties").

I. Company is in the business of marketing communications. Company's services include, but are not limited to, graphic design, marketing consulting and web design.

II. Artist is in the business of drawing. Artist's services include, but are not limited to, drawing and sketching.

III. Company or its Clients are from time to time in need of Artist's services.

IV. Company hereby enters a collaborative relationship with Artist for purposes of utilizing Artist's services on behalf of Company or its Clients.

V. In consideration for entering into this collaborative relationship with Company, Artist will receive financial compensation. Compensation amount shall be mutually agreed upon by Parties on a project by project basis prior to Artist commencing any work on behalf of Company or its Clients.

a. For work commissioned by Company, Artist will invoice Company directly.
b. For work commissioned by Company's Clients, Artist will invoice Clients directly.

VI. Artist hereby accepts such collaborative relationship with Company pursuant to the consideration as set out in paragraph V., Va. and Vb. above and subject to the terms and conditions hereinafter set out.

to bind the Company in any matters of any nature or kind whatsoever. Company understands and agrees that it shall provide Artist with guidance, assistance and direction; however, it shall place no restrictions as to time and work place of Artist.

II. The terms of this agreement will remain in effect until such time either of the Parties informs the other Party, in writing, that it is terminating the agreement.

III. Parties agree that the collaborative relationship may include an exchange of proprietary information between the Parties and between Company's Clients and Artist. Parties agree that this proprietary information will be kept confidential during the collaborative relationship and at all times following the termination of the agreement.

IV. Parties acknowledge that Parties enter this collaborative relationship each with established Clients. Parties agree not to solicit or accept work directly from each other's Clients without first obtaining permission from other Party to do so.

a. The agreement described in TERMS AND CONDITIONS paragraph 4. Shall remain in effect for a period of 2 years following the termination of this agreement

Trial Technologies, Inc., Phila

Figure 36 is an example of a contract with a call-out.

You can use almost any electronic visual on cross-examination—and the prior statement is among the most common. You can confront a witness with his own contradictory words in the form of a written or video-recorded statement.

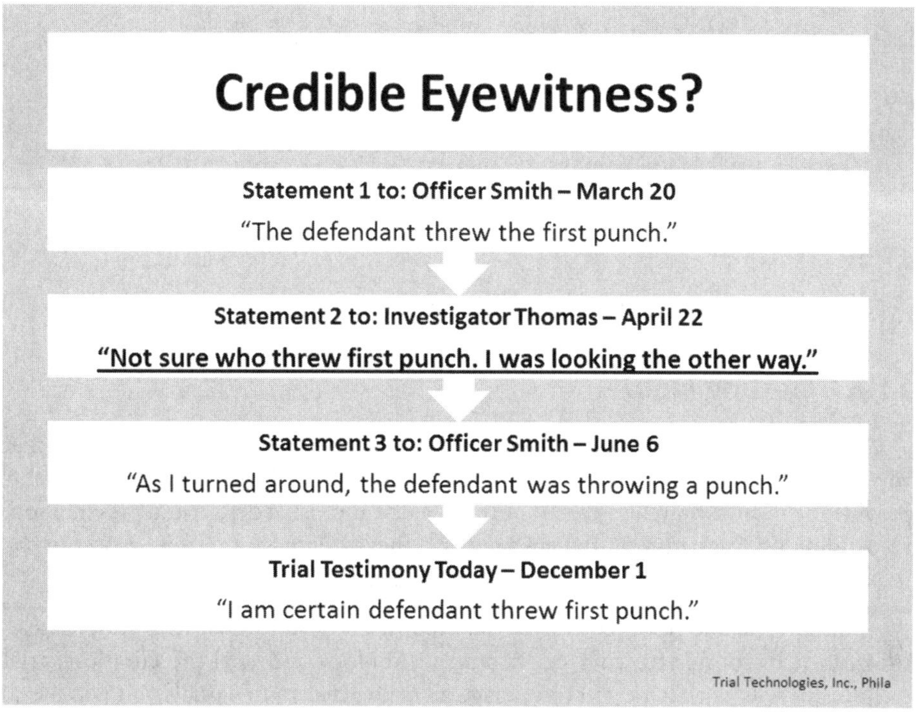

Credible Eyewitness?
Statement 1 to: Officer Smith – March 20
"The defendant threw the first punch."
Statement 2 to: Investigator Thomas – April 22
"Not sure who threw first punch. I was looking the other way."
Statement 3 to: Officer Smith – June 6
"As I turned around, the defendant was throwing a punch."
Trial Testimony Today – December 1
"I am certain defendant threw first punch."
Trial Technologies, Inc., Phila

Figure 37 is an example of a contradictory prior statement.

11.5.3.3 Dangers

It is important on direct examination for the witness to make eye contact and speak directly to the fact finder. Overusing electronic visuals on direct can impede your witness's effectiveness. Every electronic visual will capture the fact finder's attention, but it will also draw attention away from you and the witness. Once you are finished using your exhibit, it is usually best to take it down from the screen so that the fact finder will turn her attention back to the witness.

11.5.4 Damages

Proving damages is often complex, but electronic visuals can clarify and explain claims for compensation, whether tried concurrently with liability or separately in a bifurcated proceeding. A well-crafted display, perhaps as simple as a list or table, can illustrate calculations and highlight relevant facts that support a plaintiff's claim. When you are defending a claim, you can likewise use a list or table to minimize or undermine the plaintiff's argument for compensation.

ECONOMIC DAMAGES – Lost Earnings and Fringe Benefits	
Past Loss of Earnings Capacity	$406,500
Past Loss of Fringe Benefits	$90,110
Future Loss of Earnings Capacity	$2,485,320
Future Loss of Fringe Benefits	$590,800
Future Health-Related Goods and Services	$18,394,437
Total Economic Damages:	**$21,967,167**

Trial Technologies, Inc., Phila

Figure 38 is an example of a damages calculation.

11.6 Getting Help

One of the first things you will need to consider with electronic visuals is whether you are going to create your own or engage outside help. Legal graphic consultants provide the most comprehensive support for electronic visual design and presentation. Depending on the nature of the engagement, they may work on every aspect of the trial from overall strategy to courtroom technical support.

Another available resource is the trial technician, also known as a "hot-seater," who can help coordinate your courtroom technology and trial presentation. Trial technicians will work with you to manage all of the electronic visuals you will use as evidence during your trial—by setting up the courtroom with the proper equipment, displaying your exhibits and presentations during trial, and sometimes help you create and design them. One important function of the experienced trial technician is to provide multiple backup systems, thus avoiding the nightmare scenario of a disastrous midtrial crash. A trial technician can help minimize the stress of managing evidence, documents, and technology during trial, allowing you to focus on witness examinations and argument.

You must anticipate the situation where you have employed a trial technician and the opposing party has not. It is common for opposing attorneys to share equipment during trial—and it is sometimes required by the court. So if you have a technician, opposing counsel may also try to share her by asking her to bring up documents and exhibits. Although this may seem unfair, given your investment of time and money, an objection or complaint might make you seem unreasonable or petty to the jurors or uncooperative to the judge. It is therefore best to discuss and resolve this issue at the pretrial conference, so that everyone understands expectations. Your client is paying for the cost of the technician, so most judges are sympathetic to your position that you don't want to share your resources.

There are multiple factors to consider when deciding whether to retain a legal graphics consultant or trial technician, including the extent of your budget and your comfort and familiarity with electronic visuals. Professionals can usually complete such projects more efficiently than lawyers, ultimately making it cost-effective for the client. Many legal consultants, technicians, and other companies also rent out equipment.

11.7 What You Need to Display and Use Electronic Visuals

11.7.1 Courtroom Variation and Strategy

The ideal tools and methods for presenting your displays will depend on the courtroom type and its capabilities. Although you will always need to assess the courtroom in advance, you will generally be able to use most of your visuals with trial presentation software installed on a laptop or tablet, along with a projector and a screen. If sound is important for any of your visuals, verify that the courtroom is equipped with speakers, or else bring your own—and make sure they are loud enough for everyone to hear.

Some courtrooms have equipment in place, although it may not be ideal or even adequate for your needs. Some courtrooms, for example, have individual monitors for each juror, although most lawyers prefer to display their exhibits on a single large screen that will hold everyone's attention. Judges often want lawyers to use the court's equipment, even if it is outmoded, either because they are comfortable with it or want to justify its cost. You will need to decide whether using alternative equipment is a battle worth fighting.

When possible, you should discuss technology needs with opposing counsel before trial. Judges generally disfavor, and sometimes prohibit, having two separate systems in the courtroom. Additionally, you may be able to share the cost of equipment rental or purchase, which will benefit both clients.

11.7.2 Laptop Computer or Tablet Equipped with Software

11.7.2.1 Trial Presentation Software

Manage and Organize Entire Case

A laptop or tablet with trial presentation software is an effective way to collect all of your evidence and exhibits, manage large amounts of information, and present your evidence and exhibits in the most persuasive way possible. The leading programs for laptops are Sanction®, Trial Director®, and Visionary. The most common applications for tablets are Trial Director and TrialPad.

Trial software will enable you to download all of your documents, exhibits, and videos into one location, from which you can easily access and organize the digital files. When preparing for a particular witness examination, for example, you can create a folder with everything you may need during that examination, including exhibits, prior statements for impeachment, witness examination outlines, and electronic versions of any substantive evidence that you might use.

Search and Display

An important advantage of trial presentation software is that it allows you to quickly search for and find information with the click of a couple buttons. One method when using the software is to assign an identification number to each exhibit, which will allow it to be accessed quickly by typing in that number. Alternatively, you can have all of your exhibits bar-coded, which allows you to scan the bar code on a hard-copy master list and instantly bring up each exhibit.

Annotate and Change

Trials very rarely proceed exactly as planned, and the ability to adapt at the last minute is a critical skill you must develop as a trial lawyer. Trial software makes last-minute maneuvering simpler and faster than ever before. Not only is it possible to locate information quickly through easy search functions, it will take you only seconds to change, annotate, zoom in on, and highlight a portion of an exhibit or call out a specific portion of text in a transcript for impeachment.

11.7.2.2 Other Presentation Software

While trial presentation software and applications are designed specifically for litigation, you can use a laptop or tablet equipped with other software programs to create and display your electronic visuals.

Other types of software are available and easy to use. TimeMap® is a program that can create timelines. Programs that will help you create and display graphics are SmartDraw®, Adobe® Acrobat® software, Corel® WordPerfect® Office, and Microsoft® Excel®. These programs are not the comprehensive trial management systems like Trial Director and Sanction, but they can be useful tools when creating and displaying electronic visuals, especially when you only have a few graphics to display or your budget is very tight.

Although it is being used less and less because its linearity limits its effectiveness, you can also use Microsoft® PowerPoint to create and display visuals. It's difficult to make quick modifications to PowerPoint slides and even more problematic to change their order. Thus, PowerPoint is most often limited to the opening statement and closing argument, when it can be used to present checklists or element charts and be prepared well in advance. Occasionally, an expert witness may use Powerpoint to simplify her opinions.

11.7.3 Digital Presentation Podiums or Integrated Lecterns

Many courtrooms are now equipped with digital presentation podiums, usually near the center of the courtroom. You can connect your laptop or tablet to the podium to control the display and presentation of your electronic visuals, as the podiums are usually connected either to a projector or to individual monitors at counsel table, the judge's bench, and jury box. Digital presentation podiums typically contain, or connect to, most of the components that will be described below, such as document cameras, printers, audio equipment, and annotation equipment. In many courtrooms, you can also connect to the podium from ports at counsel table.

11.7.4 Digital Projector and Projector Screen

Electronic visuals can be displayed by connecting a laptop to a projector and screen. Some courtrooms have projectors that are strategically arranged for optimal viewing, but others will require you to bring your own equipment. It may be difficult in smaller courtrooms to find adequate space to project your exhibits, but you can overcome this obstacle by carefully planning the position of the projector and screen.

11.7.5 Monitors

Monitors can be used instead of, or as a complement to, a larger single screen. Some courtrooms come equipped with individual monitors for the judge, jurors, witness, and at counsel table. If you want to bring in your own monitors, most trial technicians can provide them along with other equipment. It is important, of course, to obtain the court's permission before bringing equipment into the courtroom. Equally important is to perform a test run in advance of the trial.

11.7.6 Annotation Equipment

You will often want witnesses to highlight or otherwise interact with an electronic visual. Expert witnesses frequently use this technique when explaining their testimony.

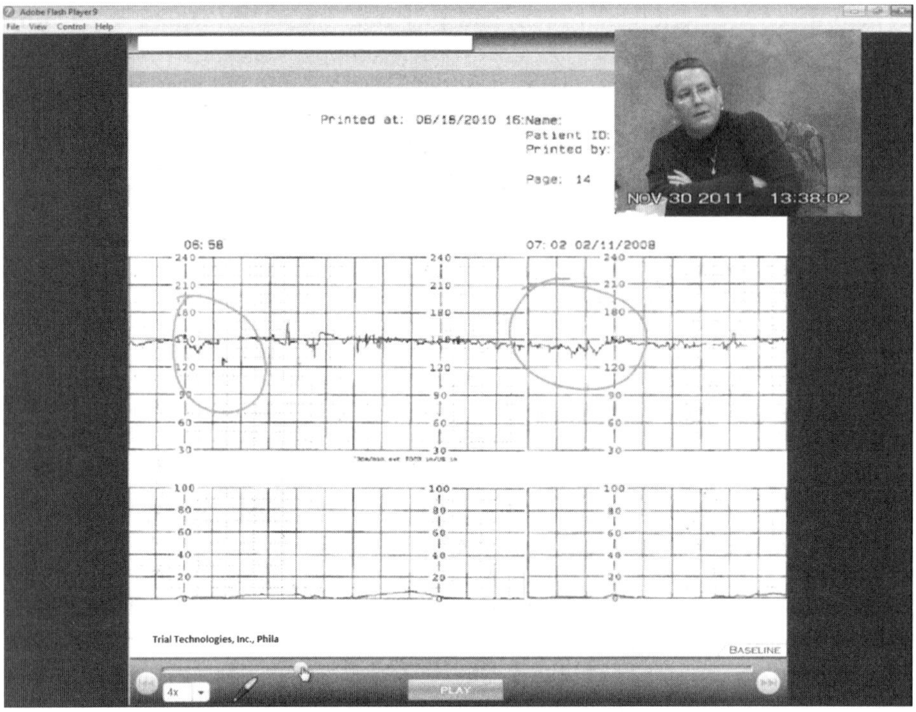

Figure 39 is an example of an expert witness slide with annotations.

When using a street diagram in an accident case, you might ask an eyewitness to identify the positions of the vehicles both before and after the collision. You can do this with annotation equipment such as touchscreen monitors, document cameras (such as the Elmo), and interactive whiteboards (such as SMART® boards).

11.7.6.1 Touch-Screen Monitors

Some monitors have annotation capabilities (as described in section 11.7.5) that allow a witness to use her finger or a stylus to mark a certain part of the display. In our fire truck case, for example, you could project a street diagram on the monitor and then ask the witness to trace an arrow indicating which way the fire truck was traveling at the time of the accident. Using her finger or a stylus, the witness can then create an image that will be projected to a larger screen or to other monitors in the courtroom. Be sure to save the annotated image so that you have the option to enter it as an exhibit.

11.7.6.2 Interactive Whiteboard

When attached to a laptop or tablet, interactive whiteboards (such as SMART boards) can display images similar to a monitor or screen while also allowing you to annotate any images projected. Additionally, a whiteboard can be used as a blank canvas on which you (or a witness) can draw a diagram, thus replacing the need for paper or flip charts.

Any images you create on the whiteboard can be saved on a computer through presentation software, printed immediately (or at a later time), and preserved as an exhibit. As part of your advance preparation, make sure that you have access to a printer in the courtroom.

11.7.7 Document Camera (Elmos)

Document or evidence cameras, most commonly referred to as "Elmos," are widely used and have, for the most part, replaced the venerable overhead projector. A document camera projects an enlargement of any document or picture. These projections can also be annotated, although that requires the witness to approach the document camera and write on the exhibit. Document cameras are frequently used as a backup system, just in case counsel's laptop or tablet malfunctions during trial. They are also handy for those occasional surprise documents provided by opposing counsel that you have not been able to download to your computer ahead of time.

A document camera can also project an enlarged image of an item of real evidence. If an expert needs to describe the markings on a bullet, for example, it would be most effective to place the exhibit under a document camera, rather than have the jurors strain to see the tiny markings themselves. Document cameras are equipped with zoom functions that allow you to increase the size of the item so its intricacies and nuances can be seen throughout the courtroom.

Document cameras have limitations. For one, they sometimes reverse the images, so counsel must make sure that documents are not shown upside down. Moreover, they can be cumbersome when one is dealing with a large number of documents during trial. To efficiently use a document camera, you must have hard copies of all of your exhibits well organized. This can be difficult to maintain throughout the trial, as you will sometimes need to shift quickly from document to document.

Chapter Twelve

Opening Statements

12.1 The Role of the Opening Statement

12.1.1 The Opening Moment

Opening statement—the advocate's first opportunity to speak directly to the jury about the merits of the case—marks the beginning of the competition for the jurors' imagination. This moment is crucial because the mental image that the jurors hold while hearing the evidence will directly influence the way they interpret it. The attorney who is successful in seizing the opening moment will have an advantage throughout the trial because the jurors will tend to view all of the evidence through a lens that she has created.

The importance of access to the jurors' imagination cannot be underestimated. We are accustomed to receiving most of our information through the sense of sight, but at trial, the jurors will obtain most of their information through the sense of hearing—the oral testimony of witnesses. They will hear descriptions and recounting of past events, but in almost all cases they will not actually see an enactment of the crucial occurrences. They will, however, envision the events as they believe them to have occurred. Each juror will summon her own mental images of the facts, objects, locations, and transactions that are described from the witness stand. The details and context of these images will, in turn, influence the juror's decision.

Consider, for example, the image that is brought to mind by the words "billiard parlor." Each person who hears that term is likely to think of a specific location that she once visited (or saw on television or in a movie) and use it as a reference in calling up a mental picture of a similar locale. Billiard parlors, in most people's experience, are probably formal, reserved, well-lighted, reasonably open, and fairly respectable. Thus, events occurring in a billiard parlor will have a certain cast to them. Jurors with this scene in mind will tend to fit the events into that image, that is, to view them in a "billiard parlor" sort of way.

On the other hand, consider the image evoked by the words "pool hall." Now many people would probably envision a place that is smoky, dark, perhaps slightly threatening, and probably a little seedy. Things happen differently in pool halls than they do in billiard parlors. Visibility is better in a billiard parlor; things happen more furtively in a pool hall. A stranger might be questioned in a billiard parlor, but a confrontation is more likely in a pool hall. In other words, the initial mental image dictates, or at least suggests, a variety of assumptions about the nature, context, and likelihood of events.

These assumptions, of course, are not graven in stone. They can be altered, dispelled, or contradicted by the evidence. Still, the creation of an initial image can be a powerful tool. Recall how Professor Harold Hill in the classic musical comedy "The Music Man" convinced the citizens of River City to purchase the instruments for a boys' band. He described their "trouble with a capital T and that rhymes with P and that stands for pool." The townsfolk listening to Professor Hill envisioned their children sinking en masse into depravity and delinquency because of the mental picture evoked by "Pool." He would not have been a quarter so persuasive if he had preached that they had "trouble with a capital T and that rhymes with B and that stands for billiards." The image just isn't that compelling.

Your task in an opening statement is to engage the jury's imagination—to help them begin to imagine the case your way. As we shall see below, this forensic task is complicated by the legal function that the opening statement plays in the conduct of the trial.

See demonstration 17 in the Visuals Appendix.

12.1.2 Legal Function

Opening statements exist to help the jury understand the evidence to be presented at trial. Of course, we hope that the evidence will be self-explanatory, but in even the best-organized cases evidence is often presented in a disjointed if not utterly discontinuous manner.

As witnesses are called to the stand, each testifies only about what he knows about the case. Thus, even the simplest narrative may be divided among many witnesses. Moreover, a single witness may have information concerning the beginning and the end of a chain of events, but may know nothing about intervening occurrences. That testimony will have to be filled in by an entirely different witness. It may not be possible to call witnesses in the most desirable or logical order due to logistical problems or unavailability. Exhibits present their own unique set of challenges since the witness necessary to lay the foundation for a document may not be the one who can adequately explain its content.

The very structure of the trial compounds the problem—the flow of direct testimony is inevitably interrupted by cross-examination. The defendant's evidence, no matter where it might reasonably fit into the overall narrative, is always delayed until after the plaintiff's entire case has been presented. The potential for confusion is great and unavoidable.

To reduce the possibility of juror confusion as a result of the manner in which evidence is introduced, the courts have developed the concept of the opening statement. At the very beginning of the trial, jurors are presented with an overview of the case so that they will be better equipped to make sense of the evidence as it is actually presented. The institutional purpose of the opening statement, then, is to ease the jury's burden by making the trial more understandable; it is not intended to give the lawyers another crack at pleading the case. For this reason, some courts have held that the presentation of an opening statement is a privilege, not a protected right, and that the privilege may be withheld in situations where opening statements will not be helpful to the jury.

Thus, we have the basis of the "nonargument" rule. The courts and commentators are virtually unanimous that opening statements may only be used to inform the jury of "what the evidence will show." Counsel may not argue the case during opening and is restricted to offering a preview of the anticipated testimony, exhibits, and other evidence. This limitation results in a highly stylized set of rules for the presentation of opening statements, and it informs almost everything else that there is to be said on the subject.

12.1.3 Advocacy

As an advocate, your governing principle in presenting an opening statement should be to use it as an opportunity to advance your theory of the case. This is not as easy, or as obvious, as it sounds.

Given the strictures placed on the content of opening statements, it may be all too easy for a lawyer to slip into complacency. Since the legal function of the opening is limited to a preview of the evidence, many lawyers take the approach of simply listing the witnesses or describing the general tenor of the expected testimony and exhibits. In other words, they discuss only what the "evidence will be." This is a serious mistake, as it squanders the potential benefits of the opening moment.

A far more useful, and equally permissible, approach is to discuss what the "evidence will show" rather than merely what it will be. The distinction is not semantic. Telling the jury "what the evidence will be" is a neutral formulation geared toward providing a simple synopsis of the trial to come. Explaining "what the evidence will show," on the other hand, requires you to consider the relationship between the expected evidence and the conclusions and outcomes that you want the jury to reach. In our intersection case, for example, the projected evidence might be that a fire truck approached the intersection and that the defendant did not stop his car. From the plaintiff's perspective, however, the evidence hopefully will show that the defendant had ample opportunity to see the fire truck, which was flashing its lights and sounding its siren, but that he was so distracted that he did not notice it.

Counsel need not feel limited to a mundane listing of the evidence to come. Rather, explain to the jury what propositions will be proven and exactly how they will be proven. As long as you avoid lapsing into argumentative form you may explicate your theory of the case. While you may not urge the jury to reach certain conclusions, you may arrange your discussion of the facts so that the conclusions are inevitable. Many tools are available to accomplish this goal. In brief, a well-developed opening statement will take advantage of some or all of the following concepts:

Choice of facts. In every opening statement you must decide which facts to include and which to leave out. While you will obviously want to emphasize the facts that you find helpful, there is also considerable risk to telling an incomplete or illogical story.

Sequencing. The order of facts may be as important as the nature of the facts. Recall the question that resulted in the downfall of the Nixon administration: "What did the President know and when did he know it?"

Clarity of description. It is one thing to mention a fact, but it is better to describe it with sufficient detail and clarity as to engage the jury in your own mental portrait.

Common sense. Common sense is used both to judge and predict outcomes. An opening statement cannot be successful if its story doesn't jibe with everyday experience. On the other hand, a jury's reflexive resort to common sense can be used to lead them to a desired conclusion. Consider an opening statement that begins this way: "The defendant woke up late; he had an important meeting to go to; the meeting was to be held far from his home; the defendant drove to the meeting." Without saying more, common sense suggests that the defendant was in a hurry.

Moral attraction. An opening statement can be made more attractive when it tells a story that people want to accept. The evidence can be described in a context of shared values or civic virtues so as to add moral force to your client's position. In the intersection case, for example, the plaintiff's evidence will be that she stopped for the fire truck. On the other hand, the evidence will show that the plaintiff knew that it was important not to get in the way of a fire engine, and so she stopped to let it pass.

In the final analysis, the most successful opening statements are those that explain exactly how you intend to win your case.

12.1.4 The Story Arc

Every trial is a story, and every story is about change and resolution. The story begins; the characters encounter conflicts or challenges; and the story ends when the tensions have been resolved. Playwrights and screenwriters refer to the "story arc," or the sweep of change that takes the characters from one condition at the beginning of the story to a different condition at the end. The story arc proceeds in the form of a narrative in which events are selected and placed in a strategic sequence so as to evoke particular values and lead to specific conclusions.[1]

1. *See* Robert McKee, Story (1997).

There are many potential story arcs in literature and film, often involving intricate characterizations, unexpected coincidences, and complex subplots. In litigation, however, there is one single arc that can be used to tell the story of every plaintiff or defendant. For our purposes it might even be called the universal story arc.

The story arc of every trial can be summarized in the following three sentences: There was a time when everything was fine. Then something terrible and disruptive happened. Now it is time to provide a remedy or restore order. In other words, every plaintiff's story begins at a time before there were any injuries. It continues through the events of the accident, or broken contract, or other disruption that has caused great harm. The story can only end when the jury (or judge) remedies the damage or rectifies the injustice. Every defendant's story (civil or criminal) begins the same way, with the terrible disruption occurring in the form of a false accusation or erroneous complaint. Once again, the story ends when the judge or jury resolves the conflict by dismissing the wrongful charges.

Opening statement is the perfect opportunity to introduce the story arc, because it allows the attorney to set out the case succinctly and persuasively. In our intersection case, for example, the plaintiff's attorney would point out that his client began her morning with great enthusiasm for the day ahead. The sun was shining, the air was clear, her health was good, and she was on her way to see a wonderful exhibit at the Art Institute. In other words, everything was fine. As she approached the intersection of Sheridan and Touhy, she saw a fire truck with its lights flashing and siren sounding, so of course she stopped her car. Then something terrible happened. The defendant failed to stop for the fire truck. Despite the lights and siren, he smashed his SUV into the rear of the plaintiff's car, sending it spinning into the intersection. Although she was wearing her seatbelt, the plaintiff's head snapped back and then forward into the steering wheel. In that moment, her life changed forever. The injuries to her back and neck were extreme and irreversible. She can no longer walk without pain or enjoy any of life's simple pleasures. She has been unable to work, and her expenses have been overwhelming. Although it will never be possible to make her whole, she has come to court for justice.

Of course, counsel will speak at much greater length about the details of the accident and the extent of the plaintiff's injuries, as well as the reasons that a jury verdict will provide restorative justice. All of those details—sequenced for maximum effect—will fit neatly into the story arc.

12.2 The Law of Opening Statements

12.2.1 The Rule Against Argument

The rule against argument is inherent in the very concept of the opening statement. Our system of law, based as it is on the production of testimony and exhibits, has no place for argument that precedes the introduction of evidence. Indeed, jurors are cautioned against discussing the case even among themselves before all of the evidence has been presented. Jurors are not supposed to begin making up their minds until they have heard all of the evidence. Therefore, the limited function of the opening statement is to create a context for the jury's understanding. Thus, argument is improper during opening statements.

12.2.1.1 Defining the Rule

The rule against argument is easier to state than to define. Moreover, application of the rule will vary from jurisdiction to jurisdiction and even from courtroom to courtroom. No matter how the rule is articulated, it is almost never hard and fast. Most judges recognize that "argument" is a relative concept and allow lawyers a reasonable amount of latitude.

As a general rule, opening statement ends and argument begins when counsel attempts to tell the jury how they should reach their decision. As long as the opening comprises only a description of the evidence, there obviously is no problem. Difficulties arise only when the advocate engages in interpretation or exhortation. You may not urge the jury to draw inferences from facts or to reach certain conclusions. You may not explain the importance of certain items of evidence or suggest how evidence should be weighed. It is improper to comment directly on the credibility of witnesses. Finally, an opening statement may not be used to appeal overtly to the jury's sense of mercy or justice.

For example, it would be proper to tell the following story to a jury during the opening statement in a personal injury case:

> Just before the accident, the plaintiff was sitting in a tavern. In less than an hour and a half he consumed at least four shots of whiskey. He bought a round for the house, and then he left. He left in his car. The accident occurred within the next twenty minutes.

It would be improper argument, however, to continue in this vein:

> The plaintiff was obviously drunk. No person could drink four whiskeys in that amount of time without feeling it. Only an alcoholic or a liar would even claim to have been sober under those circumstances.

The second paragraph violates the argument rule not only because it draws the conclusion that the plaintiff was drunk, but also because it tells the jury how to evaluate the plaintiff's anticipated testimony: "Only an alcoholic or a liar would claim to have been sober."

12.2.1.2 Guidelines

A number of guidelines or rules of thumb have been developed for determining when an opening statement has drifted into argument.

The witness test. One possible test is to question whether a witness will actually testify to the "facts" contained in the opening statement. If so, the opening is proper. If not, it has become argument. In the tavern example above, for instance, witnesses will be able to testify to the plaintiff's presence in the bar and his consumption of liquor; therefore the initial paragraph is appropriate. No such witness, however, would be allowed to testify to the conclusion that the plaintiff is a liar or an alcoholic. Accordingly, the second paragraph is impermissible.

The verification test. An alternative measure is to determine whether the content of the opening statement can be verified, the theory being that facts are verifiable while argumentative conclusions are not. Note that this analysis can be more flexible than the witness test since the comment that the plaintiff was drunk is subject to verification. On the other hand, the "alcoholic or liar" comment continues to fail under this test as well.

The "link" test. A final approach is to consider whether the opening statement contains facts with independent evidentiary value or whether the attorney has had to provide a rhetorical link in the probative chain. Again we see that the first paragraph above is just fine; it consists entirely of classic evidence. The second paragraph, however, is pure rhetoric. It becomes probative only when counsel supplies the explanation, or link, that "no person could drink that amount of whiskey without showing it."

Each of these tests is more holistic than legalistic. There are no case holdings or rules of court that detail how a particular jurisdiction will apply the rule against argument. Even a seasoned trial judge may not be able to explain exactly why an objection was sustained to some portion of an opening statement. As a practical matter, it may be best to keep in mind the principle that "argument" occurs when counsel seeks to tell the jury how they should go about reaching their decision.

12.2.1.3 Other Considerations

In addition to the words spoken and the evidence marshaled by counsel, a variety of other considerations may lead a judge to conclude that an opening statement has crossed the line into argument. Some of these are detailed below.

Tone of voice. Words that appear neutral on the printed page may become argumentative by virtue of the tone in which they are delivered. Sneering, sarcasm, volume, or vocal caricature can all transform an acceptable opening into an impermissible one.

Rhetorical questions. Rhetorical questions are inherently argumentative. Such questions can be used to suggest disbelief, as in, "What could she possibly have been thinking of?" Alternatively, they can be used as a statement of incontrovertible certainty, such as, "What other answer could there be?" In either case they strongly signal argument when used in an opening statement.

Repetition. Although an excellent persuasive device when used elsewhere in a trial, repetition can lead an opening statement into forbidden territory. In the tavern scenario above, for example, imagine that the first paragraph of the plaintiff's opening statement was embellished this way:

> Just before the accident the plaintiff was sitting in a tavern. In less than an hour and a half he consumed at least four shots of whiskey. Not two or three, but four. He bought a round for the house and then he left. He left in his car. That's right, he drove away from the tavern. He opened the car door, got behind the wheel, put the key in the ignition, started the engine, shifted into first gear, and proceeded to drive down the road. There will be two witnesses who will testify to plaintiff's consumption of alcohol. And three different witnesses will testify that they saw the plaintiff drive away from the bar in his own car.

Although each of the facts in this extended paragraph could stand as nonargumentative, some judges would no doubt consider the extreme repetition as going too far.

12.2.2 Comments on the Law

Closely related to the rule against argument is the general proscription against discussing law during opening statements. The rationale is the same. Opening statements are allowed for the purpose of organizing and previewing the evidence for the jury. Not until the end of the case will the court instruct the jurors on the law. The instructions presumably will be comprehensive and therefore will not require a preview. Indeed, it is usually impossible to predict all of the jury instructions until all of the evidence has been admitted. In any event, to the extent that the jury requires advance information about the law, this can come from the judge in the form of a preliminary instruction.

Nonetheless, it is virtually impossible for counsel to avoid some discussion of the law during any but the simplest opening statement. It is the law, after all, that determines the relevance and importance of the facts being previewed. Without some explanation of the legal issues, a jury will have no way to tell whether certain facts are significant or merely window dressing.

In a drunk driving prosecution, for example, it would obviously be permissible for the prosecutor to inform the jury that the defendant's blood alcohol level was .12 percent. Whatever test might be applied, this is clearly a provable fact that is subject to verification. It is also a fairly meaningless fact unless the jury is also informed of the jurisdiction's legal test for intoxication, which in most states is .08 percent.

Perhaps more to the point, assume that the following opening statement, consistent with the facts, was given by the plaintiff's attorney in a personal injury case:

> Ladies and gentlemen, shortly after the accident the defendant was taken to a local hospital. A blood sample was drawn, and it was analyzed for the presence of alcohol. The result was that her blood contained .07 percent alcohol. We will present the expert testimony of Dr. Adam Riback, who will testify that a blood alcohol level of .07 percent will result in the impairment of reflexes, response time, and judgment. Dr. Riback will testify that, in his opinion, blood alcohol level would significantly interfere with the safe operation of an automobile.

Note that the entire opening statement is devoted to the description of provable evidence. The material is well organized, and it will surely assist the jury in understanding the evidence of intoxication, which will probably be presented through the testimony of two or three different witnesses. There has been no mention of the law.

Defense counsel, however, might wish to give the following opening statement:

> Ladies and gentlemen, the legal limit for intoxication in this state is .08 percent blood alcohol. The defendant's blood was sampled in the emergency room within thirty minutes of the accident. The test showed that her blood alcohol level was under .08 percent, which is the level for legally operating an automobile in this state. Dr. Benjamin Fredricks will testify in this case that the defendant's blood alcohol level could not have significantly changed in the thirty minutes between the accident and the blood test. Her blood alcohol level was within the legal limit at the time of the accident.

The defendant's opening statement, to make any sense at all, must be allowed to include some information about the law. The jury cannot possibly assess the value of the other evidence without the reference to the state statute. Thus, most judges would consider this defendant's limited discussion of the law to be an acceptable part of the opening statement.

It would not be acceptable, however, for either of the parties to argue for an interpretation or construction of the law. Plaintiff's counsel could not, for example, use the opening statement to urge the jury to ignore the legal limit and concentrate on the defendant's impaired reflexes. By the same token, defense counsel could not posit that statutory intoxication is all that matters and that the jury should ignore any other evidence of inebriation. Such positions might be suitable for final argument. Neither, however, would be permissible during opening statements. In both cases the attorney is attempting to provide the jury with a method for reaching their decision rather than with a guide to understanding information as it is presented.

Most judges attempt to steer a middle course when it comes to discussion of the law during opening statements. It is almost always permissible to frame the legal issues for the jury. A sentence or two devoted to an explanation of the legal significance of the evidence will also usually be allowed. Once the discussion of the law becomes intricate, lengthy, or controversial, however, an objection will usually be sustained.[2]

12.2.3 *Persuasion*

While argument is prohibited during opening statements, persuasion is not. Indeed, persuasion is unavoidable. The test of relevance provides that evidence is not admissible unless it tends to prove or disprove some matter at issue in the case. Accordingly, few of the facts outlined in an opening statement will be "neutral." Most facts will be favorable to one side or the other. As long as counsel refrains from suggesting conclusions to be drawn from the facts, it is permissible to arrange those facts in an order that maximizes their favorable impact. Furthermore, persuasive ordering of the facts by both counsel will typically assist the jury in understanding the case because the jurors will then be able to see just how the parties' stories diverge.

The persuasive ordering of facts can be accomplished either through incremental development or through contrast. Incremental development involves the successive ordering of a series of discrete facts, each building on the last, until the desired conclusion becomes obvious. Although the facts will be related, they need not be presented in chronological order. The following example demonstrates how the plaintiff might use incremental development in our fire engine case:

> The defendant awoke at 7:00 a.m. He had an important meeting scheduled with a potential new client for 8:30 that morning. The client had not yet decided whether to hire the defendant, but the account would have been worth a lot of money. The meeting was to be held downtown, which was sixteen miles from the defendant's home. The defendant showered, shaved, dressed, and ate a quick breakfast. He went to his car, which was parked about a block away. All of this took approximately fifty minutes. By the time the defendant got to his car, it was 8:00 a.m. He had thirty minutes left before the new client was scheduled to arrive at his office.

Note that the example begins when the defendant woke up, it next skips ahead to the information about the scheduled meeting, and it then goes back to describe the rest of the defendant's morning routine. Other facts, of course, could be added to show how seriously late the defendant was and, therefore, how likely he was to drive carelessly or too fast. The point is that the individual events build on each other to explain, without saying so, why the defendant would have been driving negligently.

Contrast is the juxtaposition of contradictory facts, most often used in an opening statement to demonstrate the implausibility of some aspect of the opposing case. The defendant in the fire engine case might use contrast this way:

---

2. It should go without saying that an incorrect statement of the law is objectionable, even if made only in passing or for the purpose of framing the issues for the jury.

> The plaintiff in this case is seeking damages for pain and suffering and lost income. She claims a permanent disability. You will see medical bills offered into evidence that start with the date of the accident and continue right through to last December 10. You will also see a receipt for the purchase of a new backpack and camp stove, purchased by the plaintiff last August 17. She went to the doctor on August 15, she bought her backpack on August 17, and she went camping at Eagle River Falls on August 31. She returned to town on September 3. Her next visit to the doctor was not until October 19.

Without resort to argument, the simple contrast between the medical bills and the camping trip casts doubt on the plaintiff's allegation of permanent injury. The line between persuasive ordering and argument is crossed when counsel attempts to inject judgments, conclusions, or other means of reaching a decision into the opening statement. It is fair game to present facts showing, say, that the plaintiff requires a large judgment to be fully compensated:

> Each morning when the plaintiff wakes up, he needs assistance in getting out of bed. He cannot walk to the bathroom himself. He cannot bathe or clean himself. He cannot fix his own breakfast. If he wants to read a newspaper or a book, someone must get it for him. Each day, for twenty-four hours, he must pay a nurse or housekeeper to do all of the things that other people are able to do for themselves.

It is not fair game, however, to continue in this vein: "The plaintiff could just as easily be your own neighbor or relative; he deserves your generosity."

12.3 Structure and Elements

If a trial is a persuasive story, the opening statement is the attorney's first opportunity to tell the whole story without distraction or interruption. Not until final argument will counsel again be able to speak directly to the jury. All other communication will be filtered through the awkward, and often opaque, process of witness examination. If your theory is to be presented in its entirety, opening statement is the time to do it. Because of the conventions that control the content and form of the opening statement, it is particularly important to pay careful attention to its structure and elements.

12.3.1 Communicate Your Theory

The single most important rule for opening statements is to present a coherent theory of the case. You will, of course, have developed such a theory in your pretrial preparation since no case can be won without one. The challenge now is to communicate it clearly, succinctly, and persuasively.

Recall that a trial theory is the adaptation of a factual story to the legal issues in the case. Your theory must contain a simple, logical, provable account of facts which, when viewed in light of the controlling law, will lead to the conclusion that your client should win. In short, you will want to use the opening statement to explain to the jury why the verdict should be in your favor.

A successful theory will be built around a persuasive story. Ideally, such a story will be told about people who have reasons for the way they act; it will explain all of the known or undeniable facts; it will be told by credible witnesses; it will be supported by details; and it will accord with common sense. Thus, your opening statement should, at some point and in some manner, address all of the following elements.

What happened? The crucial events in your story will be the ones that speak to the legal elements of your claim or defense. If you represent the plaintiff in a tort case, your opening statement should contain sufficient facts from which a conclusion can be drawn that the defendant was negligent. The defendant's opening, on the other hand, should emphasize facts pointing toward his own caution or the plaintiff's fault.

Why did it happen? It is not sufficient to list the facts. A story is most persuasive when it explains why events occurred as they did. It is particularly important to explain why individuals acted as they did, since a compelling reason for an action will tend to rule out or negate alternative possibilities. For example, you may explain that the defendant in a collision case was driving slowly and carefully just before the accident. This story will be more persuasive if it can be supported with a reason. Perhaps she was returning from an antique auction, carrying an expensive and fragile chandelier in her back seat. Obviously, then, she would be inclined to be more than normally cautious. Her reason for driving slowly not only supports her version of events, but it also makes less likely a claim by the plaintiff that she careened around a corner at high speed.

Which witnesses should be believed? Trials almost always revolve around conflicting testimony, with one set of witnesses supporting the plaintiff's theory and another supporting the defendant's.[3] It is improper to argue the credibility of witnesses in your opening statement, but you may, and should, provide the jury with facts that bolster your own witnesses and detract from the opposition's. While too much background can easily clutter your opening statement and distract the jury, positive information—such as education, community ties, and family responsibility—

3. It is sometimes the case that none of the testimony is in conflict and that the jury is required only to determine the legal consequences of undisputed facts. These situations are relatively rare. Even when they do occur, the jury may be called on to determine the relative weight to be given to certain witnesses' testimony. For example, personal injury cases in which liability is clear are often submitted to the jury solely on the issue of damages. In these cases, there will often be no testimony contradicting the plaintiff's injury, but the jury will still have to decide how much weight, which is to say credibility, to give to the plaintiff's rendition of damages.

should be provided to humanize your key witnesses. Bias, motive, prejudice, and interest in the outcome of the case are always relevant to a witness's believability. Explain the facts that demonstrate your own witnesses' lack of bias; include as well the facts that demonstrate the motive or interest of the opposition. For example:

> Two experts will testify as to the cause of the fire. The plaintiff will call Fire Chief Olson, who will testify that he investigated the fire as part of his normal professional duties. Chief Olson concluded that the fire was accidental. He was not paid by either of the parties. He was simply doing his job. The defendant's expert is Dr. Jane Miller. She does not work for the city or the state—she is a private investigator. All of her income is derived from private clients. She was hired by the defendant to reach an opinion about the cause of the fire in this case, and she was paid $240 an hour to do so. She will testify that the fire was caused by arson.

How can we be sure? As should be apparent from the examples above, the persuasiveness of an opening statement, indeed the persuasiveness of virtually any aspect of a trial, is often established through details. Broad assertions can stake out territory and raise issues, but it is most often the details on which the truth will be determined. An essential element of an opening statement, then, is the judicious use of details in support of the accuracy, dependability, or believability of your facts.

Does it all make sense? Finally, the theory you present in opening, or at any other point in the trial, must make sense when it is measured against the everyday experiences of the jurors. The provision of reasons, biases, or details, no matter how compelling they are to your way of thinking, will accomplish nothing if the jurors cannot place them into a context that they understand and accept. It is meaningless to suggest that a witness should be believed because she received an "A" on her contracts exam in law school. Although that detail may make her praiseworthy in some eyes, it is not a common-sense indicator of honesty.

12.3.2 Communicate Your Theme

Your trial theme, as distinct from your theory, should be expressed in a single sentence that captures the moral force of your case. A theme communicates to the jury the reason that your client deserves to win. Thus, introducing a theme in opening is particularly effective as a persuasive matter since it can focus the jury's attention on a cognitive image that you will return to throughout the trial.

Nonetheless, using a theme in your opening statement presents some difficulty. Unlike a trial theory, a theme is intended to reflect on or interpret the evidence rather than simply to describe or outline it. Overuse or constant repetition of your theme may bring you perilously close to argument. Most judges, however, will allow the statement of a theme at both the beginning and end of an opening statement, especially when it is phrased in terms of fact as opposed to opinion or characterization.

One possible theme for the plaintiff in the fire engine case is that the defendant was "too busy to be careful." This theme can be used at the beginning of the opening as a reference point for the information about the defendant's course of conduct on the morning of the accident:

> Ladies and gentlemen, this is a case about a driver who was too busy to be careful. On the morning of the accident he woke up late. He had to be at an important meeting downtown that morning, and he had less than an hour left in which to get there.

Although there is a sense in which "too busy to be careful" is a conclusion, it is used here solely as an introduction to the facts that follow. Moreover, it is a conclusion of the sort that the rules of evidence generally allow lay persons to draw. "Busy-ness" and "carefulness" are ordinary incidents of life that are easily recognized without questionable inferences. Therefore, the theme "too busy to be careful" can almost certainly be invoked at the outset of the plaintiff's opening statement.

On the other hand, it is possible to conceive of a theme that is too tendentious for use in opening. Perhaps the plaintiff wants to use the theme that "the defendant had no business being on the road." This phrase is entirely judgmental. It will not clarify or elucidate whatever facts may follow as it is aimed strictly at invoking moral condemnation. While we all probably share a common understanding of what it means to be busy, no similar uniform meaning can be attributed to "no business being on the road." In closing argument, it will be perfectly appropriate to argue that the defendant had no business being on the road, but the phrase goes too far to use in an opening statement.

12.3.3 Use Primacy

The principle of primacy posits that in all aspects of a trial a jury will remember best those things that they hear first. The opening statement therefore provides a double opportunity to utilize primacy. The first few minutes of your opening statement constitute the "beginning of the beginning" and therefore have the potential to be among the most memorable moments of the trial. Put them to good use.

It is essential not to waste your opening moments on trivia or platitudes. Get right to the point. State your theme. Explain the most important part of your theory. Lay the groundwork for a crucial direct or cross-examination. Foreshadow your closing argument. Above all, do not spend your most precious minutes meandering through a civics-class exposition on the virtues of the American jury system.

In the fire engine case, the plaintiff might want to open something like this:

> This is a case about a defendant who was too busy to be careful. Because he failed to stop for a fire truck, he smashed his car right into the back of the plaintiff's automobile. The fire truck was flashing its lights and

> sounding its siren. All of the other drivers noticed the fire truck and stopped. Except the defendant. He had his mind on an important meeting, so he kept on driving until it was too late. Now the plaintiff will never take another step without feeling pain. Let me tell you exactly what happened.

The above opening is direct and to the point. It states theory and theme right at the outset and launches immediately into the facts that support the plaintiff's case. The three central points that the plaintiff will make are all mentioned: 1) the fire truck was clearly visible; 2) all of the other traffic stopped; and 3) the defendant was preoccupied and caused the accident.

Contrast the following example on behalf of the defendant:

> I am the attorney for the defendant, who is seated with me here at counsel table. On the defendant's left is my cocounsel. It is now our opportunity to present our opening statement. Because the evidence at trial may be introduced in a disjointed fashion, an opening statement can serve as a road map to help you understand the evidence. Imagine, if you will, the picture on the cover of a jigsaw puzzle—it helps you put together the pieces inside. And that is what I would like to do now.

The plaintiff's opening moment is obviously more persuasive. While the defendant has done a fine job of explaining the philosophy behind allowing openings, the plaintiff has begun establishing her case.

There might be a need for the defendant's approach if there were truly some possibility that the jury would not understand an opening statement without the explanatory metaphors. In fact, however, the opposite is true. The picture on the cover of a jigsaw puzzle is self-explanatory; everyone knows why it is there. You will never see a paragraph on the cover of the box explaining why the puzzlemaker provided you with a picture. In fact, you might worry about the puzzle if there were such an explanation.

Not all platitudes need to be excluded from the opening statement. There is a place in every lawyer's repertoire for a little schmaltz about the virtues of the jury system. You may wish to introduce your client and cocounsel if the judge hasn't already done so. You might even want to say a few words about the relationship between the opening statement and the rest of the trial. It is not at all wrong to do any of these things. Just don't do them first.

Two principles can guide your selection of material for the beginning of the opening statement—impact and relationship.

Impact. Your opening statement should begin with the information that you hope will have the greatest impact on the jury. What facts most support a verdict in your favor? What issues will be most hotly contested? Which witness will you rely on the most? Choose the point that you most hope the jury will take with them when they retire to deliberate.

Relationship. There will be many important evidentiary facts in most trials. Since you will want the jury to remember them all, it may be difficult to decide just which ones to begin with. This decision can be made easier if, in addition to impact, you consider the relationship of the information to some other aspect of the trial. Will the testimony of your key witness be attacked? Will you need to undermine or impeach the testimony of an opposition witness? Will your closing argument rely on certain inferences or conclusions? Use the first moments of your opening statement to begin developing the points to which you intend to return.

12.3.4 Use Issues

Your case can be only as persuasive as the theory behind it, and your theory can only be persuasive if it ties the evidence to the legal issues. Your opening statement, then, must address the legal issues in your case. Ultimately, the jury will not be asked to conclude whether a particular witness is a good person or whether events occurred in a certain order. Such decisions may be reached along the way, but they are only important to the extent that they affect the actual verdict in the case. Defense counsel may do a stunning job of convincing the jury that the plaintiff is foolish or forgetful, but she will lose her case unless she also persuades them that the defendant was not negligent.

It is imperative, therefore, that your opening statement explain to the jury why your facts are important to their decision. Although a statement of importance may seem to approach argument, recall that the opening statement's purpose is to help the jury understand the evidence. A serial presentation of facts, no matter how beautifully organized or well delivered, cannot be understood clearly without some mention of the purpose for which the evidence will be offered. Accordingly, it would be unusual for a judge to disallow a reasonable explanation of the issues toward which the evidence is directed.

Assuming that the fire engine case is being tried in a comparative negligence jurisdiction, the defense may want to show that the plaintiff was partially at fault for the accident. In her opening statement, counsel could simply list a set of facts that comprise the plaintiff's contribution to the accident and hope that the jury draws the right conclusion: the plaintiff didn't pull over; the plaintiff's brake lights were not working; and, although she claims otherwise, the plaintiff may not have been wearing her glasses. It will be more persuasive, however, and truly more helpful to the jury, if the opening first explains the import of the evidence:

> One issue in this case is whether the plaintiff herself contributed to the accident. You see, even if the defendant was negligent in some way, the law still asks whether the plaintiff was partially at fault as well. And if she

> was at fault, then any damages would have to be reduced. The evidence will definitely show that the plaintiff was at fault. When she saw the fire truck she slammed on her brakes right in the middle of the road. She didn't pull over to the side. She didn't leave a clear lane for the car that was immediately behind her. That made it impossible for the following driver, my client, to avoid the accident. Furthermore, her brake lights weren't working on the day of the accident. She knew they weren't working, but she hadn't gotten around to getting them fixed. So when she slammed on her brakes, my client had no way of knowing that she was going to make a sudden stop instead of pulling over into the parking lane.

The statement of the law is an acceptable part of this opening statement because it is correct, neutral, and closely related to the facts that follow. It is helpful because it focuses attention on the import of the facts concerning the plaintiff's driving. The evidence is going to be offered not to show that the plaintiff was generally a poor driver, but rather to show exactly how she contributed to the accident in this case.

Note, by the way, that the excerpt above does not include the disputed fact that the plaintiff wasn't wearing her glasses. Once the legal issue is used as a preface for the evidence, it becomes obvious that the plaintiff's absent glasses are not essential to the defendant's theory of the case. The defendant's theory is that the plaintiff stopped too quickly, not that she failed to see the fire truck or react in time. Therefore, the claim of missing glasses, a fact that surely would be included in any rote rendition of the negative evidence, becomes expendable. Counsel can omit the disputed, and perhaps unprovable, fact from her opening statement.

Cognition theory suggests that a jury will seldom deliberate to a conclusion on each discrete fact presented at trial. Rather, the jurors typically will attend to a series of "turning points" or crucial issues. Opening statements stand to be most effective when they anticipate these turning points and therefore comprise issue-oriented discussion of the facts.

12.3.5 Use the Evidence, Don't Just Display It

There is a world of difference between using evidence and merely displaying it. Displaying evidence is a vice most common to unprepared or disorganized lawyers, and it is frequently the result of insufficient attention to theory and analysis. While no diligent attorney would intentionally use the opening statement to list a series of facts in a purely random order, many lawyers are attracted to the allure of some seemingly natural organization. Such reference to an external guideline, chronology being the most common, is not use of the evidence, since the organizing principle is something independent of the client's litigation strategy. Use of the evidence, however, involves the purposeful ordering of the facts, as we have discussed above, in the manner most supportive of counsel's theory of the case.

12.3.5.1 The Problem with Natural Organization

"Natural" organization can be seductive. It is easy to organize an opening statement on a "witness-by-witness" basis. It is comfortable to organize an opening statement according to chronology. Ultimately, however, both of these methods may result in nothing more than a display of the evidence rather than a structure that is most persuasive under the circumstances. There is no law of nature that says that obvious principles are the most convincing or even the most understandable. An advocate defaults in her duty if she allows the accident of witness observation or the serendipitous occurrence of events to replace dynamic organization and analysis.

Avoid Witness Summaries

The "witness-by-witness" approach, in particular, is to be avoided. It is a mystery why many lawyers think that they can help the jury understand the case by naming all of the witnesses and outlining the expected testimony of each. Recall that the very purpose of the opening statement, indeed its underlying justification, is to overcome the disjointed fashion in which the witnesses will produce evidence at trial. Witness-by-witness rendition of the facts is unlikely to produce a coherent story when the witnesses take the stand and testify for themselves. This method of organization becomes no more helpful simply because a lawyer has substituted a summary of the testimony for the actual direct and cross-examinations.

Imagine that plaintiff's counsel in the fire engine case opted for the "witness" approach in her opening statement:[4]

> Ladies and gentlemen, you will hear a number of witnesses testify in this case. Let me tell you about some of them. The plaintiff will testify that on the morning of the accident she was driving south on Sheridan Road. As she approached the intersection of Sheridan and Touhy, she saw a fire truck approaching from the west. It was flashing its lights and sounding its siren, so she applied her brakes and stopped her car immediately. Suddenly another car, driven by the defendant, crashed into her from behind.
>
> Karen Dunn was a firefighter on Engine Number 9 on the day of the accident. She will tell you that the weather was clear and dry that day. She will also describe the call that her engine company received and the fact that they followed their standard procedure when they left the firehouse—flashing their lights and sounding their siren. The fire engine headed east on Touhy, in the direction of Sheridan Road.

---

4. The vignette that follows is intentionally truncated in the interest of readability. A real opening statement would obviously contain longer versions of each witness's anticipated testimony. This version, however, contains sufficient information to make the necessary point about use of the witness-by-witness approach.

> You will also hear from Nate Lipton. Nate is an auto mechanic. He will testify that just a week before the accident the defendant came into Nate's garage for some repair work. Nate advised the defendant to have his brakes relined, but the defendant was too busy. He left without having the brake job done.

The drawback of this method should be readily apparent. Even though the information attributed to each of the above witnesses was intentionally abbreviated, the opening statement quickly became boring and hard to follow. In a real opening statement, it would be necessary to flesh out the anticipated testimony in greater detail, resulting in an even more protracted, and less compelling, narrative. Moreover, as the number of witnesses increases, the disjointed nature of the opening would increase as well. As hard as it is to continue to pay attention to short descriptions of three witnesses, it would be that much harder to pay attention to longer renditions of six, ten, or more.

A still greater problem with the witness approach, however, is that it obstructs counsel's ability to develop a theory of the case. Your theory will seldom depend on which witness provides a particular piece of information,[5] but it will always depend on how the various facts fit together. In the scenario above, the witness oriented fragmentation of the story makes it impossible for the attorney to explain, or even intimate, the relationship between the presence of the fire truck and the poor condition of the defendant's brakes. While clever jurors will no doubt be able to intuit a connection, the job of the advocate is not to leave such constructions to chance. Consider the following alternative:[6]

> The weather was clear and dry on the morning of the accident. Fire Engine Company Number 9 received a call to respond to a fire, and the crew boarded their truck and left the firehouse, headed east on Touhy toward Sheridan Road. In keeping with standard procedure, they sounded their siren and flashed their lights from the moment they left the station. At that same time, the plaintiff was driving south on Sheridan. As she approached the intersection with Touhy, she saw and heard the fire truck, so she immediately applied her brakes. She had plenty of time to stop. The defendant, whose car was directly behind hers, didn't stop. At one point he slammed on his brakes, but it was too late. As hard as he hit his brakes, it did not keep him from crashing right into the plaintiff's car. You should know that the defendant's brakes were not in good repair. Only a week before he had taken his car in for some work. The mechanic told him that his brakes needed relining, but he declined to have the work done. It was less than seven days later when those same brakes proved not

5. There will be circumstances in which it is important which witness testifies to a particular fact. This situation is considered in section 12.4.2.6.
6. This vignette is also abbreviated. An actual opening statement would contain more facts, but all of the essentials are contained in this scenario.

> to be good enough to stop his car and prevent what has turned out to be a lifetime of pain for my client.

This story is far more cohesive than the witness-based account. It brings all of the vehicles together at the fateful intersection without the necessity of the jurors having to keep a running account of their whereabouts. It connects the fire engine's use of lights and siren directly to the cause of the accident. Finally, it shows that the defendant might have been able to stop his car but for the poor maintenance of his brakes. In other words, this approach to the opening statement takes what would otherwise be a nasty, but isolated, fact about the defendant and transforms it into a key supporting element of the plaintiff's theory of the case.

Be Wary of Chronology

Chronology is an obvious, natural, and often useful organizing technique for opening statements. All events in the real world, after all, occur in chronological order. Moreover, we are all used to thinking of life in chronological terms. It is for this very reason, in fact, that opening statements have become part of the trial—to allow lawyers to take individual witness accounts and meld them into a single chronological narrative.

Still it is all too easy, and sometimes counterproductive, to automatically allow chronology to establish the organization of an opening statement. Simply because events occurred in a certain order is not a sufficient reason to present them that way to a jury. This is especially the case when your story involves simultaneous, or nearly simultaneous, events that took place in different locations.

The Drawbacks of Chronology

In the fire truck case, for instance, a strict chronology might begin with the plaintiff leaving her home. The defendant probably left his home shortly thereafter, and the fire engine left the station last of all. None of this ordering should matter to either party's story, however, since the only important fact is their concurrent arrival at the fateful intersection. While it may not undermine the opening statement to detail the order in which the vehicles departed, it will certainly clutter the stories with useless, and perhaps confusing, details.

Chronology can also interfere with the logical exposition of your theory. The plaintiff's theory in the fire truck case is that she stopped for the fire engine, as required by law, but the defendant did not. The defendant was at fault because he was preoccupied and failed to keep a proper lookout. Perhaps he was speeding, and perhaps his brakes performed inadequately due to poor maintenance. The various elements of this theory both precede and follow the accident itself. For example, the defendant woke up late before the collision, but he grabbed his phone to cancel his meeting after the collision. Both of these facts directly support the theory that the defendant was in a hurry that morning. Even though they occurred at different times, they can have more impact if they are presented together.

Similarly, consider the importance of the defendant's failure to have his brakes repaired. If the opening statement were presented in strict chronology, that fact would be introduced to the jury before they had any way to measure its importance. Of course, no matter when the jury hears it, it sounds bad for the defendant to have ignored a warning about his brakes. But a chronological recitation will separate this fact from the moment of the accident, thus requiring the jury to reach back in their memories in order to recall its importance.

The brake story is most persuasive when it is added to the events of the accident, not when it precedes them. Presented first, the brake story, at best, will evoke curiosity: "I wonder why that will turn out to be important?" Presented after the account of the accident, the brake story should result in understanding: "Oh, so that is why he didn't stop in time." As an advocate you should almost always prefer to have the jury understand your theory rather than wonder about it.

The Uses of Chronology

Despite the drawbacks mentioned above, the judicious use of chronology is an essential part of every opening statement.

Chronological development should always be used to explain independent events. Every trial can be understood as a series of sub-events, which fit together to comprise the entire story. The order of addressing these sub-events is always open to determination by counsel. The sub-events themselves, however, have their own internal logic, which generally can be understood only when explained chronologically.

The fire engine case provides an excellent illustration of this principle. The plaintiff's case consists of at least the following four sub-events: 1) the collision itself; 2) the defendant's hurried morning; 3) the defendant's failure to repair his brakes; and 4) the fire department's policy of always sounding the siren on a vehicle that is responding to a call. These four elements, and of course there may be others, can be arranged in a variety of ways to make the case more persuasive. Once you have determined the overall structure however, it will make the most sense, as you reach each individual component, to detail it chronologically. Suppose that plaintiff's counsel has decided to organize her opening statement in the same order that the sub-events are given above. After going through the facts of the accident in the same sequence in which they occurred, she would proceed to develop the secondary components by relying on the chronology of each one:

> Why didn't the defendant stop when all of the other traffic did? We know that he woke up late that morning and that he had an important meeting to attend downtown, which was scheduled to begin only an hour and

> a half later. By the time he washed and shaved and went to the garage where his car was parked, he had only about thirty minutes left to get to his meeting. It was sixteen miles from his home to his office. As he headed south on Sheridan Road, every delay made him that much later for his meeting.
>
> By the time he got to the corner of Sheridan and Touhy he only had twelve minutes or so before his meeting was to start, yet he still had seven miles to go. We know that the fire truck was already at that corner, flashing its lights and sounding its siren. There is no evidence that the defendant intentionally ignored the fire truck, but he obviously didn't respond to it in time. Although at some point he hit his brakes, he still went crashing into the back of my client's car.
>
> Was there something wrong with the defendant's brakes? Could he have stopped in time if they had been working better? We know that just a week before the accident he had his car in for servicing. The mechanic advised him to have his brakes relined, but the defendant decided not to take the time to have the repair work done. He left the garage without having his brakes fixed. We also know that the fire truck gave the defendant plenty of warning. It was flashing its lights and sounding its siren. We know this because it has always been strict fire department policy to use these warning signals whenever an engine is responding to a call. And so it was that day. Engine Number 9 was responding to a call, so, as one of the firefighters will tell you herself, the lights and siren were being used with full force.

Note, by the way, the reference to the testimony of the firefighter in the paragraph about the fire truck's lights and siren. Even though the story is not being presented in a witness-by-witness fashion, it will often be helpful to refer to the source of certain evidence, particularly when you know that it will be disputed. This technique will be developed at greater length below.[7]

Although the sub-events as units are presented out of chronological order, internally each one is detailed basically as it occurred. The result of this approach is that the jury will be able to understand the context of the entire story as well as the precise nature of the individual occurrences that comprise the story.

12.3.5.2 Using Details Persuasively

As we have seen, the use of evidence in an opening statement depends on the persuasive arrangement of major propositions and supporting details. While the application of this approach will vary tremendously from case to case, the following few generalizations should prove helpful:

7. *See* section 12.3.5.2.

Big Ideas, Then Details

As a general rule, an opening statement should be organized as a series of big ideas, each of which is immediately supported by persuasive details.

As we have discussed above, jurors will tend to resolve a case on the basis of certain turning points or crucial issues. Details can be marshaled to make your version of these turning points more persuasive. For example, one major issue in the fire truck case will be whether or not the engine was sounding its siren just before the accident. If the jury decides that there was a siren, it will be more likely to bring back a plaintiff's verdict; if there was no siren, then the defendant has a better chance of prevailing. Thus, the use of the siren could be a turning point in the trial. The plaintiff's position on this issue can be made more likely through the addition of details: the fire truck was responding to a call; there is a departmental policy to use the siren whenever responding to a call; the driver of the truck was an experienced firefighter, well aware of the policy; other motorists stopped their cars.[8]

The details, however, have little meaning when offered on their own. They become important only in light of the turning point on which they are offered. The fact that the fire truck was responding to a call doesn't tell us anything about the way that the accident happened, but it does tell us that the truck was almost certainly using its siren. In the same vein, the jury will have no reason to care about the experience level of the fire truck driver until it is first informed that the use of the siren is an issue in the case. It is for this reason that details are best used to follow up or support the initial explication of a bigger idea.

Weave in the Witnesses

While the witness-by-witness approach is unlikely to result in an effective opening statement, this does not mean that individual witnesses should not be mentioned in the course of your opening. To the contrary, it is often quite important to inform the jury of the source of a specific fact or the precise nature of some anticipated testimony. The key is to weave the information about the witnesses into the narrative so that the witness references arise in the context of your theory of the case.

As we have been discussing, the use of the siren is likely to be a turning point in our fire truck case. The plaintiff says there was a siren, and the defendant says there was not. The plaintiff's opening statement can bolster her position by weaving in witness information when her narrative reaches the siren issue:

> Just as she reached the intersection, the plaintiff saw and heard an approaching fire truck. It was sounding its siren and flashing its lights. We

8. In the absence of details, the "siren question" would simply be a matter of the plaintiff's word against the defendant's. Note, then, that one value of the details is that they add persuasive force to the plaintiff's theory without relying on her own credibility. This, in turn, makes the plaintiff all the more credible, since her version of events is supported by objective facts.

> know that the siren was operating because Lieutenant Karen Dunn, the driver of the fire truck, will testify that she always sounds the siren when she is answering a call. That is fire department policy, and Lieutenant Dunn is a decorated firefighter who has been with the department for over ten years. Perhaps, for whatever reason, the defendant didn't hear the siren, but Lieutenant Dunn will testify that she is certain that she was doing her official duty—that is, using her audio and visual alarms— on the day when the accident occurred.

Used in this manner, the information about Lieutenant Dunn corroborates and strengthens the plaintiff's theory of the case. It neither stands alone as an isolated description of the witness, nor does it interfere with the flow of the narrative. Rather, it adds unapologetic support to the plaintiff's theory at the precise moment when support is likely to be most readily understood.

Raise Credibility When It Counts

Once the witnesses have been woven into the narrative, a question still remains as to when and how to deal with their credibility. Although the nonargument rule prevents counsel from commenting directly on the believability of a witness, this point can still be made quite handily with attributive details. It would be an error, however, to attend to the reliability of every witness who you mention in your opening statement.

The veracity of most witnesses is unlikely to be challenged. Building up a witness who no one is likely to tear down will only add verbiage to your opening statement and therefore violates the "anti-clutter" principle. Worse, by engaging in unnecessary damage control you run the risk of actually undermining the credibility of the witness who you are attempting to endorse.

Conversely, it is also problematic to use your opening statement to attack the credibility of a witness who has not yet testified. It is a natural instinct to want to give someone the benefit of the doubt, and if the person whose integrity you are trying to impugn is absent, you may give the impression of being disingenuous or unfair.

This is not to say that the credibility of witnesses should never be addressed in opening statements, but rather that the issue generally should be raised overtly only in fairly narrow circumstances. Passing comments on credibility typically present no problem when they are positive in nature. Plaintiff's remark that the fire truck driver was an experienced firefighter, for example, was short enough not to constitute clutter and reasonable enough not to undercut the witness. Note, however, that throwaway lines that are negative in character may still seem catty, or worse. If you are going to say something bad about someone, it is usually best to say it directly.

In any event, extended treatment of credibility is usually best left to situations where a witness is likely to be challenged or where some item of evidence is seriously in dispute.

A plaintiff who expects one of her witnesses to be attacked should consider doing some advance work to establish the witness's credibility. Once the jury has been given a reason to trust a witness, it will be more difficult for the other side to damage him. There is some risk to this, of course, because the anticipated assault may never actually materialize. Moreover, this is a tricky subject to introduce without damning the witness through faint praise. It won't help your opening statement, much less your case, to announce that "some people consider this witness to be a liar, but we will prove that he is as honest as the day is long."

Advance accreditation of a witness, then, should be accomplished in as positive a manner as possible. Humanize the witness. Give the jury a chance to come to like the witness. Explain the witness's many fine qualities. Likable people are more apt to be accepted as truthful even after negative information has been offered by the other side. Thus, the best defense to an anticipated attack, and certainly the first method to consider, is to build up the witness without any reference to the way you expect him to be maligned. Let it come as an unpleasant surprise when opposing counsel starts taking the low road against the perfectly reasonable witness you have described.[9]

On the other hand, defense counsel should almost always rise to the defense of a witness who has been disparaged during the plaintiff's opening. Particularly where you intend to rely on the witness's testimony to establish an element of your case, it is important not to allow an attack to go unanswered. If you do not defend your witness, the jury may very well infer that he is indefensible. You will have lost important ground before the testimony has even begun.

The defense of a witness's credibility need not consist of a point-by-point refutation of any charges made by the other side, although false charges certainly should be rebutted or denied. It may, however, be more effective simply to use your opening to paint a contrary picture of the witness. Consider this response in a situation where plaintiff's attorney has accused a key defense witness of shading her testimony to help out a friend:

> Plaintiff's counsel said some really nasty things about Sarah Tigre. I don't want to dignify them by repeating them, and I am not going to name-call any of the plaintiff's own witnesses. The actual evidence in this case, though, is going to show that Ms. Tigre is responsible, dependable, and honest. She was born and raised right here in town. She graduated from State University with a degree in education, and she has been a teacher ever since. Ms. Tigre works ten hours a day in an inner-city school trying

9. The issue of whether your opening statement should address negative facts about your own witnesses is discussed in section 12.4.4.

> to help kids get a better chance in life. At 3:30, when the other teachers go home, Sarah Tigre stays late supervising the drama program. On weekends she tutors kids who need some extra help. She has been named teacher of the year four times. Sarah Tigre didn't ask to be involved in this case, she just happened to be a witness. Sure, she's a friend of the defendant's, but Sarah will tell you that couldn't possibly affect her testimony. You'll see and hear Sarah Tigre, and you can judge plaintiff's charges for yourselves.

The charge of biased testimony is difficult to refute. No contrary facts can be presented, and the claim only stands to be strengthened by descent into an "is so/is not" sort of confrontation. The best approach, therefore, is often to explain why the witness couldn't possibly testify to anything but the truth.

Finally, where the trial involves seriously conflicting issues of fact, it is important to use the opening statement to stress the superior credibility of your own witnesses. In the fire truck case, for instance, the use of the siren might be a significant factual dispute. The plaintiff could deal with the question this way:

> The plaintiff heard the fire truck's siren and immediately stopped her car. The defendant has claimed that there was no siren. But you don't need to rely on the plaintiff alone in order to resolve this dispute. Lieutenant Karen Dunn will testify that she was using her siren as she always does. Lieutenant Dunn has been with the fire department for over a decade. She has no interest in this case one way or another, but she has received numerous commendations for her excellent work as a firefighter. She teaches courses at the departmental academy, and she was the first woman in the entire state to be promoted to the rank of lieutenant.

If there were no question about the siren, it would not be necessary to go into Lieutenant Dunn's background. The factual dispute, however, gives added importance to enhancing her credibility.

12.4 Content

The range of triable subjects being virtually limitless, is it possible to define what goes into a good opening statement? Of course every good opening statement, no matter what the case, contains enough information to help you win the trial, but not so much as to distract the jury or risk exploitation by the other side. The following considerations should be helpful in most trials.

12.4.1 True and Provable

Every fact that you include in your opening statement must be true and provable. We have already seen that the law limits opening statements to a preview of the evidence that will be presented once the trial begins. It is not enough, however, that some witness may be willing to make a certain statement. The ethics of our profession require that we never knowingly be involved in presenting false evidence. This stricture applies not only to offering testimony, but also to outlining the case during the opening statement.

As we discussed earlier, the concept of truth takes a very specific form in the context of the adversary system. Since the jury, or judge, is assigned the role of deciding the truth of facts, counsel is generally obligated only to present one competing version of events. An attorney does not need to subject potential witnesses to a polygraph examination or be convinced of a witness's truthfulness beyond a reasonable doubt. The attorney may not, however, present evidence known to be fraudulent. Stated conversely, while you needn't be persuaded to a moral certainty, you must have some reasonable basis for believing a fact to be true before you can offer it from the witness stand or use it during your opening statement. It does not matter how good it makes the story, it does not matter how well it fits your theory of the case, it does not matter how incontrovertible your position might be—no fact may be used in an opening statement unless it meets the "not knowingly false" test of validity.

Conversely, even assuredly true facts should not be used in an opening statement until they have been subjected to the test of provability. While there may occasionally be reasons to depart from this principle, you should, as a general rule, omit from your opening statement any fact that you are not certain you will be able to prove at trial.

An opening statement is in many ways a promise to the jury. By making a definitive statement about the future evidence, you have committed yourself to produce that evidence. If your witnesses turn out to be less conclusive than your opening statement, you may seem at best to have overstated your case. At worst, you may seem deliberately to have misled the jury. The same thing can happen when promised evidence fails to materialize, either because the court declines to admit it or because it turns out to be unavailable. Even if the jury doesn't immediately realize that there has been a gap between your opening and your proof, you can be certain that opposing counsel will point it out during final argument.

12.4.1.1 Your Central Evidence

Your strongest evidence should generally be at the heart of your opening statement. The central evidence will be a combination of: 1) the facts most essential to your case, and 2) the facts least likely to be disputed.

In the fire truck case it is central to the plaintiff's position to prove that she did indeed stop for a fire engine. The opening statement, if it does nothing else, must firmly establish in the jury's mind the presence of the truck and its use of its warning signals. Even if these facts will be disputed, they must be developed in the opening statement because the plaintiff cannot win without them.

Additionally, the plaintiff's opening statement should make liberal use of undisputed evidence even if it is not absolutely necessary to the case. The plaintiff can win the fire truck case without proving that the defendant was in a hurry. On the other hand, many of the specifics of the defendant's rushed morning cannot be controverted, which obviously makes them all the more persuasive. Thus, the plaintiff should be sure to include facts such as the time and importance of the defendant's business meeting that morning, the distance from his home to his office, the route he had to drive, his parking arrangements, and his pulling out his cell phone immediately after the collision.

12.4.1.2 Questionable Evidence

How strong or central must evidence be to gain a place in your opening statement? What should you do with evidence of dubious admissibility?

For the purpose of inclusion in your opening statement, or for later use at trial for that matter, you can regard all of your evidence as having two predominant attributes: necessity and provability. Each of these qualities, in turn, can be imagined as a continuum. The necessity level of any item of evidence can range from absolute to basically dispensable. Provability will vary to the same extent. The higher a necessity value that you assign to any fact, the less provability is required for including it in your opening statement. By the same token, evidence that is more provable can be less essential.

Note, however, that every opening statement is limited in time; you cannot, and should not, use everything. Thus, for both aspects of evidence there is a point of diminishing return. Remotely provable facts should generally be omitted no matter how important they might turn out to be. Facts only tangentially related to your theory of the case should also be left out, no matter how unquestionable they are.

Many lawyers believe that counsel should always err on the side of excluding information from the opening statement, particularly when the issue is admissibility. Why risk promising something that you will not be able to deliver? Even if you present your opening without the questionable evidence, you will still be able to offer it at trial. If it turns out to be admitted, you can make full use of it during the closing argument. This approach quite clearly minimizes the risk that your opening statement will backfire.

Some attorneys, however, are of the view that such risk aversion leads to unnecessary self-censorship. By purging your opening statement of everything that is subject to objection, you may lose the opportunity to tell the most coherent and complete story possible. Furthermore, notwithstanding your own doubts, opposing counsel may decide not to object to the evidence in question. Then you will have excluded it from your opening statement for no reason at all. Attorneys who take this position therefore place primary emphasis on the importance of the evidence and correspondingly less value on the likelihood of its eventual admission.

At this point in the discussion two caveats are absolutely necessary. First, it is unethical to use an opening statement to discuss evidence where there is no reasonable basis for admissibility. There is a line to be drawn between evidence that may be subject to objection and that which is obviously inadmissible. While one need not defer in advance to the possibility of an arguable objection, counsel cannot ethically sneak information before a jury where there is no chance of having it properly admitted. It is acceptable to run the risk of inadmissibility, but it is entirely cynical, unacceptable, and wrong to inject clearly inadmissible evidence into an opening statement.

Second, in situations where a motion in limine has been allowed, it is unethical (and perhaps contumacious) to use the opening statement to refer to evidence that has been excluded by the court. The grant of a motion in limine rules out all mention of the evidence, not simply its offer through the testimony of a witness. Many judges also make it a practice to reserve ruling on motions in limine while instructing counsel not to allude to the subject evidence during opening statements.

12.4.2 The Operative Facts

The most important part of any opening statement is its treatment of the operative facts. Facts win lawsuits. Everything else—organization, presentation, theme development—must be seen as an aid to the communication of the facts of the case.

It goes without saying that there can be no recipe for presenting the facts of a case. Each trial is unique. Some call for delicate innuendo; others may benefit from a frontal assault. Some cases rest heavily on the credibility of witnesses, while others depend on the timing of events. Often, however, the operative facts of a case will include some or all of the following.

12.4.2.1 Action and Key Events

Many cases revolve around one or more actions or key events. Most cases involving personal injury, crimes, medical malpractice, or property damage, to name only a few, require the description of a series of physical occurrences. An earlier section discussed the importance of using chronology to detail a single discrete event, as well as its frequent misuse as a device to outline an entire case.[10] This section addresses other aspects of presenting an account of the key events.

Whether representing the plaintiff or the defendant, it is important to use the opening statement to begin to paint a picture of the events in a way that helps the jury visualize the case from your client's point of view. To do this effectively you must first have created your own mental image that will, of course, be consistent with the testimony to be given later by your own witnesses. The importance of preparation cannot be overemphasized. You must know precisely how, and in what terms, your

10. *See* section 12.3.5.1.

witnesses will relate each incident. You must be familiar with all of the physical evidence, and you must, if possible, have visited the site of the events. Competent counsel should never risk the possibility of dissonance between the events portrayed in the opening statement and those that emerge from the witnesses' testimony.

In depicting events, nouns and verbs can be much more helpful than adjectives and adverbs. This may not be immediately obvious since we commonly think of modifiers as adding descriptive depth. Consider, however, which of the following accounts is more evocative of the crime. First, a short paragraph that makes maximum use of adverbs and adjectives:

> It was a heinous, horrible crime. The defendant's actions were inhuman and awful. He brutally grabbed at the victim's gold chain, fiercely yanking it away. He left an ugly, ugly bruise on the victim's neck. Unsatisfied with the proceeds of the armed robbery, the defendant then coldly and wantonly stabbed the victim twice, leaving his jacket lying in a bloody heap. It was indeed a cowardly act, taken against a defenseless victim.

Now consider a paragraph with virtually no modifiers at all:

> The defendant placed his knife against the victim's body. Without waiting, he grabbed the gold chain from the victim's neck and wrenched it until it snapped, leaving bruises on the victim's neck that didn't heal for weeks. Although he had already taken what he wanted, he twisted the knife into the victim's shoulder, turning it as he pushed, and watched as the blood welled to the surface. Then he stabbed the victim again, until blood soaked the jacket all the way through.

The second paragraph is more vivid, not only because of its slightly greater length,[11] but primarily because it describes the deeds as they occurred. In contrast, the first paragraph actually short-circuits the action by substituting value-laden modifiers for an account of the events themselves.

Of course, it would be foolish, if not impossible, to attempt to deliver an opening statement free of modifiers. Adjectives and adverbs are useful precisely because they convey compact meanings. Often they are indispensable. It is impossible to describe a red rubber ball without using the word "red."

Counsel must bear in mind, however, that modifiers frequently stand for judgments rather than for descriptions. Words like heinous, brutal, and awful or lovely, wonderful, and grand may convey the lawyer's opinion about something, but they do not depict a vision of the events themselves.

11. It inevitably takes more words to write without adjectives and adverbs since one of the functions of a modifier is to compress concepts into a single word.

12.4.2.2 The Physical Scene

The meaning and legal significance of events often depends on their location. Actions that are lawful or innocuous in one locale may become the basis of liability if they occur somewhere else. It is negligent to drive an automobile on the wrong side of the road. It may be an unfair labor practice for management to approach potential union members in their homes. It may violate a zoning ordinance to operate a law practice in a residential neighborhood. Similarly, the physical details of a particular setting may affect issues such as probability, credibility, or visibility.

It is important, therefore, to use your opening statement to set the scene for major events. While virtually all commentators agree that the scene should be set apart from a description of the action itself, there is divided opinion as to the sequence in which a scene should be described. Many lawyers suggest putting all of the details in place before going on to portray the action. In this way, the jury will already be aware of the physical details as the events unfold. Alternatively, you may describe the action first, and then go back to fill in the specifics of the setting. The theory behind this approach is that the importance of the events should be obvious, but the importance of the details will require some context to become apparent. There is no reason to care about the location of a stop sign until we know that there was a collision in the middle of the intersection.

Setting a scene involves describing a potentially unlimited number of details. Your opening statement should dwell on those details that are significant to your case while avoiding those that are merely clutter. In the fire truck case, for example, it is important for the plaintiff to note that the pavement was dry, since that would affect the defendant's stopping distance. The height of the curb, however, would be extraneous under virtually any theory of the case.

12.4.2.3 Transactions and Agreements

Most business cases involve written and oral communications far more than they do physical occurrences. In many ways, these nonphysical events may be more difficult to describe during an opening statement since there is little or no activity to depict. Nonetheless, when a case turns on the interpretation of a document or the meaning of a series of telephone calls, counsel must search for a way to bring the transaction to life.

The surest way not to bring a business transaction to life is to parse it out in minute chronological detail. It is generally far better to begin at the end. Explain the gist of the agreement and then go back to fill in only those details that are necessary to support your interpretation. There is no need, for example, to recount every telephone conversation that went into the negotiation of a purchase order. It will usually be sufficient to delineate the terms of the order itself, supported by an account of one or two crucial conversations.

It is not enough, however, simply to recite the terms of an agreement and then to point out that it was either kept or broken. While such an approach may, in the driest sense, convey your theory, it will not add moral weight to your case. Recall that your trial theme is intended to provide the jury with a reason for wanting to rule in your favor. This can only be done if you are able to explain the "rightness" of your interpretation of the contract. Why were the particular terms so important? Why was your client's reliance on the other party justified? Why will the other party's interpretation lead to chaos and disaster for the entire republic?

12.4.2.4 Business Context

Business context can be crucial to an appreciation of many agreements and transactions. Words may have specialized meanings, or unspoken expectations may be understood by all of the parties. Detailing the business context of a contract or other transaction may be the equivalent of setting the scene for an automobile accident.

Business context can include information on industry practice, course of dealings, production standards, insurability, cost of credit, lines of authority, agency, normal business hours, grievance procedures, and a host of other factors that may form the backdrop for even the simplest transaction.

12.4.2.5 Relationship of the Parties

As much as any physical detail, the past relationship of the parties can speak volumes about the merits of a case. It will add a whole new dimension to a contracts case if it is revealed that there had been a history of misunderstanding between the buyer and the seller. Past animus can be used to show motive or malice. A tradition of reliability, on the other hand, can be used to establish the reasonableness of a party's actions.

12.4.2.6 Motives and Motivations

As we have consistently seen, stories are more persuasive when they are told about people who have reasons for the way they act. An opening statement, therefore, should always attempt to stress the motivations for the parties' actions. The activity that you describe will be far more plausible if, at the same time, you are also able to explain why the people involved acted as they did.

It must be stressed, however, that the opening statement is not the time to speculate about a person's secret motives. The opening statement must develop motive in the same way that it treats everything else—through the preview of evidentiary facts. The rule against argument applies with full force, and probably then some, to the discussion of motive.

Thus, motivation must be carefully established with discrete, incremental facts. You cannot say that the plaintiff is greedy. You can point out five previous occasions on which the plaintiff sued for breach of contract, each one based on an imperceptible flaw in the goods delivered.

12.4.2.7 Amount of Damages

There are two schools of thought regarding the treatment of damages during the plaintiff's opening statement. One approach is to make the discussion of damages a significant part of the opening, explaining the nature of the injury and the amount that is being sought. The theory here is to acclimate the jury to the fact that the plaintiff will be requesting substantial monetary compensation. Where the amount sought is extremely large, many lawyers believe that it will take some time for the jury to become used to thinking about such big numbers. Thus, they like the process to begin as soon as possible.

Other lawyers believe that damage amounts will have little meaning until the jury has actually heard the evidence. It will be difficult for them to think in terms of awards until they have at least begun to make up their minds about liability. This is thought to be particularly true about big numbers, as it may make the lawyer and client seem greedy to begin talking about large verdicts before any evidence has been introduced. Lawyers who hold this view generally discuss the facts that support damages, but do not mention a specific figure. Note, however, that there is little reason not to state a precise figure for damages in, for example, a commercial case where the amount is liquidated.

Finally, a majority of defense counsel refrain from discussing damages during the opening statement. Even where the plaintiff's damage figure is inflated or unrealistic, many defense lawyers fear that they will appear to concede liability if they seem to quibble about the amount of damages right at the outset of the case. Some lawyers choose to make only a passing reference to the plaintiff's request, stating something to the effect that, "Even if the defendant was at fault, the evidence will show that the plaintiff's number is far more than would be necessary for fair compensation." Others do not even go this far. Of course, where the defendant has admitted or stipulated to liability the case will be tried only on the question of damages. Since the amount of compensation is the only issue, the defendant obviously must address it during the opening statement.

12.4.3 The Opposition's Case

It is always difficult to decide how much attention to give to the opposition's case. Plaintiff's counsel must determine whether to anticipate and respond to the expected defenses. Defendant's counsel has to consider whether and how much to react to the plaintiff's opening.

12.4.3.1 Plaintiff's Opening

Unlike final arguments, there is no rebuttal in opening statements. The plaintiff gets to address the jury only once and without the advantage of knowing what the defendant's opening will be. No matter what defense counsel says, plaintiff's attorney will not be able to respond directly until the end of the trial. This can be especially troublesome in cases where the defendant presents an affirmative defense. Since an affirmative defense, by definition, raises issues that go beyond the plaintiff's own case, the plaintiff faces a delicate problem in dealing with them during the opening statement. Should the plaintiff ignore the affirmative defense, thereby foregoing the opportunity to reply to it at the outset of the trial? Or should the plaintiff respond to the defense in advance, in essence forecasting the defendant's case?

One solution to this problem is to construct the discussion of the plaintiff's own case in such a way as to blunt any rejoinders that the defendant might raise. In a simple automobile accident case, for example, plaintiff's counsel can build up the plaintiff's level of care and skill while driving, without ever mentioning the defense of contributory negligence.

Unfortunately, not all defenses are equally amenable to this approach. Assume, for instance, that you represent the plaintiff in a sales transaction. Your client contracted to sell industrial machinery to the defendant. Your client contends that the goods were shipped, but no payment was received. There are at least three possible defenses: 1) the goods were never received due to some fault of the plaintiff; 2) they were received, but they were defective; or 3) payment was made.

To negate fully any of these claims, the plaintiff, at a minimum, must refer to the defense itself. Consider the defense of defective products. To be sure, a general statement that the goods conformed to the contract will be sufficient to stake out the plaintiff's position. But a truly persuasive story will require the plaintiff to confront and refute each of the shortcomings asserted by the defense. In the absence of this discussion in the plaintiff's opening, the jury will hear only about what was wrong with the shipment. It is conceivable that plaintiff's counsel might run through every single specification, explaining that the goods conformed across the board, but this itemization could go on forever without informing the jury of the precise issue in dispute. It would make far more sense for the plaintiff to focus her opening statement on exactly the defects claimed by the defendant.

In some cases, then, the plaintiff has little choice but to anticipate the defendant's opening statement. Here are some guidelines:

Your case first. Give primary attention to the strongest aspects of your own case. The opening statement is your opportunity to begin to capture the jury's imagination. Don't get them started imagining the things that might be wrong with your case. Accentuate the positive. To the extent possible, defenses should be treated as technicalities or annoyances.

Be certain. The process of discovery should allow you to know with some certainty exactly which defenses will be raised. There is no reason to survey all of the holes that the defendant might try to punch in your case. Concentrate on the principal defenses.

No apologies, no sneers. When it comes time to discuss the opposition's case, your tone should be firm, unapologetic, and straightforward. If you seem overly concerned or worried about a defense, it will suggest that there are indeed problems with your case. By the same token, you shouldn't sneer or be entirely dismissive; after all, you are the one who is introducing the issue. Moreover, you can't expect the jury to share your disdain for the defendant's position when they haven't even had a chance to hear it yet.

Minimize witness references. There is an inherent difficulty in predicting what the other side's witnesses are going to say. Opening statements are allowed, after all, for you to assist the jury by previewing your own evidence. Not having prepared or organized the other side's case, you would be hard put to explain how you can help the jury by guessing at what it might be.

In this vein, it has even been suggested that it is improper for counsel to preview testimony from opposition witnesses. The theory behind this position is that you may only use your opening statement to explain what you expect the evidence to show and that you cannot be certain what the opposition evidence will be. Given the reality of deposition practice and pretrial orders, however, it is obvious that in most cases you will have a good idea of just how the opposing witnesses will testify. Even if a witness ends up not being called, in most jurisdictions you will have the opportunity to call the witness yourself.

Nonetheless, it is a good idea to refer to the other side's case in summary only and to avoid direct quotations from their witnesses. There is something discordant about a lawyer predicting how opposing witnesses will testify. Additionally, there is a tremendous chance that, following such an opening, the other side's witnesses will testify differently, if only to spite you. Finally, recall that the purpose of anticipating the defendant's opening statement is to allow you to build up your own case, not to expound on the details of theirs.

There are situations where explicit quotations may be helpful. It can be devastating to read from a document that the defendant produced or to quote directly from the defendant's own deposition. The key to this approach is to be sure 1) that the quotations are accurate, 2) that they are meaningful standing alone and do not require extensive context, and 3) that you have an independent evidentiary basis for introducing them yourself.

Finally, it must be noted that the Fifth Amendment prohibits prosecutors from so much as suggesting that the defendant will testify. The Fifth Amendment does not, however, prevent the prosecutor from reading from a confession or prior statement of the defendant as long as the statement itself has not been ruled inadmissible.

12.4.3.2 Defendant's Opening

Many lawyers believe that thorough preparation includes planning every word of the opening statement in advance. This is true only to a point. While plaintiffs and prosecutors have the luxury of knowing exactly how they will open their cases, defense lawyers must be more flexible. It is a tremendous advantage to deliver the second opening statement, and defense counsel can only take advantage of this opportunity by being ready to respond to at least some aspects of the plaintiff's opening. No matter how well you have prepared your case, it is a mistake to be tied to a scripted opening statement.

Responses or rejoinders to the plaintiff's opening can be fruitful in the following situations.

Denials. The civil plaintiff's opening statement, and even more so the criminal prosecutor's, is essentially an accusation. Its entire thrust is to tell a story that accuses the defendant of negligence, breach of contract, criminal acts, or some other negative conduct. After hearing such an extended charge against the defendant, the jury's first inclination will be to ask the question, "Well, is it true?" The defendant, then, absolutely must respond with a denial. Anything short of a denial is likely to be regarded as evasion, equivocation, or worse, an admission of fault.

While defense counsel can plan to deny the plaintiff's allegations, it can be a mistake to plan exactly how to deny them. Generic denials tend to sound exactly like generic denials; they lack force because they do not meet the opposing party head-on. It can be much more effective and persuasive to pick up on the plaintiff's opening and to deny their claims using some of the same language in which they were made.

Care must be taken not to echo the insinuations of the plaintiff's charge. There is no reason to repeat all of the nasty evidence that the plaintiff claims to be able to produce. On the other hand, it is necessary to recognize that the plaintiff has made specific charges and to explain specifically how they will be rebutted.

The following is a poor example of a denial in a defendant's opening statement because it is too general to carry any weight:

> The defendant denies any and all negligence on his part. He denies that he was anything less than a careful driver, and he denies that he caused the plaintiff any harm.

Here is a worse example because it gives too much credence to the plaintiff's case:

> The plaintiff has claimed that my client was preoccupied with an important business meeting on the morning of the accident. It is their position that he was thinking about how to attract a lucrative new client instead of paying attention to the road. This is all untrue. We will prove that the accident was the plaintiff's own fault.

Here is a better example; it responds directly to the plaintiff's central claim, but it does so by building up the defendant's own case, not by reiterating the plaintiff's:

> Contrary to the plaintiff's claim, my client was anything but "too busy to be careful." We will prove that he was driving well within the legal speed limit and that he was keeping a proper and careful lookout. He had plenty of time to get to his office that morning, but the plaintiff herself stopped her car in the middle of the street rather than pulling over to the right as the traffic laws require.

Controverted evidence. It is also important to respond directly to the plaintiff's version of significant controverted evidence. Simply telling your own independent story is not sufficient—doing so will not allow you to explain why the facts in support of your version are superior. It is also risky to expect jurors to keep the plaintiff's opening in mind and then appreciate the implications of the contrary facts as you reveal them. Instead, you should make it apparent that you are contradicting the plaintiff's factual claims:

> Plaintiff's counsel claimed that my client neglected to have his brakes repaired. The facts are that he took his car in for a tune-up and the mechanic said only that he should have his brakes "looked at" within the next 10,000 miles. The evidence will show that the defendant took care of all scheduled maintenance completely according to the manufacturer's timetable and that he had no reason to think that his brakes were not functioning properly.

If defense counsel simply began talking about brakes, the jury might take it as a concession that defendant's brakes were a problem. The defense case is therefore made much stronger by pointing out how the defendant's facts contradict the plaintiff's claim.

Omissions. The absence of evidence can be as telling as the evidence itself. Defense counsel should therefore be ready to respond not only to what was said in plaintiff's opening, but also to what was not said. While it would be argumentative to accuse opposing counsel of concealing information, it is perfectly proper to point out evidentiary gaps in the plaintiff's opening statement. Assume, for example, that liability has been stipulated in the fire engine case and that it is being tried solely on the issue of damages:

> Plaintiff's counsel spoke at some length about the plaintiff's injuries. She did not, however, give you all of the facts about the plaintiff's current physical condition. The evidence will show, for example, that the plaintiff spent a weekend last summer camping at Eagle River Falls. She carried a backpack, she slept on the ground, and she hiked every day.
>
> Plaintiff's counsel did not tell you that the trip was planned for a long weekend, and she stayed the full time. It was not necessary for her to leave early. After the long weekend of roughing it, she simply went home. She didn't go to a hospital or even to her family doctor. On the other hand,

there will be absolutely no evidence in this case that the plaintiff lost any income as a result of her injuries.

Credibility. Finally, it is imperative that defense counsel reply to comments concerning the credibility of witnesses. If plaintiff's counsel trumpeted the superior credibility of her witnesses regarding a central issue or disputed fact, then you must react either by building up your own witnesses or by pointing out why and how the plaintiff's witnesses have feet of clay. Even if you did not originally intend to address credibility, you should not allow the plaintiff's position to stand unrebutted. This is even more important when the integrity of one of your own witnesses has been attacked. In these circumstances silence may be seen as a tacit admission; use your opening statement to go to bat for your witness.

12.4.4 Bad Facts and Disclaimers

Should your opening statement ever mention negative information that is likely to come out about one of your own witnesses? There is divided opinion on this issue. The traditional view is that you will appear to be hiding any bad facts that you do not mention and that you can defuse the impact of such facts by bringing them out yourself. Thus, most lawyers favor making at least a casual reference to such matters as felony convictions, admissible "bad acts," and other provable misconduct.

More recently, however, it has been suggested that jurors do not expect lawyers to say anything negative about their own witnesses and that by doing so you actually call greater attention to the damaging information. There will be time enough to respond to charges after they have actually been made; there is no need to lead the bandwagon yourself.

Whether to introduce damaging information about your own witnesses remains a matter of judgment, and no doubt the answer will differ with the context of the case. A prudent middle ground, however, is always to keep bad information, or even the suggestion of bad information, to an absolute minimum. You will want to exhibit the highest possible level of confidence and belief in your own witnesses. Thus, negative information should not be mentioned until you have laid out all of the positive facts about the witness. If you believe that you must defuse a ticking bomb, do it quickly and without fanfare.

Defense counsel, of course, does not need to wonder if any of her witnesses will be attacked during the plaintiff's opening statement. She has the advantage of going second. Thus, for defense counsel there will seldom, if ever, be a situation where it is necessary to raise damaging facts to head off the opposition. If the jury didn't get the bad news when the plaintiff opened, there should be scant reason to deliver it during the defendant's opening statement.[12]

12.4.5 Legal Issues

As was noted above, it is frequently important to use the opening statement to introduce the legal issues to the jury.[13] A statement of legal issues will put the significance of the facts into clear perspective. Explanations of the law should be brief and to the point. It is far better to weave them into the context of the story as opposed to "string-citing" all of the legal issues at once.

12.4.6 Introductions

At some point in the opening statement it will be necessary to introduce yourself, your client, and any cocounsel. Even if the judge has already introduced all of you, it is a common courtesy to do it again yourself. While there is a natural inclination to begin with introductions, they are not really important enough to warrant the use of your opening moment. It is usually better to start with a strong statement of your theory and theme and then proceed to the introductions at a natural breaking point.

12.4.7 Request for Verdict

Your opening statement should almost always conclude with a request for, or explanation of, the verdict that you will seek at the end of the trial. This request should be made in general terms: "At the end of the case we will ask you to return a verdict that the defendant was not guilty of negligence." The opening statement is not the time for a lengthy discussion of verdict forms or special interrogatories.

12.4.8 Bromides and Platitudes

There are a number of opening statement bromides and platitudes that have become venerated traditions among some members of the bar. While certain of these clichés have fallen from general use in recent years, others have taken on a life of their own, being repeated by generation after generation even though they have little, if any, intrinsic meaning. A few of the conventions have their limited uses.

---

12. It is possible, of course, that the plaintiff will introduce negative information into evidence notwithstanding the fact that it was not mentioned during the opening statement. Defense counsel should nonetheless be wary of advance disclosure during her opening. First, the plaintiff may decide not to offer the damaging evidence—or if offered, it may not be admitted. Second, much unpleasant information can be developed only on cross-examination, in which case there will be time enough to defuse it (if that is your choice) during the witness's direct. Finally, the bad facts might be introduced during plaintiff's case-in-chief, in which case cross-examination will be immediately available to the defendant, and it is unlikely to appear that the defendant was trying to conceal the material.
13. *See* section 12.2.2.

Here follows a short list of topics, phrases, and slogans that are usually best omitted from your opening statements.

The civics lesson. Some lawyers begin their opening statements with a paean to the American jury system. This invocation is unlikely to help your case since it has absolutely no persuasive value one way or the other. It may convince the jury that you are a patriotic lawyer, but it is just as likely to convince them that you have very little to say on the merits. There is a time to thank the jury for their service and to indicate your respect for the job that they are doing, but it is not at the beginning of your opening statement. The civics lesson, by the way, should be distinguished from a discussion in criminal cases of the concept of proof beyond a reasonable doubt. Reasonable doubt, unlike a generalized discourse on the jury system, is virtually always an essential element of the defendant's case that must be addressed during opening statements.

The neutral simile. It is not uncommon for a lawyer to begin an opening statement with an extended simile that is intended to explain the function of the opening. An opening statement, the jury might be told, is like the picture on the cover of a jigsaw puzzle box. Or it might be like a road map, or like the directions for programming a DVR. None of these similes is really worthwhile. They communicate absolutely nothing about your case, but they are damaging in the sense that they waste your opening moment. If your opening statement is good, the simile will be unnecessary. If your opening statement is disorganized or vague, no simile or metaphor will save it.

"Not evidence." Perhaps the hoariest opening line in the history of opening statements is the caution to the jury that "What I am about to say to you is not evidence; the evidence will be presented in the form of witness testimony, documents, and exhibits." Although this introduction is now heard less and less, it was once considered de rigueur for opening statements. Because it still survives in some quarters, the reasons for abandoning this line bear repeating. Telling the jury that your opening statement is not evidence is the rough equivalent of telling them to ignore what you are about to say. No one has ever claimed that opening statements are evidence, so there is no reason to disclaim the idea. You want the jury to pay attention to your opening; you should therefore say nothing that will tend to diminish its importance. There is one situation in which there may be some value to reminding a jury that an opening statement is not evidence. In criminal cases, the prosecution often presents a very comprehensive and compelling opening statement. Since the defense may not wish to commit themselves to putting on a case, they are often left with very little to say in response. Moreover, the defense will frequently rely most heavily on cross-examination as opposed to the development of an affirmative case. In these circumstances, it can be helpful to use the opening statement to explain that the prosecution opening, no matter how powerful it seemed, simply was not evidence. Note that in these circumstances the "not evidence" disclaimer is raised about the opposition opening, not your own.

"The evidence will show." Opening statements are limited to a description of "what the evidence will show." This rule has led some lawyers to conclude that every fact mentioned in the opening statement must be preceded with an introductory phrase such as, "we expect the evidence to show that the fire engine was flashing its lights," or "we intend to prove that the defendant had not repaired his brakes," or "there will be evidence that the defendant was already late for an important business meeting at the time of the collision." There is no harm at all in occasionally reminding the judge and jury that you are indeed forecasting evidence that is yet to come. It is hopelessly distracting, however, to use such a phrase as a preface to every item of evidence. It is entirely possible to deliver a complete opening statement without ever once saying, "the evidence will show . . . ." At most, the line should be used at wide intervals simply as an acknowledgment that the opening is a preview.

12.5 Delivery and Technique

It would be very easy to overemphasize the significance of presentational skills in delivering an opening statement. While the popular misconception may be that polished style can win trials, the truth is that well-developed facts almost always triumph over dramatics. Only once you have generated your theory of the case and organized your opening statement to present it most effectively should you turn your attention to delivery techniques. This does not mean that delivery is irrelevant, but only that the substance of the case must come first.

Recognizing the secondary role of technique, here are some useful guidelines.

12.5.1 Do Not Read

Do not read your opening statement from a prepared text. Only the most skilled professional actors can deliver a scripted speech and still appear to be spontaneous and sincere. Everyone else will seem to be stilted or labored. Your goal during the opening should be to communicate directly to the jurors, not to lecture to them from a manuscript. You will want to make eye contact, you will want to pick up on the jurors' reactions, and you will want to respond to objections and rulings by the court. Defense counsel, moreover, will want to reply to challenges, weaknesses, and omissions in the plaintiff's opening statement. A written opening statement will prevent you from doing any of these things effectively.

Much the same can be said of attempting to memorize your opening statement. While exceptional memorization is better than reading, you will still run the risk of forgetting a line (or more), of losing your place, or of being thrown off track by an objection. Very experienced lawyers may be able to deliver opening statements from memory. Novices should be wary of trying.

The best approach is to deliver the opening statement from an outline. It should be possible to list all of your major points, as well as the most important supporting details, on one or two sheets of paper. An outline will allow you to organize the material as well as ensure that you don't leave anything out, while avoiding all of the perils of reading or memorization. Although some lawyers believe that any use of notes is distracting to the jury, it is far more likely that jurors understand the need to use some notes whenever you are speaking at length. The key, of course, is for your notes to be unobtrusive. Hence, an outline as opposed to a text.

12.5.2 Use Simple Language and Straightforward Presentation

The opening statement should be reasonably straightforward and direct. It is a time to allow your facts to speak for themselves and not a time for emotional pleas or impassioned argument. In any event, the court will not allow you to make elaborate use of metaphors, literary allusions, biblical quotations, or any of the other rhetorical devices that can be so helpful during final argument.

While you should never talk down to a jury, simple language is generally the best. There is no word so eloquent that it is worth risking the understanding of a single juror. Your opening statement can be perfectly sophisticated without relying on language that you won't hear on the evening news. There is no reason to say that the defendant in the fire truck case "procrastinated" in having his brakes repaired; say instead that he "put off having his brakes fixed."[14] Most of all, do not use legalese. It isn't impressive even to lawyers, and it will tend to confuse, bore, and aggravate the jury.

12.5.3 Use Movement for Emphasis and Transition

To the extent that it is allowed by the judge, you can add considerable force to your opening statement simply by moving about in the courtroom.[15] Movement can be used most effectively to make the transition from one topic to another or to emphasize a particular point.

Movement for transition. Whenever you want to highlight a change of subjects during your opening statement, take a step or two to one side or the other. If you are standing at the lectern, your movement could be as slight as a shift to its side. By using your body in this manner, you signal to the jury that one subject has ended and another is about to begin. This motion, in turn, will have the effect of reinitiating primacy. The jury's attention will refocus, and you will then have

---

14. Readers have no doubt observed that this book does not shy away from big words. Nor should it; our language is rich, and it is made richer by the use of interesting and precise words. But writing for an audience of lawyers is one thing, and trying cases is another.

15. In some jurisdictions, counsel is required always to remain at the lectern. In a few jurisdictions, the attorneys must conduct the entire trial while seated at counsel table. Most judges, however, allow lawyers to move freely about the courtroom, especially during opening statements and closing arguments. If you are not familiar with a particular judge's practice, make a point of finding out before the trial begins.

a new "opening moment" in which to take advantage of the jury's heightened concentration and retention.

Movement for emphasis. Deliberate body movement always concentrates the jury's attention. Movement toward the jury will concentrate it even more. Whenever you reach a particularly important point in your opening statement, you can emphasize it by taking a step or two in the jury's direction. As your movement becomes faster and more purposeful, you will increasingly emphasize the point. Two caveats regarding the use of this technique should be fairly obvious: don't run and don't hover over the jury. The invasion of their space can be seen as overbearing or even threatening. Note also that your important point should not be made while you are walking—the jury might be paying more attention to your motion than to your words. Instead, use a transition sentence while you are moving toward the jury, then stop, pause a moment, and deliver your crucial point while standing perfectly still. The contrast will emphasize the issue even more.

Pacing. Pacing is bad. It distracts the jury. Far worse, it also deprives you of the ability to use movement for emphasis. If you are constantly walking back and forth in the courtroom, you cannot use a few well-chosen steps to underscore the significance of a critical detail. This can be especially crippling in an opening statement since the rule against argument otherwise severely limits your ability to accent issues for the jury.

Lectern. Most, although not all, courtrooms come equipped with a lectern. Many experienced attorneys move the lectern aside during opening statements so that nothing will stand between themselves and the jury. They either speak without using notes, or they use a few small index cards. This is an excellent approach if you are able to use it. Most lawyers, however, need more notes and are more comfortable using a lectern as home base. There is nothing wrong with speaking from a lectern, and you will not lose your case if you take a note pad with you when you deliver your opening statement. The key is to use the lectern without being chained to it. Feel free to move out to the side of the lectern or even across the courtroom, returning to your staging ground when you have finished emphasizing a point or when you need to refer to your notes.

12.5.4 Visuals and Exhibits

Your opening statement need not be confined to your words alone. Visual aids and exhibits can enormously enhance the value of your presentation.

Exhibits. Since the purpose of the opening statement is to explain what the evidence will show, you are entitled to read from or display documents and other exhibits that you expect to be admitted into evidence. If the case involves a contract, quote from the central clause. If you plan to offer a key letter into evidence, have it enlarged (either physically or electronically) and show it to the jury during your opening statement. Highlight key segments so that the jury can read along with you as you recite the opposing party's damning admission. During your opening statement, you may be able to show the jury photographs, models, maps, and charts, as well as other tangible exhibits such as weapons, machinery, or even prosthetics. There is some risk, of course, in displaying an exhibit that may not ultimately be admitted. Under modern practice, however, this problem can usually be alleviated by obtaining a pretrial ruling on admissibility.

Visual aids. In addition to displaying actual exhibits, you may also use visual aids during your opening statement. The general rule is that any visual aid must be likely to help the jury to understand the eventual trial evidence. Thus, lawyers have been allowed to show timelines to the jury or to draw freehand diagrams that will not later be offered into evidence. There are limitations, of course. The visual aids must fairly summarize the evidence, they cannot be misleading, and they cannot be argumentative. You could not, for example, produce a PowerPoint slide captioned "Three Reasons Not to Believe the Plaintiff." Visual aids should be shown to opposing counsel before your opening statement begins. You should also show visuals to the court and obtain advance permission for their use.

Other evidence. Not all exhibits are visual. It is permissible to play audio recordings during opening statements—such as legally recorded telephone conversations or 911 emergency calls—if they will later be offered into evidence. It is conceivable that creative counsel might even make use of olfactory or tactile evidence, although this possibility seems remote.

12.6 Additional Considerations

12.6.1 Motions and Objections

Objections are fairly unusual during opening statements. It may seem rude to interrupt when the other lawyer is speaking directly to the jury, and a general convention has developed that most attorneys will try to avoid objecting during opposing counsel's opening. There are times, however, when objections are called for and should be made.

12.6.1.1 Common Objections

The most common objection during an opening statement is to improper argument. Most judges will sustain this objection only when the argument is extended or over-the-top. An argumentative sentence or two will be unlikely to draw an objection and even more unlikely to see one sustained. Drawn out argument, however, should be objected to. There is no convention that allows opposing counsel to transform the opening statement into a final argument. Be particularly alert to extended argument on the credibility of witnesses.

It is also objectionable to discuss or explain the law during opening statements. Again, some brief mention of the applicable law is permissible, and in fact, unavoidable. Lengthy discourse on the law, and especially misstatement of the law, should draw an objection.

It is both objectionable and unethical for counsel to express a personal opinion during the opening statement or to assert personal knowledge of the facts of the case.[16] The purpose of this rule is to prevent attorneys from offering "facts" that will not be in evidence as well as to prevent the trial from becoming a referendum on the believability of the lawyers. This rule is intended to prevent lawyers from saying things like, "Believe me, I know what happened, and I wouldn't lie to you." It is not intended to preclude the occasional use of phrases such as "I think" or "I'm sure." An objection on this ground is most likely to be sustained when opposing counsel discusses her own investigation of the case or makes reference to her own credibility.

While opening statements are required to preview only the evidence that will ultimately come before the jury, objections usually will not be sustained on the ground that counsel is discussing inadmissible evidence. A lawyer is entitled to take a chance that her evidence will be admitted, and most judges will not rule on evidentiary objections during the opening statements. If you truly believe that evidence should be excluded, then your proper course of action is to make a motion in limine before the trial, not to raise an objection during opposing counsel's opening statement. On the other hand, it is possible that the opposition might take you completely by surprise by trying to slip some outrageously inadmissible and prejudicial tidbit into their opening statement. If that is the case, by all means object. It is unethical for an attorney to "allude to any matter that the lawyer does not reasonably believe is relevant or that will not be supported by admissible evidence."[17]

It is objectionable to refer to evidence that has been excluded via motion in limine or other pretrial ruling.

Finally, it is worth noting that there is no such objection as "That is not what the evidence will be." Opposing counsel presents her case, and you present yours. You will naturally disagree about what the evidence will show. If counsel ultimately fails to live up to the commitments given during her opening statement, then you can pound that point home during your final argument. For the same reason there is also no such objection as "Mischaracterizing the evidence." If a characterization amounts to argument, object to it. Otherwise, opposing counsel is free to put whatever spin she can on the evidence.

16. In fact, it is unethical for counsel to express a personal opinion or assert personal knowledge of the facts at any point during the trial. *See* Model Rules of Prof'l Conduct R. 3.4(e).

17. Model Rules of Prof'l Conduct R. 3.4(e).

12.6.1.2 Responding to Objections

An objection during your opening statement can be distracting. Lengthy argument, however, can be even more disruptive. Any time that you spend speaking to the court is time that you are not speaking to the jury. In all but exceptional circumstances, then, it is best to wait for the judge to rule on an objection and then to proceed.

If the objection is overruled, you may thank the court and pick up where you left off. If the objection is sustained, you must adapt your opening to the court's ruling. For example, if your theme has been declared argumentative, you must figure out a way to recast or truncate it so that you can continue to use it without objection.

Consider the "Too busy to be careful" theme that we have posited for the fire truck case. Although it is unlikely, imagine that the court has sustained an objection to the use of that phrase during your opening statement for the plaintiff. Don't ask for reconsideration or try to explain why you weren't being argumentative. A small adjustment to your opening should be sufficient:

> The evidence will show that the defendant was extremely busy on the morning of the accident. The evidence will also show that the defendant was not careful. He was busy because he had an important meeting scheduled with a new client. He was running late for the meeting, and he wanted to get there on time. We know that he wasn't careful because he kept on driving when all of the other traffic stopped for a fire truck. The truck was flashing its lights and sounding its siren, but the defendant didn't notice it until it was too late.

Finally, many judges are adept at avoiding rulings on objections during opening statements. The following scenario is not uncommon:

Counsel:	Objection, Your Honor. Counsel is engaging in improper argument.
Court:	Argument is not permitted during opening statements. Proceed.

The judge has neither sustained nor overruled the objection. What should you do? The best approach is usually to modify your opening statement slightly as an indication to the court that you understand the need to avoid argument. The judge, in effect, has cautioned you, and you should not take that as license to binge on argumentation.

12.6.1.3 Motions and Curative Instructions

Once an objection is sustained the opening statement is allowed to continue. Occasionally the offending portion of the opening statement is so damaging that the objecting lawyer must request a curative instruction from the court. This should be done primarily when opposing counsel has engaged in lengthy argument or has referred to evidence that has already been excluded.

Counsel can obtain a curative instruction by asking the court to "instruct the jury to disregard counsel's comments." Some judges then instruct the jury in rather perfunctory terms, while others actually make some effort to ensure that the jury will not consider the improper comments. In either case, the decision to request a curative instruction is a touchy one since the instruction itself might serve to emphasize exactly the point that you want the jury to disregard.

Nonetheless, in many jurisdictions you cannot appeal on the ground of improper comments during opening unless you first objected and then requested a curative instruction. Paradoxically, it is not uncommon for appellate courts then to hold that the instruction rectified any harm.

In extreme cases a motion for a mistrial can be made on the basis of improper comments during the opening statement. To warrant a mistrial, opposing counsel's improper statement must have been so prejudicial and damaging as to have destroyed irrevocably the possibility of a fair trial.

12.6.2 Bench Trials

A judge, unlike a jury, is obviously familiar with the manner in which evidence is produced at trial. Does a judge ever require help in understanding the evidence? Is there a place for opening statements in bench trials?

In all but very complex cases, judges often prefer to eliminate or severely truncate opening statements. It may be conceit, but judges tend to believe that they can follow the evidence without the benefit of a preview. Counsel, however, should be reluctant to give up opening statements. It is just as important and valuable to capture the judge's imagination as it is to begin creating a mental picture for a jury. Indeed, it may be more important to impress your image of the case on the judge since the court eventually will render its verdict without the benefit of deliberations. Even in the absence of opening statements, a jury will be composed of at least six people, all of whom will enter the jury room with different predispositions and experiences. A judge will have only her own background to rely on, and the opening statement may be your best opportunity to begin to persuade the court to see the case your way.

Nonetheless, in most jurisdictions the court has the right to forgo opening statements in bench trials. The surest way to be certain that opening statements will be allowed is to avoid abusing the privilege when it is granted. Your opening statement to the court should be particularly short, well focused, and to the point. Many of the conventions and techniques that are aimed at jurors should be eliminated when trying a case to the bench.

Judges hate long opening statements. You must do everything you can to shorten your presentation. For example, while repetition is effective in making a point to a jury, it can be deadly when opening to the court. There is seldom a need to repeat points, or to drive them home through a series of incremental steps, when your audience is a single judge. Do not omit significant details, but do not build them up in the same way that you would before a jury.

Similarly, there is certainly never any reason to go through a list of witnesses for the court. This technique has limited value in a jury trial, but it has absolutely no function in a bench trial. The judge will be able to understand who the witnesses are as they appear.

On the other hand, chronology and the ordering of facts continue to be important in bench trials. A clear picture of the occurrences will always help the judge's understanding. This applies not only to the sequence of events, but also to relationships among the various facts. If certain facts cast doubt on the credibility of a witness, tell that to the court. If a certain document will bolster or contradict a witness's testimony, tell that to the court.

Perhaps the most important consideration in opening to the court is to stress the legal issues. You should have much greater latitude in discussing legal issues in a bench trial. Tell the court what the claims and defenses are. Explain exactly how the principal facts and supporting details relate to the legal issues in the case. The judge will eventually arrive at a verdict by applying the applicable law to the proven facts. Your opening statement can be most effective if it presages this process.

12.6.3 Timing

12.6.3.1 When to Open

The plaintiff always opens at the very beginning of the case. The defendant, at least as a technical matter, usually has the option of either opening immediately after the plaintiff or waiting until the plaintiff has rested and the defense case is about to begin.

The overwhelming consensus view is that the defense should never delay opening. The plaintiff's (or prosecutor's) opening will portray their case in its strongest possible form. The defense can undermine that portrayal, and also create some discontinuity between the plaintiff's opening and the beginning of their evidence, by presenting their opening statement immediately after the plaintiff's. Delaying the defense opening will give the impression that the plaintiff's claims have gone unrebutted. On the other hand, opening at the outset of the trial will allow the jury to consider the defense position even while listening to the plaintiff's evidence. It will also create a context for defense counsel's cross-examinations.

There are only a few possible justifications for delaying the defense opening until after the plaintiff has rested. It is remotely conceivable that you might have some surprise up your sleeve that you don't want to reveal before the plaintiff has concluded its case. Alternatively, criminal defense counsel sometimes prefer to evaluate the strength of the prosecution witnesses before deciding whether to present a defense. In these situations, there may be some theoretical benefit to delaying the opening statement, although the same advantage can often be obtained by structuring an initial opening to achieve the same goals.

12.6.3.2 Multiple Parties

In cases with more than one plaintiff or defendant, the court will determine the order of opening statements. The plaintiff with the most at stake will typically be allowed to open first, followed by the others in descending order of potential recovery. Similarly, the defendant with the greatest exposure will usually be afforded the first opening statement. Other factors may also be considered, and the parties are customarily free to stipulate to some other order.

In a case with multiple defendants, it may be possible for one to open immediately after the plaintiff and for another to reserve opening until the beginning of the defense case. This approach provides the best of both worlds, although it obviously requires a fair level of cooperation among defendants. The court has discretion to grant or deny such a request.

Chapter Thirteen

Final Argument

13.1 The Role and Function of Final Argument

13.1.1 The Whole Story

Final argument is the advocate's only opportunity to tell the story of the case in its entirety, without interruption and free from most constraining formalities. Unlike witness examinations, the final argument is delivered in counsel's own words and without the need intermittently to cede the stage to the opposition; unlike the opening statement, it is not bound by strict rules governing proper and improper content. In other words, final argument is the moment for pure advocacy, when all of the lawyer's organizational, analytic, interpretive, and forensic skills are brought to bear on the task of persuading the trier of fact.

Final argument is the conclusion of the battle for the jury's imagination. Recall that opening statement marks the beginning of the attorney's efforts to help the jurors construct a mental image of occurrences, locations, objects, and transactions at issue in the case. This mental image, in turn, influences the way in which the jurors receive and interpret the evidence. At the close of the case, counsel returns to strengthen and explain the significance of those mental images.

Understanding this process should tell us something about final arguments. If counsel has been successful, the opening statement painted a picture that the jurors began to accept and internalize. The witnesses, documents, and exhibits fit neatly into that picture, reinforcing the image that counsel created. At final argument the attorney can then nail down the image by pointing out the crucial details, weaving together with witnesses' accounts, and explaining the significant connections. All three aspects of the trial—opening, witness examinations, and closing—should combine to evoke a single conception of events.

Thus, the final argument cannot be fully successful unless the preceding stages of the trial were also successful. The opening statement's mental image will not stay with the jurors unless it is sustained by evidence from the witness stand. More to the point, the final argument cannot paint a picture that is contrary to, or unsupported by, the evidence. While final argument can and should be the capstone of a well-tried case, it is unlikely to be the saving grace of a poorly tried one.

In sum, the final argument must tell the whole story of the case, but it cannot tell just any story. The final argument has to complement the portrait begun during the opening statement, and, even more important, must reflect and encompass the evidence in the case. This goal can be best accomplished only when the case is presented according to a well-defined theory.

See demonstration 18 in the Visuals Appendix.

13.1.2 Use of Theory, Theme, and Story Arc

13.1.2.1 Theory

If nothing else, the final argument must communicate the advocate's theory of the case. Some witnesses can be disregarded, some details can be omitted, some legal issues can be overlooked, but the theory of the case is absolutely essential.

The final argument, therefore, must be used to illuminate your theory. This means that you must tell the jury, or the court, why your client is entitled to a verdict. A simple recitation of facts is not sufficient. Rather, the argument should bring together information from the various witnesses and exhibits in a way that creates only one result.

To be successful, the theory presented in a final argument must be logical, believable, and legally sufficient.

Logical

A trial theory, and consequently a final argument, must be logical in the sense that the component facts lead to the desired conclusions. It is often helpful, therefore, to reason backward, starting with the end result and then providing supportive facts. In the fire engine case, the plaintiff's goal is to prove negligence. The starting point for her theory, then, is to ask which facts most strongly contribute to the conclusion that the defendant was negligent. Those facts will form the basis of the theory.

Reasoning in this manner, plaintiff's counsel will probably conclude that her strongest "theory" facts are: 1) the nature of the collision itself; 2) the presence of the fire truck; and 3) the defendant's hurried morning. Note that each fact has a logical connection to the conclusion of negligence: the collision was a classic "rear-ender," which shows that the defendant either failed to keep a proper interval or was driving too fast just before the accident. The presence of the fire truck explains why the plaintiff stopped her car and also demonstrates that the defendant failed to keep a proper lookout. The defendant's hurried morning adds proof that he was inattentive to the road.

Logic, however, is only the starting point for the final argument.

Believable

The most logical theory in the world will not win a case if the jurors don't believe it. For a theory to be sound, it must be based on facts that are likely to be accepted. Returning to the fire engine case, we recognize that the plaintiff's theory must explain why the defendant should have stopped his car. The obvious answer is the fire truck. Now imagine, however, that only the plaintiff testified that the fire truck sounded its siren. All of the other witnesses, including the firefighters, testified that there had been no siren. As certain as the plaintiff might be, the use of the siren will be a poor fact on which to ground her theory of the case; it simply will not be believed in the face of the overwhelming testimony to the contrary.

Plaintiff's counsel will have to arrive at an alternative theory to explain why the defendant should have known to stop his car. Several possibilities are immediately apparent: The defendant should have stopped once he saw the fire truck, whether it was sounding its siren or not. The defendant should have stopped because the car in front of him stopped, even if there had been no fire engine at all.

Use of the siren would certainly make the story more compelling. It enhances the defendant's negligence to imagine him ignoring the blaring alarm of a fire engine. The theory loses more than it gains, however, if it is based on an unproven or tenuous fact. There is a very real risk that the fact finder, having rejected one part of the plaintiff's theory, will go on to reject some or all of the rest.

There is no way to guarantee that the jurors will accept your final argument; the purpose of the trial, after all, is to allow the judge or jury to decide which theory is more believable. It is possible, however, to construct a rough hierarchy of reliability that will help you evaluate the value of evidence for the purpose of the final argument. As is detailed below, the most believable evidence commonly takes the form of admissions from the opposing party, followed by the undisputed evidence that you produced. Concerning disputed evidence, it is generally best to rely first on the common-sense value of the evidence and finally on the credibility of witnesses.

Admissions

For the purpose of final argument, the most "believable" information is often that which was produced by the other side. The opposing party obviously would not offer self-damaging testimony unless it were unavoidably true. Consequently, it is particularly effective to argue against a party using her own words and documents. The defendant in the fire engine case, for instance, makes an admission when he testifies that he was late for a meeting at the time of the accident. This fact passes every test of believability when used in the plaintiff's final argument:

> How do we know that the defendant was running late that morning? He said so himself. Just remember his own words. He said, "I woke up

late that morning, and I knew that I would have to hurry up to get to my meeting."

This type of argument can continue, taking advantage of points that were scored on cross-examination precisely for this purpose:

> The defendant's own words also tell us how preoccupied he was. After all, it was the defendant who testified about the importance of new clients. I'm sure you remember how he answered when I asked him if new clients mean money. He said, "Yes, that's what we're in business for." And then I asked him whether this particular new client was a valuable one, and he said, "Every new client is valuable." So there he was, late for his meeting with a valuable new client, worrying about how much money he might stand to lose.

Note that for the purpose of believability analysis, admissions need not be direct concessions, nor do they need to come in the form of testimony from the actual party. Anything can be exploited as an admission as long as it was produced by the other side. A strong closing argument can therefore make use of the opposition's witness testimony, exhibits, charts or graphs, tangible objects, or even comments made by the opposing counsel during the opening statement.

Undisputed Facts

Undisputed facts consist of the testimony, exhibits, and other evidence that you have offered and the other side has not controverted. The opposition's decision not to produce contrary evidence greatly enhances the value of such undisputed facts. While not quite so powerful as admissions from the other side, undisputed facts can provide a sturdy cornerstone for case theory and final argument:

> It is undisputed that there was a fire truck at the corner of Touhy and Sheridan. It is undisputed that the engine was answering a call. It is undisputed that other drivers slowed down or pulled over for the fire truck. It is undisputed that Lieutenant Karen Dunn was driving the fire truck. And it is undisputed that fire department policy requires the siren to be used whenever an engine company is responding to a call. The defendant may claim that there was no siren, but he hasn't even tried to deny these uncontroverted facts.

Thus, undisputed facts are helpful not only in their own right, but also because they can be marshaled to cast light on disputed evidence.

Common Sense and Experience

Admissions and undisputed facts are valuable precisely because it is impossible for the other side to take issue with them. Every trial, however, involves a core of facts and issues that are in dispute. It will be the rare final argument that can avoid entirely the necessity of explaining why the jury should prefer one version of contested facts over the other.

When key events or occurrences are in dispute, an effective final argument will first make use of common sense. As between any two stories or accounts, the jury is likely to choose the one that most closely agrees with their own experiences. In structuring an argument, then, it is essential to bear in mind the relationship between your theory of the case and the jury's sense of what will or will not ring true.

A common-sense argument can be extremely helpful, as when defense counsel argues damages in the fire truck case:

> The plaintiff claims that her life's activities have been severely limited. Now pain is a subjective thing, so no one can step inside of the plaintiff's body to see whether or not she is exaggerating. But we can look at her actions, and we can interpret them in the light of our own common sense. The plaintiff went camping last Labor Day at Eagle River Falls. She carried a backpack and slept on the ground for four straight nights. She could have gone home after a night or two, but she chose to stay for the entire trip. Is this the action of someone who is in constant pain? Is this the action of someone whose life's activities are severely limited? Can you imagine how the plaintiff might have thought about such a trip: "Well, things are difficult here at home; I guess I'll go sleep on the ground for a long weekend." I don't want to minimize the plaintiff's real injuries, but common sense certainly tells us that someone in as much pain as she claims just wouldn't go camping for four nights.

Credibility

The final method of establishing believability is to rely on the credibility of the witnesses. While credibility is important, in relative terms it is probably the weakest method of proving your version of disputed facts.

There are two problems with credibility arguments. First, they rest almost entirely on subjective impressions. While an advocate may regard one witness as enormously more credible than another, there is no way to be sure that the fact finder perceived the testimony in the same way. Second, a credibility argument asks the jury to think ill of a person, to conclude that she has omitted something, exaggerated, or even lied. Most lawyers consider it to be particularly difficult to persuade a jury to draw such adverse conclusions about any but the most disreputable witnesses. In the following example defense counsel in the fire truck case has decided to attack the plaintiff's credibility:

> The plaintiff claims that she was wearing her glasses on the morning of the accident, but you should not believe her. She has everything to

> gain from her own testimony. She wants to take a small fortune away from this case, so she obviously will tend to remember facts in the way that is the most helpful to her. If she had been wearing her glasses she wouldn't have stopped so abruptly, and the accident never would have happened.

The above argument is ineffective. The plaintiff's interest in the outcome of the case seems insufficient to persuade us that she would lie about wearing her glasses. This is not to say that counsel should always avoid credibility arguments, but only that they should be supported by admissions, undisputed evidence, or invocations of common sense. For example:

> In addition to everything else, we know that the defendant didn't bother to have his brakes fixed just a week before the accident. Nate Lipton, a mechanic who operates his own garage, testified that he told the defendant that it was time to have his brakes relined. The defendant claims that Nate only suggested that he take care of the brakes within the next 10,000 miles. Well, who are we going to believe? Nate Lipton certainly has no reason to embellish his testimony. Unlike the defendant, Nate has no stake in the outcome of this case. But there is another reason to believe Nate Lipton. The defendant admits that Nate mentioned the worn brakes, and it is undisputed that Nate Lipton has twenty years of experience as a mechanic. Our common sense tells us that no competent mechanic would open a brake drum, look at worn brakes, and then tell a driver that he could wait 10,000 miles to have them fixed. Why would Nate Lipton risk his own liability by suggesting that a customer drive out of the garage with badly worn brakes?

This credibility argument works because it is founded on the defendant's own admission as well as on common sense. In other words, the argument provides the jury with a reason to prefer the mechanic's testimony over the defendant's.

Legally Sufficient

The final component of a solid theory is legal sufficiency. The logic and believability of a final argument must lead to the desired legal result. In other words, a final argument must address the law as well as the facts.

A trial theory may be defined as the application of proven facts to legal issues. In the fire truck case, for example, the central legal issue is whether the defendant was negligent. The following might serve as an abbreviated statement of the plaintiff's trial theory:

> We have proven that the defendant was distracted and rushed on the morning of the accident. He was negligent because he failed to pay sufficient attention to the road.

A lengthier theory statement would include a definition of negligence:

> Under the law, a driver must always exercise due care and caution when operating a motor vehicle. We have proven that the defendant failed to meet that standard on the morning of the accident. A driver exercising due care wouldn't rush down the road just because he was late to a meeting. A driver exercising ordinary caution wouldn't allow himself to become so distracted that he would miss seeing and hearing a fire engine. At a bare minimum, the standard of due care and caution must call for a driver to keep his eye on the traffic around him, but the defendant didn't slow down, even though every other car on the road either pulled over or came to a stop.

In either case, the thrust of the argument is to explain not only that the defendant was wrong, but that the defendant was wrong in a way that should result in a legal consequence.

Lawyers commonly use jury instructions as a framework for discussing legal issues during final argument.[1]

13.1.2.2 Theme

A good trial theme provides an incentive for the jury (or judge) to enter a verdict in your client's favor. In addition to being logical and believable, a trial theme invokes shared beliefs and common values. Just as a theory explains why the verdict is legally necessary, the theme explains why the verdict is morally desirable.

Your trial theme should be a constant presence throughout the final argument. Unlike opening statement and witness examinations, where a theme can only be used intermittently, the entire final argument can be organized so as to emphasize your theme. You can begin with a statement of the theme and constantly return to it in each segment of the argument.

In the fire engine case, for instance, plaintiff's counsel's first words on final argument could be: "This accident occurred because the defendant was too busy to be careful." Plaintiff's attorney might then proceed through the argument by discussing issues such as the defendant's morning preparations, the accident itself, defendant's post-accident conduct, defendant's shoddy brake-repair record, and finally plaintiff's damages. At each stage of the argument, plaintiff's attorney would find a way to advert to the theme. In some situations the usage would be obvious: "The defendant didn't bother to have his brakes repaired because he was just too busy." At other points in the argument the reference might be somewhat more subtle. Consider the question of the siren:

1. The uses, and occasional misuses, of jury instructions are discussed below in section 13.4.6.

> The defendant claims that the fire engine was not sounding its siren. But the defendant's claim cannot be believed. Remember that the fire truck was being driven by Lieutenant Karen Dunn. Lieutenant Dunn, as we heard, is a decorated firefighter and the first woman ever to be promoted to lieutenant in this city. Not only is she well trained, but she now teaches courses at the fire academy. Lieutenant Dunn knows full well that fire trucks are required to sound their sirens whenever responding to a call. It is part of her job to comply with that regulation. For Lieutenant Dunn, being busy and being careful are the same thing. We know that she was careful because she was busy.

The value of the theme is its use as a moral persuader. It provides the jury a reason to want to enter the appropriate verdict. Consequently, the theme can be employed in the damages section of an argument even if its principal thrust goes to liability. Thus, the plaintiff in the fire truck case can argue damages at length, describing all of the plaintiff's injuries, disabilities, and attendant costs and expenses. Having established the nature and devastating scope of the plaintiff's damages, counsel can conclude by noting, "And all because the defendant was too busy to be careful."

As effective as the recurrent use of a theme can be on final argument, take care not to overdo it. No matter how compelling it is the first time, any single-sentence statement can become trite or bothersome if it is repeated ad nauseam. For this reason it is often wise to invoke the spirit of the theme in place of the mantra itself. For example, plaintiff's counsel in the fire truck case might describe the plaintiff's own attentiveness to the road by saying something like the following:

> She was not in a hurry that morning. She was on her way to the Art Institute, but she had over an hour until it opened. She had no reason to speed and every reason to stop as soon as she saw and heard the fire truck. There was nothing on her mind to distract her from her careful driving.

This argument employs the trial theme but does not repeat it, thus taking advantage of its moral force while avoiding an annoying echo.

13.1.2.3 Story Arc

Whether explicitly or implicitly, an advocate's final argument should take advantage of the universal story arc: At first everything was fine; the world was well ordered, and people were going about their business without interference. Then something terrible and disruptive happened; it was not the fault of my client, but she has suffered great harm (or, in the case of a defendant, is in danger of harm). Fortunately, the damage can be alleviated, or at least minimized, by entering a verdict in our favor.

The universal story arc accomplishes three important goals. First, it establishes your client as the story's protagonist—the person around whom events revolved and who therefore deserves the most sympathy and attention. Second, it takes advantage of the hard-wired human desire for equilibrium and order. The story can only end when conflicts are resolved and the protagonist (that is, your client) is restored, to the extent possible, to the peaceful state that existed before the unfair disruption. Finally, at perhaps the most critical moment of any trial, the universal arc engages the fact finder as a virtual character in the story—the "hero" who can rectify the disruption and save your client from further injustice.

The story arc is not a formula or a set outline. It is not necessary to specifically articulate its three components. Rather, it is a guide to the construction of your case—to those aspects that should be stressed and highlighted—especially in the final argument.

13.1.3 What Makes It Argument

Recall the cardinal rule of opening statements—you may not argue. In final argument, on the other hand, you may, should, and must argue if you are serious about winning your case. The gloves are off, and the limitations are removed—but what precisely distinguishes argument from mere presentation of the facts? The following are some of the most useful elements of "argument."

13.1.3.1 Conclusions

The attorney in final argument is free to draw and urge conclusions based on the evidence. A conclusion is a result, consequence, or repercussion that follows from the evidence in the case.

In our fire engine case, for example, the plaintiff will no doubt offer this evidence: the defendant woke up late on the morning of the accident; he had an important meeting to attend that morning; he did not have sufficient time to get to the meeting; he stood to lose a potential new client (and therefore a lot of money) if he arrived late.

From this evidence several conclusions may be drawn: The defendant was in a hurry. The defendant was preoccupied. The defendant was trying to plan for his meeting while driving because he wouldn't have time to plan for it after he arrived at the office. The defendant allowed his thoughts to drift to the point that he became careless and inattentive to the road.

All of the above conclusions would be permissible in argument even though there is unlikely to be direct proof of any of them. That is what makes them conclusions; they follow logically, although not necessarily, from admitted evidence. In other words, the conclusion might or might not be accurate. It is possible for a driver to be exceptionally careful even when late for a meeting. It is the force of advocacy, advanced through argument, that can lead the trier of fact to draw one conclusion as opposed to another.

Thus, it is not sufficient for a final argument to draw, or even urge, conclusions. The argument must go on to explain why the desired conclusions are the correct ones.

13.1.3.2 Inferences

While a final argument can and should include broad conclusions, it may also include the sort of narrow conclusions commonly known as inferences. An inference is a deduction drawn from the existence of a known fact. In other words, the inferred fact need not be proven as long as it is a common-sense consequence of some established fact.

Turning again to the fire engine case, assume that the defendant testified that his parking garage was located two blocks from his office. From that known fact it could be inferred that it would take him at least five minutes to walk from the garage to his office. It could further be inferred that the defendant knew how long it would take him to reach his office. Such inferences, based on a combination of proven fact and everyday experience, could be used to support the larger conclusion that the defendant was in a rush at the time of the accident.

An inference will be accepted only if it is well-grounded in common understanding. For that reason, it is often necessary or desirable to explain the basis of all but the most obvious inferences. For example, everyone will be willing to infer a child's age from knowledge of her grade in school. There is no need to explain that third graders are typically eight or nine years old. Other inferences, however, may be more complicated.

Recall the evidence in the fire truck case that the engine was being driven by a veteran firefighter. It can be inferred from this fact that the truck's siren was sounding just before the accident, but the inference will be strengthened by an explanation:

> The fire truck was being driven by Lieutenant Karen Dunn, a ten-year veteran of the force. The first woman ever to be promoted to that rank, Lieutenant Dunn did not get where she is today by being careless or by ignoring departmental rules. A fire truck is required to sound its alarm whenever it is responding to a call. This is a simple safety precaution that alerts other vehicles to clear the way. It just doesn't make sense to argue, as the defendant does, that Lieutenant Dunn would have carelessly neglected to use her siren that day at the intersection of Sheridan and Touhy.

The proven facts include Lieutenant Dunn's background and the departmental rules. The inference is that she sounded her siren on the date in question. The explanation—that the siren is a necessary safety precaution—bolsters the inference.

13.1.3.3 Details and Circumstantial Evidence

Final argument is counsel's only opportunity to explain the relevance and consequences of circumstantial evidence. Much of the art of direct and cross-examination consists of the accumulation of details that lead to a certain conclusion or result. The knowledge of the individual witnesses, not to mention trial strategy and luck, may result in the scattering of such details throughout the trial. It is during final argument that the attorney can reassemble the details so that they lead to the desired result.

In a burglary prosecution, for example, there may have been no eyewitnesses to give direct evidence against the defendant. A number of witnesses, however, might provide detailed circumstantial evidence. Perhaps one witness saw the defendant running from the scene of the crime, while another found a single shoe in the doorway of the burglarized house. Yet a third witness might have heard the defendant complaining about her need for a new MP3 player. The crime victim could testify that an expensive MP3 player was taken in the burglary. Finally, on cross-examination the defendant could be asked to try on the shoe to show that it fits.

None of these circumstantial details constitutes direct evidence of the defendant's guilt, particularly when they are adduced individually through the testimony of four or five different witnesses. They can, however, be organized into a powerful narrative leading irresistibly to conviction. Moreover, the circumstantial evidence becomes even more persuasive when all of the connections are explained in argument:

> No one saw the defendant commit the burglary, but the surrounding details point in only one direction. She was seen running, not walking, from the crime scene just after the house was robbed. That alone does not make her guilty, but it does tell us that she had a reason to run away from that house. Now consider all of the other evidence. She wanted a new MP3 player so badly that she complained about it to her friends, and the most expensive item taken in the burglary was a brand new MP3 player. It seems as though the burglar left a shoe behind that was caught in the door, and that shoe just happens to fit perfectly on the defendant's foot. It all falls together: the house was robbed, the defendant ran; she wanted an MP3 player, an MP3 player was stolen; the burglar left a shoe behind, the shoe fits the defendant. Perhaps one of these facts could be a coincidence, but all together they add up to guilt.

Trial lawyers understand that circumstantial evidence is probative and reliable. In the popular mind, however, the term "circumstantial" is often equated with doubtful or equivocal. It is therefore desirable to use final argument to explain the value and credibility of circumstantial evidence. This is frequently done by using an analogy, some of which have become all-purpose classics:

> While no one saw the defendant commit the burglary, the circumstantial evidence is overwhelming. As the court will instruct you, circumstantial evidence can be just as credible as eyewitness testimony. We can all recognize the value of circumstantial evidence based on our experiences in everyday life. For example, think of the last time that it snowed

> in the night. If you looked out on your front yard in the morning and saw footprints in the snow, you would know for sure that someone had walked across your lawn. Even if you didn't actually see anybody, the footprints were circumstantial—and absolutely reliable—evidence that someone had been there. In this case, even though no one saw the defendant, there is no doubt that she left her footprints for everyone to see.

Analogies have many other uses at trial, some of which are detailed in the next section.

13.1.3.4 Analogies, Allusions, and Stories

Analogies

An analogy can explain human conduct through reference to everyday human behavior. A witness's testimony can be strengthened or diminished by comparing her version of events to some widely understood experience or activity.

Suppose that the defendant in the fire engine case testified that he saw the fire truck, but that he did not slow down because the siren was not sounding. Plaintiff's attorney will want to characterize this conduct as unreasonable. Counsel can, of course, simply say as much: "The defendant should have slowed down, and it was unreasonable to keep driving once he saw the fire truck." From a purely legal perspective, that should be sufficient to establish negligence. It could be more persuasive, however, to use an analogy:

> The defendant admits that he saw the fire truck, but he says that there was no siren and so he did not feel it necessary to stop. Even if you believe him that he didn't hear the siren, there is nothing reasonable about conduct like that. By continuing to drive at the same speed, he was playing Russian roulette with the safety of every other driver on the road. Simple attentiveness to safety tells us that we should slow down when we see an emergency vehicle. Just because he didn't hear the siren doesn't mean that it wasn't sounding. You wouldn't expect someone to pick up a gun and fire it at somebody, claiming, "Well, I didn't see any bullets." Of course not. A gun is dangerous, and simple prudence means that you should always treat it as though it is loaded. Well, cars can be dangerous, too. As soon as he saw that fire truck, the defendant should have recognized the possibility that traffic would slow or stop. He should have recognized the possibility that it was answering a call, whether he heard the siren or not. Continuing to drive, without at least slowing down, was the equivalent of pointing a loaded gun down the road.

The above excerpt takes conduct that everyone will recognize as unreasonable and explains why the defendant's conduct falls into the same category. Counsel must be careful, however, not to use overreaching or ludicrous analogies. A careless accident should not be compared to a vicious murder or to a mass disaster.

Analogies can support testimony as well as deride it, and they can be short as well as extended. Consider the following example from defense counsel's final argument:

> Fire trucks use their sirens to tell traffic to stop. We have all seen fire engines on the street that weren't responding to calls. Without their sirens they are just part of traffic. If you look up into the sky and see an airplane flying by, you don't say, "I'd better take cover; it's going to crash."

While analogies can be very powerful, there is always the danger that they can be inverted and exploited by the other side. Thus, as long as the opposing attorney has yet to argue, counsel must take care to ensure that any analogies are "airtight." For the same reason, plaintiff's counsel often reserves the use of analogies until rebuttal when the defendant will no longer be able to reply.[2]

Allusions

An allusion is a literary or similar reference that adds persuasive force to an argument. In earlier days, before the advent of mass culture, trial lawyers' allusions were most commonly drawn from Shakespeare or the Bible. Perhaps the most frequently used quotation from Shakespeare is the suggestion that a witness "doth protest too much."[3] Today references are just as likely to be taken from motion pictures, television, popular songs, fairy tales, or, alas, advertisements. Defense counsel in the fire engine case might disparage the plaintiff's injury claim with a reference to "The Princess and the Pea":

> The plaintiff claims that her life's activities are severely limited. She says that sometimes she can't even sleep. But last Labor Day she went camping at Eagle River Falls, where she slept on the ground for four nights. Now that her case is on trial she claims that she was in pain, but the truth is that she stayed at the campground for the whole weekend. We all know the story about the princess who could feel a pea even though it was underneath a stack of mattresses. But our law doesn't allow recovery for that sort of super-sensitivity. And this plaintiff, who had no hesitation about sleeping on the ground, certainly can't complain about peas under the mattress today. You can't be a backpacker when you want to and then a princess when the time comes to try for damages.

Advertising slogans are commonly used during final argument. For all that they lack in elegance and literary merit, they have the advantage of familiarity and catchiness.

---

2. Regarding the uses of rebuttal argument, *see* section 13.2.3.
3. "The lady doth protest too much, methinks." William Shakespeare, Hamlet, Act III, scene 2, line 242.

Stories

Stories, in the form of either hypotheticals or anecdotes, can be used effectively in final argument. It is permissible to illustrate an argument with a hypothetical story as long as the story is based on facts that are in evidence. Again, from the plaintiff's argument in the fire engine case:

> Imagine what the defendant's morning was like. His alarm clock didn't go off. He woke up, looked at the clock, and began to panic. He was late, and if he missed the meeting with this new client, he would lose money and damage his position with his firm. He rushed into the bathroom to shower and shave. Maybe he cut himself, as happens so often when you hurry. Think of all the things that people do when they are rushed in the morning. No time to read the newspaper. No time to eat breakfast. No time to stop for gas, even if the tank is low. You can be sure that the defendant hurried to his car that morning. This was not the day for a leisurely drive. This was a day to push the speed limit and to run yellow lights.

This reconstruction of the defendant's morning is hypothetical in that the details are all suppositions. It is proper argument because the entire story is derived from the defendant's own testimony.

Another form of argumentative storytelling is the illustrative anecdote. An anecdote is a sort of litigator's fable or folktale, again used to elaborate on a theme in the case. Attorneys frequently draw on real or imagined family wisdom:

> My grandfather was a modest man who cared very little for life's material rewards. Although he loved other people's celebrations, he never wanted anything for himself. Especially birthday presents. "Please don't give me anything," he would say, "because every day is my birthday." When I got a little older, I asked my mother why Grandpa always said that. She told me that Grandpa once almost died from a heart attack, and after that he considered every day to be a brand new gift from God; in other words, a birthday. I always thought that Grandpa was the happiest man in the world because every day was his birthday.
>
> I think that we would all like to view life the way that Grandpa did, but the plaintiff will never be able to. She wakes up every morning in pain. Every movement must be measured and gauged. One wrong move and she risks having to spend the day in bed or even going to the hospital. She can't think of every day as her birthday because each day is hell.
>
> My grandfather had a joy in life and peace of mind that was an inspiration to everyone who knew him. More than anything else, that is the possibility that the defendant has taken from the plaintiff. She will never know simple pleasures again.

The use of the story serves to humanize the plaintiff. It is always difficult to ask for money, but to compare the plaintiff with the kindly, unassuming grandfather demonstrates both the severity of her loss and the relatively modest nature of her claim.

13.1.3.5 Credibility and Motive

Counsel may also use the final argument to comment on, and compare, the motive and credibility of witnesses. Many, perhaps most, trials involve competing renditions of past events, which the trier of fact must resolve to reach a verdict. Final argument is the only time when the attorney may confront directly the character of the witnesses and explain why some should be believed and others discounted.

Perhaps a witness for the opposing party was impeached through the use of a prior inconsistent statement or omission. While the inconsistency will to one degree or another speak for itself, the final argument can underscore just exactly how it undermines the witness's credibility. The following example is taken from the defense argument in a robbery prosecution:

> We all heard the victim claim that the robber was easily recognizable by his long hair and moustache. But just thirty minutes after the robbery he was interviewed by Officer Pinsky. At that time the robber was still at large, and the victim had every reason to give Officer Pinsky the best description he could. That description is right here in the police report. Officer Pinsky got height, weight, age, race, clothing—but not one word about long hair and a moustache. That's right, a short thirty minutes after the crime the victim didn't have a word to say about long hair or a moustache.
>
> What happened? How did long hair and a moustache get added to the description? Unfortunately, the police made a suggestion. They drove the victim around the neighborhood, pointing out "possible suspects." And to his misfortune, my client was one of the people they pointed out. He had long hair and a moustache, so those facts were added to the description at that time. I am not saying that the victim is lying, but I am saying that the second description is not reliable; it was suggested by the police. If the robber really did have long hair and moustache, the victim would have told that to Officer Pinsky right off the bat.

Witness examinations can bring out impeaching facts, and the opening statement can use apposition to contrast the credibility of different witnesses. But only on closing argument can counsel make direct comparisons. Consider the question of the siren as plaintiff's counsel might argue it in the fire truck case:

> The plaintiff told you that she stopped because she saw a fire truck, which was flashing its warning lights and sounding its siren. The defendant has

> to concede that the truck was there, but he claims that it was not using its warning signals.
>
> Well, was there a siren or wasn't there? Who should you believe?
>
> The defendant's story just isn't credible. Everyone agrees that the fire truck entered the intersection on its way to a fire scene. You have even seen the transcript of the 911 call that the truck was responding to. A fire truck would have to be using its siren under those circumstances. Only the most negligent firefighter would speed toward an intersection without sounding the siren, but this truck was being driven by Lieutenant Karen Dunn, one of the most decorated firefighters on the force. Which is more likely, that Lieutenant Dunn neglected such an elementary duty or that the defendant is wrong about the siren?
>
> The plaintiff heard the siren and stopped her car. The other drivers must have heard it as well since all of the other traffic pulled over. Of course, it is possible that the defendant testified the way he did because he simply didn't hear the siren, but that is another story. Why didn't he hear the siren? Why didn't he stop his car? For the answers to those questions we have to look at the events of his day and why he was "too busy to be careful."

Finally, motive can be argued on the basis either of proven facts or logical inferences. Counsel may tell the jury why a witness would exaggerate, waffle, conceal information, quibble, or lie. The suggested reasons need not be based on outright admissions as long as they follow rationally from the testimony in the case.

13.1.3.6 Weight of the Evidence

While the opening statement is limited to a recitation of the expected evidence, the final argument can be used to assert the weight of the evidence. Why is one version preferable to another? Why should some facts be accepted and others rejected? Why is one case stronger than the other? Consider the way in which the defense counsel in the fire truck case might argue the weight of the evidence regarding plaintiff's damages:

> The plaintiff claims extreme disability, almost all of it based on pain. But pain is an elusive concept. It cannot be seen or measured; all we have is the plaintiff's own description.
>
> But we can also look at the plaintiff's activities to see the extent of her alleged disability. We know, for example, that she went camping last Labor Day at Eagle River Falls. She put all of her gear into a backpack and stayed in a tent, sleeping on the ground for four nights. She wasn't in so much pain that she canceled the trip. She wasn't in so much pain that she couldn't carry a pack. She wasn't in so much pain that she had to come home early.

> Now she says that the camping trip was a mistake and that she was in agony the whole time. But look at the other, objective evidence. We have seen the records from her doctor; she didn't visit the doctor, or even call, until over a month after the camping trip. We have seen the records from the pharmacy; she didn't change her medication or even renew it for more than two months after the camping trip. What did she do? She took aspirin.
>
> To judge the extent of the plaintiff's alleged disability you must weigh the evidence. Evaluate the claims that she made in her testimony against the proof of her own actions and the records of her own physician and pharmacist. It is easy to claim pain, and I don't want to minimize the plaintiff's discomfort, but her own conduct makes it clear that nothing happened to limit her life's activities.

13.1.3.7 Demeanor

It is fair game in final argument to comment on a witness's demeanor. Demeanor arguments are frequently negative in nature since it is easier to characterize untrustworthy conduct. An argument that counsel's own witness "looked like he was telling the truth" may tend to seem insincere or overprotective. Negative comments, on the other hand, can be effective as long as they are adequately based on observable fact.

It is not uncommon, for instance, to remark on a witness's refusal to give a simple answer or to make an obvious concession. Similarly, counsel might mention that a witness averted his eyes or fidgeted on the stand as though hiding something. Comparable points can be made about witnesses who sneer, lose their tempers, scowl, or become impatient.

One caveat: Demeanor argument is based strictly on perception, and there is little way to ensure that counsel's perception of the witness will be the same as that of the judge or jury. Conduct that the attorney sees as evidence of deception might be regarded by a juror as a reasonable response to unfair questioning. Be careful. Demeanor argument can be best used only when the witness's behavior has been blatant and unambiguous.

13.1.3.8 Refutation

Another distinguishing feature of argument is refutation of opposing positions. Opening statements and witness examinations may recite and elicit facts that are contrary to the opposition's case, but final argument can refute them directly by pointing out errors, inconsistencies, implausibilities, and contradictions. Consider this extract from the plaintiff's final argument in the fire engine case:

> The defendant claims that he was not distracted on the morning of the accident, but that cannot be true. We know that he woke up late and

> that he had an important meeting to attend with a potential new client. New clients mean money, so missing the meeting, or even being late, could have had a devastating impact on the defendant's job.
>
> By the time he got ready for work and got to his car, he was already at least thirty minutes behind schedule. By the time he reached the corner of Sheridan and Touhy, he was still running over twenty minutes late—he still had to drive downtown, get to his garage, park his car, and proceed to his office, all in less than twenty minutes.
>
> There is no plausible way for the defendant to deny that he was preoccupied and in a hurry. His mind must have been elsewhere; certainly it wasn't on his driving. Every driver saw and heard the fire truck, but not the defendant. Every driver stopped or pulled over, but not the defendant. Those were not the acts of a careful man.
>
> One last fact shows just how absorbed the defendant was. Right after the accident he jumped out of his car and pulled out his cell phone. He called his office. That meeting was so important to him that he didn't even check to see if the other driver was hurt. That meeting was more important to him than a possible injury. No wonder it was more important to him than safe, careful driving.

13.1.3.9 Application of Law

Final argument provides the attorney an occasion to apply the law to the facts of the case. Discussion of law is extremely limited during the opening statement and all but forbidden during witness examinations, but it is a staple of the final argument. In most jurisdictions, counsel may read from the jury instructions and explain exactly how the relevant law dictates a verdict for her client.[4]

13.1.3.10 Moral Appeal

Final argument allows counsel to elaborate on the moral theme of the case. Recall that a trial theme states, usually in a single sentence, a compelling moral basis for a verdict in your client's favor. The theme invokes shared values, civic virtues, or common motivations. The theme can be stated during the opening statement and alluded to in witness examinations, but it can be hammered home in the final argument. Again, consider the plaintiff's final argument in the fire truck case:

> The defendant was "too busy to be careful." We know that from his actions and their consequences. But what was he busy doing? He was rushing to a meeting for the sole purpose of increasing his income. He was worrying about money, not about safety. It is true that he was late, but that was no one's fault but his own. And once he was late, he was

4. *See* section 13.4.6.

> so obsessed with getting to the meeting that he threw caution out the window. He was so "busy" that he didn't even care to see whether or not the plaintiff was injured. No, that business meeting was all that mattered. Well, everyone is at risk when drivers behave that way. No one is safe on the road when people care more about their meetings than they do about the way they are driving. You cannot allow someone to think that it is all right to be "too busy to be careful."

Admittedly, the moral dimension of an intersection accident is not overpowering. Cases involving crimes, frauds, civil rights violations, child custody, reckless conduct, and even breach of contract will provide more fertile ground for the assertion of a moral theme. Nonetheless, even the most mundane case can be approached from the perspective of rectitude by explaining how and why your client's position makes sense for reasons other than strict legality.

13.2 Format

In most jurisdictions, the parties' final arguments are divided into three distinct segments, which are presented in the following order: the plaintiff's (or prosecutor's) argument-in-chief, the defendant's argument-in-chief, and plaintiff's rebuttal.[5] While general principles of argument apply to all three, each segment also has its own unique set of uses, applications, and special techniques.

13.2.1 Plaintiff's Argument-in-Chief

The plaintiff (or prosecutor) must use argument-in-chief to define the issues and lay out the entire theory of the case. The plaintiff's argument-in-chief will not be successful unless it provides the jury with compelling reasons to find for the plaintiff on every necessary issue.

Because of the nature of our litigation system, the plaintiff's or prosecutor's initial argument must be comprehensive. The plaintiff in a civil case must usually prevail by a preponderance of the evidence, and the prosecutor in a criminal case must present proof beyond a reasonable doubt. In either situation, the burdened party must establish all of the elements of her cause of action. Thus, a civil plaintiff must establish all of the elements of the particular tort or contract action, and a prosecutor must prove all of the elements of the charged crime. Failing to address an element can be fatal.

5. In a few jurisdictions, the plaintiff is not allowed to argue first; thus, there are only two components: defendant's argument and plaintiff's rebuttal. The terms used to describe the components of final argument also vary from jurisdiction to jurisdiction. What we have called plaintiff's argument-in-chief, for example, is often called plaintiff's "opening," notwithstanding the potential for confusion with the opening statement. Final argument itself is also frequently referred to as closing argument, summation, or, in the United Kingdom, final address.

In contrast, and as will be discussed below in more detail, the defendant may often be considerably more selective during final argument. The defense can frequently prevail simply by disproving a single element of the plaintiff's case and therefore need not address issues as comprehensively as the plaintiff.

To counterbalance this advantage, a plaintiff's attorneys will often use the final argument to issue a series of challenges to the defendant, thus drawing the defense into a discussion of issues that they might prefer to leave alone. A prime example of such a challenge commonly arises in tort litigation, as in this abbreviated example from the plaintiff's argument in the fire engine case:

> We have seen that the defendant had a duty to drive safely on the public roadway and that he breached that duty by failing to look where he was going. There is no doubt that he struck the plaintiff's car from behind and that the accident severely injured the plaintiff. We have discussed her injuries at length, so you know just how crippling they have been. The defendant, of course, is going to tell you that the accident wasn't his fault. But the one thing he cannot deny is how much harm he caused the plaintiff. I invite the defendant's attorney to stand before you to discuss damages. If he thinks that the plaintiff wasn't hurt, let him come forward and say so.

The plaintiff can win only by establishing all of the elements of the specific tort; in negligence cases, the classic elements are duty, breach of duty, cause in fact, proximate cause, and damages. The defendant, on the other hand, can win by disproving any single element. For that reason, defendants in many cases prefer to emphasize the issues of breach of duty or proximate cause (where they think they can win) and to avoid discussing damages (where the only result might be sympathy for the plaintiff). Plaintiff's counsel in the above example sought to cut off that route by issuing a specific challenge to address damages.

13.2.2 Defendant's Argument-in-Chief

The defendant generally has substantially more latitude than the plaintiff in determining the content of the argument-in-chief. While the plaintiff must address every element, the defendant is usually free to "cherry pick," selecting only those elements or issues in which counsel has the most confidence. The defense theory, of course, must be comprehensive in the sense that it explains all of the relevant evidence, but its legal thrust may be significantly more pointed than the plaintiff's.[6]

6. A defendant is certainly not required to focus on a single element or issue. The plaintiff's case may be vulnerable in many areas, and the defendant may wish to address them all. Furthermore, concentration on one element can be risky, as that approach may concentrate too many eggs in a single basket.

The defining characteristic of the defendant's argument-in-chief is that it is sandwiched between the two plaintiff's arguments. Defense counsel must respond to the plaintiff's argument-in-chief, but will not be able to respond to rebuttal.

13.2.2.1 Responding to the Plaintiff's Argument-in-Chief

It is essential that the defense reply directly to the plaintiff's argument-in-chief. After listening to the plaintiff's prolonged excoriation of the defendant, every reasonable jury will immediately want to know what the defendant has to say in return. This does not mean that defense counsel should adopt the plaintiff's organization or respond point by point, but the defendant's argument cannot be entirely divorced from the structure that the plaintiff creates.

At a minimum, the defendant should deny the specific charges leveled in the plaintiff's argument. It is a natural human response to deny unfair or untrue accusations. The jury will expect as much from a wrongly blamed defendant. Unless there is a good reason for doing otherwise, the denial should come early in the defendant's argument.

In a more general vein, the defendant should usually devote some time to debunking the plaintiff's case. While the defense may well have an extremely strong affirmative case of its own, it is quite risky to allow the plaintiff's assertions to stand unrebutted. The precise handling of the various arguments will be discussed below in the section on organization.

Finally, the watchword for the defendant's argument-in-chief is flexibility. While the plaintiff may have the luxury of composing her entire final argument,[7] the defendant must always be alert to new issues and nuances raised once the arguments have begun. It simply will not do for defense counsel to deliver a set piece. The defendant's argument is most effective to the extent that it rebuts the plaintiff's case as presented at the end of the trial. A particularly effective device is the "reverse analogy." In the following example, assume that plaintiff's counsel used her argument-in-chief to tell a story about her modest grandfather, who took such delight in life's simple pleasures. The defense attorney can attempt to turn the story around:

> The plaintiff's lawyer spoke to us at some length about his grandfather, and it was a moving story about a straightforward man who regarded every day as his birthday. But you have to wonder what Grandpa would have thought about the plaintiff's case, which is anything but straightforward. Don't you think that Grandpa would say that anyone who goes camping for four days can't be in too much pain? And don't you think that Grandpa would say that anyone who sleeps on the ground and carries a backpack can't be too limited? And, most of all, don't you think that

7. The plaintiff, of course, will not make final preparations for the final argument until the very end of the trial. However well prepared you may be beforehand, it is still necessary to hear all of the evidence and to know which jury instructions will be given.

> Grandpa would say that no one would wait two months to see her doctor if she were really experiencing medical difficulties?

The defendant's attorney had no way of anticipating the grandfather story, but was nonetheless able to use it as an effective reverse analogy. This is not to say that defense counsel should defer preparation until the end of the plaintiff's argument, but rather that good preparation includes the ability to modify one's original plan in order to accommodate the plaintiff's remarks.

13.2.2.2 Anticipating Rebuttal

The greatest difficulty for defense counsel is knowing that she cannot speak again following the plaintiff's rebuttal. The plaintiff may comment on, criticize, or even ridicule defendant's argument, but the defendant may not respond. Defense counsel may have perfectly good answers for everything that the plaintiff says on rebuttal, but no matter. The usual rule is that the defense may argue only once.

Under these circumstances, it is extremely important that counsel do whatever possible to blunt the rebuttal in advance. One approach is to anticipate and reply specifically to the plaintiff's possible rebuttal arguments, as in this example from the defendant's argument in the fire engine case:

> This entire accident could have been avoided if the plaintiff had only pulled over instead of slamming on her brakes in the middle of the street. If she didn't cause the accident, she at least contributed to it. Now when plaintiff's counsel argues again, she may claim that there was no time to pull over. Don't believe it. There was really plenty of time to pull over. Let's look at the evidence . . . .

This approach has its drawbacks, not the least of which is the necessity of suggesting that, in fact, the plaintiff may not have had enough time to pull her car to the side. In any event, it may be just as effective to make the argument without referring to rebuttal.

Most lawyers choose to anticipate rebuttal only in the general sense, making sure to explain the phenomenon of rebuttal to the jury:

> When I am done speaking, the plaintiff's attorney will have another opportunity to argue. That is called rebuttal. Following rebuttal, however, I will not be allowed to stand before you again. The rules of procedure allow me to speak to you only once. It is not that I don't want to speak again, or that I will have no responses to what plaintiff's counsel says, but only that I will not have the opportunity to give you my responses.
>
> I have only one request to make of you. When plaintiff's counsel returns to argue, please bear in mind that, whatever she says, I will not be able to answer. I think you know from the evidence that I have answers to her

> rebuttal argument. So please keep what I have said in mind and provide those answers for me.

The timing of this aspect of the argument is important. Because it relates solely to the rebuttal, it obviously is preferable to make these remarks near the end of the defendant's argument-in-chief. On the other hand, placing them at the very end would deprive the argument of a strong finish. Thus, it is generally best to use the discussion of rebuttal as the penultimate point, saving the final moment for the most compelling substantive argument.

13.2.3 Plaintiff's Rebuttal

The plaintiff or prosecutor is generally afforded the opportunity to present the last argument. Rebuttal, therefore, is a powerful tool. The plaintiff can reply to all of the defendant's arguments and contentions, but the defendant must stand mute in response. Everyone likes to have the last word, and the rules of procedure in most jurisdictions guarantee that right to the plaintiff.

Effective use of rebuttal can be elusive. While the plaintiff's argument-in-chief can be completely planned in advance, and the defendant's argument-in-chief can be mostly planned, rebuttal must be delivered almost extemporaneously. Preparation for rebuttal typically takes place while plaintiff's counsel listens to the defendant's argument-in-chief. Nonetheless, there are certain principles that can be applied to make rebuttal more forceful and compelling. The most important principle of rebuttal is to organize it according to the plaintiff's own theory of the case.

A common approach to rebuttal is simply to make notes of the defense arguments and then to reply to the most important of them in the order in which they were delivered. This technique is easy to use, and it has the virtue of minimizing the potential for overlooking arguments. Its vice, however, is that it organizes the rebuttal according to the defendant's agenda rather than the plaintiff's. It also tends to promote a boring delivery since a rebuttal that follows this approach is likely to fall into a repetitive cadence of short paragraphs, each one beginning, "The defendant also argued . . . ."

A more effective technique involves matching the defendant's arguments to the major propositions in the plaintiff's own case. To do this, plaintiff's counsel needs only to prepare a truncated outline of the three or four most important, or hotly contested, issues in the case, leaving a blank half-page or so under each heading. In this manner, four major arguments can be spread over two sheets of paper and can be arranged in the order most advantageous to the plaintiff. Then, as defense counsel argues, plaintiff's attorney can write her notes under the appropriate heading. When it comes time to deliver rebuttal, plaintiff's counsel will have automatically organized her notes of the defendant's remarks according to the plaintiff's own structure. The rebuttal can then be delivered topically, without regard to the order of argument used by the defendant.

A second principle of rebuttal is to present the plaintiff's case in an affirmative light. Even when it is well organized, rebuttal is weakened if it becomes nothing more than a series of retorts. As with all argument, it is more effective to present the positive side of your own case, and this is particularly important when you represent the burdened party. Consequently, even in rebuttal, every position should be framed as a constructive statement of the plaintiff's own theory. Consider this short example from the rebuttal in the fire engine case:

> I would like to talk to you once again about damages. I'm sure that you remember the plaintiff's own testimony about her efforts to cope with her injuries. She has done everything possible to bring her life back to normal. She is a courageous woman who won't give up. That is why it is particularly unfair to see defense counsel trying to exploit the plaintiff's camping trip to Eagle River Falls. Of course she tried to go camping. What does the defendant want her to do, give up on life and just sit at home? Unfortunately, her efforts didn't work out. As she told you, the camping trip was pure hell. She suffered every day, and she had to stay on her back in the tent for hours at a time. Why didn't she come home early? Because she and her family had all come in the same car, and she didn't want to ruin the trip for everyone else. Sure she tried to enjoy camping. But that only proves how brave and determined she is, not that she wasn't injured.

Many lawyers attempt to save a single, devastating argument for rebuttal, on the assumption that it will be even more effective if it stands unanswered. There is, no doubt, a great deal of truth to this theory, as it deprives the defendant of all opportunity to respond. One caveat, however, is necessary. Rebuttal is technically limited to issues that were addressed during the defense argument-in-chief. If, for whatever reason, defense counsel does not raise a particular issue, then it is possible that the court will sustain an objection to its coverage on rebuttal.

Thus, it is inherently risky for the plaintiff to "sandbag" by completely omitting a subject from the argument-in-chief. Suppose, for example, the plaintiff in the fire engine case decided to defer all discussion of damages until rebuttal, thereby precluding the defendant from replying to the plaintiff's specific arguments. The defendant, in turn, could decide not to address damages at all. Some courts, then, would refuse to allow the plaintiff to raise damages for the first time on rebuttal, and the plaintiff would be entirely precluded from presenting any argument on damages.[8]

8. Note that the rule is that rebuttal may be used only to respond to issues covered during the defendant's argument-in-chief. Thus, even if the plaintiff had addressed damages during her argument-in-chief, the omission of the issue from the defendant's argument-in-chief would still technically rule out damages as a subject for rebuttal. Unlike the "sandbagging" situation, however, the plaintiff in this supposition did not forego the opportunity to discuss damages at the outset.

The rule requiring rebuttal to be within the scope of the defendant's argument is enforced with varying degrees of strictness from court to court.

13.2.4 Variations

It is always within the discretion of the court to alter the usual order of argument so as to reflect the actual burden of proof in the particular case. In cases involving counterclaims or affirmative defenses, the defendant may be allowed to present the first and last arguments or may be given a sur-rebuttal to follow the plaintiff's rebuttal. In multiparty cases the court will determine the order in which the various plaintiffs and defendants will proceed.

It is also the judge's prerogative to apportion the time for argument, although the court may not deny a party an effective opportunity to argue its case. Finally, some courts do not provide automatically for rebuttal, but rather require the plaintiff affirmatively to reserve time from the argument-in-chief.

13.3 Structure

The structure of the final argument must be developed for maximum persuasive weight. The central thrust of the final argument must always be to provide reasons—logical, moral, legal, emotional—for the entry of a verdict in your client's favor. Every aspect of the final argument should contribute in some way to the completion of the sentence, "We win because . . . ." In the broadest sense, of course, the desired conclusion should simply follow from the facts and law of the case. Few cases, however, will go to trial unless the facts are capable of multiple interpretations. Effective argument therefore places a premium on arrangement and explanation.

The use of topical organization is the guiding principle in the structure of final arguments. The following section will discuss the various methods of employing topical organization as well as the drawbacks and advantages of alternative structures.

13.3.1 Topical Organization

The importance of topical organization in final argument cannot be overemphasized. Seemingly natural methods of organization, such as chronology and witness listing, will not present the evidence in its most persuasive form. Topical organization, on the other hand, allows counsel to determine the best way to address the issues in the case. Topical organization can use, or combine, any of the following strategies.

13.3.1.1 Issues

One of the simplest and most effective forms of organization is to divide the case into a series of discrete factual or legal issues. Large issues, such as liability and damages, are obvious, but they are also so broad as to provide relatively little help in ordering an argument. It is more useful to think of issues as narrower propositions of fact or law.

In the fire engine case, for example, the plaintiff might organize the liability section of her argument according to these factual issues: 1) the defendant's hurried morning; 2) the siren; and 3) the events of the accident. The first section of the argument would emphasize the reasons for the defendant's inattention; the second segment would explain why all of the other traffic stopped for the fire truck (and why the jury should not believe the defendant's claim that there was no siren); and the third segment would finally describe the actual collision.

A fourth portion of the argument could be devoted to the legal issue of comparative fault. Plaintiff's counsel can thereby isolate and explain all of the factors that made the plaintiff's own actions reasonable and nonnegligent.

Note that this format, as opposed to strict chronology, will allow plaintiff's counsel to plan the discussions of motivation and credibility in a coherent and logical fashion.[9] All of the considerations pointing to the defendant's preoccupation can be addressed at once, including events that occurred both before (being late for the meeting) and after (rushing to call the office) the accident. Similarly, the entire "siren question" can be resolved, making it clear that the siren was sounding, before discussing the collision. Finally, counsel can address the question of comparative negligence without interrupting or detracting from the drama of the collision.

These strategies, of course, are open to question and reevaluation. Perhaps the use of the siren should be raised within the scope of the events, leaving the defendant's credibility to be addressed later. The point is that only the use of issue-based organization allows counsel to make such tactical decisions.

13.3.1.2 Elements

A second form of topical organization revolves around elements and claims. Every legal cause or defense is composed of various discrete elements. A claim of negligence, for instance, must be supported by proof of duty, breach of duty, cause in fact, proximate cause, and damages. A plaintiff can therefore develop her final argument by discussing the evidence as it supports each of the distinct elements of her cause of action. A defendant, who needs to challenge only a single element to win, can use the same form of organization, but can truncate it by focusing only on those elements that are truly likely to be negated.

9. The uses and pitfalls of chronological organization are discussed at section 13.3.1.5.

13.3.1.3 Jury Instructions

In most jurisdictions, an instructions conference is held immediately prior to the final arguments.[10] Armed with advance knowledge of the instructions that the court will give to the jury, counsel can use them to organize all, or more likely part, of the final argument.

Jury instructions must be used selectively as an organizing device. They are boring enough when read by the judge, and there is no reason to repeat them fully in their typically mind-numbing length as part of your argument to the jury. Rather, counsel should pick out several of the most important instructions and use those to develop the central points of the final argument. Thus, the plaintiff in the fire engine case might focus on the instructions dealing with due care and credibility, while the defendant might choose to use the instructions on comparative negligence and damages.

13.3.1.4 Turning Points

Modern cognitive theory tells us that jurors are likely to regard the information in a case as a series of turning points or problems. Rather than resolving the truth or falsity of every distinct fact, they are far more likely to focus on a limited number of contested issues. Once a juror decides those issues, she will be inclined to fit the individual facts into a picture that fits in with that view of reality. Thus, an attorney can persuade a jury by identifying the key turning points in the trial and explaining them in a way that agrees with the jurors' life experience and sense of reality.

Assume that the defendant in the fire engine case has raised the defense of comparative negligence and has also challenged the plaintiff's claim of damages. Defense counsel's final argument could easily be organized around turning points such as the plaintiff's failure to pull over (as opposed to merely stopping in the middle of the road) or the plaintiff's weekend-long camping trip.

Note how the turning-point approach tends to work. Defense counsel can argue (although with more details and at greater length) to the following effect:

> Everyone knows that you are supposed to pull over to the right when you see or hear an emergency vehicle. If the plaintiff stopped, but did not pull over, it must have been because she didn't have enough time to do so. That means that the fire engine's warning devices must have become noticeable only at the last moment, since the plaintiff herself would have pulled over if she had seen or heard the truck sooner. This must mean that the siren was silent, or at least inaudible, since the siren can be heard long before the fire truck can be seen.

10. In most jurisdictions, the final arguments are given before the court instructs the jury as to the law. In a few jurisdictions, however, final arguments follow the court's charge. In either situation, the attorneys know what the instructions will be before they deliver their arguments.

By persuading the jury that the plaintiff stopped in the middle of the road, defense counsel can also make progress in persuading them of the defendant's position on the siren issue. A juror who believes that the plaintiff did not pull over will look to her own life's experience for a reason or explanation and will tend to embrace other facts that make sense in that context. An inaudible or nonoperating siren provides such contextual support for the juror's conclusion that the plaintiff did not pull over. Thus, once a juror accepts that the plaintiff did not hear a siren, she will be far more likely to credit the defendant's claim that he had insufficient warning to stop his car.

13.3.1.5 Alternative Structures

Chronological Organization

Chronology is the most obvious alternative structure for a final argument. Since the events in a case manifestly occurred in a chronological order, it seems obvious to replay them in the same progression during final argument.

While chronology certainly plays an important role in final argument, it may not be the best approach to overall structure. The difficulty with chronology is that events are unlikely to have occurred in the most persuasive possible sequence. Early events can frequently be illuminated by their subsequent consequences. In the preceding section, for example, we saw the forensic relationship in the defendant's argument between proof of the plaintiff's failure to pull over and the fire engine's use (or non-use) of its siren. Told in chronological order, an argument would address the siren first; the use of warning signals obviously must have preceded the plaintiff's response. This structure, however, deprives the story of its persuasive weight since it is the failure to pull over that tends to prove the absence of a siren.

Consider, then, the following two snippets of defense argument. The first is in chronological order:

> As the fire truck approached the intersection, it flashed its lights, but it did not use its siren. The plaintiff saw the fire truck and stopped for it, but she did not have time to pull over. That is why the accident occurred. She saw the fire truck only at the last moment.

Now, the same argument presented topically:

> The plaintiff stopped her car in the middle of the street. She didn't pull over. This can only mean that the fire truck was not using its siren. Everyone knows that you must pull over as soon as you become aware of an emergency vehicle, and a siren can be heard blocks away. The location of the plaintiff's car tells us that she saw that fire truck only at the last moment.

While both arguments make the same point, the discussion is clearly more persuasive once it is freed of the chronological straitjacket. It then becomes possible to move both backward and forward in time, placing events in the most compelling order.

There can be no doubt, of course, that chronology is an essential tool in the structure of a final argument. There will come a time, or many times, in every argument when key occurrences will have to be time-ordered. Indeed, the precise sequence of events can often be the central issue in a case.

Chronology often fails, however, when it is used as the primary organizational device, as though the entire story of the case can be presented in a single order. Rather, it is best to think of the case as consisting of a series of discrete sub-stories. Each sub-story can be set out in chronological order while maintaining an overall format of topical organization.

Witness Listing

Some lawyers persist in presenting final argument as a series of witness descriptions and accounts, essentially recapitulating the testimony of each person who took the stand. This approach is unlikely to be persuasive, as it diminishes the argument's logical coherence and force. Where topical organization focuses on the importance of issues and chronological organization focuses on the real-life sequence of events, witness listing depends on nothing more than the serendipity of which witness said what. It is a lazy, and usually ineffective, method of organization.

To be sure, it will often be necessary to compare witness accounts in the course of a final argument. You may wish to demonstrate the consistency of your own witnesses as opposed to the contradictions among the opposition's. You may want to dwell on the integrity and credibility of your witnesses. Or you might want to point out the bias and self-interest of opposing witnesses. All of this can be accomplished through topical organization.

13.3.2 Other Organizing Tools

13.3.2.1 Start Strong, End Strong

The principles of primacy and recency apply with full force to the final argument. In presenting a final argument, counsel has a limited window in which to attempt to shape the jury's imagination of the acts, events, and circumstances at issue in the case. Anything that bores the jury, or distracts them from the task at hand, must be eliminated from the final argument. And it is certain that prime time—the very beginning and the very end of the argument—must be devoted to the most important considerations in the case.[11]

11. Accordingly, it is a mistake to begin the final argument with a lengthy introduction on the virtues of the jury system. It is also usually unnecessary to reintroduce counsel and clients to the jury or to dwell on your gratitude for their faithful attention to the evidence. It is sufficient to thank the jury in simple language and then to proceed to the heart of the argument. Remember that the final argument is a story. No bestseller begins with a paean to the publishing industry, and no motion picture ever starts by thanking the audience for attending.

The strength of a starting point can be measured against a number of standards, such as theory value, thematic value, dramatic impact, or undeniability. What is the central proposition of your client's theory? What aspect of the evidence best evokes your theme? What is the most emotional or memorable factor in the case? What is the opposing party's greatest concession?

In the fire engine case, plaintiff's counsel might choose to begin the final argument with a compelling restatement of her theory:

> The plaintiff was driving safely in the southbound lane of Sheridan Road. A fire truck approached the intersection from the west. It was flashing its lights and sounding its siren, so, as the law requires and as every high-school student understands, she stopped her car. All of the other traffic stopped as well, with one awful exception. The defendant kept his foot on the accelerator, never slowing down and never swerving, and he crashed his car right into the plaintiff's automobile.

Alternatively, plaintiff's counsel could start with her theme:

> This accident happened because the defendant was too busy to be careful. He was so preoccupied with his thoughts of a new client that he failed to notice what every other driver on the road saw and heard. He was so late and so rushed and so distracted that he paid no attention to the traffic all around him. He was in such a hurry to get to his office that the fire truck's emergency lights and sirens had no impact on him at all. He was so busy that getting to work became more important than ordinary caution. And make no mistake—ordinary caution would have been enough to avoid this accident completely.

Dramatic impact also works:

> In a single instant the defendant's carelessness changed the plaintiff's life forever. In one moment she went from being an ordinary, healthy, active individual to being a person who cannot take a step, lift a child, or even prepare a meal without pain.

As does undeniability:

> The one thing the defendant cannot deny is that he failed to stop for a fire engine. There is no doubt that the fire truck was there, there is no doubt that it was answering a call, there is no doubt that the other cars stopped, and there is no doubt that the defendant kept driving right into the back of the plaintiff's automobile.

The most important point is that the opening salvo in the final argument should be directed at making the jury want to decide the case in your favor. The last few minutes of the final argument should serve the same function, either summarizing the theory, highlighting the theme, driving home the strongest evidence, or painting the most compelling picture. Note that ending on a strong and memorable note is particularly important to the defendant, who will not be able to argue again following the plaintiff's rebuttal.

13.3.2.2 Affirmative Case First

Most final arguments will consist of two distinct components: developing the affirmative case and debunking the opposing party's claims and defenses. As a general rule, it is preferable to build up your own case first and then proceed to debunk the opposition.

Plaintiffs in particular should resist the temptation to begin by criticizing the defense case. No matter how weak or ridiculous the defenses, it is usually best to begin with the strong points of your own case. The plaintiff, after all, bears the burden of proof and cannot win without establishing all of the elements of an affirmative case. Thus, there is less to be gained by refuting the defense if you cannot prove your own case first. Moreover, a plaintiff who launches immediately into an assault on the defendant's case may be seen as confessing a lack of confidence in her own position. And if the jurors do not jump immediately to that conclusion, you can be sure that defense counsel will argue that precise inference: "If plaintiff's case is so strong, why did counsel begin by attacking the defense; they must be worried."

The defendant has more latitude. Having just heard the plaintiff's or prosecutor's argument, jurors are unlikely to draw any adverse inference should defense counsel begin by refuting the plaintiff's case. Indeed, most jurors will be waiting to hear the defendant's denial. Therefore, the defendant should almost always begin with a denial. After all, that is the natural response to an hour or so of the plaintiff's accusations.

Once a strong denial has been made, however, the defendant should, if possible, proceed to support it through the development of an affirmative case. That is, the defendant should usually explain why she is right before going on to explain why the plaintiff is wrong. Thus, the defendant's argument in the fire truck case might—in extremely skeletal form—proceed as follows:

> The defendant was not the cause of this accident. It was the plaintiff's fault. The defendant was driving safely and carefully, well within the speed limit. The fire engine was not sounding its siren, but as soon as he saw it, he hit his brakes and started to pull over. Unfortunately, the plaintiff chose to stop dead in the middle of the road instead of pulling to the side as the traffic laws require.

The real argument, of course, would be far longer, but the organization of the above paragraph holds true. Counsel began with a denial, demonstrated that the defendant's actions were reasonable, and went on to explain the plaintiff's own negligence.

The most frequent exception to the "affirmative case first" rule is found in criminal cases. Since a criminal defendant is not required to present an affirmative case, it is not uncommon for a defense argument to focus solely (or primarily) on the deficiencies in the prosecution's proof.

The plaintiff's (or prosecutor's) rebuttal, of course, is technically limited to refutation of the defense. Within this stricture, however, it is still advisable to frame the argument in as affirmative a light as possible.

Note finally that the "affirmative case first" rule does not mean "affirmative case only." A substantial part of most final arguments should be devoted to the weaknesses in the opposition case—just not the first part.

13.3.2.3 Cluster Circumstantial Evidence and Accumulate Details

We have seen that details can give texture and support to a theory of the case and that circumstantial evidence can establish major propositions. These small, constituent facts are often presented at different times during the testimonial phase of the trial. One witness may testify to several details, the importance of which will become apparent only in light of other evidence supplied by other witnesses. Moreover, on cross-examination counsel may deliberately separate details so as not to alert the witness to the intended thrust of the examination.

Final argument is the time for gathering details. Although the particulars may have occurred at widely different times and have been testified to by several witnesses, they can and should be aggregated to make a single point in final argument. So, for example, the plaintiff in the fire engine case will want to collect all of the details, both direct and circumstantial, that support her proposition that the defendant was preoccupied with thoughts of his important meeting:

> We know that his mind was not on his driving. Look at the details. He was late for work. He had an important meeting scheduled for 8:30 a.m., and he was still sixteen miles from downtown. He had to park his car, leave the garage, walk over two blocks to his office, and get up to the fourteenth floor. And look at what would happen if he was late. The defendant himself testified that he was meeting with a potential new client and that he hoped to land a valuable account. New clients mean advancement and raises. Losing a new client means losing money. You can't land a new client if you don't make it to the meeting. That meeting must have been the only thing on the defendant's mind. It was so important to him that the first thing he did after the accident was to pull out his phone and call his office. He didn't call an ambulance, he didn't call the police, and he didn't even check to see if the other driver was injured. No, first and foremost he cared about that new client. Everything else—driving, traffic, safety—was unimportant compared to his need to get to that meeting.

Note that the details in the above passage could have come from as many as three different witnesses and that they do not strictly follow the chronology of the accident. The argument makes coordinated use of both direct evidence (the phone call after the accident) and circumstantial evidence (the distance from the garage to his office). The argument also uses both positive (a new client means money) and negative (he didn't call an ambulance) inferences. It is the clustering or accumulation of all of these points that gives the argument its persuasive weight.

13.3.2.4 Bury Your Concessions

In the course of almost every argument it will be necessary to concede certain of the opposition's claims or facts, if only to minimize or discount them. As a corollary to the "start strong, end strong" rule, such concessions should usually be "buried" in the middle of your argument.

Suppose, for example, that your client was impeached on cross-examination with a prior inconsistent statement. At some point in your argument, you may well want to concede the inconsistency, but explain why it should be of no consequence to the outcome of the case. That is a fine strategy, but do not do it at either the beginning or the end of your argument. There are sure to be many facts that you want the jury to remember more vividly than your client's inconsistent statements, no matter how adeptly you are able to downplay their significance. In other words, bury the concessions.

13.3.2.5 Weave in Witness Credibility

We noted above that witness listing is an ineffective format for final argument. Witness credibility, on the other hand, is often a subject that must be addressed. The solution is to weave discussion of the witnesses, and their relative credibility, into the fabric of the story.

In most cases it will be sufficient to discuss witnesses only at the point that they become important to the theory of the case. So, for example, the credibility of the fire truck defendant should not form a separate section of the plaintiff's argument. There will be relatively little value to a freestanding attack on the defendant's credibility; it will seem like just that, an attack. On the other hand, jurors will be most receptive to a credibility argument at a moment when its significance is apparent:

> Let us turn to the question of the siren. There is no doubt that a fire engine's siren is a signal that traffic must stop. Ignoring a siren is definite negligence. The defendant claims that there was no siren, but he cannot be believed. He has too much at stake in this case, and he knows that the siren is a vital piece of evidence against him. And remember that Lieutenant Karen Dunn testified that she always used her siren when answering

> a call. She has absolutely no stake in this case and no reason to tell you anything but the truth. So it comes down to this—either you believe the defendant or you believe Lieutenant Dunn.

While the defendant might be unsavory and Lieutenant Dunn upstanding, it makes no sense to discuss their character traits in the abstract. By weaving the witnesses into the story, however, counsel can make full use of their disparate believability.

13.3.2.6 Damages

A special problem is raised by the issue of damages in civil cases, and especially in personal injury cases.

Most authorities agree that plaintiff's counsel should argue liability before proceeding to damages. Particularly where the damages are great or indeterminate, jurors will be more inclined to accept the plaintiff's argument once they have been convinced of liability. Stated otherwise, the desire to award damages flows naturally from a determination of liability. The converse, however, is not true. Proof of damages does not necessarily imply that the defendant was at fault.

For the same reason, defendants are often advised to address damages first, if at all. It is discordant to argue, "The defendant was not at fault, but even if he was, the damages were not so great as the plaintiff claims." The subsequent discussion of damages may be taken as a concession of liability.

Of course, many defense cases are based primarily, if not exclusively, on the issue of damages. In these cases, it should be obvious that damages should form the first, last, and most important part of the argument.

13.4 Content

The specific content of any final argument will obviously be determined by the facts and issues in the case. It is possible, however, to enumerate certain sorts of information that should be considered for inclusion in every final argument.

13.4.1 Tell a Persuasive Story

Every final argument should contain all of the elements of a persuasive story. The argument should detail the evidentiary support for counsel's theory of the case and should consistently invoke the trial theme.

We have previously discussed five substantive elements of a persuasive story: It explains all of the known facts. It is told about people who have reasons for their actions. It is told by credible witnesses. It is supported by details. And it accords with common sense.[12] These elements should be present at some point in all final arguments.

13.4.1.1 Known Facts—What Happened

A persuasive story accounts for all of the known facts. It is not premised on incomplete information, and it does not glide over or ignore inconvenient occurrences. This is not to say that a final argument must mention every minor detail in the case, but rather that it should, in some fashion, accommodate all of the established facts.

The final argument must, of course, cover the central facts of counsel's case, taking care to provide support for all of the legally necessary elements. It must also take into consideration the evidence produced by the opposing party.

Assume that the fire engine case has been tried along the lines that we have discussed in previous sections. The plaintiff has used "Too busy to be careful" as a trial theme, introducing evidence of the defendant's hurried morning. Since there was no dispute as to details such as the defendant's scheduled meeting and various travel times, these have become "known facts" in the sense that the jury is not likely to regard them with doubt or disbelief. Defense counsel might believe that these facts are inconsequential to the issue of liability; after all, people can be late for work and still drive carefully. Nonetheless, the defendant's final argument should account for these facts either by refuting them or explaining their irrelevance.

13.4.1.2 Reasons—Why Did It Happen

Explain the reasons for the actions of the parties and other witnesses. It is not enough to state that an individual did something. Rather, counsel should go on to reveal why those activities were consistent with that individual's self-interest, announced intentions, past behavior, lifestyle, or other understandable motivations. The articulation of reasons gives logical weight to the argument and can transform it from an attorney's assertion into an acceptable statement of fact.

13.4.1.3 Credible Witnesses—Who Should Be Believed

The credibility of witnesses should always be addressed on final argument. At a minimum, this means that the credibility of counsel's own witnesses should be developed in the course of establishing an affirmative case. This can usually be done subtly and indirectly, simply by providing the background information that tends to render your witnesses believable.

In cases where credibility is seriously in issue it will be necessary to take a more frontal approach.

12. The sixth, nonsubstantive, element to a persuasive story is organization.

13.4.1.4 Supportive Details—How Can We Be Sure

As we have seen throughout, persuasion often rests on the accumulation of supportive details. An essential aspect of final argument is the marshaling of details that give weight to counsel's argument.

The inclusion or exclusion of details is a tricky problem. While the right details at the right time can add an airtight quality to your case, the use of too many details (or their use to support unimportant propositions) can drag a final argument into the depths of boredom and despair. There is no single key to making judgments in this area, but it is safe to look to the following guidelines.

- Use details when important facts are in dispute. Whenever there is a disagreement about an occurrence or incident, details can effectively support your client's version of events.
- Use details when motivations are in issue. The presence (or absence) of motive can frequently be established through recourse to constituent facts. Explain why a party would want to act in a certain way. Look at the details that show the benefits of the actions' consequences.
- Use details to support an interpretation of the evidence. The meaning of certain evidence is often contested even when the underlying facts are not in dispute. Regarding damages in the fire engine case, for example, both parties will agree to the fact that the plaintiff went camping at Eagle River Falls. But how should that fact be interpreted? Does it mean that she was not really injured in the accident? Or does it mean that she is a brave woman trying to make the best of a difficult situation? Constituent details—did she stay in the tent? did she organize daily hikes? did she express reluctance about going in the first place?—may help provide the answer.
- Do not use details for unimportant reasons. The judge or jury will have a limited tolerance for details. Every time you use one detail you are diminishing the effectiveness of those that you will use later. It is therefore necessary to reserve your use of details for truly important situations. For example, you will not want to use details, even if they are available, to attack the credibility of a witness whose testimony was not damaging to your case.
- Do not use details to establish uncontested facts.

13.4.1.5 Common Sense—Is It Plausible

Perhaps the ultimate test of every final argument is plausibility. Even if an argument accounts for the known facts, gives reasons for every action, is supported by credible witnesses, and might be replete with convincing details, it still will not be accepted if it does not make sense to the jurors. Almost every other failing can be overcome or forgiven. You cannot, however, win with an implausible argument.

It is essential, therefore, that every closing argument address the subject of common sense. Explain why your theory is realistic, using examples and analogies from everyday life. Plaintiff's counsel in the fire truck case, for instance, will need to explain why the plaintiff, who claims crippling injuries, went camping at Eagle River Falls. The argument, of course, is that she did not want to be defeated by her disabilities. This argument can be strengthened by drawing on the jurors' own observations and experiences:

> It is easy to understand why someone would not want to give in to her injuries. We all know, or have seen, people who refuse to be housebound just because they are disabled. I read a story in the newspaper yesterday about a young boy who lost his right arm to cancer—but he still tried out for his high school baseball team. I'm sure that he went through a lot of pain and disappointment, but he never would have made the team if he hadn't tried. That is what the plaintiff did at Eagle River Falls. She tried to live a normal life.

"Common sense" arguments can also be used to belittle or even ridicule the opposition's case. It is every lawyer's dream that the jury will retire to the deliberation room and immediately conclude that the opposition case just doesn't stack up.

13.4.2 Tie Up Cross-Examinations

Final argument is the time to tie up the issues that were intentionally left unaddressed during cross-examination. Recall the questions that are forbidden to the prudent cross-examiner: never ask a witness to explain; never ask a witness to fill in a gap; never ask a witness to agree with a characterization or conclusion. These questions, and others like them, all risk losing control of the witness. There is a strong consensus that it is better to refrain from asking the ultimate question and to make the point instead during the final argument.

Thus, if your cross-examinations were artful and effective, you should be able to spend some portion of the final argument drawing the previously unspoken conclusions.

Assume that you represent the prosecution in a burglary case involving an alibi defense. The defendant on direct examination recited his alibi, but left an apparent gap during the crucial window when the burglary was most likely to have occurred. As a skilled trial lawyer, you knew not to go into those gaps on cross-examination for fear that the defendant would fill them in with additional information as to his whereabouts. Final argument, however, is another matter:

> We know that this burglary occurred some time during the evening of November 7. The defendant claims that he was at work that entire time. He even produced his time card, showing that he punched in at 4:00 p.m. and punched out at midnight. Other witnesses testified that they saw him

> at work at various times that night. But no one testified that they were with him during his dinner break. We know that he must have taken a break, or at least that he is entitled to one. It is the law in this state that no employee can be required to work for eight hours without a meal break of at least thirty minutes. So we have a full half hour that is unaccounted for. We know that the defendant could have slipped away, and absolutely no one testified that they were with him.

Confronted with this gap on cross-examination, a clever defendant might come up with any number of explanations as to why he didn't take a break or why he went alone. By final argument, however, it is too late. The gap stands unfilled, ready to be exploited by the prosecution.[13]

The same approach can be used with regard to explanations and characterizations. You did not ask a witness why something happened; be sure to use the final argument to tell the jury why it happened. You did not ask a witness to agree with a conclusion or characterization; be sure to use the final argument to draw the conclusion yourself.

13.4.3 Comment on Promises

Attorneys on both sides of a case will inevitably make various promises and commitments to the jury during the course of the trial. These promises may be overt, as is often the case during opening statements: "We will produce a series of documents and work records that prove that the defendant was nowhere near the scene of the crime." Or the commitments may be implicit in the theory of the case. When a plaintiff claims damages for personal injury there is obviously an implied promise of certain proof.

Whatever the case, final argument is the time for counsel to comment on promises made, kept, or broken. Point out the ways in which you fulfilled your commitments. Perhaps more importantly, and certainly more dramatically, underscore the ways in which the opposition failed to live up to their own promises. Consider the explicit promise in the alibi example used above:

> I am sure you remember defense counsel's opening statement. She told you that she would produce documentary evidence—work records—that

13. Is it unethical to use the final argument to lie in wait for a witness? Is a prosecutor entitled to obtain a conviction by depriving the defendant of an opportunity to explain himself during cross-examination? The answer lies in understanding the adversary system. The decision to refrain from asking a question on cross-examination does not deprive the witness of all opportunity to explain. The witness was free to provide whatever information he wanted during the direct examination, and opposing counsel had at least one additional opportunity to cure any defects during redirect examination. The prosecutor, or any lawyer, can fairly assume that the decision to omit a fact from direct examination means that the fact does not exist. The decision not to inquire further during cross-examination, then, at most deprives the witness of yet a third chance to elaborate. It is at least possible, if not likely, that the witness would use that chance to invent facts or obfuscate the truth.

> would prove that the defendant was nowhere near the scene of the crime. Well, the trial is now over, and all of the evidence is in. We have not seen any documentary evidence; there were no work records.

The approach needs to be modified only slightly for use with implicit commitments:

> When a plaintiff comes before you claiming injury, she makes a commitment about the proof that she will offer. You have the right to expect that she will produce evidence of the nature of the injury, that you will hear from doctors about her medical condition, or at least that you will hear from friends and neighbors about the changes in the plaintiff's life. In this case, however, there was no such proof. Of course, the plaintiff testified. But beyond her words there was absolutely no disinterested evidence that she was truly injured in any way.

Of course, the most effective final arguments are often those in which counsel is able to state: "We kept our promises, and they broke theirs."

13.4.4 Resolve Problems and Weaknesses

Final argument can be used to solve problems and confront weaknesses. No matter how well the evidentiary phase of the trial proceeded, you are sure to be left with a number of difficult or troublesome issues. Once identified, these issues can be addressed and resolved in the course of final argument.

A classic instance of such a weakness is the government's reliance on informers in drug prosecutions. Informers are assailable witnesses to begin with, and in drug cases they are often further sullied with histories of their own substance abuse. Recognizing the problems created by relying on such witnesses, prosecutors have developed over the years an almost standardized, and extremely effective, final argument approach. In its barest form it goes something like this:

> It is true that a number of the prosecution witnesses were informers and former drug users. They aren't the most upstanding citizens in the world. It was not the prosecution, however, who chose them as witnesses. The defendants chose these people as witnesses when they set out to sell illegal and dangerous drugs. Who can we expect to serve as witnesses to drug deals? Not clergymen, not doctors, not solid citizens or civic leaders. No, drug deals take place in a shadowy world that is populated by petty criminals and addicts. Those were the people who were present for this transaction, and those were the witnesses whom we had to call to the stand.

There are several schools of thought as to the best timing for addressing weaknesses or problems. Some authorities believe that weaknesses should never be addressed unless the opposing side raises them first. Others believe that at least certain weaknesses should be dealt with "defensively," on the theory that the sting can be preempted by discussing the issue first.

The decision is not always simple. Plaintiffs' attorneys have the choice of dealing with weaknesses during either argument-in-chief or rebuttal. Thus, they can either initiate the discussion or they can wait to see whether the defense brings up the issue during its argument-in-chief. Defendants, on the other hand, must be more wary. Even if the plaintiff (or prosecutor) omits a problem area from the argument-in-chief, it might still be exploited mercilessly on rebuttal.

Because the jury's deliberation does not depend solely on the final arguments, there may ultimately be some weaknesses that must be addressed whether the opposition mentions them or not. Assume that the plaintiff's attorney in the fire engine case delivered the entire final argument without mentioning the plaintiff's camping trip and that the subject was also omitted from the defense argument. Should the plaintiff's counsel rejoice and refrain from mentioning the subject in her rebuttal argument? The jury, after all, heard the evidence, which was damaging to the plaintiff's case. There is no guarantee that they will not consider it, or even base their verdict on it, once they retire to the jury room. Because the evidence was both harmful and easily counteracted, it is probably wisest for plaintiff's counsel to make sure that the topic is covered during final argument. Since counsel's ability to discuss the issue on rebuttal is limited by the scope of the defense argument, the best approach might well have been to address the issue during the plaintiff's argument-in-chief.

13.4.5 Discuss Damages

The trial of a civil case can usually be divided into the conceptual areas of liability and damages. Although liability is the threshold issue, it is a mistake to underestimate the importance of damages. Unless the trial has been bifurcated, plaintiffs in particular should devote a significant portion of the final argument to the development of damages.

It may be helpful to think of damages as comprising a "second persuasive story" in the case. Once liability has been established, damages can be addressed using all of the persuasive story elements that we have discussed above. Counsel should account for the known facts that bear on damages, give the reasons for the actions of the people involved, address the credibility of the specific witnesses, delineate the crucial details, and explain why the requested damage award accords with common sense.

There are two significant aspects involved in most arguments for damages—method and amount. It is important to explain to the jury precisely how damages have been (or should be) calculated. It is also usually important to request a specific amount rather than leaving the award to the jurors' guesswork.

Some defense attorneys prefer to avoid or minimize the issue of damages, reasoning that any discussion may be seen as an implicit admission of liability.[14] Many lawyers, however, choose not to "roll the dice" on liability, concluding that a reduced damage award is the next best thing to winning the case outright. When discussing damages, defense lawyers have a choice. You may simply rebut the plaintiff's damage claim, or you may present a competing estimate of your own. The decision will rest on the circumstances of the particular case. Note, however, that the presentation of a competing damage estimate may run a greater risk of seeming to concede liability.

13.4.6 Use Jury Instructions

Some part of every final argument should be devoted to the court's forthcoming jury instructions as well as to the elements of the claims and defenses in the case. Jury instructions can be extremely important in the way that the jurors decide the case, and it is to counsel's advantage to invoke some of the instructions during argument.

Care must be taken, however, not to overuse or dwell on the instructions. The charge to the jury is universally regarded as one of the most boring parts of the trial, and there is not much value in simply giving the jurors a lengthy advance notice of the instructions to come. The instructions should be used strategically as further evidence of your client's right to prevail on key issues in the case. Thus, discussion of the instructions should not form a single, extended part of the final argument. Rather, they should be used throughout the argument, read or referred to at the points where they can accomplish the most good.

Assume, for example, that the plaintiff in the fire engine case called an expert economist to testify to the plaintiff's expected future losses. The defense, on the other hand, did not produce expert testimony for fear of crediting the plaintiff's claim to damages. Assume also that the court agreed to give the standard expert witness instruction to the jury: they may reject all, or any part, of the testimony of expert witnesses, and the credibility of experts should be judged in the same manner as any other witness. As defense counsel approaches the issue of damages during her final argument she will therefore want to make use of the expert witness instruction. The defendant's final argument, then, might go as follows:

> It is true that the plaintiff offered the testimony of Dr. Staffilino, an economist. But, as the court will instruct you, you may discount or reject any part of Dr. Staffilino's testimony. You do not need to accept what he said just because he is an expert, and the facts of this case show that the plaintiff was not really injured that severely. As the court's instructions will make clear, expert witnesses can make mistakes, or even be biased, just like any other witness.

14. Defense lawyers often seek bifurcated trials to avoid this problem.

Thus, counsel can use the instruction to place the court's imprimatur on her position discounting the value of the expert witness.

Jury instructions are particularly useful when it comes to discussing the elements of the various claims and defenses. It is imperative that the plaintiff persuade the jury that she has established all of the legal elements of her claim. Since the concept of "legal elements" can often be confusing, it is frequently quite helpful to simply run through the court's instruction on elements, explaining at the same time the manner in which each requirement has been satisfied.

In similar fashion, the defendant can use the court's instruction to focus on one or more elements to show that they have not been satisfied by the evidence.

13.4.7 Use Verdict Forms

In addition to jury instructions, the court will also provide the jurors with a set of alternate verdict forms. One of these forms will be the paper that the jury actually fills out as its official verdict in the case.

Use the verdict forms in your final argument. Show the jurors the form that you want them to use and explain how you want them to fill it out. You may persuade the jurors that you are entitled to win the case, but that will do you little good if, by mistake, they end up entering the wrong verdict.

13.4.8 Introductions and Thanks

By final argument it should be unnecessary to reintroduce yourself and your cocounsel to the jury. If, for some reason, you believe that renewed introductions are called for, make them short.

You should, at some point, thank the jury for their time and attention. They have truly fulfilled an important civic duty, sometimes at considerable personal cost or inconvenience, and their importance should be recognized. It is, on the other hand, all too easy to overdo the acknowledgments. Lengthy encomiums to the jury system will quickly become cloying. Even worse are declarations of abject gratitude where counsel feels compelled to confess that the trial has been a boring ordeal. A simple statement of thanks on behalf of yourself and your client is usually sufficient.

13.5 Delivery and Technique

Final argument is generally regarded as the advocate's finest hour. It is the time when all of the skills—no, the arts—of persuasion are marshaled on behalf of the client's cause. While a polished delivery will not rescue a lost cause, a forceful presentation can certainly reinforce the merits of your case.

Most of the persuasive techniques that we have discussed previously, and especially those used in opening statements, also have their applications in final argument.

13.5.1 Do Not Read or Memorize

It is a mistake to write and read your final argument. As we noted in the chapter on opening statements, only the most skilled actors can truly appear natural while reading from a script. Memorization is only slightly more likely to yield an unaffected presentation, and it carries the extreme additional risk that you will forget your place or leave out a crucial part of the argument.

In addition to the purely forensic drawbacks of reading and memorization, the advance scripting of a final argument deprives you of the ability to respond to opposing counsel or to last minute rulings by the court.

The most effective final arguments are those that are delivered from an outline. The use of an outline allows you to plan your final argument, to deliver it with an air of spontaneity, and to adapt to the arguments of the opposition.

Do not be reticent to use notes during final argument. It is all well and good to speak without notes if you are able to do so, but it is far better to refer to a page or two on your pad than it is to omit a crucial argument. Even if you are capable of arguing without notes, you should still use the outline method of preparation rather than writing out and memorizing a speech.

13.5.2 Movement

A certain amount of body and hand movement will enliven your final argument and increase the attentiveness of the jurors. Gestures can be used to emphasize important points or to accent differences between your case and the opposition's. Body movement can also be used for emphasis or transition. Pausing and taking a step or two will alert the jury that you are about to change subjects. Moving toward the jury will underscore the importance of what you are about to say. Moving away from the jury will signal the conclusion of a line of argument. Note that body movement can only be used effectively if you avoid aimless pacing. Constant movement not only distracts the jury, but it also deprives you of the ability to use movements purposefully.

Some courts require counsel to stand planted at a lectern or even seated at a table, but most allow the attorney to move fairly freely about the courtroom. Many authorities suggest that the use of a lectern places an obstacle between counsel and the jury. While this may be true, it is easily possible to overstate the importance of abandoning the lectern. Use it if you need it.

13.5.3 Verbal Pacing

The speed, tone, inflection, and volume of your speech can be important persuasive tools. Changes in speed, tone, inflection, and volume can be used to signal transitions and to maintain the jurors' attention. It is important, of course, to avoid speaking too quickly or too loudly.

The pacing of your speech can be used to convey perceptions of time, distance, and intensity. If you describe an event rapidly, it will seem to have taken place very quickly. If you describe it at a more leisurely pace, the time frame will expand. In similar fashion, rapid speech will tend to magnify intensity and reduce distance. Slower delivery will reduce intensity and increase distance.

13.5.4 Emotion

There are different schools of thought regarding the use of emotion in final argument. Many lawyers believe that emotion has little place at any point during the trial, while others believe that emotion can communicate as effectively as logic or reason. There is a clear consensus, however, that false emotion will backfire. Insincerity has a way of showing through, and there is little that is less persuasive than an overtly insincere attorney.

The best approach to emotion is to save it for the times when you are discussing the moral dimension of your case. There is no reason to wax passionate over the date on which a contract was signed. It is understandable, however, to show outrage or resentment toward a party who intentionally breached a contract, knowing that it would cause great harm to another.

The absence of emotion may be taken as a lack of belief in the righteousness of your case. What reasonable person would be unmoved when discussing crippling injuries to a child or perjury by the opposing party? There will be points in many trials that virtually call out for an outward display of feeling, and a flat presentation may be regarded as an absence of conviction.

13.5.5 Visuals

As with opening statements, visual aids can be extremely valuable during final argument. Counsel is generally free to use any exhibit that has been admitted into evidence and also to create visual displays solely for the purpose of final argument. Any item that has been admitted into evidence may be used during final argument. Thus, documents may be read out loud, displayed electronically, or enlarged. Counsel can highlight key passages in important documents or can array various documents side by side. This last technique is particularly useful to demonstrate relational concepts such as contradiction or continuity.[15]

Physical evidence other than documents may also be used during final argument. Counsel may exhibit items such as weapons, models, photographs, samples, and anything else that has been admitted by the court. Counsel may also use the evi-

15. *See* chapter eleven concerning the use of electronic visuals in final argument.

dence to conduct demonstrations and reenactments, as long as they are consistent with the testimony in the case. In criminal cases, for example, it is common for the prosecutor to show the jury precisely how a weapon was held and used.

Counsel has wide latitude to create visual aids specifically for use during final argument. The only restriction on the use of such materials is that they must be fairly derived from the actual evidence. Visual aids may be "argumentative." In fact, it may be best to think of them as argument in graphic or physical form.

Thus, it is perfectly legitimate for an attorney to use a blackboard or marking pen to write in large letters "THREE REASONS NOT TO BELIEVE THE PLAINTIFF," and then to fill in three columns of reasons for discounting the plaintiff's testimony. Since counsel could obviously tell the jury the reasons not to believe the plaintiff, she may also write them down. In other words, anything that could be spoken may also be illustrated.

More sophisticated visual aids can take the form of charts, graphs, overlays, computer animations, and enlargements.

13.5.6 Headlines

A headline announces where the argument is going next. Just as newspapers use headlines to pique the interest of readers, so can they be used to focus the attention of jurors during final argument.

A headline can take the form of a simple statement, a rhetorical question, or a short "enumeration." The defendant in the fire truck case, for example, might use a headline as brief as the following headline when turning from liability to damages:

> Now let us look at the plaintiff's claim for damages.

Alternatively, defense counsel might choose to make the transition more argumentative:

> Having seen how weak the plaintiff's position is on liability, let's turn to her damages claim.

Or the headline can be used to emphasize the importance of the coming subject:

> As I told you during the opening statement, the real heart of this case is damages. I want to show you now just how inflated the plaintiff's claim really is.

Rhetorical questions can also be useful, as in this example from the plaintiff's argument in the fire engine case:

> What could lead a person to drive so carelessly?

Or, more elaborately:

> How could the defendant have missed seeing the fire engine, when every other car on the road saw it and stopped?

Finally, the technique of "enumeration" might be the most effective of all. Every teacher, and probably most students, will recognize this phenomenon. As soon as the lecturer announces that there are "three reasons" or "four rules" or "six characteristics," every person in the room begins to take notes. It seems that little serves to concentrate the mind more than the onset of a numbered list. This approach can also be used in final argument:

> The defendant was negligent in three different ways.

Or,

> There are four basic flaws in the plaintiff's claim for damages.

Or,

> There were three different moments at which the defendant could have avoided this accident. Let me explain them to you.

The technique of enumeration is particularly effective when it is used in conjunction with a visual aid. Do not simply tell the jury that the defendant violated three "rules of the road." Write the numbered headlines down in bold letters or project them on a screen.

13.5.7 Simple, Active Language

The chapter on opening statements contains a substantial discussion of the persuasive use of simple, active language.[16] The same rules apply equally to final arguments, with the additional proviso that simple, active language may be applied in argumentative form.

One further point should be made. There is a strong temptation during final argument to use judgmental or conclusory terms such as heinous, brutal, deceptive, unfair, virtuous, naive, and the like. Although usually not permitted during opening statements, such language is allowed on final argument. Nonetheless, counsel would do well to remember that conclusory adjectives and adverbs tend to be less persuasive than active nouns and verbs. It is one thing to assert that a crime was heinous, and quite another to describe its awful, vivid details.

13.6 Ethics and Objections

The rules of ethics, evidence, and procedure combine to place a number of very real, though definitely manageable, limits on what can be said during final argument.

16. *See* section 12.5.2.

13.6.1 Impermissible Argument

13.6.1.1 Statements of Personal Belief

It is improper and unethical for an attorney to "assert personal knowledge of facts in issue . . . or state a personal opinion as to the justness of a cause, the credibility of a witness, the culpability of a civil litigant or the guilt or innocence of an accused."[17]

The purpose of this rule is twofold. First, it prevents lawyers from putting their own credibility at issue in a case. The jury is required to decide a case on the basis of the law and evidence, not on their affinity for or faith in a particular lawyer. While every advocate strives to be trusted and believed, it subverts the jury system to make an overt, personal pitch.

Moreover, a statement of personal belief inevitably suggests that the lawyer has access to off-the-record information and therefore invites the jury to decide the case on the basis of evidence not in the record. Consider the following:

> I have investigated this case thoroughly. I have spent hours with my client, and I have visited the scene of the accident. I could tell, just from talking with her, how seriously she has been injured. Believe me, I would not take up your time if my client were not telling the truth. I have handled many other cases of this type, and I can honestly say that this is one of the strongest plaintiff's cases that I have ever seen.

Here, the lawyer has not merely asked for the jury's confidence. Counsel has impliedly asked the jury to enter a verdict on the basis of out-of-court interviews and previously tried cases.

The rule against statements of personal belief is an important one. It should not be demeaned by a too-literal interpretation. It is difficult to purge your speech entirely of terms such as "I think" or "I believe." While good lawyers will strive to avoid these terms, it is not unethical to fall occasionally into first person references. Similarly, it is unnecessary to preface every assertion with statements such as "the evidence has shown," "we have proven," or the like.

It is unethical to ask the jury to decide the case, or any issue in the case, on the basis of its trust in counsel. Thus, the following argument for the plaintiff in the fire truck case is permissible, though some of its language would better be avoided:

> The defendant must have been worried about how late he was for his meeting. We have heard from the defendant's own mouth that his parking garage is almost three blocks from his office. It would take an average person about ten minutes to park his car and walk that far. I think that he also had at least another half hour or so of driving to do. Put the times

17. *See* Model Rules of Prof'l Conduct R. 3.4(e).

> together, and you will see that he was at least twenty minutes late. That was enough to distract him from his driving.

The personal statement in the above example is really nothing more than an inference from the evidence. Of course, things would be different if counsel used an exaggerated tone of voice or series of gestures to emphasize personal belief as opposed to a conclusion drawn from the trial evidence.

On the other hand, this argument is definitely improper:

> I know that it would take at least ten minutes to walk from the defendant's parking garage to his office. I work downtown, and I have walked that distance many times myself. Believe me, it is at least a ten-minute walk.

Here it is clear that counsel is asserting personal knowledge, not admitted evidence, as a basis for the desired conclusion.

13.6.1.2 Appeals to Prejudice or Bigotry

It is unethical to attempt to persuade a jury through appeals to racial, religious, ethnic, gender, or other forms of prejudice. It is a sad fact of life that some jurors can be swayed by their own biases, but lawyers cannot and should not seek to take advantage of this unfortunate phenomenon.

An appeal to prejudice asks the jury to disregard the evidence and to substitute an unreasonable stereotype or preconception. Thus, such arguments violate the rule against alluding to "any matter that the lawyer does not reasonably believe is relevant or that will not be supported by admissible evidence."[18]

The mention of race, gender, or ethnicity is not always improper. It would, for example, be permissible to refer to a party's race if it is relevant to identification by an eyewitness.

On the other hand, it is definitely unethical to make racial or similar appeals implicitly or through code words. An argument based on bigotry cannot be saved through subtle language.

13.6.1.3 Misstating the Evidence

While it is permissible to draw inferences and conclusions, it is improper intentionally to misstate or mischaracterize evidence in the course of final argument. Accordingly, defense counsel in the fire truck case could portray the plaintiff's camping trip as follows:

> The plaintiff admits that she went camping at Eagle River Falls. She did all of the things that ordinary campers do. She carried a pack, she slept

18. *See* Model Rules of Prof'l Conduct R. 3.4(e).

> on the ground, she went hiking. In other words, she willingly undertook all of the strains, exertions, and activities of backpacking. No one made her take that trip; she did it for recreation. Of course, she told a different story here on the witness stand. The only possible conclusion is that she has exaggerated her claim for injuries.

To be sure, the above example is replete with characterizations, but they are fair characterizations. Even if no witness actually testified that the plaintiff went camping voluntarily, it is a reasonable inference that "no one made her take that trip."

The following argument, on the other hand, definitely appears to misstate the evidence:

> The plaintiff was an enthusiastic and carefree camper. She carried the heaviest pack in the family, and she insisted on chopping the wood and pitching the tent. She would have gone camping again the next weekend, but her family couldn't keep up with her.

These are, by and large, assertions of fact, not simply inferences. (While the statement that the plaintiff was an "enthusiastic" camper might be seen as an inference, the statements concerning the "heaviest pack" and the plaintiff's desire to go camping the next weekend are clearly presented as proven facts.) They may not be made in final argument unless they are supported by the record.

Although the rule against misstatements and mischaracterizations is plain enough, judges, for obvious reasons, are usually loath to invoke it. No one is capable of remembering all of the evidence that was admitted at trial, and the line between allowable inferences and forbidden mischaracterizations is difficult to draw. Opposing counsel are, after all, expected to disagree about the content and interpretation of evidence. Thus, judges often try to refrain from ruling on objections based on the misstatement rule. Instead, the court's typical response to an objection is merely to remind the jury that they are the sole judges of the evidence and that they should rely on their own memories rather than on counsel's presentation.

Nonetheless, in truly egregious situations a judge can and will sustain an objection to argument that misstates the evidence. What is more, appellate courts have been known to reverse judgments in situations where the prevailing attorney's argument strayed too far beyond the record.

Two lessons should be drawn concerning the "misstatement" rule. First, evidence should not be misstated. The courts' general reluctance to resolve questions raised by the rule should not be taken as license to ignore the rule. Second, the "misstatement" rule should not be used as an excuse to make spurious objections, to interrupt opposing counsel's argument, or to quibble over the meaning of the evidence. Objections should be made, but only when opposing counsel has seriously and prejudicially departed from the record.

13.6.1.4 Misstating the Law

In most jurisdictions, attorneys may use final argument to explain the relevant law, to discuss the jury instructions, and to apply the law to the facts of the case. Counsel may not, however, misstate the law or argue for legal interpretations that are contrary to the court's decisions and instructions.

Thus, defense counsel in a criminal case could not argue that the jury must acquit the defendant "if there is any doubt whatsoever, no matter how insignificant or far-fetched it might be." By the same token, the prosecutor could not argue that a reasonable doubt only exists if the jury "is persuaded that there is a good chance that the defendant is not guilty." In both of these examples, the attorneys offered definitions of reasonable doubt that are not found in any jurisdiction.

Courts vary in the degree to which they allow lawyers to paraphrase or summarize the law. Attorneys in some jurisdictions are given relatively free rein to argue, while others permit counsel only to read the jury instructions.[19]

Counsel is never free, however, to ask a jury to ignore or disregard the law. Although the potential for jury nullification plays an important role in both our civil and criminal justice systems, it is not a device that can be actively invoked by counsel. You may hope that the jury will refuse to apply a harsh, unfair, or inequitable law, but you may not urge them to do so.

13.6.1.5 Misusing Evidence

When evidence has been admitted only for a limited or restricted use, it is improper to attempt to use it for any other purpose. Suppose, for example, that the ownership of an automobile is at issue in a case. The court has allowed evidence that the defendant maintained insurance on the vehicle, ruling that while the existence of liability insurance is generally inadmissible, it can be received to show agency, ownership, or control.[20] Thus, the following argument is permissible, in keeping with the limited admissibility of the evidence:

> We know that the defendant owned the automobile, because she paid for the insurance on it. You have seen the policy, signed in her own handwriting. No one would sign up and pay for insurance on a car that she did not own.

This argument, on the other hand, is improper:

> We have all seen the insurance policy. The defendant in this case carried over $300,000 in liability insurance—you can see it right there in black

19. In yet other jurisdictions, counsel is not permitted to read the jury instructions, but may paraphrase them.
20. *See* FED. R. EVID. 411.

> and white. She can afford to pay for the damages, and she should pay for the damages.

The Federal Rules of Evidence contain many examples of the limited admissibility doctrine. Rule 404 provides that character evidence may not be admitted to prove actions in conformity with a person's character, but it may be used to prove motive, opportunity, intent, or preparation. Subsequent remedial measures, under Rule 407, cannot be admitted as proof of negligence, but they may be offered to prove the feasibility of precautionary measures. Offers of settlement or compromise are generally inadmissible, but Rule 408 does not require their exclusion if offered to prove the bias or prejudice of a witness.

In each of these situations, final argument should only employ the evidence for the purpose for which it was admitted. Finally, it should go without saying that counsel may not use, or attempt to use, evidence that was excluded by the court.

13.6.1.6 Appeals to the Jurors' Personal Interests

An appeal to the jurors' personal interests invites the jury to decide the case on a basis other than the law and evidence. So, for instance, it is improper for defense counsel to tell a jury that a large verdict will raise taxes or insurance rates. Similarly, plaintiff's counsel cannot argue that an inadequate verdict will result in increased welfare payments. Other predictions as to the potential consequences of a verdict may be equally objectionable. Thus, a prosecutor cannot argue that an acquittal will increase the crime rate or endanger the citizenry.

A specific form of this principle is the so-called "Golden Rule," which prohibits counsel from asking the jurors to envision themselves in the position of one of the litigants. The following is an excerpt from a classic forbidden argument:

> The plaintiff in this case lost his right arm in an industrial accident. You must now determine how much money is necessary to compensate him for his loss. Let me ask you this question: How much money would you want if it had been your right arm? If someone offered you $1,000,000 to have your arm crushed, would you take it? Would you accept $2,000,000?

Such arguments obviously appeal to the jury's sympathy. They also ask the jurors to decide the case on the basis of their own self-interest, as though they were the people actually affected by the outcome of the case.

For much the same reason, counsel cannot refer to the possibility of reversal on appeal, pardon, parole, or other potentially curative measures. Such arguments appeal to the jurors' self-interest by inviting them to avoid making the hard decisions themselves.

13.6.1.7 Appeals to Emotion, Sympathy, and Passion

While there is an emotional side to virtually every trial, counsel may not use final argument to ask the jury to decide the case on the basis of sympathy or passion. Impermissible appeals to passion are often found when counsel dwells on some dramatic, but barely relevant aspect of the case, such as the nature of a plaintiff's extreme injuries when only liability is at stake.

We have already discussed the unethical nature of inflammatory arguments based on racial, religious, ethnic, and gender prejudice. Equally objectionable, although perhaps less offensive, are arguments that appeal to local chauvinism or stereotypical concepts of wealth, education, political affiliation, physical appearance, and the like.

13.6.1.8 Comments on Privilege

It is unethical for the prosecutor in a criminal case to comment on the defendant's invocation of the privilege against self-incrimination. The prosecutor can neither point out nor ask the jury to draw any adverse inference from the defendant's decision not to testify or present evidence.

Jurisdictions are divided as to the rule in civil cases. In some states, it is permissible to ask the jury to draw an adverse inference from a party's invocation of a privilege. Here is an example of such an argument:

> I am sure that you remember the cross-examination of the plaintiff. I asked him where he was going on the morning of the incident, and he said that he was on his way to see the doctor. But he refused to answer when I asked why he was going to the doctor. He invoked what is called the physician-patient privilege. Now, the plaintiff had the right to invoke that privilege, and the court ruled that he did not have to answer my question. But I ask you, why was the defendant afraid of telling us the reason that he needed to see a doctor? What was he hiding? What is the awful secret? If it had just been an ordinary visit—a sore throat or the flu—you can be sure that he would have told us. So there must have been something about the visit that hurt his case.

In other states, however, the above argument would not be allowed since it would be regarded as infringing on the party's right to assert the privilege in question. Whichever approach a jurisdiction takes, the same rule will usually apply to all privileges: attorney-client, physician-patient, husband-wife, clergy-penitent, and others. It is conceivable, however, that a court would allow counsel to comment on the assertion of one privilege but forbid it concerning the invocation of another. Familiarity with local practice is therefore essential.

13.6.1.9 Exceeding the Scope of Rebuttal

The proper scope of rebuttal was discussed previously.[21] It is objectionable to attempt to argue new matters on rebuttal.

13.6.2 *The Protocol of Objections*

13.6.2.1 Making Objections

Objections during final argument follow the same general pattern as objections during witness examinations. Counsel should stand (unless local practice differs) and state succinctly the ground for the objection. There is usually no need to present argument unless requested to by the court.

Some attorneys believe that so-called speaking objections should be employed during final argument, to ensure that the jury understands why counsel is objecting. Following this approach, you would not simply say, "I object, your Honor, counsel is misstating the evidence." Instead, the objection might go as follows:

> I object, your Honor. There was absolutely no evidence to the effect that the plaintiff carried the heaviest pack on that camping trip. In fact, she testified that her children had to help her with her pack every day.

This is not good form, and it may draw a rebuke from the court. Speaking objections should not be used to score substantive points with the jury. A far better approach is simply to make the identical point during counsel's own argument. There is some justification for defense counsel to make extremely limited use of speaking objections during the plaintiff's rebuttal since the defense attorney will not have the opportunity to argue again.

In any event, most attorneys attempt to avoid objecting during opposing counsel's final argument. It is considered a common courtesy to allow opposing counsel to speak uninterrupted. Moreover, the overuse of objections may result in the interruption of one's own final argument. This does not mean, of course, that seriously improper arguments should be tolerated.

It is unethical to make spurious objections simply for the purpose of interfering with opposing counsel's argument.

13.6.2.2 Responding to Objections

The best response to an objection is often no response. An objection disrupts the flow of final argusment, and an extended colloquy with the court will only prolong the interruption. A dignified silence will usually be sufficient to allow the court to rule and to impress the jury with the basic rudeness of the interruption.

---

21. *See* section 13.2.3.

Once the court rules, whether favorably, unfavorably, or inscrutably, counsel should simply proceed by adapting the argument to the court's ruling.

13.6.2.3 Cautionary Instructions

When an objection to final argument has been sustained, the judge will usually caution the jury to disregard the offending remarks. If the court does not give such an instruction on its own motion, objecting counsel should consider asking for one. The downside, of course, is that a cautionary instruction may only serve to emphasize the content of the objectionable argument. Nonetheless, some jurisdictions require that counsel request such an instruction in order to preserve the issue for appeal.[22]

In extreme cases, and especially where a cautionary instruction may only exacerbate the situation, a motion for a mistrial may be appropriate.

13.7 Bench Trials

Most of the techniques discussed above can be used in both bench and jury trials. Judges, however, are famously impatient with long final arguments. Counsel should therefore strive to keep final arguments as short as possible in bench trials. Most of the adaptations discussed in the chapter on opening statements apply equally to final arguments. In brief, counsel should be particularly alert to legal issues and standards when arguing to the court. The judge is likely to have followed and understood the evidence, but will still want to know how the law should be applied to the facts of the case. It is permissible to cite case law during final argument to the bench. Finally, be prepared for the court to ask questions.

22. Paradoxically, appellate courts often hold that a cautionary instruction has cured the negative impact of an improper argument.

Chapter Fourteen

Jury Selection

14.1 Introduction

Jury selection is one of the least uniform aspects of trial advocacy. The procedures used to select and qualify jurors differ widely from jurisdiction to jurisdiction. In some courts, the attorneys are little more than observers, while in others they are given wide latitude to question the panel of potential jurors. The trend for many years, however, has been to restrict, if not eliminate, attorney participation. While this is most often done in the name of efficiency, it is also a response to perceived abuses. Many lawyers have seen jury selection as an opportunity to begin arguing the case, or even to introduce evidence surreptitiously. Others have engaged in all manner of obsequious behavior aimed at currying favor with the jurors. As a consequence, the heyday of attorney-conducted jury selection now seems past. In some highly publicized trials, the process may still occasionally consume weeks or months, but the reality is that jury selection has been de-emphasized in many parts of the country. It is likely that this will continue to be the case.

In truth, it was never really possible to "select" a jury. Even in the most lenient jurisdictions the best that counsel could generally accomplish was to deselect or disqualify a certain number of potential jurors. Today, the goals of jury selection can be summarized as: 1) eliminating jurors who are biased or disposed against your case; 2) gathering information about the eventual jurors to present your case effectively; and 3) beginning to introduce yourself, your client, and certain key concepts to the jury.

As restricted as jury selection may have become, however, it does remain the one aspect of the trial when counsel can interact with and obtain direct feedback from the jurors. At all other moments in the trial, one can only observe and infer the jurors' reactions. During jury selection, even when it is conducted solely by the court, it is possible to learn directly from the jurors themselves. If this precious opportunity is to be preserved, lawyers must use it wisely and fairly.

14.2 Mechanics of Jury Selection

14.2.1 Terminology

Jury selection is markedly different from other aspects of the trial, and it has developed a lexicon of its own.

The "venire" or venire panel is the group of citizens from which juries are to be chosen. The venire, also called the jury pool, is typically assembled from lists of registered voters, licensed drivers, or other adults. Jurisdictions vary widely as to an individual's term of service on the venire. Some courts utilize a "one day or one trial" system in which potential jurors are released after one day unless they are seated on a jury. The more traditional approach, still employed by many courts, is to require potential jurors to be available for a set period of time, ranging from a week to a month.

"Voir dire"[1] is the process of questioning venire members by either the court or the attorneys (or both) to select those who will serve on a jury.

In the course of voir dire counsel may seek to disqualify potential jurors. This is done by making a challenge. A "challenge for cause" is an objection to the venire member's qualifications to sit on the jury either because she does not meet certain statutory requirements or because she has revealed significant bias or prejudice in the course of questioning. A challenge for cause must be ruled on by the court and may be objected to by opposing counsel. There is no limit on the number of potential jurors who may be challenged for cause.

"Peremptory challenges," sometimes known as strikes, may be exercised without cause. The parties are typically allowed to excuse a certain number of potential jurors without stating their reasons. Except in the case of apparent racial or other discriminatory motivation, peremptory challenges must be allowed. The number of peremptory challenges available to each party is determined by statute or court rule.

In most states there are statutory exemptions that allow individuals to decline jury service. Traditionally, many occupational groups were exempt, including lawyers, physicians, dentists, clergy, and even embalmers. In many states, most of these automatic exemptions have been eliminated. Note that an exemption does not disqualify a person from serving on a jury, but only allows her the privilege of opting out. Even in the absence of an exemption, venire members can request to be excused from service on the basis of hardship.

There are also minimal statutory qualifications for jury service. While these differ from state to state, they typically include the ability to understand English, as well as an age requirement. Convicted felons are also frequently disqualified from jury service.

1. Juror voir dire should not be confused with witness voir dire as described in section 9.2.3.1.

14.2.2 Questioning Formats

The voir dire of potential jurors may be conducted by the judge, the attorneys, or both. As noted above, the right of counsel to participate in jury voir dire has been greatly limited in many jurisdictions. Nonetheless, some state systems still permit wide-ranging attorney voir dire. In a large number of federal courts, the current practice is for the judge to conduct the entire voir dire, allowing counsel only to submit written questions which the court may use or discard. This model saves time and avoids abuses, but it is subject to the criticism that a judge's questions will necessarily be fairly superficial. The judge, after all, cannot possibly know as much about a case as the attorneys and is unlikely to be attuned to all of the possibilities for uncovering subtle prejudices.

Finally, a growing number of courts have adopted a mixed approach in which the judge conducts the primary voir dire, but the attorneys are allowed to ask supplemental questions. This format attempts to accommodate both the court's need for efficiency and counsel's interest in participating in the voir dire.

14.2.3 Timing and Order of Voir Dire

The timing and exercise of challenges is determined in large part by the format for questioning the venire members.

14.2.3.1 Preliminary Statements

In all three questioning formats it is typical for the judge to make a preliminary statement to the entire venire panel, describing the voir dire process, the nature of the case, and the issues involved, and perhaps introducing the parties and their attorneys. In systems where attorney questioning is permitted, the lawyers may also be allowed to make preliminary remarks, or at least to introduce themselves and their clients if the judge has not already done so.

14.2.3.2 Size of the Venire Panel

The number of venire members brought to the courtroom should exceed the total needed for the jury as well as the total number of peremptory challenges available to all of the parties. Assume, for example, that our fire engine case is to be tried by a jury of six, with two alternates, and that the local rules of court allow three peremptory challenges for each party. Thus, the minimum size for the venire would be fourteen. It is possible, however, that some venire members will be challenged for cause; others may request to be excused for reasons of hardship or personal convenience. Consequently, it is likely that the voir dire will begin with a panel of at least twenty or twenty-four. In controversial or highly publicized cases, the initial panel may need to be much larger.

14.2.3.3 Questions to the Entire Panel

Many courts begin the voir dire with a series of inquiries to the entire venire panel. These questions typically require only "yes" or "no" responses and seek to develop information relevant to the particular case. Some judges have a standard set of questions, but most will also accept suggestions from counsel.

Venire members are asked to raise their hands if the answer to any question is "yes." Are you related to any of the attorneys or parties?[2] Do you or members of your immediate family work in the aerospace industry? Have you ever been the victim of a crime? Have you ever been asked to cosign for a loan? Venire members who raise their hands may be asked follow-up questions by the court. In jurisdictions where the attorneys participate, the follow-up questions may come during the lawyers' voir dire.

The court may also ask the entire panel whether anyone requests to be excused by reason of hardship or whether any of the potential jurors falls under a statutory exemption.

Jury questionnaires may also be used to direct questions to the entire venire panel. In a large number of jurisdictions, every venire member is asked to fill out a card providing information such as address, occupation, age, marital status, and the like. In some courts, the attorneys are also allowed to fashion a more detailed questionnaire containing questions relating to the specific trial. Such questionnaires are subject to court approval and are most likely to be used in particularly complex cases.

14.2.3.4 Questions to Individual Jurors

The questioning of individual jurors, either by the court or by counsel, may follow several models.

The jurors may be questioned one by one with the exercise of challenges following immediately. In extremely sensitive or highly publicized cases, such questioning may take place in the judge's chambers.

It is more common for the venire to be questioned in groups. Frequently, twelve prospective jurors are seated in the jury box for voir dire. Sometimes smaller groups of four or six are questioned at one time.

14.2.3.5 Exercising Challenges

The timing for the exercise of challenges is governed by the approach used for questioning the venire members. When jurors are questioned singly, as noted

2. The court, of course, will name the attorneys and parties, perhaps also asking them to stand at this point. In addition, the court may also ask whether any of the potential jurors are related to certain named witnesses.

above, challenges (either peremptory or for cause) are usually expected to follow immediately.

A variety of challenge sequences can be used when potential jurors are questioned as a group.

One approach is to question the venire in groups of four. Once the questioning is finished, either by the court or by the attorneys, counsel is first asked whether there are any challenges for cause.[3] The plaintiff (or prosecutor) is usually asked to make her challenges first. Defense counsel may object to the challenge and may also ask to conduct additional voir dire aimed at demonstrating that the juror can be fair. The judge will rule, either excusing or retaining the juror. Then the procedure is reversed, with the defense challenging and the plaintiff being given the opportunity to object.

If a challenge for cause is allowed, the excused juror will be replaced by another member of the pool who will then be questioned in like fashion.

Once all challenges for cause have been ruled on, the attorneys will then have the opportunity to exercise peremptory challenges. Again, the plaintiff and defendant will alternate. Unlike challenges for cause, there are no objections to peremptory challenges other than on the basis of unlawful discrimination.[4] Excused jurors will be replaced with jurors from the pool, who will then be questioned. This process continues until there are no further challenges and the proper number of jurors has been seated.[5] The questioning will then begin again with another group of four. Variations on this approach are also used with groups of six or twelve.

Most lawyers prefer to make their challenges at a sidebar conference to avoid offending the remaining members of the panel. If the judge requires challenges to be announced in open court, this should be done as politely as possible. Peremptory challenges can be made quite obliquely: "Your Honor, we request that Mr. Roth be thanked for his time and excused from further service." Challenges for cause will require more explanation, but they should still be courteous.

Note that courts vary as to the finality of an attorney's statement that she does not wish to exercise a challenge. In some jurisdictions, counsel must present a challenge at the earliest possible time; otherwise it is waived forever. In other courts, it may be permissible to "re-invade" the panel, usually because opposing counsel subsequently exercised a challenge. Following this approach, if plaintiff's counsel "passes" a group of jurors, she may only challenge one later if defense counsel has challenged a member of the same group.

3. In some jurisdictions, the plaintiff questions the jurors and must then present any challenges for cause, followed by the defendant's questions and challenges. In other jurisdictions, both parties complete their questioning before either is given an opportunity to raise challenges.

4. Concerning the impermissible use of peremptory challenges, *see* section 14.5.3.

5. Depending on the jurisdiction, jurors who are not challenged are referred to as having been seated, accepted, or "passed."

An alternative approach, widely used in federal courts, is the "strike" system. Under this method, the entire venire panel is questioned before any challenges are heard. The attorneys and the judge then meet out of the presence of the venire. The court first hears challenges for cause. Once these are decided, the attorneys take turns stating their peremptory challenges. The first twelve (or six) unchallenged panel members will constitute the jury. The necessary number of alternates will be selected in the same fashion. In some jurisdictions, the attorneys will simultaneously submit written strikes, rather than alternating.

14.2.3.6 Preserving Error

What happens when the court erroneously denies a challenge for cause? In most jurisdictions, the denial of a challenge for cause cannot be the basis of an appeal unless the challenging party has exhausted its peremptory challenges.

14.3 Planning and Conducting Voir Dire

In systems where lawyer participation is permitted, voir dire must be planned as carefully as any other aspect of the trial. Your areas of inquiry must be designed to obtain the maximum amount of useful information without overstepping the boundaries set by the court.

Bear in mind that a successful voir dire will accomplish at least three goals. First, it will allow you to uncover grounds to challenge jurors for cause. Second, it will provide you with enough information to make wise use of your peremptory challenges.

Finally, a well-conducted voir dire will give you a basis for adapting your trial strategy to best appeal to the jurors in the case. For example, suppose that voir dire in the fire truck case disclosed that one of the jurors had worked her way through college as an electrical inspector. While this information is unlikely to cause either party to want to challenge her, it does suggest that she will probably be receptive to arguments based on precision or safety standards. Thus, the plaintiff might want to use an analogy in her final argument to the effect that the defendant "broke the rules" when he failed to have his brakes repaired.

14.3.1 Permissible Inquiries

It is almost always permissible to question potential jurors on their backgrounds, work histories, and life experiences. In this vein, it is common to ask jurors about their past involvement with the legal system; their membership in civic, political, social, religious, and other organizations; their hobbies, reading interests, and other pastimes; their families and education; their business experience; and other similar topics.

It is also permissible to inquire as to the jurors' knowledge of or relationship to the parties, lawyers, and witnesses involved in the case. It is fair to ask about family relationships, friendships, business arrangements, debtor-creditor relationships, professional acquaintances, employment, or investment relationships.

Many courts likewise allow counsel to ask jurors about their attitudes and possible preconceptions or prejudices concerning legal and factual issues in the case. Thus, assuming relevance to the case, jurors can be questioned about their attitudes toward issues such as capital punishment, welfare, seat belt laws, or medical treatment. It is expected, for example, that defense counsel in criminal cases will ask potential jurors whether they understand the concepts of the presumption of innocence and proof beyond a reasonable doubt. Most courts draw the line, however, when purported questions about jurors' attitudes spill over into indoctrination or argument.[6]

Finally, it is almost always proper to inquire into an individual's exposure to pretrial publicity.

14.3.2 Question Form

Most authorities suggest that voir dire questions be asked in very open, nonleading form. Suggestive questions circumscribe the potential juror's answer and are therefore unlikely to result in much usable information. Open questions, on the other hand, have the potential to open a window on the juror's outlook or point of view. Consider the following examples. First, a suggestive question:

Counsel: Do you get the local newspaper?

Juror: Yes, I read it every morning.

Now an open question:

Counsel: What magazines, newspapers, or blogs do you read?

Juror: I get the morning paper, and I also subscribe to *Motor Sport* and *Car and Driver*. I read a couple of car blogs every day.

By the same token, narrow questions are unlikely to uncover much about a potential juror's true attitudes. Consider these scenarios:

Counsel: Are you prejudiced against people who receive public assistance?

Juror: No, I'm not prejudiced against anybody.

6. *See* section 14.5.2.

As opposed to:

Counsel:	What do you think about public assistance?
Juror:	I suppose that it's necessary, but an awful lot of people get it just because it's easier than working.

Another reason to avoid leading questions is that they are almost certain to make the venire members uncomfortable. No one likes to be cross-examined. And no matter how gentle we think we are, leading questions will probably feel like cross-examination to potential jurors.

14.3.3 Stereotypes and Generalizations

The early literature on jury selection was typified by its reliance on ethnic, class, and racial stereotypes. North Europeans were considered to be conservative and prosecution-oriented in criminal cases. Latins and Mediterraneans were thought to be emotional and therefore sympathetic to plaintiffs in personal injury cases.

Most of this thinking has long since been abandoned. Virtually all modern research indicates that there is far more diversity within ethnic groups than there is between groups and that ethnicity is a very poor predictor of complex attitudes. This is not to say, however, that characteristics such as race, class, or gender are entirely irrelevant to jury selection. Recall from the discussion of opening statements that every advocate seeks to have the jury create a mental image that is helpful to her case.[7] That task is made far easier when at least some of the jurors have had personal experiences similar to those that counsel wishes to evoke.

A fact of contemporary life is that group identity can often be used as a proxy for certain life experiences. One obvious example is discrimination. While most Americans will say that they object to discrimination, members of minorities are far more likely to have seen or felt it directly. Thus, a lawyer whose case depends on proof of discrimination will no doubt want minorities on the jury. This is not because minorities are inherently generous or sympathetic, but rather because it is more likely that they will comprehend the proof.

The use of group identification as a proxy for experience is not limited to minority groups. Union members, for example, will be more likely to understand concepts such as going on strike or the importance of paying dues, should those issues be relevant to a trial. Older people may have more experience with certain types of medical treatment; parents can be expected to have more relevant knowledge in cases involving children.

Closely related is a concept that might be called "affinity selection." Much psychological research suggests that jurors will be more likely to credit the testimony of persons who are like themselves. Following this theory, lawyers will want jurors

7. *See* section 12.1.1.

who most resemble their clients and principal witnesses. To the extent possible, counsel would also want to exclude jurors who might be the counterparts of the opposing party or significant adverse witnesses. Tactical advantages notwithstanding, it is improper to use peremptory challenges to exclude minorities from juries.[8]

14.3.4 Juror Profiles

Jury selection often calls for snap decision making, requiring counsel to exercise (or waive) peremptory challenges on short notice with far less than perfect information. In jurisdictions where the judge conducts all or most of the voir dire, counsel may be left with dozens of unanswered questions, yet will still have to decide whether or not to strike a particular juror. Even in courts that allow wide-scale lawyer questioning, the exercise of peremptory challenges will still call for large amounts of intuition, guesswork, and seat-of-the-pants reckoning.

Faced with a daunting task under even the best of circumstances, many lawyers develop "juror profiles" to aid their decision making. This process involves creating a list of attributes that you would want in your "perfect juror." To do this, one must consider both the facts and circumstances of the case and the characteristics of your client and principal witnesses. For example, the facts of our accident case suggest that the plaintiff's perfect juror might be someone whose work requires careful attention to rules, as well as someone who has experienced and overcome physical injuries. Recall also that one of plaintiff's key witnesses will be Lieutenant Karen Dunn, who will testify to fire department procedures. The plaintiff will therefore want jurors who will identify with Lieutenant Dunn and who may resent an aggressive cross-examination of her; perhaps relatives of firefighters or women who have succeeded in traditionally male occupations.

In addition to profiling the preferred juror, it is also necessary to imagine a "nightmare juror," the one whom you absolutely must avoid. For our intersection plaintiff, the juror from hell would probably be young, male, self-reliant, a lover of fast cars, and a successful entrepreneur. Such a juror would be inclined to identify with the defendant and be skeptical of the plaintiff's damage claims.

Both lists will go on and on. And, of course, no single juror will ever combine all of the desired traits and experiences. Most real people will possess both positive and negative characteristics, sometimes abundant quantities of each. Thus, the profiles will always necessarily involve some degree of rank ordering. Should the plaintiff strike a young, male entrepreneur—who also happens to be the brother of a female firefighter?

Jury consultants (see below) often prepare extensive "scoring" systems that assign positive and negative point values to each listed characteristic. In that manner, the profiles become virtual equations: plug in the values, try to keep the high scorers, and

8. *See* section 14.5.3.

strike the low ones. When well-devised through sophisticated survey instruments and demographic data, these systems may be quite accurate. Otherwise, they may amount to little more than intuition painted by numbers.

In the absence of a qualified and proficient consultant, then, lawyers may best use profiling as a sort of shorthand, keeping ready track of important information until the time comes to reach a decision. In doing so, it is important to keep in mind that every human being is a multifaceted individual. Even the best, most rigorous attitudinal survey can only tell you what a specific person is likely to think; no profile can tell you how an actual individual will actually react to actual evidence and argument. Thus, it is entirely possible that an entrepreneurial race car driver might turn out to be the plaintiff's best juror or that a feminist firefighter might end up being her worst.

In short, jury selection is ultimately an exercise in interpretation. A well-conceived profile can be a useful template, but not a substitute for judgment.

14.3.5 Jury Consultants

It is now possible to retain a consultant to assist with jury selection. There is a broad range of available services. Some consultants are professional psychologists who will sit at counsel table during voir dire to assess the venire members' responses and body language. Others are social scientists who will conduct surveys to determine the ideal juror profile. Some will assemble "shadow juries" or focus groups for pretrial preparation so that various arguments can be tried out on demographically representative samples.

Whatever their specialty, jury consultants are usually expensive. As a consequence, they are generally used only in big-budget cases.

14.4 Voir Dire Strategies

Whether voir dire will be restricted or extensive, its value can always be maximized through careful planning. The first step is to understand your own goals. The selection process can be used to educate yourself about the jury panel, to develop (or counteract) challenges for cause, to test the panel's reactions to aspects of the case, to obtain commitments to fair treatment, and to begin the process of developing rapport with the jury.

Each goal carries its own implications for the conduct of voir dire.

14.4.1 Gathering Information

The legal justification for voir dire is to allow counsel to obtain information about the venire panel so that a fair jury may ultimately be seated. In an age of cynicism, many advocates will announce that they really want an unfair jury—one that is biased in their favor and against their opponents. Be that as it may, the process itself is truly more designed to eliminate bias than it is to perpetuate it. The calculation is simple. With relatively few peremptory challenges at your disposal, you cannot hope to determine which jurors will serve in your case. The best you can do is to choose several who will not sit.

Your first goal, therefore, should be to assure your client a fair trial by identifying those potential jurors who, for whatever reason, cannot be objective about your client's case.

14.4.1.1 Identifying Bias and Preconceptions

Most people want to be fair. Most people think they are fair. Nonetheless, each of us views new data in light of our prior life's experiences. The sum of those experiences may exert an enormous influence over how new facts will be understood or perceived.

For example, one issue in our intersection case is whether the fire truck was sounding its siren immediately prior to the accident. Since departmental regulations required the use of the siren, it would be difficult to convince, say, a military officer that the regulation was not followed on the date in question. Thus, a soldier with command responsibility would be a "biased" juror in the sense of coming to the case with a settled preconception about the likelihood of certain events. On the other hand, a different member of the venire panel might once have worked in an environment where "rules were made to be broken." Quite apart from any conscious favoritism, that juror would have an entirely different outlook on the question of the siren's use.

Discovering a juror's set of preconceptions is a subtle and difficult task, requiring delicate probing of the person's lifestyle, relationships, education, and personal history. Most important, you have to know what you are looking for. What sort of information will help you decide whether to keep or strike an individual juror? The facts you need will almost always be case-specific, turning on considerations of evidence, inference, and personality. As always, a good way to start thinking is by considering your theory and theme.

In the fire engine case, one component of the plaintiff's theory is that the defendant was late for an important business meeting, and, because he was distracted, he failed to notice that traffic had stopped for a fire truck. The plaintiff, therefore, will want jurors who are receptive to this theory. She will look for jurors who are especially responsible, punctual, careful. She will want to excuse jurors who are casual, absent-minded, or more easygoing about their obligations. Of course, this information cannot be gathered directly. Imagine an interchange like this:

Q: Are you a responsible person?

A: Why, no, I am not.

Obviously that will never happen. People almost universally think of themselves as responsible, and those who do not are unlikely to admit it. To obtain reliable information, counsel will have to consider the elements of responsibility and then look for indicators. Obvious questions would go into the potential juror's educational and work history. Additional inquiries (with some follow-up) might include:

> Q: Have you ever been in a position where you supervised other people? Tell me about it.
>
> Q: Have you ever been in a situation where you had to depend on someone else to get something done? To be on time? How did they handle it? How did you?
>
> Q: Deadlines make a lot of people nervous; how do you feel about them?

Some of these questions are trivial, but a resourceful advocate will easily be able to come up with more and better keys to the potential juror's thoughts and attitudes.

14.4.1.2 Identifying Affinity

Many psychological studies have shown that jurors are more likely to believe witnesses they like or with whom they have something in common. While this affinity link can usually be overcome, it is obviously preferable to begin the trial with an advantage in this area. Some aspects of affinity are apparent, such as age or gender. Other aspects are readily available, such as occupation, marital status, education, or address. Still other possibilities require more in-depth probing.

Consider all of the characteristics of your client and major witnesses. Which of these will become known to the jury? Is your client a parent? A jogger? A gourmet cook? A self-made professional? Also consider your client's overt personality traits. Is he aloof and short-spoken? Shy? Humorous? Go through the same analysis for the opposing parties and their major witnesses. While you would not want to dismiss a juror simply because he and the opposing party share the same hobby, the information might be helpful in deciding borderline cases. If you are down to your last challenge, and you truly can't decide which of two jurors to strike, why take a chance on the one who belongs to the same alumni association as the other side's most important witness.

Finally, remember that affinities can be transferred. The defendant in the fire truck case would not want to see a firefighter on the jury. Nor would he want the spouse, parent, sibling, best friend, sweetheart, or next-door neighbor of a firefighter. Nor would he want someone whose life had been saved by a firefighter, or someone who, as a child, had spent every free afternoon hanging around the firehouse. The only way to find out about these relationships is to ask.

14.4.1.3 Planning for Trial

The final reason to gather information is not to eliminate potential jurors, but rather to educate yourself about the jurors who end up sitting in your case. You will want to gather as much information about them as possible: Who are they, what do they care about, what have they done in their lives, what are their families like, who are their friends, what important decisions have they made?

The answers to these questions, and dozens of others like them, can help you shape your arguments so that they will be as persuasive as possible. For example, if you have learned that one of your jurors is an MBA who plays racquetball, you will avoid making disparaging comments about yuppies, no matter how great the temptation to tweak the opposing party.

14.4.2 Challenges for Cause

You may also use voir dire to develop (or counteract) potential challenges for cause. Because a fair and impartial jury is an essential element of due process, each party is entitled to an unlimited number of challenges for cause.

14.4.2.1 Developing Challenges for Cause

In most jurisdictions, statutes or court rules set out the minimum qualifications for jurors. Most courts use screening systems so that individuals who fail to meet the basic requirements are excluded from venire panels. You may nonetheless come across jurors who are disqualified by reason of age, residence, or inability to communicate in the required language. These jurors may be excused for cause.

Jurors may also be excluded on the ground of bias. In the context of jury selection, "bias" means something more than simple bent or inclination; rather, it refers to an inability to serve as an impartial juror. The standard is usually a high one.

Sometimes, of course, the need to disqualify a juror may be obvious. The juror may be closely related to one of the parties or may have had an important experience quite similar to the events at issue in the case. For example, many courts will automatically exclude crime victims from cases that involve comparable offenses. By the same token, it may be possible to excuse jurors who belong to affected occupational groups—say, insurance adjusters from personal injury cases or nurses from medical malpractice trials. Nor is it unusual for members of the venire panel to disqualify themselves, stating that some element of the case would make it impossible for them to be impartial.

Nonetheless, jurors need not be removed for cause merely because they have some similarity to one of the parties or because they have had a passing exposure to the facts of the case. Thus, a challenge for cause will often have to be developed through further questioning once a possible premise for disqualification has been discovered.

Looking again at the fire truck case, recall that one of the primary witnesses for the plaintiff will be the fire department's first-ever female lieutenant. The defendant, of course, wants to avoid jurors who will identify too closely with this witness. Imagine, then, this interchange between defense counsel and a prospective juror:

Q: Do you have any close relatives who are firefighters?

A: Yes, my daughter is a firefighter in another state.

At this point a challenge for cause will almost certainly be denied. Although it may seem likely that the juror would be predisposed to accept a firefighter's testimony, there is no reason to think that the juror would not be able to decide the case fairly on its facts. More questioning is needed before a court will excuse the juror (in the absence of a peremptory challenge).

Q: Would you mind telling us how your daughter came to be a firefighter?

A: Well, it's something that she always dreamed of doing. There's still a lot of prejudice against women in those positions, but she set her mind to it and she succeeded.

Q: Did she have to overcome any special obstacles?

A: She sure did, but she just decided that she would be twice as good as everybody else.

Q: This case is going to involve testimony from the first female fire lieutenant in our community. Do you think that she may have had to overcome the same sort of obstacles as your daughter?

A: I would think so.

Q: Because of your own experience with your daughter, do you think that you might have some special insight into the career of another woman firefighter?

A: Probably, now that you mention it.

Q: Would it be fair to say that you might be especially sympathetic to the challenges facing women in today's fire departments?

A: That would be fair.

Q: Now, thinking of your daughter and what she went through, is it possible that you might feel uncomfortable listening to testimony that a woman fire lieutenant failed to follow regulations?

A: I might. It would depend on the testimony.

Q: Well, let me ask you this. What do you think someone else might think about your reaction to a woman firefighter's testimony?

A: I suppose they might think that I'd be on her side.

Q: Given that, do you think it might be better for you to sit on a different trial, one that doesn't involve an issue so close to home?

A: I guess that I would be more comfortable on a different case.

At this point a challenge for cause would get a more sympathetic hearing from the court. Still, it is not a sure thing. The juror's comfort level, though important, is not the ultimate determinant of a challenge for cause. The question is whether the juror can be fair and impartial. Thus, either plaintiff's counsel (or the court, depending on the judge's own approach) might attempt to rehabilitate the potential juror.

Q: I'm sure you understand that this case has nothing to do with your daughter.

A: Of course.

Q: So would you do your best to listen to the testimony in this case and evaluate it fairly, without thinking about your daughter?

A: I certainly would.

Q: Does that mean you could put aside your pride in your daughter's accomplishments and give these parties a fair trial based on the evidence in this case?

A: I'm sure that I could.

Following this questioning it will be up to the judge to decide whether or not to allow the challenge for cause. Some judges will deny all challenges unless the juror virtually admits an inability to be fair. Other courts are more lenient, excusing jurors whenever there is a reasonable basis for inferring bias.

14.4.2.2 Presenting Challenges for Cause

No matter how skillfully done, a challenge for cause always has the potential to embarrass or offend the potential juror. For this reason, lawyers prefer to make such challenges at sidebar or in chambers. Not every judge is accommodating, however, so it is often necessary to present challenges in open court.

In these circumstances tact is essential. The manner in which you present the challenge may be taken as an affront by the subject juror or by others on the panel. Thus, you should not announce:

> We challenge Mr. Levitt, who is clearly too prejudiced to serve impartially in this matter.

Rather, try something kinder and gentler, such as:

> We move that the court excuse Mr. Levitt for cause and release him to serve on a different jury.

The court, of course, might not immediately agree with your assessment of the juror. You may therefore find yourself having to be more explicit about why the person is too biased to serve on the jury. Moreover, your opponent might well be primed to argue loudly and extensively (and in the presence of the entire venire panel) that you are being unfair yourself in impugning the integrity of so fine, objective, and impartial a citizen as the upstanding Mr. Levitt. In this uncomfortable situation there are three important things to bear in mind.

First, it is never too late to ask for a sidebar. Though the court has required you to make your challenges in open court, the judge might nonetheless be willing to hear argument outside the presence of the panel.

Second, no purpose can be served by abandoning diplomacy in the presence of the venire panel. Do not argue that the potential juror is a bad or bigoted person. Argue instead that his expressed views and experiences will make it impossible for him to decide the case objectively. The distinction is not trivial; it is the difference between a personal attack and a fair request. (On the other hand, do not be so polite as to concede your point, and remember that your argument will also constitute your record on appeal.)

Finally, be aware that no matter how well justified, you still might lose the challenge for cause. For this reason, many lawyers insist that you should never make a challenge for cause unless you have at least one remaining peremptory challenge available to remove the juror even if the judge will not do it for you.

14.4.3 Testing Reactions

A further strategy is to use voir dire as a means of testing jurors' reactions to aspects of the case. The purpose here is not to begin your argument or indoctrinate the juror, but rather to get an initial read on whether your anticipated positions are likely to make sense to the jury.

For example, the key to the defense in the fire truck case might well be to attempt to minimize the plaintiff's damages. Defense counsel might therefore want to ask each juror a question such as, "Do you think that people ever exaggerate their injuries?" The answers are all likely to be equivocal, "Some people do, some don't; I would have to hear the evidence." But the jurors' manner of answering the question could well give counsel some insight into how they, collectively, might accept an argument that the plaintiff was not injured as badly as she claims.

Of course, anything you learn may also educate your opponent. Try to be subtle.

14.4.4 Obtaining Commitment

It is often thought that certain parties, in certain circumstances, begin each trial with a natural persuasive advantage. Conversely, other parties begin with a handicap no matter what the articulated standard of proof. For example, criminal defendants, personal injury defendants (particularly in cases involving serious injuries), large corporations, and lawyers either suing or being sued by their clients, all can typically expect to face an uphill battle. Consequently, many lawyers for such parties use voir dire as an opportunity to gain a commitment from each juror to be fair and to follow the law.

In criminal cases, it is standard practice for defense counsel to emphasize the presumption of innocence and to underscore the prosecution's burden of proof beyond a reasonable doubt. Many defense lawyers conclude by asking for every juror's pledge to honor and apply that standard.

In a similar vein, a lawyer in civil cases might ask jurors to "give a corporation the same fair treatment that you would give to an individual." In personal injury cases, jurors will probably be asked if they understand that liability and damages are separate questions and that a severely injured plaintiff is not automatically entitled to damages. To the opposite effect, plaintiff's counsel in a medical malpractice case might ask jurors to agree not to give extra weight to a doctor's testimony.

14.4.5 Developing Rapport

Voir dire is your only opportunity to converse directly with the members of the jury panel. You can speak to them during your opening statement and final argument, but you cannot ask them questions, and they cannot answer you. Moreover, first impressions tend to be lasting impressions. Thus, it is essential to regard voir dire as your best opportunity to begin to develop a positive relationship with the jury.

Often the best way to make a good impression is to avoid making a bad impression. Never talk down to the venire panel, never overwhelm them with lawyerisms, never appear frustrated, never argue with a potential juror, never insult or mock a potential juror, and always attempt to make eye contact.

Almost every study of juror perceptions concludes that jurors are most receptive to lawyers who are well-organized, knowledgeable about the facts of the case, confident, authoritative, and polite.

Of course, you will do everything in your power to avoid inconveniencing or embarrassing members of the venire panel. You will not ask deeply probing questions unless they are clearly related to some objective in your case. You will not exhaust the panel (or any member) by dwelling on minutia or pointless details. If your questions are going to be unavoidably embarrassing, you will ask the court to conduct the voir dire in chambers. You will be unfailingly considerate, even to jurors whom you intend to excuse. Remember, the members of the venire panel may have spent hours or days together before they ever were introduced to you. Members of the panel may have become quite friendly so that an affront to one might be taken personally by others.

14.5 Ethics and Objectionable Conduct

As was noted above, the conduct of voir dire has been subjected to increasing supervision by the courts. Here follows a survey of behavior that has been held unethical or improper.

14.5.1 Contact with Venire

Direct or indirect contact with the venire panel is unethical.[9] This is true when the contact is made for the purpose of gathering information, and it is doubly true when it is done in order to influence their opinions.

14.5.2 Improper Questioning

Many courts consider it improper to use voir dire as a means of arguing the case or indoctrinating the jury. While such a "persuasive" approach was once widely advocated, it is now generally frowned upon by most judges.

It is particularly unethical and objectionable to use voir dire as a means of presenting inadmissible evidence. For example, it would be wrong for plaintiff's counsel in a personal injury case to proceed in this manner:

Counsel: Could you be fair to the defendant even though he is a business broker who earns over $100,000 a year?

Or,

Counsel: Would you be influenced by the fact that the defendant is heavily insured?

While each of these questions is ostensibly designed to ascertain the juror's ability to be fair, in reality they are intended to exert improper influence on the outcome of the case.

It is permissible to inquire as to jurors' understanding and acceptance of the law, but counsel cannot use voir dire to misstate the law or to suggest an incorrect standard. Defense counsel in a criminal case could not ask this question:

9. *See* Model Rules of Prof'l Conduct R. 3.5(b).

Counsel: Do you understand that the defendant cannot be convicted if you hesitate, even for half a second, to believe that he committed the crime?

Similarly, the prosecutor could not make this inquiry concerning the burden of proof:

Counsel: Do you understand that hundreds of defendants are convicted in this courtroom every year, so the standard cannot be that hard to satisfy?

It is likewise improper to use voir dire to begin arguing factual inferences or legal conclusions or to mischaracterize evidence in the guise of a predicate for a question.

Thus, in our accident case it would be wrong for plaintiff's counsel to ask an argumentative question such as the following:

Q: If the evidence shows that the defendant was late for an important business meeting, do you think that might mean he was more likely to be a little distracted or careless?

Similarly, the next question asks the venire to accept an inaccurate statement of evidence:

Q: The evidence will show that the defendant tried to drive through an intersection ahead of a fire truck that was responding to an alarm. Do you think that such conduct is ever justified?

Some lawyers may be tempted to pry into venire members' personal lives by asking unnecessarily embarrassing questions. While a certain amount of intrusion is inherent in the voir dire process, this should not be taken as license to invade a juror's zone of privacy.

Appeals to prejudice are as unacceptable during voir dire as they are at any other stage of the trial.

14.5.3 Impermissible Use of Peremptory Challenges

Peremptory challenges cannot be used for the purpose of excluding racial minorities from jury service. This rule applies to both the prosecution[10] and defense in criminal cases and to all parties in civil cases.

10. Batson v. Kentucky, 476 U.S. 79 (1986); Georgia v. McCollum, 505 U.S. 42 (1992); Edmonson v. Leesville Concrete Co., 500 U.S. 614 (1991); J.E.B. v. Alabama, 511 U.S. 127 (1994).

If it appears that peremptory challenges are being used in a racially discriminatory manner, the court must hold a *Batson* hearing to determine whether there is a legitimate, nonracial basis for the challenge.

The U.S. Supreme Court has extended the *Batson* rule to challenges based on gender, so that a minihearing may be necessary if it appears that one party has attempted to use peremptory challenges to exclude either female or male jurors. Lower courts have also applied the *Batson* rule to cases of religious or ethnic discrimination.

14.5.4 Making Objections and Motions in Limine

Objections may be raised in the course of voir dire just as in any other phase of the trial. Should opposing counsel stray from permissible questioning it is appropriate to alert the court:

> Objection, your Honor, these are not proper voir dire questions.

Or,

> We object, counsel is arguing his case.

It may sometimes be necessary to be more specific:

> Your Honor, the defense objects to the plaintiffs' incorrect statement of the burden of proof.

If opposing counsel is adept at voir dire, the questioning of jurors may seem very much like a personal conversation, with lawyer and juror engaged in a friendly chat. In those circumstances, an objection, no matter how well founded, may be taken as a rude interruption. Thus, most attorneys try to keep voir dire objections to a minimum and if necessary, to keep them brief and polite.

On the other hand, an unskilled or overbearing opponent may step across the line separating advocacy from respect or good taste. The jury system does not profit when attorneys offend, frustrate, or anger members of the panel, particularly when the questions have no apparent relationship to the issues in the case. While it might be tempting to watch such a lawyer alienate the venire, the better tactic is probably to rescue the potential juror with an objection:

> Objection, your Honor, to the irrelevant and unnecessarily personal nature of counsel's questioning.

It is also possible to direct a motion in limine to the voir dire process. In many cases, particularly in jurisdictions where wide-open questioning is the norm, the court may be disinclined to limit voir dire in advance. So, for example, it could be difficult to prevail on a motion to prohibit "argumentative" questions or questions that seek to "indoctrinate the panel." While such questions are improper, most judges will probably want to hear the actual voir dire before ruling. Of course, if opposing counsel has a reputation for abusing voir dire, then the motion should be made, supported by compelling facts.

Motions in limine are most likely to be successful when aimed at specific lines of questioning or specific items of evidence. So, for example, a court very well might allow a motion to prohibit all references to a disputed scientific test, an excluded document, or certain inflammatory evidence of questionable admissibility. A court might also direct counsel to refrain from questioning the venire in areas with great potential for prejudice—such as race, sex, or mental illness—depending on the relevance to actual issues in the case.

INDEX

E

F

G

H

I

M

Q

U

V